Rise of the New World Order:
The Culling of Man

J. Micah'el Thomas Hays

This book was conceived, researched, written and edited by the author. This is my first attempt at a book and my editing certainly isn't professional grade, but the information you need in order to know what is really happening in our world is contained within, so please keep this in mind when you are reading what I have assembled here.

You will probably have to read this book more than once in order to fully "awaken", that is, to fully connect all the dots in your own mind of what I'm laying out. The dots **do** connect. Just to be clear, some of the information in the front of this book will make more sense after learning more about those aspects contained later in the book. Each time you read this book through, the connections will become more and more crystal clear, until you see things in our world aren't really as they seem.

This book is not to be taken lightly for certain. What is in this book is highly disturbing and it was never my intent to scare or anger anybody, but it is what it is. The contents within are the definitive explanation of a real-life nightmare that instead of going to sleep to, you wake up to. You awaken to the reality of living in the New World Order, which is the transitional phase from free humanity to the Luciferian one world government of the End Times described in Biblical prophecy.

I did my exacting best to bring current the ongoing Biblical events that occurred after the delivery of the Book of Revelation, those events related to the Biblical prophecy of the End Times and the arrival of the Antichrist. I think you will find what I'm laying out to be unnerving to say the least.

I want to thank the patriotic truth seekers who have contributed their time, thoughts, research, words and lives over many years in order to try and wake humanity up to the dire threat of the New World Order. I challenge anyone to dispute as untrue what I have laid out in these pages, and any hollow attacks on me **without addressing the facts contained herein** will fall to the bottom. If someone else could come up with a more definitive explanation than the conclusions I've come to as to why the world is such a messed up place, I'd like to see it.

After awakening to the facts contained here within, I was called back into God's service after living most of my life as a militant atheist. What is contained in this book was more than ample evidence for me to believe there is something much more powerful than mankind running the show here on Earth.

When I learned about what's happening behind the curtains of the world stage today, that which is contained in this book, I had an overpowering urge to educate myself about all aspects of it until I got to the bottom of it, and I **did**. Upon being one of the very few who were able to see the forest for the trees, I was compelled to warn others by using as many of the **facts** available as I could get together. Those that willingly ignore the facts in this book are going to suffer terribly in the very near future, much worse than those who know what is really going on and have prepared themselves and their loved ones.

I must apologize to my loving family for neglecting them during the composition of this book, and at the same time thank them for being patient enough with me to allow the thousands of hours of work that went into the construction of this book. I never wanted kids when I was younger because this world was such a messed up place, and now it's even worse, but I knew in my heart if I ever did have kids that I'd have to do whatever I needed to do to make this world a better place for them, and to give them the promising future they deserve. They don't deserve to inherit the nightmare that is contained in this book.

Besides divine intervention forcing my hand, the motivation to put what I learned into writing was to warn my family, friends, and countrymen of perilous times to come, and to prepare for them. I simply would not be able to live with myself knowing what I know and not at least try to "wake up" the people I love and care about. The people close to me, who really know my character, know that I wouldn't lie to them about something as serious as what we are going to go over. Writing this book was never a choice for me, but a task I feel I was assigned a long time ago. A lot of odd things have happened in my life, and looking back on them now they make sense with regards to what came together here.

When I first went to start writing this book, I would stare for days into a blank, yellow note pad wondering where to even begin to come up with an outline to guide me. I just started writing down the facts that I knew about what was going on and who was involved. Those pages of facts soon turned into categorized computer files with hundreds of facts and notes in each one. Those files were then consolidated into an outline and first draft, and evolved into what you are reading right now.

I've logged 7 years and well over 6,000 hours into research and writing this book, so know for certain that this isn't something that just got haphazardly thrown together and slapped up on some website. What is described in this book should have you at full attention, front and center, as the single most important situation in your life of what you should be aware of and preparing for. This is not a drill, this is the real deal.

My loving mother passed away shortly after the first draft of this book, but she knew what it was about on more than one level. She knew about the existence of the New World Order, what it was all about, and was proud that I wasn't afraid to speak up on behalf of my beliefs. I've never known a more spiritual, caring, and loving person in my entire life. It is in her loving and caring spirit that this book comes forth. Love you, mom. I miss you every day.

"The world is a dangerous place to live; not because of the people who are evil, but because of the people who don't do anything about it."
-Albert Einstein

The Culling of Man

Foreword

Right off the bat let me explain why Old Glory is displayed upside down on the cover. A nation's flag, when displayed upside down, is a distress signal in time of war. **We are a nation in distress, and we are under attack right this moment.** We are at war with unseen forces that you have no idea even exist. We are in a war against the proponents of a secret plan hatched thousands of years ago to enslave the world. The modern day incarnation of this "Great Plan" is aptly and deceptively named the "New World Order". If they called it what it really is, the "Enslavement of Mankind", you probably wouldn't want to go along with it, so they gave it a catchy name to mask their intentions. I'm going to show you where, when and why this plan was initiated and who nurtured it along through history all the way to this very day. Today we are very near to the completion of this grand conspiracy. If you are a Biblical scholar and ever wondered how the Luciferian one world government prophesized in the Bible was going to come about, I'm going to show you how it is unfolding right under your nose today. I'm going to lay out for you what this "Great Plan" is and who's running it today, so that you will be taken out of the darkness you have been kept in all your life and into the light of the truth.

> *"You will know the truth, and the truth shall set you free"*
> -Jesus Christ

Regardless of whether or not you believe in God, if you feel our elected officials aren't doing the job we elected them for and that our country is going down the tubes, this book is for you. It is going to explicitly explain why our federal government is a corrupt joke that doesn't work.

This book was never meant to tell you the entire truth of how life really works, but it will certainly change the way you view the world and life in general. This book is meant to be an alarm clock to wake you up to the fact that things aren't really as they seem, and you better be prepared to do some homework of your own after reading what I've got to say. I'm not asking you to believe what I'm going to say, so much as I don't want you to deny it **before you've done your own research.**

"Condemnation before investigation is the highest form of ignorance."
-Albert Einstein

In recent years the rise of suppressed information coming out of the internet has broken the disinformation barrier put up by those striving to fulfill the Great Plan. Thanks to the (currently) unfiltered information flowing from the internet, the masses of people concerned enough to want the truth are now privy to what our world leaders and the despotic forces behind them have been up to for the last few thousand years.

It is a <u>fact</u> that there is a concerted effort by these people to destroy our country and our present way of life.

The knowledge now erupting from the internet has blown the lid off of the secrecy of the Great Plan. The conspiracy is right there in plain sight for those to see if you know where to look, as they literally hide it right in front of your face. This is why right this second the conspirators are plotting the means to bring about censure of this specific type of information in the name of "fighting domestic terrorism". The time is short for you to use the internet to fully and independently educate yourself and others before the stream of free-flowing information is shut off forever.

This book could have been broken up into well over 100 individual books as there is so much information to know, but neither you nor I would have the time for it. Please keep the following statement in mind, even writing it on a piece of paper to remind you of it as you go through the contents of this book: **I would request of you to look at this book as a research outline of subjects you need to look in to, with just enough information given about each topic for you to get the gist of what is going on. There is much more to the story of every single component in this book than what I am telling you, but I included**

everything I thought was the most relevant in the time and space of a single book.

For the most part, any subjects or statements in this book can be verified or further researched by a quick search on the internet via Google or Bing search engines. Although I did include a bibliography of some very important books I took information from, much of this book was pulled and cross-referenced from the internet. **I want you to do your own research and make up your own mind as to what the real truth is---don't blindly believe anyone, including me.** Bottom line, the truth does not fear investigation, and if I can be proven wrong on anything I've written I'd welcome the correction. Nobody wants the absolute truth as badly as I do, and that's what I was after in this book.

The information contained herein is potentially life-changing and must be read with an open mind. Think of your mind as a parachute: it doesn't work properly unless it's open. Unless you're willing to put everything you think you know temporarily on hold and open up to the possibility that we've been lied to and intentionally misled all of our lives, then this book isn't for you. If it is the truth that sets you free, then it is lies that put you in bondage. You will need to unlearn a lot of the poisonous propaganda that has been fed to you all of your life through organized religion, the political system, and the Mainstream Media, all of which were put in place by the proponents of the Great Plan.

Most people these days suffer from what is called "normalcy bias", also known as the "ostrich effect". The normalcy bias causes otherwise smart people to underestimate or deny the possibility of oncoming disaster or danger. Since it hasn't happened to them before, they can't fathom it happening in the future, and they don't take the appropriate measures to head off a coming danger, or at least prepare for it.

As you are reading this right now, sinister forces are conspiring behind the scenes of the world stage to bring about the end of the world as you know it. There are bad things to come very soon, and there will literally be Hell on Earth in a very short time. You need to know what is **really** going on and prepare the best you can for it.

If this book begins to become widely circulated, the proponents of the Great Plan will unleash their wolves in the Mainstream Media and will scream "conspiracy theory" at this book, when it is in fact a nonfictional, critical examination and presentation of world history and the facts in general of what is happening in the world today.

There have literally been hundreds of books written about the Great Plan/New World Order to try and warn humanity, but all have for the most part have fallen on deaf ears. I hope to end that drought of truth with your help, you, the person holding this book and reading this right now.

It is very specific in the Bible that in the End Times a Luciferian (Satanic) one world government will rise up and take over the world, and I'm going to show you that that is exactly what is unfolding today behind the scenes. I'm going to build a case in this book and factually prove this.

This is why the last century has been the most violent and horrific in the world's history---and will get worse. Much worse. **Biblical-proportion-style worse.**

The proponents of the Great Plan have covered their tracks well by doing everything possible to discredit and malign the Bible, while at the same time following its script of prophecy to a "T". If you are knowledgeable in Biblical prophecy this book will have you at full attention.

It matters not what you believe when it comes to matters of God and religion. It matters what **they** believe---the people running the Great Plan--- and what game plan **they** are following and executing, and **they** are following an agenda specifically outlined and foretold in Biblical prophecy, both Old and New Testaments.

Our enemy is not a race or religion, but a spiritual movement that encompasses all races and religions under a single banner: The Great Plan, aka The New World Order.

> *"About the time of the end, a body of men will be raised up who will turn their attention to the Prophecies, and insist upon their literal interpretation, in the midst of much clamor and opposition."*
> *-Sir Isaac Newton, 1642-1727*

I don't believe the Great Plan is real because I'm a Christian; it is the other way around: I am a Christian because I **know** the Great Plan is real, and it is nearing its completion right now.

The diabolical people who are the proponents of the Great Plan know everything about **you**. Now it's time you learned everything about **them**.

This is the story of the Great Plan ......and the coming **culling of mankind.........**

The Secret Covenant

An illusion it will be, so large, so vast it will escape their perception.

Those who will see it will be thought of as insane.

We will create separate fronts to prevent them from seeing the connection between us.

We will behave as if we are not connected to keep the illusion alive.

Our goal will be accomplished one drop at a time so as to never bring suspicion upon ourselves.

This will also prevent them from seeing the changes as they occur.

We will work together always and will remain bound by blood and secrecy.

Death will come to he who speaks.

We will keep their lifespan short and their minds weak while pretending to do the opposite.

We will use our knowledge of science and technology in subtle ways so they will never see what is happening.

We will use soft metals, aging accelerators and sedatives in food and water, also in the air.

They will be blanketed by poisons everywhere they turn.

The poisons will be hidden in everything that surrounds them, in what they drink, eat, breathe and wear.

We will create medicine that will make them sicker and cause other diseases for which we will create yet more medicine.

We will render them docile and weak before us by our power.

Their minds will belong to us and they will do as we say. If they refuse we shall find ways to implement mind-altering technology into their lives.

We will use fear as our weapon.

We will establish their governments and establish opposites within.

We will own both sides.

They will perform the labour for us and we shall prosper from their toil.

Our families will never mix with theirs.

Our blood must be pure always, for it is the way.

We will make them kill each other when it suits us.

We will keep them separated from the oneness by dogma and religion.

We will control all aspects of their lives and tell them what to think and how.

We will guide them kindly and gently letting them think they are guiding themselves.

We will foment animosity between them through our factions.

When a light shall shine among them, we shall extinguish it by ridicule, or death, whichever suits us best.

We will make them rip each other's hearts apart and kill their own children.

They will bathe in their own blood and kill their neighbours for as long as we see fit.

We will benefit greatly from this, for they will not see us, for they cannot see us.

We will continue to prosper from their wars and their deaths.

We will make them live in fear and anger.

We will use all their tools we have to accomplish this.

The tools will be provided by their labour.

We will make them hate themselves and their neighbours.

We will always hide the divine truth from them, that we are all one.

This they must never know!

Drop-by-drop; drop-by-drop we will advance our goal.

We will take over their land, resources and wealth to exercise total control over them.

We will deceive them into accepting laws that will steal the little freedom they will have.

We will establish a money system that will imprison them forever, keeping them and their children in debt.

When they shall ban together, we shall accuse them of crimes and present a different story to the world for we shall own all the media.

When they shall rise up against us we will crush them like insects, for they are less than that.

They will be helpless to do anything for they will have no weapons.

We will recruit some of their own to carry out our plans, we will promise them eternal life, but eternal life they will never have for they are not of us.

The truth will be hidden in their face, so close they will not be able to focus on it until it's too late.

Oh yes, so grand the illusion of freedom will be, that they will never know they are our slaves.

When all is in place, the reality we will have created for them will own them.

Their minds will be bound by their beliefs, the beliefs we have established from time immemorial.

But if they ever find out they are our equal, we shall perish then. This they must never know.

If they ever find out that together they can vanquish us, they will take action.

They must never, ever find out what we have done, for if they do, we shall have no place to run. No one shall give us shelter.

This is the secret covenant by which we shall live the rest of our present and future lives, for this reality will transcend many generations and life spans.

This covenant is sealed by blood, our blood!

-   unknown

Chapter 1

WELCOME TO THE NEW WORLD ORDER

"The very word "secrecy" is repugnant in a free and open society; and we are as a people inherently and historically opposed to secret societies, to secret oaths and secret proceedings. The high office of the President has been used to foment a plot to destroy the American's freedom and before I leave office, I must inform the citizen of this plight."

-John F. Kennedy, murdered by the proponents of the Great Plan for standing up against them

"I am concerned for the security of our great nation; not so much because of any threat from without, but because of the insidious forces working from within."

-General Douglas MacArthur

"I know no safe depository of the ultimate powers of society but the people themselves; and if we think them not enlightened enough to exercise their control with a wholesome discretion, the remedy is not to take it from them, but to inform their discretion by education."

-Thomas Jefferson

"We must speak more clearly about sexuality, contraception, about abortion, about values that control population, because the ecological crisis, in short, is the population crisis. Cut the population

by 90% and there aren't enough people left to do a great deal of ecological damage."

-Henry Kissinger, member of the Council on Foreign Relations, Bilderberg Group, Club of Rome and Trilateral Commission, and alleged 33rd degree Freemason

"This is a terrible thing to say. In order to stabilize world population, we must eliminate 350,000 people per day. It is a horrible thing to say, but it's just as bad not to say it."

-Jacques Cousteau in an interview with the UNESCO Courier, November 1991

Why do you think our economy, our government, our society, and the world in general are so completely messed up, and getting worse year by year, generation after generation?

So chaotic......so corrupt.......so perverted......

The economy has been on a virtual roller coaster ride since the beginning of the 20th century, and in the year 2013 we're mired in the worst economic downturn since the Great Depression. Our federal government is so corrupt it has degenerated into a punch line on a late-night TV monologue. It seems that no matter who we vote for, the size, power, and corruption of government continue to grow. To most people something is terribly wrong with our political establishment but they can't seem to put their finger on it.

Our society is permeated with immoral filth. Degenerate pornography, drugs, immorality and gutter-behavior are the norm on the radio, TV and movies. We are living in a depraved world and getting worse every year like clockwork.

We're not evolving anymore as a society.....we're DE-volving, and our country and the world are headed for a carefully crafted self-implosion, beginning with the big economic crash that is still to come. The crash of 2008 and even the Great Depression will seem like a walk in the park compared to what is just around the corner.

For there exists an insidious, invisible evil all around us. It is all-encompassing, all-permeating, and currently controls how we as humans live our lives, and how we will live them in the future. This evil power running the show today in the United States is the same dark force that has been steering humanity for thousands of years.

I'm talking about living in the world orchestrated, manufactured, and guided by the proponents of the Great Plan and the multinational corporations they control that influence your life as you know it. The products you eat, wear, watch, listen to, look at and are mesmerized and hypnotized by. Exxon. Facebook. Google. Bank of America. Microsoft. General Electric. Chase. Disney. Apple. McDonalds. Visa. Coca-Cola. Pfizer. And right on down the globalist corporate line.

The Great Plan consists not only of the controllers of these gigantic corporations, but controllers of many higher educational establishments, the Mainstream Media and political think tanks. Entrenched Congressmen who have sold their souls and our country down the river for "favors" are also involved. The front man of the Great Plan, the President of the United States, is hand-picked before any election ever occurs. He is put in place to sign Executive Orders that circumvent our elected Congress and subvert the Constitution, creating entities of doom like FEMA in order to override our Constitutional rights, and also to pass Police State legislation like the Patriot Act so they can legally wage war against those patriotic Americans who would oppose their plans.

> *"None are more hopelessly enslaved than those who falsely believe they are free"*
> *-Goethe*

Welcome to the New World Order. You are currently living in its transitional phase from a planet of sovereign nations to a borderless one world government controlled by the wealthiest, most diabolically evil people in the world.

To put it in simple terms, the New World Order is the corporate takeover of humanity, which is also the exact definition of **fascism.** You aren't going to like who they want for their future fascist leader either, but we'll get to that soon enough.

I talked about the "normalcy bias" or "ostrich-effect" earlier that grips people when confronted with facts that are contrary to what they were taught to believe, **or want to continue to believe**. Most people have been conditioned from birth by the Mainstream Media to have built in "slides" that shut down the mind's critical examination process when it comes to certain sensitive or controversial topics. "Slides" is a CIA term for a conditioned type of response which short-circuits a person's rational thinking process and terminates debate or examination of the topic at hand. For example, the mention of the word "conspiracy" often solicits a slide response with many people. After all, no conspiracies are real, right?

Do not allow this to happen to **you**. Your family, friends, livelihood and your way of life are in imminent danger because of the "Great Plan" revealed in this book. What I'm going to show you is an urgent, life-threatening matter that is going to affect you and your family in a very bad way, very soon.

I'm going to lay out a monstrous conspiracy that exists against mankind and has for millennia. I've meticulously researched the various components of the Great Plan, and condensed the facts of the most pertinent components into a book you can read in a couple of days as opposed to spending years of research trying to nail down exactly what is going on. This is the book I wish I'd had years ago to dispense to me what is really going on. I certainly would have led a drastically different life had I known the truth of what is really going on.

You've always known in the back of your mind that something wasn't quite right in the world, but you just couldn't put a finger on it, could you? Well, I'm going to tell you exactly what's been going on behind your back, under your nose, and right in front of your face. By reading this book you have obligated yourself to the ingestion of the "red" pill, and you will know the ugly truth.

It's time to expose the root cause of 95% of the problems in the world. Nearly if not all of them have been intentionally orchestrated by the people running the Great Plan: Corrupt governments. Endless wars. Rampant drug abuse. A never-ending economic roller coaster. Immorality and degeneracy everywhere you turn in society. These are the intentional effects of the Great Plan/New World Order agenda. Their ultimate goal is to degenerate the economies, governments and societies of the individual countries, causing them to self-destruct, and whatever's left at the end will willingly fall into the waiting hands of their "savior", the one world government that will rise from the ashes.

The very last people on Earth you would want to try and save us are the people who intentionally caused the problems to start with, but that is exactly what they are setting us up for.

These people aren't shy about their agenda either. If you go looking for it, it is all there to find in official government and private documents and publications. They just don't ever put it in the Mainstream Media for you to see.

> *"The individual is handicapped by coming face-to-face with a conspiracy so monstrous he cannot believe it exists. The American mind simply has not come to a realization of the evil which has been introduced into our midst."*
> *- J. Edgar Hoover, first head of the FBI, speaking of the existence of the Great Plan*

There are perilous times coming, and those who don't know what is going on are going to suffer terribly, much worse than those who DO know what is going on and have made the necessary preparations.

It is time for you to wake up and take on some hardcore responsibility about this pressing, urgent matter. You need to absorb and act on the facts and circumstances I'm going to lay out herein. You will probably need to read this book **multiple times** for the truth to sink in, and each time it is gone through, the curtain that is the facade of our manufactured reality will be lifted just a little more, until you can truly visualize what is really happening. You will view the world in a whole new light.

This book is not only for Americans of every walk of life, but for humanity, so that they may know the truth of what is really going on with our world. The patriotic citizens of the United States need to take special heed of my words as we have been targeted in particular by the Great Plan's conspiracy of calculated manipulation, hatred and loathing.

We've been taken for a ride:

> *"We are grateful to The Washington Post, The New York Times, Time Magazine and other great publications whose directors have*

attended our meetings and respected their promises of discretion for almost forty years. It would have been impossible for us to develop our plan for the world if we had been subject to the bright lights of publicity during those years. But, the world is now much more sophisticated and prepared to march towards a world government. The supranational sovereignty of an intellectual elite and world bankers is surely preferable to the national auto-determination practiced in past centuries."

-David Rockefeller, member of the Council on Foreign Relations, co-founder of the Bilderberg Group, the Club of Rome, and the Trilateral Commission. He is the current head of the Rockefeller oil and banking dynasty and a master of the Great Plan to the extreme

You didn't actually think that our Presidents are self-made men who started with nothing and miraculously became President, did you? Our Presidents are selected and groomed years in advance by the diabolical proponents of the Great Plan.

Once you start cross-referencing family blood lines, names, business relationships, and memberships in the secret and semi-secret societies, you will find that it is the "usual suspects" time and again calling the shots. The same secret societies and the same personalities that populate them. The same families. The same bankers. The same politicians. The same CEOs. Right on down the globalist line. It is the equivalent of a global organized crime syndicate, and since they make the rules, they literally are getting away with murder.

"Since I entered politics, I have chiefly had men's views confided to me privately. Some of the biggest men in the United States, in the field of commerce and manufacture, are afraid of something. They know that there is a power somewhere so organized, so subtle, so watchful, so interlocked, so complete, so pervasive, that they better not speak above their breath when they speak in condemnation of it."

-Woodrow Wilson, 28th President of the United States, referring to the Great Plan

Right now, I want you to take **30 seconds** and really think about your family and how much you really love them, and what kind of future you want for them. Think about your kids, grandkids, and right on down the line. Your wife. Your husband. Your parents. Your family. Your friends. Everybody you care about and love. They are **all** in harm's way because of this "Great Plan" to enslave the world at **any** cost.

As you digest the information in this book, remember that your actions henceforth will either contribute to the solution and a bright, hopeful future for the next generations..........or you will contribute to the problem and help expedite the Great Plan along to completion. The end result of the path we are currently on is a dark, destitute, and meager existence for your loved ones---they would curse us forever for not standing up to the tyranny that is the New World Order.

> *"The real menace of our republic is this invisible government which like a giant octopus sprawls its slimy length over city, state and nation. Like the octopus of real life, it operates under cover of a self created screen....At the head of this octopus are the Rockefeller Standard Oil interests and a small group of powerful banking houses generally referred to as international bankers. The little coterie of powerful international bankers virtually run the United States government for their own selfish purposes. They practically control both political parties."*
> *-New York City Mayor John F. Hylan, 1922*

Forget everything you've ever learned or been told by the Mainstream Media about our reality, because it is for the most part a pack of lies, distractions, and deceptions.

> *"The ruling class has the schools and press under its thumb. This enables it to sway the emotions of the masses."*
> *-Albert Einstein, on how the proponents of the Great Plan steer humanity*

It has been said that truth passes through three stages. The first being denial. The second being violent opposition. The third being widespread acceptance of the proclaimed truth as common knowledge. As you read this book, keep in mind that you will probably fall into one of those three categories. One group of people will vehemently deny what I am saying is true, and pass it off as lunacy---**without checking the facts for themselves**. Another group will be greatly distressed to this kind of information being released, threatening their fake-reality bubble. Rather than pay attention to the facts, **they will take great pains to discredit me and my message**. That is, they will attack the messenger instead of address the facts of the message. The last group, respectively, will sit back and say to themselves *"I knew it all along. I knew there was something just not right in the world, and this is it."*

"The real rulers in Washington are invisible, and exercise power from behind the scenes."
-Supreme Court Justice Felix Frankfurter, 1952

With the advent of the internet over the last few years, all manners of suppressed information suddenly have a direct outlet to the general public. Quite literally, information that has been kept secret for thousands of years is suddenly spilling out within only a very few years' time and "they" aim to stop it. Members of Congress have openly discussed an internet "switch" they could turn off if they needed to in the name of "homeland security". That is, if enough people begin to find out about this stuff they could potentially foment a revolution against the Great Plan, and the proponents of it will do everything in their power to quash this.

This book is the brutally honest explanation of the **New World Order,** and this is the primary directive of this book: to expose their plans and let you know what is going on so you can research it yourself and prepare for what is to come before they pull the plug on this type of information.......**and they WILL pull the plug, mark my words.**

"Some even believe we (the Rockefeller family) are part of a secret cabal working against the best interests of the United States, characterizing my family and me as 'internationalists' and of conspiring with others around the world to build a more

*integrated global political and economic structure – one world, if
you will. If that's the charge, I stand guilty, and I am proud of it."*
- *David Rockefeller, from his published memoirs*

On the surface, the notion of a one world government might not be
such a bad thing. That is until you find out the truth of who is currently
pushing its agenda and who intends to run it when it gets in place. If you
are a caring and compassionate human being, you will **want** to know the
truth such that you can help your family, your neighbor, and your fellow
humanity. We are all in this together.

They have used the Mainstream Media, which they own and control,
to brainwash you into thinking everything is all right.

It's not.

*"In a time of universal deceit, telling the truth is a revolutionary
act"*
- *George Orwell, author of '1984' and proponent of the Great Plan*

You and I both know beyond a shadow of a doubt that the people
running the federal government of the United States are corrupt from
the top to the bottom, but you have no idea just how corrupt and ill-
intentioned the monstrosity really is that our puppet politicians have
built into the present-day federal government. **Keep in mind that the
government is not our enemy**. Government is merely a tool that is as
malignant or benign as whoever is wielding it---just like a gun. Right
now the people who have bought and paid for our federal government
are the ones wielding the gun of governmental tyranny, and **they are
firing on us right now.**

Our "elected" United States government is a facade, bought and paid
for by a financial pyramid scheme that was pushed into legalization by
the Great Plan conspirators in 1913. These conspirators are none other
than the ancestors of the current-day owners of the privately-held Federal Reserve. That's right, **PRIVATE OWNERS** of the Federal Reserve.
The Federal Reserve, **incorporated in 1913**, is not part of our federal
government and is a legally chartered, for-profit corporation. Not only
this, but they are, for the most part, untouchable by law. The only thing

federal about the Federal Reserve is its intentionally deceptive name. It is the private bank of our federal government, and it is a **for-profit banking corporation with dividend-collecting Class A shareholders.**

> *"Give me control of a nation's money supply, and I care not who makes its laws."*
> *-Mayer Amschel Rothschild, founder of the Rothschild Banking Dynasty in the mid-1700's. His descendents are majority-owners of the Federal Reserve today.*

How does the Federal Reserve tie into the Great Plan and the one world government? We will get into that, and you will see the connection as clear as day.

Again, **the Federal Reserve is NOT a part of the federal government**---it is a privately-owned, for-profit international banking corporation that supplies our government, country and citizens with the money that we use in our economy.

The "Fed" is a CARTEL of privately-owned member banks---mostly owned by Europeans in fact---who deal in secret over the control of our economy, and by default our government........and our lives. See how that works?

> *"I am a most unhappy man. I have unwittingly ruined my country. A great industrial nation is controlled by its system of credit. Our system of credit is concentrated. The growth of the nation, therefore, and all our activities are in the hands of a few men. We have come to be one of the worst ruled, one of the most completely controlled and dominated governments in the civilized world. No longer a government by free opinion, no longer a government by conviction and the vote of the majority, but a government by the opinion and duress of a small group of dominant men."*
> *-Woodrow Wilson, 28th U.S. President, and the one who signed the Federal Reserve Act in 1913 that authorized the creation of the privately-owned Federal Reserve*

The Founding Fathers of our nation warned us time and time again, explicitly I might add, to watch out for this particular group of pirates and what they would do if we let them get control of our ship.

They warned us multiple times about the dangers of letting a privately-owned central bank (the Federal Reserve) issue our money instead of having the Federal Government Issue it---as **MANDATED** in the Constitution. You never hear them teach this fact in the public school system, and you will soon know why.

An oppressive foreign central bank was the primary excuse for declaring our independence from Great Britain in 1776:

> *"The colonies would gladly have borne the little tax on tea and other matters had it not been that England took away from the colonies their money, which created unemployment and dissatisfaction. The inability of colonists to get power to issue their own money permanently out of the hands of George the III and the International Bankers was the PRIME reason for the Revolutionary War."*
>
> *-Benjamin Franklin*

What is happening with our money system right now in our country is **ILLEGAL** according to our Constitution.

Article 1, Section 8 of our Constitution reads: (only) **Congress shall have the power to coin money, and regulate the value thereof.** Period. End of story.

> *"I believe that banking institutions are more dangerous to our liberties than standing armies. Already they have raised up a money aristocracy that has set the government at defiance... If the American people ever allow private banks to control the issue of their currency, first by inflation, then by deflation, the banks will deprive the people of all property until their children wake-up homeless on the continent their fathers conquered... The issuing power should be taken from the banks and restored to the government to whom it properly belongs. The modern theory of*

the perpetuation of debt has drenched the earth with blood, and crushed its inhabitants under burdens ever accumulating".

-Thomas Jefferson, second President of the United States and author of the Declaration of Independence

You will find these warnings among many, many others from politicians throughout the United States' history. They never tell you about these warnings in school or in the Mainstream Media because you are not going to be told what you are not supposed to know. It has never been explained to you in the public schools how our money system really works....all by the direction of the Great Plan.

"I see in the near future a crisis approaching that unnerves me and causes me to tremble for the safety of my country; corporations have been enthroned, an era of corruption in High Places will follow, and the Money Power of the Country will endeavor to prolong its reign by working upon the prejudices of the People, until the wealth is aggregated in a few hands, and the Republic is destroyed. I feel at this moment more anxiety for the safety of my country than ever before, even in the midst of war. The government should create, issue, and circulate all the currency and credit needed to satisfy the spending power of the government and the buying power of consumers. The privilege of creating and issuing money is not only the supreme prerogative of government, but it is the government's greatest creative opportunity. The financing of all public enterprise, and the conduct of the treasury will become matters of practical administration. Money will cease to be master and will then become servant of humanity."

-Abraham Lincoln

I can tell you right now that there is the highest probability that we will never pull out of the recession/depression we are in as of the beginning of 2013. We are soon going to experience the horrific crash of the runaway pyramid-scheme freight train coming down the tracks we have been warned about for over 200 years. When our dollar crashes in the near future and hyperinflation sets in, you will know the true meaning of not only the word "depression", but "tyranny".

"History records that the money changers have used every form of abuse, intrigue, deceit, and violent means possible to maintain their control over governments by controlling money and its issuance."
– James Madison, 4th President of the United States

If we are to have any hope of a promising future, you need to learn our suppressed history---the events that happened that they didn't want you to know about. The stuff that was intentionally left out, covered up, or flat-out lied about in the schools. You need to learn why we had so much death and destruction in the 20th century. It was all to enable the progression of the plan of world domination, the Great Plan.

There are millions of others who are awake to what is really going on, and there is an established movement against it on the internet, but we need all hands on deck to pull our country out of the death rattle we are in right now. We've got to come together or we are done for. They've exploited our differences over the millennia and used them to divide and conquer us. They have caused us to wage war and murder each other for their Great Plan. The New World Order is an enemy to all of humanity. There is nothing in it for you and your family except poverty and generations of slavery to come, and that's if they allow you to live. They have purposely put us under the National Debt to crush our future and turn us into true slaves to the masters of the Great Plan. Free humanity is on its last leg with one last chance to rise up and beat them, and that chance starts by waking up and rallying the patriotic citizens of the United States of America. We've got to awaken the giant that is American Patriotism. It is our only hope to unite to defeat them.

Do you remember how patriotic and energized everybody was right after 9/11 happened? If everybody was awake to what was going on, that's how our country would be like, instead of the whole "Me Me Me" attitude that permeates our society these days.

*"It is the system of nationalist individualism that has to go....
We are living in the end of the sovereign states....In the great
struggle to evoke a Westernized World Socialism, contemporary
governments may vanish....Countless people...will hate the New
World Order....and will die protesting against it."*
    -H.G. Wells, proponent of the Great Plan, in his book "The New
World Order", 1940

These people mean business, and you are going to see all the stops
they've fiendishly pulled off over the years to promote the advancement
of their agenda. Our precarious future lies in our suppressed history.
I can't emphasize enough how important it is to understand what has
happened in the past that they have hidden from us.

If you think you are wealthy and have plenty of money to ride out
any type of economic storm that may be coming, you are dead wrong. If
you think that a one world government might not be such a bad thing,
you are even more wrong. There will only be two classes of people after
the coming storm: the oligarchs and the serfs. If you have $100 million
in the bank, it will be rendered worthless in a matter of days after the
Federal Reserve's gigantic pyramid scheme comes crashing down and
hyperinflation wipes out all but 1% of the 1% of the richest men on the
planet. It is impossible for a bank to issue money with no backing and not
run into hyperinflation. History has shown this over and over again to be
a FACT, and this is exactly what is going to happen.

If you think Bill Gates is the richest man in the world, you are mistaken. There are personal fortunes controlled by the European Rothschild and American Rockefeller clans in the multi-TRILLIONS of dollars,
divested into hundreds of tax-free foundations. They wield this wealth
and power against us behind the scenes---pulling the puppet strings of
our governments and guiding us towards completion of the Great Plan.

Money is power, huge money is huge power, and unlimited money is
unlimited and omnipotent power. This is what the **PRIVATE OWNERS
OF THE CENTRAL BANKS OF THE WORLD POSSESS RIGHT NOW**---an
unlimited money supply for their private owners to use as they wish..........
and they are wishing to fulfill the Great Plan of world enslavement.

"This present window of opportunity, during which a truly peaceful and interdependent world order might be built, will not be open for too long — We are on the verge of a global transformation. All we need is the right major crisis and the nations will accept the New World Order."
-David Rockefeller, speaking at the United Nations, Sept. 23, 1994

The world's wealthiest and most powerful banking families banded together in the late 1700's to monopolize the wealth of the world, and thereby the power, and are attempting to bring all of humanity under a fascist-socialist based one world government that they intend to be masters of forever. This is the gist of the Great Plan today: **Dominate the world by controlling all the money.**

When they crash the United States dollar, and they will, we will fall into utter chaos........and the nationwide martial law and FEMA camps that they have been preparing and legislating for us in our very own Congress will be activated.

It is their intent to completely bankrupt and crash, and thereby discredit, the Federal Government of the U.S. This will be the primary reason they will use to dissolve our country and have it come under United Nations rule. The United Nations, which I will show you, was started by the proponents of the Great Plan, and is the skeleton of the tyrannical one world government that they are plotting will one day completely run the planet. No more country. No more freedom. No more patriotism. No more fun.

The total collapse of our country and subsequent fall into the waiting hands of the one world government has been meticulously planned for generations, and will happen very soon unless we do something about it.

"We shall have World Government, whether or not we like it. The only question is whether World Government will be achieved by conquest or consent."
-James Paul Warburg, son of Paul Warburg (the chief architect of the creation of the Federal Reserve) speaking to the United States Senate on February 17, 1950

It is their goal to not only ensure their power and place in society forever by creating hegemony so large and powerful it could never be overthrown, but to take control of the entire planet---and their descendents will carry on their legacy of tyranny forever.

This plan has been in motion for thousands of years; guided through the ages by various occult secret societies—and the original Great Plan is followed to this day. They are nearing the completion of their master plan to take over the entire planet, and you will probably see it come to fruition in your lifetime.

These diabolical masterminds orchestrate events like 9/11 terrorism and anthropogenic (man-made) Global Warming/Climate Change schemes to intimidate and coerce humanity----just like steering a ship..... right onto the rocks.

They utilize what is called the Hegelian Dialectic to steer the societies they control, which is a societal mind-control game of problem-reaction-solution.

This is how the Hegelian Dialectic they employ works: The puppet masters covertly plot and initiate a problem for humanity, mankind reacts just as predicted, and then the evil ones introduce the course of action they originally wanted---disguised as the solution to the "problem" that they created to start with. A main arterial of this is called a "false flag" operation, by which a violent incident such as an assassination or terrorist attack is staged in order to facilitate military or governmental action that wouldn't have been agreeable to the public otherwise.

The Hegelian Dialectic has been used by the proponents of the Great Plan to start nearly every war since our country's inception, and we will go over this later in detail.

With all of this said, we do not live in a "free" country right now---the United States of America---we don't.

Right this second, you and I don't live in a free country, and that is a **fact**. We are nothing more than indebted wage-slaves working on a plantation owned by the masters of the Great Plan.

Let me explain:

"Since March 9, 1933, the United States has been in a state of declared national emergency (martial law)....Under the powers

delegated by these statutes, the President may: seize property; organize and control the means of production; seize commodities; assign military forces abroad; institute martial law; seize and control all transportation and communication; regulate the operation of private enterprise; restrict travel; and, in a plethora of particular ways, control the lives of all American citizens.

A majority of the people of the United States have lived all of their lives under emergency rule. For 40 (now 80) years, freedoms and governmental procedures guaranteed by the Constitution have, in varying degrees, been abridged by laws brought into force by states of national emergency....from, at least, the Civil War in important ways shaped the present phenomenon of a permanent state of national emergency."

- Senate Report, 93rd Congress, November 19, 1973

What's all this martial law business about?

In the aftermath of the Civil War, the people running the federal government were facing a big dilemma. Up until this time, Congressmen were actually liable for their decisions and the actions of the federal government...just like it **should** be. It was structured like a "general partnership" in that way. In order to hurriedly rebuild the Union, the liability of going against the Constitution by the Congressmen needed to be negated in order to declare Martial law upon the people in the South.

History shows that many terrible atrocities were committed "in the name of rebuilding the Union." Liability from lawsuits that would surely come from the actions they wanted to undertake were too much for the Congressmen to bear. It was proposed that the government should form a corporation to shield the Congressmen from personal liability.

So they did.

Our Congress was coerced into forming a private corporation named "The District of Columbia", better known as Washington, D.C. On February 21, 1871, our Congress passed the "District of Columbia Organic Act of 1871", establishing the federal government as a corporation. The purpose of this corporation was to carry out the business needs of the government under the martial law aftermath of the Civil War---and everything else that was to follow, because they never rescinded the legislation, leaving our federal government in place as a corporate entity.

The District of Columbia, which is a ten mile square parcel of land, is a completely separate entity from the United States of America. **It is a legal corporation sitting on its own sovereign land.**

(As a side note, the name "Columbia" is highly significant, so keep this in mind for later in the book.)

The Act was passed, D.C. was incorporated, and carpetbaggers were then sent down to help "rebuild". This was called the Reconstruction Era. **We have been ruled by this legal corporation ever since.**

Upon changing from a body of representatives elected by the people (pre-D.C.) to a corporation, our country changed from utilization of Common Law (God's law) to Marine Admiralty Law (King's law), and as such **we went from being a free and sovereign people to OWNED ASSETS of United States Inc.** When we are electing the President of the United States, it is really electing him for the position of CEO of United States Inc.

To make a long story short, once our country and its people were beholden to the corporation called Washington, D.C., the proponents of the Great Plan set in motion to put this corporation into debt---to them.

It took them years of work, but an integral mechanism of the Great Plan, the Federal Reserve System, was finally coerced into place in 1913. The proponents of the Great Plan intended to facilitate their intentions of United States world domination by **creating out of thin air** and **LOAN-ING** all the money that was needed for the United States government to be built into the monstrosity it is today. What the Federal Reserve did and does today amounts to nothing more than government-sanctioned counterfeiting. The Federal Reserve then intentionally crashed the economy less than 20 years after their inception, causing the Great Depression, and **foreclosed** on the collateral that USA Inc. put up to borrow said monopoly money. What collateral would that be you ask? You and I and our entire country's people, possessions and land.....and this is the truth. Our entire country was foreclosed on in 1933 over worthless monopoly money the proponents of the Great Plan created out of thin air.

"It is well enough that people of the nation do not understand our banking and monetary system, for if they did, I believe there would be a revolution before tomorrow morning."
-Henry Ford, speaking of the misery the Fed caused Americans via the Great Depression

It only took the Federal Reserve 20 years to officially bankrupt USA Inc., and in 1933 the United States Federal Government was dissolved by the Emergency Banking Act, March 9, 1933, 48 Stat. 1,Public Law 89-719; with the Federal Government declared by President Franklin D. Roosevelt as being bankrupt and insolvent.

Less than one month later, on April 5, 1933, Roosevelt signed **Presidential Executive Order 6102**, the gold confiscation order. All interest due to the Federal Reserve since its creation 20 years earlier in 1913 was stipulated to be paid to the Federal Reserve **in gold**, and the government was bankrupt and out of gold to pay them with—so they took the American people's gold to give to this corrupt entity. Of course they didn't really take the gold for nothing, they gave the people pieces of paper that they were told was worth something---the same worthless pieces of paper we use for dollars today.

There was a stipulation that the interest was to be paid to the Federal Reserve in gold, but there was no stipulation in the Federal Reserve Act for our country ever paying back the principle and getting out of debt. Apparently they weren't expecting us to ever pay that back, and under their system it is **impossible to pay it back.** Don't you ever forget that the borrower is **always** subservient to the lender, and we are under the thumb of the owners of the Federal Reserve right now, today.

Two months later, on June 5, 1933, Congress passed House Joint Resolution 192. HJR 192 was passed to suspend the gold standard we had been on prior to the bankruptcy and override the gold-as-money clause in the Constitution. **According to the Constitution, all United States currency was to be in the form of gold or silver.** HJR 192 effectively bypassed the Constitution, allowing the Federal Reserve to take total control over the country via the money they were creating out of thin air— called "fiat" currency and not backed by silver and gold---and dictating by law that their Monopoly money was now legal tender. **This** is very important to understand, because this law dictated that the Fed <u>did not need to have on hand the same amount of gold as was being issued in paper dollars.</u> It detached our money from being tied to something that has tangible worth, gold, to being a free-floating commodity unto itself that was being "manufactured" by the corporation called the Federal Reserve. President Nixon furthered the damage to our dollar, and ultimately our economy, in the early 70's by taking the country off the "gold standard" altogether, immediately sending us into high inflation.

What the Federal Reserve is doing today is explicitly against what it states in our Constitution about money and how the economy is supposed to operate. Again, in Article I, Section 8, Clause 5 of the Constitution it states "..... **The Congress (not the Fed) shall have power... to coin money, and regulate the value thereof......**" It also states in Article I, Section 10, Clause 1 that "**.... no state shall...coin money; emit bills of credit; make anything but gold and silver coin a tender in payment of debt....**" This was put in the Constitution by our Founding Fathers to prevent exactly what happened in 1933---a hostile takeover of the country by a select few diabolical men.

> *"We have, in this country, one of the most corrupt institutions the world has ever known. I refer to the Federal Reserve Board. This evil institution has impoverished the people of the United States and has practically bankrupted our government. It has done this through the corrupt practices of the moneyed vultures who control it".*
>
> *-Congressman Louis T. McFadden in 1932, who was subsequently assassinated for speaking out against the Federal Reserve*

By controlling not only the Federal Reserve in the United States, but also the other central banks of the Western nations such as the Bank of England in Great Britain, the Bundesbank in Germany, and others, and by control of the international money entities such as the International Monetary Fund (IMF), the Bank of International Settlements (BIS), and the World Bank, the proponents of the Great Plan effectively have control over the world right now by default.

They run the show according to the golden rule: Whoever controls the gold (money) makes the rules.

Money is power, and if you control **all** the money, you have **all** the power.

Now that they have the unlimited power they needed, it is their intention to inflict upon humanity an all-encompassing and tyrannical one world government.

Once in place and empowered, the one world government they will control fully intends on forcing upon every human on the planet the following actions:

1. **The abolishment of all individual nations' governments and borders**
2. **The abolishment of all private property**
3. **The abolishment of all inheritance**
4. **The abolishment of all Patriotism**
5. **The abolishment of all Religion---except the one they will offer**
6. **The abolishment of all family and marriage**
7. **The culling of mankind down to a more manageable number of not more than 500 million.**

"A total world population of 250-300 million people, a 95% decline from present levels, would be ideal."

-Ted Turner, Audubon magazine interview 1996, founder of CNN, Club of Rome/Bilderberg Group member, major United Nations donor and supporter, and big time proponent of the Great Plan

In 1979, some of the American proponents of the Great Plan went as far as to erect a monument in Georgia laying out their plans for the world called the Georgia Guidestones. Erected anonymously by a secret source of financing, the Guidestones have engraved in eight different languages on four giant monoliths ten "commandments" for humanity. Also referred to as the "American Stonehenge", their plans for humanity are laid out like commandments from a god, their god. The "commandments" read as follows:

1. *Maintain humanity under 500,000,000 in per-*
   petual balance with nature.
2. *Guide reproduction wisely - improving fitness and diversity.*
3. *Unite humanity with a living new language.*
4. *Rule passion - faith - tradition - and all*
   things with tempered reason.
5. *Protect people and nations with fair laws and just courts.*
6. *Let all nations rule internally resolving ex-*
   ternal disputes in a world court.
7. *Avoid petty laws and useless officials.*
8. *Balance personal rights with social duties.*
9. *Prize truth - beauty - love - seeking harmony with the infinite.*
10. *Be not a cancer on the earth - Leave room*
    for nature - Leave room for nature

Several things are obvious of their intentions by the erection of this monument. The messages engraved on the Georgia Guidestones deal with four major subjects: (1) The need for a one world government, (2) Population and reproduction control, (3) The environment and man's relationship to the natural world, and (4) Spirituality/Religion.

Limiting the population of the earth to 500 million will require the elimination of over nine-tenths of the world's 7 billion people. **That's over 90% that need to be culled for those keeping track at home.** From the quotes I've given and more to come, the global elite don't have a problem telling us that they want most of us dead, and that's a fact, hence the name of this book.

The American Stonehenge's reference to establishing a world court foreshadowed the creation of the International Criminal Court in 2002. The Guidestones' emphasis on preserving nature precipitated the environmental movement of the 1990s. The reference to "seeking harmony with the infinite" reflects the current effort to replace Judeo-Christian beliefs with a new spirituality---the so-called New Age movement that was founded by confirmed Luciferian Helena Blavatsky, a dedicated proponent of the Great Plan.

The goals laid out on the Georgia Guidestones mirror the Great Plan-dictated, United Nations-produced "Earth Charter"—which was compiled under the direction of Mikhail Gorbachev, Maurice Strong, and founder/organizer Stephen **Rockefelle**r---all Great Plan proponents. .

The Earth Charter, launched in the year 2000, coincidentally espouses the exact same issues as on the Guidestones: control of reproduction, global government, the not-only-importance of nature but the supremacy of it and the environment over mankind, and a new-age religion. The similarity between the ideas engraved on the Georgia Guidestones and those projected in the Earth Charter reflect the common origins and goals of both, the Great Plan.

In order to officially certify the goals of the Great Plan to the ignorant masses, the Carter Administration of the late 1970's appointed an official governmental task force to "study" the effects of mankind on the world. In other words, it was intended to be an official government decree on how to begin legislating the Great Plan into global law.

This taxpayer-funded group procured a two-volume document called the "Global 2000 Report". This was presented to President Carter and then Secretary of State Edward S. Muskie. Its purpose was to project global socio-economic trends for the next twenty years, and indicated that the resources of the planet were not sufficient enough to support the expected dramatic increase in the world's population.

This report called for the population of the United States to be culled to less than 100 million people by the year 2050, this in a Federal Government-commissioned report.

This is a deadly-serious matter. The proponents of the Great Plan want the United States to crash and burn and our citizens dead in order to implement their agenda.

The proponents of the Great Plan pledge no loyalty to any flag, nation, creed, race or religion. The only loyalty they have is to the Great Plan agenda. The only thing that is standing in the way of their New World Order is the existence of a strong United States.

Do you ever wonder why you have never heard of any of this stuff I'm talking about before?

It is because you are not told what you are not supposed to know. Besides the actual proponents of the Great Plan, the only people that know what is really going on are the people who knew something wasn't right and went looking for the truth. At this point, the truth-seekers like me are akin to a mosquito trying to bring down an 800 pound gorilla. Right now, there is little hope for my country or my countrymen's future.

They own and/or control the world's central banks, the Mainstream Media, most of the biggest global corporations, nearly all of the oil and energy sources, and most of the governments of the world, and you are purposefully kept in the dark so you won't resist what they are planning for the future.

The puppet masters of Planet Earth purposefully keep you in a naïve bubble---this is the only way they can advance the Great Plan.

Very few of our elected politicians who found out about the Great Plan have dared to tell the truth about what is going on, let alone stand up to it. A number of the ones that did coincidentally ended up dead and no longer a threat. The United States Federal Government is morally and economically bankrupt. Our children will inherit a national debt so large it can never be repaid, and that was the point of the Federal Reserve to start with: to use, enslave and destroy the United States of America.

I can honestly say that I believe the American Dream is dead at this point, as our children will inherit the tyranny to enforce paying the National Debt and the austerity measures that go with it.

When the Federal Reserve pyramid scheme collapses and the integrity of our dollar with it, you will know what I have said is the truth. They are building FEMA concentration camps all across the country right now in preparation of the coming martial law after the financial collapse and you probably didn't even know that, or don't care or won't care....until it is too late.

Land of the free and home of the brave?

It's more like land of the SHEEP and home of the SLAVE.

Wake up America..........before it's too late.

Chapter 2

GOD VS RELIGION

It is a fact that religion of one form or another has been used for millennia to govern and control mankind, and the same holds true today. There was always a great question mark in my mind when it came to not only believing in God, but how could there be so many different religions. In my mind they were either all right or all wrong---there couldn't just be one right and the rest wrong. I just figured they were all wrong. I held this position for most of my life until the weight of the evidence I have gathered in this book began tipping the scales and I could no longer deny the existence of God.

I never liked the "Big Bang Theory", which basically states that in the beginning there was nothing---which then exploded, but I had no viable substitution for the Big Bang to explain how we got here. I now believe that there had to have been a supernatural beginning to the universe, you just can't get something out of nothing without some "outside persuasion", something you could only call supernatural.

I also particularly had trouble believing that mankind as he is today evolved from apes---without some outside intervention. Mankind as we know him today for the most part appeared out of nowhere in ancient Sumeria about 6,000 years ago, complete with agriculture, advanced tools, religious beliefs, and a civilized society. This gap in time between cavemen and modern man's beginnings in Sumeria is the "missing link" you probably have heard about. I believe in evolution to a point, as evidenced by the fossil records, but there is beyond a shadow of a doubt more to mankind's reality than this.

After the exhaustive research and interpretation of the facts that are in this book, I could come to no other conclusion than God exists. Then the scales tipped even further until I could no longer deny that Jesus Christ was a real entity on the Earth for a very short period of time. I believe He was sent here by the Creator God to not only give us guidance in the proper way to live, the way God intended us to live as stewards of the Earth and each other, **but to explicitly warn us of a great evil in our midst and what was to happen as a result of this evil.** I'm talking about the Great Plan here, and Jesus Christ did more to warn us about it, where it came from, and who is running it than any other man in history.

Written 2,000 years ago, the entire Book of Revelation in the New Testament is Christ warning us through a man named John what was to happen in the future and what to watch out for.....and who the evil ones were, the proponents of the Great Plan. After I was awakened to the Great Plan and embarked on my quest for the ultimate truth of what was really going on, it was troubling to me as an atheist doing research why the people spearheading the information war against the Great Plan were nearly all proclaimed Christians. It just wasn't making sense at all that people smart enough to acknowledge the facts surrounding the New World Order and that it is an imminent threat to us were dumb enough to fall for that religious mumbo-jumbo---or so I thought.

Whether you are an atheist, Jew, Christian, or any other religion or agnostic or just a plain old don't-label-me human being, this book aims to shed some light on the real truth of life on Earth as we know it today. Do not let my position as a servant of the Most High God get in the way of you doing some objective thinking and research of your own when you are done going over the information contained herein. The Great Plan affects every single person on this planet, and soon for the worse.

To be quite blunt, what is happening with regards to the Great Plan/ New World Order is exactly as prophesized in the Bible. What is going on has to do with the dark side of the supernatural guiding mankind down the path to complete enslavement, which will ultimately turn into the End Times as described in the Bible. That dark supernatural force is the stuff that most of our various religions were born of. My numbers aren't exact to be sure, but starting about 4,000 +/- years ago, different forms of "idol worship" and pantheistic (multi-deity) religions began to appear in order to lead mankind astray from our Creator, the Most High God, so the Great Plan could advance towards its end goal. These included Sun/Moon god worship and worship of inanimate idols such as Baal and Moloch. Later on this evolved into the Egyptian/Greek/Roman/Indian/etc. pantheons of gods. All of these various religions sprang from one diabolical man, who was literally the first incarnation of the Biblical "Antichrist". His Biblical name was King Nimrod and right now you are living under his Great Plan to rule the world. **He is also regarded as the original founder of the modern day Freemasons**, insert conspiracy theory here.

Now, again, this is very important, so I want your undivided and full attention **right now, right this SECOND!** Before proceeding from here, you've got to remember how important it is to keep an open mind when evaluating what I'm going to lay out. You have been conditioned by the corrupted school systems and Mainstream Media to have immediate doubt and pan anything that is "outside the box"......**and THAT is the main reason why we are in such deep trouble right now.** People blindly accept that all that they are taught or hear from our corrupted school system and Mainstream Media is all there is to the story. You have been trained to think that our public schools and the Mainstream Media represent the general sentiment of the population---**THEY DO NOT**. The school system in the United States and the Mainstream Media are compromised tools of the Great Plan, complete with a pre-programmed agenda that is presented as public sentiment. In particular, the Mainstream Media is intentionally guiding us down the path towards acceptance of their goal of a one world government.

One cannot begin to understand what is going on with the world today without taking a journey back in time, to see how and where this nightmare began, the Great Plan. The Bible, I believe, is a Divine guide for mankind and the best source to shed light on what is happening. The Bible, albeit penned by the hand of man, is such a complex story with intricately intertwined prophecies and characters that, in my opinion, it could only have come from supernatural inspiration.

Not only this, but books of the Bible that give even greater insight into past and future events were removed altogether, including the book of Enoch, which is a very important work in my opinion. The Book of Enoch was contained in the Dead Sea Scrolls, which were written before

Jesus Christ was born, and is quoted by Christ's own half-brother Jude in his New Testament epistle, giving it credence. The prophet Enoch is highly renowned by the proponents of the Great Plan, and there are reasons for this. The Book of Enoch lets too much out of the bag about what has happened in history and what is to happen in our future. Our mortal masters just could not allow this, and this is why it was removed from the present day version of the Bible. The proponents of the Great Plan have used their power over time to corrupt religion and even the Bible to turn them into tools of oppression and control by the hands of the proponents of the Great Plan.

Do I believe the Bible should be taken literally? Yes and no. I think the personal understanding of interpreting what it is saying is directly related to how in tune you are with God. I think you also have to use a dose of common sense when interpreting what it says. Do I believe the Earth is only a few thousand years old as some followers of the Bible do? Absolutely not. I believe in facts. I believe that the Earth is 4.5 billion years old as science has proven it is, and so on and so forth. I have my own views and interpretations to be sure, but we're going to keep it as simple as possible for this book's sake and not get too much into what can be better explained in another book, perhaps an addendum to this one.

I guess the main thing to remember when viewing what is going on today, is that religion has been used for the longest time to guide and control humanity, not on behalf of God, but in the interest of power, tyranny, and the dark forces acting on our planet: The Great Plan. Some of my fellow brothers and sisters in the truth movement who are atheist claim that religion was put in place by the Great Plan proponents millennia ago to purely to control mankind. I would offer the counterpoint to this that not only does it state numerous times in the Bible to fight and expose evil, but it literally tells us intimate details of the Great Plan I'm sure they didn't want us to find out about. I don't think the proponents of the Great Plan would have not only outed themselves, but recommended to their serfs to rise up against them, but to be willingly subordinate to them.

"Who will stand up for me against evildoers? Who will take his stand for me against those who do wickedness?"
-God, Psalm 94:16

There is no true separation of church and state in this country, the United States, but there is the illusion that there is. This is why churches are tax-exempt organizations under the United States government. This is why our money is stamped "In God We Trust". This is why you put your hand on the **Bible and swear to God** that you will tell the truth if you ever go to court---a government institution. This is why the President of the United States swears an oath to uphold our Constitution on a Bible---so help him God.

The phrase "separation of church and state" does not appear anywhere in the Constitution, and that is a fact.

Unfortunately for us, the great religious institutions of this world have been usurped by evil, and are purposefully leading us down the path to tyranny.

The allegations and convictions of rampant pedophilia in the Catholic Church, for example, are only the tip of the iceberg when it comes to the worldwide corruption of religious institutions.

It is important for the sake of this book to immediately address the two major players among the organized religions tangled up in opposition to the Great Plan: Judaism and Christianity. I knew this was going to be a prickly pear to address, since I have many good friends who are Jews and Catholics especially, but just know that what I'm going to lay out is only meant to enlighten all parties of what is really going on in the world.

Onward we go.

Chapter 2/A

JUDAISM

It has been rumored and even outright accused by some that there is a Jewish conspiracy to take over the world, so we are going to address this right off the bat. This conspiracy theory is intentionally promoted by the proponents of the Great Plan to muddy the waters of truth and also to incriminate the Jews of this accusation with such propaganda as the Protocols of Zion. Just as the Jews were made the scapegoat by Hitler for Germany's problems, so again will the proponents of the Great Plan blame them over what is coming down the tracks. Hitler was one of the greatest leaders of the Great Plan, and I will prove this later in this book.

I will tell you right now that the Great Plan is **not** a Jewish conspiracy, but there are "Jews" who are part of the Great Plan through their membership in the Babylonian Mystery Religion, just as there are "Christians" and "Mormons" and "Buddhists" etc. who are members. The members of the Great Plan hide behind various religious fronts when in reality they all belong to the same occult religion behind the scenes. The Babylonian Mystery Religion was in fact started by a diabolical tyrant named **King Nimrod**, who we will go over in depth shortly.

I myself thought that there was a Jewish conspiracy to take over the world for a long time, because that is the sentiment of a good-sized segment of the population whether people want to admit it or not. Throughout my life I've randomly come across people, who when we got to talking about politics and the state of the world, were of the position that there was a Jewish conspiracy in place to run the United States, if not the world.

This was my view during my years as an atheist. I harbored mixed feelings towards Jewish people because of my lack of knowledge of the existence and mechanisms of the Great Plan and the true origin of Judaism. Let's take the Protocols of Zion for example.

If you read the Protocols of Zion, and correctly interpret what they are saying, it seems that everything that is in them has come true, is coming true, or is apparently going to come true. This is because they were composed, in my opinion, by the people running the Great Plan a couple of hundred years ago, predating the alleged true source of the Protocols, fictitious works published in the mid-1860s as red herrings. If you go through the Protocols of Zion and substitute the word "Great Plan" for "Jew", you will have in front of you the virtual blueprint of the Great Plan to take over the world.

The fact that they represent a plan to take over the world that was matching up to exactly what is going on was maddening to me, and was one of the primary reasons I thought there was a Jewish conspiracy going on. That was one of the two main goals of them letting the Protocols out to start with: to put the Great Plan out there in the public realm so that if any member of the Great Plan tried to go public with the plan, he would immediately be shouted down as an anti-Semitic conspiracy theorist. Just like today, they like to hide their intentions right in front of our faces. The second goal was to create a red herring to implicate the Jews, who in reality have no hand in it. Hitler used the Protocols as a propaganda tool to go after the Jews over Germany's economic problems, the same type of problems we are going to be dealing with shortly, chiefly hyperinflation.

The Jews trace their roots back to the Biblical Abraham, who is the origination of God's Earthly opposition to King Nimrod's Great Plan to take over and enslave the world. This is the origination of the whole "chosen people" stuff you may have heard of. This is very, very important to understand, so pay close attention here: Abraham was chosen by the Creator God to represent Him and His values in the time of King Nimrod's rule, which was an occult-filled, depraved and evil world. In the extra-Biblical work , The Book of Jasher there are details of an encounter between Abraham and King Nimrod over this very issue. The Jews are hated by the proponents of the Great Plan because they represent humanity's original opposition to it through Abraham, and are a modern day reminder of it.

This was the single, hardest chapter of this book to research and contemplate an understanding of what I believe is the truth, because so much has been put out there to intentionally muddy up the water of what is really going on. I feel the guidance I have received will stand up to the scrutiny it will certainly come under by all parties concerned. It was never my desire or choice to be one to try and clarify the matter of the "Jewish conspiracy", but it was necessary in order to get to the truth in what is going on.

So. Who exactly are the Jews? Let's do a little crash course in Biblical history here:

The Jews of today are those people following the religious practices of the last remaining "intact" tribe of the original 12 tribes of Israel, which is the tribe of Judah, **and/or** those who are considered a Jew by bloodline. According to the Bible, the original 12 tribes of Israel were established by the 12 sons of a man named Jacob, who had his name changed by God to "Israel". Jacob/Israel is the son of Isaac, who was in turn the son of the Biblical Abraham. Abraham and his descendents were chosen by God to be His beacon of light, truth, and morality after the organization and implementation of King Nimrod's Babylonian Mystery Religion, aka the formalized Great Plan. God made a pact with Abraham that if he were to follow Him in worship instead of the pagan ideals put forth by Nimrod that He would reward him and his ancestors with prosperity, which He did. These "chosen people", today known as the Jews, are the decedents of Abraham and the Biblical Hebrews.

Down the timeline after Abraham, when his decedents strayed from God into paganism they fell out of God's favor and struggled. When they were just and right with God, no one could stand against them and they were prosperous. It was after the fall of King Solomon around 930 B.C. that the tribes of Israel, the Hebrews/Israelites, were split apart into two separate entities: the tribes of Judah and Benjamin in the southern part of Israel, and the balance in the north. This is how it stayed until around 730 B.C. when the Assyrians invaded and dispersed the northern 10 tribes. All of the tribes except the tribe of Judah were scattered and dissolved into the general population of the known world at the time.

This is where the Jewish/Judaic (tribe of Judah) line of heritage comes from. Judaism is the modern day continuation of the religious practices of the ancient Biblical Hebrews.

Abraham is also the patriarch of Jesus Christ, Moses, Elijah, and the rest of the Bible prophets. So, in effect, the modern day Jews are the "honorary" representatives of God's original plan for His followers, the Hebrews, through Abraham. The reason I use the word "honorary", and that is certainly not meant to disrespect Judaism, is that it is my position that with the arrival, ministry, death, and resurrection of Jesus Christ, the true path to the Most High God is now through Jesus Christ and not through Judaism. Some Jews also believe this to be true. They are called Messianic Jews, so you can still hold onto those deeply rich Jewish traditions **and** believe in Jesus Christ.

Here are two quotes from the last book of the Bible, the Book of Revelation, which tell us **exactly** what is going on with regards to the "Jews" who are involved in the Great Plan. Even though they were written two thousand years ago, they are more relevant today than ever:

Revelation 2:9 I know thy works, and tribulation, and poverty, (but thou art rich) and I know the blasphemy of **them which say they are Jews, and are not, but are the Synagogue of Satan.**

Revelation 3:9 Behold, I will make them of the **Synagogue of Satan, which say they are Jews, and are not, but do lie;** behold, I will make them to come and worship before thy feet, and to know that I have loved thee.

Even though this part of the Book of Revelation was written as a warning to the Christians at the time of its authorship, it is also meant to be applicable to what is happening today, as what was said should also be interpreted as a metaphor, much like other passages of the Bible. What was pertinent then is even more so today. What these two quotes are telling us is that there are people who are claiming to be Jews and hiding behind the label of "Jew" but are really followers of Lucifer (Satan). It is so important for us to comprehend this that **Jesus Christ tells us the exact same thing twice** in order to drive home the point, and that is to beware the fake Jews who are doing the work of Satan, alongside the fake Christians, etc. These are the Synagogue of Satan "Jews" who follow

King Nimrod's Babylonian Mystery Religion, which is the Great Plan. It is **this** group of fake "Jews" who control a large part of world finance, but certainly not all of it, and they are today the main driving force of the Great Plan due to a single family of Synagogue of Satan "Jews" named the Rothschilds, more on them in a little while.

If the Jews, the Torah-following, God-of-Abraham worshipping Jews, would realize the real truth of what is happening within their ranks, they would (hopefully) stand up to those who say they worship the Most High God but really are Luciferians (Satanists), and I'm talking about the Rothschilds and their Great Plan ilk.

The #1 harbinger of the prophesized Luciferian one world government and the End Times to follow was the resurrection of Israel in 1948---this is clearly stated in the Bible. Israel had to be resurrected for the rest of the End Times prophecies to fall into place. **Israel was in fact resurrected by the actions of the Rothschilds to initiate the End Times and I will prove this later in these pages.**

Those who know the Bible intimately will find this book to be quite an alarm clock about what is going on right under our noses, as it is all according to the script(ure).

Spearheading the plan to keep a lid on the facts of what is happening is the ADL, or Anti-Defamation League. The ADL was founded in 1913 by the proponents of the Great Plan. **This is the same year the Federal Reserve was set up and that was not a coincidence by a long shot.** It was founded not to protect the Jews, but to shield the Synagogue of Satan and the financial Ponzi scheme they were setting up via the Federal Reserve. **The main purpose of the ADL is to shout down anybody, by screaming "anti-Semitism", who would question the existence and the legality of the Federal Reserve. The Fed is primarily owned and controlled by Synagogue of Satan "Jews". The privately-owned and for-profit central banking system is the engine of the Great Plan.**

The ADL actually accomplishes the exact opposite of its stated mission of protecting the Jews, as it explicitly and intentionally groups the good Jews together with the Synagogue of Satan "Jews". The people running the ADL at its upper echelon know exactly what is going on, while the people within its organization doing the busy work under their corrupted guidance think they are working for a just cause. The ADL has nothing to do with standing up for the Jews and everything to do with making sure people won't learn about or speak up about the truth---about the fake "Jews" hiding within the Jewish community. What they are doing is muddying the waters with intentional controversy to divide the good Jews against the rest of the population. Any attack upon the Synagogue of Satan "Jews" is reacted to by the ADL as an attack upon **all** Jews, and with the help of the Mainstream Media the Great Plan controls, this hoax is brainwashed into the minds of the ignorant masses.

The Synagogue of Satan is working with other various factions of the Great Plan towards the one world government, including the upper echelon of the Vatican and an entire network of secret and semi-secret organizations that we will go over.

Chapter 2/B

ROMAN CATHOLICISM

We're going to turn our attention to the Vatican now, as their upper echelon is working in concert with the Synagogue of Satan and other various factions of the Great Plan.

The entire Great Plan power structure is shaped like a pyramid, with the inner circle of the followers of the Babylonian Mystery Religion at the very top of the compartmentalized system, and unknowing, naive humanity at the base---you and me---holding the whole thing up. Between us and them we have the societal system they own and control: banking, the economy, government, media, energy resources, multi-national corporations and organized religion.

On December 25, 2005, the current head of the Vatican, Pope Benedict XVI, in his annual Christmas speech at the Vatican, flat-out called for a New World Order, and he meant the one we are talking about in this book. We're going to go back in time here to see how and why the Vatican is willingly part of the Great Plan.

I want to make one thing crystal clear here before we go forward. I'm not throwing the average God-fearing/following/respecting Catholic under the bus here. I don't doubt for a second the sincerity of the average Catholic's faith, only that they have been deceived **as all of us have** through the agenda of the Great Plan.

After the death of Jesus Christ, His ministry began to spread slowly at first, but then like wildfire across the land. At this time, the Roman Empire was omnipotent, and ruled the entire known world with an iron fist. The leaders of Rome, the emperors and their upper echelon, were all followers of the Great Plan. This is **why** they were in power. They worshipped an entire pantheon of gods, including counting the emperors as gods who were to be worshipped. It was rulers like Caligula, whose turn at the tiller of power was defined by violence, murder, torture, pedophilia and incest, who lorded over the Roman Empire immediately after the death of Christ. It is these types of people who ruled the Roman Empire right up until the time it took over Christianity in the 4th century and became the "Holy" Roman Empire, and those practices continue right to today. This is the root cause of all the rampant sexual misconduct permeating the Catholic Church.

As the faith and belief in Christ began to grow amongst the slaves and others of the Roman Empire, the Roman aristocracy could see the writing on the wall that Christianity was going to be a force that would challenge or even overthrow their authority. They decided, instead of competing with it for power, to co-opt the Christian movement and incorporate it into their form of governmental control. They knew their days ruling the world were going to be numbered if they didn't act. Prior to this decision, those found to be practicing Christians were summarily fed to the lions for the amusement of the pagan masses.

In approximately 313 A.D., Roman emperor Constantine established himself as the first authoritative leader of the Christians, the first "pope" if you will. This led to the birth of the Vatican a dozen years later.

The pagan Roman Empire was thereby transformed into the **Holy** Roman Empire. They melded Jesus and the events surrounding his prophetic coming with the Babylonian Mystery Religion, creating Roman Catholicism.

In order to get the ignorant but substantial masses to go along with this, who were used to pantheistic worship, a new "pantheon" was set up. This is where you get the practice of Catholics praying to different entities other than God even today: Mother Mary, St. Peter, and a host of other "saints". These entities are also displayed in statues that are also prayed to.

The Second Commandment explicitly states:

"You shall have no other gods before Me. You shall not make for yourself an idol, or any likeness of what is in heaven above or on the earth beneath or in the water under the earth."
-Exodus 20:3, 4

The Catechism of the Council of Trent, convened by the Vatican in the mid 1500's, states the following:

"It is lawful to have images in the Church, and to give honor and worship unto them..."

This action by the Vatican effectively **nullified** the Second Commandment. They had no authority to do this.

To further the melding of Christianity to paganism, the Vatican, around 336 A.D., officially placed the celebration of Christ's birthday on the same day that is also the original Sun god's birthday, **King Nimrod's** (re)birthday---December 25.

Any learned Bible scholar will tell you that Christ was not born on December 25th, but was probably born in the fall season, according to various verses given in the New Testament.

The Vatican is also responsible for corrupting the celebration of the rise of Christ from the dead, now called Easter, **which is also based on King Nimrod's Babylonian Mystery Religion.**

The Vatican was born of evil, and has been promoting evil since its inception around 325 A.D. This was the start of "organized" Christianity, the form of which turns people off to "Christians" today.

This is very important to understand: Rome has ruled Europe and the world, for the most part, since before and after the death of Christ. It is only with the recent rise in power of the Freemasonic wing of the Great Plan, over the last 250 years or so, that their power has been challenged. The Vatican ultimately chose to side with the Masonic wing behind the scenes, while maintaining an anti-Masonic stance up front. This is evidenced by the Rothschild/Vatican banking relationship of over 200 years, while at the same time the Vatican refused to recognize the State of Israel's existence until 1993. **This is the year the Vatican officially**

buried the hatchet and formally joined forces with the Freemasons to work to complete the Great Plan.

Here are some prime examples regarding the Vatican and their Luciferian Great Plan agenda to separate Man from God:

According to the Ten Commandments, God dictated to His followers to honor the seventh day of the week:

> *"Remember the Sabbath day by keeping it holy. Six days you shall labor and do all your work, but the seventh day is a Sabbath to the Lord your God. On it you shall not do any work, neither you, nor your son or daughter, nor your manservant or maidservant, nor your animals, nor the alien within your gates. For in six days the Lord made the heavens and the earth, the sea, and all that is in them, but he rested on the seventh day. Therefore the Lord blessed the Sabbath day and made it holy."*
> *-Exodus 20:8*

The seventh day of the week is **SATURDAY**. This is why today if you look at a calendar, Sunday is shown as the first day of the week and Saturday is the seventh day, the Sabbath Day. This is why Jews today pay respect to God on **Saturday**. In order to further separate mankind from God and subjugate him, the Vatican, over a number of years, gradually changed the Sabbath for Christians from Saturday to Sunday. This was set in motion by Emperor Constantine, through the Sunday Law of March 7, 321 A.D. This law reads as follows: **"On the venerable Day of the Sun let the magistrates and people residing in cities rest, and let all workshops be closed."** The "Day of the Sun" is a reference to Sun worship, which in fact originated with King Nimrod.

The Council of Laodicea added to the substituting of the Sabbath from Saturday to Sunday in A.D. 364. The council acknowledged the Sabbath as Saturday, but also gave recognition to Sunday. Canon 29 stipulated: **"Christians shall not Judaize and be idle on Saturday but shall work on that day; but the Lord's Day they shall especially honour, and, as being Christians, shall, if possible, do no work on that day. If, however, they are found Judaizing, they shall be shut out from Christ."**

The Council of Trent, already noted here for sanctifying idol worship, was when the Vatican officially changed the Sabbath from Saturday to Sunday in the mid-1500's.

Was the Sabbath changed by Christ? Is there a passage to be found in the New Testament moving the Sabbath sanctioned by God Himself from Saturday to Sunday? Certainly not. Such a momentous alteration to God's divine law would have been explicitly mentioned in the New Testament, but no such ordinances are to be found. There is not a passage in the entire Bible which sanctions any change in the Sabbath day. Another deception to drive a wedge between man and God and just a part of the Great Plan.

This action by the Vatican effectively nullified the Fourth Commandment. They had no authority to do this.

The Unholy Roman Empire teaches all kinds of blasphemy, including that a Christian's soul must burn in purgatory after death until all of their sins have been purged. To speed up the purging process, money may be paid into the coffers of the Vatican so a priest can pray for an earlier release of the sinner's soul. Not only that, but the Vatican allows "indulgences"---which is prepayment for sins not yet committed. This is absolute blasphemy, again with no Biblical passages to back any of this up.

God's word is clearly against the doctrine of purgatory, and especially for trying to buy your way into God's good grace instead of directly asking for forgiveness from God. According to the Bible, Christ came to forgive us for being who we are as humans, the things we do that we know deep in our hearts we shouldn't, end of story.

Another blasphemy by the Unholy Roman Empire was by creating something called the "Mass", which they tell their followers is a continual sacrifice of Christ.

This is a completely heretic act.

The Catholic Encyclopedia states the following:

"In the celebration of the Holy Mass, the bread and wine are changed into the body and blood of Christ. It is called transubstantiation, for in the Sacrament of the Eucharist the substance of bread and wine do not remain, but the entire substance of bread is changed into the body of Christ, and the entire substance of wine is changed into his

blood, the species or outward semblance of bread and wine alone remaining." (Vol. 4, pg. 277, Article: "Consecration")

The Vatican teaches that **the Holy Mass is a literal eating and drinking of the flesh and blood of Christ.** The priest supposedly has the power to change the bread and wine into the body and blood of Christ. This is a complete and utter abomination unto God, and is in reality an occult black magic act and practice, which shouldn't be surprising since the Great Plan is the origination of the occult.

Let's be very clear here so you understand how the Vatican is driving yet another wedge between mankind and his God. Drinking blood is PURELY a Black Magic/Occult/Luciferian practice, and by partaking in this occult ceremony you are supremely blaspheming God. Why are Catholics pretending to do this occult and evil ceremony as a religious Christian ceremony? **Because the upper echelon of the Vatican are Luciferian followers of the Great Plan, and always have been, and still are today.**

Besides all of the above listed perversions of God's will, the Unholy Roman Empire has been behind all kinds of other wholesome goodness over the last seventeen hundred years or so, not in the name of God, but in the name of the Great Plan.

I probably don't need to tell you the evil committed by the Unholy Roman Empire throughout such events as the Crusades, the Inquisition, etc. However, we are going to go over some specifics of just how sadistically evil the people running the show were and are still today.

I used to **despise** Christians for the evil acts "they" had been responsible for over the centuries, especially knowing what happened in the Middle Ages. Little did I know the real truth behind the matter, and hopefully your eyes are beginning to open that things are not at all how they seem.

The legendary Crusades were only about **gaining and maintaining wealth and power, and had nothing to do with the values and teachings of Jesus Christ.**

And then there's what was called the "Inquisition".........

In 1233, Pope Gregory IX pronounced the official beginning of the Inquisition to root out heresy in the land under control of Rome, and dispatched sadistic monks to carry it out. These were literally Luciferian priests of the Great Plan. The horrific atrocities they executed can only be described as Satanic, and so far removed from how Jesus Christ taught we should treat each other that it just boggles the mind that people can't see this stuff for what it really is---pure evil.

These evil, depraved monks decided that the best way to determine if someone was a heretic was to **torture them extensively and creatively**------just like Jesus would have wanted, right?

Just to illustrate how evil the people running the Unholy Roman Empire are, here are some of the persuasive "gadgets" the Inquisitors came up with to commit their evil acts, all with the approval of the Vatican and in the name of (blaspheming) Christ. Not only this, there is not a doubt in my mind that while performing these horrific acts they were also conducting occult rituals, which is the foundation of the Great Plan:

The Judas Chair: This was a large, pyramid-shaped seat. The accused heretic was placed on top of this chair, with the point inserted into their anus or vagina, then very slowly lowered onto the point with ropes and weights. The effect was to gradually stretch out and cause duress to the opening of choice in an extremely painful manner.

The Head Vice: The Inquisitors would place the heretic's head in a specially fitted vice, then tighten until the teeth and bones were crushed, with the victim's eyes usually popping out of the skull.

The Pear: A large, bulbous-looking gadget that is inserted---again---into the Inquisitor's orifice of choice—the mouth, anus, or vagina. A lever on the device causes it to slowly expand while being inserted, until points emerge from the tips and pierce the victim from the inside.

The Wheel: Pretty straightforward. The offending "heretic" was strapped to a large wheel and then their limbs are smashed to pieces with an iron bar. The shattered arms and legs were then weaved like rope in between the wheel spokes to form a macabre piece of art.

Methods of execution weren't any less gruesome at the hands of the Inquisitors. Burning at the stake was the most common form of death, but the Inquisitors also employed other sick and twisted forms of killing the condemned "heretics".

Among these were:

Sawing: Heretics were hung upside down and were sawed in half starting at the genital area.

Disembowelment: A small slit was cut in the heretics gut, and his intestines were drawn out slowly and deliberately to keep the victim alive as long as possible......nice.

If the Vatican was smart, they'd fire up the Inquisitions again to look into all of the pedophilia problems that they just can't seem to shake.

This brings us now to a covert, highly funded and highly secretive Vatican organization named the Society of Jesus, or the Jesuits for short. Also nicknamed the "Black Assassins", they are the behind-the-scenes foot soldiers helping to ensure and promote the Unholy Roman Empire's place in the Great Plan/New World Order.

Founded in 1534 by practicing occultist Ignatius Loyola, the upper echelon of the Jesuits are Luciferians, and the vast majority below them believe they are doing good works---same as the Freemasons today.

Ignatius Loyola loved to spend time studying books about the various dead saints. In fact, he aspired to find ways to be able to communicate with these dead saints, which of course is Necromancy---an occult Luciferian practice. During the years of 1525-1528 he put into writing his new spiritual outlook on life based on his occult work, and called these writings *The Spiritual Exercises of Ignatius Loyola*.

The Society's founding principles are contained in the document *Formula of the Institute*, written by Loyola.

Jesuits are regarded for their work in education, founding schools, colleges, universities and seminaries, intellectual research, and cultural pursuits, and for their missionary efforts. Of course all these efforts hide the true nature of their purpose: propagating the Great Plan pursuits of the Unholy Roman Empire.

The head of the Jesuits, also known as the Superior General, is often referred to as the "Black Pope". "Black" in the sense used here means "secret/occult". The Black Pope is in charge of commanding not only the Jesuits, but Vatican fraternal organizations such as the Knights of Malta, the Knights of Columbus, and others. Anyone belonging to any of these **organizations is doing the work of the Great Plan and not the work of Christ, no matter what they are told or believe.**

The Vatican has long denied the alleged occult role of the Jesuits and especially the existence of the insidious "Jesuit Extreme Oath of Induction". Make no mistake, the oath I am going to show you is real, and it has been around since at least the early 1700's.

The text of the Jesuit Extreme Oath of Induction was meticulously recorded in the Journals of the 62nd Congress, 3rd Session, of the United States Congressional Record (House Calendar No. 397, Report No. 1523, 15 February, **1913**, pp. 3215-3216).

The text was subsequently torn out of the Congressional Record by an anonymous agent but not before it was copied word for word by several researchers, including Ian Paisley for the European Institute of Protestant Studies.

According to Paisley, the Blood Oath was also quoted by Charles Didier in his book "Subterranean Rome" (1843), translated from the French original. And Fr. Alberto Rivera, who escaped from the Jesuit Order in 1967 and died in 1997, confirmed before his untimely and suspicious death that the induction ceremony and the text of the Jesuit Oath were real and identical to what appeared in the 1913 Congressional Record.

Before the Oath is performed, Paisley paints a sinister picture of the private ceremony. This quote is as recounted in Didier's book and Fr. Rivera's recollections:

"When a Jesuit of the minor rank is to be elevated to command," said Paisley, "he is conducted into the Chapel of the Convent of the Order, where there are only three others present, the principal or Superior standing in front of the altar. On either side stands a monk, one of whom holds a banner of yellow and white, which are the Papal colors, and the other a black banner with a dagger and red cross above a skull and crossbones, with the word INRI, and below them the words IUSTUM NECAR REGES IMPIUS. The meaning of which is: It is just to exterminate or annihilate impious or heretical Kings, Governments, or Rulers."

"Upon the floor is a red cross at which the postulant or candidate kneels. The Superior hands him a small black crucifix, which he takes in his left hand and presses to his heart, and the Superior at the same time presents to him a dagger, which he grasps by the blade and holds the point against his heart, the Superior still holding it by the hilt, and thus addresses the postulant."

At this point, the Jesuit General-Superior Speaks and the Blood Oath is administered. The following is a copy of the text of the Oath as it appeared in the 1913 Congressional Record:

(The Superior speaks, and please note how often this oath refers to the **Masons**:

My son, heretofore you have been taught to act the dissembler: among Roman Catholics to be a Roman Catholic, and to be a spy even among your own brethren; to believe no man, to trust no man. Among the Reformers, to be a Reformer; among the Huguenots, to be a Huguenot; among the Calvinists, to be a Calvinist; among other Protestants, generally to be a Protestant; and obtaining their confidence, to seek even to preach from their pulpits, and to denounce with all the vehemence in your nature our Holy Religion and the Pope; and even to descend so low as to become a Jew among Jews, that you might be enabled to gather together all information for the benefit of your Order as a faithful soldier of the Pope. You have been taught to plant insidiously the seeds of jealousy and hatred between communities, provinces, states that were at peace, and to incite them to deeds of blood, involving them in war with each other, and to create revolutions and civil wars in countries that were independent and prosperous, cultivating the arts and the sciences and enjoying the blessings of peace; to take sides with the combatants and to act secretly with your brother Jesuit, who might be engaged on the other side, but openly opposed to that with which you might be connected, only that the Church might be the gainer in the end, in the conditions fixed in the treaties for peace and that the end justifies the means. You have been taught your duty as a spy, to gather all statistics, facts and information in your power from every source; to ingratiate yourself into the confidence of the family circle of Protestants and heretics of every class and character, as well as that of the merchant, the banker, the lawyer, among the schools and universities, in parliaments and legislatures, and the judiciaries and councils of state, and to be all things to all men, for the Pope's sake, whose servants we are unto death. You have received all your instructions heretofore as a novice, a neophyte, and have served as co-adjurer, confessor and priest, but you have not yet been invested with all that is necessary to command in the Army of Loyola in the service of the Pope. You must serve the proper time as the instrument and executioner as directed by your superiors; for none can command here who has not consecrated his labours with the blood of the heretic; for "without the shedding of blood no man can be saved". Therefore, to fit yourself for your work and make your own salvation sure, you will, in addition to your former oath of obedience to your order and allegiance to the Pope, repeat after me:

(Text of the Oath:)

I_____ , now in the presence of Almighty God, the blessed Virgin Mary, the blessed St. John the Baptist, the Holy Apostles, St. Peter and St. Paul, and all the saints, sacred host of Heaven, and to you, my Ghostly Father, the superior general of the Society of Jesus, founded by St. Ignatius Loyola, in the pontification of Paul the Third, and continued to the present, do by the womb of the Virgin, the matrix of God, and the rod of Jesus Christ, declare and swear that His Holiness, the Pope, is Christ's Vice-Regent and is the true and only head of the Catholic or Universal Church throughout the earth; and that by the virtue of the keys of binding and loosing given to His Holiness by my Savior, Jesus Christ, he hath power to depose heretical Kings, Princes, States, Commonwealths, and Governments, and they may be safely destroyed. Therefore to the utmost of my power I will defend this doctrine and His Holiness's right and custom against all usurpers of the heretical or Protestant authority whatever, especially the Lutheran Church of Germany, Holland, Denmark, Sweden and Norway, and the now pretended authority and Churches of England and Scotland, and the branches of same now established in Ireland and on the continent of America and elsewhere and all adherents in regard that they may be usurped and heretical, opposing the sacred Mother Church of Rome. I do now denounce and disown any allegiance as due to any heretical king, prince or State, named Protestant or Liberal, or obedience to any of their laws, magistrates or officers. I do further declare the doctrine of the Churches of England and Scotland of the Calvinists, Huguenots, and others of the name of Protestants or Masons to be damnable, and they themselves to be damned who will not forsake the same. I do further declare that I will help, assist, and advise all or any of His Holiness's agents, in any place where I should be, in Switzerland, Germany, Holland, Ireland or America, or in any other kingdom or territory I shall come to, and do my utmost to extirpate the heretical Protestant or Masonic doctrines and to destroy all their pretended powers, legal or otherwise. I do further promise and declare that, notwithstanding, I am dispensed with to assume any religion heretical for the propagation of the Mother Church's interest; to keep secret and private all her agents' counsels from time to time, as they entrust me, and not to divulge, directly or indirectly, by word, writing or circumstances whatever; but to execute all that should be proposed, given in charge, or discovered unto me by you, my Ghostly Father, or any of this sacred order. I do further promise and declare that I will have no opinion or will of my own or any mental reservation whatever, even as a corpse or cadaver (perinde ac cadaver), but will unhesitatingly obey each and every command that I may receive from my superiors in the militia of the Pope and of Jesus Christ. That I will go to any part of the world whithersoever I may be sent, to the frozen regions north, jungles of India, to the centers of civilization of Europe, or to the wild haunts of the barbarous savages of America without murmuring or repining, and will be submissive in all things, whatsoever is communicated to me. I do further promise and declare that I will, when opportunity presents, make and wage relentless war, secretly and openly, against all heretics, Protestants and Masons, as I am directed to do, to extirpate them from the face of the whole earth; and that I will spare neither age, sex nor condition, and that will hang, burn, waste, boil, flay, strangle, and bury alive these infamous heretics; rip up the stomachs and wombs of their women, and crush their infants' heads against the walls in order to annihilate their execrable race. That when the same cannot be done openly I will secretly use the poisonous cup, the strangulation cord, the steel of the poniard, or the leaden bullet, regardless of the honor, rank, dignity or authority of the persons, whatever may be their condition in life, either public or private, as I at any time may be directed so to do by any agents of the Pope or Superior of the Brotherhood of the Holy Father of the Society of Jesus. In confirmation of which I hereby dedicate my life, soul, and all corporal powers, and with the dagger which I now receive I will subscribe my name written in my blood in testimony thereof; and should I prove false, or weaken in my determination, may my brethren and fellow soldiers of the militia of the Pope cut off my hands and feet and my throat from ear to ear, my belly be opened and sulphur burned therein with all the punishment that can be inflicted upon me on earth, and my soul shall be tortured by demons in eternal hell forever. That I will in voting always vote for a Knight of Columbus in preference to a Protestant, especially a Mason, and that I will leave my party so to do; that if two Catholics are on the ticket I will satisfy myself which is the better supporter of Mother Church and vote accordingly. That I will not deal with or employ a Protestant if in my power to deal with or employ a Catholic. That I will place Catholic girls in Protestant families that a weekly report may be made of the inner movements of the heretics. That I will provide myself with arms and ammunition that I may be in readiness when the word is passed, or I am commanded to defend the Church either as an individual or with the militia of the Pope. All of which I,_____, do swear by the blessed Trinity and blessed sacrament which I am now to receive to perform and on part to keep this my oath. In testimony hereof, I take this most holy and blessed sacrament of the Eucharist and witness the same further with my name written with the point of this dagger dipped in my own blood and seal in the face of this holy sacrament.

(He receives the wafer from the Superior and writes his name with the point of his dagger dipped in his own blood taken from over his heart.)

(Superior speaks:)

You will now rise to your feet and I will instruct you in the Catechism necessary to make yourself known to any member of the Society of Jesus belonging to this rank. In the first place, you, as a Brother Jesuit, will with another mutually make the ordinary sign of the cross as any ordinary Roman Catholic would; then one crosses his wrists, the palms of his hands open, and the other in answer crosses his feet, one above the other; the first points with forefinger of the right hand to the center of the palm of the left, the other with the forefinger of the left hand points to the center of the palm of the right; the first then with his right hand makes a circle around his head, touching it; the other then with the forefinger of his left hand touches the left side of his body just below his heart; the first then with his right hand draws it across the throat of the other, and the latter then with a dagger down the stomach and abdomen of the first. The first then says Iustum; and the other answers Necar; the first Reges; the other answers Impious. The first will then present a small piece of paper folded in a peculiar manner, four times, which the other will cut longitudinally and on opening the name Jesus will be found written upon the head and arms of a cross three times. You will then give and receive with him the following questions and answers:

From whither do you come? Answer: The Holy faith.

Whom do you serve? Answer: The Holy Father at Rome, the Pope, and the Roman Catholic Church Universal throughout the world.

Who commands you? Answer: The Successor (Black Pope) of St. Ignatius Loyola, the founder of the Society of Jesus or the Soldiers of Jesus Christ.

Who received you? Answer: A venerable man in white hair.

How? Answer: With a naked dagger, I kneeling upon the cross beneath the banners of the Pope and of our sacred order.

Did you take an oath? Answer: I did, to destroy heretics and their governments and rulers, and to spare neither age, nor sex, nor condition; to be as a corpse without any opinion or will of my own, but to implicitly obey my Superiors in all things without hesitation or murmuring.

Will you do that? Answer: I will.

How do you travel? Answer: In the bark of Peter the fisherman.

Whither do you travel? Answer: To the four quarters of the globe.

For what purpose? Answer: To obey the orders of my General and Superiors and execute the will of the Pope and faithfully fulfill the conditions of my oaths.

Go ye, then, into all the world and take possession of all lands in the name of the Pope. He who will not accept him as the Vicar of Jesus and his Vice-Regent on earth, let him be accursed and exterminated.

Although the Freemason upper echelon and the Vatican both work on their ends of fulfilling the Great Plan, they had always been competing entities, jockeying for the highest position they could on the Luciferian pyramid of power. They are now conjoined in their quest to complete the Great Plan.

The Vatican, via the Jesuits, was also responsible for creating the "ratlines" that smuggled all of the best, and most diabolical, evil, depraved scientists who tortured millions out of Nazi Germany and into the waiting hands of the U.S. government---to be put to use for our own weapons/technology/space programs within our military.

That was how NASA was created---using Nazi scientists and technology. Our own government named this "Operation Paperclip".

Scores of other Nazi kingpins were given fake passports and sprinkled all up and down Central and South America by the Vatican. Why Central and South America? Because those countries are primarily Catholic and are for the most part controlled by the Vatican. Sure they have punitive dictators and puppet democracies running the countries, but the common denominator is that they ultimately get their marching orders from the Vatican. The infamous Dr. Josef Mengele, aka Dr. Death, died a free man living on the beach in Brazil thanks to the Vatican.

Good stuff, right? Just like Jesus would have wanted, right? **HELL NO!**

The Unholy Roman Empire, aka the Vatican, has done everything in its sordid history to distance mankind from God.....and closer to evil. The further away you get from what God wanted us to be, the closer you get to the dark, occult forces of the universe. If you are a true believer in God and Jesus Christ, the most respectful thing you can do for God is to **leave** the Catholic Church immediately.

You do not need **any** type of religious affiliation to believe in and do right by God. The form of Christianity propagated by Rome is an abomination of what Christ had intended for us. You've got to wake up.

Chapter 2/C

MORMONISM

I'm not going to spend a lot of time on Mormonism, but its founders were players in the Great Plan. I want to briefly shine a light on the Church of Latter Day Saints founders, because it is important to understand how widespread the Great Plan goes.

The founders of the Church of Jesus Christ of Latter Day Saints, aka the Mormons, were all in on the ancient plan of world domination, King Nimrod's Great Plan. Joseph Smith, along with Hiram Smith and Brigham Young, were the key figures behind the creation of the Mormon religion in 1830, and they were allegedly all **33rd degree Freemasons**. A 33rd degree Freemason is a confirmed Luciferian and follower of the religious aspect of the Great Plan. The three formed their "church" as a front for occult activity, and to open another front against humanity in the name of the Great Plan.

So, are you beginning to see a pattern here? The Luciferian proponents of the Great Plan have, over time, set up shop within their opposing sides' camps to cover their tracks. Within Judaism you have the Synagogue of Satan, largely represented by practicing Cabalists, and within Christianity you primarily have the upper echelon of the Unholy Roman Empire and Mormonism. Pretty slick, eh?

The doctrine of Mormonism teaches the age-old tenet of the Great Plan that man can evolve into a god. This is the bottom-line doctrine of every pagan religion, and is also the core belief of the Babylonian Mystery Religion, the very first pagan religious system.

Many, many witnesses have come forward with horrific tales of alleged mind control, torture, and human sacrifices that have taken place at the temple headquarters in Salt Lake City, Utah over the years. The temple itself is adorned with all kinds of occult symbols, such as the all-seeing eye, pentagrams, and other Masonic symbolism that has no place in a Christian house of worship, betraying the church's true foundation and mission.

The early Mormon Church had access to Rothschild money through their Freemasonic connections in the Great Plan, and it has been alleged that they received the funding they needed to build the Mormon empire through Kuhn-Loeb bank, who also funded the Russian Revolution and Adolph Hitler's rise to power.

On a separate note but also pertinent to letting you know what is going on, the founder of the Church of Scientology, L. Ron Hubbard was also in on the Great Plan. He was a member of the Luciferian Ordo Templi Orientis Freemasonry lodge, and modeled his teachings and symbols in his work after confirmed 33rd degree Freemason Aleister Crowley, the infamous Satanist who headed the OTO organization at the time of Hubbard's membership.

L. Ron Hubbard was involved with the occult and Black Magic and, in fact, described the evil Crowley as **"a very good friend of mine."** Although I could find no information regarding his status, I firmly believe that Hubbard was also a 33rd degree Freemason. Keep Aleister Crowley's name in mind for later in this book, for he heavily influences our society today from beyond the grave.

Chapter 3

THE GREAT PLAN

Now that you are aware that we are being guided along a specific agenda, we are going to go back in time to see when and where the Great Plan for the global enslavement of mankind originated.

To be perfectly clear, the Great Plan in the year 2013 is a single, all-encompassing conspiracy, thousands of years in planning and executing. It is not the Jews. It is not the Catholics. It is not the Freemasons, etc. It is comprised of components of all of them and more, banded together under what they themselves describe as Luciferianism.

Again, although I believe the Bible is of divine inspiration, I also believe a good deal of the contents are parables/metaphors. I firmly believe that this is why Christ often spoke in so many parables: To explain the actions and will of God in simple, layman's terms so the average man could understand the point of what was trying to be relayed. Keep in mind that man was a much simpler being back then and even up until comparatively recent times. There are multiple warnings to mankind regarding the Great Plan throughout the Bible, with the most comprehensive being the last book of the Bible, the Book of Revelation, which tells us about the (then) future culmination of the Great Plan.

With that said, I want to go to the **first** book of the Bible, Book of Genesis, to see how the Great Plan was set in motion. But, before we even do that, I need to explain to you exactly who or what Satan is.

Satan/the Devil is not some guy in a red suit with red skin and a tail, horns, and brandishing a pitchfork. If he was to appear to you in this dimension as a physical being, he would be the most handsome and even beautiful being you've ever seen in your life. Satan and the rest of the "angels" and "demons" in the Bible are all interdimensional beings and have distinct personalities, being either benign, like an angel, or neutral/ malignant like a demon. Satan is an interdimensional being with godlike (lower "g") intelligence and powers, originally created by God to be his right hand man---for lack of a better term---but he is not God's opposite. For comparison sake the opposite of Satan would probably be considered the Archangel Michael.

Satan was given a tremendous amount of power by God, doing great things for God at one time. It is even possible that he had a hand in the creation of the 3-dimensional universe we live in. This would explain the Freemasons reverence of the "Grand Architect of The (3D) Universe", or GATU, with the upper, upper echelon of Freemasonry being practicing Satanists.

The Bible tells us that Satan rules over this planet until the return of Jesus Christ to smite the New World Order and reclaim Earth for God.

> "We know that we are from God, and the whole world lies in the power of the evil one."
> -John 5:19

> "Now is the judgment of this world; now will the ruler of this world be cast out."
> -John 12:31

> "In whom the god of this world hath blinded the minds of them which believe not, lest the light of the glorious gospel of Christ, who is the image of God, should shine unto them."
> -2 Corinthians 4:4

> "Wherein ye once walked according to the course of this world, according to the prince of the powers of the air, of the spirit that now worketh in the sons of disobedience."
> -Ephesians 2:2

"Be sober-minded; be watchful. Your adversary the devil prowls around like a roaring lion, seeking someone to devour."
-1 Peter 5:8

"And the great dragon was thrown down, the serpent of old who is called the devil and Satan, who deceives the whole world; he was thrown down to the earth, and his angels were thrown down with him."
-Revelation 12:9

"For our struggle is not against flesh and blood, but against the rulers, against the powers, against the world forces of this darkness, against the spiritual forces of wickedness in the heavenly places."
-Ephesians 6:12, if you substitute "interdimensional" for "heavenly", you will better understand the realm from which these entities, Satan and the fallen angels/demons, are operating from

Satan, as all interdimensionals and humans alike, was given free will. Satan felt he had been doing so well for God that he began to get a big head over it, something we call pride, and apparently felt unappreciated. He ultimately decided that he could rally a bunch of God's angels, 1/3 of them according to the Bible, and try to overthrow God. Well, this obviously didn't work out, and I believe that this event happened as a result of, and immediately after, the seeding of mankind as we know him today on Earth approximately 6,000 years ago. I'm certainly not saying that this is when the Earth was created, but I believe this is when mankind as we know him today was planted here.

According to the proponents of the Great Plan themselves, this grand scheme started in the Garden of Eden and is literally responsible for the "fall of man". It is their position that God was unjust, keeping mankind naïve of his own power and potential and trapped in the Garden of Eden, which is another metaphor I believe, to be forever subservient to Him. They believe that Satan, metaphorically as a serpent, revealed to mankind the truth of man's potential to become gods themselves over the Earth and "live forever" through acquisition and implementation of **knowledge.** Satan interjected not to help mankind, but to spite God.

When mankind, or more accurately the people following the Luciferian Great Plan, reached this "god" status they would theoretically no longer need God as they would have complete control over everything on Earth, including being able to reincarnate themselves and live forever. In their minds this would set mankind free of his domineering Creator. This is the metaphorical partaking of the fruit from the "Tree of **Knowledge**" by Adam and Eve in Genesis, and that is the crux of the Great Plan, also called the Luciferian Philosophy: If mankind, or **a certain sect** of mankind, were to gain enough knowledge, they would become gods themselves. This is represented in the Book of Genesis:

> *"For God knows that in the day you eat from it (the Tree of Knowledge) your eyes will be opened, and you will be like God, knowing good and evil."*
> *-Satan, Book of Genesis 3:5*

Before mankind was tripped up by Satan, all he knew was *good.* It never entered into his mind to try and advance to god-status himself. Now that the seed of megalomania and disobedience was planted in mankind by Satan, man learned how to rebel against God and could discern that there really was a difference between good and evil.

It is particularly important to read very carefully what is said in the Bible in the section where the basis of the Great Plan is revealed. The whole of chapter 3 in the Book of Genesis has to do with the Luciferian initiation of the Great Plan, it was that important to address it within the first pages of the Old Testament.

> *Then the LORD God said, "Behold, the man has become like one of Us, knowing good and evil; and now, he might stretch out his hand, and take also from the tree of life, and eat, and live forever"*
> *-Book of Genesis 3:22*

The culmination of the implementation of what was revealed through the "Tree of Knowledge" leads to the "Tree of Life", which is ascension to immortality/godhood. The "Tree of Life" and the pursuit of its fruits of personal godhood is the basis of Cabbalism, an occult belief system started by the Synagogue of Satan, which we will go over later in this chapter. The "Tree of Knowledge/Tree of Life" concept---being the basis of the original Great Plan---was also carried with the dispersed workers from King Nimrod's Tower of Babel to Egypt, the Far East and other areas, where it shows up conceptually as how man can become a god unto himself. The visual representations of these metaphors also show up in various ancient religions. The Tree of Life is particularly important to Hinduism and Buddhism. Eastern religion mysticism/occult knowledge is highly regarded by the proponents of the Great Plan. This is powerful evidence of the original dispersing of King Nimrod's occult religious practices. Not only this, but the concept of man's quest for eternal life is the central theme of an ancient novel called "*The Epic of Gilgamesh*", written in ancient Mesopotamia, aka Babylon. According to some researchers, this book and its central character, Gilgamesh, are based on the life and aspirations of King Nimrod. I also believe this to be the case.

> "When the gods created mankind, death for mankind they allotted, life they retained in their own keeping."
> -The Epic of Gilgamesh

God didn't want His special creation, the humans, to be aspiring gods themselves. He wanted obedient worshippers doing what He intended for us to do when we were put here: be stewards of the Earth, take care of it and each other, and honor God for what He has given us. God is God and man is man, but Satan set a certain section of mankind---his followers in other words---down that rebellious path in a quest for godhood, causing the fall of mankind across the board. If the human race were to be left unchecked, they would eventually rise up to godlike-status on Earth, which is almost where we are today. If you were to look at a line graph of man's status in terms of intelligence/scientific achievements/inventions/etc. over the last 6,000 years, the last 100 or so years it would be in a sharp, vertical ascent straight up compared to the previous millennia of man's existence. Our knowledge of how things work has increased exponentially as these past hundred or so years have ticked by, and even more so with the advent of the computer age.

This passage from the Book of Daniel, telling of the signs of the End Times, might shed some light on the subject:

"But as for you, Daniel, conceal these words and seal up the book until the end of time; many will go back and forth, and knowledge will increase."
-Book of Daniel, 12:4

The reference to "many will go back and forth" means rapid-speed worldwide travel at will by the masses, which is possible today, but not 100 years ago. The reference to "knowledge will increase" should be self-explanatory, as we are in the steep ascent to man becoming a god on Earth.

There is only room for **one** God, and it is spelled out very clearly with the very first of the Ten Commandments: **"Thou shall have no other gods before Me"**. I could go on and on about this, but just know that this is how the concept of the Great Plan originated. King Nimrod just took the idea to the next level, incorporating it into the Babylonian Mystery Religion he created that rules the world today.

Now, God could just as well snap His fingers and make the proponents of the Great Plan vanish forever and there would truly be peace on Earth, but that would be against allowing "free will" to operate. Each and every one of us is being tested on this Earth and in this life, and each and every one of us has God-given free will to do what we want to---as long as we are not living in a police state that is, which is coming soon. The Earth and mankind are almost like God's little experiment, giving mankind the freedom to either worship Him and do what He intended us to do, or not to. It is my conclusion that life on Earth is basically a test for each and every human on the planet, to see if we use our free will for good or bad, and this will be reflected in what happens to your life-essence (your soul) after your 3D space suit, the physical vehicle for your interdimensional soul, has expired.

So going forward from the start of the Book of Genesis, I'm not going to take the time in this book to go into what happened before the "Great Flood", just know that mankind's departure from what God wanted out of us was expedited at this time by the help of "fallen angels", the so-called "Watchers" from Genesis 6:2, the Book of Enoch, and other religious sources. Again, more in-depth topics like this will be addressed in an addendum to this book, but just to let you know what is coming in the near future: What we call Extra-terrestrials today (ETs) were called angels, fallen angels, Watchers, and demons in Biblical times, and they have been interacting with humans ever since we were put here, with both good and bad intentions.

The proponents of the Great Plan are conditioning us about what is to come and you probably don't even know it. Pay special attention to a man named Steven Greer and his organization called the **Disclosure Project**, which is seeking to indoctrinate the public for what is to happen regarding the "ETs". I will elaborate more on this at the end of this book, as it is very important to understand. If you ever wondered how the Great Pyramids were built, the giant statues of Easter Island erected, or any of the other ancient wonders of the world were constructed, most if not all of them **impossible** to build with today's modern cutting-edge engineering and machinery, you now know the answer of how they got here. The engineering and construction that went into the pyramids, for example, were far too advanced for as primitive of people that existed that long ago. Only beings with highly advanced intelligence, methods and motivations could have orchestrated the precision construction of the Great Pyramids and other ancient wonders. We have been visited before, we are being visited now, and those same interdimensionals that were responsible for building these structures will be making a grand appearance and soon. The proliferation of UFO sightings/abductions/events/etc. over the last few decades is testament to what is coming.

According to the Bible, after the "Great Flood" event, civilization was virtually non-existent except for Noah, his family, and the creatures on the Ark. Here again, I believe that the "Great Flood" is possibly a metaphor for the supernatural sterilization of the Earth by God or His representatives to rid the world of DNA-corrupted beings, aka Nephilim, created by the malevolent interdimensionals. I also believe other humans were reintroduced along with Noah's kin to reestablish mankind on Earth.

The first man to break away from God and again follow the Luciferian Doctrine after the sterilization process was Noah's great grandson named King Nimrod, mankind's first "king". He is the man responsible for putting together the game plan of what needed to be done in order to elevate man to god-status, which is the exact gist of the Great Plan.

His game plan has been held tight to the chest like any good plan, this is one of two reasons why the occult secret societies were originally spawned. The other reason for the creation of the occult secret societies was to use group-conscious occult ceremonies to communicate with the malevolent interdimensionals for insight on completing the Great Plan. This was the foundation of the Babylonian Mystery Religion.

This "Great Plan" was passed down via occult secret societies over centuries and millennia behind the scenes of the various great civilizations of history: Babylon/Sumeria, Egypt, Greece, Rome, and everything in between. The people running the show today are for the most part the same occult group of people who follow the Babylonian Mystery Religion and have been running civilization since the days of King Nimrod.

Today, 95% of the goals of the Great Plan are public, and they have actually been letting it out for decades their intentions of destroying the USA and forming a one world government. The 5% of the plan that is still secret is contained by the modern day masters of the Great Plan and are the upper echelon, 33rd degree and higher, of the modern day incarnation of the Luciferian Babylonian Mystery Religion called Freemasonry. The other 95% of the orchestration of the Great Plan is right out in the open for anyone who cares to open their eyes to see, represented by The Royal Institute for International Affairs, the Council on Foreign Relations, the Bilderberg Group, the Club of Rome, the Trilateral Commission and the United Nations. These are all organizations started and controlled by the masters of the Great Plan. Nearly **all** influential congressmen, Presidents, and corporate kingpins belong to these groups and follow their globalist New World Order agenda and that is a **fact.** The agendas of these organizations are in the public arena, but intentionally never get broad media coverage due to a blackout by the privately-owned Mainstream Media. The same people who started and control these 6 organizations also own and control the Mainstream Media, hence the complete absence of this type of information in the main public arena.

You are going to see in this book the extent of evil we are really up against. It is literally like a giant octopus that has its tentacles wrapped around the entire Earth---dominating the planet as a whole since the pinnacle of the British Empire, which then morphed into the American Empire. Soon our country's dominance over the world will be (further) melded with the United Nations, and the metamorphosis from the American Empire into the Luciferian one world government will be complete.

There are very, very few major political or financial events that the Great Plan **hasn't** been involved in orchestrating or manipulating to further their goals. Nearly if not all wars, political assassinations, economic cataclysms, etc. are the result of the machinations of the Great Plan.

After gaining control of the British Empire through their takeover of the Bank of England in the early 1800's, the Rothschild Banking Dynasty and their co-conspirators of the Great Plan were able to seize control of the United States via their treacherous founding of the Federal Reserve in 1913. Whoever controls the issuance of a nation's money via the central bank in effect rules the country through the power of money. This is why it explicitly says in our Constitution that our Congress and not a private for-profit corporation should control issuance and management of our currency. That way the people, not the bankers, reap the benefits of its issuance. Now that they had control of the United States, they used the private Federal Reserve to create the money to loan to our federal government in order to build up the United States into the warmongering terror machine we know today. The trillions in profits reaped by the Military Industrial Complex went directly into the pockets of the proponents of the Great Plan, and continue to do so today.

> "In the councils of government, we must guard against the acquisition of unwarranted influence, whether sought or unsought, by the military industrial complex. The potential for the disastrous rise of misplaced power exists and will persist."
> -President Dwight D. Eisenhower, stated in his farewell address to the nation, Jan. 1961

This is why the U.S. has military bases in nearly every country in the world today, not in the name of democracy as we are told, but according to the agenda of the Great Plan. Our military is not out there protecting our freedom; they are spreading the tyranny of the Great Plan.

With the enormous amount of money they controlled through the Federal Reserve, they were able to buy up, hand-pick, and guide "their" people into political power to get the results they wanted across the board. They have literally controlled our country ever since 1913. It doesn't matter who is steering our ship, the Democrats or Republicans, these groups respective politicians all belong to the same "95%" control groups, and all push the same New World Order agenda **because it is the agents of the Great Plan who are put in place to start with**, and **that** is a fact.

If you want to find out if a President, Supreme Court Justice, Congressman or multinational corporation kingpin is working for you, me and America **or** the Great Plan, all you have to do is find out if they belong to any of the "95% public" control groups such as the CFR or Bilderberg Group. If they belong to these groups **and** are confirmed 33rd degree Freemasons or higher, you know they are extremely powerful personalities......and highly evil.

Nearly all of our nations powerful career politicians are in on the plan, bought out by the illegal and un-Constitutional money created by the Federal Reserve---this is why they were promoted to the job to start with: to help bring in the New World Order. They are all aware of the Great Plan to a certain degree, but most not as aware as **you** will be by the end of this book, and actively promote it because they enjoy belonging to the power elite and the huge and easy money that goes with it. These people have literally sold their souls for power in this lifetime, and they will regret it in the end. The entrenched politicians are usually *lawyers* to start with when their political careers begin, but go on to make incredible amounts of money as a willing part of the Establishment. What they are after even more than money, however, is power. Power over other humans. This makes them feel like the "gods" they aspire to become right now, and they love every Mainstream Media minute of it. They literally get off on it.

"Power is the ultimate aphrodisiac."
-Henry Kissinger, CFR, Bilderberg Group, Club of Rome, and Trilateral Commission member and alleged 33rd degree Freemason

A small number of the highest and most important ranking politicians and corporate kingpins are alleged to be 33rd degree Freemasons---or married to 33rd degree Freemasons. Freemasonry at the 33rd degree level and **higher** is actually a religion, the modern day religious incarnation of King Nimrod's Babylonian Mystery Religion, which is the worship of Satan. The reason I keep saying "alleged" 33rd degree Freemason is that I personally have no way to prove that. I wasn't there at their 33rd degree initiation and neither were you or anybody else that would talk about it and live if they were there to witness it. That is the whole point of a secret society, blood oaths of secrecy until death, be it natural causes or at the hands of your fellow secret society members.

What we do have, however, are various Masonic "prophets" who flat out admit to not only being 33rd degree Freemasons, but admitting that at the 33rd degree you literally are pledging yourself to the worship of Satan. We will go over this soon here, but various sources have claimed that prolific leaders of our time in political, religious and social worlds are 33rd degree Freemasons. I certainly wish that someone with the needed resources would investigate the backgrounds of the various alleged 33rd degree Freemasons and compile a report of truth, but a concerned guy can only wish at this point. Once you see as we go along here how intertwined the families and people running the New World Order today are with Freemasonry, I think you'll agree that Freemasonry is the modern day housing of the Great Plan.

The proponents of the Great Plan have been very busy over the last century or so. Manufacturing money out of thin air to fund their conquest for a one world empire. Resurrecting Israel in preparation of the End Times and appearance of the Antichrist. Guiding themselves towards godhood through science. Plotting an agenda to fulfill the prophecy of the Bible. These are the roles they chose to play. These are the roles these family bloodlines have filled throughout history moving the agenda forward and we're very near the end of the Bible story right here today.

The kicker of all this is that the proponents of the Great Plan have been deluded by Satan into believing they can change the ending of the Bible story. What is going to happen in our future has already happened on God's watch, and the end result will truthfully be as told in the Book of Revelation, with the return of Jesus Christ and His entourage to smite the Great Plan and take control of our world back from the forces of darkness.

Unfortunately for you, me and everyone else, between now and then is going to get downright **ugly**.

Chapter 3/A

KING NIMROD AND THE BABYLONIAN MYSTERY RELIGION

So, who is this man King Nimrod who has been revered by the proponents of the Great Plan for thousands of years, who has heavily influenced your life since birth, who is going to subject you and your family to great danger in the near future, **and who you've probably never even heard of before reading this book?** King Nimrod is an extremely significant character, as you are going to see, and his legacy has been intentionally hidden for thousands of years.

Although there are many elaborate stories and legends about Nimrod, particularly in Jewish Midrash and even the Islamic holy book the Koran, let's go back to the first book of the Bible, Book of Genesis to start with:

> *"Cush was the father of Nimrod, who became a mighty warrior on the earth. He was a mighty hunter before the LORD; that is why it is said, "Like Nimrod, a mighty hunter before the LORD." The first centers of his kingdom were Babylon, Uruk, Akkad and Kalneh, in Shinar."*
> *-Genesis 10:8-10*

According to the Bible, King Nimrod was the great-grandson of Noah, and is credited with establishing the first major civilization after the Great Flood, beginning his rule **roughly** around 2,200 B.C., lasting until **roughly** 2,000 B.C.

When it says in the Bible that Nimrod, which means "rebellious one", was a mighty hunter, it is not particularly talking about hunting animals. Nimrod was a hunter of men's souls. That is, it was his goal to corrupt as many souls in God's eyes as he could in order to get them to follow the Great Plan he was orchestrating.

Today's meaning of the term "Nimrod" is foolish, stupid, or idiotic---an obvious deception to hide from us the real meaning of who or what Nimrod really was, and how influential he really is.

King Nimrod not only organized the Great Plan into action after the flood, there are multiple stories of Nimrod having various interactions with the Biblical Abraham. If you know your Bible, you know Abraham to be the one who made a pact with God to be His beacon of light in a dark and depraved society, Nimrod's ancient Babylon. Nimrod and Abraham were polar opposites, which is reflected in how the Luciferians run the planet today.

King Nimrod was also the first man to individually rule and have complete control over the entire known world at the time, truly the very first "one world government". He is also said to be the first "king" ever, and also the first king to wear a crown to signify his greatness.

A highly regarded Jewish historian from the 1st century A.D. named Titus Flavius Josephus had some interesting things to say about King Nimrod:

> *"Now it was Nimrod who excited them to such an affront and contempt of God. He was the grandson of Ham, the son of Noah, a bold man, and of great strength of hand. He persuaded them not to ascribe it to God, as if it were through his means they were happy, but to believe that it was their own courage which procured that happiness. He also gradually changed the government into tyranny, seeing no other way of turning men from the fear of God, but to bring them into a constant dependence on his power. He also said he would be revenged on God, if he should have a mind to drown the world again; for that he would build a tower too high for the waters to reach. And that he would avenge himself on God for destroying their forefathers.*

Now the multitude were very ready to follow the determination of Nimrod, and to esteem it a piece of cowardice to submit to God; and they built a tower, neither sparing any pains, nor being in any degree negligent about the work: and, by reason of the multitude of hands employed in it, it grew very high, sooner than anyone could expect; but the thickness of it was so great, and it was so strongly built, that thereby its great height seemed, upon the view, to be less than it really was. It was built of burnt brick, cemented together with mortar, made of bitumen, that it might not be liable to admit water. When God saw that they acted so madly, he did not resolve to destroy them utterly, since they were not grown wiser by the destruction of the former sinners; but he caused a tumult among them, by producing in them diverse languages, and causing that, through the multitude of those languages, they should not be able to understand one another. The place wherein they built the tower is now called Babylon, because of the confusion of that language which they readily understood before; for the Hebrews mean by the word Babel, confusion..."

The Tower of Babel is a legendary structure, and it was of King Nimrod's doing. The tower was actually what is called a "ziggurat", which is a religious temple. Temples like these were built all over the world after the scattering of mankind from the Tower of Babel, with the people taking their Nimrod-inspired pagan beliefs with them.

"Now the whole world had one language and a common speech. As people moved eastward, they found a plain in Shinar and settled there.

They said to each other, "Come, let's make bricks and bake them thoroughly." They used brick instead of stone, and tar for mortar. Then they said, "Come, let us build ourselves a city, with a tower that reaches to the heavens, so that we may make a name for ourselves; otherwise we will be scattered over the face of the whole earth."

But the LORD came down to see the city and the tower the people were building. The LORD said, "If as one people speaking the same language they have begun to do this, then nothing they plan to do will be impossible for them. Come, let us go down and confuse their language so they will not understand each other."

So the LORD scattered them from there over all the earth, and they stopped building the city. That is why it was called Babel—because there the LORD confused the language of the whole world. From there the LORD scattered them over the face of the whole earth."
-Genesis 11:1-9

It is especially important to understand what God says in this line **"If as one people speaking the same language they have begun to do this, then nothing they plan to do will be impossible for them."** This is God Himself acknowledging that that the Great Plan was indeed in motion and if man is left unchecked he will eventually ascend to godhood on Earth. Now that the Earth is nearly reunited under the New World Order, and mankind's knowledge has accelerated to light speed, bringing man ever closer to godhood/immortality, God is again going to step in and scuttle those plans as he did once before, because **humans were not put here to become gods.** Only this time, it will be for good, and this is where the term called "End Times" comes into play. It will not be the end of the world; it will be the end of mankind's independent reign over the Earth, with God's designated Representative Jesus Christ taking over the show from Satan and the Great Plan.

King Nimrod's plans went south a few thousand years ago when God threw a monkey wrench in the works and confused the language of the tower's workers. According to the Bible, since the workers couldn't communicate, the tower went unfinished and the workers grouped together and moved away according to their respective assigned languages. This is supposedly how the different languages used today came about, and how mankind was dispersed across the planet. As the people moved away, they took King Nimrod's pagan/pantheist religious practices with them, which at thier root are Sun worship. Nearly all pagan religions trace their roots back to Nimrod's Babylonian Mystery Religion. The term "mystery religion" means that it is a religion in which the true meaning of it is hidden from the general public. You only learn the truth of what it really is about as you rise up the ranks through various and increasingly more sinister initiations to prove that you can be entrusted with the group's secrets.

King Nimrod's name has morphed over time, as he was reinvented whenever a "new" pagan religion was set up, which were always based on ones that came before. He has also been known as Baal, Osiris, Moloch, Zeus, Kronos, Dionysus, Hermes, Saturn, St. Valentine and on and on. All of these trace back to Nimrod. Nimrod was the only "real" entity out of all of these, being a human, and the rest are merely representations of this man who once ruled over ancient Babylon.

Babylon was the first great city to exist, was the first "kingdom", and was the capital of the first great civilization as well. Babylon is mentioned over 250 times in the Old Testament, **second only to Jerusalem in significance in Holy Scripture**---this is how important Nimrod, Babylon, and the Babylonian Mystery Religion are to the Bible story, the prophecies, and what is happening in the world today.

Although Babylon is hardly mentioned in the New Testament, as Babylon had not been an empire for over 500 years at the time of its writing, it is mentioned in the **future tense** in the Book of Revelation numerous times. Jesus Christ knew all about the Great Plan and warns us of it, and this is pointedly represented in the Book of Revelation talking in future tense of Babylon as both a city/country and the political/religious system it represents. Remember, it was Jesus Christ who gave John the visions of what is contained in the Book of Revelation.

> *"And there followed another angel, saying, Babylon is fallen, is fallen, that great city, because she made all nations drink of the wine of the wrath of her fornication."*
> *-Book of Revelation, 14:8*

> *"And the great city was divided into three parts, and the cities of the nations fell: and great Babylon came in remembrance before God, to give unto her the cup of the wine of the fierceness of His wrath."*
> *-Book of Revelation, 16:19*

"And upon her forehead was a name written, MYSTERY, BABYLON THE GREAT, THE MOTHER OF HARLOTS AND ABOMINATIONS OF THE EARTH."
-Book of Revelation, 17:5

"And the ten horns which thou sawest upon the beast, these shall hate the whore, and shall make her desolate and naked, and shall eat her flesh, and burn her with fire."
-Revelation 17:16

"And he cried mightily with a strong voice, saying, Babylon the great is fallen, is fallen, and is become the habitation of devils, and the hold of every foul spirit, and a cage of every unclean and hateful bird. For all nations have drunk of the wine of the wrath of her fornication, and the kings of the earth have committed fornication with her, and the merchants of the earth are waxed rich through the abundance of her delicacies."
-Book of Revelation, 18:2-3

"Standing afar off for the fear of her torment, saying, alas, alas, that great city Babylon, that mighty city! For in one hour is thy judgment come."
-Book of Revelation, 18:10

"And a mighty angel took up a stone like a great millstone, and cast it into the sea, saying, Thus with violence shall that great city Babylon be thrown down, and shall be found no more at all."
-Book of Revelation, 18:21

Now, why is Babylon referred to as being of the feminine in Revelation? It turns out that King Nimrod was not alone in his formalizing of the Great Plan. His wife, a former prostitute named Queen Semiramis, was the one who probably concocted the idea of integrating the Great Plan with a secret religious system, and assumed the role of spiritual leader as counterpart to Nimrod's role as political leader. For all intents and purposes, Semiramis is equally important to Nimrod within the Babylonian Mystery Religion.

Semiramis' name has also **morphed** over time, and her titles over the ages have included Astarte, Eastre (*Easter*), Ishtar, Isis, Ashtoreth, Venus, Queen of Heaven, the Great Mother, Mother Goddess, Mother Earth, Mother Nature, and dozens if not hundreds of others. **All of these are variations of Queen Semiramis, wife of King Nimrod.**

The religion they started is a counterfeit of the prophecy of Jesus Christ, and is tied to astronomy/astrology. Upon their deaths Nimrod was deified to his subjects as the Sun, and Semiramis as the Moon.

In other words, **King Nimrod was in fact the first Sun god**, and all other Sun gods that came after were based on his representation, including the Sun god Apollo of the Greek pantheon of Gods. This is very telling, because in the Book of Revelation it states:

> *"And they had a king over them, which is the angel of the bottomless pit (the Abyss), whose name in the Hebrew tongue is Abaddon, but in the Greek tongue hath his name Apollyon."*
> -Book of Revelation, **9:11**

Apollyon in Greek means **Apollo**, who again was the designated Sun god of ancient Greece. **Apollo was the Greek representation of King Nimrod.** Now read the above passage again, and take special note of the number of the passage 9:11 to remember later in this book, **9:11**.

> *"The beast, which you saw, once was, now is not, and will come up out of the Abyss and go to his destruction. The inhabitants of the Earth whose names have not been written in the book of life from the creation of the world will be astonished when they see the beast, because he once was, now is not, and yet will come."*
> -Book of Revelation, 17:8

Between the above two passages, Jesus Christ is telling us that the infamous **Beast** of the Book of Revelation, also known as the **Antichrist**, is really a resurrected **King Nimrod.** He will return to once again rule over the political and religious system he started thousands of years ago. If you think this is impossible, just ponder our advances in genetics and cloning over the last few years. If a sample of Nimrods' DNA was somehow preserved down through the generations of occult secret societies, you could easily have a "Jurassic Park" situation unfold. Think about it. We're not talking about fossilized remains that are millions of years old here. We are only talking about a few thousand years of time. This is also why I believe the pharaohs of Egypt were so carefully mummified, preserved so that one day their DNA could be intact enough to bring them back to life.

Nimrod's kingdom predates Egypt's pharaoh's rule, and it was a contingency of his followers that founded and lorded over the great ancient Egyptian civilization. I believe King Nimrod's DNA was brought there and hidden away, carefully mummified in a secret chamber among the Great Pyramids. Based on the legend of Osiris, it is my opinion that this part of his body was his reproductive organ, knowing the perverted way the proponents of the Great Plan operate. According to Egyptian legend, Osiris, or at least part of him, was the first Egyptian to be mummified. Egypt is also the origination of the obelisk, which is a representation of the male phallus. This is why I believe there is an Egyptian obelisk in front of the Unholy Roman Empire's Vatican and Washington, District of **Columbia** (Washington Monument), with both entities following the Great Plan and thus paying tribute to King Nimrod's mummified DNA sample that will be used to bring the original Sun god back to life.

A very interesting thing happened in the mid to late 1990s. The Tomb of Osiris (Nimrod) was actually discovered near the Great Pyramids. The tomb and sarcophagus were breached, but it was never let out if they found anything significant in the grave. It is also alleged that no less than the US military was on hand closely overseeing and guarding the excavation, it was that important. It is my belief that the proponents of the Great Plan are now in possession of King Nimrod's DNA sample, and he could theoretically be alive right this second. Advanced technologies hidden away in federal government black ops labs are typically 20 years or so ahead of what is let out to the general public, so I believe they definitely had the means to bring Nimrod back to life immediately upon getting their hands on his DNA.

This is also the probable reason for the eye of Osiris/Horus (Nimrod) being on top of the pyramid on the back of our nation's Great Seal, and also on the back of our one dollar bill. Nimrod's DNA has been in Egypt since ancient times, and the eye represents Nimrod watching over his Great Plan from the Abyss, with his DNA right there at the pyramids, waiting to be brought back to life so he could again rule the world using the system he put in place millennia ago.

It says in the Bible that Satan himself will empower the Antichrist, probably meaning that it will take Satan's supernatural power to retrieve Nimrod's soul from another dimension, **the Abyss noted above**, and put it in his newly resurrected body, truly bringing Nimrod back to life and fulfilling the goal of the Great Plan all along: for man to become a god on Earth and "live" forever like gods through knowledge, i.e. modern day DNA/genetics technology.

And on a side note here, this is why mankind's ultimate achievement of all time, the race to and landing on the moon, was named the "Apollo" space program. This was the ultimate demonstration at that time of mankind's advancing knowledge and the final drive towards godhood via the Great Plan. They paid direct homage to Nimrod via his pseudonym Apollo. This is also why the first space shuttle ever launched was named Columbia. Columbia is another name for Queen Semiramis, and it was her turn to be honored by the proponents of the Great Plan.

The gist of the story of Nimrod and Semiramis is that it is a counterfeit of the story of the prophesized Messiah, who finally showed up as Jesus Christ. In a nutshell, the story goes that Semiramis was Nimrod's **mother**, who he incestuously married. Nimrod died at some point of his reign, and Semiramis bore a son not long after---allegedly supernaturally conceived by the deified Nimrod and born **on December 25th**. She claimed that her newborn son was an "immaculate conception" by the Sun god Nimrod, and that the baby was the promised seed, the "savior'", as promised by the Creator God to the people after the Luciferian-incited "fall of man". This baby was named Tammuz.

The date of December 25 was ceremoniously picked because this has to do with the Winter Solstice. December 25th is the day that the Sun begins to rise higher in altitude against the horizon in the Northern Hemisphere, resulting in longer days. In the occult world this is meant to represent the return of the Sun, which is Nimrod reincarnated as Tammuz.

This counterfeit prophecy by the Babylonian Mystery Religion of an immaculate conception by a god of the savior of mankind predates all others that followed, and has been replicated over and over though the ages in other pagan systems. In Egyptian mythology it was Isis and her son Horus. In Hinduism it is Devaki and her son Krishna. In Buddhism it is Maya and Buddha. There are untold others, many with birthdays on December 25—as with the original Semiramis/Tammuz.

You are probably going to be a little unnerved about the **fact** that the two biggest holidays for Christians, Christmas and Easter, **are based on King Nimrod's Babylonian Mystery Religion:**

> "The real origin of Christmas goes back to ancient Babylon. It is bound up in the organized apostasy with which Satan has gripped a deceived world these many centuries! In Egypt, it was always believed that the son of Iris (Egyptian name for "Queen of Heaven") was born December 25th. Semiramis also bore the title "Queen of Heaven" - and she was Nimrod's mother. Paganism celebrated this famous birthday over most of the known world for centuries before the birth of Christ.
>
> Nimrod started the great organized worldly apostasy from God that has dominated this world until now. Nimrod married his own mother, whose name was Semiramis. After Nimrod's death, his so-called mother-wife, Semiramis, propagated the evil doctrine of the survival of Nimrod as a spirit being. She claimed a full-grown evergreen tree sprang overnight from a dead tree stump, which symbolized the springing forth unto new life of the dead Nimrod. On each anniversary of his birth, she claimed, Nimrod would visit the evergreen tree and leave gifts upon it. December 25th, was the birthday of Nimrod. This is the real origin of the Christmas tree."
>
> -"The Plain Truth About Christmas", David J. Stewart

> "December 25 was highly honored and recognized by Nimrod's supporters...Many centuries later this pagan custom was "Christianized" as being the birthday of Christ."
>
> -"The True Origin of Christmas and Other Holidays", The Gilead Institute of America

"Nimrod was a great grandson of Noah. Nimrod became a "mighty tyrant in the face of Jehovah." Much of the Babylonian worship was carried on through mysterious symbols - thus the "Mystery" religion. This system of idolatry spread from Babylon to the nations, for it was from this location that men were scattered over the face of the earth (Gen. 11:9). As they went from Babylon, they took their occult worship and its various mystery symbols with them."

-"Babylon: Mystery Religion", Ralph Woodrow

Every Christmas when you buy a Christmas tree, exchange gifts, or burn a Yule log, you are partaking in the Luciferian (Satanic) Babylonian Mystery Religion and you didn't even know it.

"Traditionally, a yule log was burned in the fireplace on Christmas Eve and during the night as the log's embers died, there appeared in the room, as if by magic, a Christmas tree surrounded by gifts. The yule log represented the sun-god Nimrod and the Christmas tree represented himself resurrected as his own son Tammuz. So our Christmas tree -- and our yule log -- have tremendous meaning, but not a Christian meaning. The yule log is the dead Nimrod, human ruler of ancient Babylon, who was eventually deified as the sun incarnate, and hence a god. The Christmas tree is mystical Tammuz, the slain god come to life again"

-"After Armageddon", John A. Sarkett,

"Jesus Christ was NOT born on December 25. But December 25th can be traced back to Genesis and a man named Nimrod. Nimrod was the founder of a great false religious system that began in ancient Babylon that has always opposed the truths of God. It's time we face facts! This world is deceived, just as God prophesied it would be (Rev. 12:9). Satan is the power behind this deception. Satan has successfully pawned off the old customs of the Babylonian mystery religion as being pleasing to Jesus Christ."

-*"Why Christmas is (Not) So Important to God", Carl Hilliker and Mark Jenkins, December 2002 article in The Trumpet*

I hope you're beginning to see that we've been grossly misled as to how things really are and who is pulling the strings behind the scenes in the world today.........

> *"Christmas as a pagan holiday traces back thousands of years before to a man named Nimrod, founder of ancient pagan Babylon. Babylon's false worship is found today in every nation and in some aspect in nearly all religions, including present day Christianity "*
> -*"Christmas Unwrapped", from the History Channel, by Alan Mansager*

> *"December 25th was celebrated as Nimrod's birthday. Generally, all mankind is fast asleep, dreaming this old Babylonian dream."*
> -*"The Story of Nimrod, As It Relates To Christmas and Easter", Wilhelm J. Wolfaardt,*

> *"Egyptian and Babylonian antiquities identify Nimrod's mother as Semiramis, and his birthday was celebrated on 25th December. Thus began the worship of Semiramis and the child-god, and the whole paraphernalia of the Babylonian religious system. The Roman Pagans used to celebrate the birthday of their child-god on 25th December, and the Roman Catholic Church sought to win over as many people as possible to nominal Catholicism by proclaiming the same day to be the birthday of Jesus. So the Pagans had no difficulty worshipping the Catholic Madonna and child. They were seen as yet another manifestation of the Babylonian Queen of Heaven (Semiramis)and her son (Nimrod). The Pagans made no compromises, they didn't need to, they just continued their Pagan worship within the church. While it's easy to knock the Catholic Church because of their Maryolatry, the Protestants cannot be left off the hook. The Protestant Reformation dispensed with only a part of the Babylonian system of worship. The celebration of Christmas,*

inherited from the Roman Catholic Church, via Pagan Rome, via Egypt, via Babylon, is still practiced as the most important event in the Protestant Christian calendar, so from that point of view the Protestants are as much into Paganism as the Catholics. The Christmas tree is specifically a Babylonian symbol. On Christmas Eve the Yule Log is thrown onto the fire.On Christmas Day there is the tree, covered in decorations and surrounded with presents, representing the resurrected Nimrod of Babylon."
     -*"The True Meaning of Christmas", Mike Gascoigne, 1996*

Now, let's take a look at the hero of Christmas, **Santa**, now that you've got your blinders off.

The real reason Santa is magic and can transform himself into fire to go up and down the chimney is because he is meant to be a modern day representation of a Sun god....**namely King Nimrod**. All the way back from ancient times, fire is viewed as the earthly representation of the Sun. **Nimrod** is the one who, from ancient times, Biblical times, has to do with the evergreen tree and presents left for his followers. Santa is just a modernized version of Nimrod.

The red-colored suit Santa (anagram for **Satan** by the way) wears is representative of fire, which of course is ultimately representative of the Sun god King Nimrod. This is where the Christmas colors of red and green come from: red = fire, which is Nimrod as the Sun, while green = Tammuz as the evergreen tree.

This is the same Santa who is full of magic, can see you when you're sleeping, knows when you're awake, etc. He also has a list of those who are either in his favor, or not. In reality, those on the "nice" list are those who ignorantly toe the line of the New World Order masters and don't question anything that is going on. Those on the "naughty" list are those who would oppose the Luciferian New World Order and the Police State that Nimrod's minions are setting up in the United States as you read this. We'll go over what gets you put on the 'naughty list' towards the end of this book.

Santa is also sometimes referred to as St. Nick. "Nicolas" is the Greek version of the name Nimrod, and another name for Satan/the Devil is "old Nick". Out of all the possible names for Santa, it just happens to be

St. "Nick"? There is also reference to the "Nicolaitans" as being enemies of Jesus Christ in the Book of Revelation. Knowing what I know now I don't believe for a second that it is a coincidence that Santa was bestowed the title of St. Nick.

It seems the more pagan and materialistic we've become, the more important and magical-feeling Christmas has become. This is because it is based on supernatural occultism. That magical feeling you get around Christmas is the result of group-conscious thought paying homage to the original Sun god, the mastermind of the Great Plan, King Nimrod. That feeling you get is literally **real black magic working on you**, and it is similar to being on some sort of mind-altering drug.

Let's shine the light of truth on **Easter** now:

> *"Lent, Easter and Christmas are of Babylonian origin."*
> *-"Easter and Christmas paganism 2000 B.C. to date", Edward* Stevens

Easter was originally the celebration of the resurrection of Tammuz, and this is a **fact**. It has absolutely nothing to do with Christ's resurrection. This is very important to understand.

According to Babylonian legend, Tammuz was born on December 25 but was later slain by a wild boar, and through the weeping of Semiramis he sprang back to life in the Spring on Easter as the vegetation.

Easter falls immediately after the observance of the forty days of Lent. According to legend, when Tammuz died, the followers of Semiramis joined her in grieving over the death of her son Tammuz for forty days. This was later Christianized by the Unholy Roman Empire as Lent. The practice of observing the death and resurrection of Tammuz is even noted in the Old Testament:

> *"Then he brought me to the door of the gate of the Lord's house which was toward the north; and, behold, there sat women weeping for Tammuz."*
> *-Ezekiel 8:14*

So how do the "Easter rabbit" and "Easter eggs" fit into this equation?

The rabbit is well known as a symbol of fertility. Semiramis is also known as the goddess of fertility.

The egg is also a symbol of fertility, and was allegedly a sacred symbol in ancient Babylon due to a fable about the goddess of fertility, Semiramis. They believed a huge egg fell from Heaven into the Euphrates River, and out of this egg the goddess Semiramis (Eastre) was hatched. The egg came to symbolize the goddess "Eastre", **which is also where the name "Easter" comes from.**

Not only is everything about Christmas and Easter we just reviewed complete blasphemy, but by establishing "Holy" days associated with imaginary characters that turn out not to be true, this intimately affects a child's view of God. They were lied to about two of their most beloved heroes, Santa and the Easter Bunny, so how are they supposed to believe in another invisible being that they can't see but are told is real? Just another diabolical scheme by the Great Plan to drive a wedge between mankind and God.

Halloween is also based on the Babylonian Mystery Religion, and when you Google and cross-reference this, you will see I am telling the truth.

> *"The first Halloween ritual was celebrated thousands of years ago in the post-Flood world in Mesopotamia (now called Iraq). While we do not know the exact name of this ancient festival, we do know that it involved worship of fire and serpents; astrology; witchcraft; magic; communicating with the spirits; and human sacrifice. The first of these festivals was instituted by Nimrod at the Tower of Babel. Nimrod was a mighty leader of the Babylonian people and he persuaded them that he was a god who had come down to earth and as such, was to be worshipped. The Babylonian people worshipped him under a variety of names and titles such as Samas – the Sun God, Marduk, Merodach, Ninus, Bel / Baal, Attis – the list is practically endless. Nimrod, along with his wife, founded what the Bible refers to as Mystery Babylon – a pagan, false religious system that included worship of many gods and goddesses, fire, serpents, the sun and moon, and the planets."*
> *-"Traditions: The Real Origins of Halloween", J. R. Terrier, 2007*

"The Bonfires of Halloween - were originally called - "bone" Fires - "Sacrificial victims were led through the streets of the village by "MASKED" Celtic priests, the Druids, who ceremonially offered the victims to the Lord of Death, Satan. From the death agonies of the "living" victim placed on the altar of sacrifice, the priests divined the future of the village from the way the soul departed the body. This custom originated in BABYLON where the Babylonian priests' prayed to the symbolic deity - Nimrod. The victims were furiously consumed by the roaring flames, and in the morning, all that was left were the bones and ashes. Today without realizing it, people everywhere practice a similar ritual during the Harvest Festival, not as "bone fires," but as "bon fires."

-"The Dark Night of the Soul: Halloween", Lampholder Newsletter, October 1998

"When we think about the history of Halloween we generally trace its roots back to the time of the Druids in England, Scotland and Ireland. In truth, its roots go much further back than that. The celebration of the "Lord of the Dead" (later known as Halloween) can be traced to ancient Babylon and to the trinity worship of Nimrod, the sun god and his son Tammuz, and the Queen of heaven Semiramis, wife of Nimrod, mother of Tammuz. When Julius Caesar entered the British Isles he was amazed to find that the Druids had adopted the complete Chaldean (Babylonian) system -in almost its pure form. In these gruesome ceremonies, the bodies of the victims were often eaten by the priests. It is interesting to note that the Chaldean (Babylonian) word for priest is "Cahna" and the word for lord is "Baal" hence, "Cahna-Baal" or priests of Baal (Nimrod) from which we derive our English word for the eaters of human flesh, cannibal."

-"Halloween, the Counterfeit "Last Great Day", Carl R. Dillenback

"Have you ever wondered where the heinous pagan worship rituals of the Druids originated? I have. As it turns out it goes all the way back to Nimrod, who built Babel or Babylon. He conceived a one world government model in rebellion against Jehovah-God

and went about to establish a one world government in the land of Shinar - which is today known as Iraq. Nimrod instituted a pagan worship system that rejected the Lord God Jehovah. Instead the primary false god worshipped was Nimrod - called Baal (Syrian & Phoenician), Bel (Assyrian), Moloch or Moloch (Ammonites), Ra or Re (Egyptian) to name just a few. Here is why that is important. The American Book of Days says, "Many of Halloween's customs are derived from the ancient Baal Festivals."
-The History of Halloween, Pastor David L. Brown, Ph.D., 1998

"From ancient Babylon, this diabolical mystery religion and the pagan rituals associated with it spread to Egypt, Asia, North and South America – all over the world. As Halloween, it is now firmly entrenched in mainstream, modern society where it has become high on the list of many people's favorite celebrations. Dressing in scary costumes and going trick-or-treating are only a few of the customs of our traditional Halloween celebration which come to us right from the world of the occult and paganism."
-Traditions: The Real Origins of Halloween, J. R. Terrier, 2007

Believe it or not, **Valentine's Day is also based on King Nimrod**. The mascot of Valentine's Day, the bow-wielding Cupid looking to shoot someone in the heart, is meant to represent Nimrod, the "mighty hunter" of the days of ancient Babylon.

I'll leave the nuts-and-bolts information on Valentine's Day for you to discover. Just go to Google search and type in "Valentine's Day Nimrod" and you will see the truth of the origin of Valentine's Day.

So. All of our Holidays are based on this one guy, the guy who founded the Babylonian Mystery Religion that runs the world today. All of these days are called "Holidays", which is short for "Holy Days". Another terrible deception, as they should really be called **Unholy** days. As disturbing it is to say, **by celebrating any of these days you are in actuality blaspheming God, and that is the 100% truth.**

From this moment forward, whenever those holidays are celebrated by the unknowing masses, you will know the real truth behind them, the real truth of the matter.

What you just read is the gist of what you need to know about King Nimrod/Semiramis/Tammuz/Babylonian Mystery Religion to get you pointed in the right direction. The Great Plan completely and utterly dominates the world as you are hopefully beginning to see. This man King Nimrod is going to be brought back to life and a modernized Babylonian Mystery Religion will be the religious/political system of the End Times. There is nowhere on the face of the Earth you can go to get away from it, so you might as well educate yourself about it and what the Great Plan's agenda for the future holds......if they get their way.

You aren't going to like it.

Chapter 3/B

OCCULTISM AND EMPIRE

After King Nimrod and Semiramis faded into Biblical history, their legacy stayed alive under the umbrella of pantheism, meaning multiple-god worship. Pantheism for the masses in itself is not direct worship of Satan; this is always reserved for the upper echelon of the Great Plan. The people would not fall for direct worship of Satan, as this would by default substantiate the existence of God---who they should be worshipping. As long as Satan and his minions can deceive mankind into worshipping something other than the Most High God, then his goal of corrupting man in the eyes of God is satisfied.

Throughout history up until today, it is only the elites of the Great Plan who knew who their religious practices were paying homage to: **Satan.** It is the supernatural power emanating from the entity Satan and other interdimensionals that guides Nimrod's followers to the forefronts of societal power. Today, the religious aspect of the Luciferian Great Plan primarily rests on the shoulders of the upper, upper, **upper** echelon of the secret society called the Freemasons, those of the 33rd degree and higher, and secondly with the upper echelon of the Unholy Roman Empire. The people running the planet are quite open to the fact that they worship Satan/Lucifer--- I'm going to show you this in their own words in the next chapter.

The various Freemasonic "prophets" such as Albert Pike, Helena Blavatsky, Alice Bailey, Manly P. Hall, and others all confirm the Luciferian doctrine known as the Great Plan rests upon the shoulders of the 33rd degree and higher Freemasons of today, and that

the Freemasons are the modern day torchbearers of King Nimrod's Babylonian Mystery Religion.

Although it is not taught in our history-sterile schools, it is the people who follow and execute the Great Plan who are always in power. It is because these people are consistently the most ruthless, vile, perverted, wicked, bloodthirsty, backstabbing and diabolical of all---those who live and breathe evil. This is also why all the great societies and empires of world history fell---they became too evil under their guidance and basically cannibalized themselves. We are going through this in the United States right this second.

When you analyze the facts, you will find that the entire Western Civilization as we know it had its foundations in the Great Plan/Babylonian Mystery Religion. All of the great civilizations of history were pantheistic, not monotheistic like Judaism or Christianity, and pantheism originated with King Nimrod and the Babylonian Mystery Religion.

These megalomaniacs create and rule empires based on powerful ancient occult knowledge that has been passed down over millennia. They establish an empire; lose control of the runaway freight train of degeneracy they created and then gorged on, and then attempted to keep their creation from crashing and burning to the ground through implementation of a police state. It always without fail ends like this, and **the United States is on this same path right now, right this second.**

Although their empires always end up disintegrating, the occult Great Plan **doesn't** and is passed on to the next empire, starting again in a new location, always trying to get to the end goal of the Great Plan: turning themselves into gods over their empire by corrupting it and specifically turning the society into a rebellion against the Most High God. After the United States falls, the next empire up to bat will be the prophesized one world government, the one to end them all.

Again, all great empires of the past were, **without question**, centered on pagan/pantheistic worship---which were again derived from King Nimrod's model known to you now as the Great Plan, and to be more precise should be called the **Occult** Great Plan.

Since you may have some confusion as to what the term "occult" really means, let's look at a definition of the word.

The word "occult" is derived from the Latin word occultus, which means **clandestine, hidden or secret.** The terms "esoteric" and "arcane" have very similar meanings, and the three terms are interchangeable, being used extensively by the various Freemasonic prophets to describe their religious beliefs.

Occult practices include black magic, alchemy, extra-sensory perception (ESP), astrology, spiritualism, necromancy, and divination among other supernatural involvements. All of these practices and more are contained within the religious aspects of the Great Plan. Occultism and its concepts can be found in the belief structures of paganism, Gnosticism, Hermeticism, Wicca (the Druids), Cabbalism, Theosophy, Satanism, Thelema, and many others.

For all intents and purposes, occultism is synonymous with Luciferianism, and is in direct opposition to the direction of the Most High God. Here is what God has to say about the occult:

> "When you enter the land the LORD your God is giving you, do not learn to imitate the detestable ways of the nations there. Let no one be found among you who sacrifices their son or daughter in the fire, who practices divination or sorcery, interprets omens, engages in witchcraft, or casts spells, or who is a medium or spiritist or who consults the dead. Anyone who does these things is detestable to the LORD; because of these same detestable practices the LORD your God will drive out those nations before you. You must be blameless before the LORD your God. The nations you will dispossess listen to those who practice sorcery or divination. But as for you, the LORD your God has not permitted you to do so."
> -Deuteronomy 18:9-14

Now, we're not talking about Harry Potter-type make-believe magic here. We are talking about the real deal: black-magic-invoking-human-sacrificing-blood-drinking-demon-conjuring-evil. If you believe in God, you, by default, automatically open your beliefs to the existence of magic, etc., especially when it says in the Bible that this stuff is real and we are not "permitted to do so" as the above Biblical quote reads.

Again, to drive the importance of this point home here, the reason God speaks out against this stuff is because it is **real.** That is why it is **oc-cult,** or **"secret knowledge"**. That is, the truth of this supernatural power is hidden from the general public because it is real and it is being used against us in order to advance the agenda of the Great Plan. Remember what "supernatural" really means: not of our world, the "natural" world. The 3D world we live in. It has to do with interacting with dimensions of reality that are not in our realm. I know this is deep stuff, but please keep your mind open at least until you've read this entire book to see how bad of a spot we've been put in.

It is of the supernatural, and utilizing the supernatural to advance man's path to godhood on Earth that was taught to mankind by the original fallen angels hundreds of years before the Great Flood event, the Watchers. Perhaps you have heard the term "sacred geometry". This has to do with the occult and the hidden knowledge and use of symbols and geographic locations to conjure supernatural knowledge/favors from these evil forces. If you go on the internet to Google Images and type in "sacred geometry", the vast majority of the images that show up are pentagrams, hexagrams, and variations of the image of the "Tree of Life". The "Ouija Board" is a good example of using symbols to conjure/invite spirits via the supernatural. If you willingly invite them into your sphere of consciousness and offer up symbols showing your sincerity, they will be more than happy to come into this dimension and interact with you. This occult knowledge of how to tap into the supernatural has been passed down through the ages all the way to today's Freemasonic elite. The upper echelon of the Great Plan have this occult thing down to a venerable science: they are the ultimate masters of the occult. The upper echelon of Freemasons are highly revered by the actual "Satanism" community, according to compelling testimony from former Satanists who did a one-eighty and ran for their lives to God and Christ to save their souls. This is why throughout the Bible, God tells his followers to avoid the occult like the plague: it was born of evil, by evil, only to be used for evil.

I could spend literally hundreds of pages here talking about the various empires such as the Egyptian, Medo-Persian, Greek, Roman empires and everything in between and how they followed various incarnations of the Babylonian Mystery Religion/ Great Plan, rose up to ultimate power, and then met their demise, but that would take too long. **Way too long**. It is enough to know that every one of them without exception rose and fell because they were ruled by occultists following the Great Plan and the society was corrupted and fell---just like what we are in the midst of today in our country, the USA.

Since you now know how these empires were raised up and then fell, let's focus briefly on the "recent" secret societies that were instrumental for keeping the Great Plan moving forward since the time of Jesus Christ coming to explicitly warn us of it. You've got to keep in mind, the occult has been just what the name implies---a secretive movement. These people didn't let out much documentation for future generations to discover and use against them, holding their cards tight to their chest. I'm just going to tell you the most pertinent parts of what has happened, as to tell you everything would be too much to contain in a single book. To be sure, you will have plenty of homework to do when you are done with this book.

For the most part, prior to the arrival of Jesus, the Great Plan was able to exist unchallenged in the upper echelons of the ruling political forces of the day and was semi-secret---as people gleefully followed the deviant path they were always led down, just like today in America. With the coming and ministry of Jesus Christ, people were suddenly offered a different path to go down for spiritual fulfillment, one of goodness instead of the usual moral debauchery.

After Christ's time, Christianity began to spread like wildfire. After the Roman Empire co-opted Christianity to use it as a tool to rule over the ignorant masses, the occult aspects of the Great Plan were largely forced underground.

"The rise of the Christian Church broke up the intellectual pattern of the classical pagan world. By persecution of this pattern's ideologies it drove the secret societies into greater secrecy; the pagan intellectuals then reclothed their original ideas in a garment of Christian phraseology, but bestowed the keys of the symbolism only upon those duly initiated and bound to secrecy by their vows."

-Manly P. Hall, 33rd degree Freemasonic "prophet" in his book "The Secret Destiny of America"

This is where two different factions of the Great Plan came into being. The original one being flat out Babylonian Mystery Religion Luciferianism ran chiefly by the Synagogue of Satan, and the second being the same Babylonian Mystery Religion-with-a-Christian-façade, the Unholy Roman Empire. Both of these branches were ruled by individual competing factions of the Great Plan. The Vatican in fact tried to stamp out the other through the elimination of the Knights Templar, and then again later through the Inquisition. There is no love between these two groups, only the same bloodthirsty, backstabbing grab-all-you-can power hungry megalomaniacs. Bad news for us, as I told you, is these two groups have now merged and is just one more sign we are on the fast track to bad times ahead.

So, let's keep this moving along and go over the infamous Knights Templar.

Aside from the Unholy Roman Empire, the competing aspect of the Great Plan stayed largely underground for over a thousand years, driven deep under by the Vatican, until an organization called the Knights Templar came onto the scene in the year 1119. Another very significant event happened shortly after the founding of the Templars: the written form of the Synagogue of Satan's Cabbala appeared. The Cabbala is often referred to as "Jewish mysticism", when is should be more accurately called Synagogue of Satan mysticism, or just flat out Great Plan occultism, which is where it really originated.

Varying accounts place the composition of the Book of Zohar, the central text of Cabbalism, anywhere from the 2nd to 14th century CE. I believe it appeared early in the existence of the Templars. Putting the Cabbala, which represents a large part of the supernatural aspect of the Great Plan, into writing to be consumed by the masses was the next logical step for the proponents of the Great Plan, as this would draw more followers into their circles of power and further bring supernatural influence over the world.

The Cabbala/Kaballah consists of coded esoteric writings, unable to be properly deciphered without occult knowledge, and, again, is the earliest written form of the supernatural aspect of the Great Plan. Unless you were in the upper echelon of the Great Plan and/or an experienced occultist, you would have no clue how to interpret what the Cabalistic writings were truly saying. This is also where the term "cabal" comes from, which means:

1. A group of conspirators or plotters, particularly one formed for political purposes.
2. A secret plot or conspiracy, especially a political one
3. An exclusive group of people

Does this definition sound like today's proponents of the Great Plan, secretively plotting to bring in their one world government and elevate themselves up as gods over us? I would resoundingly say **"yes"**.

According to Cabbalists themselves, their teachings date back and began with Adam and the fall of man, and claim to contain occult knowledge from Moses, Solomon, and others. Moses himself was raised an occultist until age 40 when he struck down the soldier who was whipping a Hebrew slave and realized his destiny was to serve the Most High God. King Solomon, although in God's service to start, went astray and ended up participating in the occult, which caused his and Israel's downfall. In fact, the best challenge to the Great Plan came with Israel's heyday of King Solomon. But he was turned away from God to the occult and fell out of God's favor, eventually coming back to God for redemption. King Solomon was quite an interesting character, building Solomon's Temple as a tribute to God and then falling and turning it into a house of the occult, which ultimately caused the breakup of Israel. Solomon was able to use the power granted to him by God to do some pretty crazy stuff, including allegedly the summoning of various interdimensionals to help him construct the temple. Solomon is arguably the most highly regarded figure save for Nimrod in Freemasonry, and it is part of the Great Plan to rebuild Solomon's Temple, the most important temple ever built to the Lord, and supremely blaspheme God by Nimrod ruling the world from it when he returns. This is according to both Freemasonry and the Bible.

King Solomon is widely regarded in black magic circles as the greatest sorcerer of all time---and at the same time regarded as the wisest man in the Bible, except for Jesus Christ of course.

The Cabbala also describes in detail the many "angels and demons" that inhabit the spiritual realm...**and how to conjure them into service for the Cabbalist.** The Cabbala gives its followers a literal road map of the occult, which it calls the "Tree of Life". The Tree of Life is the representation of man becoming a god unto himself, being immortal and never "dying". Remember, this is represented not only in Cabalism, Hinduism, Buddhism, etc., but originated in the Book of Genesis in the Bible:

> *"Behold, the man has become like one of Us, knowing good and evil; and now, he might stretch out his hand, and take also from the Tree of Life, and eat, and live forever "*
> *-God, Genesis 3:22*

A large percentage of Satanic occult groups over history have based their beliefs upon the Cabbala, and this speaks volumes of the true Luciferian nature of Cabbala.

Cabbalism is also the spiritual interpretation of various esoteric symbols and emblems, such as the all-seeing eye.

Webster's Collegiate Dictionary defines Cabbala as:

"1. A kind or system of occult theosophy or mystical interpretation of the Scriptures among Jewish rabbis and certain medieval Christians. 2. Secret or esoteric doctrine or science, in general: occultism: mystic art: mystery."

The following definitions give further clarity to the above definition of the Cabbala, by better defining "occult" and "occultism":

Occult: **Of, pertaining to, concerned with, or designating alchemy, magic, astrology and other arts and practices involving use of divination, incantation, magical formulae, etc.**

Occultism: **Occult theory or practice; belief in hidden or mysterious powers and the possibility of human control of them.**

Albert Pike, revered as one of if not the greatest Freemasonic "prophet" of all time, also stresses the fundamental importance of the Cabbala to Freemasonry:

> *"All truly dogmatic religions have issued from the Kaballah and return to it; everything scientific and grand in the religious dreams of all the Illuminati, Jacob Boeheme, Swedenborg, Saint Martin, and others, is borrowed from the Kaballah; all Masonic associations owe to it their Secrets and their Symbols."*
> *-Albert Pike, "Morals and Dogma," page 744*

Now that you have a little background on the Cabbala, let's get back to the Knights Templar, who used the Great Plan and the power handed to them via the Cabbala to nearly take over the world. It was not time for Lucifer's New World Order yet, however, which is why it was destined to fall.

The "Poor Fellow-Soldiers of Christ and of the Temple of Solomon", aka the Knights Templar, were founded as a "Christian" military organization 1119 by 9 French knights, with the purpose of escorting pilgrims to the Holy site in Jerusalem and elsewhere. They got their name from the location of their headquarters: **the ruins of Solomon's Temple.** Solomon's Temple is **extremely** important to both Biblical prophecy and the Great Plan as this is the location where the Antichrist is ultimately to rule the world from. This is why the Temple of Solomon plays such a visible and important role in Freemasonry today.

Varying accounts aside, the Templars either discovered the contents of the basis of Cabbala that were hidden inside Solomon's Temple, or the knowledge was brought into their circle by the Synagogue of Satan, or a combination of the two. Either way, it ended up as the Knights Templar employing the supernatural power contained in Cabbala to guide the rise of their empire up to the point where it ultimately threatened the other arm of the Great Plan, the Unholy Roman Empire, for supremacy over the land.

The Knights Templar swung in under the radar and were officially endorsed by the Vatican around 1129 and they quickly became the favorite charity throughout the Roman Empire. A huge amount of money was soon pouring into their coffers, and non-combatant members of the Templars soon were managing a large economic infrastructure throughout Europe. They are to be credited with forming the **first international banking cartel, and are the forefathers of our modern banking system.** They are the ones who came up with the concept of **issuing paper receipts for actual gold and silver** for the pilgrims and others to travel about with on their journeys---making them less likely targets for robbers in search of gold and silver bullion. The pilgrims deposited their gold/silver with a local Templar "bank" before leaving on their journey and received a document indicating the value of their deposit. They then used this document upon arrival in the Holy Land to retrieve their funds.

Our use of checks is based on their system. Not only this, but it is certain in my mind that the Templars were generating "checks" for themselves to use that had no money to back them, **exactly like what happens today in our modern banking system.** This is called **fractional reserve lending, and every bank in the world practices this <u>treachery with full blessings from our co-opted national governments.</u>** The Templars created the prototype of domination-by-banking that powers the Great Plan today. This is partially why the Knights Templar are so highly revered by the Freemasons, and they **are** revered.

The Knights Templar acquired vast tracts of land, both in Europe and the Middle East. They owned and managed farms and vineyards. They built churches and castles, and were involved in manufacturing, import and export. In other words, they were becoming quite a powerful force in Europe and beyond. They established satellite headquarters in England, Scotland, France, Spain and Portugal.

The Templars even had their own fleet of ships, and at one point even owned the entire island of Cyprus.

Thanks to occult guidance, the Templars' power grew at an astonishing rate. And grew. And grew. What was also growing were the stories circulating that the Knights Templars upper echelon were not Christians, but Luciferians who engaged in all sorts of satanic activity including worshipping a demonic entity known as Baphomet, blood sacrifices, and homosexual activity. Homosexual acts in the context of what the Knights Templar were doing, and what the proponents of the Great Plan engage in today, have little to do with being "gay" and everything to do with what is called Luciferian "sex magick", something we will go over in a little while. The official seal of the Knights Templar showing two male riders on one horse, allegedly showing their allegiance to a vow of poverty, is most likely a reference to the "homosexual" sex magick rituals they were using in black magic rituals. The sex magick rituals were not only used for occult purposes, but were used as blackmail against any Templar seeking to rat out or leave the organization---just like the people running the show use today. Remember, the Vatican's Inquisition was going on during the time of the reign of the Templars, and anyone even rumored to be involved with the occult or homosexuality was liable to be tortured and executed.

Blackmail or not, the stories of the occult activities of the Knights Templars were gradually and uncontrollably leaching out into the society they were now dominating. In 1307 King Philip of France, deeply in debt to the Knights Templars, took advantage of the situation and ordered all Knights Templars in France to be arrested, tortured and executed. Incidentally, this event took place on Friday, October 13, 1307, which is allegedly why Friday the 13th is unlucky. Another example of facets of the Great Plan permeating our society like the "Holidays".

Under pressure from King Phililp, Pope Clement V finally ordered the disbanding of the Knights Templar permanently in 1312.

The Templars' Sovereign Grand Master, Jacques DeMolay, was tried, convicted and burned at the stake, and their temples shut down. Today, the Freemasons pay tribute to the legacy of the one-time masters of the Great Plan, the Knights Templar. The Freemasonic youth group today is named the "DeMolays". The highest ranking of the York rite of Freemasonry is called the "Knights Templar" degree, and so on and so forth.

The coinciding abrupt disappearance of a major part of the European money base that was held in their banks, namely gold coins and bullion, gave rise to speculation and legends about the Templars and where they and all that money went. A large portion of them in fact escaped the wrath of the Unholy Roman Empire. It was time for the occultists to go back into hiding and regroup, taking the wealth accumulated and hidden by the Knights Templar with them. **Huge** quantities of gold disappeared along with the living members of the Knights Templar right into thin air. It is alleged that the upper echelon of the persecuted Templars took all gold in their possession and fled to Scotland, becoming the origin of what is known today as the **Scottish Rite of Freemasonry. The Scottish Rite is the dominant form of Freemasonry and the one used to orchestrate control of the world from behind the scenes today.**

This brings us to the next public face of the Great Plan.........the Rosicrucians.

Evidence directly from the leading Masonic prophet of our time states that the surviving Knights Templar merged with other occultists in the early 1300's, combining forces to form the Order of the Rose-Croix, or simply the Rosicrucians.

For evidence of this, we go again to Albert Pike's book "Morals and Dogma", and again as a reminder, Albert Pike is considered the premier "prophet" of Freemasonry and the book "Morals and Dogma" is considered the modern day Bible of Freemasonry:

> *"The successors of the Ancient Adepts Rose-Croix, abandoning by degrees the austere and hierarchal Science of their Ancestors in initiation, became a Mystic Sect, uniting with many of the Templars, the dogmas of the two intermingling, and believed themselves to be the sole depositaries of the secrets of the Gospel of St. John, seeing in its recitals an allegorical series of rites proper to complete the initiation."*

By the early 1600s, more than three hundred years had passed since the Knights Templar had been "abolished". As a result, the proponents of the Great Plan once again decided to test the waters to see how the public would respond to its occult philosophies by taking the Rosicrucians public.

For obvious reasons, they could not share their real history linking them to the Great Plan, so they created a story explaining their origins around a mythical character by the name of Christian Rosenkreuz---yet another in a long line of deceptions orchestrated by the proponents of the Great Plan.

This fictitious tale was published in a document known as the *"Fama Fraternitatis,"* which the occultists circulated throughout Europe. The story relates how Rosenkreuz traveled to Syria and then Egypt to study the occult. After he had learned from all of the great masters of occult philosophy in the Middle East and Northern Africa, he returned to Europe to spread his newly-found occult knowledge throughout the land. But as the story went, he was unfavorably received across the land and returned home to Germany where he was to establish a society based on his teachings.

According to Albert G. Mackey's "Encyclopedia of Freemasonry", referring to Fama Fraternitatis: **" the fiction was readily accepted as a truth by most people, and the invisible society of Rosenkreuz was sought for with avidity by many who wished to unite with it."**

This well calculated move by the proponents of the Great Plan allowed them to monitor Europe's reaction to the occult without revealing their true identity or the names of its members, but at the same time creating a renewed interest in the occult throughout Europe.

The Rosicrucians knew that if they were to progress towards their goal of a Luciferian one world government and fulfill the Great Plan, they would need to go public to enlist the support of many minions across the entire world.

In the proven tradition of the Knights Templar, the Rosicrucians decided to take on the outward appearance of good deeds to mask the evil which they were secretly plotting from within the upper echelon of their organization, and under this disguise they merged with and took over the benign stone mason guilds of Europe.

Thereafter, the stone masons, who actually worked with stone and chisel, became known as Operative Masons, as they were actually blue-collar-type workers employed in the building profession. The occultists, who were then as today white collar criminals, which took over the guilds, became known within the guilds as Speculative Masons.

The stone mason's guilds in Europe were a natural front for the occultists, as the Knights Templars before them had been great builders, and their history of being involved with stone work went all the way back to King Nimrod and the Tower of Babel. It was a perfect front on all levels.

With the construction of cathedrals on the decline in the 1600's, the stone mason's guilds were also on the decline and in danger of going extinct. With the guilds and the Rosicrucians in need of each other, the partnership was sealed, and the mason's guilds over decades of time became known as speculative guilds---after the occultists who ran them---and they were soon flooded with other budding occultists looking to join in. The presence of actual people in the mason guilds who worked with stone came to an end with the advent of something you have heard of called Freemasonry.

This transition culminated in the forming of the world's first Freemasonic Grand Lodge in London in 1717. By way of this gradual takeover, the torch of the Great Plan had been passed from the Templars to the Rosicrucians, and then to the newly-public "Freemasons". By the time of the founding of the first Freemasonic lodge, most if not all guild masons were now considered "speculative" Masons.

Chapter 3/C

FREEMASONRY

A great deal of deception regarding the origins of Freemasonry and its role in the world stage today has intentionally been manufactured lately in an attempt by the Great Plan-controlled Mainstream Media to cloud the waters of truth. You now know the real truth of the origin of Freemasonry, but let's expand on your newly-gained knowledge.

Freemasonry today at its **lower levels** is more of a "good ol' boys" network geared toward advancing the careers of fellow Freemasons through business contacts with other Freemasons. It has nothing what-soever to do with blue collar stoneworkers and everything to do with white collar businessmen looking to join the Brotherhood to gain insider contacts to further their careers.

The proponents of the Great Plan use the **upper levels** of Freemasonry to pull the strings from behind the scenes of our national governments, international banks, and multi-national corporations. This is because Freemasonry, at its upper, upper echelon of degrees, is the primary mod-ern day housing of the ancient Babylonian Mystery Religion, secondarily resting with the upper echelon of the Unholy Roman Empire. **It is only the upper 1% or less of all Freemasons that know what the true intent of their organization historically was and is**. The multitudes of lower rank-and-file Masons, mostly "Blue Lodge" Masons, have no idea they are being used as pawns to help set up a one world government.

The proponents of the Great Plan rarely, if ever, recruit from the lower levels of Freemasonry. All of their upper echelon minions consist of the various bloodline families who have always been involved with the

Luciferian secret societies and those rogue independent personalities who have proven themselves highly valuable to their agenda.

Point of fact, nearly all Freemasons are in fact honorable men who believe their organization is for good and wholesome causes, at least this is what they are coerced to think. **This harkens back to both the Knights Templar and the Rosicrucians putting up a diabolical façade to fool people into believing they are only dedicated to good deeds and to question them is nonsensical when in fact a great deception has taken place yet again.**

There is also a direct connection I want to immediately reveal between Freemasonry and the ancient Babylonian Mystery Religion, and that is the fact that Freemasonry regards King Nimrod as the first Freemason for his "masonry prowess" he employed in undertaking the construction of the Tower of Babel. **This is a carefully planted deception, trying to hide the true nature of Nimrod's significance within Freemasonry.** This is also an implication of King Nimrod as the head architect of the Great Plan, for if you tie all of the symbolism involved in Freemasonry such as the hexagram, the all-seeing eye, the obelisk, and on and on it all goes back to Nimrod and the occult Babylonian Mystery Religion. I would say that the varying quotes of the Freemasonic "prophets" we will go over, fully admitting Lucifer is the god of the Freemasons, should convince you of the true evil intent of the people running the Freemasonic Great Plan and their goal of a Luciferian one world government, exactly as stated in the Bible.

As recently as the spring 2006 issue of *Freemasonry Today* (a sanctioned Masonic publication) we are publicly told that King Nimrod, not King Solomon, was the first head of Freemasonry:

> *"The universal sentiment of the Freemasons of the present day is to confer upon Solomon, the King of Israel, the honor of being their first Grand Master. But the legend of the Craft had long before, though there was a tradition of the Temple in existence, given, at least by suggestion, that title to Nimrod, the King of Babylonia and Assyria. It had credited the first organization of the fraternity of craftsmen to him, in saying that he gave a charge to the workmen whom he sent to assist the King of Nineveh in building his cities."*

Do you see the deception on the part of *Freemasonry Today* to imply that it is Nimrod who first organized a fraternity of stone workers that gives him his status within Freemasonry?

Not only is Nimrod considered to be the first Freemason and Masonic leader, some initiates of Freemasonry are required to take the "Oath of Nimrod". Are you beginning to connect the dots on this? The Oath of Nimrod is part of the initiation process for the "Indentured Apprentice", which is the first degree of Freemasonry. The oath reads as follows:

Apprentice Degree (1st).

I, _____, do in the presence of El Shaddai and of this Worshipful Assembly of Free Masons, Rough Masons, Wallers, Slaters, Paviors, Plaisterers and Bricklayers, promise and declare that I will not at any time hereafter, by any act or circumstance whatsoever, directly or indirectly, write, print, cut, mark, publish, discover, reveal, or make known, any part or parts of the Trade secrets, privileges, or counsells of the Worshipful Fraternity or Fellowship of Free Masonry, which I may have known at any time, or at any time hereafter shall be made known unto me.

The penalty for breaking this great oath shall be the loss of my life.

That I shall be branded with the mark of the Traitor and slain according to ancient custom by being throtalled, that my body shall be buried in the rough sands of the sea a cable's length from the shore where the tide regularly ebbs and flows twice in the twenty-four hours, so that my soul shall have no rest by night or by day–

(Candidate Signs his name)

Freemasonry spread quickly after the establishment of the first formal lodge in 1717, and by the late 1700s, this front-organization had become well known for their good and charitable works---being viewed with favor by the general public, ala the Templars and Rosicrucians remember.

With a formal organization for their millennia-old plan back in the public eye, the Luciferians were again free to aggressively pursue their ambition of taking over the world.

For the vast majority of Masons, Freemasonry is a continuous parade of deceptions. Most Lodge leaders do not realize that they are deceiving their members. For the most part, they are simply reciting the same things they have heard and said, over and over, assuming that they are right and good. However, the upper echelon deliberately deceives the Masons under them. Most men who join have no idea that their initiations consist of solemn blood oaths with implications of their death if they reveal any secrets.

Masons do in fact take blood oaths, but are told that they are only symbolic, being part of tradition. They participate in rituals that they don't understand the ancient meaning of, assuming that they must be alright because their Masonic friends have done it.

> *"Part of the symbols are displayed there to the initiate, but he is intentionally misled by false interpretations. It is not intended that he shall understand them; but it is intended that he shall imagine he understands them. There must always be a commonplace interpretation for the mass of initiates, of the symbols that are eloquent to the Adepts. (33rd degree Masons or higher)"*
> -"Morals and Dogma", Albert Pike

Simply put, Freemasonry is an **organization within an organization**. One part of the organization is deliberately lied to and misled with false interpretations and only exists as a facade to the general public. The lower level Masons think they are working for a just and honorable cause, while the other part of the organization, the upper echelon, knows the spiritual truth of Freemasonry and its origins and goals.....the Great Plan.

Freemasonry at its highest level is a **religion**. It is the modern day incarnation of the **Babylonian Mystery Religion** of King Nimrod and Queen Semiramis. Masons meet in temples, such as the Scottish Rite Temple. They have an altar and there is a "holy book" on it. They have prayers, deacons, and religious titles for their leaders, such as High Priest and Worshipful Master. They say that they bring men from spiritual darkness to spiritual light. Although Freemasonry is in fact a religion, most Masons deny this fact because they simply don't know the truth of the Great Plan. One of the requirements of being a Mason is belief in a Supreme Being. They just don't tell you which god they really worship at the pinnacle of leadership when you first join, which again is Satan.

Once a man makes it through the first three Freemasonic rites, he becomes a Master Mason and is eligible to join the Scottish Rite or the York Rite. It is mainly contained within the upper echelon of the Scottish Rite the ultimate secrets of the Great Plan. I believe that it is called the Scottish Rite because that is allegedly where the persecuted Knights Templars fled after the Unholy Roman Empire moved to quash them. Scottish Rite Masonry has twenty-nine more degrees after "Master Mason". Each of these degrees includes initiation, with a blood oath. A Thirty-Second Degree Mason is a man who reached the Third Degree (Master Mason) in his local Lodge, and then went through twenty-nine more degrees in the Scottish Rite to attain the title of "Sublime Prince of the Royal Secret". Now, I wonder just what the "Royal Secret" could be......

Once a Scottish Rite Mason reaches the top of the pyramid of Freemasonry, they are eligible to become a 33rd degree Freemason. This level of Masonry is by invite only from those Masons who are already 33rd degree or higher. Keep in mind that the 33rd degree is only the first of the Luciferian degrees, and the occult ladder goes much higher.

Membership initiation into the Thirty-Third Degree allegedly includes drinking wine, symbolic of blood, out of a human skull and taking a solemn oath that their primary allegiance is to the other Thirty-Third Degree Masons and those Masons above them in rank---whose allegiance is to Satan.

Another outgrowth of the Freemasonic circle is an organization in the United States called Skull and Bones. This is a private fraternity of sorts, based at Yale University, and is the proving grounds for Americans who wish to work for the Great Plan. Also referred to as the "American Illuminati", the full name of the organization is the "Skull and Bones Brotherhood of Death". Sounds like a wholesome group, right? No, I suppose not. Their membership parallels and overlaps that of the 33rd degree Masons in terms of their placement in government and business. It is my opinion some of the members of Skull and Bones are also 33rd degree Masons, but since they don't call these things "secret societies" for nothing, information about this has not been forthcoming. Nonetheless, some of the Skull and Bonesmen are virtually on equal footing with the 33rd degree Masons in terms of the Great Plan pecking order. We'll go over Skull and Bones in more detail shortly.

So. In 1992 it was Skull and Bonesman George Bush Sr. vs. (alleged) 33rd degree Freemason Bill Clinton for the Presidency of the United States. In 1996 you had (alleged) 33rd degree Freemason Bob Dole against (alleged) 33rd degree Freemason Bill Clinton. Next it was Skull and Bonesman George W. Bush vs. (alleged) 33rd Degree Freemason Al Gore. Then it was Skull and Bonesman Bush vs. Skull and Bonesman John Kerry. Are you understanding this? We don't select or elect any of our Presidents. They are hand-picked and groomed for the job years in advance according to their membership status in the Luciferian secret societies and their willingness to follow the agenda of the Great Plan.

I need to again address the use of the term "alleged" 33rd degree Freemason. Freemasons have a habit of not airing their secrets in public under threat of death, including who is a member of the upper echelon of Freemasonry.

What I do know is that you do not have to rise up the ranks of Freemasonry to become a 33rd degree. You can have ranks 1-32 bestowed upon you in a single ceremony, and then take the 33rd degree initiation. Doing it this way subverts years of involvement in the lodges and therefore minimizes the exposure of the most important Freemasons to other, lower-level Masons who might confirm these peoples involvement with Freemasonry. This is how, I believe, they keep a lid on who the 33rd degree Masons are. Masonic prophets like Albert Pike, Manly P. Hall, and the like have no problem publicly stating that they are 33rd degree Masons and the fact that they worship the entity Satan, as you shall soon see, but to have a sitting President who is publicly known as a 33rd degree Freemason would endanger their program.

> "Masonry, like all the Religions, all the Mysteries..., conceals its secrets from all except the Adepts and Sages, or the Elect, and uses false explanations and misinterpretations of its symbols to mislead those who deserve only to be mislead...Truth is not for those who are unworthy or unable to receive it, or would pervert it."
>
> -Albert Pike, 33rd degree Freemason, from his occult masterpiece Morals and Dogma

If I ever had the resources to fully investigate various claims of our elected officials' status as 33rd degree Freemasons, I certainly would. Regardless of what rank of Freemasonry, if any, of the people on the list below, their true intentions are betrayed regardless of their position on the religious end of the Great Plan through Freemasonry. Most of our elected Senators, Congressmen, Supreme Court Justices, and everybody on the President's Cabinet including the President hold membership cards in one or more of the various Round Table steering groups we'll go over later in this book. These steering groups were factually started and controlled today by the masters of the Great Plan.

Here is a list commonly found on the internet of famous 33rd degree Freemasons. There is strong evidence that some of these men are of the 33rd degree, and some I can find nary a clue to their status in Freemasonry. Again, detailed investigations into the backgrounds of these and other people who are deciding how we are going to live our lives should be initiated immediately to determine their status, if any, within Freemasonry, aka King Nimrod's Luciferian Great Plan.

- Founding Father George Washington
- Benjamin Franklin
- Paul Warburg (founder of the Federal Reserve)
- Al Gore
- Newt Gingrich
- President Clinton
- President Gerald Ford
- President Lyndon Baines Johnson (LBJ)
- President Harry Truman
- President Franklin D. Roosevelt
- British Prime Minister Winston Churchill
- Joseph Stalin (yes the above three, who led the allies in WW II, were all alleged 33rd degree Freemasons)
- British Prime Minister Tony Blair
- Aleister Crowley (self-confessed Satanist)
- Walt Disney (occult themes in kids movies, started "Club 33"--- a secret Masonic club located on the Disneyland property, and the only place in the "Magic Kingdom" that serves booze)

- Filmmaker James Cameron (Avatar was pro-New World Order)
- Rev. Jesse Jackson
- Karl Marx (the creator of Communism)
- H.G. Wells, author of *The New World Order*
- And on and on and on...............

There are degrees above the 33rd, and these are reserved for the most advanced occultists, those who are master practitioners of black magic, etc. We'll talk briefly about these degrees when we get to talking about a man named Aleister Crowley, nicknamed "the most evil man of the 20th century".

One more thing to talk about that is central to both the Great Plan/ Freemasonry and what is stated in Biblical prophecy to happen right before the End Times, and that is the rebuilding of Solomon's Temple in Israel.

It is their intention to gain control of the Islamic Temple Mount in Jerusalem, which was built atop the ruins of King Solomon's Temple. After assuming control of this highly coveted piece of land, they will demolish the Islamic Temple and rebuild Solomon's Temple. According to Biblical prophecy, once the Temple is rebuilt, the Masonic Christ, better known as the Antichrist, who you now know as a resurrected King Nimrod, will make his appearance and the ultimate Hell on Earth will follow.

King Solomon was quite the interesting character, and again is highly revered by the Freemasons not only because he built the prophetic Temple that he transformed into an occult temple, but because of his masterful power in the occult circles of the day. Part of his life was spent honoring the Most High God and part of it was spent paying homage to the pagan gods of his many foreign wives, which is the following of Nimrod's Babylonian Mystery Religion and by default is worship of Satan.

Solomon is credited by occultists with mastering the use of the "Seal of Solomon" for occult ceremonies, which is the most powerful esoteric symbol in black magic/witchcraft and also known as a hexagram. **This is where the term putting a *_HEX_* on someone comes from**. You are using a hexagram in an occult ceremony to request the supernatural forces to interact in our dimension and cause someone harm. You may also know this symbol better as the **"Star of David"** which adorns the modern day Israeli flag. Symbols such as the hexagram originated in occult black magic circles and can be renamed but not **repurposed**. The very reason that symbols such as the hexagram or pentagram (5-sided star, also a black magic symbol) are in existence was because they were originally used millennia ago during occult rituals to interact with "demons". These symbols serve the same evil purposes today, only covertly. The term "Star of David" is an intentional deception by the masters of the Great Plan, and has nothing to do with King David. Before it was repurposed at the Star of David, it was called the Seal of Solomon. The use of the hexagram, in fact, actually predates King Solomon and was originally known as the Star of Rephaim, which is representative of the worship of the planet Saturn. Tracing the origin of the hexagram even further back and it appears that it originally was a symbol representing **King Nimrod.** The fact that the Luciferian occult symbol for the Antichrist is on the Israeli flag today is a **RED FLAG** betraying who is really running not only Israel these days, but the world. **The Star of David has nothing to do with Judaism and everything to do with the occult and the Great Plan of Nimrod**.

The hexagram is arguably the most influential and powerful occult symbol in the world. In fact, it is so significant that the Synagogue of Satan bloodline who largely controls the world's money supply today, the European Rothschilds, took their name directly from it. **Their name is the literal translation of the symbol of the occult hexagram.**

Mayer Amschel Bauer, the patriarch of the Rothschild Banking Dynasty, changed his last name in the 17th century to depict the red hexagram "star" (or shield) which he had hung as his identifying symbol on the front door of his goldsmith shop in Germany. This marked the beginning of the family of "Red Shield" or Rothschild. The Rothschilds are the heads of both the Synagogue of Satan and the Great Plan today, and their name is synonymous with the hexagram, and this is why there is a hexagram on the flag of Israel today. It is by direct action of the Rothschild family that Israel came back into existence, and we will go over the facts of this and you will see this to be the truth.

The hexagram is also the official insignia of the Freemasons today, although veiled. By removing the horizontal lines of the hexagram, you are left with a near perfect image of the positioning of the Freemasonic square and compass. This follows along perfectly with the Great Plan's use of symbols to mean one thing to most people, but to the adepts of the Great Plan, that same symbol has a completely different and esoteric meaning. The unfinished Freemasonic symbol of the hexagram, aka the symbol of Nimrod, directly symbolizes both the unfinished Great Plan---also represented by a pyramid sans capstone---and the unfinished Temple of Solomon, the future seat of a resurrected Nimrod. Once the New World Order is firmly established and the Temple of Solomon rebuilt, it will be time for the Antichrist/Apollyon/Nimrod to make his appearance and take his throne once again.

It is also highly probable that the hexagram is representative of the mark of the beast. The number 666 can easily be extracted from the geometry of the hexagram. The mark of the Beast has to do with commerce, according to the Bible, **and this mark is today on nearly every product you buy and you didn't even know it.** Go right now to your cupboard and grab a box of cereal, a bottle of water, or any packaged product, which pretty much encompasses anything you would buy these days. Look on it for the recycling emblem--- the three arrows forming a pyramid shape. Look very carefully at the center of this pyramid. Do you see the hexagram? Although there are slight variations, the original recycle emblem creates a **perfect hexagram in the center.** This is why it was selected over all competing designs, and was very possibly planted to appear to be a coincidence. All other recycling emblems are based on this original design, incorporating a hexagram in the middle. This is an intentional marking of the products you buy today with the mark of the Beast.....Nimrod.

I've got two more loose ends to throw in here as we wrap up our *brief* discussion of Freemasonry. It again has to do with our space program, which was the pinnacle of our advanced knowledge at the time.

The single runway at Kennedy Space Center in Florida is called **Runway 33**, where the **Apollo** moon missions **and** the first space shuttle **Columbia** launched from.

Also, alleged 33rd degree Mason and 2nd man on the moon Buzz Aldrin **factually** claimed the moon for the Freemasons in an occult ceremony he performed by himself while he was standing on the moon.

Google it. You'll be amazed.

Chapter 4

DAWN OF THE NEW WORLD ORDER

The "New World Order" is the transitional phase between sovereign nations and a one world government run by the Luciferian global elite under Satan and his human representative King Nimrod/the Antichrist. This is exactly what is prophesized in the Bible, this is exactly the goal of the Great Plan, and this is exactly what is unfolding before us today. They are **very close** to achieving their objective. You probably don't understand yet how bad this will be for us, but by the end of this book you will have learned all of the most important moving parts of it and how they interlock to form a pyramidal, compartmentalized conspiracy run by a very few Luciferian families, and to the ultimate benefit of only a few thousand of the people involved with bringing the one world government in. They have all jockeyed or are jockeying for position in it right now, to live under it and benefit from it in the times to come.

If what they were trying to do was for the good of humanity, they would be doing it out in the open instead of behind closed doors, under the veil of secrecy. Only evil acts are done in the dark, away from concerned eyes.

The story of the Great Plan coming into its end goal of the New World Order is such that one cannot explain it to the layman to the point of him or her understanding it without a fully rehearsed 24-hour speech. It is such a vast, interconnected web of deceit that the only way to explain it is to lay out all aspects of it, showing how the dots all connect. So this is what you are holding in your hand, from me: My written speech that will take you about 24 hours straight to read.

The reason it takes so long to explain it is the same reason why someone could be called a "conspiracy nut" by piping off about only one element of it. Without knowing all of the elements and the facts behind them, you can't even begin to visualize the real conspiracy, and it's easy to pass off people ranting about the Federal Reserve or 9/11 or New World Order-anything as lunacy and then go back to the personal non-reality bubble most people these days reside in.

Now that we've **briefly** gone through how the Great Plan began and how it was carried forward from ancient to modern times, we are going to go into some greater degree of detail regarding the significant players and events of the last 300 or so years that have brought us to the doorstep of the New World Order.

Time has been on the side of the 6,000 year old Great Plan, and they have moved their agenda along slowly and covertly enough so as not to arouse suspicion from the population at large. That's not to say that people haven't been trying to call this conspiracy out for millennia. Even the warnings of God's prophets and Jesus Christ Himself throughout the entire Bible have for the most part fallen on deaf ears. You are holding in your hands as dire of a warning as I was able to manifest, and hopefully you understand this warning at this point.

Only independent-type thinkers have been able to step outside of the proverbial box over the years and view what is happening without blinders. The result of those thinkers has been a crescendo of books, lectures and video presentations trying to warn the world of what is going on----along with an even greater crescendo of denial and mud-slinging from the Establishment-owned Mainstream Media shouting them down and labeling the truth as "conspiracy theory". This has successfully discredited the truth movement to a point where it has been for the most part an effort-in-vain, much to the detriment of humanity.

I aim to change that, and I won't beat around the bush here: **I need your help**. I am just one man who is standing against the Beast. I need your help if we are to have any hope of a promising future for our kids and humanity in general.

The general public has been brainwashed by the media to not only **not** think outside the box they've been put in, but to ridicule those that do as crazy. *"Don't go outside your box. It's not safe out there".* You know what? It's **not** safe out there, and it's because you and everyone else won't get out of their damn box and speak up for what's right, fair and true.

I will tell you that the only people that are crazy are those people who diligently stick their heads in the sand because they are afraid that their reality bubble will burst if they actually were to know what is really going on. By doing this you are allowing the New World Order agenda of pure tyranny to march forward unchallenged and unabated. By doing this you are being complacent in the face of imminent danger to you, your country, your family, and your way of life.

Again, I don't want you to take my word regarding anything I've said, but to check for yourself the facts of what I'm relating. This is what I did when I first began to come into contact with various claims about the various different components surrounding the New World Order. Investigate. Cross-reference. Investigate some more. Fire-test. Cross-reference. Lather. Rinse. Repeat. You get it. Eventually you are going to see how the facts just don't lie about what is really going on, what I'm telling you in this book.

We're going to go over now, briefly, how the central control mechanism, the modern day financial/banking system, was put in place and by whom. We're also going to go over in some detail what organizations were created by the modern day proponents of the Great Plan in order to bring their ancient blueprint of control to fruition, and also review the central characters who were major contributors to the advancement of the Great Plan, now being openly called the New World Order by its proponents.

Chapter 4/A

THE ROTHSCHILD BANKING DYNASTY

"I care not what puppet is placed on the throne of England to rule the Empire, the man that controls Britain's money supply controls the British Empire, and I control the money supply."
-Nathan Rothschild, son of Mayer Amschel (Bauer) Rothschild

The Synagogue of Satan's Rothschild Banking Dynasty is deeply rooted in the Great Plan and this one particular European family lord over it today.

There are two factors that will show that they are today's principal controllers of the Great Plan. The first one is because they have primary control of the world's central banking institutions, which can be factually traced through the history of the founding of the various global banking institutions. The IMF, World Bank, Bank of International Settlements, the Federal Reserve, the Bank of England, and on and on and on are principally owned and controlled by the Rothschilds and their lesser minions.

Whoever controls a nation's currency controls the country's economy, and by default controls the country.

The second factor is that they had a hand, and were probably also the initiators, in the founding of a new secret society to take the baton and run the Great Plan to its completion: The infamous **Illuminati.**

A ton of disinformation has been put forth by the Mainstream Media regarding the existence of the Illuminati over the last few years, and this coincides with the factual information regarding their founding and motives that have been leaked out through the internet. You can forget everything you think you know about the Illuminati, I'm going to tell you the bottom-line truth of the matter, because I've taken the time and had the guidance to get to the bottom line.

We will go over the Illuminati in the next chapter, and we will keep our discussion of the Illuminati pertinent to the facts, unlike what has been put forth by the Mainstream Media.

*****I'm going to once again remind you, the reader, that for the most part what you are reading is as brief of a summary as possible on each respected subject to inform you of the importance of said subject in this book and its relationship to the unfolding New World Order. If this were not the case, this book would be tens of thousands of pages long and would not be completed in time to warn people of what is really going on in the world.*****

Now, with that said, let's keep moving forward through the timeline of the Great Plan.

Mayer Amschel Bauer, the Rothschild Banking Dynasty's patriarch, was born in Frankfurt, Germany in 1743, the son of Moses Amschel Bauer, a banker and goldsmith.

Mayer Amschel's father, Moses, had a goldsmithing business, and was a buyer and seller of gold and silver bullion. In other words, he was a "money changer" of the same type referred to in the Bible. The **only time** Jesus Christ ever used violence in His ministry on Earth was the one time He physically turned over the tables of the money changers in the temple and chased them out of the building for ripping off the Jews over the temple tax.

Moses Bauer hung above his business door a sign depicting a **red hexagram**, or "Star of David/Seal of Solomon/Star of Rephaim/Star of Nimrod", which you'll remember is the most significant occult symbol used in black magic. In the context that Bauer was using it, the terms "star" and "shield" are synonyms, and the shop became known as the "Red Shield (star)" goldsmith shop. The German word for "red shield" is Rothschild. The name Rothschild literally translates to "**Red Hexagram**".

The Rothschilds adopted this powerful occult symbol as the symbol of their name, and thus changed their name from Bauer to Rothschild. This was the birth of the infamous House of Rothschild.

Upon his father's death, Mayer Amschel Rothschild took over the family business and began to build it---buying competing coin shops and locally consolidating his business. Soon they were the premier dealers in gold and silver bullion in all of Europe.

Amschel was an aggressive, tenacious businessman, and after establishing his business in gold trading and banking, he expanded to antiques, wineries, and the importing of manufactured materials from England. The Rothschild family began to amass a huge fortune for the time.

Rothschild's status as the premier gold dealer in Europe landed him a spot in 1769 as a court agent of Germany's Prince William IX of Hesse-Kassel (Germany). Prince William IX inherited his father's fortune upon his death in 1785, and his was the largest private fortune in all of Europe at the time. Some of this money had come from Great Britain paying for the use of 16,800 of his father's Hessian soldiers to try and stop the revolution in America. This money was never given to the troops, and fell into Prince William's possession upon his death.

In 1785, Amschel and his wife Gutele moved their entire family, five sons and five daughters, to a five story dwelling they were to share with another Synagogue of Satan member, the Schiff family. In 1865, The Schiffs' not-yet-born grandson Jacob would move to New York and in 1917 he would become the mastermind behind the funding of the Bolshevik Revolution in Russia, more on this later.

As they came of age, Amschel sent his sons to the major capitals of Europe to open branch offices of the family banking business. Amschel, stayed in Frankfurt, Salomon was sent to Vienna, Austria. Nathan was sent to London. Karl went to Naples, Italy, and Jakob went to Paris.

Although all the sons became successful bankers under Amschel Sr., **Nathan Rothschild** exhibited a superior intellect and skill in the banking business. When he got to London, he became a merchant banker and began to cement ties between the House of Rothschild and the existing Bank of England, the British equivalent of our Federal Reserve and also a privately-held, for-profit bank. Rothschild didn't own the Bank of England at this point, but his foot was in the door.

In June, 1806, as Napoleon's troops pushed their way into Germany, Prince William fled to Denmark, leaving his money with Amschel Rothschild. History records that Rothschild was enlisted by the Prince to take care of his banking affairs in his absence, and Rothschild hid William's ledgers, which revealed a list of debtors and the interest required from them, and 600,000 pounds ($3,000,000), to keep Napoleon from confiscating it.

Buderus von Carlhausen, the treasury official who handled William's finances, was given "power of attorney" and he in turn made Rothschild his chief banker, responsible for collecting the interest on the royal loans. Napoleon, now running the show in Germany, decreed that all debts being paid to Prince William were to go to the French Treasury instead, and offered a 25% commission on any debts that he would collect. Rothschild refused to cooperate, as he himself was making more money taking care of the Prince's financial affairs as he continued to collect the debts and commissions for the Prince.

Circumstances of the Napoleonic Wars allowed the Rothschilds to execute a plan which would guarantee them the financial control of Europe, and soon the world. It began with taking advantage of the outcome of the Battle of Waterloo. Early in the battle, Napoleon appeared to be winning, and the first secret military report to London communicated that fact. However, upon reinforcements from the Prussians, the tide turned in favor of Lord Wellington and Great Britain.

On Sunday, June 18, 1815, a man named Rothworth, a courier of Nathan Rothschild was on the battlefield observing the fight. Upon seeing that Napoleon was going to be beaten, he went by horse to Brussels, then to Ostende, and for 2,000 francs, got a sailor to get him to England across stormy seas. When Nathan Rothschild received the news on June 20th, he informed the British government that Napoleon was **winning---when in fact he was losing. So, with everyone believing Wellington to be defeated, Rothschild immediately began to sell all of his stocks on the English Stock Market in order to crash it.** Everyone else followed his lead---exactly as planned---and also began selling, causing stocks to plummet to practically nothing.

In the last minutes of the trading day, Nathan Rothschild's agents secretly began buying up nearly all the stocks at rock-bottom prices. On June 21, at 11:00 PM, Wellington's envoy, Major Henry Percy showed up at the War Office with his report that Napoleon had been crushed in a bitter eight hour battle, losing a third of his men. **The stock market soared the next day, giving the Rothschild family complete control of the British economy due to their new ownership of so much of**

its companies' stock. Through their diabolical actions in the stock market that fateful day, they also now held a majority interest of shares in the Bank of England---giving them total control over the British economy. They only held minority interest, if any, of the stock of the Bank of England before this incident. After it, they were the virtual owners of it. The Rothschilds hold controlling interest in the Bank of England to this day.

This is pertinent information to show the tenacity of the Rothschilds, and the amount of financial power the Rothschilds began to wield not only over Great Britain but the world. Again, the Rothschilds are also responsible for the treacherous founding of the United States' privately held central bank, the Federal Reserve, **and they also own controlling interest in it to this day.** They are therefore the true masters of the United States. The Rothschild Banking Dynasty is the backbone of the Luciferian New World Order. They are the pinnacle of mankind's evil actions against God on this Earth.

After Napoleon's defeat, Prince William returned to resume his rule in Germany, and the Rothschilds were sitting fat as the richest bankers in the world, and they only increased their fortune and therefore their power as time marched on.

Two years after the coup of the London stock market in 1817, France, in order to get back on their feet again after Napoleon's defeat, secured loans from a French banking house in Ouvrard, and from the Baring Brothers in London. The Rothschild cabal, fresh off the culling of the British economy, saw their chance to get a death grip on France, and in October 1818, Rothschild agents began buying huge amounts of French government bonds, which caused their value to increase. On November 5th, they were then **dumped** on the open market, creating a financial panic as their value plummeted. As France's stock market valuation disintegrated, the Rothschilds again bought up millions of shares of French companies for pennies on the dollar. Thus, the Rothschilds gained financial control of France through majority ownership of a large number of its native corporations' stock.

This was the beginning of the House of Rothschild, which controlled a fortune estimated to be well **over $300,000,000 in the early 1800's**---an absolutely astounding amount of wealth at the time. This wealth has only increased as a large portion of it was in banking, which always appreciates due to interest charged.

The Rothschilds began to invest heavily in all aspects of commerce, and soon the Rothschild Banking Dynasty spanned Europe with railroads, invested in coal and ironworks, financed England's purchase of the Suez Canal, paid for oil exploration in Russia and the Sahara Desert, financed the czars of Russia, supported Cecil Rhodes' diamond monopoly in Africa, aided France in creating an empire in Africa, financed the Hapsburg monarchs, and saved the Vatican from bankruptcy---among other financial endeavors. Just unbelievable the number of financial pies they had their fingers in way back then.

In the United States, through their American and European agents, they financed Rockefeller's Standard Oil, Carnegie Steel, and Harriman's Railroad---and were silent partners in all. Werner Sombart, in his book "The Jews and Modern Capitalism", said that from 1820 on, it was the **"age of the Rothschild"** and concluded that there was **"only one power in Europe, and that is Rothschild."** In 1913, the year they founded the Federal Reserve, the family fortune was estimated to be **over two *billion* dollars.**

After patriarch Mayer Amschel Rothschild died on September 19, 1812, his will allegedly spelled out specific guidelines that were to be maintained by his descendants:

1) All important posts were to be held by only family members, and only male members were to be involved on the business end. The oldest son of the oldest son was to be the head of the family, unless otherwise agreed upon by the rest of the family, as was the case in 1812, when the diabolical Nathan was appointed as the patriarch.

2) The family was to intermarry with their own first and second cousins, so their fortune could be kept in the family, and to maintain the appearance of a united financial empire. For example, his son James (Jacob) married the daughter of another son, Salomon.

3) Rothschild ordered that there was never to be "any public inventory made by the courts, or otherwise, of my estate ... Also I forbid any legal action and any publication of the value of the inheritance."

The closeness of the Rothschild brothers under their father Amschel is seen in a letter from Salomon Rothschild to his brother Nathan on Feb. 28, 1815, **"We are like the mechanism of a watch: each part is essential. "**

This closeness is further seen in that of the 18 marriages made by Mayer Amschel Rothschild's grandchildren, 16 were contracted between first cousins.

The great poet-philosopher Heinrich Heine once said, **"Money is the god of our time, and Rothschild is his prophet."**

The actual amount of money they control today is unknown, due to the fact that they hide their wealth within tax-exempt organizations and in secretive off-shore and Swiss banking accounts---all of which are free from the prying eyes of humanity. The "public" wealth they profess to have only numbers in the low billions of dollars. In other words, Bill Gates and Warren Buffet are not the richest men on the planet by a long shot.

There is plenty of documented evidence that the House of Rothschild, along with other, lesser-empowered International Bankers, have used their tremendous wealth to initiate and finance both sides of every war since the American Revolution. They have literally been responsible for the slaughter of hundreds of millions of innocent people.

The main Rothschild headquarters are located in an area in the heart of London, England, within the financial district known as "The City of London". This is a sovereign piece of land, and at the same time has corporate status, that is separate from Great Britain, controlled for the most part by the Rothschilds and their ilk. This is the exact same setup that exists for our nation's capital, Washington D.C. A sovereign piece of land that has corporate status. Well guess who owns both corporations? You got it. Not only this and not to be left out, the Unholy Roman Empire sits on its own piece of sovereign land also, Vatican City.

All major British banks have their main offices within the City of London financial district, along with branch offices for 385 foreign banks, including 70 from the United States. It is here that you will find Great Britain's private central bank, the Bank of England, also the British Stock Exchange, Lloyd's of London, the Baltic Exchange (shipping contracts), Fleet Street (home of publishing and newspaper interests), the London

Commodity Exchange (to trade coffee, rubber, sugar, textiles, etc), and the London Metal Exchange. It is virtually the financial hub of the world, even more so than New York City, and is the home base of the Rothschild Banking Dynasty.

Just how were the Rothschilds able to pull all of this off? Well, they just happened to mastermind the creation in 1776 of an organization you may have heard of: **the Illuminati.**

Amschel Rothschild, the patriarch, had one more endeavor besides worldwide monopolization of wealth. He was able to put together a group of fellow occultists and pool their resources to form a secretive and domineering financial empire known as the Illuminati. It was through the Illuminati that the Rothschilds were to leverage their immense wealth and power to influence world affairs and move the Great Plan forward by leaps and bounds in a comparatively short amount of time, orchestrating their agenda through the Freemasonic secret society.

The decedents of the Illuminati families exist today and are as real as a heart attack, so unlearn what you have been brainwashed into believing about them. The final stage of the Great Plan that the Illuminati took the reins of in 1776 is nearing completion.

Chapter 4/B

THE ILLUMINATI

"By this plan we shall direct all mankind. In this manner, and by the simplest means, we shall set in motion and in flames. The occupations must be allotted and contrived, that we may in secret, influence all political transactions ... I have considered everything and so prepared it, that if the Order should this day go to ruin, I shall in a year re-establish it more brilliant than ever."
-Adam Weishaupt, mastermind of the Illuminati

Occultist Adam Weishaupt (1748-1811), was Professor of Canon (Vatican) Law at Ingolstadt University in Bavaria, and proclaimed the birthday of his project known as the Illuminati as May 1, 1776. The Illuminati had been in the process of coming together for 5 or 6 years before this, but the reason this particular day was picked as the birth of the Illuminati is because it is an occult holiday known as **Beltane**. Beltane is the occultist's New Years Day, with all new occult endeavors aspiring to begin on this unholiest of days. This is also why Communists celebrate Mayday, which is also on May 1---in honor of the founders of Communism and occultists-in-chief the Illuminati. It was the Illuminati who planned, funded and orchestrated the rise of Communism, which we will go over soon.

Weishaupt was originally born into a Jewish family, with his father a rabbi, but "abandoned" Judaism when his father died, and converted to Unholy Roman Catholicism after being raised by Jesuits. He then defected from Catholicism and embraced his true occult calling. Ultimately his only allegiance was to the Great Plan.

". . . it was this same remembrance, preserved, or perhaps profaned in the celebrated Order of the Templars, that became for all the secret associations, of the Rose-Croix, of the Illuminati, and of the Hermetic Freemasons, the reason of their strange rites, of their signs . . . and, above all, of their mutual devotedness and of their power."

-Albert Pike, 33rd degree Freemasonic "prophet", from his book 'Morals and Dogma'

Enlisting in its initial membership the highest ranking, most influential and most wealthy Freemasons (occultists) of the time, the secret society within a secret society was born called the **Illuminated Seers of Bavaria** or "Illuminati" for short. The path to the completion of the Great Plan was "illuminated" by the guidance of their god Satan, their god, who is also referred to as "the light bearer". The entity called Satan showed them (illuminated) the plan of action to undertake by which they would be able to take over the world and complete the Great Plan, hence their name the "Illuminati". The main path of action needed to be taken was to install Illuminati-owned central banks in all of the Western nations.... which they did. Money is power, and through the control of the nation's money systems the Illuminati would by default control the nations themselves. This is exactly where we are at today.

The Illuminati allegedly began as 13 families, and the heads of those families still run it today. Out of those original 13 small families, however, grew dozens and hundreds and thousands of descendents who today are a large number of people in politics at the federal level, the people running all the international banks, owners and heads of huge multinational corporations, and etc. etc. etc. They are all in place to promote the Illuminati agenda, which is globalism. This is factually why most of our Presidents of the U.S. are related—even Obama, tracing their shared ancestry back to European royalty. European royalty today and in the past are full-fledged participants of the Great Plan.

The original families' descendents also head up and staff covert organizations you will come to know such as the Council on Foreign Relations, the Bilderberg Group, the Club of Rome, and the Trilateral Commission.

Again, much disinformation about the true origin and agenda of the Illuminati has been intentionally put forth by Hollywood and the Mainstream Media lately as a result of Pandora's Box of truth that was opened via the independent internet truth seekers. Do your own research as I have and you will see why they are so desperate to muddy up the waters regarding the Illuminati. Contrary to what you may have heard, the Illuminati are real, and the organizational hierarchy they began in the 18th century exists today, carried forward in time by the bloodline families who run it and the cronies they have been able to hire with the immense amount of money under their control.

With the backing of the growing Rothschild international banking network, the occultists, through the Illuminati-Rothschild money power, now had the financial means to carry out their evil plans. As a result of the Rothschilds' money power, the occultists were able to regain the banking prominence---**and therefore the political power**---that they once held under the **Knights Templar**.

The Illuminati decided to use the existing occult-themed Freemasonry lodges and members as a front, and for all intents and purposes **the Illuminati pulled off a hostile takeover of Freemasonry.** There were already high-ranking Freemasons when the Illuminati officially formed in 1776, but by infiltrating their own agents, the Illuminati were able to gain total control of the highest levels of Freemasonry, and therefore of Freemasonry itself. The Illuminati basically took over the highest degrees, 33rd and above, and in effect were a secret society within a secret society. Freemasonry was already the modern day incarnation of the Great Plan, but it needed to be super-charged with a fiat money system ala the Knights Templar in order to be expedited to the finish line, hence the creation of the Illuminati and involving the money master Rothschild Banking Dynasty.

In 1782 in Wilhelmsbad, Bavaria (Germany) at the first meeting of the newly formed Masonic Congress of Wilhelmsbad, Weishaupt's Illuminati were able to certify their position among the European Freemasonic lodges as the new undisputed leaders of the Great Plan.

By the time of the third Masonic Congress in 1786, the Illuminati controlled all of the Masonic lodges across Europe, and they revealed **their stated goals for the world** at this meeting as this:

1.) Pantheism (Babylonian Mystery Religion) for the higher degrees; atheism for the lower degrees and the populace.

2.) Communism of goods, women, and general concerns. Remember, back in those days, women were considered second-class citizens and virtually the "property" of the men who took care of them.

3.) The destruction of the Church and in particular all forms of Christianity, and the removal of all existing human governments to make way for a one world government.

However, all was not well within the Illuminati power ranks and some started to quit the organization. Some even started to talk, and this was the beginning of the end of the Illuminati as they had been operating, at least of having their operations semi-public and vulnerable to attrition.

In October 1783, Joseph Utzschneider, a lawyer who had dropped out of the Illuminati in August, presented to the Bavarian Duchess Maria Anna a document which detailed the activities and goals of the Illuminati.

He had an ax to grind because he felt he had been promoted too slowly, and was constantly prodded to prove his loyalty to the organization.

The Duchess took the information and gave it to the Duke of Bavaria. It is through actions like this that have been passed down in history to us that we have been allowed access to the goals of the Illuminati.

Duke Karl Theodore Dalberg, the Elector Palatinate of Bavaria, after discovering from the Utzschneider document that the goals of the Illuminati were to take over the world by overthrowing all civil government, issued a proclamation on March 2, 1785 identifying the Illuminati as a branch of the Freemasons, and ordered that their Lodges be shut down.

The government launched an offensive against the Illuminati by initiating judicial inquiries at Ingolstadt. In an attempt to preserve the secrecy of their motives, the Illuminati allegedly burned many of their documents.

However, the Bavarian government was able to seize many of their papers when they raided the **Freemasonic lodges.**

Weishaupt felt the heat coming and fled across the border into Regensburg, settling in Gotha, where he found refuge with another Illuminati member, the Duke of Saxe-Gotha.

In April, 1785, Utzschneider was able to convince three other members of the Illuminati to come forward with information. They were fellow professors at the Marienburg Academy who had doubts about the validity of the organization's principles *when they discovered that they would receive no mystical powers. This is because the true occult power of the supernatural is solely reserved for the top tier echelon of the Luciferians, the Illuminati.*

They were also disgruntled over Weishaupt's arrogance lording over the Illuminati. **Professors Cossandey, Grunberger, and Renner went before the Bavarian Court of Inquiry on September 9, 1785, where they supplied valuable information, such as membership lists, and revealed the Illuminati's aims and goals, which they consolidated into the following six points:**

1. Abolition of the Monarchy and all ordered government.
2. Abolition of private property.
3. Abolition of inheritance.
4. Abolition of patriotism.
5. Abolition of the family, through the abolition of marriage, all morality, and the institution of communal education for children.
6. Abolition of all religion.

The purposes of these six points were to divide the people politically, socially, and economically, and to weaken countries to the point where they were ready to accept a one world government to take care of the problems that the Illuminati had caused to start with.

The disgruntled ex-Illuminati testified that **"all religion, all love of country and loyalty to sovereigns, were to be annihilated..."**

The government pardoned all public officials and military leaders who publicly admitted membership. Those who didn't, and were discovered to be members, lost their rank and standing, were removed from office, and societally blacklisted as traitors.

The actions of the Bavarian government barely had any effect on the in-motion plans of the conspirators however.......

Weishaupt, during the government investigation into the Illuminati, was preparing to set his plans into motion for the French Revolution, which was slated to begin in 1789. In July of 1785, he instructed Xavier Zwack, one of the Illuminati's most prominent leaders, to put their plans in book form. **This book contained not only the plans for the execution of the French Revolution, but also contained a history of the Illuminati and many of their ideas for expansion and future endeavors.** A copy of this book was sent by a courier, identified as Jacob Lanze, to Illuminati members in Paris and Silesia.

However, after leaving Frankfurt and riding through Regensburg on horseback, Lanze was struck by lightning and killed. **The local authorities found the documents and turned them over to the Bavarian government, which further fueled the importance of their investigation of the Illuminati's conspiratorial activites. This is another source of the factual plans set into motion by the Rothschild banking dynasty and their Illuminati co-conspirators. These are the exact same plans they follow today.**

Zwack, whose name was on Renner's list that was handed over to the Bavarian authorities, had his house in Landshut searched by the police in October 1785 and all his papers relating to the Illuminati were seized. He was immediately dismissed from his position as a lawyer for the government. Many books, documents, papers and correspondence were discovered including over 200 letters written between Weishaupt and the members of the Illuminati which dealt with matters of the highest secrecy. The following year more information was taken from the houses of Illuminati members Baron Bassus and Count Massenhausen. **Among the confiscated documents were tables which contained their secret codes and symbols, secret calendar, geographical locations, insignias, ceremonies of initiation, recruiting instructions, statutes, a partial roster of members, and nearly 130 official seals from the government which were used to counterfeit state documents.**

Suffice it to say, all of this information shed even more light on the Illuminati and what they were up to, and the danger first realized by the government had now become a full-blown national emergency.

In 1786 the Bavarian government gathered together all of the confiscated documents and published them in a book called *"Original Writings of the Order and Sect of the Illuminati"*, which was circulated to every government and crowned head in Europe, including France, to warn them of the impending danger from this **highly funded, highly motivated, and highly secretive occult organization.**

The leaders of the Illuminati who appeared before the government's Court of Inquiry **testified** that the organization was dedicated to the overthrow of church and state. However, these revelations and the publication of their documents **did little to alert the public because of their <u>unbelievable claims</u>.**

Remember from the start of this book, the first couple lines of the Secret Covenant????.........

"<u>An illusion it will be, so large, so vast it will escape their perception. Those who will see it will be thought of as *insane*."</u>

Or how about FBI chief J. Edgar Hoover's blunt statement regarding the New World Order conspiracy:

"<u>The individual is handicapped by coming face-to-face with a conspiracy so monstrous he cannot believe it exists. The American mind simply has not come to a realization of the evil which has been introduced into our midst."</u>

With the release of the government's tell-all book on the Illuminati, new measures were immediately taken by Bavarian government officials. The leaders of the conspiracy were arrested and formally interrogated, then forced to renounce the Illuminati. The final blow came on August 16, 1787, when Duke Dalberg of Bavaria issued his final proclamation against the Illuminati. Anyone found guilty of recruiting members were to be **executed**, while those who were recruited, **would have their property confiscated and then be deported.**

Zwack, who was banished, sought sanctuary in the Court of Zweibrucken, where he was later appointed to an official position in the principality of Salm-Kyburg. He contributed to the Illuminati movement in Holland, and was later summoned by Dalberg, as the government tried to deal with the problem of fugitives who might attempt to reorganize the Illuminati.

Zwack immediately fled to England.

On November 15, 1790, the heat kept coming and another edict was announced against the members of the organization. **Anyone found to be an active member was to be put to death.** The following year a list of 91 names of alleged members was compiled. **They were hunted down and executed.** This persecution didn't end until **1799** when Dalberg died.

The "apparent" demise of the Order of the Illuminati was a minor setback, who continued to operate unabated underground, just as they do today.

Weishaupt wrote:

> *"The great care of the Illuminati after the publication of their secret writings was to persuade the whole of Germany that their Order no longer existed, that their adepts had all renounced, not only their mysteries, but as members of a secret society."*

Point of fact, Weishaupt was more motivated than ever, and wrote:

> *"By this plan we shall direct all mankind. In this manner, and by the simplest means, we shall set in motion and in flames. The occupations must be allotted and contrived, that we may in secret, influence all political transactions ... I have considered everything and so prepared it, that if the Order should this day go to ruin, I shall in a year re-establish it more brilliant than ever."*

The Illuminati soon grew into a worldwide network by infiltrating and using the Masonic lodges as a front, and have been behind nearly **EVERY** major political event since their inception---keep this in mind as we go over the various wars and other major historical events that happened by their clandestine guiding hand later in this book.

Chapter 4/C

THE UNITED STATES OF BABYLON

"There is a Destiny which has the control of our actions, not to be resisted by the strongest efforts of Human Nature. The preservation of the sacred fire of liberty, and the destiny of the republican model of government, are justly considered as deeply, perhaps as finally staked, on the experiment entrusted to the hands of the American people."

-George Washington, alleged 33rd Degree Freemason, 1st President of the United States

This chapter was particularly distressing to put to paper, and it caused a mental block that delayed the release of this book for many long weeks. As a fiercely patriotic American who bleeds Red, White, and Blue, it was really unnerving as to the extent that we have been lied to about how things really are in the world, and especially the true nature of why the United States is even in existence. However, our quest for the truth does not fear investigation or revelation, and that is what this book is about: Getting at the truth, no matter how disturbing.

Here is what I believe to be the truth: Our country was created and set into motion to become a resurrected version of King Nimrod's ancient Babylon. The Great Plan's agenda was to raise us up to be the most powerful country in history, use that power to set up a global police state though the Unites States military, and then intentionally crash and burn our country—turning over the prefabricated infrastructure of the world police state to the waiting New World Order/one world government, which right now is housed within the United Nations.

People have been perplexed that an entity as powerful as the United States, the most powerful and influential country in the history of man, isn't mentioned at all in the Bible. Well, I believe it is. This is because the United States is really the "Babylon" detailed in the End Times prophecies. The one that is the most powerful nation in history across the board, which then self-destructs and is physically destroyed by outside factions. **This is also why we currently house the first incarnation of the one world government, the United Nations.**

We were intended to end up not only as the most powerful country in terms of military and financial might, but also powerful in terms of our moral debauchery. I'd say we have met those goals, as these things have come to pass, and now that we have achieved them, our time as king of the hill is almost up---all according to plan. We are on the downward slide towards the end of the United States right this second. No other country will crash harder or descend deeper into pandemonium as the United States after the big financial crash occurs as a result of the Federal Reserve Ponzi scheme.

The founding of the United States was orchestrated by the guiding hands of the proponents of the Great Plan, and we are going to go over two distinct sections in this chapter. The first section is going to be the sum total of evidence that the Freemasonic elite orchestrated the founding of the United States with the express intent of it becoming a modern day Babylon.

The second section is going to discuss how the descriptions of the End Times entity called "Babylon", chiefly described in the Book of Revelation but also in other sections of Biblical prophecy, matches perfectly with the United States today. Again, this is why the United States is not mentioned in Holy Scripture, as the title of the United States is listed as Babylon. The usage of the term "Babylon" or "Mystery Babylon" means not only a municipality similar to the kingdom of ancient Babylon, but the religious-political system that enabled Babylon to be rebuilt, represented by the Babylonian Mystery Religion, the Great Plan. This is the missing piece in Biblical prophecy concerning the United States role in the End Times events. We're going to have significantly contributed to the End Times occurring, but our country will be gone and the land significantly ruined. I believe this will come about not by nuclear destruction, but by a technology-based weapon known as HAARP that we will go over towards the end.

Not a city or country has existed since the original Babylon, the original "one world government", that could match its original recipe of human debauchery, political power, military might, and general domination of the countries (world) around it. Knowing what we know about the Bible and its use of metaphors, you are going to see that the United States **is** the "Babylon" described in the End Times prophecies of the Bible.

Alleged 33rd degree Freemason George Washington, along with alleged 33rd degree Freemason Benjamin Franklin and other confirmed prominent Freemasons at the time were central characters to the plot of the founding of the United States. It is also alleged that the plans for the American Revolution were fomented through the existing Masonic lodges at the time, and I would tend to believe it.

Through gathering and analysis of the evidence available, it appears that there was also a hostile takeover of Freemasonry from within by the Illuminati, and the Freemasons in America were against it as it was a European movement that they were largely left out of.

America is the greatest military, political, economical-powerhouse society the world has ever known. There is no way that a few square miles of desert in the middle of Iraq are going to supplant New York City and the U.S. as the financial hub of the world, nor would it replace Hollywood as Moral Debauchery, Inc.

It would have been too obvious a sign of the End Times to rebuild Babylon where it was located in the past, so they resurrected it as the United States.

By interpreting the Bible literally, most people have missed Babylon being resurrected right before their eyes. Some Biblical scholars believe that the Babylon referred to in the Book of Revelation is the Roman Empire that existed at the time of its writing, but this is simply not the main point being relayed here. The events happening during the writing of Revelation were a microcosm of events to come relating to the End Times.

Now let's go over the evidence showing that the United States is the new Babylon, and that it has been used to help fulfill the Great Plan.

Let's start with a quote from **certified** 33rd Degree Freemason Manly P. Hall, the most revered Freemasonic "prophet" of the 20th century:

"European mysticism was not dead at the time the United States of America was founded. The hand of the mysteries controlled in the establishment of the new government for the signature of the mysteries may still be seen on the Great Seal of the United States of America. Careful analysis of the seal discloses a mass of occult and Masonic symbols chief among them, the so-called American Eagle. ... the American eagle upon the Great Seal is but a conventionalized phoenix... Not only were many of the founders of the United States government Masons, but they received aid from a secret and august body existing in Europe which helped them to establish this country for a peculiar and particular purpose known only to the initiated few. The Great Seal is the signature of this exalted body—unseen and for the most part unknown—and the unfinished pyramid upon its reverse side is a trestleboard setting forth symbolically the task to the accomplishment of which the United States Government was dedicated from the day of its inception."

The "Great Seal" that Hall is talking about is the Great Seal of the United States, **which is factually full of Masonic/Great Plan symbolism.** We'll go over this in detail when we get to reviewing the design of the United States' one dollar bill. Just know that the seal of our country, since its inception, was intended to show Masonic control of our country. In Masonic circles of the Great Plan, they refer to the United States as the "new Atlantis", which is code for "New Babylon".

Here is another quote from Hall:

"For more than three thousand years, secret societies have labored to create the background of knowledge necessary to the establishment of an enlightened democracy among the nations of the world ... Men bound by a secret oath to labour in the cause of world democracy decided that in the American colonies they would plant the roots of a new way of life. Brotherhoods were established to meet secretly, and they quietly and industriously conditioned America to its destiny for leadership in a free world.

On the reverse of our nation's Great Seal is an unfinished pyramid to represent human society itself, imperfect and incomplete. Above floats the symbol of the esoteric orders, the radiant triangle with its all-seeing eye. ... There is only one possible origin for these symbols, and that is the secret societies which came to this country 150 years before the Revolutionary War. There can be no question that the great seal was directly inspired by these orders of the human Quest, and that it set forth the purpose for this nation. ..."

- Manly P. Hall, from his book "The Secret Destiny of America"

Now, it is my contention that the Illuminati exercised a hostile take-over of Freemasonry right around the time of the founding of the United States. Remember, both the Illuminati and the United States were "born" in 1776.

So, with that said, let's back history up a bit to the late 1700s and see what was happening in the infancy of these United States regarding the actions of the Illuminati.

In 1785, the **Columbia** Lodge of Freemasonry was established by the Illuminati in New York City, and the Illuminati have been operating in the United States ever since. **This was the first Illuminati-controlled Freemasonry lodge in the United States**, the rest before this one were still aligned with the "original" Freemasons running the Great Plan. Among its members were Governor DeWitt Clinton, Horace Greeley (politician and editor of the New York Daily Tribune), Charles Dana, and Clinton Roosevelt (the ancestor of Franklin D. Roosevelt).

The name **"Columbia"** is very special to the Illuminati, as it is another name for **Queen Semiramis**. This is where the term Washington, D.C. (District of **COLUMBIA,** aka District of the Illuminati/Great Plan) comes from. Also important titles with their term "Columbia" in it: **The first space shuttle was named "Columbia"; you have Columbia Broadcasting Service, CBS, with the Freemasonic "all-seeing eye" for their logo, Columbia records---also with the "all-seeing eye" for their logo. Then you have Columbia Pictures and their logo is a mountain (pyramid) with the rays emanating from the top ala the "all-seeing eye", etc. The "all-seeing eye" is purely a Freemasonic/ Great Plan symbol, and this is a fact.**

What's the first thing you see at the start of a Columbia Pictures movie? A lady, holding a flame, with a sun burst effect behind her head... she looks just like the *Statue of Liberty*.

THE STATUE OF LIBERTY was, in fact, conceived by Freemasons, financed by Freemasons, accepted by Freemasons, and installed by Freemasons in a Freemasonic ceremony. The Statue of Liberty was intended by the Masons to be a representation of King Nimrod's wife, Queen Semiramis. The Statue of Liberty is literally the "whore of Babylon" described in the Book of Revelation, watching over the blossoming New Babylon at its 100th anniversary.

The Statue of Liberty in New York harbor was presented in 1884 as a gift from the French Grand Orient Temple Masons to the Masons of America in celebration of the centenary of the rebirth of Babylon.

She is holding the Masonic "Torch of Enlightenment", which is representative of man's quest for knowledge in order to become gods themselves on Earth.

The cornerstone plaque on the statue records how it was factually laid in a Masonic ceremony......perfect.

Clinton Roosevelt, listed as one of the first members of the Columbia Lodge above, put out a book in 1841 called *"Science of Government Founded on Natural Law"*, in which he quoted:

> *"There is no God of justice to order things aright on Earth, if there be a God; he is a malicious and revengeful being, who created us for misery."*

Roosevelt's book was a blueprint of the conspiracy to eliminate the U.S. Constitution and to destroy the country based on the principles of Weishaupt. It contained the detailed plan for the **New Deal** and the **National Recovery Act** that was implemented 92 years later by his direct descendant and alleged 33rd Degree Freemason **President Franklin D. Roosevelt.**

Roosevelt referred to himself and other members of the Columbia Lodge as the "enlightened ones", and referred to the U.S. Constitution as a "leaky vessel" which was "hastily put together when we left the British flag" and in need of revision as it gave the American people too much freedom.

The Illuminati weren't going to wait for the U.S. to turn into Babylon; they were instead going right for the throat of the world and usurping the reins of the Great Plan from the American faction of Freemasons.

This is my bottom line position of a hostile takeover of Freemasonry/ the Great Plan by the Illuminati: The main worldwide body of Freemasonry, led in American by George Washington, Benjamin Franklin (both alleged 33rd degree Freemasons) and others orchestrated the formal founding of the United States. At this same time, the Illuminati were executing a hostile takeover of European Freemasonry and wanted to start right in on taking over control of the U.S. from the American contingency of Freemasons. They knew it was being founded as the New Babylon and they wanted immediate control over it.

The actions of the Illuminati were considered dangerous to our fledgling country by people in the know, and the warnings about their activities were soon coming fast and furious.

On July 19, 1789 David Pappin, President of Harvard University, issued a stern warning to the graduating class concerning the Illuminati's blossoming influence on American politics and religion.

In April of 1793, France sent their ambassador, Edmond Genet, to the U.S. so he could collect money owed to France that was loaned to help finance the American Revolution. However, his real reason for being here was to gain political favor for France and most important to his mission, spread the doctrine of the Illuminati, which he did through the establishment of "Democratic Clubs".

George Washington stated that the Democratic Clubs **"...would shake the government to its foundations"**, an obvious reference to what would happen to the United States if it fell into the hands of the Illuminati.

John Quincy Adams, oldest son of the 2nd President, John Adams, who became our 6th President in 1825, said that these Democratic Clubs were **"so perfectly affiliated with the Parisian Jacobins that their origin from a common parent cannot possibly be mistaken."** The Parisian Jacobins were in fact the representatives of the Illuminati in France.

Because of the Illuminati threat, both Washington and John Adams lobbied Congress to pass the "Alien and Sedition Act" which was **"designed to protect the United States from the extensive French Jacobin conspiracy, paid agents of which were even in high places in the government."**
This quote by George Washington himself says it all:

"It is not my intention to doubt that the doctrine of the Illuminati and the principles of Jacobinism had not spread in the United States. On the contrary, no one is more satisfied of this fact than I am. The idea that I meant to convey, was, that I did not believe that the Lodges of Freemasons in this Country had, as Societies, endeavored to propagate the diabolical tenets of the first, or pernicious principles of the latter (if they are susceptible of separation). That Individuals of them may have done it, or that the founder, or instrument employed to found, the Democratic Societies in the United States, may have had these objects; and actually had a separation of the People from their Government in view, is too evident to be questioned."
-George Washington, first President of the United States of America

In order to infiltrate the Masonic lodges in Europe, Adam Weishaupt had originally enlisted the aid of a British fellow, John Robison. Robison was a professor of Natural Philosophy at Edinburgh University in Scotland, a British historian, and Secretary-General to the Royal Society of Edinburgh.

When he went to Germany to meet with Weishaupt, he was given the Illuminati's revised conspiracy plans to study, in order to expand their influence in Great Britain. Robison didn't agree with their principles of a worldwide socialistic government, and verbally warned American Masons in 1789.

John Robison was so disturbed by what was revealed to him by Weishaupt that he wrote and published a book to expose the organization in 1798 called *"Proofs of a Conspiracy Against All Religions and Governments of Europe, Carried On In the Secret Meetings of Freemasons, Illuminati, and Reading Societies".*

He wrote:

> *"I have observed these doctrines gradually diffusing and mixing with all the different systems of Freemasonry till, at last, an association has been formed for the express purpose of rooting out all the religious establishments, and overturning all the existing governments of Europe."*

So, what Robison was saying here is that he was witnessing the Illuminati-takeover of Freemasonry, didn't like it, and acted to try and stop it through his book exposing them. This again lends credence to the theory that the Illuminati's hostile takeover of Freemasonry was disputed by those who either weren't in the Illuminati's Freemasonic power circle, or were just flat out against it.

Also, that same year, 1798, Abbé Augustin Barruel, a French patriot, published his *"Memoires pour servir a l'Histoire du Jacobinisme"* or translated to English, ***"Memoirs Illustrating the History of Jacobinism".***

Both of these books sought to warn the fledgling United States about the Illuminati conspiracy, ***but the warnings were not taken seriously by the population at large.***

A small percentage of patriotic Americans **were** concerned, and an Anti-Masonic political party was actually founded in the early 1800's as a third political party to try and expose/fight Masonic influence in our country. Convincing people there was a grand conspiracy afoot was another matter, and the Anti-Masonic party fizzled out with no impact upon the Great Plan.

We are now going to go over the balance of the evidence that the Freemasons were responsible for the founding of the United States, and control it today.

Let's start with the occult layout of the geography entailing the area within our nation's capital, Washington, D.C. (Remember, District of **Columbia**).

A Freemasonic architect was commissioned to design the street plan for Washington D.C, and every federal building in our nation's capital bears a Masonic plaque. There are many occult symbols to be found shaped out of the roadways in our nation's capital---examples of this can easily be found on the internet at Google images.

The Washington Monument, the Capitol Building, Statue of Liberty, White House, etc. were all initiated with a Masonic ritual laying of the first cornerstone.....and this is a <u>fact.</u>

Washington Monument itself is an occult symbol for the male phallus, an obelisk, and has been since the time of the ancient Egyptians---a probable dedication to Nimrod. Not only is there a symbol of a male phallus in the middle of our capitol, but a dome atop a building signifies the female reproductive parts, with the domed U.S. Capitol building filling that role. There is a lot of odd sex-ritual stuff that goes on within the protocols of Freemasonry, but this is also why there is an occult obelisk in Vatican City facing the domed Vatican, laid out exactly as in D.C.

Let's now go briefly to what it says in the Bible about "Babylon" as an entity in the End times.

Of the 354 mentions of Babylon in the Bible, 342 are in the Old Testament. There is nothing relevant referring directly to "Babylon" in the New Testament until you come to the Book of Revelation, where it is referred to in the future tense over and over as the spiritual pied piper leading the world to apostasy.

Here are but a handful of dozens of references to "Babylon" in the End Times, with every one describing the United States of today:

-*Superpower among nations (Jeremiah 50:23)*
-*Most recent of nations to become the world's superpower (Jeremiah 50:12)*
-*Multicultural (Jeremiah 50:37)*
-*Wealthy among nations (Jeremiah 51:13; Revelation 17:4)*
-*Leader in world trade and economics (Revelation 18:13)*
-*Influential in many countries (Jeremiah 51:13)*
-*Loud voice in the world (Jeremiah 51:55)*
-*Strong defenses (Jeremiah 51:53)*
-*Idolatrous lust for false gods and other material things (Jeremiah 50:38)*
-*Revels in epicurean pleasures (Revelation 18:4)*
-*Sins piled as high as heaven (Revelation 18:5)*
-*Blinded by pride (Revelation 18:7; Jeremiah 50:24; 1 Thessalonians 5:3)*

*- Sits upon many waters=2 oceans, the Gulf of Mexico, the Great Lakes (Revelation 17:1, 15). The original city of Babylon is **landlocked**.*
-Etc., etc., etc.

Like I said earlier, you've got some homework to do regarding not only the state of our country, but the state of the world under the Great Plan. This little problem isn't going to go away, and will, in fact, only grow worse as time marches on.

Chapter 4/D

THE FRENCH REVOLUTION

Before I get into this section, you've got to remember this very important detail: there is no loyalty within the ranks of the Great Plan. The people who are running it are diabolical and treacherous in nature, always scheming and ready to stab another in the back to move up the ladder of the Luciferian hierarchy. The Unholy Roman Empire-division of the Great Plan controlled France at the time of the French Revolution. The Illuminati needed to get rid of the religious rule in favor of democratic rule, where they would easily be able to control the puppet public officials just like they do today with kickbacks and "favors" like high-paying speaking arrangements, lucrative book deals, donations for re-election, etc. The Illuminati didn't care if they were "on the same Luciferian side" as the Vatican---they were looking to move their end of the ancient plan along and were going to challenge the Unholy Roman Empire for control of France.

The Illuminati had infiltrated France by 1787 through French orator and revolutionary leader **Count Gabriel Victor Riqueti de Mirabeau.**

Mirabeau introduced Illuminati principles at the Paris Masonic Lodge, and they were readily accepted as the path to Freemasonic world domination.

The French Freemasons, under the influence of the Illuminati, committed themselves to a plan for overthrowing the King's government, which again was under Vatican control at the time. Under the guise of liberty and equality, the lower level Masons were convinced they were ending the autocratic regimes in order to have government by and for the people, which is the exact opposite of what the Illuminati were really planning. The lower level Masons were deceived in order to get them to help what the upper echelon was plotting, just like today.

Many revolutionary leaders in France joined the Illuminati, who had eventually infiltrated all 266 Masonic lodges by 1789, even though the lower degree Masons weren't aware of the Luciferians at the top calling the shots, again, just like today.

The Illuminati began to create situations in order to create dissention among the people. A good example of this today being the false left/right paradigm our political system currently resides under. The false left-right system forces people to choose from the apparent lesser of two evils instead of a person who would really effect change for the better in our country.

The plan was set in motion and the Duke of Orleans, an Illuminist, instructed his agents to buy up as much grain as they could. The French people were then led to believe that the King had intentionally caused the shortage. This caused starvation among the citizens of France. Then under the Illuminati's guiding hand, fellow conspirators in the government helped create runaway inflation. These carefully planned situations manipulated the people like puppets into turning against a king whose reign had actually strengthened the middle class before the Illuminati stepped in.

The Illuminati had infiltrated the Masonic Lodges to such an extent that they had ceased operating under the title of "Freemasons" and instead started calling themselves "The French Revolutionary Club."

Their ranks were swelling with revolutionaries, and when the Grand Lodge near Paris needed a larger meeting place, they began using the hall of the **Jacobin's Convent**. This revolutionary group of 1,300 people emerged on July 14, 1789 as the **"Jacobin Club"**. The Illuminati founded and controlled this club, and were directly responsible for fermenting the activities which developed into the French Revolution. These are the exact same Jacobins that we just went over whose presence in the fledgling United States caused such concern to George Washington among others.

Weishaupt put a radical Jacobin at the helm of the revolution in 1791, Maximilien Francois Marie Isidore de Robespierre, and he was closely maintained under control of Weishaupt and the Illuminati.

The monarchy under the Vatican had ruled France for many centuries, **but starting in April of 1789 it only took <u>three years</u> of the Illuminati's meddling influence to fall.**

During the revolution, the Jacobins oversaw the carrying out of a plan which called for the population to be reduced by one-third to one-half, murdering over 300,000, including the execution of King Louis and his family. Those French citizens arrested who responded with the proper Masonic hand signs were the only ones spared if the revolutionaries were to come upon them. The great culling of the citizens during this time was done to insure the stability of the new French Republic.

Charles Maurice de Talleyrand, who became the Catholic bishop of Autin in 1788, orchestrated a radical reorganization of the Church under Weishaupt and was excommunicated by the Pope. He then became a deputy to the National Assembly. The Jacobins controlled the National Assembly and, **Count Gabriel Victor Riqueti de Mirabeau, the one who brought the Illuminati to France to start with, became France's leader in late 1789, the same year the revolution started**. Mirabeau acted as a leader of the Third Estate, or common people, until his death in 1791.

In August, 1792, after the overthrow of the government, the tri-colored banner was replaced by the red flag of social revolution.

All actions of the revolution were orchestrated by the Illuminati through the Jacobins they controlled, right down to the official end of the revolution on July 28, 1794, when revolution commander Robespierre was publicly executed by guillotine to ensure he wouldn't cause trouble for his bosses and newly-crowned masters of France, the Order of the Illuminati. Although the Illuminati's Jacobins were disbanded as the end of the revolution was in sight, and the Illuminati went back into the shadows, they continued to hold onto power using the power of money, just as they do today in the U.S., from behind the scenes.

It's a dog-eat-dog world within the ranks of the New World Order with loyalty to none but the implementation of the Great Plan. They used Robespierre until he was no longer of use and then used him one last time, having him executed as a sign of capitulation to the newly formed French republic. Once the people actually **felt** like they controlled their own destiny, they were much more easily manipulated by the Illuminati, much like the citizens of the United States are today.

Chapter 4/E

NAPOLEON

This brings us to the next chapter of France's dealings with the influence of the Illuminati: Napoleon Bonaparte.

Vicomte de Barras, a member of the Illuminati and also a member of the newly formed French National Assembly, took a shining to 24 year old Napoleon Bonaparte, who was leading French forces against the English and Spanish at Toulon in 1793. Barras was appointed as Commander-in-Chief of the French military by the Illuminati-controlled National Assembly and wielded great power in the government. He was able to parlay this position into a spot as a member of the five-man Directorate which then began to govern France, and was viewed by the people as the most powerful political figure in France at the time.

This Illuminist decided that Napoleon would be a great candidate and workhorse for the Illuminati, and chose Napoleon to lead France's military forces.

Unfortunately for them, Napoleon was a rogue with a mind of his own.

Much to the chagrin of the Illuminati, Napoleon used his charisma and influence of "his" military forces to overthrow the Directorate and became the Emperor of France.

Napoleon then went on a war-spree across Europe---the Napoleonic Wars--- bringing about total disruption to the Illuminati's plans. He also put the final dagger into the heart of the waning Unholy Roman Empire, installing his brother Joseph as the King of Naples in 1806. After conquering Spain in 1808, he moved his brother Joseph from Italy to Spain, and replaced him in Italy with his brother-in-law Murat. Napoleon's brother Louis was made King of Holland, and another of his brothers named Jerome was crowned as King of Westphalia (Germany).

Napoleon was doing exactly what the Illuminati had set out to do---conquer Europe; the only problem was that he wasn't on their side anymore.

"When a government is dependent upon bankers for money, they and not the leaders of the government control the situation, since the hand that gives is above the hand that takes. Money has no motherland; financiers are without patriotism and without decency; their sole object is gain."
- Napoleon Bonaparte

When France invaded Russia in 1812, however, this went badly for Napoleon and signaled the coming end of his reign of conquest, at least for the time being. From 1812 to 1814, Napoleon fought the War of the Sixth Coalition. The Sixth Coalition, consisting of Austria, Prussia, Russia, Sweden, the United Kingdom, and a number of German States defeated Napoleon, drove him out of Germany, and invaded France. The Coalition defeated France and exiled Napoleon to the island of Elba, Italy. Less than a year later, Napoleon escaped Elba, reunited his army, and set off to conquer Europe once again.

The Illuminati saw the handwriting on the wall this time, and if they didn't act soon, Napoleon would once again set the Great Plan back by years. They began to fight back tenaciously. Nathan Rothschild, the Illuminati's main money master, bankrolled the opposition to Napoleon, sending money to Lord Wellington in Spain to shore up his resources.

As a side note, **don't forget how Nathan Rothschild was able to parlay his information regarding Napoleon's last battle into control over the British stock market.**

Upon his defeat at Waterloo in 1815, Napoleon was exiled, again, this time to the island of Saint Helena in the south Atlantic which is where he died in 1821.

All of the territories held by France under Napoleon were returned to the countries whose borders they fell under, and France's borders were returned to their original 1792 location.

After the Napoleonic Wars, the Illuminati thought that Europe would be tired of the fighting and the killing, and would accept any solution to have peace, including surrendering their sovereignty.

Through the Congress of Vienna (1814-15), the Illuminati hoped to create the first "United Nations"---the foundation for the one world government they were ultimately after.

From September 1814 to June 1815, the powers of the allied coalition, who were the winners of the Napoleonic Wars, met at the Congress of Vienna along with a large number of rulers and officials representing smaller states.

It was the biggest political meeting in European history, with its intent to solidify the Illuminati's growing control over Europe.

Another reason for the convening of the Congress of Vienna was to establish Switzerland as a "forever neutral" country that the Illuminati could store and hide their burgeoning wealth, safe from the hands of future inter-warring nations. This is the exact reason Switzerland has always remained a "neutral" country.

Many of the European governments were in debt to the Rothschilds (Illuminati), so the Illuminati figured they could use that as a bargaining tool to get the countries to capitulate to a unified Europe.

The Russian czar saw through the façade of the planned European federation, recognizing it as an Illuminati ploy to grab power, and would not go along with it. With that in mind, on September 26, 1815, the **"Treaty of Holy Alliance"** was signed by Czar Alexander I of Russia, Francis II of Austria, and Frederick William III of Prussia to counter what the Illuminati were trying to accomplish with the Congress of Vienna.

The head of the Rothschild banking dynasty, Nathan Rothschild, loathed the Czar for his actions, and dreamed of the day that his family would get revenge by destroying the Czar and his family for this outrage of standing in the way of the Great Plan. The Illuminati had their revenge, which they accomplished 100 years later in 1917 through the Bolshevik Revolution.

Chapter 4/F

GIUSEPPE MAZZINI

After the death of Adam Weishaupt in 1830, the Illuminati began looking for another central leader who was also a Masonic occultist like them. Alleged 33rd degree Freemason Giuseppe Mazzini fit the bill after showing off his prowess in wrestling Italy away from the Unholy Roman Empire and basically handing it over to the Illuminati. Mazzini founded a group of revolutionaries called Young Italy in 1831 one year after Weishaupt died. Their goal was to free Italy from the control of monarchy and the Pope. They succeeded, and Mazzini was honored as a patriot in Italy. However, in the process of liberating Italy, the bloodletting organization known as the Mafia was born. Yes, this is correct: **The Mafia is an Illuminati-affiliated organization and is still a part of their network today.**

In the beginning of their operations, the Young Italy revolutionaries needed money, and they:

> *"...supported themselves by robbing banks, looting or burning businesses if protection money was not paid, and kidnapping for ransom. Throughout Italy the word spread that "Mazzini autorizza furti, incendi e attentati," meaning, 'Mazzini authorizes theft, arson, and kidnapping.' This phrase was shortened to the acronym, M.A.F.I.A. Organized crime was born."*
>
> *-John Daniel, "Scarlet and the Beast," Vol. I., pages 330-331*

Mazzini was selected by the Illuminati to lead their organization, and took the reins of their worldwide operations beginning in 1834.

During his leadership, Mazzini enticed an American occultist and Freemason named Albert Pike into joining the upper echelon of the Illuminati. When invited by Mazzini he readily agreed to join. Pike was then made head of Illuminati operations in the U.S. Mazzini could sense an extra-powerful occult nature about Pike and tasked him to write an occult book that guided the transition from average high-ranking mason into a top-ranking Illuminati mason, that of the 33rd degree. Pike then penned what is considered the modern-day Freemasonic "Bible" called **Morals and Dogma.** This book was used by the Illuminati as a "pied piper" to bring the Freemasonic lodges in the United States under their control, where before the Illuminati had operated mainly out of the Columbia lodge.

It is because of the deception that exists within their organization between the tiny upper echelon and the vast majority below that most Freemasons vehemently deny the evil intentions of their fraternity. Since the vast majority never progress pass the third degree, let alone to the Luciferian 33rd degree, they would not be aware of the real purpose behind Freemasonry, the fulfillment of the Great Plan.

Here, I'll let Albert Pike himself clarify, from his book *"Morals and Dogma"*:

> *"Masonry, like all the Religions, all the Mysteries, Hermeticism and Alchemy, conceals its secrets from all except the Adepts and Sages, or the Elect, and uses false explanations and misinterpretations of its symbols to mislead those who deserve only to be misled; to conceal the Truth, which it calls Light, from them, and to draw them away from it."*

When instructing Pike how the book should be developed, Mazzini wrote the following to Pike in a letter dated January 22, 1870.

> *"We must allow all the federations to continue just as they are, with their systems, their central authorities and their diverse modes of correspondence between high grades of the same rite,*

organized as they are at the present, but we must create a super rite, which will remain unknown, to which we will call those Masons of high degree whom we shall select. With regard to our brothers in Masonry, these men must be pledges to the strictest secrecy. Through this supreme rite, we will govern all Freemasonry which will become the one international center, the more powerful because its direction will be unknown."

Mazzini basically wanted to customize the process for an initiate becoming a 33rd degree Freemason in order to ensure the pledge would be fully under the Illuminati's influence and control. In 1871, Pike published the 861 page Masonic handbook known as ***"Morals and Dogma of the Ancient and Accepted Scottish Rite of Freemasonry."*** It is now and has been since the publication of this book, part of the rites for an aspiring 33rd degree Freemason who has reached the 32nd degree, called a "Shriner", to read and accept as his belief the content of Morals and Dogma. Contained within this occult masterpiece is the revelation that Lucifer is the god of the Freemasons and the Great Plan.

In another letter, dated August 15, 1871, Pike wrote to Mazzini upon completion of his master work, *Morals and Dogma*:

"We shall unleash the Nihilists and the Atheists, and we shall provoke a formidable social cataclysm which in all its horror will show clearly to the nations the effect of absolute atheism, the origin of savagery, and of the most bloody turmoil. Then everywhere, the citizens, obliged to defend themselves against the world minority of revolutionaries, will exterminate those destroyers of civilization, and the multitude, disillusioned with Christianity, whose deistic spirits will from that moment be without compass, anxious for an ideal, but without knowing where to render its adoration, will receive the pure light through the universal manifestation which will result from the general reactionary movement which will follow the destruction of Christianity and atheism, both conquered and exterminated at the same time."

After Mazzini's death on March 11, 1872, Pike allegedly took over worldwide operations of the Illuminati. The trail following who was individually running the Illuminati becomes a bit clouded after Pike's passing, but from what I've gathered I believe the Rothschilds now personally hold the reins of Illuminati leadership through a family tribunal.

Chapter 4/G

ALBERT PIKE

"That which we must say to the crowd is: 'We worship a God, but it is the God one adores without superstition.' To you, Sovereign Grand Inspectors General (33rd Degree Masons), we say this, that you may repeat it to the Brethren of the 32nd, 31st, and 30th degrees: 'The Masonic religion should be, by all of us initiates of the high degrees, maintained in the purity of the Luciferian doctrine.

If Lucifer were not God, would Adonay, or 'Adonai,' Hebrew for the word 'Lord' which refers to Jehovah, the God of Abraham, which they avoided using, whose deeds prove his cruelty, perfidy, and hatred of man, barbarism and repulsion for science, would Adonay and his priests calumniate him? Yes, Lucifer is God, and unfortunately Adonay is also God. For the eternal law is that there is no light without shade, no beauty without ugliness, no white without black, for the absolute can only exist as two Gods: darkness being necessary to light to serve as its foil as the pedestal is necessary to the statue, and the brake to the locomotive...

...Thus, the doctrine of Satanism is a heresy; and the true and pure philosophic religion is the belief in Lucifer, the equal of Adonay; but Lucifer, God of Light and God of Good, is struggling for humanity against Adonay, the God of darkness and evil."

-Albert Pike, July 14, 1889, in a statement to the 24 Freemasonic Supreme Councils of the world who were meeting in Paris on this day

Albert Pike (1809-1891) was an occultist and confirmed 33rd degree Freemason who ultimately became the leader of the U.S. branch of

Scottish Rite Masonry, and alleged head of the Illuminati. The Scottish Rite of Freemasonry houses the greatest details and plans of the Great Plan today.

Pike held the title "Sovereign Pontiff of Universal Freemasonry", and was called by Freemasons worldwide as the "Prophet of Freemasonry" and the "greatest Freemason of the nineteenth century". Albert Pike was a diabolical genius, and able to read and write in 16 different languages among other feats of intellectualism. He also had what is common to the various Freemasonic "prophets", and that is a "spirit guide". He allegedly had a mystical bracelet he could use to contact these otherworldly spirits for guidance in his life. What the New Age crowd and the Freemasons call "spirit guides" are referred to as demons in the Bible, and I would more accurately call them interdimensionals in today-speak.

Albert Pike was born on December 29, 1809 in Boston, attended Harvard and became a lawyer, then later served as a Brigadier-General in the Confederate Army. He was appointed by the Confederacy to be the Indian Commissioner in order to create an army of Indian warriors. He became Governor of the Indian Territory and succeeded in creating an army consisting of Chickasaws, Comanches, Creeks, Cherokees, Miamis, Osages, Kansas, and Choctaws. He became known to them as the "faithful pale-face friend and protector."

The savagery of their attacks under the sadistic Pike forced Jefferson Davis, the President of the Confederacy, to soon disband the Indian army. After the Civil War, Pike was found guilty of treason and jailed only to be pardoned by President Andrew Johnson on April 22, 1866 who met with him the next day at the White House. On June 20, 1867 Scottish Rite officials including Pike allegedly bestowed upon Johnson the 4th - 32nd degrees of Freemasonry and weeks later received the 33rd degree initiation.

Gen. Albert Pike is the only Confederate general with an honorary statue on federal property in Washington, DC. He was honored, not as a commander or even as a lawyer, but as Southern regional leader of the Scottish Rite of Freemasonry. The statue stands on a pedestal near the foot of Capitol Hill, between the Department of Labor building and the Municipal Building, between 3rd and 4th Streets, on D Street, NW.

"..Thirty-third degree Freemason Albert Pike (1809-1891), the man destined to develop the Luciferian Doctrine for the Masonic hierarchy, could not accept that Lucifer and Satan were the same personality. While teaching his beliefs to a select few in the Supreme Council, Pike became the most powerful Mason in the world. Although an obscure general in the Confederate Army during the American Civil War, he was hardly inconspicuous in Freemasonry. From 1859 until his death in 1891, Pike occupied simultaneously the positions of Grand Master of the Central Directory at Washington, D.C., Grand Commander of the Supreme Council at Charleston, S.C., and Sovereign Pontiff of Universal Freemasonry. He was an honorary member of almost every Supreme Council in the world, personally receiving 130 Masonic degrees. Pike also was one of the most physically and morally repulsive individuals in American history. Weighing well over three hundred pounds, his sexual proclivity was to sit naked astride a phallic throne in the woods, accompanied by a gang of prostitutes. To these orgies he would bring one or more wagon loads of food and liquor, most of which he would consume over a period of two days until he passed into a stupor. In his adopted state of Arkansas, Pike was well known as a practitioner of Satanism. Portraits of his later years show him wearing a symbol of the Baphomet around his neck."

-John Daniel, from his book on Freemasonry entitled **Scarlet and the Beast**

Pike was the Grand Master of a Luciferian group known as the Order of the Palladium/Sovereign Council of Wisdom, which had been founded in Paris in 1737. Palladism had been brought into the Great Plan from Egypt by Pythagoras in the fifth century B.C., and it was this cult of Satan that was introduced to the inner circle of the Masonic lodges in the early 1800's.

Albert Pike and other Masonic occultists established the New and Reformed Palladian Rite of Freemasonry, also known as the Supreme Council. This Order contained two degrees: 1) Adelph and 2) Companion of Ulysses (or Companion of Penelope for female initiates). Pike, along with Mazzini, Lord Palmerston, and Otto von Bismarck intended to use the Palladian Rite to create an umbrella group that would tie all Masonic groups together.

In addition to founding the Supreme Council/Palladian Rite in Charleston, South Carolina, Pike established Supreme Councils in Rome, Italy (led by Mazzini); London, England (led by alleged 33rd degree Freemason Lord Henry Palmerston); and Berlin, Germany (led by alleged 33rd degree Freemason Otto von Bismarck). He set up 23 subordinate councils in strategic places throughout the world, including five Grand Central Directories in Washington, DC (North America), Montevideo (South America), Naples (Europe), Calcutta (Asia), and Mauritius (Africa), which were used to gather political and societal information. In other words, these were global Illuminati "think tanks". All of these branches have been used for orchestrating Illuminati activities ever since.

In his book, *"Morals and Dogma"*, Pike states:

"Every lodge is a temple of religion, and its teaching instruction in religion... Masonry is the successor to the Mysteries (Babylonian Mystery Religion)."

"The primary tradition... has been preserved under the name of the Kaballah by the priesthood of Israel (Synagogue of Satan)"

"All truly dogmatic religions have issued from the Kaballah and return to it; everything scientific and grand in the religious dreams of the Illuminati, Jacob Boeheme, Swedenborg, Saint Martin, and others is borrowed from the Kaballah; all Masonic associations owe to it their secrets and their symbols."

"Though Masonry is identical with the ancient Mysteries, it is so only in this qualified sense: that it presents but an imperfect image of their brilliancy, the ruins of their grandeur .."

"Masonry, successor to the Mysteries (Babel, Mythras, Tammuz, Whicka, etc.) still follows the ancient manor of teaching."

"The true name of Satan, the Kabalists say, is that of Yahweh reversed; for Satan is not a black god. For the initiates this is not a Person, but a force, created for good, but which may serve for evil. It is the instrument of liberty and free will."

These are only a small handful of quotes from Great Plan proponent Albert Pike. You have heard enough about this famous Freemasonic "prophet" in this space, so onward we go.

Chapter 4/H

ROCKEFELLERS AND ROBBER BARONS

"The drive of the Rockefellers and their allies is to create a one-world government combining super capitalism and Communism under the same tent, all under their control.... Do I mean conspiracy? Yes I do. I am convinced there is such a plot, international in scope, generations old in planning, and incredibly evil in intent."

-Congressman Larry P. McDonald, publicly talking about the Great Plan/New World Order plot in 1976. He was a vocal opponent of the Great Plan while a Congressman and was killed in the Korean Airlines 747 that was conveniently shot down by the Soviets in 1983. Of course, this was certainly no coincidence as you probably now realize.

"I don't want a nation of thinkers. I want a nation of workers."

-John D. Rockefeller, patriarch of the Rockefeller oil and banking dynasty

"Some even believe we (the Rockefeller family) are part of a secret cabal working against the best interests of the United States, characterizing my family and me as 'internationalists' and of conspiring with others around the world to build a more integrated global political and economic structure – one world, if you will. If that's the charge, I stand guilty, and I am proud of it."

- David Rockefeller, from his book "Memoirs"

Now I'm going to introduce you to the "American Rothschilds", and the second wealthiest family in the world, the Rockefellers.

The Rockefeller family, as it is infamously known today, began its ascent up the financial ladder with its founding patriarch John D. Rockefeller, and also to a lesser degree his brother, William Rockefeller.

In 1870, John founded the Standard Oil Company and aggressively ran it until he officially retired in 1897. Standard Oil began as an Ohio partnership formed by John D. Rockefeller, his brother William Rockefeller, and a few other much less relevant people. The Rothschilds knew the importance of this emerging energy source and began to finance Rockefeller's relentless march towards a total oil monopoly in the United States from their coffers at the National City Bank of Cleveland. The Rothschilds have been intimately involved with the Rockefellers ever since---becoming lifelong partners of theirs behind the scenes. They knew that having control over such an up-and-coming energy source as oil would pay off in the future, and today the oil of the world is controlled by the Rockefeller/Rothschild-owned oil corporations of Royal Dutch Shell, Exxon/Mobil, Chevron, BP, and the rest. Sure the Saudis and the rest "own" the oil in the ground, but it is the continued monopoly over the extraction, refinement, and distribution by these companies which helps to further enrich and thereby empower the Illuminati crowd.

As kerosene and gasoline grew in importance, Rockefeller's wealth soared, and he became the "world's richest man" and first American worth more than a billion dollars.

Rockefeller realized early in the game that the oil refinery business, which could offer great profits in a short time, was at the mercy of uncontrolled competition. His solution was simple: crush all competition by any and all means possible, and with Rothschild backing this is exactly what he did.

> *"Competition is a sin."*
> *-John D. Rockefeller*

The above quote is the same strategy as was applied to the founding of the Federal Reserve. Former banking adversaries such as Rockefeller, J.P. Morgan, and the Rothschilds buried the hatchet amongst their competing interests in the banking business to come together for the common good, **their** common good, and form a monopoly over the monetary system of the United States. That is exactly what they have today: a monopoly over our money.

The Rockefeller dedication to a total oil monopoly is legendary in American history. Rockefeller embarked on a campaign of coercing all competing oil refineries out of business. He worked from a number of fronts to accomplish this. First, he would send a minion, not known to be working for Rockefeller, with an offer to buy the competing refinery for a low price, but offering cash up front. If the offer was refused, the competitor would then come under attack from a competing Rockefeller refinery which greatly undercut his price, driving him out of business.

If this technique were to fail, Rockefeller would then embark down the route of intimidation and violence, beating the rival workers as they went to and from their jobs, or burning or blowing up the competing refinery.

The Rothschilds sent their personal representative, Jacob Schiff, to Cleveland to help Rockefeller plan further expansion. At this time, the Rothschilds controlled 95% of all railroad mileage in the United States, through the J.P. Morgan Company and Kuhn Loeb & Company according to Department of Commerce figures for the year 1895.

The infamous J.P. Morgan, forever immortalized as the "tycoon" from the game Monopoly, was merely another of Rothschild's agents in the United States, sent here from Great Britain to help them monopolize the wealth of our entire country to help fulfill the Great Plan and plunge us into a totalitarian one world government.

"In March 1915, the J.P. Morgan interests -- the steel, shipbuilding, and powder interest, and their subsidiary organizations -- got together 12 men high up in the newspaper world and employed them to select the most influential newspapers in the United States and sufficient number of them to control generally the policy of the daily press ... They found it was only necessary to purchase the control of 25 of the greatest papers. An agreement was reached; the policy of the papers was bought, to be paid for by the month; an editor was furnished for each paper to properly supervise and edit

information regarding the questions of preparedness, militarism, financial policies, and other things of national and international nature considered vital to the interests of the purchasers."
- U.S. Congressman Oscar Callaway, 1917

Schiff worked out an elaborate rebate deal for Rockefeller by setting up a dummy corporation, South Improvement Company. These rebates ensured that no other oil company could survive in competition with the Rockefeller firm. The scheme was later exposed, but by that time Rockefeller had plowed under all competitors and achieved a virtual monopoly over the oil business in the United States.

During the next half century, John D. Rockefeller was routinely caricatured by socialist propagandists as the epitome of the ruthless capitalist, while in reality at this exact same time he was one of the **principal financiers** of the world Communist movement.

Despite the fact that it was actually the House of Rothschild who had achieved worldwide financial control, the fury of the American public was directed exclusively against its two principal representatives in the United States: John D. Rockefeller and J.P. Morgan. One of the few revelations of the actual state of affairs appeared in **Truth** magazine, December 16, 1912, which pointed out that:

> ``Mr. Schiff is head of the great private banking house of Kuhn, Loeb & Company, which represents the Rothschild interests on this side of the Atlantic. He is described as a financial strategist and has been for years the financial minister of the great impersonal power known as Standard Oil."

The real conspirators were and always have been the European Rothschilds, who are the capstone of the Illuminati global power structure.

Because of the concealment of the Rothschilds' power in the U.S., it was a relatively simple matter for the American public to accept the "fact" that the Rockefellers were the preeminent power in this country.

To shield his wealth from federal taxes John D. created the Rockefeller Foundation, a web of affiliated tax-exempt organizations that today effectively dictates their agenda to the political, religious and educational entities of our country.

The Rockefeller Foundation has a tradition of financially supporting Ivy League and other major colleges and universities over the generations, including Yale---home of the Skull and Bones Brotherhood of Death fraternity, which we will go over. The Rockefeller's financial support is considered by them an investment, with the intent of using these schools to "farm" the up and coming generations of people who will support the Great Plan through placements in existing corporations, banks, government, etc.

The Rockefellers were also involved in many large construction projects in America, **including <u>donating the land</u> to build the first incarnation of the one world government, the United Nations.**

They were also involved with the founding of the Federal Reserve, of which their Chase Manhattan Bank is one of the founding private banks making up the Federal Reserve cartel. They also were co-founders of the Council on Foreign Relations, the Bilderberg Group, the Club of Rome and the Trilateral Commission. These are four of the preeminent Illuminati global steering organizations that we are going to go over in detail in chapter 6.

In 1981, Robert McNamara retired as head of the World Bank. At a dinner in his honor in Washington, David Rockefeller made the following revealing statement:

> *"The world that we have worked to construct is threatened. The gravity of this moment, when Mr. McNamara and others are about to leave their posts while a new administration re-examines American foreign aid policy, is great. If we are going to save the international institutions we have put in place, the moment is now or never, for the struggle between the old guard and the new is going far beyond the struggle for capital appropriations. It is going to endanger the new world order which we have based on the alliance between Wall Street and Washington.*
>
> *While we men of firms and banks organize international channels of economy and raw materials, the government is now building its own diplomatic and economic bridges between*

Washington and foreign governments. By our methods, our governments contribute to the stability and economic growth of the world, our multinationals benefit, and when it is necessary, they contribute their political support. Now radical conservatives are attempting to destroy all that in seeking first and foremost to serve the national interests of the United States".

With regards to J.P. Morgan, he was just another Rothschild shill. J.P. Morgan was merely a front man, so the Rothschilds could continue to stay in the shadows, out of the public eye.

The Morgans of Great Britain were friendly competitors with the Rothschilds and were socially close to them. Junius Morgan's London-based firm was saved from financial ruin in 1857 by the Bank of England over which the Rothschilds held control. Junius' son, Juliet Pierpont Morgan, better known as J.P. Morgan, was sent to the United States to act on behalf of the Rothschilds. With the financial backing of the richest family on the planet, he couldn't lose.

J.P. Morgan went to great lengths to appear totally American, but was in reality a British Rothschild agent. The Rothschilds backed him at every corner, helping him build up a gigantic banking and corporate empire that they actually held majority interest in.

As Rockefeller became flush with oil money, he decided to enter the banking business and started his own bank, Chase Manhattan bank, known today as **Chase** Bank. This entry into the field of banking was not welcomed by Morgan, and they became fierce competitors. Eventually, they decided to minimize their competition---remember, competition is a sin---by entering into joint ventures. In the end they worked together, along with their Rothschild backers, to create a national banking cabal called the Federal Reserve System of the United States.

Upon J.P. Morgan's death it was factually revealed that he only owned about 20% of his "interests" and the remainder was held by the Rothschilds.

The Rockefellers and their allies have a vested interest in seeing the United States fall as the #2 ranked family of New World Order royalty. Their drive to destroy the United States and usher in the New World Order is purely traitorous and a stab in the back to the people and country of the United States, the very people they made their money off of. The proponents of the Great Plan have not a shred of loyalty to their countries of origin, as they want all countries to fall under the borderless one world government. Their only loyalty is to the fulfillment of the Great Plan.

Chapter 4/I

COMMUNISM

"The Evil One is the satanic revolt against divine authority, revolt in which we see the fecund germ of all human emancipations, the revolution. Socialists recognize each other by the words, 'In the name of the one to whom a great wrong has been done.' Satan is the eternal rebel, the first freethinker and the emancipator of worlds."

- Mikhail Bakunin, Russian anarchist and Satanist, good friend of Karl Marx

The Illuminati had a hand in the creation of Communism through their afilliate Karl Marx, and were behind the communist Russian Revolution in 1917. The Illuminati were involved with Marx because he was an alleged 33rd degree Freemason, with worldwide Freemasonry under Illuminati control at this time. The tenets of Communism are virtually identical to the philosophy espoused by the Illuminati to take over the world. This is also why May 1, which is both the highly important occult holiday of Beltane **and** the anniversary of the "birthday" of the Illuminati, is celebrated in Russia in relation to the start of Communism.

Today, **1/3 of the entire world** lives under atheistic Marxist Communist rule. Communist rule is like living in a country that has been fully converted to the New World Order-style of government they want for the entire world: **Socialism under a 24/7 police state with no freedom of speech, religion, right to protest, right to own guns, right to own private property, etc.**

"From the days of Spartacus (Adam) Weishaupt to those of Karl Marx, to those of Trotsky, Bela-Kuhn, Rosa Luxembourg and Emma Goldman, this world-wide conspiracy ... has been steadily growing. This conspiracy played a definitely recognizable role in the tragedy of the French Revolution.

It has been the mainspring of every subversive movement during the nineteenth century; and now at last this band of extraordinary personalities from the underworld of the great cities of Europe and America have gripped the Russian people by the hair of their heads, and have become practically the undisputed masters of that enormous empire.

There is no need to exaggerate the part played in the creation of Bolshevism and in the bringing about of the Russian revolution by these international and for the most part atheistical (Synagogue of Satan) Jews. It is certainly a very great one; it probably outweighs all others. With the notable exception of Lenin, the majority of the leading figures are (Synagogue of Satan) Jews."

-Winston Churchill, alleged 33rd degree Freemason, speaking frankly about the Great Plan

Karl Marx, the father of Communism, was a Synagogue of Satan, 33rd degree (alleged) Freemason and documented **Satanist.** Before we talk about Marx, let's talk briefly about his mentor, Synagogue of Satan member and documented **Satanist** Moses Hess. Hess was also the mentor to Marx's co-creator of the Communist Manifesto, Friedrich Engels who was an atheist and also, of course, an alleged 33rd degree Freemason.

Moses Hess wanted to wipe out every trace of God that existed in human society. It was Hess' view that the new socialist society of the future could not exist if people still believed in God. Hess wanted the people living under his ideal socialist society to be obedient to the **state,** not **God.**

Hess is also the real "father" of the political movement called Zionism, not Theodore Herzl. In 1862, Hess published a book he called *Rome and Jerusalem - The Last National Question.* In this book he proposed the foundation of a Jewish nation in Palestine. He also proposed that the Jews establish a socialist agrarian system there that would allow them to find "redemption through the land." These are both central tenets of Zionism. As a Satanist and participant of the Great Plan, it was his aim to reestablish Israel not to benefit the Jews, but in preparation of the coming Antichrist, the mastermind of the Great Plan, King Nimrod.

The Communist Manifesto was published in 1848 by Hess' protégés Karl Marx and Fredrick Engels. This is the source from which the Communist philosophy was born.

Do you find it odd that both Marx and Engels were Satanists, and by default believed in God, but pushed atheism in the Communist Manifesto? This strategy is, again, to lead the people away from the one true God, the ultimate source of power in the universe. **Remember, 1/3 of the world lives under the Luciferian system of government created by Marx and Engels.**

Make no mistake about it, Marx was a Satan worshipper. Marx's favorite daughter Eleanor even went on to marry a fellow Satanist named Edward Eveling.

The House of Rothschild solidified their financial control over Europe in the 1800's, and was then ready for the next phase of the Great Plan: Communism (socialism) for the entire world, of which the Illuminati would sit atop of from behind the scenes, just like they do today.

To kick off this next phase of the ancient Great Plan, the Illuminati decided to implement Communism in Russia. They chose Russia for two reasons: the large population within its borders, and secondly **for revenge against the Czarist royal family for refusing to participate in the Congress of Vienna**---the Illuminati's very first attempt at uniting Europe/Russia as a first step towards a one world government.

To pull this off, they enlisted the help of Synagogue of Satan member and alleged 33rd degree Freemason Nikolai Lenin. Lenin was a Russian revolutionary and student of Marx who himself was out for revenge against the Czar after his older brother, Alexander, was hung in 1887 along with four comrades for conspiring to assassinate Czar Alexander II, the grandfather of Nicholas II.

> *"We must combat religion. The spread of atheism is our chief task. Communism abolishes eternal truths, religion & morality"*
> *-Nikolai Lenin*

During his teenage years, Lenin admired Mikhail Bakunin (see quote at beginning of this chapter), who was a follower of Weishaupt's Illuminati principles and a Satanist.

In 1903, in London, Lenin initiated a split in the Russian Social-Democratic Workers Party, which was completed in 1912, and became known as the All Russian Communist Party in 1918, and finally just the "Communist Party" that ruled now-socialist Russia. Russia was now the world's first socialist state, a milestone for the Great Plan.

""...Lenin was sent into Russia ... in the same way that you might send a vial containing a culture of typhoid or of cholera to be poured into the water supply of a great city, and it worked with amazing accuracy. No sooner did Lenin arrive than he began beckoning a finger here and a finger there to obscure persons in sheltered retreats in New York, Glasgow, in Berne, and other countries, and he gathered together the leading spirits of a formidable sect, the most formidable sect in the world... With these spirits around him he set to work with demoniacal ability to tear to pieces every institution on which the Russian State depended."
-Winston Churchill

In 1905, while Russia was engaged in the Russo-Japanese War, the Communists tried to get the farmers to revolt against the Czar, but they refused. Many of the leaders, including Lenin and the revolutionary Leon Trotsky were exiled.

After this aborted attempt, the Russian Czar deposited $400,000,000 in the Chase Manhatten Bank, National City Bank, Guaranty Trust Bank, the Hanover Trust Bank, and Manufacturers Trust Bank in the United States, and $80,000,000 with the Rothschilds in Paris. He did this because he knew who was behind the growing revolutionary movement, and hoped by engaging in a business relationship with the Illuminati to end it. By placing his money within the confines of the Illuminati banks, he fully expected them to back down.

Well, he was dead wrong. This only motivated them even more to overthrow the Czar so they could keep his money, which they did.

Marx, Lenin, Trotsky, and Stalin. The revolutionary activities of all these men were financed by British, French, German, and American international bankers; all of them dominated by the House of Rothschild.

The Illuminati has been in control of Russia ever since. The entire Cold War was a façade to rally America around a common cause, that Russia was our enemy, and for the Military Industrial Complex to be spawned and turn the United States into a military power unlike any other in history---all to be used by the Illuminati as the "enforcement arm" of their agenda to take over the world.

A book by author Antony Sutton called **Western Technology and Soviet Economic Development** intricately details how United States and European-based banks and corporations provided Lenin with the technology and money his group needed to overthrow the Czar and control the Russian people. Besides this book, there is plenty of hard evidence out there tying the Rothschild Banking Dynasty, aka the Illuminati/Great Plan/New World Order banking interests, to financing and organizing the rise of Communism in Russia, and this is all you need to know from me about it at this time.

Chapter 4/J

SKULL AND BONES
BROTHERHOOD OF DEATH

There are a handful of Illuminati-backed college fraternities in the U.S., but we are going to focus on the most influential and nefarious of them all: The Yale chapter of the Skull and Bones Brotherhood of Death.

Sounds like a real wholesome organization, doesn't it? There are other illuminized fraternities preying upon our most promising young Americans, such as Yale's other two lesser-influential secret societies, "Scroll and Key", and "The Wolf's Head Society".

Ivy League secret society-themed fraternities, and very specifically the Skull and Bones, were created with one purpose in mind: To find likeminded people and put them on the path to help create the New World Order after they graduate and enter into the work force.

Skull and Bones is located at Yale University in New Haven, Connecticut. The society's alumni organization, which owns the fraternity's real property and oversees the organization, is the Russell Trust Association, named for General William Huntington Russell. Russell co-founded Skull and Bones with classmate Alphonso Taft. Taft's son William Howard Taft, also a "Bonesman", ended up as our 27th President of the United States.

In 1823, Samuel Russell, William H. Russell's cousin, established Russell and Company for the purpose of acquiring opium in Turkey and smuggling it to China. Many of the great American and European family fortunes were built upon the smuggling of opium to China in the 1800's.

Russell and Company's Chief of Operations was Warren Delano, Jr., grandfather of President Franklin Delano Roosevelt. Other Russell partners included John Cleve Green, who financed the founding of Princeton; Abiel Low, who financed construction of **Columbia** University; Joseph Coolidge; and the Perkins, Sturgis and Forbes families.

Johan Fitche, who headed the University of Berlin until 1817, was a disciple of the Illuminati and heavily influenced Skull and Bones co-founder William Russell. It was Fitche's philosophy that the children of Germany should be taken and raised by the State in order to be told what to think and how to think it, a core concept of Communism.

George Wilhelm Friedrich **Hegel** took over Fitche's chair at the University Of Berlin in 1817, and was a professor there until his death in 1831.

William Huntington Russell, Samuel's cousin, studied in Germany under Hegel in 1831 until his death.

To Hegel, our world exists as a world of reason. The state is "absolute reason" and the citizen can only become free by worship and obedience to the state. Hegel called the state the "march of God in the world" and the "final end". This final end, Hegel said, **"has supreme right against the individual, whose supreme duty is to be a member of the state."** Both fascism and communism have their philosophical roots in Hegelianism. Hegelian philosophy was very popular and influential during William Russell's time in Germany.

The **"Hegelian Dialectic"** is based upon the ideas of Hegel, and has been used to gradually help steer the world towards implementation of the New World Order. The Hegelian Dialectic is also often referred to as the **"problem-reaction-solution"** principle.

It goes like this:

1) The people running the government wish to pass otherwise unpopular legislation, so it creates or exploits a problem and blames it on others

2) The people react as planned by asking the government for help---willing to give up their rights for some sort of solution to the fabricated problem

3) The government offers the solution that was planned long before the crisis arose

With these teachings and philosophy under his belt, William Huntington Russell returned to Yale in 1832, and formed a senior society with Alphonso Taft. Class valedictorian Russell, along with fourteen others, became the founding members of "The Order of Skull and Bones Brotherhood of Death".

Fifteen juniors are tapped each year by the seniors to be initiated into the next year's group of Bonesmen. The main initiation procedure consists of the initiate to sit alone, naked, in a coffin, with the 15 senior Bonesmen gathered around him. He is told to masturbate while at the same time recounting his entire sexual history to the elder Bonesmen, which is to be used against the initiate by the Order if he should ever stray from their "flock". Other initiation ceremonies also take place including mock human sacrifice. Once indoctrinated into the program, Bonesmen are swore to a lifetime of secrecy, with death at the hands of fellow Bonesmen for speaking about the inner workings of the organization. This is why it is called the "Brotherhood of Death". This is the same type of threat doled out in Masonic blood oath ceremonies: If you speak about secrets revealed to you, you die.

The family names on the Skull and Bones roster should be familiar to some of you: Lord, Whitney, Taft, Jay, Bundy, Harriman, Weyerhaeuser, Pinchot, Rockefeller, Goodyear, Sloane, Stimson, Phelps, Perkins, Pillsbury, Kellogg, Vanderbilt, Bush, Lovett and so on.

When fellow Bonesmen George W. Bush and John Kerry were competing for the United States Presidency in 2004, both were asked by the late Tim Russert on "Meet the Press" about their membership in this secretive organization, and their non-compliance to speak about it was very brunt. These interviews are currently available on YouTube and their reactions when asked about their membership in Skull and Bones are very telling. They were both **extremely** uncomfortable when the subject was brought up.

One more thing about Skull and Bones, and you will have heard the gist. Under the Skull and Bones official logo of a skull with crossbones, is the number "322". This refers to the passage in the Old Testament, Genesis, verse 3:22, which states **"And the Lord God said, Behold, the man is become as one of us, to know good and evil; and now, lest he put forth his hand, and take also of the tree of life, and eat, and live forever".** God stated this after he found that Eve had been told of a path to godhood by Satan, the forbidden "Tree of Knowledge", and had also shared this information with Adam. What the placement of the numbers 322 within their insignia is saying, is that under Satan's influence, the members of Skull and Bones were to be shown the path to godhood by following the Great Plan. This is through their affiliation with the Illuminati.

Chapter 4/K

MADAME HELENA BLAVATSKY

Madame Helena Petrovna Blavatsky (1831-1891) is one of the top Great Plan "prophets" and the founder of the religion known as Theosophy. Theosophy is the origin of the **"New Age"** movement, although most people involved in New Age practices don't have a clue about what Theosophy is and how their particular New Age beliefs tie in to it. The true root of the New Age movement is the Great Plan belief that the entity known to all as Satan is really an angel of light and he is the one who deserves our worship and allegiance.

> *"One of the most hidden secrets involves the so-called fall of Angels. Satan and his rebellious host will thus prove to have become the direct Saviours and Creators of divine man. Thus Satan, once he ceases to be viewed in the superstitious spirit of the church, grows into the grandiose image. It is Satan who is the God of our planet and the only God. Satan (or Lucifer) represents the Centrifugal Energy of the Universe, this ever-living symbol of self-sacrifice for the intellectual independence of humanity. "*
> *- H.P. Blavatsky, from her magnum opus and Adolph Hitler's favorite book "The Secret Doctrine"*

In my estimation, Blavatsky's "The Secret Doctrine" is on equal footing to "Morals and Dogma" by Albert Pike as the most important modern Great Plan/Freemasonic book, and remember, both of these occult works praise Satan as their god. Blavatsky's first book, "Isis Unveiled" is also highly revered by the Freemasons. The entity Satan has been the overlord of the Great Plan since antiquity, but only now are his followers allowed to not only admit this fact but promote it through the media they now control.

Although she was a woman and not eligible to become a Freemason, Freemasons of her time hailed her books as pure genius, and there are multiple quotes attributing praise on her from many high-ranking Freemasons of her day. They even went to the trouble when she was alive of giving her an honorary degree of Masonry to show their respect for her teachings. If she was a man, she would have easily been a 90th degree Freemason, a literal deacon of Satanic black magic. She was a real-life "wicked witch" to be certain, full of malevolence and hatred towards Jews, Christians, humanity in general, Jesus Christ and the Most High God.

> "The Secret Doctrine" and "Isis Unveiled" are Madame Blavatsky's gifts to humanity, and to those whose vision can pierce the menacing clouds of imminent disaster it is no exaggeration to affirm that these writings are the most vital literary contribution to the modern world. No more can they be compared with other books than can the light of the sun be compared with the lamp of the glowworm. The Secret Doctrine assumes the dignity of a scripture, . . ."
>
> -Manly P. Hall, 33rd degree Freemasonic "prophet"

Madame Blavatsky sprang from an occult family, and had progressed to a "spiritual medium" by the time she was a teenager. She worshipped Satan and his company of demonic spirits all of her life. Satan was the inspiration for her to write many books about the occult---the words even being channeled to her by a demonic entity, a "spirit guide" named Kuthumi.

Blavatsky's two most influential books, **Isis Unveiled** and **The Secret Doctrine** were written by what is called "automatic hand", which is when a demonic entity puts words into your head that are then transferred to paper, and then turned into a book. This is also how Albert Pike wrote **Morals and Dogma**, and how other Masonic prophets composed their greatest works, via interdimensional guides.

> *"The Celestial Virgin which thus becomes the Mother of Gods
> and Devils at one and the same time; for she is the ever-loving
> beneficent Deity...but in antiquity and reality Lucifer or Luciferius
> is the name. Lucifer is divine and terrestial Light, 'the Holy Ghost'
> and 'Satan' at one and the same time."*
> -Helena Blavatsky, The Secret Doctrine

Blavatsky and alleged 33rd degree Freemason Colonel Henry Steel Olcott (1832-1907) together founded the Theosophical Society in 1875. Theosophy is a religion, the worship of Lucifer, and **one of its three main objectives** is the formation of an all encompassing one world pagan religion that rejects the monotheistic religions of Judaism and Christianity. Theosophy is basically a reformulation of the Babylonian Mystery Religion tailored to fit a new generation of occultists, which is today's New Age movement.

The **second** objective of Theosophy is the declaration of the universal brotherhood of mankind and the need for a **one world government**.

The **third** objective of Theosophy is to encourage people to tap into the **spiritual, occult powers that exist in <u>every</u> <u>single</u> <u>human</u> <u>being</u> and to use these to personally transcend to godhood on Earth.**

Thomas Edison was one of her most famous followers. He learned to meditate and accessed the occult power she promoted. That was the probable source of his genius and the force behind his career. On the opposite side at the time of Edison you had Nikola Tesla, a devout Christian, who for the most part blew Edison's doors off in the invention department. Tesla was the one who invented the form of electricity you use in your home and the world today, among many other invetions. Why is it that Tesla's inventions were covered up and Edison's trumpeted in our modern day history books? Is it because God showed off His true power over the Great Plan in granting so much futuristic knowledge to Tesla? Tesla was literally a thousand years ahead of his time. This, I believe, is one of the two main reasons Tesla has been blacklisted from our school history books. The other reason will become apparent towards the end of this book, as his research will again have a profound impact on us very soon.

Margaret Sanger, the founder of Planned Parenthood; Helen Keller (she designated the sign language hand sign for "love" as the occult devil-horns hand symbol); Elvis Presley; and T.S. Eliot are other notable Theosophists among other famous people you probably have heard of who followed, sometimes unknowingly, the Luciferian doctrine.

> *"In this case it is but natural... to view Satan, the Serpent of Genesis, as the real creator and benefactor, the Father of Spiritual mankind. For it is he who was the "Harbinger of Light," bright radiant Lucifer, who opened the eyes of the automaton created by Jehovah, as alleged; and he who was the first to whisper: "in the day ye eat thereof ye shall be as Elohim, knowing good and evil"—can only be regarded in the light of a Saviour..."*
> *-Helena Blavatsky, referring to verse 3:22 of Genesis in her book The Secret Doctrine*

Although Blavatsky was patently anti-Jewish, she was a follower of Kaballah and references its influence in her books. This adds to the weight of evidence that Kaballah originated through the Synagogue of Satan, her co-followers of Lucifer.

> *"Lucifer represents.. Life.. Thought.. Progress.. Civilization.. Liberty.. Independence.. Lucifer is the Logos.. the Serpent, the Savior."*
> *"Once the key to Genesis is in our hands it is the scientific and symbolic Kabbala which unveils the secret. The Great Serpent of the Garden of Eden and the "Lord God" are identical ... When the Church, therefore, curses Satan, it curses the cosmic reflection of God ...*
> *For it is he who was the "Harbinger of Light," bright radiant Lucifer, who opened the eyes of automaton (Adam) created by Jehovah, as alleged; and he who was first to whisper, "In the day yea eat there of, ye shall be as Elohim, knowing good and evil" -- can only be regarded in the light of a Saviour. An "adversary" to Jehovah ... he still remains in esoteric truth the ever loving "Messenger"... who conferred on us spiritual instead of physical immortality ...*

> *Satan, or Lucifer, represents the active ... "Centrifugal Energy*
> *of the Universe" in a cosmic sense ... Fitly is he ... and his adherents*
> *... consigned to the "sea of fire," because it is the Sun ... the fount of*
> *life in our system, where they are petrified ... and churned up to re-*
> *arrange them for another life; that Sun which, as the origin of the*
> *active principle of our Earth, is at once the Home and the Source of*
> *the Mundane Satan... "*
> *-Helena Blavatsky*

Blavatsky coined the official motto of the Theosophical Society as **"There is no religion higher than truth"** and the official insignia of her Theosophical Society was a **hexagram** with an ankh in the middle of it, surrounded by a serpent, with a **swastika** at the top. Again, the hexagram is very important to the members of the Great Plan and is arguably the most important occult symbol in existence. The ankh gives a nod to the ancient Egyptian occult contributions to not only Theosophy but the Great Plan. The significance of the swastika is to represent the Eastern religions that created it. The swastika is actually a representation of the Sun, which in occult religion is of course meant to represent Nimrod.

After the founding of the Theosophical Society, she went on to form an occult magazine called *Lucifer* in London in 1887.

Blavatsky died in 1891, but her New Age spiritualism lives on today and its roots can be traced back to her in virtually every New Age belief today. In 1907, Annie Besant took over as head of the Theosophical Society, later allegedly earning an honorary 33rd degree in Co-Masonry.

Blavatsky was highly influential on the next Great Plan "prophet" to come along, also a woman: Alice Bailey.

Chapter 4/L

ALICE BAILEY

Alice Bailey was a Theosophist who took up where Madame Blavatsky had left off in terms of receiving demonic channeled messages that turned into lengthy occult books. Her books are considered just as important as Blavatsky's to the New Age movement. In 1920 Alice married another Theosophist, alleged 33rd degree Freemason Foster Bailey. Foster Bailey was also her co-conspirator in founding what was originally called the **Lucifer** publishing company in 1922 to help distribute her occult books. In 1923 they started "The Arcane School" to teach disciples how to further the Great Plan through the melding of all religions. Due to public outcry regarding the overt reference to their Luciferian agenda, they shortened the name of their publishing company to Lucis Trust, which still operates today, pumping out hundreds of various New Age books. The Lucis Trust also publishes and distributes **United Nations** books and propaganda, and maintains the meditation room inside the UN.

Bailey, through her demonic "spirit guide" Djwhal Kuhl, gives us great insight as to the Freemasons affiliation with the ancient Great Plan:

> "The Masonic Movement is the custodian of the Law, the holder of the Mysteries, and the seat of initiation... a far more occult organization than can be realized... intended to be the training school for coming advanced occultists."

Alice Bailey also tells us through channeled information from her spirit guide the truly evil agenda of Freemasonry:

"There is no question therefore that the work to be done in familiarizing the general public with the nature of the Mysteries is of paramount importance at this time. These mysteries will be restored to outer expression through the medium of the Church (New Age/one world religion) and the Masonic Fraternity... When the Great One (Nimrod/Antichrist) comes with his disciples and initiates we shall have the restoration of the Mysteries and their exoteric presentation as a consequence of the first initiation."

Bailey was an ardent proponent of the Great Plan, and her numerous quotes can be attributed to her view that a one world government was a desired goal.

"What we need above all to see—as a result of spiritual maturity—is the abolition of those two principles which have wrought so much evil in the world and which are summed up in the two worlds: sovereignty and nationalism."

In Alice Bailey's book called *"Education for a New Age"*; she says that in the new age, **"World Citizenship should be the goal of the enlightened, with a world federation and a world brain."**

In other words, the New Age = the religious aspect of the New World Order

Regarding the founding of the fledgling United Nations before her death in 1949, she had this to say:

"Evidence of the growth of the human intellect along the needed receptive lines (for the preparation of the New Age) can be seen in the "planning" of various nations and in the efforts of the United Nations to formulate a world plan... From the very start of this unfoldment, three occult factors have governed the development of all these plans. Within the United Nations is the germ and seed of a great international and meditating, reflective group - a group of thinking and informed men and women in whose hands lies the destiny of humanity. This is largely under the control of many fourth ray disciples, if you could but realize it, and their

point of meditative focus is the intuitional or Buddhic plane - the plane upon which all hierarchical activity is today to be found".

To facilitate the prophesized one-world religion, aka the New Age movement, Alice Bailey and her husband Foster Bailey started a group called "World Goodwill" - an official non-governmental organization within the United Nations.

The stated aim of this group is: **"to cooperate in the world of preparation for the reappearance of the Christ".**

They aren't talking about the **good and loving "Christ" here either**. They didn't say Jesus Christ; they said *"the Christ"*. They are talking about the Masonic Christ....known to you and me as the Biblical Antichrist, and known to them by names such as Nimrod, Osiris, Apollo, etc.

World Goodwill is closely connected to the Illuminati and its minions. Authors and participants in its various conferences read like a CFR or Bilderberg roster, including numerous Rockefeller family members and the nefarious (alleged) 33rd degree Freemason and card-carrying Synagogue of Satan member Henry Kissinger, among many other elitists promoting the NWO.

Chapter 4/M

ADOLPH HITLER

When I started digging into this New World Order business, I have to admit, I was shocked to find out about Hitler's occult background that has been suppressed by the truth-sterile school system and the Mainstream Media. I was not surprised that Hitler was a participant of the Great Plan, and Hitler actually believed that he was going to be the one to complete it, but I was certainly all the more unnerved as I connected the dots to what his religious beliefs **really** were and **who** it was that funded him into power.

Keep in mind when reading this section that I am just giving you the gist of the story, as all chapters in this book, and due diligence for further information is up to you, the reader.

Hitler's early life certainly gave no indication of his future as the fascist leader of Germany. After failing for the most part in high school, he left and began to live as a vagrant on an orphan's pension which came from his father's service as a customs official among other income. He wanted to become an artist, but simply didn't have the artistic talent needed to get him into any of the better art schools at the time. Born and raised a Catholic, Hitler rejected those traditions in his teens and began to lead a hedonistic lifestyle. This set him down the path towards the awaiting tentacles of the Great Plan. Hitler is painted by the history books as a Christian, when in reality he was anything but; another carefully planted deception by the Great Plan. He was actually a ***Theosophist and espoused Theosophical ideals.*** Here are just a few of Hitler's quotes/ thoughts about Christianity, which are the exact same ideals put forth by the founder of Theosophy, Madame Blavatsky, who hated Jews and Christians in particular:

"Christianity is a religion that defends the weak and the low"

"It is purely Jewish and oriental in origin"

"It forces people to bend their backs to the sound of church bells and crawl to the cross of a foreign god"

"It began 2000 years ago among sick, exhausted, and despairing men who had lost their belief in life"

"The Christian tenets of forgiveness of sin, resurrection, and salvation are plain nonsense"

"The Christian of mercy is a dangerous, un-German idea"

"Christian love is a silly concept because love paralyses men"

"The Christian idea of equality protects the racially inferior, the ill, the weak, and the crippled."

Searching for a purpose in life, he spent a large amount of time in the Hofberg Library in Vienna, delving into books about the history of the occult and Eastern religions. Eastern religions, such as Hinduism in particular, are held in high esteem by the members of the Great Plan for their occult contributions, and are reflected in particular by Madame Blavatsky and Alice Bailey throughout their literary works.

Hitler was highly motivated to learn the mysterious powers contained within the occult and had experimented using some Eastern religion meditation techniques. This was far too slow a progress for him, and he wanted to learn as much as quickly as possible about the secrets of the occult. Around the age of 21, a book dealer named Earnest Pretzsche allegedly introduced Hitler to a psychedelic drug containing the hallucinogenic mescaline. This produced clairvoyant visions that made Hitler believe he had opened the door to the gaining of super-natural powers, powers he could use for his own nefarious purposes. He allegedly also experimented with other hallucinogenics in his quest for knowledge and power.

The upper echelon of the Great Plan has always used mind-altering drugs during black magic ceremonies to open portals in their minds to "demons", and Hitler had stumbled upon this.

Some years later Hitler got involved with the Thule Society in Munich, who had the same dedication to gaining occult powers as he did.

The Thule Society was an occult group in Germany largely based on the teachings of---drum roll please---Madame Blavatsky. Blavatsky's book *"The Secret Doctrine"* was allegedly one of Hitler's favorite books, and I don't doubt this because the Theosophy-based occult Thule Society was later transformed by Adolf Hitler into the **National Socialist German Workers' Party (Nazi Party).**

Blavatsky is also where Hitler and the Nazis not only got the idea to use the **swastika** as their emblem, but also to label the Jews with the **hexagram** who were destined for the concentration camps. **It is my belief that the reason the Jews were being marked with hexagrams was to verify the intention to use them as human sacrifices to Lucifer and the other occult gods, the *interdimensionals*, who are literally the power behind the occult.** Both of these occult symbols are contained within Blavatsky's symbol of Theosophy as we went over already.

One of the founders of both the Thule Society **and** the Nazi Party was occult master Dietrich Eckart. Eckart was a dedicated **Satanist** and one of the seven founding members of the Nazi Party. Eckart claimed to be the initiator of Hitler into the secrets of Luciferianism and is quoted as saying on his deathbed in 1923: **"Follow Hitler. He will dance, but it is I who have called the tune! I have initiated him into the 'Secret Doctrine;' opened his centres in vision and given him the means to communicate with the Powers. Do not mourn for me: I shall have influenced history more than any German."**

From the beginning of their association, Eckart allegedly believed Hitler was the **Antichrist,** and Hitler dedicated the second volume of

Mein Kampf to Eckart. Eckart was that important of an influence on Hitler.

It is through the Luciferian Thule Society that Hitler received his "Aryan supremacy" and eugenics teachings, **which are the exact same ideals taught by Blavatsky. Hitler was literally following the program of the Great Plan as laid out by Madame Blavatsky via her own demonic interactions that were transferred into her books by automatic writing.**

Hitler jumped on board the Great Plan train when he ventured into the occult. Some people are naturally more receptive to supernatural/occult influence and power than others, and Hitler was gifted in this particular ability. Once on the inside track of the occult through the Thule Society, Hitler was careful to try and cover the tracks of his occult dealings. Hitler made various public statements to try and diffuse the existence of occult influence within the Nazi Party, even disparaging it. Keep in mind that although the "official" Nazi policy was to exterminate the Freemasons along with the Jews, this was a front and only applied to those lower ranking Freemasons who were NOT the fellow occultists involved with the Great Plan----which is about 99.9% of them.

Hitler even became a member of another, even more sinister occult group called the Vril Society. According to the English writer, Lord Bulwer-Lytton, who named the society, Vril was the occult power that woke up man's ability to possess superhuman qualities.

The Vril Society counted two other very important people besides Hitler among their membership, and who later would become infamous Nazis---Hermann Göring and Heinrich Himmler.

The most evil of Hitler's entire inner circle was without a doubt Heinrich Himmler. He was the grandmaster of several secret societies and allegedly had satanic and black magic masses organized in several different old castles around Germany. As head of the dreaded SS, Himmler was chiefly responsible for much of the terror which was created by the Third Reich, including the abominable experiments performed on imprisoned Jews and others by the infamous Dr. Death, Josef Mengele.

I'm going to go over briefly the truth of the matter that the Illuminati did in fact finance Hitler, but I will leave it to you to do your own research into this further. I suggest starting with a book called **Wall Street and the Rise of Hitler**, by Prof. Anthony Sutton.

This book details that GM, General Electric, ITTC, Ford Motor, Chase Manhatten bank, Morgan Guaranty Trust, Exxon, and other American companies financed Adolph Hitler and provided him the weapons and supplies to wage WWII.

Another smoking gun is the fact that President George W. Bush's grandfather, the late US senator Prescott Bush, was a director and shareholder of companies that profited from their involvement with the financial backers of the fledgling Nazi Germany.

Brown Brothers Harriman (BBH), one of many of Prescott's "employers" acted as a US base for the German industrialist, Fritz Thyssen, who financed Hitler in the 1930s before falling out with him at the end of the decade. Bush was also the Director of the New York-based Union Banking Corporation (UBC) that represented Thyssen's US interests. Thyssen owned the largest steel and coal company in Germany and grew rich from Hitler's efforts to re-arm Germany between the two world wars.

You've got to remember that after World War I, Germany was in ruins, both economically and physically. They needed huge money to rebuild and fell right into the hands of the Rothschild money cabal.

Prescott Bush's Union Banking Corporation assets were in fact <u>seized</u> in 1942 under the Trading with the Enemy Act.

Among other easily verifiable facts showing the Illuminati were backing Hitler was the fact that the Rockefeller's were selling oil to Hitler via Spain to fill the gas tanks of Hitler's Luftwaffe air force and the Panzer division of tanks that were rolling all over Europe.

As a proponent of the Great Plan, Hitler was indeed the enemy of the Jews. Hitler's holocaust and massacre of the Jews was the perfect ploy to generate the worldwide sympathy needed to initiate the rebirth of Israel, all per plan.

The seed for Israel coming back into existence was in fact planted in 1917 by the **Rothschilds**. This happened with the creation of the Balfour Declaration.

Lionel Walter Rothschild, eldest son of the diabolical controller of the Bank of England, Lord Nathan Rothschild, was a close friend of Zionist Chaim Weizmann. Lionel worked to formulate the draft declaration for a

Jewish homeland in Palestine with Weizmann. Weizmann was a Zionist leader, President of the Zionist Organization, and the first President of the State of Israel upon reunification.

On November 2, 1917, Rothschild received a letter from the British foreign secretary, Arthur Balfour, addressed to his London home at 148 Piccadilly. In this letter the British government declared its support for the establishment in Palestine of "a national home for the Jewish people". This letter became known as the Balfour Declaration, and was ultimately used by the Rothschilds to force Britain's and the Allies' hand after WW II into reforming Israel---**by United Nations' mandate of course**.

Arthur Balfour was chosen to be part of the Great Plan's **"Round Table Group"** in 1891, and with Illuminati financial backing went on to became Prime Minister of Great Britain in 1902.

In a nutshell, Lionel Rothschild, who was tied intimately to the federal government of the United States through their control of the newly-founded United States Federal Reserve, offered to bring the United States into WW I on the side of the British in exchange for the British supporting the creation of a reunited Israel. They accepted, the U.S. was brought in, and the allies won WWI. However, due to the inability of the proponents of the Great Plan to establish a legitimate "one world government" body that was needed to sanction the re-creation of Israel, namely the League of Nations, the re-creation of Israel would require one more terrible war. The ritual sacrifice of millions of Torah-abiding Jews by Hitler was orchestrated in order to generate the worldwide sympathy to convince the nations of the world to capitulate to a "Jewish homeland".

With Israel now back on the world stage, it was full steam ahead for the proponents of the Great Plan to finalize the path to fulfillment of the Bible prophecies, and the heralding of the New World Order. I have a high degree of respect for Jews and the State of Israel as the homeland of the Bible events, but the resurrection of Israel is **factually** the #1 harbinger of the dawn of the End Times.

Chapter 4/N

ALEISTER CROWLEY

As we're going down the list here of the most influential people and families of the last 250 or so years who had a hand in the progression of the Great Plan, it is important to show that universally they were all connected with **Freemasonry**, which is the modern day stronghold of the Great Plan to bring in the New World Order, aka the Biblically prophesized one world government.

Confirmed 33rd degree Freemason Aleister Crowley (1875–1947) was referred to in his home country of Great Britain as "the wickedest man alive", as Crowley once bragged to have ceremonially sacrificed "over 150 children in one year" among other demonic acts. **He was allegedly also a 90th degree Misraim rite Freemason, a black magic echelon of Freemasonry.**

> "For the highest spiritual working one must accordingly choose that victim which contains the greatest and purest force. A male child of perfect innocence and high intelligence is the most satisfactory and suitable victim. But the bloody sacrifice, though more dangerous, is more efficacious; and for nearly all purposes human sacrifice is the best. In the Sacrifice during Invocation, however, it may be said without fear of contradiction that the death of the victim should coincide with the supreme invocation."
>
> -Aleister Crowley, from the book he wrote by automatic hand, **Magick in Theory and Practice**, talking about how effective it is

to use human sacrifice as a vehicle to interact with the demonic entities. 'Supreme invocation' equates to the male sexual climax

Crowley was also allegedly a "pansexual" meaning sexual attraction to people of all genders. In other words, he engaged in homosexual activity but didn't particularly consider it "gay" sex but pansexual sex, and more accurately "ritual" sex to be used during black magic ceremonies. **A lot of of the people running the world also have this exact same view as we are going to go over.**

Referring to himself as "the Great Beast" from the Book of Revelation, Aleister Crowley allegedly had his first mystical experience with the supernatural in Sweden in December of 1896, this according to numerous Crowley biographers. This particular incident had to do with Crowley's first sexual experience with a man, the beginning of his pansexuality. This is far too deep of a topic for this book and will be better addressed in the addendum to this book, but sex and particular sexual acts can be used to interact with the supernatural realm, the same as mind-altering drugs, animal/human sacrifices, chanting certain sounds or syllables, aligning candles/fire/torches in occult symbols such as the pentagram/hexagram, etc. It is my belief that all of these particular actions that have been passed down over the millennia are based in blaspheming the Creator God to the maximum amount possible in order to cause a supernatural opening or "rip" in our 3D time-space continuum---briefly allowing the interdimensionals access into our world. **When you put all of the actions I listed together and more in one place at one time is when the real supernatural sparks fly.**

Crowley was incidentally raised in the strictest Christian household, and when Crowley's father died at age 11, it was his anger towards God over his death that triggered his descent into evil. He explored any and all avenues of blaspheming God, and it is through this dogged determination to spite God to the maximum degree that he was able to supernaturally formulate his philosophies and write his books which are considered occult masterpieces. This man Crowley has had a tremendous influence on our society and contributed greatly to the moral degeneration and resulting societal collapse that is currently well underway.

Aleister Crowley enrolled at Trinity College in Cambridge in England in 1895 until age 21 when his trust fund kicked in. He then quit school to devote himself to a life of complete hedonism...and the occult.

In 1898 Crowley was initiated into the occult Freemason-founded **"Hermetic Order of the Golden Dawn"**, the beginning of his affiliation with various occult groups. This group arguably had the biggest influence on 20th century occultism.

In 1904, Crowley began to receive supernatural revelations from an interdimensional entity he called "Aiwass", who was supposedly a messenger from the Egyptian god **Horus**, who himself is a representation of **Tammuz/Nimrod**. Over a period of only 3 days, Crowley wrote by "automatic hand" the book entitled *"The Book of the Law"*, which is widely used in occult circles today.

Aiwass told Crowley that a new age had dawned for mankind and that he was a prophet. Crowley's crowning statement, ***"Do what thou wilt shall be the whole of the law"*** was revered by the counterculture movement in the 60's, morphing into ***"If it feels good, do it"*** and ***"Do you own thing".*** These are all variations of Crowley's original hedonistic Luciferian philosophy.

Crowley went on to pen other occult books through channeling this Aiwass entity, even creating his own religion based on his beliefs and teachings from this evil being, called Thelema.

Not only this, but Crowley, who was also a talented artist, drew a sketch of another supernatural being named "Lam" he called his guru and it turns out **his alleged guru looks exactly like all modern-day depictions of a *"grey"* alien.** Keep in mind that this was many years before people knew what "aliens" were even supposed to look like. Again, what you and I would call aliens today were called demons in ancient times and they are not creatures from another world as we are deceptively led to believe, but interdimensional entities full of malevolence towards the Creator God's personal project, mankind.

In 1910 Crowley joined the O.T.O., the Ordo Templi Orientis. The O.T.O. is the highest ranking Luciferian Freemasonic organization in the world. Crowley in fact took it over in 1921 and then proceeded to rewrite the Temple's doctrine to best fit his Satanic intentions. Crowley introduced the practice of male-on-male sex magic into O.T.O. as one of the initiations into the highest degrees of the Order, for he believed it to be the most powerful and effective way of immersing people in black magic and supernatural interaction short of human sacrifice.

Now take a minute and reflect how the homosexual lifestyle and sodomy in general is being shoved down our throats today in the Mainstream Media and you can probably begin to see the handwriting on the wall by the proponents of the Great Plan.

There is much more to explore and say about Aleister Crowley, including such facts as that he was a personal tutor of Aldous Huxley, one of the godfathers of the 60's movement. Crowley was also good friends with L. Ron Hubbard, the founder of Scientology, among other talking points.

Chapter 4/O

MANLY P. HALL

"The Secret Doctrine and Isis Unveiled are Madame Blavatsky's gifts to humanity, and to those whose vision can pierce the menacing clouds of imminent disaster it is no exaggeration to affirm that these writings are the most vital literary contribution to the modern world. No more can they be compared with other books than can the light of the sun be compared with the lamp of the glowworm. The Secret Doctrine assumes the dignity of a scripture."

-Manly P. Hall, 33rd degree Freemasonic "prophet", talking about his and Hitler's favorite books

Manly P. Hall (1901-1990) was the leading Masonic philosopher of the 20th century, with none more revered since Albert Pike. The most useful information you need to know about him comes directly from Hall himself in his numerous quotes spelling out many pertinent details of the Great Plan. The following quotes come from his highly revered Masonic composure, ***"The Secret Destiny of America"***, and keep in mind that this is just from **<u>one book:</u>**

"In this way, the old dream of the philosophic empire descended from the ancient world to modern time. Secret societies still exist and regardless of the intemperance of the times, they will continue to flourish until the quest (*Great Plan*) is complete. For more than three thousand years, secret societies have labored to create

the background of knowledge necessary to the establishment of an enlightened democracy among the nations of the world."

"Histories are generally written about the men who prominently influence the events that make history; little is written--though it might be of greater interest--about those shadowy figures who seem always to stand behind the men who make history."

"On the reverse of our nation's Great Seal is an unfinished pyramid to represent human society itself, imperfect and incomplete. Above floats the symbol of the esoteric orders, the radiant triangle with its all-seeing eye.... There is only one possible origin for these symbols, and that is the secret societies which came to this country 150 years before the Revolutionary War. ... There can be no question that the great seal was directly inspired by these orders of the human Quest, and that it set forth the purpose for this nation."

"There exists in the world today, and has existed for thousands of years, a body of enlightened humans united in what might be termed, an Order of the Quest. It is composed of those whose intellectual and spiritual perceptions have revealed to them that civilization has secret destiny ... The outcome of this 'secret destiny' is a World Order ruled by a King with supernatural powers (*Antichrist/Nimrod*). This King was descended of a divine race; that is, he belonged to the Order of the Illumined for those who come to a state of wisdom then belong to a family of heroes-perfected human beings."

"And so it is from the remote past, from the deep shadows of the medieval world as well as from the early struggles of more modern times, that the power of American democracy has come. But we are only on the threshold of the democratic state. Not only must we preserve that which we have gained through ages of striving, we must also perfect the plan of the ages, setting up here the machinery for a world brotherhood of nations and races."

Here is another telling quote about the Great Plan from Hall's book, "The Secret Teachings of All Ages":

"European mysticism was not dead at the time the United States of America was founded. The hand of the mysteries controlled in the establishment of the new government for the signature of the mysteries may still be seen on the Great Seal of the United states of America. Careful analysis of the seal discloses a mass of occult and Masonic symbols chief among them, the so-called American Eagle. ... the American eagle upon the Great Seal is but a conventionalized phoenix... Not only were many of the founders of the United States government Masons, but they received aid from a secret and august body existing in Europe which helped them to establish this country for a peculiar and particular purpose known only to the initiated few. The Great Seal is the signature of this exalted body—unseen and for the most part unknown—and the unfinished pyramid upon its reverse side is a trestleboard setting forth symbolically the task to the accomplishment of which the United States Government was dedicated from the day of its inception."

The following quotes taken from Hall's **"The Lost Keys of Freemasonry"** shine even more light on the Luciferian Great Plan and their quest for godhood on Earth:

"Man is a god in the making. And as the mystic myths of Egypt, on the potter's wheel, he is being molded. When his light shines out to lift and preserve all things, he receives the triple crown of godhood."

"Masonry is a university, teaching the liberal arts and sciences of the soul to all ... It is a shadow of the great Atlantean Mystery School, which stood with all its splendor in the Ancient City of the Golden Gates, where now the turbulent Atlantic rolls in unbroken sweep ... . When the Mason learns that the key to the warrior on the block is the proper application of the dynamo of living power, he has learned the mystery of his Craft. The seething energies

of Lucifer are in his hands and before he may step onward and upward, he must prove his ability to properly apply energy."

Yet one more quote from Hall gives us what you already now know about Freemasonry, from a master of Freemasonry himself in his book **"Lectures on Ancient Philosophy":**

"Freemasonry is a fraternity within a fraternity -- an outer organization concealing an inner brotherhood of the elect ... it is necessary to establish the existence of these two separate and yet interdependent orders, the one visible and the other invisible. The visible society is a splendid camaraderie of 'free and accepted' men enjoined to devote themselves to ethical, educational, fraternal, patriotic, and humanitarian concerns. The invisible society is a secret and most August [defined as 'of majestic dignity, grandeur'] fraternity whose members are dedicated to the service of a mysterious arcannum arcandrum [defined as 'a secret, a mystery']."

There are **many more quotes attributed to Hall** that you can research for yourself, but it was his various quotes regarding the Great Plan which give him the reverence he was bestowed upon by his fellow Freemasons.

Chapter 4/P

BOHEMIAN GROVE AND RITUAL SEX "MAGICK"

"The faggiest Goddamn thing I've ever seen"
-President Richard Nixon, after attending the Bohemian Grove event

B ohemian Grove is a **men-only** 2,700 acre resort/campground nestled among towering redwood trees in Monte Rio, Northern California.

Once a year every July since the late 1800's, around 2,000 of the most highly influential men in the world gather at this spot for two weeks to covertly meet regarding world affairs....and to hold occult rituals.

The Bohemian Grove attendees list has included every Republican and numerous Democratic Presidents since 1923, many federal government cabinet officials and directors/CEOs of multinational corporations including heads of the biggest banks in the world. Also, high-ranking military officials and contractors, oil company chairmen, Federal Reserve board members, and Mainstream Media personalities are attendees on a regular basis.

Past and present attendees of the Bohemian Grove gathering reads like a "who's who" of the world's power elite. These attendees include David Rockefeller, Gerald Ford, Ronald Reagan, Richard Nixon, George H.W. Bush, George W. Bush, Barack Obama, John McCain, Dick Cheney, Donald Rumsfeld, Alan Greenspan, Walter Cronkite, Newt Gingrich, Alexander Haig, Jack Kemp, Malcolm Forbes, Henry Kissinger, Colin Powell, John Major, William F. Buckley, William Randolph Hearst, Jr., Caspar

Weinberger, George Schultz, former C.I.A. director William Casey, and Helmut Schmidt.

In fact, Helmut Schmidt, former German Chancellor says in his own autobiography, *"Men and Powers: A Political Retrospective"*, that political, industrial, and financial leaders from all over the world travel to Bohemian Grove every summer. He goes on to talk about similar occult men's groups in Germany where they do druidic rituals, but states that Bohemian Grove is his favorite place to participate in these occult rituals. He also goes on to say that he is a member of the Council on Foreign Relations, the Trilateral Commission and the Bilderberg group. He also unequivocally says that he has been an active proponent in pushing a one world government, aka the New World Order.

There are hundreds more names you would recognize, but this is enough to mete out credibility that the people who attend this Luciferian gathering are the ones running the planet.

On the first Saturday of the camp, an elaborate ritual called the Cremation of Care is held just after dinner. It begins with the procession of a group of men, dressed in red pointed hoods and red robes, very akin to KKK regalia, of whom some play a funeral dirge while others carry torches. **Remember, these are the people who run the world who are participating in this ritual.** These men also carry an open coffin containing a body made of a black fabric-covered wooden skeleton. This is referred to as "the body of care", symbolizing the concerns and woes that the important men of the world attending the Bohemian Grove ceremony supposedly must bear in their daily lives. The effigy of "care" is placed atop a stone alter in front of a 40-foot tall statue of Moloch---the owl god originally created as one of the images/idols representing a character you now know as **King Nimrod**. The official insignia of the Bohemian Club, the owners of Bohemian Grove, is also an owl, aka Moloch.

This effigy is then lit on fire. This "cremation of care" symbolizes that for the next two weeks, the attendees need not have a care in the world for the moral and sexual debauchery they are about to undertake.

For many years, a recording of the voice of club member Walter Cronkite was used as the voice of The Owl during the ceremony. Walter Cronkite, who Americans turned to for news and trusted for decades, was a proponent of the one world government and an upstanding participant of the Great Plan. I've even seen video of him making the following statement after receiving an award for his efforts to promote the one world government:

> "It seems to many of us that if we are to avoid the eventual catastrophic world conflict we must strengthen the United Nations as a first step toward a world government patterned after our own government with a legislature, executive and judiciary, and police to enforce its international laws and keep the peace. To do that, of course, we Americans will have to yield up some of our sovereignty. That would be a bitter pill. It would take a lot of courage, a lot of faith in the new order. But the American colonies did it once and brought forth one of the most nearly perfect unions the world has ever seen. Pat Robertson has written in a book a few years ago that we should have a world government, but only when the Messiah arrives. He wrote, literally, any attempt to achieve world order before that time must be the work of the devil. Well, join me. I'm glad to sit here at the right hand of Satan."

This is **why** Cronkite was promoted to his particular position in the media to start with: **To promote the Great Plan.**

Now remember, these are the people running our country and the world that are going to Bohemian Grove to partake in occult black magic rituals, including depraved sex ceremonies and acts. The reason they are able to keep this stuff out of the public eye is not only because they control the media, but that what is really happening is so unbelievable that it is able to keep its own secret through the sheer outrageousness of the truth.

And this is just at Bohemian Grove we're talking here, let alone what these people are doing very privately in smaller, more intimate groups around the world all year, every year. It is at Bohemian Grove that the power players of the New World Order annually gather and partake in occult black magic ceremonies and ritual acts of sodomy with bussed-in male prostitutes. It is literally a giant orgy of sodomy, drugs, backroom business deals, and the general contempt for God and society as a whole. And when it comes to sex with male prostitutes, being homosexual/

sexually attracted to men is incidental to these people. They are only after the sodomy-sex part of it, because by engaging in sodomy as a ritual black magic act, these people are able to interact with demonic entities. They've been doing this exact thing for thousands of years and continue to do it to this day in occult rituals.

Sex and reproduction are held in the highest regard by God, and humans have been elevated such that sex is also a highly spiritual experience. By intentionally mocking the human sexual act through sodomy, bestiality, pedophilia, etc., this is how the evil ones are able to blaspheme the Most High God and come into contact with His enemies as a reward. This is also why Aleister Crowley introduced sodomy as the highest form of achieving seniority in the highest Satanic Freemasonry organization in the world, the O.T.O./Ordo Templi Orientis. When a male is engaged in the act of sodomy, at the point of orgasm when the brain is feeling like what men know it feels like during orgasm, the mind feels like it's in a different world, and that's because it is. This is far too deep of a subject to get into in this book, but just know that this is what these people are after when they are participating in this behavior: engaging in sodomy during occult rituals in order to interact with the supernatural for personal gain. This is also why sodomy is pushed so hard in the Mainstream Media these days. The more sodomy in society, the more evil they are able to bring into our world, because the general populace is unknowingly channeling negative energy that is being harnessed by the power elites running the New World Order.

The Supernatural, Satan and sodomy are intricately intertwined. This is in fact where the term "sodomy" originated---from the Biblical cities of Sodom and Gomorrah. These two cities became so wickedly sexually depraved and evil in the eyes of the Creator God, such an affront to how the Lord had intended us to behave, that He decided to wipe those centers of evil from the face of the Earth.

Sodomy, by definition, is **"anything but vaginal intercourse between a man and a woman",** so this spans all forms of sex, including oral, anal, bestiality, BDSM, pedophilia, and other sex acts.

This is the exact reason there were multiple stories of "homosexual" activity among the Knights Templar. They were using sodomy to channel evil for personal gain, and used it to help gain the power the occultists once wielded through Nimrod's ancient occult Great Plan.

This is also why the Vatican can never seem to shake off its ongoing pedophilia problems. The evil starts at the top and permeates the entire organization, that is how the Great Plan works and the Vatican's system is rooted in the Great Plan.

In the first manifestations of the Great Plan after ancient Babylon, sodomy was popularized in the society at large. Worshippers of Baal, who is **Nimrod** remember, erected shrines and temples of male prostitution. Roman Emperors Nero, Caligula, and Commodus engaged in incest, sex with boys, bondage, sexual torture and a variety of other evil behavior. This is also documented common behavior among the Egyptian pharaohs and their entourage. Alexander the Great was also a documented pedophile who loved little boys. These are all leaders who ascribed to the Great Plan. In Greece's heyday, pedastery was commonplace and if you **weren't** bisexual you were thought of as odd.

The people who run the Great Plan today engage in the exact same behavior as the people running the Great Plan have for thousands of years, and that is the cold, hard truth.

> *"Judah did evil in the eyes of the LORD. BY THE SINS THEY COMMITTED THEY STIRRED UP HIS JEALOUS ANGER MORE THAN THOSE WHO WERE BEFORE THEM HAD DONE. They also set up for themselves high places, sacred stones and Asherah poles on every high hill and under every spreading tree. There were even male shrine prostitutes in the land; the people engaged in all the detestable practices of the nations the LORD HAD DRIVEN OUT BEFORE THE ISRAELITES."*
> *-1 Kings 14, Old Testament*

This is referring to the land of Judah under King Solomon's son Rehoboam's rule. King Solomon, who tried to please God **and** partake in the occult at the same time, let the original Israel get so wicked that there were ordained male prostitutes for the express intent of conjuring evil within the Temple of Solomon, which was supposed to be the Most High God's House of Holiness. Solomon turned it into a house of evil, and this is why God originally split up Israel, only to be reunited again at the start of the End Times---which is where we are at today.

Not only is it male-on-male sodomy in particular they are using to channel evil, the most effective way to channel those dark forces is by combining sodomy with pedophilia and human sacrifice/blood drinking. The reason for this is to supremely blaspheme the Creator God in the absolute, most extremely worst way possible. By doing this, the malevolent "demons" grant them favors because it pleases them to provoke God.

Again, the Aleister Crowley quote, which describes killing a young boy at the moment of orgasm for the maximum blasphemy possible:

"For the highest spiritual working one must accordingly choose that victim which contains the greatest and purest force. A male child of perfect innocence and high intelligence is the most satisfactory and suitable victim. But the bloody sacrifice, though more dangerous, is more efficacious; and for nearly all purposes human sacrifice is the best. In the Sacrifice during Invocation, however, it may be said without fear of contradiction that the death of the victim should coincide with the supreme invocation (*the moment during orgasm*)."
-Aleister Crowley, Magick in Theory and Practice

I was forever impacted one night I happened to be watching T.V. and heard actor Corey Feldman's story of "vultures always being around him and the other child actors" that would sexually abuse them. These vultures are the Hollywood contingency of the Luciferian Great Plan. I would call on those victims like Feldman to come forth with the truth of what has happened so that they can not only heal, but to drag this Luciferian BS out into the open. Some of the worst of the worst of the proponents of the Great Plan are the people wielding power in Hollywood today. These are the same people ultimately in charge of the programming and propaganda coming out of the Mainstream Media, and now you know why our media across the board is filled with degenerate filth and anti-Christian, anti-American sentiment. They want to degenerate and crash our country; it is part of the plan.

The entire Establishment's apple cart was almost upset a few years ago over a scandal called "Boys Town" which was quickly swept under the mat by the Mainstream Media. More than a few Congressmen were about to be exposed as pedophile sodomites when it all just kind of went away.

As I'm writing this right now there is some sort of pedophile scandal smoldering in Europe with regards to European royalty and politicians, all participants of the Great Plan.

And while we're talking about sex and its overall impact on society and therefore our lives, let me tell you that with the advent of the internet, pornography has reached a whole new level of degeneracy to impact the masses. Exploitation of humans to churn out the pure, concentrated evil that is online pornography in the 21st century, and the effect is has on the people who watch it, has reached Biblical proportions. We're not talking about innocently finding your dad's Playboy in the bathroom here. The level of degeneracy the internet brought about is disturbing to say the least, and certainly a harbinger of the fall of our society. Today, children unmonitored on the internet have access to any type of sex imaginable with just a few clicks of a mouse, where only 20 years ago this kind of EZ access was an impossibility.

OCCULTISM=LUCIFERIANISM=SATANISM

Henry Luce, the founder of *Time, Life, Fortune, Sports Illustrated,* and other influential magazines, was initiated into the ranks of the Great Plan through his membership in the Skull and Bones Brotherhood of Death. He was later also a member of the Bilderberg Group and the Council on Foreign Relations, both semi-public Great Plan steering organizations. His periodicals not only influenced society, but they also didn't mince words with what was happening in society, even throwing it in the face of the American public.

The headline of the cover of the June 19, 1972 issue of Luce's *Time* magazine reads: **The Occult Revival: Satan Returns**

They were only stating what was happening in society at the time. After the social upheaval in the 1960s, saying you belonged to the occult or were a practicing Satanist suddenly wasn't the worst thing in the world to the newly conditioned American public.

The Bible plainly states that the people who populate the upper echelon of King Nimrod's Babylonian Mystery Religion, aka the Great Plan, aka the New World Order, are black-magic-practicing, human-sacrificing, blood-drinking, pedophile-sodomite Satan worshippers, whose goal is to enslave the world under a one world government, ultimately unveiling the Antichrist, which they call the Masonic Christ/Resurrected Nimrod/Osiris/Apollo/etc.....and to **beware** of them.

What is happening right now with the orchestration of what the Great Plan has pulled off is exactly as told in Biblical prophecy, throughout the Bible, both Old and New Testament. This is why I was transformed from a hardcore atheist to a convinced Christian. There are explicit warnings about these **exact** people, and is in fact the cornerstone of Biblical prophecy. The very reason Jesus Christ was sent by the Creator God to start with was for good men and women of **all** races, creeds, colors, etc. to have a path to God, giving them an "out" of the spiritually unfulfilling life following the path blazed by the Great Plan. The culmination of the New Testament contained in the Book of Revelation is literally Jesus Christ returning to Earth to fight and defeat the resurrected King Nimrod and his minions. That's it, that's the bottom line.

Hopefully by this point in this book you have been enlightened that warning humanity of the Great Plan was one of the main purposes of the Bible. If, instead of God, it was the proponents of the Great Plan who concocted the Bible, they would have certainly left out the parts explicitly implicating them as the evildoers. Realizing this fact was the crucial turning point transforming me from an atheist to believing in God. The fact that the people currently running the planet, the Luciferian Great Planners, not only believe in God but hate Jesus Christ in particular with a passion, was very incriminating to me. They don't passionately hate Buddha, or Krishna, or whoever. It is always **Jesus Christ** they direct their hatred towards, because it is He and no other who is scheduled to come back and kick their butts, to put it bluntly.

The proponents of the Great Plan do in fact believe in God, but choose to worship Satan with the excuse that Satan, being created by God, is just another facet of God, and this is revealed through the writings of the modern day Freemason prophets we just went over.

It is the people running the Great Plan today that have been deceived worst of all, and if any of them were to read this book I would say to them that **it is never too late to turn your life around and to live a fulfilling life as a good, decent and compassionate human being who sees the value in human life, and who would be genuinely appreciated by humanity instead of despised by those who know the real truth of the matter.**

Unfortunately, by demonstrating how extreme they can blaspheme the Creator God, the occultists are rewarded by those spiritual entities who are God's and mankind's enemies. You could say they are even addicted to interacting with these beings. It is by glorifying Satan and his demonic entourage, animal/human sacrifice, and sex magick rituals that they accomplish this blasphemy.

There is a special chemical called adrenochrome that is generated in the blood of human sacrifice victims, and this is used by the Luciferian elite as a powerful mind-altering drug. The more the victim is terrorized/tortured/sexually abused the more of this substance is generated through the synthesis of adrenaline. The Luciferians then kill the victim and drink this drug-laden blood, which metaphysically alters their minds and puts them in the spiritual realm with demonic entities. This was one of the main purposes of the human sacrifice/blood drinking ritual to start with.

The proponents of the Great Plan from ancient times have always sacrificed humans, drank their blood, ate their flesh, and without question were involved in pedophilia/sodomy as a way of paying tribute to the malevolent spirits. Whereas before a lot of these ceremonies took place in public, particularly the human sacrifices, the people running the Satanic show today just do it covertly in clandestine black magic/occult circles. I'm not talking about your Presidents or Congressmen per se, although I'm sure some of them have been involved in this over time. I'm talking mainly about the heads of the families running the Great Plan today, known simply as the Illuminati, who really steer our country and literally pick our President and then tell him what to do....or else.

The Biblically prophesized one world government is **supposed** to be Satanic. Hopefully you now see that it is unfolding right before your eyes.

> "It is generally agreed that the biggest single influence in the modern expansion of ritual magic, and the occult explosion in general, in the Western world, was the Golden Dawn. This magical fraternity, founded by Freemasons at the end of the 19th century, developed a complex ritual system with ten degrees of initiation relating to the Cabalistic Sephiroth."
>
> - Janet and Stewart Farrar, world renown witches, from their book "The Life and Times of A Modern Witch". They also wrote "A Witches Bible Complete"

We talked about even higher degrees of Freemasonry, above the "enlightened" status of the 33rd degree level where some of our Presidents, Prime Ministers, media moguls, and industrial titans exist. Let me re-emphasize that the ONLY way to get to the 33rd degree of Freemasonry or higher is that you either have to be born into one of the Luciferian bloodlines of the Illuminati, or you have to be INVITED to join them, after displaying that you are capable of perpetrating the kind of evil they want and need out of you.

This brings us to briefly discussing the levels of Freemasonry above the 33rd degree---the super-secret esoteric, Luciferian degrees. 99.9999% of lower-ranking, blue lodge Freemasons don't even know these exist. This is where the hardcore Satanists aspire to dwell. The "Church of Satan" and people who partake in that organization and others like it are amateurs compared to what the Illuminati upper echelon partake in: direct contact with the entity Satan. The Illuminati/Freemasons are **highly** regarded in Satanic circles as the scientists/engineers of the occult world.

We already went over that to become a 33rd degree Mason you need to agree that Satan is the god of the Freemasons/Babylonian Mystery Religion/Great Plan/New World Order. The higher degrees are achieved through wicked murder rituals, pedophilia, bestiality and sodomy-based sex, and that is enough for you to know from me. This is why Satanist Aleister Crowley proudly boasted of being a 90th degree Mason, when most people in his day had not a clue what that really meant.

These higher levels of Freemasonry are the degrees that really get involved with interacting with malevolent supernatural beings. There is a reason that the Illuminati are all Luciferians and practice these black magic rituals and everything that goes along with that: the supernatural forces of evil are **real**, and they draw their power to control the world through these supernatural beings and always have since the days of King Nimrod and even before.

For all intents and purposes, the "Illuminati" are Satan's current primary minions on Earth. They are the pinnacle of Satanism. The Illuminati are the people that "run of the mill" Satanists look up to as the ultimate echelon of closeness to Satan. The **very reason** they are called the Illuminati, is that they have received the light of Lucifer, which literally translates to and means "light bearer". He personally guides them and they have therefore become "illuminated". The "Illuminated Seers of Bavaria", remember? These higher rites of Freemasonry above the 33rd degree are called the Misraim rites, rising up to the 90th degree, and are primarily populated by the upper echelons of the Illuminati.

If you think things are bad in the world right now, you have no idea of what is coming and how bad they will really get. They are going to get worse and fast, and we will go over this in more detail at the end of this book, and what you should do to prepare yourself and your family.

Think about it: 300 years ago occultists were put to death for conjuring demons. Today they are given tax-free status by our government as churches, the Church of Satan for example, and nobody gives them a second thought to what they are really promoting because society has been completely distracted and corrupted.

> *"As it was in the days of Noah, so it will be at the coming of the Son of Man"*
> *-Jesus Christ, talking about how deviant, corrupt, and violent society will be just prior to His return*

If you know your Bible, and even if you're not religious, you may have at least heard that the reason God destroyed humanity the first time was because humanity got so wicked. The reason man got so wicked and forced God's hand was because he was taught wickedness by the first batch of troublemaking interdimensionals or "fallen angels", the Watchers. This is described briefly in the Book of Genesis. The Book of Enoch documents how these entities taught men all kinds of sinful activity such as how to invoke the supernatural by blaspheming God. This exact same batch of ultra-evil beings are due to be released in the End Times to once again wreck havoc on the Earth.

The ever-increasing tales of alien abductions, crop circles, and UFOs/aerial phenomenon are, to me, indicative that they have recently been allowed to venture out of their spiritual prison to influence our 3D world. The year of the first widely reported UFO sightings in the New Babylon came in the year 1947, near Mt. Rainier in Washington State. The infamous Roswell incident occurred in 1947 also. What else happened around this time? The resurrection of Israel in 1948, which again is the #1 sign of the beginning of the End Times. We are even being prepared for what is to come though something called "The Disclosure Project" and I suggest you look into what they are telling us in advance in order to prepare you to go along with what they are planning for us. I believe the Great Deception near the end Times mentioned in the Bible has to do with some sort of "alien" invasion or other supernatural interaction with humanity. The reason it says that God sends this deception is that it is God who has to let these malevolent beings out of their interdimensional jail in order for them to show up here and mislead us.

> *"And for this cause God shall send them strong delusion, that they should believe a lie."*
> *-2 Thessalonians 2:11*

Chapter 5

MONEY=POWER

"Give me control of a nation's money and I care not who makes its laws."

- Mayer Amschel (Bauer) Rothschild, patriarch of the Rothschild Banking Dynasty

"The central bank is an institution of the most deadly hostility existing against the Principles and form of our Constitution. I am an Enemy to all banks discounting bills or notes for anything but Coin. If the American People allow private banks to control the issuance of their currency, first by inflation and then by deflation, the banks and corporations that will grow up around them will deprive the People of all their Property until their Children will wake up homeless on the continent their Fathers conquered."

*-Thomas Jefferson (this describes where we are at **today** under the Federal Reserve)*

"The few who understand the system will either be so interested in its profits or be so dependent upon its favours that there will be no opposition from that class, while on the other hand, the great body of people, mentally incapable of comprehending the tremendous advantage that capital derives from the system, will bear its burdens without complaint, and perhaps without even suspecting that the system is inimical to their interests."

-The Rothschild brothers of London, writing to associates in New York, 1863.

"The money power preys on the nation in times of peace, and conspires against it in times of adversity. It is more despotic than monarchy, more insolent than autocracy, more selfish than bureaucracy. It denounces, as public enemies, all who question its methods or throw light upon its crimes."
- Abraham Lincoln

Hopefully you recall from earlier how the Federal Reserve System of the United States of America is not a governmental entity but is in fact a privately-owned, for-profit corporation. The people who own that corporation are also the people pulling the strings of the New World Order agenda, using the money they control through the Fed to expedite the Great Plan to completion. It is not a coincidence that the Fed is owned by the Illuminati and their minions, it is in fact an integral part of the Great Plan.

Complete control over the world's financial system is the primary route through which the Illuminati are able to implement the completion of the Great Plan, and we are getting **damn** close to completion. If they are able to get this tyrannical one world government fully in place, it literally sets the clock in motion for the arrival of the Antichrist, King Nimrod 2.0, and quite literally the end of the world as we know it. Even if you consider yourself an atheist, the agenda the proponents of the Great Plan follow is precisely spelled out for all of humanity in Biblical prophecy.

It is unfolding before our very eyes....

Now, money **is** power, and when you have governmental authorization to create unlimited amounts of money, you can literally create unlimited amounts of power out of thin air. By a numerical entry on a computer screen, the Illuminati can **legally** create as much money as they want to. Since they, the Illuminati, took us off the gold standard in 1933, they have in fact had the power to create as much money as they want and it is all legally sanctioned by our Illuminati-corrupted federal government.

The amount of money they control is astounding. They could be doing so much good with it, but instead they use it for their diabolical plans of the global enslavement of mankind.

It is critical for you to understand how the banking system in our country and the world **really** works, and I'm talking purely the facts here. It is going to seem too simple to be true, but the system put in place by the bloodline families of the Illuminati---who for all intents and purposes own and control nearly the entire world banking system---was explicitly designed to rob us of our money and put us in debt to this group of Luciferians promoting the Great Plan's agenda.

"The process by which banks create money is so simple that the mind is repelled."
-John Kenneth Galbraith, Economist

"Money is the most important subject intellectual persons can investigate and reflect upon. It is so important that our present civilization may collapse unless it is widely understood and its defects remedied very soon."
- Robert H. Hemphill, former credit manager, Federal Reserve Bank of Atlanta

Money today is a commodity. The scarcer it is, the more valuable it is. The more of it that is "printed", or created by entering the amounts onto a computer screen, the less it is worth. It is very simple math. When the Fed prints a lot of money, you get what is called "inflation". This is the exact definition of inflation in fact: the inflating of the amount of money in the money supply. More inflating = the dollar is worth less because there is more of them in circulation. It's factually just simple math.

The private owners of the Federal Reserve are loaning the United States government money they don't physically possess so they can charge us interest and take profits they haven't earned and don't deserve. They intentionally row the economy up and down by inflating and then deflating the currency, and since they know what is coming in advance, the bloodline families who own the Federal Reserve are able to make appropriate investment decisions and siphon wealth off us that way also.

"All the perplexities, confusion and distresses in America arise not from defects in the Constitution or confederation, nor from

want of honor or virtue, as much from downright ignorance of the nature of coin, credit, and circulation."
    -John Adams, in a letter to Thomas Jefferson

Right now the Illuminati are finishing their money scheme swap for a huge amount of the material possessions on Earth. They took all that money they made out of thin air and used it to buy up huge stores of gold and other precious metals, tangible assets like corporations and mortgage-backed securities. They also used it to build up the global military infrastructure they need to enforce the one world government police state.

They are turning their Monopoly money into tangible assets right now and have been since 1913. When the pyramid scheme comes crashing down in the next few years, you will be left holding worthless Monopoly money while they are left holding trillions of dollars worth of physical, tangible assets including your house if you owe on it and are unable to make payments because of a decimated economy.

The financial crash in 2008 is absolutely, unequivocally nothing at all compared to what is soon to come. As the United States grip over the world economy slowly slips away, and people no longer view the U.S. dollar as a good investment, the value of the dollar will begin to erode. Slowly at first, but surely, the dollar will be worth less and less in shorter and shorter amounts of time. From that point it is merely a death watch for the dollar to crash, hyperinflation to set in, and what's left of the United States will be finished. There will be rioting. There will be concentration camps. There will be martial law---and worse. We will talk at the end of this book about how to prepare for this coming calamity. The government knows it is coming and has made preparations for it that we will go over, most of it having to do with a governmental entity called FEMA.

"I believe that banking institutions are more dangerous to our liberties than standing armies. Already they (the Illuminati) have raised up a moneyed aristocracy that has set the Government at

defiance. The issuing power should be taken from the banks and restored to the people to whom it properly belongs."
    -Thomas Jefferson

And lastly, pay special attention to what President Lincoln says in the following quote about privately owned central banks and who should really be in charge of our money system:

"The Government should create, issue, and circulate all the currency and credits needed to satisfy the spending power of the Government and the buying power of consumers. By the adoption of these principles, the taxpayers will be saved immense sums of interest. Money will cease to be master and become the servant of humanity."

Chapter 5/A

HISTORY OF MONEY

Money. You can't live without it, everybody needs it, and you never seem to have enough of it. At least this is how the world currently operates under the Great Plan.

There has been a need for "money" or something tangible that could be traded or exchanged for goods and services for millennia. In the earliest history of mankind, it was all about bartering: Trading particular items for different items that were needed.

The first items to be used as money were staples of the day: cattle, grain, weapons, basically anything that had tangible value. This worked fine for millennia, but as humans advanced, they came up with new ways to accomplish bartering, and "money" was invented.

Around 1000 B.C. the Chinese were the first to make metal coins to be used as currency, and around 700 B.C., the Lydians became the first people of the Western world to make coins made of metal to be used as a medium for exchange.

Countries throughout the known world were soon minting their own coins with specific values. Metal was used because it was readily available, easy to work with and could be recycled into new money as it wore out.

Since coins were given a certain value, it became easier to compare the cost of items people wanted, and thus facilitated trade.

With the introduction of paper currency and non-precious coinage, "commodity" money---which means the coins actually had material value unto themselves such as silver or gold---evolved into "representative" money; the metal "slugs" we call coins today. This meant that what money itself was made of no longer had to be very valuable. .

All the way from ancient times into the twentieth century, the majority of world currencies were based on commodity money through the use of silver and gold.

Due to the results of the Great Depression, the majority of the world's private gold reserves in the form of coins and bullion at the time were taken up by the Illuminati-owned central banks of the Western world, and the commodity money was replaced by representative or "fiat" money---which is only worth something because the government says it's worth something. In other words, **the money is only as valuable as the word and the credit of the government backing it.**

We continued to use silver from the Great Depression era on, until 1964, when the United States government ceased to make our coins out of 90% silver---which meant they actually had value to them. Now our coins are made of copper and zinc and have value in name only.

Money today is given value by a government decree, accompanied by enforceable legal tender laws. By law the refusal of "legal tender" money in favor of some other form of payment is illegal.

Fiat money made of paper is now being replaced by computerized fiat money---so in effect we are heading down a road where no money at all changes hands between humans---it all happens in cyberspace under the control and watchful eyes of the Illuminati-owned central banks of the Western world. This ever-growing control and monitoring of our money and how we spend it will eventually give rise to what the Bible calls "the mark of the Beast", where no human may buy or sell anything without the permission of the one world government and the one world ruler, the Beast, King Nimrod.

Chapter 5/B

FRACTIONAL RESERVE LENDING

We're now going to go over how fractional reserve lending works, which is how a majority of the money in use today in the world is created.

Money first originates with the central banks, but what happens after it leaves the central banks and goes into the national banking system is pure madness. It is nothing more than a **giant pyramid scheme**, that if you or I tried to execute, we would be thrown instantly in jail. This isn't a problem, however, when you literally own and control the government.

Fractional reserve lending historically came about in 16th century Europe, but I believe it actually originated with the earlier masters of the Great Plan, the Knights Templar, and I'll leave it at that.

As trade increased dramatically, it became cumbersome, not to mention dangerous, for merchants to lug around large quantities of gold. So, instead they would deposit their gold with a known goldsmith and get a receipt for the gold. These receipts would then be traded around instead of the gold---with the merchants knowing that they could go and get the actual, physical gold whenever they wanted.

Here's how it went awry back then, just as today: The goldsmiths noticed that hardly any merchants ever came to exchange their receipts for the physical gold---they were just using the receipts for their gold to trade with. The goldsmiths caught on to this fact and started loaning out the gold they held for the merchants to other businesses and private parties, and collected interest on the money that they really should have kept locked up in their vault.

Not only this, but they began to generate receipts for gold that they didn't even possess, just like today.

This was the start of fractional reserve banking, and it is how the banking system works today. There are many, many, MANY more "receipts" (dollars) than there is anything tangible, such as gold, to back them up with. This is a VERY important method of societal manipulation you need to understand here, and it will be worth reading and re-reading this section on money until the seriousness of this scam sinks in.

Fractional-reserve banking is fully sanctioned by the corrupted federal governments of the world, in which banks keep only a fraction of their deposits in reserve as cash and other highly liquid assets, and lend out the remainder. This fraction they keep in the "vault" is usually only about 10% of total deposits. This means if everybody that had money in a particular bank went to withdraw their money, only 10% of the money that is spoken for by the general public would be available for withdrawal.....and that is the truth. And even worse, that 10% is not sitting in the vault, it is only numbers on a computer screen representing the 10% reserve.

Your money is not really there, it exists only as numbers on a piece of paper, a computer screen, or in your mind.

By the mechanism of its action, the practice of fractional reserve banking greatly expands the money supply beyond what it would otherwise be---and this creates artificial growth and retraction cycles in the economy, or "bubbles" and "busts". Today, this is called the "business cycle" and the public has been led to believe that this is a natural occurrence, **when in fact it is a <u>contrived</u> occurrence**. The owners of the Federal Reserve know which way the cycle is going to go before it happens and make appropriate investment decisions. The reason they are able to do this is **because it is their intentional actions that are causing these cycles to start with**. It is legalized insider trading, there is no other term for it.

Because of the prevalence of fractional reserve banking, the broad money supply of most countries is a multiple much larger than the amount of base money created by the country's central bank. That multiple (called the money multiplier) is determined by the reserve requirement or other financial ratio requirements imposed by a nation's central bank.

Central banks like our Federal Reserve are the entities that mandate reserve requirements that require banks to keep a minimum fraction of their demand deposits as cash reserves---again, usually around 10% and this number exists only in cyberspace, not as stacks of cash in a bank's vault. This both sets a limit to the amount of money creation that occurs in the commercial banking system, and ensures that banks have enough ready cash to meet normal demand for withdrawals.

Now, this is where fractional reserve lending gets tricky, and unbelievable, so follow closely:

Let's say "Edward" goes to Bank of America and gets a loan for $10,000 for whatever---the usage by Edward of this money is irrelevant to our scenario. He takes his check for 10 grand from Bank of America and takes it to another bank across the street he has an account at, Chase Bank. Chase takes his deposit and credits his account. Chase is then able to take $9,000 of the $10,000 deposit and loan it out---keeping $1,000 not in the vault, but "on hand" in the form of a mere computer entry. Let's say a man named "George" walks in right after Edward and borrows that 9 grand, and takes it to another bank he has an account at across the street, Bank of America, and deposits the money. The process then can repeat itself nearly indefinitely---creating purely monopoly money back and forth just between these two banks. This is a very simple analogy, but it is a fact. Not only do situations like this happen, but then you throw in a second, even more maddening situation: **How the "money" came into existence in the first place.**

The money at the base of this pyramid scheme was literally created out of nothing---through a mere ledger entry back in 1913 by the Federal Reserve. This "money", which came from nothing and is backed by nothing, is called "fiat" currency. Fiat currency is money that is not backed by gold or silver, which was the sole intent of inventing paper money to start with.

Today our money is not backed by gold or silver, and is only worth something because the government tells us it is. This "money" that originates today with a Federal Reserve computer entry---if you even want to call it money---**IS THEN LOANED at FACE VALUE PLUS INTEREST TO**

OUR FEDERAL GOVERNMENT. You and I are paying **National Debt interest** to the Illuminati on monopoly money that they created out of thin air. It is complete financial enslavement, there is no other word for it, and slavery was the intent by the proponents of the New World Order all along.

Again, under the Federal Reserve System, when a new dollar is issued, we pay taxes to pay for the dollar as the principal (debt) **plus** interest on the created-out-of-nothing dollar. We as American taxpayers pay for each new dollar twice, and who gets the money? The Illuminati banksters who control this money. According to the Constitution, the taxpayers should only pay taxes for the paper, ink, and printing costs of new money, and should reap the benefits of its usage. Why should we give Luciferian international bankers the right to create money out of thin air and screw us over? That is exactly what is happening.

And that's not even the worst part. We are hit with the hidden tax called inflation---which is the intentional devaluing of our money. The Federal Reserve has to constantly pump more base money into the economy in order to cover the interest and principle on the original money "loaned" out to the government plus the INTEREST on the INTEREST of said monopoly money. And then they have to print more money to pay the interest on the interest on the interest. It is a total scam, engineered to enslave us and the world as a whole, and this is a fact.

Chapter 5/C

U.S. CENTRAL BANK HISTORY

All money for a particular country originates with what is called a central bank. A central bank can either be government-owned, or privately-owned. Our Constitution **mandates** that our country's central bank be **government owned**, and therefore benefits our citizens instead of a small group of greedy men. There has been a tug-of-war between the U.S. citizens and the Illuminati since the inception of our country over who got to issue our nation's currency, and the power has changed hands between the government and the Illuminati several times. The Bank of the United States (1816-36), an early attempt at a privately-owned central bank, was abolished by non-Illuminati-puppet President Andrew Jackson, who believed that it threatened the nation.

> "The bold effort the present bank had made to control the government, the distress it had wantonly produced...are but premonitions of the fate that awaits the American people should they be deluded into a perpetuation of this institution or the establishment of another like it."
> -Andrew Jackson, who the Illuminati attempted to assassinate over his abolishment of their central bank scam

Abraham Lincoln, although it is never taught in our corrupt public school system, fought a legendary battle with the Illuminati bankers during the Civil War over who was going to issue the money to fight the war. Lincoln followed the Constitution and issued money through the federal government, allowing him the financial power to win the war and save our country.

"The money powers prey upon the nation in times of peace and conspire against it in times of adversity. The banking powers are more despotic than a monarchy, more insolent than autocracy, more selfish than bureaucracy. They denounce as public enemies all who question their methods or throw light upon their crimes. I have two great enemies, the Southern Army in front of me and the bankers in the rear. Of the two, the one at my rear is my greatest foe."

*-Abraham Lincoln, who the Illuminati **did** assassinate for defying them*

The power to issue our nation's currency fell back into the hands of the Illuminati with the creation of the privately-held Federal Reserve System in 1913, and this is where we will pick up the story of central banking in the United States.

Chapter 5/D

THE FEDERAL RESERVE SYSTEM

"We have, in this country, one of the most corrupt institutions the world has ever known. I refer to the Federal Reserve Board. This evil institution has impoverished the people of the United States and has practically bankrupted our government. It has done this through the corrupt practices of the moneyed vultures who control it".

-Congressman Louis T. McFadden, 1932. He was later poisoned after two previous assassination attempts after pressing for an investigation into the Federal Reserve's actions regarding the Great Depression

In order for the Illuminati to fully implement their plan for world control, they were going to have to harness the growing power of their resurrected Babylon. Remember, money equals power, and whoever controls the money has the power. The way to get the money power under their control was to finagle in a privately-owned central bank for the United States that would be under their control.

The United States had managed to do without a central bank since the days of Andrew Jackson in the 1830's, who had abolished the central bank during his presidency.

I am one of those who do not believe that a national debt is a national blessing, but rather a curse to a republic; inasmuch as it is calculated to raise around the administration a moneyed aristocracy dangerous to the liberties of the country. Gentlemen, I

have had men watching you for a long time and I am convinced that you have used the funds of the bank to speculate in the breadstuffs of the country. When you won, you divided the profits amongst you, and when you lost, you charged it to the bank. You tell me that if I take the deposits from the bank and annul its charter, I shall ruin ten thousand families. That may be true, gentlemen, but that is your sin! Should I let you go on, you will ruin fifty thousand families, and that would be my sin! You are a den of vipers and thieves. I intend to rout you out, and by the grace of the Eternal God, will rout you out.
    -Andrew Jackson, 7th President of the United States

The country had been doing just fine economically, and there was absolutely no reason for a private central bank. That is, until the time came that the Illuminati felt it was time to make their move and take the Great Plan to the next level. In order to pull this off, they employed the program of the Hegelian Dialectic we already talked about, which is problem-reaction-solution. They were going to have to create problems within the independent banking system, which they already largely controlled---but could have 1000x the control of the U.S. if they had a privately-held central bank to operate out of. They began to pull the levers of trickery and created banking panics by starting rumors about bank failures. The Illuminati knew that they had to spook the public into believing that they needed a private central bank for national economic stability, and they did just this via a financial false flag.

According to Congressman Charles Lindbergh, Sr., the "Money Trust" (Illuminati) caused the national banking panic in 1907, and thereby forced Congress to create a National Monetary Commission in 1908. **Headed by Senator Nelson Aldrich, father-in-law of card-carrying Illuminati member John D. Rockefeller, Jr., the Commission recommended creation of a privately owned central bank.**

Of **course** they did.....

In order to convince Congress and the public at large that the establishment of a private central bank was a good thing, the following plan of action was laid down in a clandestine meeting at Jekyll Island in Georgia.

(The following is from G. Edward Griffin's book about the founding of the Federal Reserve, *"The Creature From Jekyll Island"*)

The purpose of the meeting at Jekyll Island:

1. **How to stop the growing influence of small, rival banks and to insure that control over the nation's financial resources would remain in the hands of those present;**
2. **How to make the money supply more elastic in order to reverse the trend of private capital formation and to recapture the industrial loan market;**
3. **How to pool the meager reserves of all the nation's banks into one large reserve so that at least a few of them could protect themselves from currency drains and bank runs;**
4. **How to shift the inevitable losses from the owners of the banks to the taxpayers;**
5. **How to convince Congress that the scheme was a measure to protect the public.**

According to Griffin, and all other sources I've researched, the new central bank was to be "hidden" from the public, with the following goals of the new central bank by the proponents of the Great Plan:

1. **Do not call it a cartel nor even a central bank.**
2. **Make it look like a government agency.**
3. **Establish regional branches to create the appearance of decentralization, not dominated by Wall Street banks.**
4. **Begin with a conservative structure including many sound banking principles knowing that the provisions can be quietly altered or removed in subsequent years.**
5. **Use the anger caused by recent panics and bank failures to create popular demand for monetary reform.**
6. **Offer the Jekyll Island plan as though it were in response to that need.**
7. **Employ university professors to give the plan the appearance of academic approval.**

8. **Speak out against the plan to convince the public that Wall Street bankers do not want it.**

The representatives who attended and formulated the plan to install the Federal Reserve were as follows:

- Nelson W. Aldrich, Republican Senator, Freemason, married into Illuminati family through the Rockefellers
- A. Piat Andrew, Assistant Secretary of the Treasury, Freemason
- Benjamin Strong, head of JP Morgan's Bankers Trust and later to become the chairman of the Federal Reserve, not a Freemason---just a Rothschild/Illuminati front man
- Henry P. Davison, Sr, partner at JP Morgan, not a Freemason---another Illuminati puppet
- Paul M. Warburg, representative for the Rothschilds and Warburgs in Europe, and partner in Kuhn, Loeb & Company, headed the meeting and was the architect of the Federal Reserve System, alleged 33rd degree Freemason
- Frank A. Vanderlip, President of National City Bank in New York, representative for John D. Rockefeller, alleged 33rd degree Freemason
- Charles D. Norton, President of 1st National Bank in New York, not a Freemason---just a another Illuminati front man

Not only did they come up with the blueprint for the Federal Reserve at this meeting, they also came up with a plan to make sure their newly-indentured servants were forced to pay up to their newly-crowned slave masters......the **Federal Income Tax**, which was also passed in 1913 and this is a fact. The Federal Reserve was created to bankrupt our government and thereby enslave the United States citizens by putting us on the hook to the Illuminati for the debt. The Income Tax and the IRS were created to enforce the payments on the enormous debt that was soon to come. See how that works?

Two of the ten planks of Karl Marx's "Communist Manifesto" literally are the creation and operation of a private central bank, **and** a graduated income tax---both **ILLEGAL** in our country according to the U.S. Constitution.

In order to get their plan for a central bank/income tax through though, the Illuminati needed an absolute puppet in the driver's seat to cement their plan. They found this man in our 28th President, Woodrow Wilson.

Woodrow Wilson was elected President and took over in 1913, having beaten incumbent William Howard Taft, who had vowed to veto legislation establishing a central bank. To divide the Republican vote and elect the relatively unknown Wilson, J.P. Morgan and Co. poured money into the candidacy of former President Teddy Roosevelt and his Progressive Party. This effectively split the Republican vote and ensured Wilson's---and the Illuminati's---victory.

Although Wilson was naïve to the true workings of the political world, he was smart enough to utter the following quote in 1913 regarding the men who brought him to Washington and were running the show:

"Since I entered politics, I have chiefly had men's views confided to me privately. Some of the biggest men in the United States, in the field of commerce and manufacture are afraid of something. They know that there is a power somewhere so organized, so subtle, so watchful, so interlocked, so complete, so pervasive, that they better not speak above their breath when they speak in condemnation of it."

He of course was referring to the proponents of the Great Plan, the Illuminati.

Though unconstitutional, as only "The Congress shall have Power... To coin Money, regulate the Value thereof..." (Article I, Section 8, U.S. Constitution) the Federal Reserve Act was passed in the House of Representatives under the guise of "needed banking reform" on September 18, 1913. More than forty important differences in the House and Senate versions remained to be settled after getting through the House of Representatives, and the opponents of the bill in both houses of Congress were led to believe that many months would tick by before the Conference bill would be ready for consideration.

The Congressmen prepared to leave Washington for the annual Christmas recess, assured that the Conference bill would not be brought up until the following year. Now was time for the Illuminati's minions to act and act fast. In a single day, they ironed out all forty of the disputed passages in the bill and quickly brought it to a vote in the Senate. The Senators, wanting to leave for Christmas recess, passed the bill without even analyzing it....just like they do today.

On Monday, December 22, 1913, the bill was passed by the House 282-60 and the Senate 43-23.

"This [Federal Reserve Act] establishes the most gigantic trust on earth. When the President signs this bill, the invisible government of the monetary power will be legalized....the worst legislative crime of the ages is perpetrated by this banking and currency bill. From now on, depressions will be scientifically created"
-Congressman Charles A. Lindbergh, Sr., 1913

The bill was signed by President Woodrow Wilson on December 23, 1913. Years after he signed the Federal Reserve Act, Wilson lamented:

"I have unwittingly ruined my country. A great industrial nation is controlled by it's system of credit. Our system of credit is concentrated in the hands of a few men. We have come to be one of the worst ruled, one of the most completely controlled and dominated governments in the world-- no longer a government of free opinion, no longer a government by conviction and vote of the majority, but a government by the opinion and duress of small groups of dominant men."

Although called "Federal," the Federal Reserve System is factually privately owned by member banks, these banks of course owned by the Illuminati families. The Fed makes its own policies, and is not subject to oversight by Congress or the President. As the overseer and supplier of our nation's currency, the Fed gave the already-in-place Illuminati banks access to public funds, which enhanced their lending capacity even further.

"The financial system has been turned over to the Federal Reserve Board. That Board administers the finance system by authority of a purely profiteering group. The system is Private, conducted for the sole purpose of obtaining the greatest possible profits from the use of other people's money"
-Charles A. Lindbergh Sr.

The ten major shareholders of the Federal Reserve Bank System are ALL Illuminati owned or controlled banks. Since the Fed itself won't tell us which banks own it, we have to go off of cross-referenced listings of the owners from the internet, which are: Rothschild: London and Berlin; Lazard Bros: Paris; Israel Seiff: Italy; Kuhn- Loeb Company: Germany; Warburg: Hamburg and Amsterdam; Lehman Bros: New York; Goldman Sachs: New York; Rockefeller Chase Manhattan: New York.

Most of the banks that dominate the United States economy **aren't even from the United States**. This is treason of the highest degree, and the Federal Reserve must be eliminated by the citizens of the United States before it is too late. The Great Depression, which was intentionally caused by the Illuminati, is small potatoes compared to what is coming when their gigantic pyramid scheme comes crashing down.

"The Federal Reserve banks are one of the most corrupt institutions the world has ever seen. There is not a man within the sound of my voice who does not know that this nation is run by the International bankers. Some people think the Federal Reserve Banks are the United States government's institutions. They are not government institutions. They are private credit monopolies which prey upon the people of the United States for the benefit of themselves and their foreign swindlers."
-Congressman Louis T. McFadden

Suppose the United States government wants to borrow a billion dollars. The government issues a fancy looking piece of official paper called a "bond" for this amount, much as a water company does when it wants to raise money for a new pipeline or a new dam. The government delivers this bond for the billion dollars to the Federal Reserve Bank. The Federal Reserve Bank takes the bond and writes an order to the Department of Printing and Engraving to print the billion dollars' worth of bills. After about two weeks or so, when the bills are printed, the Department of Printing and Engraving ships the bills to the Federal Reserve Bank, which then writes a check for about two thousand three hundred dollars to pay for printing the billion dollars' worth of bills. The Federal Reserve Bank then takes the billion dollars and lends it to the United States government, and the people of the country pay interest at an exorbitant rate each year on this money, which was created out of nothing.....the owners of the Federal Reserve Bank put up **nothing** to issue this money, no gold....nothing. The process I just described is all done electronically these days, with no paper changing hands whatsoever.

"The new law will create inflation whenever the trusts want inflation...they can unload the stocks on the people at high prices during the excitement and then bring on a panic and buy them back at low prices...the day of reckoning is only a few years removed."
-Charles A. Lindbergh Sr.

That day came a mere 16 years after the 1913 founding of the Federal Reserve, in 1929, when the big stock market crash happened and the Great Depression ensued. This was eerily reminiscent to the way Nathan Rothschild crashed the English stock market and took control of Great Britain 100 years earlier. It was a little different here, in that the crash was engineered over years to happen, and that the entire group of Illuminati were involved and not just a single player. All of the Illuminati insiders knew what was coming and quietly exited the market just before the crash. When the market crashed, they jumped in and scooped up millions---if not billions---of shares of our American corporations for pennies on the dollar---and they have controlled our country and multinational corporations ever since.

It only took the Illuminati **20 years** after establishing the Federal Reserve to bankrupt the United States government. On the heels of the

Great Depression, the United States Federal Government, an incorporated entity, was declared by President Roosevelt to be bankrupt and was dissolved by the Emergency Banking Act, on March 9, 1933, essentially turning over the country to the Fed.

On April 3, 1933, under Presidential Executive Order number 6102, the Federal Government began confiscating all privately held Gold in the United States, under threats of fines and imprisonment, in order to turn it over to the Illuminati. You see, one of the terms of passing the Federal Reserve Act in 1913, was that the Fed was to be paid the interest on the money it was creating out of nothing with **GOLD BULLION**. This was the "Gold Clause" in the wording of the Federal Reserve Act. Since the federal government was bankrupt and out of gold, they took ours and gave it to the Luciferian Illuminati crooks. They were kind enough to "buy" it from the Americans, though, and gave them monopoly fiat money in the form of Federal Reserve notes for it----which again, the Federal Reserve created out of thin air at no real cost to them.

On June 5, 1933 Congress passed the Joint Resolution To Suspend The Gold Standard and Abrogate The Gold Clause (since they had just confiscated America's gold anyways)---taking us off the gold standard and fully onto purely "fiat" money. Now the Illuminati were completely in the driver's seat of the United States' future. If you look at a dollar bill from before 1933, it says "payable in gold". If you look at a dollar bill after 1933, it says that it is "legal tender"---which means it is just worthless paper backed by nothing tangible. Since taking us off the gold standard, the only thing that gives our money value is how much is in circulation and how credible our Federal Government is. The more the Federal Reserve creates, the less it is worth, and this is how we are going to get into a hyperinflation mess here very soon---the crashing of the pyramid scheme.

Since the Federal Government didn't have any assets to forfeit to the Illuminati, they assigned the private property of their "economic slaves", the U.S. citizens and their country's land and assets, as collateral against the un-payable federal debt. They pledged the unincorporated federal territories, national parks and forests, birth certificates (you), and non-profit organizations, as collateral against the federal debt.

Wright Patman (1893-1976) was a Democratic representative from Texas, who served in the U.S. Congress from 1929 to his death on March 7, 1976. He was chairman of the House of Representatives Committee on Banking and Currency for 40 years. For 20 of those years, he continually introduced legislation to repeal the Federal Reserve Banking Act of 1913. This is exactly what Presidential candidate Ron Paul did for a number of years, and this is the very reason his character was assassinated and marginalized in the Mainstream Media when he first ran for President in 2008. He was trying to help us, but was labeled a crackpot by the MM assassins.

Here are excerpts from what Patman said on September 29, 1941, as reported in the Congressional Record of the House of Representatives (pages 7582-7583):

"When our Federal Government, that has the exclusive power to create money, creates that money and then goes into the open market and borrows it and pays interest for the use of its own money, it occurs to me that that is going too far. I have never yet had anyone who could, through the use of logic and reason, justify the Federal Government borrowing (from the Fed) the use of its own money... I am saying to you in all sincerity, and with all the earnestness that I possess, it is absolutely wrong for the Government to issue interest-bearing obligations. It is not only wrong: it is extravagant. It is not only extravagant, it is wasteful. It is absolutely unnecessary.

Now, I believe the system should be changed. The Constitution of the United States does not give the banks the power to create money. The Constitution says that Congress shall have the power to create money, but now, under our system, we will sell bonds to commercial banks and obtain credit from those banks.

I believe the time will come when people will demand that this be changed. I believe the time will come in this country when they will actually blame you and me and everyone else connected with this Congress for sitting idly by and permitting such an idiotic system to continue. I make that statement after years of study.

We have what is known as the Federal Reserve Bank System. That system is not owned by the Government. Many people think that it is, because it says 'Federal Reserve'. It belongs to the private banks, private corporations. So we have farmed out to the Federal Reserve Banking System that is owned exclusively, wholly, 100 percent by the private banks — we have farmed out to them the privilege of issuing the Government's money. If we were to take this privilege back from them, we could save the amount of money that I have indicated in enormous interest charges."

I'm going to keep harping on this, because it is critical to understand this: The Federal Reserve is a private monopoly of our money supply operated for the benefit of the proponents of the Great Plan, all under the guise of protecting the public interest from "evil bankers". What happened is, in reality, the exact opposite of this. It was put in place by evil bankers to turn us into slaves, and to give the Illuminati the money power they needed to take the Great Plan to completion. The Illuminati families who own our Federal Reserve are in fact, by definition, the most evil people on the planet, and they are in total control of our country.

If **you** could accurately predict future interest rates, inflation and deflation, you would know when to buy or sell stocks and make a bundle of money---just like the Illuminati. This is just another way they fleece us. The Federal Reserve has secret meetings to determine future interest rates and the amount of money to be inserted or taken out of the economy. The Securities Exchange Commission (SEC) by law, supposedly stops insiders from profiting by privileged information. However, also by law, they have no idea who is in on the Fed's secret meetings. The Federal Reserve has never been audited, and its operations are 100% a secret kept from the public. It is the Fed that decides if we are going to go into a boom or bust period in the economy, and the people on the inside know this in advance and profit from it.

"In the United States we have in effect two governments... We have the duly constituted Government, and then we have an independent, uncontrolled and un-coordinated government in the

Federal Reserve System, operating the money powers which are reserved to Congress by the Constitution."

-Chairman of the House Banking Committee Wright Patman, 1964

I'll close this chapter on the Federal Reserve with this fact: 4 out of 5 of our patriotic Presidents who opposed a privately-held central bank while in office were assassinated: Abraham Lincoln, James Garfield, William McKinley, and John F. Kennedy. **These were the only U.S. Presidential assassinations in history**. They were all murdered by the Illuminati. The fifth, Andrew Jackson, miraculously survived his attempted assassination when BOTH of the assassin's pistols jammed....

Chapter 5/E

MASONIC SYMBOLISM ON OUR MONEY

The New Babylon's government-sanctioned currency is the "dollar", and it is the most widely used and recognized currency in the world. There are no Egyptian pyramids in the United States, so why is there one on the back of our nation's currency unit, the one-dollar bill? You already know the answer to that question at this point, right friend?

The proponents of the Great Plan have so little regard for their slaves, and feel that their agenda is so far enough along that it cannot be stopped, that they had the gall to put their occult Freemasonic-Great Plan symbolism right in front of your face on our money.

The occult design of our dollar bill was first debuted in 1933, **celebrating the exact same year** the Federal Reserve, aka the proponents of the Great Plan, took possession over the country.

Coincidence? No, unfortunately not.

Not the five, ten, twenty, or any other denomination of dollars, but the one dollar bill, because that is the representative unit of the money system that was used to build up the political/economic/military power of New Babylon...the "dollar". What the Federal Reserve did in a nutshell was to give the U.S. government a credit card with no limit. To make the payments and interest on this credit card, the Fed simply generated more money and loaned it to our federal government. Uncle Sam then went on a military spending spree and the United States (New Babylon) conquered the world once again. The story of what has happened and what they are trying to do is literally right on our money, via the imagery of the Great Seal of the United States.

That's right, on our one dollar bill. I want you to take note because it is also important that this story is on the back and not the front of the one dollar bill, the "hidden" side of the dollar.

Take one out of your pocket right now and look at it. There is, in my opinion, only one significant image regarding the symbolism of the Great Plan on the front of the dollar. This is the image of alleged 33rd degree Freemason George Washington, who was a full-fledged participant of the Great Plan, and who is admired by most unknowing Americans. The Illuminati-owned Federal Reserve put him on there to pay homage to the fact that he was indeed working to fulfill Nimrod's vision of a New World Order.

However, when you turn it over to see the "reverse" of the dollar, which means the other side of it, you will see both sides, the obverse (front) and reverse (back), of the Great Seal of the United States on display for all to see. Pay attention now to what I just said: **The Great Seal is the official seal to the entire world of our country, the United States of America.** No other country on the planet has such overt occult display of the numerous symbols of the proponents of the Great Plan, and this is because the United States is literally a reincarnated version of King Nimrod's Babylon.

After the non-Jacobin/Illuminati branch of Freemasons placed the occult symbolism on the Great Seal when it was finalized in 1782, the **reverse** side of it remained hidden from the public for 150 years until alleged 33rd degree Freemason and Theosophist Henry Wallace convinced fellow 33rd degree (alleged) Freemason FDR to put it on the back of the one dollar bill to announce to the world that they were firmly in control of the United States in 19**33**.

Looking at the back of the dollar you may recognize the "all-seeing eye" of Osiris/Horus (Nimrod) on top of the Egyptian pyramid that we have already talked about, but there is much more Masonic/Great Plan symbolism that is hidden in plain sight.

To begin with, the Great Seal, and therefore also our money, is replete with the number 13.

Yes, there were 13 original colonies, and the reason there were 13 and not 12 or 14 is that the number 13 is very special to the occultists running the world. Hopefully you will understand that the number 13 was very important to the most significant of our founding fathers, being that the most influential were high-level Freemasons, and this is **why** there were 13 original colonies to start with. In occult numerology, the number 13 represents depravity and rebellion against authority, and in particular, God's authority over us. This is also why there were 13 families who comprised the original Illuminati, not 12, not 14......13. The number 13 is incredibly significant to the occult beliefs of these people. It absolutely does have to do with the occult, and that is the main point of them using various numbers like they do.

So, viewing the reverse (the back) of the dollar bill, you can see both sides of our country's official seal. It is the obverse, or "front" of this very seal that is displayed on the front of the President's podium when he is speaking publicly. Little do you know that the back of that placard hanging on the podium, the "reverse" of our Great Seal, is, again, intended to show who is really running the country from behind the scenes: the proponents of the Great Plan.

"The combination of the Phoenix (*changed to a bald eagle now*), the pyramid, and the all-seeing eye is more than chance or coincidence. There is nothing about the early struggles of the colonists to suggest such a selection to farmers, shopkeepers, and country gentleman. There is only one possible origin for these symbols, and that is the secret societies which came to this country 150 years before the Revolutionary War. Most of the patriots who achieved American independence belonged to these societies, and derive their inspiration, courage, and high purpose from the ancient teaching. There can be no question that the great seal was directly inspired by these orders of the human Quest, and that I set forth the purpose for this nation as that purpose was seen and known to the Founding Fathers."

-Manly P. Hall, **confirmed** *33rd degree Freemasonic "prophet"*

At the left side of the back of the dollar, within the circle, is the back or "reverse" side of the Great Seal of the United States. Again, you always see the front part of the Seal on the Presidential podium, but the back of the seal---the "hidden" part, just like the role of the Great Plan in our lives--- shows an incomplete Egyptian pyramid with the All-seeing eye staring at you. The Freemasons tell us publicly that this is the "eye of providence", which they say means the eye of "God", but they fail to discern that the god they are referring to is the original Sun god King Nimrod, the founder of the Great Plan.

Now, staying at the left side of the back side of the bill here, within the reverse side of the Great Seal: Over the top of the pyramid spells "Annuit Coeptis". This is Latin, and means "He (Nimrod) looks with favor upon".

Under the pyramid spells "Novus Ordo Seclorum". This is also Latin and translated means "A new secular order", or also could be translated as "A new order of the ages"....or.....**the New World Order**. Put the two statements together, and you will see what they are talking about. They are announcing what is happening right in front of your face, and only their fellow occultists are able to look at these symbols/words and how they are used, and what context, and know the truth of what is being said and what is going on.

When the Illuminati fully took the reins of the United States government in 1933, and therefore its hard working citizens, they thought they had the tiger by the tail and arrogantly announced it and placed it right in front of your face that exact same year.

OK. Staying on the back of the dollar at the left side, the pyramid within the circle has-guess how many-**13** layers of bricks. This is, again, meant to represent the powerful occult number 13. Yes it is unlucky to **you**, but not to these occultists, remember that. The Roman numerals underneath the 13-layer pyramid add up to 1776---not meant to represent the year of our country's independence, which was in fact 1783. 1776 was the year that the birth announcement of the resurrected Babylon was sent out via the Declaration of Independence, and this is why that number is on there---paying homage to the Great Plan. They were announcing the birth to the world, via the Declaration of Independence, of the United States, which they fully knew was intended to be New Babylon. Their prophecy on this matter was certainly precise, wasn't it? The United States turned out to be the most powerful, corrupt, raunchiest, filth-infested entity in history, comparable only to the original Babylon, and that was the goal.

Also please note on the back of the dollar that the pyramid is incomplete, as the floating eye of Horus (Nimrod) within the triangle sits above the pyramid. This signifies that the plan is not yet complete, but is **close** to completion. The "all-seeing eye" is Nimrod watching over his resurrected Babylon from the spirit realm, waiting to be "reborn" via the technology created right here in the New Babylon.

Remember the genetic cloning stuff we talked about? I honestly believe that the Illuminati are running around with or know the location of King Nimrod's DNA sample. This is why there was a big push in ancient Egypt to mummify the pharaohs—so they could also be brought back to life someday. Only when the New World Order/one world government is fully in place, and the technology in place to bring Nimrod (Antichrist) back to life from the dead, and he has been brought back to life, will their plan be complete. Well, they are ever-nearing having the first part of that equation in place, and I believe they probably already have the second part of that equation solved, or are damn close. The third part could very well have happened, and King Nimrod, aka the Antichrist, is possibly alive right now. We are extremely close to the apocalyptic events happening on the Earth described in the Book of Revelation, among other Holy writ.

Panning across the dollar from left to right, at the center of the dollar it says "IN GOD WE TRUST". Hopefully you know now what god that is. Certainly not the Most High God. It is the god of Babylon, King Nimrod, and this statement is on all of our money, both paper and coin. For a country that supposedly has a separation of church and state, don't you find that a bit odd that a purely religious statement is on our money? It is because there **is** a separation between the one true God and Nimrod's New Babylonian government. There is **no separation** between the god on our money, Nimrod, and the New Babylon; they are one and the same.

Now, pan to the right side of the back of the bill and within the circle is contained the obverse, or front of the Great Seal. **Again**, this is the side you see when the President is speaking from the podium to the citizens of New Babylon. On the front of the Seal you see an eagle---which represents the United States. It wasn't always the eagle that represented the U.S. It was changed to the eagle in 1841, from the all-too-obvious Freemasonic symbol of the Phoenix, and this is a fact. **The original phoenix**

was meant to represent <u>Babylon</u> rising from the ashes, resurrected as the <u>United States</u>.

It's hard to count these without a magnifying glass or microscope, but there are 32 feathers on the eagle's right wing, meant to represent the 32 degrees of formal rites in the Scottish rite of Freemasonry. There are 9 tail feathers---meant to represent the 9 degrees of formal rites in the York rite of Freemasonry. Both Scottish and York rite have---as invite only---the 33rd degree, with the York Rite jumping from 9th degree directly to the Luciferian 33rd degree, and this is reflected in the 33 feathers of the eagle's left wing. The significance of the left wing here, in my opinion, can be construed to be meant to signify that the Great Plan conspiracy is a "left wing" or "socialist" conspiracy---and that is exactly their goal: worldwide socialism under King Nimrod.

Now, look above the eagle's head: you will see **13** stars in the shape of---not the Star of David remember---the Star of Rephaim, which is probably actually the Star of Nimrod, at least a 3,000 year old occult symbol used in black magic rituals. The placement at the top of the front of our seal of this symbol signifies that the occult Great Plan runs the show in New Babylon.

The occultists certainly did not assemble **13 *pentagrams***, which are also black magic symbols, in the shape of a ***hexagram*** as a coincidence.

Staying on the right side of the back of the dollar, within the front of the Seal of the U.S., we have **13** leaves in the olive branch, **13** bars and stripes in the shield, **13** arrows in the right claw, and **13** letters in "E Pluribus Unum" on the ribbon---all in tribute to the proponents of the Great Plan who own and control the United States through the Federal Reserve's monopoly over our money supply.

Chapter 5/F

FEDERAL INCOME TAX/IRS

Do you like looking at your pay stub and seeing how much money Uncle Sam is extracting from you via income tax withholding to throw into the black hole that is our National Debt? There was no need for a personal income tax prior to 1913, as there was plenty of money to run the country coming in from corporate taxes. However, with the passage of the Federal Reserve Act in 1913, a way was needed to put the American public on the hook for what the proponents of the New World Order were going to do in the years to come. By providing the federal government with unlimited credit in 1913 via the fiat money the Federal Reserve was now legally authorized to create out of thin air, this allowed the feds to spend more money than they were taking in via corporate and the newly enacted income taxes.

I'm going to tell you something right now that you may not believe, but is 100% true: **There is no law in existence <u>anywhere</u> in the IRS tax code or elsewhere that says you have to pay income tax to the Federal Government of the United States of America.** The income tax is a completely voluntary tax, but you are led to believe that it is mandatory. A mandatory, graduated income tax completely violates the Constitution. What our Constitution mandates is that all personal taxes collected by the government must be apportioned, which in a nutshell means equally collected and equally distributed back to the people.

Not only is there no law requiring you to pay income tax, the Sixteenth Amendment "authorizing" the implementation of the income tax **was never ratified by the states.** The federal income tax is a **complete**

fraud perpetrated on the naïve citizens of the United States via the agenda of the Great Plan.

Not only is it an illegal tax, the graduated income tax in place in this country is also one of Karl Marx's ten planks of Communism, first published in 1848.

The IRS is literally the collection agency of the Federal Reserve, and that is the truth. The Fed buys our bonds and needs money in the treasury to pay them interest, which comes from you and me via illegal personal income taxes. Most of the corporations that formerly funded the federal government have long ago moved to offshore holding corporation-status and don't pay into the system. The profiteers of these offshore corporations then put all of their taxable income into tax-free foundations or secret Swiss accounts, further avoiding the funding of our nation's government. The naïve citizens of the United States are left all alone to shoulder the burden of bankrolling the New Babylon.

A national income tax was declared unconstitutional in 1895 by the Supreme Court, so a constitutional amendment was proposed in Congress by none other than ...**Senator Nelson Aldrich**, the main Congressional proponent and puppet of the Illuminati who helped put the Federal Reserve in place.

As the Sixteenth Amendment was presented to the American people at the time, it seemed reasonable. The American public would be liable for income tax on only one percent of income under $20,000, with the assurance that it would never increase. Those making more than 20k were subject to a progressively increasing tax. Fast forward 100 years to 2013 and the IRS can confiscate almost 40% of your earnings through this tax. As our National Debt climbs, you can rest assured that these rates will not be going down, but up as they tighten the noose on their slaves.

You would think the ultra rich proponents of the New World Order such as the Rockefellers would have fought against this income tax tooth and nail, but they were actually the ones behind it. You will understand this well in a couple of sections here when we go over the creation of the "tax-free foundations" that they came up with right around this time to explicitly shield their wealth, and therefore their power, from the income tax.

Chapter 5/G

THE GLOBAL BANKING CABAL

"The Federal Reserve Bank of New York is eager to enter into close relationship with the Bank for International Settlements.... The conclusion is impossible to escape that the State and Treasury Departments are willing to pool the banking system of Europe and America, setting up a world financial power independent of and above the Government of the United States....The United States under present conditions will be transformed from the most active of manufacturing nations into a consuming and importing nation with a balance of trade against it."
- Rep. Louis McFadden, Chairman of the House Committee on Banking and Currency quoted in the New York Times, June 1930. At the end of 2012, our national trade deficit stood at $540 billion.

Now I'm going to discuss the central banks for the ENTIRE WORLD that the proponents of the New World Order have set up, that the individual nations' central banks, like the Federal Reserve, will ultimately answer to. Their conspiracy is a global one, and in order to control the entire globe, it necessitates controlling all of the world's money through one entity. They do not have a single entity as of yet, they have three entities: The Bank for International Settlement (BIS), the International Monetary Fund (IMF), and the World Bank. These three will probably be merged into one giant global bank after the United States' dollar spins into hyperinflation and the big banking crash occurs, which as of early 2013 is not very far off.

Let's begin by talking about the first one of these to come into existence, the BIS. Now, keep in mind that I could go on for dozens of pages describing each one of these privately-held agencies, so for the sake of keeping this book to a readable length, I will just give you an overview of the facts.

To start with, the BIS is housed in a building that was intentionally meant to look like the most famous artist's rendition of the Tower of Babel. This was not a coincidence by a long shot, as the people running the show are again paying homage to Nimrod.

The BIS meets once a month in Switzerland, home of the untouchable "Swiss bank accounts" you probably have heard of, where the elite hide a lot of their electronic wealth. Each of the dozen or so visiting members from the largest central banks around the world has his own office at the BIS with secure telephone lines to his home country.

The membership of this private "club" is restricted to a handful of powerful men who determine daily the interest rate, the availability of credit, and the money supply of the banks in their own countries. They include the governors of the U.S. Federal Reserve, the Bank of England, the Bank of Japan, the Swiss National Bank, and the German Bundesbank among others.

The Bank of International Settlements was originally established in May 1930 by bankers and diplomats of Europe and the United States to collect and disburse Germany's World War I reparation payments.

Although the BIS was organized as a commercial bank with publicly held shares, its immunity from government interference (and taxes) in both peace and war was guaranteed by an international treaty signed in The Hague in 1930.

Since the BIS also provided a safe and convenient repository for the gold holdings of the European central banks, it quickly evolved into the bank for central banks. As the world depression deepened in the Thirties and financial panics flared up in Austria, Hungary, Yugoslavia, and Germany, the governors in charge of the key central banks feared that the entire global financial system would collapse unless they could closely coordinate their rescue efforts. The obvious meeting spot for this collective effort was the BIS, where they regularly met anyway to facilitate gold swaps and war-damage settlements.

After World War II, the BIS reemerged as the main clearing house for European currencies and, behind the scenes, the favored meeting place of central bankers. When the United States dollar came under attack in the 1960s, massive swaps of money and gold were arranged at the BIS for the defense of the American currency.

The BIS is the main worldwide money-organizing group of the three, and is by far the most secretive and powerful.

The latter two entities, the IMF and World Bank, are more of a "public face" for the global banking scheme, and came about through the Bretton Woods system in July of 1944.

The Bretton Woods system refers to the international monetary regime that dominated global finance from the end of World War II until the early 1970s. Taking its name from the site of the 1944 conference, the Bretton Woods system set up a system of rules, institutions, and procedures to regulate the global monetary system. The planners at Bretton Woods established the International Monetary Fund (IMF) and the International Bank for Reconstruction and Development (IBRD), which today is known simply as the World Bank.

The IMF and the World Bank were designed to work together, with the IMF acting as the judicial/executive branch mediating between the member countries and running the show, while the World Bank was to be exactly what it was called---the bank for the entire world, providing endless fiat money to war-ravaged and underdeveloped nations for economic development, all for a price of course. The World Bank has taken in as collateral for these loans entire countries' supplies of natural resources in the process. Through the use of the Illuminati-controlled CIA, puppet governments were set up all over the third world nations of the world in order to control the governments receiving these loans---in order to ensure they defaulted on them. This pushed the countries further in the hole and in debt to the proponents of the New World Order.

One of the main reasons for Bretton Woods was to establish global exchange rates tied in to a physical commodity, gold, in order to establish some sense of stability in the world markets after the Illuminati-induced chaos of the Great Depression and World War II. To set up this stability, they tied only the U.S. dollar to the value of gold, and all the other world currencies would be in turn tied to the dollar. In order to facilitate the

New World Order, they needed to get trade moving freely, VERY freely, in order to bring down the big industrialized nations by transferring jobs out of the high-paying Western nations and into the slave-wage third world nations. This would have a twofold effect for them: it would destroy the powerful Western country middle-class who would be their biggest threat to world domination, and it would topple the Western power structure, sending the world into a power vacuum that a global government, the New World Order, would fill just nicely.

In order to help this along, organizations such as the World Trade Organization, the G20, and trade agreements such as NAFTA and GATT were implemented, and have done a pretty good job of their primary goal of transfering manufacturing from the United States to Third World sweat-shops, and knocking the U.S.A. off the high-and-mighty manufacturing perch we once stood upon.

By the early 1970's, the Illuminati were ready to light the fuse on their now worldwide fiat-money pyramid-scheme, and On August 15, 1971, the United States pulled out of the Bretton Woods Accord taking the US off the Gold Exchange Standard. The 25% gold reserve requirement for Federal Reserve Notes was ended in 1971, when President Nixon totally removed the dollar from any gold basis. Since 1971, the value of the dollar has been strictly based on supply and demand of the dollars themselves.

This allowed the dollar to "float". Shortly thereafter, Britain followed, floating the pound sterling. The industrialized nations followed suit with their respective currencies. In anticipation of the fluctuation of currencies as they stabilized against each other, the industrialized nations also increased their reserves by printing money, or "inflating", in amounts far greater than ever before. The result was a depreciation of the value of the US dollar like never before, as well as the other currencies of the world. **This is why there was massive inflation in the 1970's---culminating with the Federal Reserve having to ratchet up interest rates to around 20% circa 1980-1981 in order to put the brakes on the runaway inflation freight train.** They came close at that time to crashing the dollar, but the Illuminati weren't quite ready to implode the economies of the world just yet. Unfortunately for the people alive right now in 2013, they are **now ready** to let the pyramid collapse and you're going to see quite the financial disaster in the coming months and years.

They needed a scheme of such massive fraud that the world would not be able to dig themselves out of the black hole, and would have to capitulate to a single world currency under control of the proponents of the Great Plan. This scheme was hatched during the Clinton administration, when Clinton, an alleged 33rd degree Freemason and bonafide Illuminati henchman, repealed the Glass-Stegall Act, also known as the Banking Act of 1933. In the wake of the wild speculation that helped fuel the fire that caused the stock market crash in 1929 and the Great Depression, patriotic Congressmen took it upon themselves to regulate the banks that had contributed the gasoline to turn the small fire into a raging inferno that engulfed the entire world. The Glass-Stegall Act was put in place in response to the climate of corruption, financial manipulation and insider trading which led to more than 5,000 bank failures in the years following the 1929 Wall Street crash. It also prohibited commercial banks, brokerage firms, hedge funds, institutional investors, pension funds and insurance companies from investing/speculating in each other's businesses. It also established the Federal Deposit Insurance Corporation or FDIC for short.

After Clinton repealed Glass-Stegall in 1999, the Illuminati's wolves on Wall Street headed straight for the hen house that was the American Middle Class by creating something called "derivatives". The term "derivative" means just that---its value is derived from something else----usually another derivative in the way they used them. Derivatives are paper-based investments......based on paper-based investments...... based on paper-based investments......right on down the line until you finally run into the tangible thing that thousands and millions of these mini-pyramid schemes were based on. The black hole that was created by these derivatives still exists----the gaping debt hole has only been temporarily plugged as of the writing of this book. I've run into estimates that the black hole may be up to a **$1.5 quadrillion dollar debt abyss** that is literally going to suck the entire global economy into it and this event will cause such an upheaval that civilization as we know it will probably end, and the Luciferian one world government will rise out of its ashes.

It actually came out in the Mainstream Media during the financial crisis of 2008 that Bank of America alone was sitting on $50 trillion worth of derivatives exposure. This is just one of many, many huge international banks playing with fire via derivatives. Only 20 of these banks with the same exposure as B.O.A. adds up to one quadrillion dollars, and there are way more than 20 international banks involved, so we are talking about an absolutely huge sum of financial liability. A literal black hole of electronic money-debt just waiting to swallow up the present day economic systems of the world.

Mark my words; this is going to happen in the very near future and it will be ugly. I will go over how to prepare for this as best as possible at the end of this book.

Chapter 5/H

THE TAX-EXEMPT FOUNDATIONS

"The Council on Foreign Relations, another member of the international complex, financed by the Rockefeller and Carnegie Foundations, overwhelmingly propagandizes the globalist concept. This organization became virtually an agency of the government when World War II broke out. The Rockefeller Foundation had started and financed certain studies known as the War and Peace Studies, manned largely by associates of the Council; the State Department, in due course, took these studies over, retaining the major personnel which the Council on Foreign Relations had supplied."

-Rene Wormser, author of "Foundations: Their Power and Influence", 1958

Intermarrying between Great Plan family members does well to contribute to keeping their money, and therefore their power, retained within the Illuminati ranks. However, the primary avenue through which the global elites grow and retain their power is through the various tax-free foundations they set up and control. By "donating" their billions to their tax-free foundations, they give up ownership of the money, but still retain all the power that that money enables them by directing how their foundations use that money. **Not only this, but the media they control hails them as humanitarians, when in fact they are using the money for the exact opposite purposes.**

Nearly every significant action implemented by the proponents of the Great Plan in the 20th century and beyond to compromise the integrity of American society and seize the reins of world power have been directed and financed, either wholly or partially, through the elite's tax-exempt organizations, which have been brainwashed into public opinion as benefactors of our society.

The revolving door cross-pollination that occurs between these pro-New World Order tax-free foundations, the multinational corporations, the New World Order steering groups we will discuss next chapter, and the United States federal government is rampant and treasonous. Although I am just giving a bare-bones summary here, it would only take a couple of hours of your time to research this topic to find what I say is indeed the truth.

With the means to loan enormous sums to the government (the Federal Reserve), a method to make payments on the debt (income tax), and an escape from taxation for the wealthy (tax-free foundations), all that remained in the year 1913 was an excuse for the federal government to start borrowing giant sums of money. By some incredible "coincidence," one year after the founding of the Fed in 1913, World War I began in 1914, and after American participation national debt rose from $1 billion to $25 billion.

The American public, and therefore their elected officials (at least some of them) began to wake up to the fact that these giant foundations and their billions of dollars worth of influence were not doing the work they were granted tax-free status for, which was to act in the best interests of the country and humanity in general.

In 1952 a Congressional Committee to investigate the tax-free foundations was created, called the Cox Committee, led by Rep. Eugene E. Cox, a Democrat from Georgia. Its stated purpose was to find out:

"...which foundations and organizations are using their resources for purposes other than the purposes for which they were established, and especially to determine which such foundations and organizations are using their resources for un-American and subversive activities or for purposes not in the interest or tradition of the United States ."

Cox made the discovery that officers and trustees of some of these suspect foundations were in fact **Communists**, and that grants had been doled out to Communists or Communist-controlled organizations both in the United States and abroad.

Cox "coincidentally" died during the investigation in December of 1952 and the facts were glossed over in a cover-up by Congressmen who were pro-New World Order.

Immediately after Cox's death, patriotic members of the 83rd Congress commissioned Congressman B. Carroll Reece in 1953 to continue where Cox had left off and investigate the tax-exempt foundations to determine why they had financed Communist organizations. The Reece Committee ended up discovering:

1. *In 1915 the Carnegie Endowment for International Peace launched a propaganda program to force the United States into World War I.*

2. *Many of our large foundations were actively promoting Communism and socialism.*

3. *The Rockefeller Foundation financed Dr. Alfred Kinsey' badly flawed study of human sexuality, and his effort to undermine the moral standards of our nation.*

4. *The* Rockefeller *Foundation, the Carnegie Education Foundation, and the Ford Foundation had used their grant making power to take over American education and force our colleges and universities to abandon their religious beliefs and moral standards.*

5. *The foundations influenced State Department policy and were largely responsible for bringing communism to China.*

6. *The foundations were working to undermine our constitutional form of government.*

Reece's Special Committee to Investigate Tax Exempt Foundations uncovered evidence that foundations were financing civil rights groups, liberal political groups, political extremist groups, and supporting revolutionary activities throughout the world. The Committee reported:

> "Substantial evidence indicates there is more than a mere close working together among some foundations operating in the international field. There is here, as in the general realm of social sciences, a close interlock.
>
> The Carnegie Corporation, the Carnegie Endowment for International Peace, the Rockefeller Foundation and, recently, the Ford Foundation, joined by some others, have commonly cross-financed, to a tune of many millions ... organizations concerned with internationalists, among them, the Institute of Pacific Relations, the Foreign Policy Association (which was "virtually a creature of the Carnegie Endowment"), the Council on Foreign Relations, the Royal Institute of International Affairs and others ... and that it happened by sheer coincidence stretches credulity."

On August 19, 1954, Reece summed up his investigation with this statement:

> "It has been said that the foundations are a power second only to that of the Federal Government itself ... Perhaps the Congress should now admit that the foundations have become more powerful, in some areas, at least, than the legislative branch of the Government."

The investigation came to an abrupt halt in 1955 after funding was withheld by bought-and-paid-for pro-New World Order congressmen.

Rene Wormser, the counsel for the Reece Committee, later wrote "Foundations: Their Power and Influence."

In his book, Wormser says:

> "The chief motivation in the creation of foundations has long ceased to be pure philanthropy--it is now predominantly tax avoidance.... The increasing tax burden on income and estates has greatly accelerated a trend toward creation of foundations as

instruments for the retention of control over capital assets that would otherwise be lost...."

According to Rep. Wright Patman, a U.S. Congressman and chair of the United States House Committee on Banking and Currency in a report in 1962 to the 87th Congress, it is because of the existence of the elite's foundations that **"only one-third of the income of the nation is actually taxed."** The rest of it is dumped tax-free into these Illuminati-controlled organizations to be literally used against us.

These accumulations of tax-exempt billions place an even heavier burden on taxpayers. By protecting trillions of dollars from taxation, the tax-exempt organizations thereby force taxpayers to take up the slack in order to bankroll all that government demands, or at least the interest payments on our federal credit card to the Federal Reserve.

Chapter 6

STEERING THE NEW WORLD ORDER

The proponents of the Great Plan have a handful of semi-secret organizations that are their "public face", even though most people
have no idea they even exist, and if they do know they exist don't know
what their real function is. All of these entities were created and funded
by those who are pushing for a one world government, and the exact
same people who own the Federal Reserve, IMF, World Bank, started
the United Nations, organized the European Union, started all the major
wars, etc. etc. ad nauseum. The relationship between all these groups,
besides being run by the Illuminati families, is demonstrated not only
by their common objective of forming a one world government under
their control, but by their funding via the tax-free foundations and
multi-national (global) corporations. Again, within these organizations
we have the rampant cross-pollination of New World Order personnel.
Members and officials of the Round Table groups are also officials in the
various federal governments of the world, the international corporations
(mainly banking), and the tax-free foundations, and all routinely migrate
between the four with no scrutiny from the media that they control or
the public at large, which they also control.

As their plans near the finish line, the amount of people needed
to finish the job of organizing and installing a one world government
was simply too large to keep concealed within the upper echelon of the
Freemasons. They needed to take the lower-level organizational aspects
of the Great Plan "public" to accommodate the growing numbers of "pro-
globalists" on their payroll. A vast majority of the people involved in

these Great Plan steering groups have no idea they are actually helping to promote the completion of a plan to take over the world thousands of years in the making, let alone the fact that it is guided by Luciferians of the most evil sort. This is why I don't believe people like Bill Gates, Oprah Winfrey, Mark Zuckerberg, or any other famous personalities have any real idea of what kind of evil they are helping to promote through being members of these various organizations.

We're going to go over these various groups now, all started, funded and controlled by the proponents of the Great Plan.

Chapter 6/A

THE ROUND TABLE GROUPS

So what are the "Round Table" groups you're probably wondering? The term "Round Table Groups" is not a formal term, just a general term to group together the various New World Order steering organizations that were created and funded by the proponents of the Great Plan. These groups were the latest innovation of the Illuminati beginning in the late 1800's going into the home stretch of the creation of a one world government.

Again, as the size and scope of the job of bringing in a one world government grew, so needed to grow the amount of people necessary to run it and at the same time keep the masses in the dark about what was really going on. The one man who could probably be credited with getting these groups up and running is named Cecil John Rhodes, an alleged 33rd degree Freemason.

In 1877, Cecil John Rhodes laid out his own plans to unite the world under a New World Order:

> "At the present day I become a member of the Masonic order I see the wealth and power they possess, the influence they hold, and I think over their ceremonies and I wonder that a large body of men can devote themselves to what at times appear the most ridiculous and absurd rites without an object and without an end.
> The idea gleaming and dancing before one's eyes like a will-of-the-wisp at last frames itself into a plan. Why should we not form a secret society with but one object: the furtherance of the British

Empire and the bringing of the whole uncivilized world under British rule for the recovery of the United States for the making the Anglo-Saxon race but one Empire."
-Cecil Rhodes' book "Confessions of Faith"

Rhodes, who was in **fact** financially backed by the Rothschilds, acquired enormous wealth by developing diamond mining properties in Africa, founding the legendary DeBeers diamond company. At one time, DeBeers controlled **90% of the entire world's diamond market**, although that number has since slipped a bit. The African country of Rhodesia was not only founded by Rhodes but named after him, and was part of the British Empire at one time. After gaining independence from Great Britain, Rhodesia was split into two countries, Zambia and Zimbabwe.

Rhodes was a member of the British "Fabian Society", counting among its more influential members Andrew Carnegie, of Carnegie Steel, and H.G. Wells, author of the "The New World Order". The Fabian Society stated that world socialism was inevitable, and that there would be a difficult and painful transition period for mankind in the near future.

"Countless people ... will hate the new world order ... and will die protesting it. When we attempt to evaluate its promise, we have to bear in mind the distress of a generation or so of malcontents, many of them quite gallant and graceful-looking people."
-H.G. Wells

The Fabian Society was, for all intents and purposes, the first "Round Table" group member, and being that it was only a "semi-secret" society, served as the model for the future Round Table Groups. The stated mission of the Fabian Society was to extend the British Empire to include the entire Earth---ruled under a "New World Order", hence the title of Wells' book of the same name. It was the Fabian's intent, that the transition to one world government was to be carried out gradually so as not to arouse suspicion, with appropriate indoctrination of the populace, until the system was fully in place. The official mascot of the society was the **turtle**, meant to represent that a slow, gradual shifting over to a one world government was necessary in order to get the unknowing masses to cooperate.

When Rhodes died in 1902 he donated his fortune---placed with the British Rothschilds---to establish a Rhodes scholarship program at Oxford University in England to carry out the ideas formulated within the Fabian Society, which **is** the implementation of the Great Plan/New World Order. The scholarships were to go to promising young men from the British colonies and the United States, with the majority going to Americans, like alleged 33rd degree Freemason Bill Clinton among others.

During the past century, over 4,600 young men have been sent to Oxford as Rhodes scholars to be indoctrinated in socialism and world government and then sent out to bring about these goals to reality. Rhodes scholars work in government, the international banking cartels, the boards of global corporations, the tax-free foundations, the Supreme Court, the media, major universities, the United Nations, and the various Round Table Groups among others promoting a one world socialist government.

Rhodes planted the seeds of the Round Table groups before he died, and these groups play a vital role in how the proponents of the Great Plan run the world today. Rhodes was viewed within the Illuminati circles as the "new Weishaupt" for his controlling nature, his high intelligence, and his vision for the future of the world under the Great Plan. His appointed successor, alleged 33rd degree Freemason Lord Alfred Milner, continued Rhodes work after his death.

The Round Table Groups, as they are generally called today by the Truth Movement are as follows: the British Royal Institute for International Affairs/RIIA (founded 1919), the Council on Foreign Relations/CFR (the U.S. version of the RIIA founded in 1921), the Bilderberg Group (1954), the Club of Rome (1968), and the Trilateral Commission (1973). Each succeeding group was added as the conspiracy grew in size and scope in order to maintain orderly control of it. These are the organizations through which Western nations governmental policies are formulated by the Illuminati today. The CFR literally is the "Establishment" you probably have heard referred to over the years. All of these organizations are run by the Illuminati to facilitate the bringing in of the Luciferian New World Order.

Chapter 6/B

"TRAGEDY AND HOPE"

"The powers of financial capitalism had another far-reaching aim, nothing less than to create a world system of financial control in private hands able to dominate the political system of each country and the economy of the world as a whole. This system was to be controlled in a feudalist fashion by the central banks of the world acting in concert, by secret agreements arrived at in frequent meetings and conferences. The apex of the systems was to be the Bank for International Settlements in Basel, Switzerland, a private bank owned and controlled by the world's central banks which were themselves private corporations. Each central bank...sought to dominate its government by its ability to control Treasury loans, to manipulate foreign exchanges, to influence the level of economic activity in the country, and to influence cooperative politicians by subsequent economic rewards in the business world."

- Dr. Carroll Quigley, Professor of History at Georgetown University

Dr. Carroll Quigley is recently best known as Bill Clinton's professor of history at the Foreign Service School of Georgetown University, and it was Quigley who wrote the letter of recommendation for Bill Clinton to be a **Rhodes Scholar**. Quigley also taught at Princeton and at Harvard, but that's not what makes him extremely relevant to the workings of the New World Order.

Carroll Quigley was a confirmed socialist who believed the world could be a better place if the educated elite ruled. The proponents of the Great Plan allowed Quigley to go through thousands of their secret documents housed at the CFR in the attempt to put together a history of their plans for world domination, to be viewed only by the proponents of the Great Plan. Dr. Quigley felt that the public wouldn't have cared if this information was released, and in fact revealed the game plan of the elite when the elite didn't want it publicized.

Far from wanting to hide this "network", as he called it, Quigley was actually quite proud of it, and unbeknownst to the Illuminati crowd he worked for and hung out with, Quigley published a book in 1966 outing their plans for world domination. I'll let him cut their throat with this quote directly from his mouth:

> *"I know of the operations of this network because I have studied it for twenty years and was permitted for two years, in the early 1960's, to examine its papers and secret records. I have no aversion to it or to most of its aims and have, for much of my life, been close to it and to many of its instruments. I have objected, both in the past and recently, to a few of its policies...but in general my chief difference of opinion is that it wishes to remain unknown, and I believe its role in history is significant enough to be known."*

This did not sit well at ALL with the proponents of the New World Order, and the book was subsequently pulled from the shelves, but not before many patriots got their hands on the content and spread it around, keeping it alive in order for us to view today.

The book was 1,300 pages of nothing but outing the Great Plan, and was entitled *"Tragedy and Hope: A History Of The World In Our Time".* You can buy this book today, right now, on Amazon.com, and if you have any doubt as to what I am saying in this book, I highly encourage you to get your hands on this book and read it.

"These people (*the Illuminati*) are the hope of the world, and all who resist them represent tragedy" is a quote attributed to Quigley---hence the title of his book, *Tragedy and Hope.*

Quigley felt the Great Plan had advanced far enough that not only could it not be reversed, it needed to be bled out into the society so people would get used to it, that is, having the elites running the planet by servitude of the rest. Quigley either was naïve to it, or intentionally ignored the Luciferian aspects of the Great Plan, so his book is by no means a complete review of what is really happening in the world. It is just another part of the Great Plan puzzle.

Chapter 6/C

ROYAL INSTITUTE FOR INTERNATIONAL AFFAIRS/COUNCIL ON FOREIGN RELATIONS

*"The Council on Foreign Relations (CFR) is "the establishment."
Not only does it have influence and power in key decision-making
positions at the highest levels of government to apply pressure
from above, but it also announces and uses individuals and groups
to bring pressure from below, to justify the high level decisions for
converting the U.S. from a sovereign Constitutional Republic into a
servile member state of a one-world dictatorship."*
-Former Congressman John Rarick, 1971

The first "official" Round Table Group that was created is the RIIA, or The Royal Institute for International Affairs, and was created in 1919. This secretive and highly exclusive group is where the "Chatham House Rule" originated, the secrecy rule subsequently adopted by all other Round Table groups. This rule states that there are no records kept of the contents of the meetings by individual members, no notes taken, and not a peep uttered about the proceedings to the outside world.

Until the formation of the CFR in 1921, the RIIA was a joint British/ American organization with offices in both Britain and the U.S. It was realized that to effect maximum pressure on the U.S. State Department to bend to the will of the proponents of the Great Plan, and thus maximum influence on the U.S. role in global affairs, that it was necessary to create an American version of the RIIA, the Council on Foreign Relations, or CFR. Nearly every influential politician at the federal level of our country is a member of the CFR, and this is a fact you can take to the bank. This is an Illuminati founded/funded/operated organization, **whose stated mission is to merge the United States into the coming one world government.**

The CFR's bi-monthly publication *"Foreign Affairs"* doesn't even try to hide the fact that they are pro-New World Order. All of these issues are currently available on the CFR website for purchase, lucky us.

You see, they hide their agenda from us...sort of, but if you go looking for evidence of their agenda it is right there for anyone to find. They just keep this stuff out of their controlled Mainstream Media, which is why most people are kept in the dark and clueless about these matters. Americans are not unlike mushrooms in this aspect: we are kept in the dark, and fed a constant diet of **bullshit.**

Let's concentrate on the CFR, aka the Eastern Establishment or just plain old "the Establishment", since they are the main ones pulling our strings in the United States..........

"The most powerful clique in these (CFR) groups have one objective in common: they want to bring about the surrender of the sovereignty and the national independence of the U.S. They want to end national boundaries and racial and ethnic loyalties supposedly to increase business and ensure world peace. What they strive for would inevitably lead to dictatorship and loss of freedoms by the people. The CFR was founded for "the purpose of promoting disarmament and submergence of U.S. sovereignty and national independence into an all-powerful one-world government."
-Harpers, July 1958

"It's good to be back at the Council on Foreign Relations. I've been a member for a long time and was actually director for some time. I never mentioned that when I was campaigning for re-election back home in Wyoming (laughs)."
-former Vice President Dick Cheney addressing the CFR at the Ritz Carlton hotel in Washington D.C. on February 15, 2002

The reason Mr. Cheney doesn't make light of the fact he is in the CFR back home in Wyoming is because if the people in Wyoming knew what he was really up to, they would probably hang him high in a tree by the neck.

The Council on Foreign Relations was incorporated as the American branch of the RIIA in New York on July 29, 1921. Founding members included Woodrow Wilson's personal Illuminati handler, alleged 33rd degree Freemason "Colonel" Edward House---a confirmed Rothschild agent. The balance of the chief founding members reads like an Illuminati checklist: J.P. Morgan, John D. Rockefeller, Paul Warburg (architect of Federal Reserve legislation), Otto Kahn, Jacob Schiff....ah heck, you get the picture. Always remember, the trail always, always, ALWAYS traces itself back to the European Rothschild banking dynasty, who are the masters of the Illuminati, and the Illuminati families which they teamed up with. The Rothschild family to this day run the Great Plan and are undisputed overlords of it through the sheer amount of money they control. By running the Great Plan the Rothschilds in effect run the world. They are Luciferians to the extreme, the living, breathing Synagogue of Satan on Earth.

Col. House, a socialist, wrote in his book, *"Philip Dru: Administrator: A Story of Tomorrow"*, that he was working for **"Socialism as dreamed of by Karl Marx."** In this book, House tells of a "conspiracy" which would gain control of both political parties and use them as instruments in the creation of a socialist world government, which is exactly where we are headed today. Both parties today are merely instruments of the CFR, with both parties marching us forward to a New World Order. During a Presidential election, both opposing candidates are working out of the CFR offices and get their marching orders from them by consensus of the ruling body of the CFR. Nearly all of the corrupt gang of D.C. career politicians are fully in on this scheme, having been bought off by the agents of the Federal Reserve working behind the scenes through "favors" in the form of cushy high-paying speaking engagements, placement of family members in prominent jobs, backroom-dealt favors, and on and on. It is extremely easy to research these people's lives, and books should be written about all of them to expose them for their despicable behavior against the people they are supposed to be representing and protecting.

The founding president of the CFR was John W. Davis, J.P. Morgan's personal attorney, while the vice-president was Paul Cravath, also representing the Morgan interests.....which were really the Rothschild interests of course.

The roster of CFR members is thoroughly impressive. We are talking about the people who are literally running the world. Its current membership, all 4,000 or so of them, is like reading a "who's who" of the elite politicians, media, financiers, businessmen, and educators. From the CFR come over **90%** of the people in the State Department and key positions in the Executive Branch of our nation's government, and they are all under control of the Illuminati's Council on Foreign Relations.

Multinational corporations who are corporate-sponsor members? Goldman Sachs, JP Morgan Chase bank, Bank of America, Chevron, Exxon/Mobil, General Electric, Citibank, American Express, Nike, Shell Oil, Boeing, Airbus, Alcoa, Toyota, Coca-Cola, DeBeers, Federal Express, Google, IBM, Merck, Pfizer, and the list goes on, and on, and on.

"The New World Order will have to be built from the bottom up rather than from the top down...but in the end run around national sovereignty, eroding it piece by piece will accomplish much more than the old fashioned frontal assault."
-CFR member Richard Gardner, writing in the April 1974 issue of the CFR's journal, Foreign Affairs.

Chapter 6/D

THE BILDERBERG GROUP

"We are grateful to the Washington Post, The New York Times, Time Magazine and other great publications whose directors have attended our meetings and respected their promises of discretion for almost forty years... It would have been impossible for us to develop our plan for the world if we had been subjected to the lights of publicity during those years. But, the world is now more sophisticated and prepared to march towards a world government. The supranational sovereignty of an intellectual elite and world bankers is surely preferable to the national auto-determination practiced in past centuries."

- David Rockefeller, addressing the Bilderberg Meeting, June 1991, Baden, Germany

As their plans continued to grow in scale, a new globalist organization was needed to help keep the New World Order locomotive on the tracks: The Bilderberg Group.

In 1954, the most powerful men in the world met at the inaugural meeting of the Bilderberg Group, hosted by the Dutch royal crown and the **Rockefeller** family in the luxurious Hotel Bilderberg in Oosterbeck, Holland. For an entire weekend they debated the best ways to expedite the bringing in of the planned one world government. When it was over, they decided to meet once every year to exchange ideas, discuss pertinent international affairs, and ensure the Great Plan was moving ahead as planned.

They named themselves the Bilderberg Group, and it has become the pinnacle of the Round Table world power groups. Since 1954, about 130 hand-picked representatives of the elite have gathered yearly in a luxurious hotel somewhere in the world arrogantly plotting the subversion and silent takeover of constitutional governments everywhere.

Here is a SMALL sampling of the past elitist membership or attendees at Bilderberg meetings: David Rockefeller, Henry Kissinger, Lloyd Bentsen, Helmut Kohl, Prince Charles, Prince Juan Carlos I of Spain, Queen Beatrix of the Netherlands, Katharine Graham, Alice Rivlin, Gerald Ford, Bill and Hillary Clinton, Dan Quayle, Donald Rumsfeld, Colin L. Powell, John Edwards, Bill Bradley, Bill Richardson, Christopher Dodd, Dianne Feinstein, Kathleen Sebelius, Alexander Haig, Ralph E. Reed, George Stephanopoulos, U.S. Treasury Secretary Timothy F. Geithner, George Soros, Paul Volcker, Alan Greenspan, and Ben Bernanke (former and current Chairmen of the Federal Reserve), World Bank president Robert Zoellick, H. J. Heinz II (CEO of H. J. Heinz Company), Peter A. Thiel (Co-Founder, PayPal), Eric E. Schmidt (Chairman and Chief Executive Officer, Google), Lloyd Blankfein (CEO of Goldman Sachs), Rupert Murdoch, Donald E. Graham (Chairman of the Board of The Washington Post Company), William F. Buckley, Jr. (founder of National Review and former host of Firing Line), Peter Jennings, George Will, Lesley Stahl, Bill D. Moyers, Bill and Melinda Gates, and many others. The list includes prominent persons in politics, the military, financial institutions, major corporations, academia, and the media. A great many of these people have been tricked into believing that a one world government is a good thing, while obviously being unaware of the Luciferians who are really running the show at the top.

Why are the WTO and G8 meetings carried in every newspaper, given front page coverage, with thousands of journalists in attendance, while not a single one covers the Bilderberg Group meetings even though they are annually attended by Presidents of the International Monetary Fund, The World Bank, Federal Reserve, chairmen of the 100 most powerful corporations in the world such as DaimlerChrysler, Coca Cola, British Petroleum, Chase Manhattan Bank, American Express, Goldman Sachs, Microsoft, Vice Presidents of the United States, Directors of the CIA and the FBI, General Secretaries of NATO, American Senators and members of Congress, European Prime Ministers and leaders of opposition parties, top editors and CEOs of the leading newspapers in the world?

The answer is very simple: because they own and control the Mainstream Media and you are not told what you are not supposed to know.

Chapter 6/E

THE CLUB OF ROME

"The Earth has cancer and the cancer is Man."
-Club of Rome, Mankind at the Turning Point, 1974

"... the resultant ideal sustainable population is hence more than 500 million but less than one billion."
-Club of Rome, Goals for Mankind, 1976.

The next entry into the Round Table Group was the Club of Rome, which was conceived during "The Conference on Conditions of World Order". This meeting was held from June 12-19, 1965 at the Villa Serbelloni in Bellagio, Italy, sponsored by the Congress for Cultural Freedom, with a grant from the Ford Foundation and the American Academy of Arts and Sciences.

Three years later in April, 1968, a think-tank of financiers, scientists, economists, politicians, heads of state, and industrialists from ten different countries again met in Italy, at **David Rockefeller's private estate** in Bellagio, Italy, at the request of Aurelio Peccei. Peccei was an Italian industrialist who had close ties to Fiat and the Olivetti Corporation. He claimed to have solutions for world peace and prosperity, which could be accomplished through a one world government. The Club of Rome (COR) was initially established with a membership of 75 prominent scientists, industrialists, and economists from 25 countries.

"Democracy is not a panacea. It cannot organize everything and it is unaware of its own limits. These facts must be faced

squarely. Sacrilegious though this may sound, democracy is no longer well suited for the tasks ahead. The complexity and the technical nature of many of today's problems do not always allow elected representatives to make competent decisions at the right time."
-Official quote from the Club of Rome

The Club of Rome's first publication, titled *"The Limits to Growth"*, was published in 1972 and dealt with the Illuminati-propagated issue of worldwide overpopulation. It stated that **"If the world's consumption patterns and population growth continued at the same high rates of the time, the earth would strike its limits within a century."**
The book, which sold 12 million copies in 27 languages, described their vision for the world:

"We believe in fact that the need will quickly become evident for social innovation to match technical change, for radical reform of the institutions and political processes at all levels, including the highest, that of world polity. And since intellectual enlightenment is without effect if it is not also political, The Club of Rome also will encourage the creation of a world forum where statesmen, policy-makers, and scientists can discuss the dangers and hopes for the future global system without the constraints of formal intergovernmental negotiation."

For the most part, the Club of Rome is a high-powered, Illuminati-funded think-tank, functioning as a research institute on economic, political, and social problems. The COR claims **"there is no other viable alternative to the future survival of civilization than a new global community under a common leadership,"** aka the one world government.
Their website claims:

"The Club of Rome's mission is to act as a global catalyst of change that is free of any political, ideological or business interest. The Club of Rome contributes to the solution of what it

calls the world problematique, the complex set of the most crucial problems- political, social, economic, technological, environmental, psychological and cultural- facing humanity. It does so taking a global, long term and interdisciplinary prospective aware of the increasing interdependence of nations and the globalization of problems that pose predicaments beyond the capacity of individual countries."

On September 17, 1973, they released a report called the *"Regionalized and Adaptive Model of the Global World System"* which was prepared as part of the "Strategy for Survival Project". This revealed the COR's goal of dividing the world into **ten** political/economic regions... which in turn would fall under a single global authority, the one world government.

The same plan was published in a Club of Rome book called *"Mankind at the Turning Point"*, which said:

"The solution of these crises can be developed only in a global context with full and explicit recognition of the emerging world system and on a long-term basis. This would necessitate, among other changes, a new world economic order and a global resources allocation system..."

We better go back and see what the Book of Revelation says about the COR's proposed ten regions, aka the "ten kingdoms" of the End Times:

"And the ten horns which thou sawest are ten kings, which have received no power as yet but receive power as kings one hour with the beast. These have one mind, and shall give their power and strength unto the beast."
-Rev. 17:12-13

Chapter 6/F
THE TRILATERAL COMMISSION

A ll that leaves for us to look at within the Round Table Groups, is
the **David Rockefeller**/Zbigniew Brzezinski-created Trilateral
Commission, being founded in 1973. The official insignia of the Trilateral
Commission is a cleverly disguised "666", which you can check for yourself on Google Images.

> *"This regionalization is in keeping with the Tri-Lateral Plan
> which calls for a gradual convergence of East and West, ultimately
> leading toward the goal of one world government. National
> sovereignty is no longer a viable concept."*
> *-Zbigniew Brzezinkski, Co-founder of the Trilateral Commission
> and **National Security Advisor** to President Carter. Currently
> Barack Obama's **Foreign Policy Advisor**. Also a professor at
> **Columbia** University from 1960 to 1989 as head of the Columbia
> Institute on Communist Affairs*

The Trilateral Commission was officially founded on July 1, 1973.
Its founder and primary financial backer was card-carrying Illuminati
member David Rockefeller, longtime chairman of the Rockefeller family-
controlled Chase Manhattan Bank and virtual overlord of the Rockefeller
family's global corporate empire. At the time of the founding of the TC,
David Rockefeller was **Chairman of the Council on Foreign Relations**.
No surprise there, right?

"The gradual shaping of a community of the developed nations would be a realistic expression of our emerging global consciousness; concentration on disseminating scientific and technological information would reflect a more functional approach to man's problems; both the outlook that would gradually replace the institutionalized religious, ideological, and intensely national perspectives that have dominated modern history."
  - *Zbigniew Brzezinkski*

One of the most obvious reasons for creation of the Trilateral Commission is simply to deflect attention away from the CFR as the New World Order gained momentum coming out of the turbulent---by Illuminati design mind you---1960's. People started waking up a little bit and started throwing around terms like "the establishment" and "the man". "Fight the power", etc.

"The technetronic era involves the gradual appearance of a more controlled society. Such a society would be dominated by an elite, unrestrained by traditional values."
  - *Zbigniew Brzezinski*

Rockefeller's idea for establishing the Trilateral Commission emerged after he had read a book entitled *"Between Two Ages"* written by pro-New World Order scholar, Prof. Zbigniew Brzezinski of Columbia University.

In his book, Brzezinski proposed an alliance between North America, Europe and Japan.

"Resist as it might, the American system is compelled gradually to accommodate itself to this emerging international context, with the U.S. government called upon to negotiate, to guarantee, and, to some extent, to protect the various arrangements that have been contrived even by private business."
  - *Zbigniew Brzezinski*

In other words, it was necessary for the international elites, Illuminati and otherwise, to band together to protect their interests, and to ensure, in the developed nations, that political leaders were brought to power who would ensure that the global financial interests of the Rothschilds, Rockefellers and the balance of the world oligarchy would be protected over those of the rest of humanity.

"Many of the original members of the Trilateral Commission are now in positions of power where they are able to implement policy recommendations of the Commission; recommendations that they, themselves, prepared on behalf of the Commission. It is for this reason that the Commission has acquired a reputation for being the Shadow Government of the West."

- Journalist and Trilateral Commission researcher Robert Eringer

Ronald Reagan was very vocal in his disdain for anyone who was involved with the Trilateral Commission before he was elected President in 1980. He was critical of Jimmy Carter for being a TC member and for the fact that there were nineteen Trilateral Commission members in the Carter administration.

Reagan stated that, if elected, he would investigate the Trilateral Commission. He even went so far as to say that he would never allow George Bush Sr. a place in his administration because Bush was a Trilateral and a CFR member. Reagan was allegedly threatened with media blackmail if he did not accept Bush as his running mate in order to keep the Illuminati presence in the White House, and also to tame his outspoken views of the Trilateral Commission.

Investigative researcher and patriotic American Brian Quig wrote in 1991:

"Goldwater's Administrative Director Tom Dunlevy... was an insider at the 1980 GOP convention... I will always remember the very words of Tom Dunlevy following my protest of the selection of George Bush for VP. They were etched into my mind. "We didn't like that either. It was a deal with the Devil. Henry Kissinger and Gerald

Ford, present at the convention as agents of David Rockefeller, assured Reagan the presidency if he accepted Bush on the ticket. Otherwise Rockefeller would swing the election to Carter."

Brian Quig mysteriously died in 2005 in a freak accident.....in which he was run over by a truck after many years of trying to expose the workings of the New World Order.

Conservative author and political commentator Cleon Skousen spoke with Reagan at the convention, both before and after the Bush decision, and related how Reagan told him how Kissinger and Ford, with the support of Walter Cronkite, coerced him. According to Skousen these are Reagan's very words **"They showed me the brush by which I would be tarred if I did not go along."**

Not only did Reagan bring in Bush but he never again uttered a word against the Trilateral Commission or the CFR. In 1981, Reagan's transition team of 59 people was composed of twenty-eight CFR members, ten members of the Bilderberg group, and at least ten Trilateral Commission members.

Remember how Reagan got shot just under three months after being sworn in? On March 30, 1981, "crazed" gunman John Hinckley Jr. shot Reagan, with CFR/Trilateral Commission/Skull and Bonesman/Bohemian Grovesman/alleged 33rd degree Freemason/former CIA director George Bush Sr. in the driver's seat as Vice-President to take over the Presidency?

Reagan miraculously survived and was then allegedly promoted to 33rd degree Freemason status in order to ensure whose team he was indeed working for.

Remember, the guy waiting in the wings to take over the country if Reagan died is the same George Bush whose father **Prescott Bush had helped to finance Adolph Hitler's war machine.**

Well, those are the Round Table Group members in a nutshell. All founded, financed and controlled by the usual suspects, the same ones who own the Federal Reserve, founded the UN, and basically run the world: The modern day masters of the Great Plan.

Chapter 7

METHODS OF MADNESS

If it is possible to do it, and it will further their death grip over the world, the proponents of the New World Order have no reservations about poisoning us, brainwashing us, intimidating us, giving us a subpar education, falsely imprisoning us, and finally assassinating us if all else fails to bring the United States crashing down and its citizens under one world government compliance.

Nearly every major think tank you can research is actively involved in bringing about ways to further the Great Plan agenda.

Finding ways to dumb us down, tranquilize us, amuse us, confuse us, poison us, distract us, etc. ad nauseum is the name of the game, and we're going to go over many of the ways they influence us to keep us from discovering the truth of what is happening and then acting upon it.

The more they can influence us, the more power they are able to gain over us. It is a vicious cycle which is cannibalizing the United States as I speak.

Your body and mind are like a giant sponge that takes in and metabolizes both physical and mental input. The more poison they can get you to put in your body, and the more lies and propaganda they can inject into your mind, the more compromised you're going to be and less likely to resist what direction they are taking us, which is straight into a Luciferian one world government, and that is a fact.

Chapter 7/A

VOTING MACHINE FRAUD

L et's start off with the people who we "elected" to drive our country straight into the ground....

Campaign donations and clandestine actions from pro-New World Order entities aside, we've got a terrible issue we need to address, and that is a legitimate, factual concern about voting machine fraud. The proponents of the Great Plan have pulled out all the stops to advance their agenda, and have left no avenue uncompromised to complete their mission.

Think about this: The 50 states in the USA are divided into over 3,000 counties. Ohio, for instance, is divided into 88 counties, Iowa is divided into 99 counties, and so on. In approximately 1% of these counties, there are paper ballots which are hand counted properly, the way all of our counties should be counting our ballots. This respectable 1% consists of about half of the counties in New Hampshire---the *"Live Free or Die"* state---and a very few, very small counties scattered throughout the rest of the United States.

In 99% of the other compromised counties, the Democratic and Republican controlled Boards of Elections make sure that the ballots are commandeered from the neighborhood precincts as the polls close their doors. This is to make sure that the neighborhood citizens and other watchdog-patriots do NOT have a chance to count, or at least spot-check, their own votes. Such counting or spot-checking by the citizens would make centralized computer vote-rigging impossible. This is why the Illuminati, who today control both the national Democratic and Republican parties through the CFR, vehemently oppose any such citizen participation at the neighborhood precinct level. This is because centralized counting is the common feature of **all** governments trying to rig elections.

> *"Those who cast the votes decide nothing. Those who count the votes decide everything."*
> *-Joseph Stalin, alleged 33rd degree Freemason, candidly speaking the truth*

In these 99% of USA counties, citizens are forced to use either computer or machine methods of casting a ballot. Vote counting is wide open for fraud this way. The Democratic and Republican parties at the county level delegate the "counting" to one of a small handful of privately-owned companies which count 99% of the votes in United States national elections in complete secret, with no independent verification or audit.

Currently the four companies which are delegated the power to count the votes in the USA were Election Systems & Software, Diebold, Hart, and Sequoia. The local county election boards use armed guards to make sure the citizens, candidates, and reporters cannot see what these private companies are doing to the ballots in the "counting room" on election night. Since 1973, the powers behind the RNC and the DNC have arm-twisted, persuaded, and bullied the local governments in most counties in the USA to unconstitutionally delegate the vote counting to these four mysterious companies. By 1988, the counting companies had consolidated their control over 49 states, and half of New Hampshire.

The private companies controlling the ballots are given a direct feed to a team of manipulators which represent a pool of the AP wire service and the major TV Networks, all under Illuminati control.

The vote-fraud cartel was further empowered through the implementation of the criminal "Help Americans Vote Act" of 2002 or HAVA, which should really be called the "Helping the New World Order by Computer Fraud" Act.

HAVA appropriated **$4 billion** of our money to entice the state and county election offices to implement computer "vote-counting" systems from basically three major companies, Diebold, Sequoia, and Election

Systems & Software. These systems provide for no paper trail and no citizen checks and balances. Most people have no idea how their vote is counted, and I'm here to tell you as of right now under this system, your vote doesn't count.

The patriotic organization "Citizens for a Fair Vote Count" has estimated that it would take no more than $400 million dollars per election to hand count every vote on every ballot in the United States. Because the New World Order proponents and their Mainstream Media insist on easily rigged elections, all you hear is how we can't possibly afford the expense of a hand count.

Bullshit.

We spend hundreds of BILLIONS of dollars supporting out world military empire. Billions of dollars were just spent on just the promotion and advertising for the 2012 Presidential election alone. Why would billions of dollars be spent for a job that only pays $400,000 year unless someone else besides the President is going to benefit? You already know the answer to that. We can easily fund an honest and accountable vote-counting system by the people, for the people; to ensure that who we want running the country is who gets into power. This is the only way we are going to get our foot in the door and get some real "change" in this country.

So, in a nutshell, it's either paper ballots/hand counting for an honest election and real change, or corrupted centralized computer counting by the proponents of the New World Order and the usual suspects stay in office...over and over and over, pushing our country further and further under water.

Which would you prefer?

Chapter 7/B

TAVISTOCK INSTITUTE

A lthough the Round Table groups we just went over exist to advance the agenda to bring in the New World Order, those groups themselves need guidance as to WHAT to do to help foster the transformation. This is where diabolical think tanks like the Tavistock Institute come in to play.

> *"There will be in the next generation or so a pharmacological method of making people love their servitude and producing dictatorship without tears so to speak. Producing a kind of painless concentration camp for entire societies so that people will in fact have their liberties taken away from them, but will rather enjoy it, because they will be distracted from any desire to rebel by propaganda, or brainwashing, or brainwashing enhanced by pharmacological methods. And this seems to be the final revolution."*
> *- Aldous Huxley, student of Aleister Crowley, member of the Tavistock Group, California Medical School, 1961*

The Tavistock Institute is **very** influential in the way the proponents of the Great Plan pull the strings of American society.

Created at Oxford, England in 1921 with funding from the Royal Institute of International Affairs, yes the same RIAA Round Table Group member we just discussed, with later funding from (*ahem*) the **Rockefeller Foundation**, the Tavistock Institute for Human Relations is the nerve center for the global manipulation of human consciousness. The

Tavistock Institute works hand-in-hand with the tax-free foundations to create societal policy ideas, and then feeds them to the Round Table Groups for execution.

Not long after Tavistock was set-up by co-founder John Rawlings Rees and others, it became the core of Britain's Psychological Warfare Bureau. Tavistock also played a crucial role in the creation of the OSS, the precursor to the CIA. Tavistock was also behind the formation of NATO.

Today, Tavistock operates through a vast network of satellite think tanks, non-governmental organizations, universities, and media organizations to influence public opinion, while breaking down the moral fabric that has held the West together using scientifically-created techniques of manipulation. An important role that Tavistock has played in the modern day corporate world, via the National Training Laboratories, is the sponsoring of group sensitivity and diversity programs designed to erase a person's individuality so that they become a "team player". Tavistock and their minions are responsible for the PC movement that has infected our country.

The fact is, "political correctness" is all about creating and fostering uniformity. Political Correctness is a Tavistock-initiated and promoted idea to shut down dissension, making people too afraid to speak their minds. Individualism is one of the biggest obstacles in the way of the New World Order. They want a public that is predictable and conditioned to do as it's told without question, and you can't have that in a non-PC environment.

Tavistock portrays itself as a non-political, non-governmental organization, but this is simply not true when you look at how deeply entrenched it is with governments and organizations connected to government worldwide.

The Tavistock Institute is headquartered in London. Its prophet was alleged 33rd degree Freemason Sigmund Freud, and Tavistock's pioneering work in behavioral science along Freudian beliefs established it as the world nerve center of the New World Order ideology.

Tavistock Foundation techniques have a single goal: to break down the psychological strength of the individual, rendering him helpless to stand up and oppose his New World Order masters.

Any technique which helps to break down the family unit and traditional principles of religion, honor, patriotism and "normal" sexual behavior is used by the Tavistock scientists and doctors as weapons against good and decent humanity.

Through the Stanford Research Institute, Tavistock also controls the National Education Association, which directly influences the public school system curriculum.

The Institute of Social Research at the National Training Lab brainwashes the leading executives of business and government to follow the globalist agenda of the New World Order.

The implementation of powerful mind-altering drugs is also a common Tavistock strategy. The infamous MK Ultra program of the CIA, in which unsuspecting CIA officials were given LSD and their reaction studied like guinea pigs, resulted in several deaths. The U.S. Government had to pay millions in damages to the families of the victims, but the culprits were never indicted. The program originated when Sandoz AG, a Swiss drug firm, owned by S.G. **Warburg** Co. of London, developed Lysergic Acid. Franklin D. Roosevelt's advisor, James Paul **Warburg**, son of Paul **Warburg** who wrote the Federal Reserve Act, and nephew of Max **Warburg** who helped to finance Hitler, set up the Institute for Policy Studies to promote the drug. The result was the LSD "counter-culture" of the 1960s.

It is a FACT, that one of the CIA's main objectives upon inception was the trafficking of narcotics into our country in order to alter societal values, and they continue to do that to this day. Narcotics trafficking is a staple of Illuminati operations and always has been since the Opium Wars of the mid-1800s. This has a two-pronged purpose, the first of which is attacking the United States societal system though mass ingestion of mind-altering substances by the citizens and the resulting side effects of that. The second is to fund CIA "black ops", which are operations done by the CIA that aren't supposed to ever be found out about by you and me, completely off the financial books/records of the government, most of which are intended to benefit the advancement of the Great Plan.

The principal guiding agency of the CIA, the Institute for Policy Studies, was in fact funded by New World Order proponent James Paul **Warburg**.

It was literally through intentional actions of operatives within our federal government that brought about the entire 60's counterculture and launched the downward deviant spiral the United States is in today.

So what are some of the most influential Tavistock Institutions operating in and influencing the United States today?

The Brookings Institution dedicates its work to what it calls a "national agenda." They wrote President Hoover's program, took credit for President Roosevelt's "New Deal", the Kennedy Administration's "New Frontiers" program, and President Johnson's "Great Society." Brookings has been advising the United States Government how to conduct its affairs for the past 70 years and is still doing so to this day.

Another of the main institutions established by Tavistock in the United States was the National Training Laboratories (NTL). Founded in 1947 by members of Tavistock, the NTL had as its explicit purpose the brainwashing of leaders of our government, educational institutions, and corporate bureaucracies into the Great Plan agenda, and then using these "leaders" to either themselves run Tavistock group sessions in their organizations or to hire other similarly trained group leaders to advance the agenda.

From the mid-1950s onward, the NTL put the majority of the nation's corporate leaders through such brainwashing programs, while running similar programs for the State Department, the Navy, the Department of Education, and other sections of the federal bureaucracy. There is no firm estimate of the number of Americans who have been put through this process in last 50 years at either NTL, or as it is now known the NTL Institute for Applied Behavioral Sciences, which is based in Rosslyn, Virginia, or its West Coast base of operations, the Western Training Laboratories in Group Development, or in various satellite intuitions. The most reliable estimate is in the several millions.

One of the groups that went through the NTL mill in the 1950s was the leadership of the National Education Association, the largest organization of teachers in the United States. Thus, the NEA's outlook has been "shaped" by Tavistock, through the NTL. In 1964, the NTL Institute became a direct part of the NEA, with the NTL setting up "group sessions" for all its affiliates. With funding from the Department of Education, the NTL Institute drafted the programs for the training of the nation's primary and secondary school teachers, and has a hand as well in developing the content of educational reforms, including OBE or Outcome Based Education.

Also under Tavistock is the University of Pennsylvania, Wharton School of Finance & Commerce. One of the "brain trusts" of Tavistock, Wharton has become one of the more important Tavistock groups in so far as "Behavioral Research" is concerned. Wharton attracts clients such as the U.S. Department of Labor, which teaches how to produce "cooked" statistics at the Wharton Econometric Forecasting Associates Incorporated. Wharton's "Econometric Modeling" is used by every major Illuminati-controlled company in the United States and Europe, including the International Monetary Fund, the United Nations, and the World Bank.

The Institute for the Future, another Tavistock satellite group and funded by the tax-free Ford Foundation, predicts and prepares for a long-range agenda. The Institute for the Future predicts what it believes to be changes that will be taking place in time frames of fifty years. They decide what is to be viewed as normal and what is not, and prepares position papers to steer governmental policy in the direction towards a one world government.

The Institute for Policy Studies, the same we just went over, is another of the major outlets of Tavistock policy. The IPS has shaped and re-shaped United States policies, foreign and domestic, since it was founded by James P. **Warburg** and other Rothschild entities in the United States. The IPS was incorporated in 1963 by Marcus Raskin and Richard Barnett, both highly trained Tavistock Institute graduates. The objectives of IPS came from an agenda laid down for it by the Tavistock Institute, one of the most notable being to create the "New Left" as a grass roots movement in the U.S Through its many powerful lobbying groups on Capitol Hill, the IPS relentlessly pressures Congressmen to bend to their agenda. The IPS has a network of lobbyists, all supposedly operating independently but in actuality acting cohesively, so that Congressmen are pummeled from all sides by seemingly different and varied lobbyists. In this way, the IPS was, and is still, able to successfully sway individual Congressmen and Senators to vote for the New World Order agenda.

The IPS became, and remains to this day, one of the most prestigious think tanks controlling foreign policy decisions, which we, the people, foolishly believe are those of our law makers.

Another Tavistock infestation in our country I need to make you aware of is the Rand Research and Development Corporation, or simply known as the Rand Corporation. Specific Rand policies that became operative include our ICBM program, prime analyses for U.S. foreign policy making, instigator of various space programs, U.S. nuclear policies, corporate analyses, hundreds of projects for the military, and the CIA in relation to the use of mind altering drugs like LSD.

There are literally THOUSANDS of highly important companies, government institutions and organizations that make use of Rand's services. To list them all would be impossible. Among Rand's specialties is a study group that predicts the timing and the direction of a thermonuclear war, plus working out the many scenarios based upon its findings.

That's probably enough to pique your interest of the Tavistock Institute, there is much more to learn about them, but not here.

Chapter 7/C

MAINSTREAM MEDIA CONTROL

"In March, 1915, the J.P. Morgan interests, the steel, ship building and powder interests and their subsidiary organizations, got together 12 men high up in the newspaper world and employed them to select the most influential newspapers in the United States and sufficient number of them to control generally the policy of the daily press in the United States.

These 12 men worked the problems out by selecting 179 newspapers, and then began, by an elimination process, to retain only those necessary for the purpose of controlling the general policy of the daily press throughout the country. They found it was only necessary to purchase the control of 25 of the greatest papers. The 25 papers were agreed upon; emissaries were sent to purchase the policy, national and international, of these papers; an agreement was reached; the policy of the papers was bought, to be paid for by the month; an editor was furnished for each paper to properly supervise and edit information regarding the questions of preparedness, militarism, financial policies and other things of national and international nature considered vital to the interests of the purchasers."

- Congressman Oscar Callaway, Second Session, 64th Congress of the United States of America, U.S. Congressional Record February 9, 1917

There are many, many avenues that the proponents of the Great Plan use to attack our bodies and minds in order to keep us progressing down the path to the one world government. Their big gun is the

Mainstream Media---which is completely and unequivocally under their control, machine gunning you daily with rounds and rounds of NWO-scripted propaganda.

Six globalist corporations, all controlled by pro-New World Order interests, control **all** the mainstream media in the U.S. Remember, the very essence of a globalist corporation is the fostering and promotion of globalism in order to increase sales. Therefore, the people that own these corporations that pump out the news and information in the United States have absolutely no vested interest in protecting **our** best interests. These powers-that-be dictate nearly everything you see and hear. They use this highly-coveted direct access to subliminally condition you and the rest of the public to respond favorably to their plans. Subliminal programming bypasses normal analytical logic and quite literally brainwashes you. They use subliminal techniques to over-sexualize us, make us greedy and materialistic, superficial, shallow, anxious, passive, helpless and unquestioning. They condition us to label those who question the "norm" and seek answers as conspiracy theorists, nut-jobs, racists, or left/right wing wackos. We truth-seekers have valid questions, arguments, and evidence that anyone who is a rational thinker should investigate for themselves before coming to any conclusion about who is steering our ship. This is especially true given the preponderance of evidence I'm laying out in this book that there is a grand conspiracy afoot to destroy our country and take over the world.

Remember David Rockefeller's quote from the Bilderberg meeting?

"We are grateful to The Washington Post, The New York Times, Time Magazine and other great publications whose directors have attended our meetings and respected their promises of discretion for almost forty years. It would have been impossible for us to develop our plan for the world if we had been subject to the bright lights of publicity during those years. But, the world is now much more sophisticated and prepared to march towards a world government. The supranational sovereignty of an intellectual elite and world bankers is surely preferable to the national auto-determination practiced in past centuries."

We just talked about this, but don't you think it's a bit odd that when the most powerful people on the planet get together to meet to discuss the most important matters in the world at the annual Bilderberg meeting, that not a peep about it is mentioned in the Mainstream Media? It is always plastered all over the media when the WTO meets, or when the G8 or G20 or whatever meets, or any other even semi-significant global meeting happens.....but never the Bilderberg meeting? When the most powerful people on the planet get together to meet in strict secrecy you better believe they are plotting something, and that something is a **one world government**.

The Mainstream Media in our country gets its marching orders from the CFR and that is a fact, and the MM is heavily represented at the CFR. Personalities you know such as Tom Brokaw, Diane Sawyer, Walter Cronkite, and the rest of the national news celebrities are all members of and toe the line of the CFR masters.... and therefore the Great Plan. If they didn't, they wouldn't be getting their cushy $20 million a year salaries to keep their mouths shut and only say what they are told to say.

"We live in a dirty and dangerous world. There are some things the general public does not need to know and shouldn't. I believe democracy flourishes when the government can take legitimate steps to keep its secrets, and when the press can decide whether to print what it knows."
-Katherine Graham, Washington Post publisher and CFR member, wiping her feet on the 1st Amendment

It has only been very recently with the advent of the free-flow of information out of the internet that the formerly ignorant masses were allowed to view the hidden agenda of the New World Order.

The Mainstream Media serves multiple functions for the Illuminati. First, it distributes information that they want you to believe is "real" news, when in fact it is usually only partial truth or outright lies. Secondly, the MM assists in the cover-up of information that has leaked out through sources not under their control. Today, that is mainly the damning information about their plans now pouring out of the internet. In other words, "damage control". Thirdly, the Mainstream Media functions as a weapon to assassinate the character and credibility of those who expose the practices of the proponents of the Great Plan. This was clearly evident when anti-Federal Reserve/New World Order agenda, non-Establishment member Ron Paul made waves in 2008. He was portrayed as crazy for such radical ideas as bringing our troops home and ending our current program of worldwide tyranny, and also eliminating the Federal Reserve. Also, the MM acts as a firewall to prevent information detrimental to the Illuminati's control from reaching the public. Besides owning controlling blocks of stock, the Illuminati keep a lid on their plans by threatening to withhold advertising dollars from the corporations they control if networks dare to air controversial material, effectively keeping them in line. Finally, they act to continually reinforce "mainstream" accounts of current and historical events. The Mainstream Media essentially serves as a primary tool for social conditioning and mind-control.

One of the most recent ways they have employed to dispel the rumors of the New World Order and other pertinent "conspiracies" is by putting this stuff directly into the mainstream media, the TV and movies as plot lines. After all, if it's on TV or a movie it can't possibly be real right? Unless it comes from a "documentary" on TV or the movies then it's all fake, right? They are playing the public like a fiddle. You don't believe that they can play us like fiddles? When was the last time you were at a movie and cried. Or were scared. Or laughed. Or got mad. Those emotions you felt are a direct result of pre-planned scripts to elicit the exact feelings they wanted out of you. This is where the Tavistock Institute and their satellite organizations are so very valuable to the Great Planners to muddy up the water of what is really happening.

Mind control, in fact, is the **only** way the proponents of the Great Plan can manipulate 7 billion people without them rising up and hanging them all. By some estimates, the number of people working within the Great Plan and benefitting enough financially to go along with it is only around 10,000. So there you have it: 13 Luciferian families rule the world, with around 10,000 underlings helping them control 7 billion mind-controlled wage-slaves. I believe this to be a pretty good assessment of the truth.

Control of the mind has long been one of the **un**-holy grails that the Illuminati have been after for a very long time. They seem to be doing an excellent job of it, judging by how far they have been able to covertly advance the Great Plan right under humanity's nose. They saturate television with predictive, repetitive programming, violence, sex, murder, torture and other tactics designed as a coordinated attack on the minds of the masses, in order to achieve a total degeneration of society. We have all heard of stories and seen images of people being attacked, raped, injured or in distress and are totally ignored by bypassing members of the public. We have been conditioned **not to get involved**. We are told to wait until directed by the government to act on behalf of our fellow man, and submit and do whatever we are told, as we move into our future existence as programmed slaves.

This has been done lately with the bombardment of television with these ridiculous "reality" shows---that have absolutely NOTHING to do with reality, but they are pushing them as reality to mess your mind up.

The explicit intention of the reality shows is clearly to not only make money from the humiliation and suffering of unsuspecting people, but to inflict a false sense of reality upon the viewers of these shows to detach them from the "real" reality that is going on around them.

The Illuminati are Luciferians, let me reemphasize that, and that is why the media these days is saturated with pro-occult imagery. People laugh it off as harmless entertainment, and it has been made "cool" by the people in control of the system, all done in order to further humanity along the path to the Luciferian one world government, and this is a fact. This is why there are so many occult themes in movies and TV today. Not only are they promoting the occult, all manners of degeneracy are on the table and promoted by the Mainstream Media: "potty humor", which revolves around sodomy and excrement, anti-Christian imagery and messages, promoting disrespect for American values and the family unit in general. Christianity bashing is practically considered an art form in Hollywood. Bash any other group and the ACLU would be up in arms.

Just as in the movie "The Wizard of Oz", the Mainstream Media is the "curtain" which prevents us from understanding that the real controllers behind it are think tanks, the Federal Reserve, the Wall Street gang, and the tax-exempt complex---all representatives of the proponents of the Great Plan.

Another primary role of the mainstream media is to project the illusion of a two-party political system. The grass roots Democrats and Republicans have their philosophical differences at the starting line, but as you move up the party ladders these differences become less and less distinguishable until finally the ladders disappear behind the CFR-managed news curtain and come together at the top of the power-pyramid under the direct control of the Illuminati.

"Think of the press as a great keyboard on which the government can play."
-Dr. Joseph Goebbels, Nazi Propaganda Minister

In 1983, Ben Bagdikian published *"The Media Monopoly",* which warned that continuing deregulation of the media under Ronald Reagan's FCC was allowing the media to be bought and controlled by an ever-shrinking number of corporate owners. Once called an"alarmist," the book is now considered a classic, because all its predictions have come true. In 1985, there were 50 corporations who owned and controlled what you were seeing and hearing in America. By 1992, the number of corporations controlling the media in the United States had fallen from 50 to 20.

Now there are **six** that control 95% of what you see and hear in the United States: **General Electric** (owns NBC, Universal Pictures, among others), **Walt Disney** (owns ABC, ESPN, Touchstone, Miraxmax, Pixar, among others), **News Corporation** (owns Fox, National Geographic, Wall Street Journal, 20th Century Fox, among others), **Time-Warner** (owns HBO, Cinemax, Cartoon Network, TBS, TNT, America Online, MapQuest, Moviefone, Warner Bros. Pictures, Castle Rock and New Line Cinema, and more than 150 magazines including Time, Sports Illustrated, Fortune, Marie Claire and People Magazine, among others), **Viacom** (owns MTV, Nickelodeon, VH1, BET, Comedy Central, Paramount Pictures, among others), **CBS** (Home of the all-seeing-eye logo, owns CBS Television, Showtime, book publisher Simon & Schuster, 29 television stations, and CBS Radio, Inc, which has 140 stations, among others).

All six of these companies are CFR corporate members, and their executives regularly attend CFR meetings and execute CFR policy. Just a reminder, the entire purpose of founding the CFR was to merge the United States into King Nimrod's one world government.

> *"There is no such thing at this date of the world's history, in America, as an independent press. You know it and I know it... The business of journalists is to destroy the truth, to lie outright... We are the tools of rich men behind the scenes. We are jumping jacks, they pull the strings and we dance. Our talents, our possibilities and our lives are all property of other men. We are intellectual prostitutes."*
> *-Journalist John Swinton, New York Press Club 1953*

There is no such thing as left or right wing media, it's all corporate-controlled Illuminati-dictated media designed to divide and conquer us, and they are doing a masterful job of it. The entire left-right paradigm is a farce. It is a distraction, and it is a disgrace. It pits Americans against Americans---but it doesn't matter who wins, we always lose and they and their agenda always win the way it is set up right now.

The proponents of the Great Plan also use the media to perform grand experiments on us. Probably the most famous of these, that most people don't even know was a psyops experiment, was the "War of the Worlds" radio broadcast. Written by alleged 33rd degree Freemason H.G. Wells, also author of the book *"The New World Order"*, the War of the Worlds radio broadcast went out over the airwaves at 8:00 PM Eastern Standard Time, on the evening of October 30, 1938, the night before Halloween. An estimated six million Americans listened to the famous Orson Welles broadcast, which described an extraterrestrial invasion from Mars. An estimated one million people ran into the streets of New York and rioted. This experiment was, in fact, funded by the **Rockefeller Foundation** in an attempt to see how the public would react to a simulated alien invasion. You see, a simulated alien invasion is one of the rumored means by which the Illuminati intend to trick mankind into accepting the New World Order/one world government.

With the masses of sheeple willfully distracted by the many avenues of entertainment and "news" foisted upon them by the Mainstream Media, no one is spending valuable time looking at the national deficit and the trillions of dollars that are owed to banks in foreign countries, that we as the taxpayers are on the hook for. Who owns these banks, and who intentionally got us into the financial mess to start with? The exact same elite group of wealthy individuals running the media today to cover it up until it's too late.......the proponents of the New World Order.

We've been had.

Chapter 7/D

EDUCATION CONTROL

Another New World Order agenda item you need to know about and look into further is our country's abysmal educational system. We already went over how the National Education Association is affiliated with the Tavistock Institute, and was originally funded by the **Rockefeller** foundation, but the corruption of our children's education, and our country's future, goes way past that.

John Dewey of **Columbia** University, considered the father of the American Education System, **was a New World Order proponent**. He believed that children do not go to school to develop individual talents but rather are to be prepared as "units" in an organic society. He was an avowed atheist and socialist, and the first president of the American Humanist Society, a New Age-oriented group.

Dewey also co-authored 1933's Humanist *Manifesto*, which called for a "synthesizing of all religions" and "a socialized and cooperative economic order." John Dewey is also credited with creating the Dewey Decimal System, by which libraries are organized today. In other words, he was a very influential individual on our school system.

Under the influence of the NEA the test scores of our children have consistently been sliding for years compared to the rest of the developed nations and now sit at around number 18 or so out of 36 industrialized nations. This is also in no small part thanks to George W. Bush signing off on the "No Child Left Behind" act in 2002 right on the heels of 9/11.

No Child Left Behind (NCLB) is a federal law that provides money for a small amount of extra educational assistance for poor children in return for perceived improvements in their academic progress. Under the U.S. Constitution, the states have the primary responsibility for public education. However, if states want to receive federal NCLB funds, they must agree to this recent law's requirements. In a time of diminishing and often depleted state coffers, not to mention increasing disregard for our Constitution, states have little alternative but to comply. The result is continued build-up of big centralized government, and a subpar education for the future citizens of America. In a nutshell, what NCLB does is require the states to set their own standards for scholastic achievement and then must meet those goals to get the federal money. So....what do you think the vast majority of the schools do now? They set the bar **LOW** so they can ensure that they meet/surpass these goals and stay on the federal government teat. This is a disaster of a policy, and is just one more way the Illuminati are forcing the United States to dig its own grave.

Political correctness and "tolerance" towards all religions, races, creeds, sexual orientations, etc. is the modern day mantra of the educational system in the United States and emphasis on these line items is placed above the reason the kids should be there to start with: learning reading, writing, and arithmetic and excelling at these three so that the U.S. might have a bright future. I'm certainly not saying it is bad to respect other humans that are different that you or I, but it is up to the family and community to teach these things and not a taxpayer-funded government entity.

Chapter 7/E

OIL CONTROL

Not only do the modern day proponents of the Great Plan own and control the majority of the world's central banks and the Mainstream Media, but they control nearly all of the energy in the form of oil. This was accomplished through the Rothschilds backing of the Rockefeller's aggressive ambition to set up a global oil monopoly in the late 1800's. We already went over that, but just know that the next time you buy gasoline for your car, if you are buying Exxon, Chevron, Mobil, Texaco, Union 76, Shell, or Arco, you are sending money directly to the Illuminati. In other words, every time you fill up your car the Illuminati gains more money and therefore more power. Get it?

We'll go over this more later, but the proponents of the Great Plan are also the ones who are promoting the environmental movement to fight additional oil exploration. This keeps the oil prices artificially high and their monopoly turning out the maximum profits possible, while keeping humanity under their financial thumb.

Here is an interesting tale for you to consider, and this is a 100% true story. There once was a genius named Nikola Tesla, who was a fierce competitor of Thomas Edison's in the late 1800's/early 1900's. Edison was running his newly founded General Electric Corporation, and Tesla worked for G.E.'s competition....Westinghouse. Tesla was a profound inventor whose story has largely been stricken from the public record because of his many unique and beneficial-to-mankind inventions, inventions that the Illuminati wanted for themselves. There is one particular invention that got him in big trouble with the Illuminati at the peak of his creative endeavors: the Tesla free-energy coil.

After inventing AC electricity, which stands for alternating current and is how electricity is transmitted and used worldwide today, Tesla sold his AC invention to George Westinghouse---his boss at the time---for one million dollars. Tesla then went to work building his dream project: a free energy generator he was going to give for free to mankind.

Tesla spent his remaining funds on his other inventions and culminated his efforts in a major breakthrough in 1899 at Colorado Springs by transmitting 100 million volts of high-frequency electric power wirelessly over a distance of 26 miles, at which he lit up a bank of 200 light bulbs and ran one electric motor. The method he would use to produce this wireless power was to employ the earth's own resonance with its specific vibrational frequency to conduct AC electricity via a large electric oscillator. With this version of his Tesla coil, Tesla claimed that only 5% of the transmitted energy was lost in the process. Tesla didn't have much of that million dollars left after he paid off the investors in his AC program and out of funds yet again, he turned to JP Morgan to fund the project, not knowing what a truly evil man Morgan was and whose interests he really represented.

When J.P. Morgan agreed to fund Tesla's project on Morgan's terms, construction on a huge structure was started and almost completed near Wardenclyffe in Long Island, NY. Looking like a huge wooden oil derrick with a mushroom cap, it rose into the sky a total height of 200 feet. Apparently there was some sort of misunderstanding as the project moved along and Tesla told Morgan it was his full intention to use the device to offer free energy to humanity. Morgan was furious, as this would have enabled mankind to get out from under the Illuminati's energy-control stranglehold and prosper, and would have drastically reduced the power of the Illuminati energy monopoly.

Morgan withdrew his support to the project in 1906, and eventually the structure was dynamited and brought down in 1917. Tesla was a great man and never much cared about how much money his inventions were worth---only whether or not they would benefit mankind. He died penniless in 1947. Upon his death the federal government confiscated all of his blueprints, diagrams, writings, etc. with the excuse that they were too dangerous to fall into the wrong hands. Who's worse hands could they have fallen into other than the Illuminati who now are using his inventions against us? Not only does the technology exist for **unlimited cheap/free energy**, but it is being suppressed by the Illuminati in order to maintain their energy monopoly.

Another point of fact, right now, as you read this, the technology exists for automobiles to run on liquid hydrogen---the same fuel that powers the space shuttle. Derived from the electrolysis of water, when burned in an internal combustion engine liquid hydrogen burns completely clean---emitting only water vapor out of the exhaust pipe with no harmful emission whatsoever. Do you think, though, with humanity firmly in their grip via their worldwide oil monopoly that the Illuminati are going to allow this technology to reach the masses? Not if they can help it. They will challenge my assessment of liquid hydrogen, saying it takes too much energy to electrolyze water to create liquid hydrogen. That is where the Tesla Coil/cheap energy generator could easily remedy this.

It is the Luciferian Rockefeller/Rothschild/Illuminati/New World Order consortium who not only control the output and distribution of all the oil that is polluting our planet, AND are the ones suppressing the "clean" technologies that would correct this, but they are the ones pushing the environmental movement through the UN in order to create and control both sides of the equation. I will talk about this later, but "man-made" global warming is a manufactured fraud designed to destroy the industrialized nations of the world through tyrannical cap-and-trade "pollution taxes" issued and enforced by the Illuminati-founded and controlled United Nations. You probably know who Al Gore is, right? The former Vice-President under alleged 33rd degree Freemason President Bill Clinton? The same Al Gore who made "An Inconvenient Truth" about how man-made global warming is going to destroy us all? The same Al Gore who is also an alleged 33rd degree Freemason doing the bidding of the Illuminati? In the 1970's, the big environmental scare was global COOLING, and that is a fact. You really need to open your eyes and see how badly we are being taken for a ride. It is all about cooking up ways to divide us, to conquer us, and to control us.

Chapter 7/F

ILLEGAL IMMIGRATION

One of the primary goals of the New World Order is the merging of sovereign nations into a borderless one-world community under United Nations rule.

Although the proponents of the Great Plan are pushing Muslim/Arab immigration into the European Union to destabilize their societies and weaken them, we're going to concentrate on illegal immigration into the United States, primarily from Mexico.

Let me say this right off the bat before we proceed: **Being against illegal aliens coming into our country is not a racist ideal as the Mainstream Media pushes**. The flood of illegal aliens coming into our country are primarily from the country of Mexico, and **Mexicans are not a race but a nationality**. Just because they happen to have brown skin does not make it racist to speak up about this as you have been conditioned to believe. If it were Russia to our southern border and white illegal Russians were pouring into our country it would not be nearly as touchy of an issue, but the Mainstream Media uses the color of the Mexicans' skin to try and quash those who speak out against illegal immigration as racists. Note also that we don't have any problem with illegal immigration from Canada whatsoever, but if we did I would also be speaking up about that. Over my life I have had many Mexican friends from my 20+ years in the construction trades, and they are as hardworking of a people as any, with most being devout Christians, albeit misguided through their following of the Unholy Roman Empire's paganized Christianity.

I don't blame the Mexican people one bit for trying to attain a better life for themselves and their loved ones. Mexico is a third world country, and their standard of living is much lower than ours. By our corrupted federal government intentionally under-manning our southern border and flooding our country with illegal third worlders, and giving them liberal access to our taxpayer-funded social services, it has the effect of being one more straw thrown on the back of the citizens of the United States in order to break us down in order to absorb us into the one world government. Thanks to a politicized misinterpretation of the 14th Amendment to our Constitution, if an illegal alien from any country births a child on United States soil that baby is considered a citizen of the United States, and that baby and its mother are automatically entitled to taxpayer-funded social services that they had no participation in contributing to, further putting us in debt and deeper on the hook to the Illuminati bankers.

A strong United States with a thriving middle class is the biggest stumbling block that exists to the ushering in of the Great Plan's one world government, and America's middle class must be destroyed in order for the United States to fall. The United States **will** fall and the New Babylon will merge into the one world government if we fail to act. They are already virtually one in the same today, with the United Nations operating out of our country right now, excusing the horrendous worldwide atrocities the New Babylon sees over.

By intentionally under funding/staffing the securing of our southern border and flooding the United States with third world illegal aliens, the proponents of the New World Order accomplish the following:

-it helps to divide the United States, pitting the legal citizens against the illegals, balkanizing it, and especially pitting the whites against the "minorities"---creating racial tensions to further distract and divide the country

-illegal labor helps to bring down the prices of labor in general, and therefore bringing down the standard of living of the United States

-it helps to increase government spending across the board to deal with it, further putting the governments into debt to the Illuminati bankers

-it helps to water down our sense of patriotism by forcing a new and foreign culture upon us

-It helps to further their goal of a borderless, integrated race of man and world---the one world government is a government of the world with no sovereign nations and no borders.

There is no society that can indefinitely allow a relentless flood of illegal aliens to contravene its laws, violate its sovereign borders, overwhelm its infrastructures and social systems, and degrade employment opportunities for its own people. The massiveness of the illegal invasion is contributing to the destruction of our culture, language and way of life. I don't know if you've noticed lately, but a large percentage of the signs in the multinational corporations you frequent are in both English **and Spanish**. Why not French or German? Because we don't have millions of French or German speaking people illegally flooding into our country.

As evidenced by the pro-illegal alien marches, the pro-illegal alien contingency wants to maintain their allegiance to Mexico. They want jobs, free social services and they want all the rights of American citizens---but none of the responsibilities.

There are currently over **23 million illegal aliens and probably millions more than that occupying our country today with 10,000 more a day entering the United States.** 99% of these illegal aliens are Catholics and follow the Vatican's marching orders, including not believing in or using birth control. These are the "undocumented immigrants" that the Vatican and their satellite charities aid and abet. One must wonder if 23 million Hindus or Muslims or Buddhists were to illegally invade America, would the Vatican still be loudly advocating for their legalization? This is just the Unholy Roman Empire doing its part in bringing down the U.S.

Take an educated look and you will see what the future holds in store for the United States. We are slowly devolving into a socialist state that is sinking under the horrendous weight of forced multi-culturalism, multi-lingualism and entitlements for the lawless. Those illegals who flaunt their desire for the reconquista of our land, waving their Mexican flags while they blatantly glorify their disdain for acculturation and assimilation into our language and culture, need to be expelled IMMEDIATELY.

The illegal aliens are already demonstrating where their allegiance lies by their disrespect for our country. There is no mystery here---they don't bother to hide it and literally shove it in our faces.

If you haven't heard of a racist organization called La Raza, you should look into it. La Raza literally means "the race" and refers to the intentional flooding of the United States southwest with so many illegal Mexicans that the native citizens of the U.S. will be forced out, and those lands lost during the Mexican-American War will be retaken purely though Mexican repopulation. They call these states the territory of "Aztlan" and are working diligently to fulfill this goal.

The cost of this unarmed invasion is in the hundreds of billions of dollars a year---and you and your family are footing the bill. We are sinking under the weight of the taxpayer burdens to the tune of $46.7 billion dollars to fund just one executive order by the treasonous President Clinton, Executive Order 13166, that requires multi-lingualism everywhere and everyplace. This is the main reason why you see so many signs, descriptions on food products, etc. in Spanish. **It was mandated by law.**

What the proponents of the Great Plan are initially after is a merging of the United States with Canada and Mexico, under what has been proposed as the NAU, or North American Union. This is similar to the European Union, and also the African Union, which you probably have never heard of but plans for this merging exist today.

Under the North American Union, it will spell the end of the United States without fail. A borderless union will allow the Mexicans to flood in by the millions and we will no longer be a melting pot of immigrants, we will be a Latino country in less than 20 years at the third-world country rate they reproduce given our generous social services.

A 2010 national census suggests that by the year 2040, Latinos, as a result of illegally-entered Mexicans, will be the majority population in the United States as it is if current trends continue. In the year 2012 it was reported by the U.S. Census Bureau that non-white births had for the first time in history surpassed white births in the United States, largely as a result of the illegal invasion from Mexico.

Illegal immigration: just one more way the proponents of the New World Order are attacking the naïve citizens of the United States.

Chapter 7/G

ASSASSINATIONS

"The bold effort the present (central) bank had made to control the government ... are but premonitions of the fate that awaits the American people should they be deluded into a perpetuation of this institution or the establishment of another like it."
-Andrew Jackson, Seventh President of the United States

Another method employed by the proponents of the New World Order, when all else fails, is assassinating those leaders who would stand against them. **Virtually every assassination and attempted assassination of our Presidents was the result of Illuminati action, and was the result of sitting Presidents messing with the Illuminati's central banking scam.**

Early in our country's history, the Illuminati employed a special agent of theirs to help found and run their newest central bank in the U.S. This was the **second** central bank set up by the Rothschilds after the Congress refused to renew the charter of the **first** central bank that the Rothschilds had set up, called the First Bank of the United States. Child prodigy Nicholas Biddle, born in 1786 in Philadelphia, was the point man for the Illuminati to create a second central bank in the United States. Biddle was a genius, and graduated from the University of Pennsylvania at the age of 13, and from Princeton at 17. Biddle moved to and lived in France from the ages of 19 to 24. He ultimately came under the guiding wing of Great Britain's **Nathan Rothschild**. A central bank in America was instigated by the Rothschilds and their agent Biddle in 1816, and in

1822, under President James Monroe, Biddle became president of the Second Bank of the United States, an Illuminati-owned bank.

In 1828, immediately upon his election as the new President of the United States, President Andrew Jackson began an investigation of the Second Bank of the United States. Jackson knew that banks played an important role in the United States' economy, but he believed the Second Bank of the United States held too much power and could wield it at any moment to ruin the U.S. economy if they didn't get their way politically.

President Jackson argued that the bank was privately owned with stockholders from foreign nations who had political agendas at odds with the United States' best interests....exactly like what we have today in the Federal Reserve. That is, their allegiances were with foreign countries and foreign agendas. Not only this, it explicitly stated in the still-freshly-printed United States Constitution that the power to create the nation's money supply lies with our Congress. Jackson viewed foreign ownership of our money supply as a matter of national security, and he was 100% correct.

> *"You are a den of vipers and thieves. I intend to rout you out, and by the grace of the Eternal God, will rout you out. I am ready with the screws to draw every tooth---and then the stumps."*
> *-Andrew Jackson, speaking to Biddle and his banking cronies on his goal of taking the money power away from the Illuminati*

The battle raged between Jackson and the Illuminati and by 1832 when Jackson was up for re-election, the Illuminati agents tried to get a renewal Bill for the bank passed. But Jackson vetoed the bill and made a speech concerning the event, saying:

> *"More than 8,000,000 of the stock of the bank is held by foreigners who are more dangerous than the military power of an enemy."*

Biddle had many Congressmen and Senators financially beholden to him, and he wielded great political power. He deliberately created a banking panic and a depression for the purpose of frightening the voters and blaming it on President Jackson. Biddle was later arrested and charged with fraud, but his powerful protectors shielded him from Jackson's attempts at justice.

In 1832 Jackson ran for re-election and, despite the fact that the Illuminati bankers poured **$3,000,000**, a huge amount of money at that time, into Henry Clay's campaign to defeat him, he was re-elected as a champion of the people.

Jackson was thereby successful in destroying the Bank by vetoing its 1832 re-charter by Congress and by the withdrawing of U.S. funds beginning in 1833.

Obviously none of this was sitting well with the Illuminati, and when President Jackson was leaving the Capitol out of the East Portico after the funeral of South Carolina Representative Warren R. Davis, Richard Lawrence, an unemployed and "deranged" housepainter from England, stepped out from hiding behind a column and aimed a pistol at Jackson which misfired. Lawrence then pulled out a second pistol---which also misfired. Lawrence was then disarmed and restrained by none other than Davey Crockett, among others.

Richard Lawrence gave the doctors several reasons for the shooting. He said he had recently lost his job painting houses and blamed Jackson. He claimed that with the President dead, "money would be more plenty", a reference to Jackson's struggle with the Bank of the United States, and that he "could not rise until the President fell."

After his "act", he was not surprisingly declared insane at trial. Don't buy for a minute the propagandized historical take that this man was insane----he was just another minion of the Illuminati.

Next up to bat against the Illuminati bankers was our sixteenth President of the United States, Abraham Lincoln, and he unfortunately lost his life for crossing them.

As the country was engulfed in Civil War, Lincoln made the following statement of fact:

"I see in the near future a crisis approaching. It unnerves me and causes me to tremble for the safety of my country. The money powers preys upon the nation in times of peace and conspires against it in times of adversity. It is more despotic than a monarchy,

more insolent than autocracy, more selfish than bureaucracy. It denounces, as public enemies, all who question its methods or throw light upon its crimes. I have two great enemies, the Southern Army in front of me & the financial institutions at the rear, the latter is my greatest foe. Corporations have been enthroned, and an era of corruption in high places will follow, and the money power of the country will endeavor to prolong its reign by working upon the prejudices of the people until the wealth is aggregated in the hands of a few, and the Republic is destroyed."

During the Civil War, President Lincoln needed money to finance the war from the North. The Illuminati-owned banks in New York, who Lincoln first went to, were going to charge him 24% to 36% interest. Lincoln was disgusted and went away greatly distressed, for he was a man of principle and would not think of plunging his beloved country into a debt that the country would find impossible to pay back. However, the Confederacy took them up on it, and this is how the South was financed.

President Lincoln was advised to get Congress to pass a law authorizing the printing of full legal tender Treasury notes to pay for the War effort, as this was not only authorized in the Constitution, but was mandated by it. Lincoln immediately recognized the great benefits of this part of our Constitution. At one point he wrote:

"We gave the people of this Republic the greatest blessing they have ever had - their own paper money to pay their own debts..."

The Treasury notes were printed with green ink on the back, so the people called them "Greenbacks"; this is the origination of this term.

Lincoln printed over 400 million dollars worth of Greenbacks, money that he ordered to be debt-free and interest-free money in order to finance the War. He printed it, paid it to the soldiers, to the U.S. Civil Service employees, and bought supplies for war.

Shortly after that happened, "The London Times" printed the following:

"If that mischievous financial policy, which had its origin in the North American Republic, should become indurated down to a fixture, then that Government will furnish its own money without cost. It will pay off debts and be without a debt. It will have all the money necessary to carry on its commerce. It will become prosperous beyond precedent in the history of the civilized governments of the world. The brains and the wealth of all countries will go to North America. That government must be destroyed, or it will destroy every monarchy on the globe."

The Illuminati bankers obviously understood the repercussions of this act. The main thing that is a threat to their power and the agenda of the Great Plan is sovereign governments printing interest-free and debt-free paper money. They knew it would break their power if they didn't control the money supply.

After this was published in *The London Times*, the British Government, which was controlled by the Illuminati through the Bank of England, moved to support the Confederate South, hoping to defeat Lincoln and the Union.

After this action, they were intentionally confounded by two things:

First, Lincoln knew the British people, and he knew that they would not support slavery, so he issued the Emancipation Proclamation, which declared that slavery in the United States was abolished. At this point, the Illuminati could not openly support the Confederacy because the British people simply would not stand for their country supporting slavery.

Second, President Abraham Lincoln was made aware that the Tsar of Russia, Alexander II (1855-1881), was also having problems with the Rothschild banking cabal as he was refusing their continual attempts to set up a central bank in Russia. The Tsar decided to give Lincoln some unexpected help. The Tsar issued an edict that if either England or France actively intervened in the American Civil War and helped the South, Russia would consider such action a declaration of war, and take the side of Lincoln and the Union. To show that he was serious, he sent part of his Pacific Fleet to a port in San Francisco and another part to New York. The Russian navy then became a threat to the ships of the British navy which had intended to help the South. This of course just added fuel to the fire of the ax the Illuminati had to grind with the Czar and his family, culminating in the end of Czarist rule in Russia and the establishment of Communism as you read earlier.

> *"The Government should create, issue, and circulate all the currency and credits needed to satisfy the spending power of the Government and the buying power of consumers. By the adoption of these principles, the taxpayers will be saved immense sums of interest. Money will cease to be master and become the servant of humanity..."*
> *-Abraham Lincoln*

As you know, the North won the War, and the Union was preserved. The United States remained as one nation.

Of course, the proponents of the Great Plan were not going to capitulate that easy, for they were determined to put an end once and for all to Lincoln's interest-free, debt-free Greenbacks. Lincoln was assassinated by an agent of the Illuminati, alleged 33rd degree Freemason John Wilkes Booth, shortly after the war ended in retribution for his stance against the agenda of the Great Plan.

Soon thereafter, Congress revoked the Greenback Law and enacted, in its place, the National Banking Act. The national banks were to be privately owned and the national bank notes they issued were to be interest-bearing. The Act also provided that the Greenbacks should be retired from circulation as soon as they came back to the Treasury in payment of taxes.

The next Illuminati-defiant President didn't last nearly as long as Lincoln or the others. President James A. Garfield, the 20th President of the United States and who lasted only 100 days in office, stated **two weeks** before he was assassinated in 1881:

> *"Whoever controls the volume of money in our country is absolute master of all industry and commerce...when you realize that the entire system is very easily controlled, one way or another, by a few powerful men at the top, you will not have to be told how periods of inflation and depression originate."*

As a Congressman, he had been chairman of the Appropriations Committee and was a member of the Banking and Currency Committee. In other words, he had a working knowledge of how the Illuminati bankers operated, and how what was happening was against the Constitution.

Unfortunately, he was killed before he had time to stir them up some real trouble......

It was not only Presidents who stood up and went against the wishes of the Illuminati. There were other patriotic Americans in history who paid the price for challenging the proponents of the New World Order.

Congressman Louis McFadden, House Committee on Banking and Currency Chairman (1920-31), stated:

> *"When the Federal Reserve Act was passed, the people of these United States did not perceive that a world banking system was being set up here. A super-state controlled by international bankers and industrialists ... acting together to enslave the world ... Every effort has been made by the Fed to conceal its powers but the truth is — the Fed has usurped the government."*

On the floor of the House of Representatives, McFadden is credited with the following statement:

> *"Mr. Chairman, we have in this Country one of the most corrupt institutions the world has ever known. I refer to the Federal Reserve Board and the Federal Reserve Banks, hereinafter called the Fed. The Fed has cheated the Government of these United States and the people of the United States out of enough money to pay the Nation's debt. The depredations and iniquities of the Fed has cost enough money to pay the National debt several times over. This evil institution has impoverished and ruined the people of these United States, has bankrupted itself, and has practically bankrupted our Government. It has done this through the defects of the law under which it operates, through the maladministration of that law by the Fed and through the corrupt practices of the moneyed vultures who control it."*

After he lost his congressional seat in 1934, he remained in the public eye as a vigorous opponent of the Illuminati's financial system; that is, until his sudden death.

There were two previous attempts on Louis McFadden's life. Two bullets were fired at him on one occasion, and later he was poisoned at a banquet.

McFadden was finally done in by another poisoning attack after attending a different banquet in New York City on October 3, 1936.

One last assassination we will go over and you will get the picture. These assassinations happened not by random acts or coincidence by "crazed gunmen", but because of the single common denominator that all of these patriotic gentlemen were against a privately-held central bank operating the United States money supply for their own personal gain.

Since November 22, 1963 when JFK was assassinated, many different theories as to why and by whom he was murdered have been bandied about.

I'm going to give you the real reason as to why he was murdered now, and after taking in what I've given you so far, you will know this is the truth.

President Kennedy was originally installed as a typical puppet President, just like we have today and have had since the days of Lincoln. The Illuminati, knowing that Kennedy was from an elitist family and "one of them", thought that he would toe the line of the Establishment and not deviate from their plans to destroy America and usher in a one world government.

Well, that all went out the window after he was elected President, and if they would have known that at the beginning he would never have made it to the Presidency.

Although he did many things to buck the Great Plan, including trying to end the war in Vietnam, on June 4th, 1963, President Kennedy signed Executive Order 11110, which further amended Executive Order 10289 of September 19th, 1951. This gave Kennedy, as President of the United States, legal clearance to authorize creation of money outside the Federal Reserve. This money was to belong to the people of the United States, an interest and debt-free money as mandated by the Constitution.

He ordered the printing of "United States Notes" as opposed to "Federal Reserve Notes", circumventing the Federal Reserve's "authority".

Kennedy issued $4,292,893,825 of Treasury-issued, not Fed issued, cash money in $5 bills. It was patently obvious that Kennedy was out to scale back and then eliminate the Federal Reserve System. You can get one of these $5 bills from a rare coin dealer and view for yourself that across the top it does not say "Federal Reserve Note"; it says "United States Note", as all of them should and would if we were following the Constitution, which we're not.

Only a few months later, In November of 1963, Kennedy was assassinated. You can view the videos on YouTube of the moments immediately before he was shot, of the Secret Servicemen being **CALLED OFF** from his motorcade so the gunman, or gunmen possibly, would have a clear shot. I don't know who shot him for sure, or if there was more than one gunman, but it is a moot point. I do know who was behind it, and now you do too: the Illuminati.

No reason was given, of course, to the American Public for anyone wanting to commit such an atrocious crime. But for those who knew anything about money and banking, it made perfect sense, especially if you knew the history of patriotic Presidents being killed by the Illuminati banksters.

It is interesting to note that only **one day** after Kennedy's assassination, all the United States notes which Kennedy had issued, were called back out of circulation. All of the money President Kennedy had created was then destroyed.

Alleged 33rd degree Freemason Lyndon Baines Johnson was immediately sworn in as the new President, and the Great Plan was back on track in the New Babylon.

Chapter 7/H

FDA

Why are Americans so damn fat and unhealthy? We're not THAT inactive and lazy are we? Why does our society have so many medical problems that we didn't have 30 years ago? The foods we eat are laced with pesticides and other poisonous substances, but most of us don't think twice about eating them. We live longer than the generations before us, but our golden years are dominated by trips to the doctor for more pills, treatments, and surgeries than can possibly make sense. When my grandma died a few years ago she was taking a mountain of pills everyday just to "stay healthy", and it was all paid for by the federal government, further pushing us into the debt abyss. It's almost like some corrupt entity is intentionally steering us down a preplanned, golden year's hypochondriac road.

There is such an entity, and it is one of the cogs of the New World Order system. This cog is a corrupt and bloated federal bureaucracy that is in charge of making sure what is put into our bodies is supposedly safe---the federal Food and Drug Administration. Believe you me; the FDA is fully under the New World Order's control matrix in order to help facilitate our destruction. I'm going to go over a handful of products in the next few chapters deemed "safe" by the FDA, when in fact they are the exact opposite of that, and downright dangerous to our well-being.

It is not uncommon knowledge in D.C. that if you "do your time" at the FDA and act in a favorable manner towards the huge pharma companies that a lucrative job working at these same drug companies is virtually guaranteed in your future. The Illuminati's tentacles of financial influence over all aspects of our lives should be as plain as day to you at this point in this book. The Federal Reserve. Mainstream Media. Big Oil. Big Pharma. All are majority or outright owned and controlled by the proponents of the New World Order.

There are many, many insidious ways that the Illuminati-controlled multinational corporations are cutting financial corners with our food supply, adding addictive flavor enhancers, and generally poisoning us. This includes lacing our foods with high fructose corn syrup, nitrites, pesticides, bovine growth hormones, and the like---all in the name of increasing their profits at our expense with the full knowledge of the federal government that these compounds also serve to make us lethargic, unhealthy, and beholden to Big Pharma to cure us when our biological systems collapse from ingesting all these toxic substances in our food and water.

Humans in health distress are less likely to have the motivation to rise up against the New World Order agenda, and this particular plan of attack starts at the FDA.

Let's look at the FDA itself first, and then we'll go over some of the major health offenders that are allowed into our food supply.

In a poll conducted in 2007, Consumer Reports found the following with regard to the public's view of the Food and Drug Administration:

* *96 percent agreed the government should have the power to require warning labels on drugs with known safety problems. As Consumer Reports explains, "Right now, the Food and Drug Administration must negotiate safety warning labels with a drug maker."*

* *84 percent agree that drug companies have "too much influence over the government officials who regulate them." More than two-thirds of those surveyed are concerned that drug companies actually pay the FDA to review and approve their drugs. It's a situation that turns drug companies into the "customers" of the FDA, and the customer is always right, right? Right.*

* *92 percent agree that pharmaceutical companies should disclose the results of ALL clinical trials, not just the ones with positive results that they*

wish to publicize. Currently, drug companies can bury negative drug trials, and the FDA has in fact been caught conspiring with drug companies to keep negative drug data secret from the public.

* 93 percent think that the FDA should have the power to demand follow-up safety studies from drug companies. Currently, the FDA has no authority to require follow-up safety studies on drugs after they are introduced to the market. This is a serious oversight shortfall, given that many problems with drugs only appear after widespread use, as patients are widely used as guinea pigs in any new drug launch.

* 60 percent agreed that doctors and scientists with a financial conflict of interest should not be allowed to serve on FDA advisory boards. Currently, doctors who earn hundreds of thousands of dollars each year in "consulting fees" from drug companies are not only allowed to vote on the recommendations for FDA approval of their drugs, there is not even any FDA requirement to disclose such conflicts of interest.

New rules proposed by the FDA would reduce this level of corruption by allowing doctors to receive a maximum of $50,000 per year from companies impacted by their decisions. This would have the effect of making the FDA numerically less corrupt than it is now, but still tolerating blatant conflicts of interest. It would, in all true definition of it, set a "bribery ceiling."

* 91 percent said they had seen a drug advertisement on television or in print---a victory for Big Pharma accomplished by the FDA legalizing such ads in 1998. 26 percent said they asked their doctor for a brand-name medication after learning about it from an advertisement. The purpose of this advertising blitz is purely to increase sales of drugs, not -- as is claimed by Big Pharma and the FDA -- to "educate" patients about medical treatments and medicines.

* 75 percent agreed that the allowing of drug advertising has resulted in the over-prescribing of pharmaceuticals. Fifty-nine percent said the government should restrict pharmaceutical advertising, and 26 percent said they "strongly agree" with such restrictions on pushing drugs in public---which is all they are really doing.

More than half of those surveyed said they are currently taking prescription drugs, indicating that more than half of American adults are now on drugs. Forty percent said they have experienced a negative reaction (negative side effect) from taking prescription medications.

Most side effects go unreported, and there is currently no enforced legal requirement that doctors or drug companies report newly discovered side effects to the FDA.

The United States is the **only** industrialized nation in the world that allows drug companies to advertise directly to consumers. It was legalized in 1998 by the FDA, following political pressure and influence from the drug companies who knew that being able to push brand-name drugs through advertising would result in windfall profits. Some drugs are sold at markups as high as **300,000%** over the cost of their manufacturing expense, with most subsidized in some form or another by the taxpayers, aka you and me.

Pharmaceuticals are now the 4th leading cause of death in America. According to the Journal of the American Medical Association, prescription drugs currently kill approximately **100,000** Americans each year.

Synthetic opiates such as Percocet, Oxycodone, Hydrocodone, and the like easily find their way into our middle and high schools, introducing our kids to "drugs" at an even earlier age than ever. The best way to protect Americans from these dangerous, deadly products is to call for and enact reforms that end the medical racket currently being jointly operated by the FDA and Big Pharma such as Pfizer, Merck, Glaxosmithkline, etc.

Unfortunately, many of the very lawmakers who would vote on such legislation are, much like FDA advisors, "on the take" via lobbyist favors from the very same pharmaceutical companies that stand to be impacted by their vote.

The FDA is NOT looking out for our best interests. Remember Merck's Vioxx? Merck knew damn well that the amount of profits they were reaping at the time would outnumber the amount of dollars in claims they would have to pay out, so they kept it on the market even after knowing it was deadly. Closer FDA oversight would have easily prevented this.

The FDA has repeatedly banned and confiscated herbs and nutritional supplements that compete with prescription drugs, and conducted armed raids on alternative medicine clinics, confiscating computers, threatening alternative health practitioners, and scaring away patients from healthy alternatives to Big Pharma's assembly line of harm.

The FDA also censors scientific information about the benefits of natural foods like cherries by threatening cherry growers with legal action if they did not remove scientific information about cherries from their websites, and has pursued and shut down companies selling natural-based, genuine cancer treatments that probably work as good or better as anything on the market right now.

The FDA knowingly approved harmful food additives for widespread use in the food supply, like Aspartame, which we will go over here soon, and allowed the continued legal use of harmful, cancer-causing food additives in the national food supply such as sodium nitrite, which is in all processed meats today.

The FDA also refused to ban a poisonous artificial fat from the food supply (hydrogenated oils/trans fats) for decades, even though the World Health Organization urged member nations to outlaw the substance in 1978. Hydrogenated oils have proliferated into our processed food supply and continue to harm us all today.

Taking all of this poisoning on the FDA's watch into consideration, is it any wonder that we are now the most chronically diseased population that has ever been recorded in the history of mankind? There is not a population on Earth other than ours that has suffered from diseases like we do in the United States today. You would have to be asleep at the wheel to not think that there's a correlation between the government-approved poisons we are ingesting, the diseases we are getting as a result, and the medical bills to treat them.

We're the #1 nation in the world per capita in terms of jail incarceration, mental disorders, obesity, diabetes, cancer, and a host of other health issues, and we have the HIGHEST health care costs per capita. We have in our country the most expensive drugs in the world. We have more doctors and health care professionals per capita than any country in the world. How in the HELL is this possible unless we are being sabotaged from within?

Not only is the FDA corrupt from top to bottom, a lot of the consumer chemicals that that you come into contact with everyday fall not under the FDA but the EPA---and have little to no oversight. Since the Toxic Substances Control Act (TSCA) became law in 1976, the number of chemicals in commercial products has increased from 60,000 to 80,000, yet the EPA has required testing on only 200 and restricted only 5. Under this act, chemicals are presumed safe unless proven otherwise, and that is a tough case to prove given the corruption in our government.

Case in point: formaldehyde. Formaldehyde is used extensively in building products these days, mostly in a product called OSB---oriented strand board. I've been in the building trade all my life, and I will tell you for a fact that most new houses are nothing but formaldehyde gas chambers. The floors, walls, roof, siding, and even framing components, along with the interior trim are full of formaldehyde, and this is a fact. Some people are literally surrounded by formaldehyde in these new homes. There have been studies linking exposure to formaldehyde to cancers, asthma, and other illnesses, but do you think anything will be done about it?

The FDA is a completely corrupted organization that is supposed to be looking out for us but instead the people working there look out for themselves and how many financial favors can be done for them down the road, financially and otherwise. It always traces back to the corrupting power of money, with the ultimate corrupt money power being the Federal Reserve.

It is imperative for you to be extremely vigilant about what you and your family are putting into your bodies, especially your children, whose developing biological systems are extremely vulnerable at a young age.

Chapter 7/I

FLUORIDE

We as Americans have been brainwashed since birth that fluoride is good for you and a necessary component of good dental health. Nothing could be farther from the truth.

Let's start with that glass of water from the local water municipality your kids were drinking this morning with their breakfast--or the juice or other processed beverage that was mixed from concentrate with municipality water for that matter. There is about a 70% chance that it was intentionally poisoned with fluoride. That's right, fluoride. The same fluoride that is in your toothpaste is often added to our public water supplies, with the deceptive cover of being in the name of the fight against tooth decay.

This is a completely malevolent **lie**.

Fluoridation of the public water supply is one of the main avenues of attack the proponents of the Great Plan use to break down the minds of the general populace of the United States in particular, such that we may be molded into the mindless wage slaves they covet. An alert, intelligent and informed American Public they want not. Repeated doses of minute amounts of fluoride will in time reduce an individual's power to resist domination by slowly poisoning and tranquilizing the brain, thus making him or her submissive and less likely to rise up against their New World Order masters.

Contrary to what you may believe or are led to believe, fluoridation of water in the United States is a relatively new thing. Fluoridation became an official policy of the U.S. Public Health Service in 1951, and by 1960 water fluoridation had become widely used in the U.S. By 2006, 69.2% of the U.S. population on public water systems was ingesting fluoridated water.

Both the Germans and the Russians added fluoride to the drinking water of prisoners of war during World War II to make them subdued and docile. Do not believe the government when they tell you it is harmless to ingest---it isn't.

The reason they push Fluoride so hard in the United States is because the patriotic citizens of the Unites States are the single biggest threat to the completion of the Great Plan. Most Western European countries water supplies are **not** fluoridated and have experienced the same decline in dental decay as the US as dental care education/technology has improved. Europe has already been for the most part indoctrinated into socialism in preparation of one world government rule, and now every option is being used in order to trip up the United States.

Fluoride is one of the most poisonous, toxic chemicals on the face of the Earth. Fluoride is the principle ingredient in **rat poison**----it is this effective of a poison. The amount of poisonous fluoride in a typical tube of fluoride toothpaste is **sufficient to kill a small child if it were consumed all at once.** This is why it implicitly states on the back "**If more toothpaste than would normally be used for brushing is ingested, contact a poison control center immediately**".

One of the truths of fluoride the American public needs to understand is the fact that the fluoride we ingest is nothing more than a hazardous waste by-product of the nuclear and aluminum industries. By *selling* it to water companies to put in our water, this eliminates the costly need to properly dispose of toxic waste. In addition to being the primary ingredient in rat and cockroach poisons, it is also a main ingredient in anesthetic, hypnotic, and psychiatric drugs---such as Prozac, as well as military NERVE GAS.

Even though only 70% of the population receives fluoridated water, the other 30% aren't able to escape the "web of fluoride" because fluoridated water is also used to make some bottled waters, beers, soft drinks, energy drinks, juices, and others. If you don't want to ingest fluoride, you shouldn't have to. They already offer fluoride supplements you can buy if you really want to put poison in your body. **If they really wanted to** put something in the water that is good for your health they would be adding <u>vitamins</u>, but they don't because that would actually be good for you, and that is <u>not</u> on the Great Plan agenda.

The following letter was received by the Lee Foundation for Nutritional Research, Milwaukee Wisconsin, on 2 October 1954, from a research chemist by the name of Charles Perkins. He wrote:

"I have your letter of September 29 asking for further documentation regarding a statement made in my book, "The Truth about Water Fluoridation", to the effect that the idea of water fluoridation was brought to England from Russia by the Russian Communist Kreminoff. In the 1930's Hitler and the German Nazis envisioned a world to be dominated and controlled by a Nazi philosophy of pan-Germanism. The German chemists worked out a very ingenious and far-reaching plan of mass-control which was submitted to and adopted by the German General Staff. This plan was to control the population in any given area through mass medication of drinking water supplies. By this method they could control the population in whole areas, reduce population by water medication that would produce sterility in women, and so on. In this scheme of mass-control, sodium fluoride occupied a prominent place.

Repeated doses of infinitesimal amounts of fluoride will in time reduce an individual's power to resist domination, by slowly poisoning and narcotizing a certain area of the brain, thus making him submissive to the will of those who wish to govern him.

The real reason behind water fluoridation is not to benefit children's teeth. If this were the real reason there are many ways in which it could be done that are much easier, cheaper, and far more effective. The real purpose behind water fluoridation is to reduce the resistance of the masses to domination and control and loss of liberty."

When the Nazis under Hitler decided to go to Poland, both the German General Staff and the Russian General Staff exchanged scientific and military ideas, plans, and personnel, and the scheme of mass control through water medication was seized upon by the

Russian Communists because it fitted ideally into their plans to communize the world."

I was told of this entire scheme by a German chemist who was an official of the great I.G. Farben chemical industries and was also prominent in the Nazi movement at the time. I say this with all the earnestness and sincerity of a scientist who has spent nearly 20 years' research into the chemistry, biochemistry, physiology and pathology of fluorine --- any person who drinks artificially fluorinated water for a period of one year or more will never again be the same person mentally or physically."

-Charles E. Perkins, Chemist, October 2, 1954

Here is another letter that needs to be quoted at length as well to help corroborate Mr. Perkin's testimony. This letter was written by a brilliant scientist named Dr. E.H. Bronner. Dr. Bronner was a nephew of the great Albert Einstein, served time in a WWII prison camp and wrote the following letter printed in the *Catholic Mirror*, Springfield, MA, January 1952:

"It appears that the citizens of Massachusetts are among the 'next' on the agenda of the water poisoners.

There is a sinister network of subversive agents, Godless intellectual parasites, working in our country today whose ramifications grow more extensive, more successful and more alarming each new year and whose true objective is to demoralize, paralyze and destroy our great Republic ---- from within if they can, according to their plan --- for their own possession.

The tragic success they have already attained in their long siege to destroy the moral fiber of American life is now one of their most potent footholds towards their own ultimate victory over us."

Fluoridation of our community water systems can well become their most subtle weapon for our sure physical and mental deterioration. As a research chemist of established standing, I built within the past 22 years 3 American chemical plants and licensed 6 of my 53 patents. Based on my years of practical experience in the health food and chemical field, let me warn: fluoridation of drinking water is criminal insanity, sure national suicide. DON'T DO IT!!

Even in very small quantities, sodium fluoride is a deadly poison to which no effective antidote has been found. Every exterminator knows that it is the most effective rat-killer. Sodium Fluoride is entirely different from organic calcium-fluoro-phosphate needed by our bodies and provided by nature, in God's great providence and love, to build and strengthen our bones and our teeth. This organic calcium-fluoro-phosphate, derived from proper foods, is an edible organic salt, insoluble in water and assimilable by the human body; whereas the non-organic sodium fluoride used in fluoridating water is instant poison to the body and fully water soluble. The body refuses to assimilate it.

Careful, bonafide laboratory experimentation by conscientious, patriotic research chemists, and actual medical experience, have both revealed that instead of preserving or promoting 'dental health', fluoridated drinking water destroys teeth before adulthood and after, by the destructive mottling and other pathological conditions it actually causes in them, and also creates many other very grave pathological conditions in the internal organisms of bodies consuming it. How then can it be called a 'health plan'? What's behind it?

That any so-called 'Doctors' would persuade a civilized nation to add voluntarily a deadly poison to its drinking water systems is unbelievable. It is the height of criminal insanity!

No wonder Hitler and Stalin fully believed and agreed from 1939 to 1941 that, quoting from both Lenin's 'Last Will' and Hitler's Mein Kampf: "America we shall demoralize, divide, and destroy from within.

Are our Civil Defense organizations and agencies awake to the perils of water poisoning by fluoridation? Its use has been recorded in other countries. Sodium Fluoride water solutions are the cheapest and most effective rat killers known to chemists: colorless, odorless, tasteless; no antidote, no remedy, no hope: Instant and complete extermination of rats.

Fluoridation of water systems can be slow national suicide, or quick national liquidation. It is criminal insanity ------- treason!!"
Signed,
Dr. E.H. Bronner, Research Chemist, Los Angeles

The public outcry by Dr. Bronner and others precluded the fluoridation of public water systems, but soon thereafter, the Food and Drug Administration allowed this deadly poison to be put in the water, and then toothpaste, and our dentists were systematically brainwashed into providing fluoride treatments to their many patients.

Independent scientific evidence over the past 50 plus years has shown that fluoride shortens our life span, promotes various cancers and mental problems, and most importantly, makes humans stupid, docile, and subservient, all from one little additive to the water.

Just recently there have been governmental public warnings not to give children under 6 months old anything with fluoride, especially mixing fluoridated water with instant formula. Those with tiny body mass, small liver, small kidneys and a developing brain are affected the most by the poisonous fluoride coming out of the tap.

Not only this, but all of that fluoridated water coming into and being used in your house is sent right back out into our environment through the drain pipes in your house. This is complete madness.

In 1952 a slick PR campaign rammed the concept of water fluoridation through our Public Health departments and various dental organizations. Honest scientists who have attempted to blow the whistle on fluoride's dangers have consistently been black listed, and have never received the attention they fairly deserve in the compromised national media.

The Centers for Disease Control and Prevention has acknowledged the findings of many leading dental researchers, that the mechanism of fluoride's benefit is **TOPICAL---not SYSTEMIC**. That is, you don't have to swallow fluoride to kill the bacteria on your teeth. As the benefits of fluoride are topical (fluoride IS poison and serves to kill the bacteria on your teeth), and the risks are systemic, the best use of fluoride to help prevent tooth decay is to deliver the fluoride directly to the tooth in the form of toothpaste. The minute amount of bacteria killed as fluoridated water passes over your teeth when you drink it is insignificant next to what happens to your body when it is ingested and runs its destructive course through your body.

If you want to poison an entire population, there's no easier way than to put it into the water supply. And if you really want to make sure everyone is poisoned, you would pass laws that mandate the adding of this poison into the water supply, such as fluoridation laws. Many of these laws exist today.

There's absolutely no good science behind any of the arguments for drinking fluoride. Even if they were using genuine natural fluoride, there are no studies that show the ingestion of fluoride decreases the incidence of tooth decay in modern society. Yet this myth persists in the dental community, and the American Dental Association stands firmly behind this national poisoning agenda. They will call anybody who disagrees with it a "nut," and they will say that all the water must be fluoridated, all in the name of fighting tooth decay.

I could literally go on and on about the factual evidence showing toxic side effects from fluoride ingestion, but we need to keep this book moving. I highly suggest that you do your own research on fluoride, as all topics in this book, for your own version of truth on the matter.

Chapter 7/J

VACCINES

You have probably seen your child's nurse insert a syringe into a large vial, extract a particular vaccine, and then leave a substantial amount of vaccine in the original container. If you've witnessed this seemingly benign procedure, you've seen how vaccine manufacturers are not only saving money at the expense of public health, but they are intentionally contributing to the poisoning of the citizens of the United States.

In order to store larger amounts of vaccine at a lower cost, companies started offering "multi-dose units" while adding preservatives, in the form of **mercury**, to prevent contaminations. That way, doctors can open and close a vaccine container and keep the vaccine sterile while assuring the public that those contaminants are quickly killed by the preservative, **a form of mercury called Thimerosal.**

Most if not all those vaccines your kids have been forced to get since they were born are loaded with Thimerosal, and that is a fact.

Mercury in the form of Thimerosal is the preservative of choice for vaccine manufacturers. First introduced by Eli Lilly and Company in the late 1920s, the company began selling it as a preservative in vaccines in the 1940s. Thimerosal contains 49.6 percent mercury by weight and is metabolized into ethylmercury and thiosalicylate. Mercury is the principle agent that kills vaccine contaminants---and brain cells.

The United States Department of Defense classifies mercury as a hazardous material that could cause death if swallowed, inhaled or absorbed through the skin---sounds like it's ok to inject into our kids though, right? Studies indicate that mercury tends to accumulate in the brains of humans after they are injected with these poisoned vaccines. Mercury poisoning has been linked to cardiovascular disease, autism, seizures, mental retardation, hyperactivity, dyslexia and many other nervous system conditions.

That might explain why thimerosal was eliminated in most countries years ago. In 1977, a Russian study found that adults exposed to ethylmercury, the form of mercury in thimerosal, suffered brain damage years later. As a result of these findings, Russia banned thimerosal from children's vaccines in 1980. Denmark, Austria, Japan, Great Britain and all the Scandinavian countries have also banned the preservative. **But why hasn't the U.S.?** It's because we are being intentionally attacked from all sides by the proponents of the Great Plan. If the U.S. is strong, the one world government will never be allowed to rise over it. If we fall, they can and will merge us into a one world government.

Infants are particularly vulnerable to the toxic Thimerosal. Some vaccines, such as vaccines for hepatitis B, contain as much as 12.5 micrograms of mercury per dose. That's more than 100 times the EPA's upper limit standard when administered to infants, but that doesn't matter because vaccines fall under the corrupted FDA's jurisdiction.

Scientists are finding stronger and stronger links between thimerosal and neurological damage. One report by Dr. Vijendra Singh of the Department of Pharmacology at the University of Michigan found a higher incidence of measles, mumps and rubella vaccine (MMR) antibodies in autistic children.

The National Vaccine Information Center in Vienna, Virginia, has noted a strong association between the MMR vaccine and autistic features. Reporting similar findings, the Encephalitis Support Group in England claims that children who became autistic after the MMR vaccine started showing autistic symptoms as early as 30 days after vaccination.

When the FDA finally formally released this information in 1999, the news came too little too late for some parents. The damage had already been done to millions of kids.

Autism affects 500,000 to 1.5 million Americans and has grown at an annual rate of 10 to 17 percent since the late 1980s. California found a 273 percent increase in autism between 1987 and 1998. Maryland reported a 513 percent increase in autism between 1993 and 1998 and several dozen other states reported similar findings. Some scientists say the estimated number of cases of autism has increased 15-fold---1,500 percent--- since 1991, the year when the number of childhood vaccinations doubled by the mandate of the CDC.

One in every 2,500 children was diagnosed with autism before 1991, **one in 166** children now have the disease.

This increase in reported autism cases directly parallels the increase in the number and frequency of thimerosal-containing vaccinations administered to infants. As of today, children are given as many as 21 immunizations in the first 15 months of life---most if not all containing Thimerosal.

So why isn't Congress doing anything about this nightmarish problem? Hopefully by now you know that our Congress has been completely usurped by the Great Plan and has been since the inception of the Federal Reserve. Our Congress has actually AIDED vaccine manufacturers, on the pretense of "security" reasons. In 2002, a mysterious piggyback on the 2002 Homeland Security bill **freed drug companies of liability in lawsuits regarding thimerosal.** Then-House Majority Leader and upstanding CFR member Dick Armey told CBS News he snuck the amendment in to keep vaccine makers from going out of business. Armey claimed it was a matter of national security.........**"We need their vaccines if the country is attacked with germ weapons."**

Yeah. THEIR germ weapons. There is a substantial body of suppressed evidence, of which I won't go into here for time and space sake, that all of the latest "plagues" that are menacing mankind like SARS, AIDS, the bird flu, etc. were actually manufactured in our government's military labs and turned loose on the world for their own societal experiments. Our military has a long and sordid history of doing stuff like this---with Congress' permission no less---and I suggest you look into this further if you doubt what I say. By scaring the public into rushing to get the mercury-laden bird flu vaccine, they are treating us as guinea pigs.

Not only this, but it has been proven by the truth movement that there are some really odd substances being put in the vaccines besides Thimerasol. Formaldehyde, aluminum, various additional biological agents you would be shocked at, and other toxic substances are added if you look into the truth behind the vaccines they give us.

Chapter 7/K

ASPARTAME

So......... how's that Diet Coke treating you these days? Or that piece of chewing gum? Or those Flintstone vitamins your kids are eating? Or that sugar-free Jell-O? Or that "diet anything" for that matter? Chances are better than not that that anything you are ingesting that is called "diet" or "sugar-free" is loaded with a poisonous compound called aspartame---better known as NutraSweet---and that's just the stuff that is labeled to tip you off. Most chewing gums these days have aspartame in them and **aren't** labeled as "sugar free", so be vigilant for your kids' sake.

Aspartame is one of if not the most dangerous food additives in existence, and more and more products containing it are rolled out every year in the name of "health". Aspartame pretty much scrambles your brain so you have to spend extra mental effort just to keep up with life—let alone question it. Mix up a batch of aspartame-loaded sugar free Jell-O with some fluoridated water; feed it to the kids after a trip to the doctor for some mercury-contaminated vaccines and you can see we are literally surrounded by poisons, all by design of the proponents of the Great Plan.

Aspartame was discovered by accident in 1965 when James Schlatter, a chemist of G.D. Searle Company, was testing an anti-ulcer drug. Schlatter inadvertently smeared his hand with liquid aspartame from a flask. He licked his thumb clean and was surprised by how sweet it tasted. The compound ended up being 200 times sweeter than sugar per volume. It contained virtually no calories and tasted more like sugar than other sweeteners: ideal for the growing diet consumables market. Sales of Aspartame in 2012 were in the multi-billions of dollars, with Aspartame added to over 6,000 food products globally.

It took 16 years from Schlatter's discovery for his company, US drug giant Searle, to win FDA approval for the sweetener. Searle's safety research was one of the main sticking points that resulted in the 16 year time frame. Doubts over its safety prompted a special investigation by the FDA, which discovered some of the tests were "seriously flawed". A senior FDA toxicologist told a Congressional committee: **"At least one test has established beyond any reasonable doubt that aspartame is capable of producing brain tumors in animals."**

We're talking about a substance so toxic that even the corrupt FDA was speaking up about it to Congress!

In 1981 an internal memo from three FDA scientists advised against approval of NutraSweet. That year President Reagan fired the FDA commissioner and gave the job to Dr. Arthur Hull Hayes. Three months later aspartame was cleared for consumer use.

It was originally approved for dry goods on July 26, 1974, but objections filed by neuroscience researcher Dr. John W. Olney and consumer attorney James Turner in August 1974 as well as investigations of G.D. Searle's research practices caused the FDA to put approval of aspartame on hold on December 5, 1974. Aspartame was finally approved for dry goods in 1981 and for carbonated beverages in 1983. In 1985, biofood engineering giant **Monsanto** (remember that name) purchased G.D. Searle. We're going to discuss Monsanto again here in a couple of chapters.

According to researchers and physicians studying its adverse effects, aspartame accounts for over **75 percent** of the adverse reactions to food additives reported to the FDA. Many of these reactions are very serious including seizures and death. A few of the **90** different documented symptoms and side effects listed in the report as being caused by aspartame include: Headaches/migraines, dizziness, seizures, nausea, numbness, muscle spasms, weight gain, rashes, depression, fatigue, irritability, tachycardia, insomnia, vision problems, hearing loss, heart palpitations, breathing difficulties, anxiety attacks, slurred speech, loss of taste, tinnitus, vertigo, memory loss, and joint pain. The following chronic illnesses can be triggered or worsened by ingesting of aspartame: Brain tumors, multiple sclerosis, epilepsy, chronic fatigue syndrome, Parkinson's disease, Alzheimer's, mental retardation, lymphoma, birth defects, fibromyalgia, and diabetes.

Aspartame is a compound made up of three separate chemicals: aspartic acid, phenylalanine, and methanol. **These compounds individually are toxic, let alone combined.** It is absolute madness that this is allowed into our foods, foods your kids eat every day. Do you like giving your kids poison to drink in their water and poison to eat in their food? That is exactly what you're doing.

Let's take a look at each one of these 3 components of Aspartame a little more in depth, shall we?

Dr. Russell L. Blaylock, a professor of neurosurgery at the Medical University of Mississippi, put together a book thoroughly detailing the damage that is caused by the ingestion of excessive aspartic acid from aspartame. Blaylock makes use of almost 500 scientific references to show how excess free excitatory amino acids such as aspartic acid and glutamic acid (about 99 percent of monosodium glutamate (MSG) is glutamic acid) in our food supply are causing serious chronic neurological disorders and a host of other acute symptoms.

Aspartic acid acts as a neurotransmitter in the brain by speeding up the transmission of information from neuron to neuron. Too much aspartic acid in the brain kills certain neurons by allowing the influx of too much calcium into the cells. This influx triggers excessive amounts of free radicals, which kill the cells. The neural cell damage that can be caused by excessive aspartic acid is why it is referred to as an "excitotoxin." It literally "excites" or stimulates the neural cells to death.

Aspartic acid is an amino acid. Taken in its free form (unbound to proteins) it significantly raises the blood plasma level of aspartic acid. The excess aspartic acid in the blood plasma shortly after ingesting aspartame leads to a high level of those neurotransmitters in certain areas of the brain.

The excess aspartic acid slowly begins to destroy neurons. The large majority (75 percent or more) of neural cells in a particular area of the brain are killed before any clinical symptoms of a chronic illness are noticed, and by then the damage has been done. A few of the many chronic illnesses that have been shown to be contributed to by long-term exposure to excitatory aspartic acid damage include Multiple Sclerosis, memory loss, hormonal problems, hearing loss, epilepsy, Alzheimer's disease, Parkinson disease, hypoglycemia, AIDS, dementia, neuroendocrine disorders, brain lesions, and a host of other problems, **and this is just from ONE of the THREE components of aspartame.**

The second component of aspartame that attacks your health is Phenylalanine. Phenylalanine is an amino acid normally found in the brain. Persons with the genetic disorder phenylketonuria (PKU) cannot metabolize phenylalanine. This leads to dangerously high levels of phenylalanine in the brain, sometimes lethal. It has been shown that ingesting aspartame, especially along with carbohydrates, can lead to excess levels of phenylalanine in the brain even in persons who do not have PKU.

This is not just a theory, as many people who have eaten large amounts of aspartame over a long period of time and do not have PKU have been shown to have excessive levels of phenylalanine in the blood. Excessive levels of phenylalanine in the brain can cause the levels of seratonin in the brain to decrease, leading to emotional disorders such as **depression**. It was shown in human testing that phenylalanine levels of the blood were increased significantly in human subjects who chronically used aspartame.

Even a single use of aspartame raises the blood phenylalanine levels. In his testimony before the U.S. Congress, Dr. Louis J. Elsas showed that high blood phenylalanine can be concentrated in parts of the brain and is especially dangerous for infants and fetuses. **He also showed conclusively that phenylalanine is metabolized much more efficiently by the rodents used in the clinical experiments required by the FDA to get approval than by the humans who would end up ingesting it as consumers.**

One account of a case of extremely high phenylalanine levels caused by aspartame was recently published in the *"Wednesday Journal"* in an article titled "An Aspartame Nightmare". A man named John Cook was drinking six to eight diet drinks every day. His symptoms started out as memory loss and frequent headaches. He began to crave more aspartame-sweetened drinks. His condition deteriorated so much that he experienced wide mood swings and violent rages. Even though he did not suffer from PKU, a blood test revealed a phenylalanine level of 80 mg/dl. He also showed abnormal brain function and brain damage. After he kicked his aspartame habit, his symptoms improved dramatically.

The third component of the 3-pronged spear that is aspartame is Methanol. Methanol, commonly known as wood alcohol, is a deadly poison.

Methanol is synthesized from aspartame when it is heated to above 86 degrees Fahrenheit, which of course happens when it enters your body, which is 98.6 degrees. This also occurs when an aspartame-containing product is heated, such as the preparation calls for in sugar-free, aspartame-laced Jell-O, or when used in cooking of any manner.

Methanol breaks down into formic acid and formaldehyde in the body---not good stuff in other words. Formaldehyde is the deadly neurotoxin we talked about a little while ago that is in a large number of building materials these days.

An EPA assessment of methanol states that methanol **"is considered a cumulative poison due to the low rate of excretion once it is absorbed. In the body, methanol is oxidized to formaldehyde and formic acid; both of these metabolites are toxic."** The EPA recommends a **limit** of consumption of 7.8 mg/day. A one-liter aspartame-sweetened soft drink beverage contains about **56 mg of methanol**. Heavy users of aspartame-containing products consume as much as 250 mg of methanol daily or **32 times the EPA "safe daily limit"**.

Symptoms from methanol poisoning include headaches, ear buzzing, dizziness, nausea, gastrointestinal disturbances, weakness, vertigo, chills, memory lapses, numbness and shooting pains in the extremities, behavioral disturbances, and neuritis. The most well known problems from methanol poisoning are vision problems including misty vision, progressive contraction of visual fields, blurring of vision, obscuration of vision, retinal damage, and blindness. Formaldehyde is a known carcinogen, causes retinal damage, interferes with DNA replication and causes birth defects.

Due to the lack of a couple of key enzymes, humans are many times more sensitive to the toxic effects of methanol than animals. Therefore, tests of aspartame or methanol on animals do not accurately reflect the danger for humans. As pointed out by Dr. Woodrow C. Monte, director of the food science and nutrition laboratory at Arizona State University, **"There are no human or mammalian studies to evaluate the possible mutagenic, teratogenic or carcinogenic effects of chronic administration of methyl alcohol."**

He was so concerned about the unresolved safety issues that he filed suit with the FDA requesting a hearing to address these issues. He asked the FDA to **"slow down on this soft drink issue long enough to answer some of the important questions. It's not fair that you are leaving the full burden of proof on the few of us who are concerned and have such limited resources. You must remember that you are the American public's last defense. Once you allow usage (of aspartame) there is literally nothing I or my colleagues can do to reverse the course. Aspartame will then join saccharin, the sulfiting agents, and God knows how many other questionable compounds enjoined to insult the human constitution with governmental approval."**

Shortly thereafter, the Commissioner of the FDA, Arthur Hull Hayes, Jr., approved the use of aspartame in carbonated beverages. **He then left for a lucrative position with G.D. Searle's public relations firm, aka the company that was manufacturing Aspartame at the time!**

The troops of Desert Storm were "treated" to large amounts of aspartame-sweetened beverages. Many of them returned home with numerous disorders similar to what has been seen in persons who have been chemically poisoned by formaldehyde.

In a 1993 act that can only be described as diabolical, the FDA approved aspartame as an ingredient in numerous food items that would **always** be heated to above 86 degrees Fahrenheit as part of the preparation process, such as diet or low-cal TV dinners.

These are the three components of aspartame. And now for the icing on the aspartame cake, the **byproduct** of aspartame metabolism in the body: DKP (diketopiperazine)

The presence of DKP is the end result of the chemical reactions the body goes through while breaking down the poisonous aspartame. DKP has been implicated in the occurrence of brain tumors, among other health concerns.

G.D. Searle conducted animal experiments on the safety of DKP. The FDA found numerous experimental errors occurred, including **"clerical errors, mixed-up animals, animals not getting drugs they were supposed to get, pathological specimens lost because of improper handling."**

Aspartame is a neurotoxin and also classified as an "excitotoxin", and is addicting on many levels. By the time you have a diet soda and a piece of chewing gum in the morning, another diet soda, gum, and a low-carb processed lunch at noon, you easily may have just ingested five doses of man-made poison, and you've still got over half your day to go, not to mention the fact that the diet sodas were probably made with fluoride-spiked water.

Chapter 7/L

MONOSODIUM GLUTAMATE

Yet another way the unknowing masses have their physical and mental health compromised is through rampant use by international corporations of a neurotoxin/excitotoxin called Monosodium Glutamate, or MSG. MSG contributes directly to obesity, hypertension, and a host of other health problems such as seizures, ADD/ADHD, heart palpitations, tremors, and many other symptoms that are harmful and even fatal.

Think about this now: that handful of MSG-laden Doritos, Cheetos, or similar snack chips you are putting in your kids' lunches every day **is probably the cause of their diagnosed ADD/ADHD** for which you are now giving them **another poison**, Ritalin, to combat symptoms while not removing the original source of the problem, the chemical-laden chips.

MSG started out innocently enough, but now it is added to thousands of food products to not only make them taste better, but to get you literally addicted to them and boost the multinational corporations' bottom line.

For thousands of years kombu and other seaweeds have been added to foods in Japan to enhance flavor. In 1908 a Japanese scientist discovered that the active ingredient in kombu is glutamic acid and from there the use of its sodium salt, monosodium glutamate, began in Japan. During the Second World War, American quartermasters came to the realization that Japanese army rations tasted great. Following the war, they introduced monosodium glutamate, the flavor enhancing excitotoxin in the Japanese rations, to the food industry and the world-wide use of processed, free glutamic acid began to explode---much to the detriment of mankind.

The multinational corporations have found that manufactured free glutamic acid, chiefly in the form of monosodium glutamate (MSG), but also found in hydrolyzed vegetable proteins, etc., when added to our processed foods, makes the blandest, cheapest, and most-unhealthy foods taste wonderful. By putting MSG in as much of the processed food as they can, it allows them to use cheaper ingredients in an increasingly competitive world.

Since MSG is cheap and enhances so wonderfully the flavor of bland and tasteless foods, such as many low-fat and vegetarian foods, manufacturers are eager to go on using it and do not want the public to realize any of the inherent dangers. Not only does it make bland ingredients taste better, the MSG actually gets you "high"---making the food you eat that contains it addicting. Why is it so hard to eat just a few Doritos or Cheetos? They are chock full of MSG, and this is a fact.

Glutamic acid is a neurotransmitter that excites more than our taste buds. It stimulates the neurons in our brain. This electrical charging of neurons is what makes foods with MSG or other substances that naturally contain MSG not only taste good, but make us feel good. Unfortunately however, the free glutamic acid can cause problems in many people and the side effects of MSG consumption are downright dangerous.

The risk to infants, children, pregnant women, the elderly and persons with certain chronic health problems from excitotoxins are great. Even the Federation of American Societies for Experimental Biology (FASEB), which usually understates problems and typically mimics the FDA party-line, recently stated in a review that:

> "It is prudent to avoid the use of dietary supplements of L-glutamic acid by pregnant women, infants, and children. The existence of evidence of potential endocrine responses, i.e., elevated cortisol and prolactin, and differential responses between males and females, would also suggest a neuroendocrine link and that supplemental L-glutamic acid should be avoided by women of childbearing age and individuals with affective disorders."

Because there was so much concern about MSG, the FDA actually commissioned a study to be conducted by FASEB. The study resulted in a 350 page report completed on July 31, 1995. The research determined that MSG consumption can result in the following side-effects: elevated heart rate, extreme rise or drop in blood pressure, angina, circulatory problems, muscular swelling, joint pain/stiffness, neurological problems, depression, dizziness, disorientation, anxiety, hyperactivity in children, seizures, sciatica, migraines, gastrointestinal issues, IBS, respiratory problems, and the list goes on and on.

So why doesn't the FDA require warning labels on foods with MSG in them? For the same reason that there are none on aspartame, and the same reason there is fluoride in the water, and mercury in the vaccines, etc. etc. ad naseum. We have in the United States today a completely corrupted federal government, completely taken over by the money power generated by the Illuminati-owned Federal Reserve and unabashedly pushing the agenda of the Great Plan.

Glutamic acid, the active component in MSG, is also **hidden** in ingredients under about 40 different names.

These **ALWAYS** contain MSG---just to warn you---so if you see any of these on the ingredients of a particular product, you know it contains this dangerous excitotoxin: Glutamate, Monosodium glutamate, Monopotassium glutamate, Glutamic acid, Calcium caseinate, Gelatin, Textured protein, Hydrolyzed protein (any protein that is hydrolyzed), Yeast extract, Yeast food, Autolyzed yeast, Yeast nutrient.

These **OFTEN** contain MSG or **create** MSG during processing: Artificial flavors and flavoring, natural flavors and flavoring, natural pork flavoring, bouillon, natural beef flavoring, stock, natural chicken flavoring, broth, malt flavoring, barley malt, malt extract, seasonings (the word "seasonings"), carrageenan, soy sauce, soy sauce extract, soy protein, soy protein concentrate, soy protein isolate, pectin, maltodextrin, whey protein, whey protein isolate, whey protein concentrate, anything protein fortified, protease, protease enzymes, anything enzyme modified, enzymes, anything ultra-pasteurized, anything fermented.

So. MSG is an excitotoxin that is addicting. It literally gives your body a rush. Next time you reach for those Cheetos, Doritos, or virtually any other "snack food", check the ingredients for MSG. You might see the real reason they are betting you that you "can't eat just one" or "Once you pop, you can't stop".

You literally **can't**....

Chapter 7/M

MISC. DRUGS, ETC.

Many, many, MANY drugs have proliferated in our society since the 1960's, most of them legal with a prescription, and many of them detrimental to our society. I could certainly go on for pages and pages about all the various legal "recreational" drugs and what they do, but you know they are there. You know they are bad for us. You know they are addictive and damaging to the individual, the family, and to society at large.

These days, prescription painkillers are fast supplanting "illegal" drugs as the go-to drug-of-choice for young people. Easy to acquire and cheap, more people are killed by prescription drugs than illegal drugs. Check the local recovery hospitals and they are filled with the ranks of oxycodone addicts.

Not only are these tiny pills readily available to our youth, they are often used by the unknowing masses, both young and old, in combination with **alcohol**. This has a disastrous two-fold effect. The first is that the narcotic-based pills magnify the alcohol high to the point it can easily kill you, whether it be in a car wreck or flat out putting you to sleep forever.

The second and even worse effect is that most of the painkillers are in the form of a combo-drug, combining the narcotic oxycodone with **acetaminophen** for a better painkilling effect.

I don't know how many people I've come across in my life and warned once I found out that they had a prescription for Vicodin, Percocet, or any other drug cocktail where some form of opiate is combined with acetaminophen. If you take these concoctions that contain acetaminophen, which also goes by the brand name Tylenol, and consume alcohol of any quantity, the acetaminophen reacts with the alcohol and **turns into deadly poison for your liver**. This is why most liver transplants are needed: not from years of alcohol abuse, but from a single/multiple use combining alcohol and acetaminophen. It absolutely **obliterates** your liver.

There should be a huge warning on the fronts of the Tylenol bottles to alert the public to this fact. Do you think it will ever get done? It would need FDA approval of course. Who has the bigger lobby when it comes down to it? Humanity, or the mega-pharmaceutical companies with the FDA in their pocket?

How about the fact that over 5,000,000 children are diagnosed with ADHD every year in our country and prescribed Ritalin or a similar drug? The reason these kids are starting to behave like this is because they are bombarded with poisons from all sides from the time of infancy. Throw in a pre-programmed agenda of degenerate kids TV programs with subliminal messaging and there you have it folks. If parents actually paid attention to what their kids are being exposed to and guarded them from it, whether it be internet porn, or drugs, or fluoridated water, or violent video games, or MSG-laden Cheetos, or corruptive television shows, etc., etc., most of these kids would be fine. All of these things add up and begin to affect people in negative ways, especially kids. This is the real reason we are suddenly seeing kids go crazy with guns and shooting up schools.

What most parents don't seem to realize is that Ritalin is a powerful mind-altering drug, and a potentially addictive one at that. Ritalin is actually a powerful stimulant, with an effect similar to ingesting cocaine. The entire point of prescribing Ritalin is so the body overloads with drug-fueled energy and becomes tired, and then more relaxed. In other words, it slows the kid down by over-energizing and running down his system. What this does is create an easy to brainwash robot for the one world government agenda.

With the Ritalin-zombie crowd safely squared away, the Illuminati are free to take care of the "non-conformists" through flooding our country with alcohol and illegal drugs. Do you know why those beer and liquor companies spend so much money on advertising? If they didn't brainwash you into intentionally putting yourself into a drug-induced stupor, you probably wouldn't. This is why tobacco advertising is illegal today. Society rose up against cigarettes like they should against alcohol, hydrocodone, Ritalin, and all the rest of the BS being foisted upon us.

And then you've got the big guns of brain destruction. Extremely powerful mind altering substances such as heroin, cocaine, meth, LSD and others serve to corrupt your mind, body and soul, allowing demonic influence to come into your life, and I'm speaking from experience here. Even marijuana now days has literally been engineered to be hundreds of times more powerful than what our parents or grandparents were smoking in the 60's. The illegal import and domestic manufacture of these drugs by both Mafia and CIA operatives goes a long ways towards funding underground "black ops", which is code for doing the bidding of the Illuminati. Always remember, the Mafia's vast drug cartels are under Illuminati control via their founder, Giuseppe Mazzini.

The United Nations Office for Drug Control and Crime Prevention generally describes the production, trafficking and sales of illicit drugs as a **$400-billion-a-year industry**. It's like paying them to dumb us down to make it easier for them to enslave us. Literally.

Chapter 7/N

GMO FOODS

This chapter was a quick add-on as I was wrapping this book up, so I'm going to keep it very short, but I felt it was too important to leave out until we talked again as this is a ticking time bomb in people's stomachs.

It is my opinion that it will be proven in a few years that eating GMO (genetically modified) foods will be comparable to smoking in terms of the average number of people who get cancer and die from ingesting them, which is nearly the entire country. You need to be very aware that right now I guarantee you are eating GMO foods and had no clue. Nearly the entire food supply in the United States has been infected with GMO food products. Even if you shop at Whole Foods or other "organic" food stores, it was independently found by the group Organic Spies that 20-30% of the food at Whole Foods contained GMO products. GMO foods are one of if not the chief reason for the explosion in the organic foods movement. We're going to quickly talk about corn and corn products in the USA for **one**, **single** example.

Europe is moving right now to ban GMO corn because it is scientifically proven to be very dangerous to eat, and yet they are still able to keep the Americans in the dark about it through a cooperated media blackout of the issue. I will tell you right now, that most breakfast cereals today are made of GMO corn, and you can't make what they did to it un-GMO, and your body is reacting to digesting something that is literally "unnatural". They tweaked the corn's genetics in a way that the corn now has the power to create "natural" insecticide, making the spraying for bugs unnecessary. This **saves** Mother Earth and kills **you**, and I believe there will be a coming explosion of cancer in the United States from this. Remember, corn is just **one** GMO crop of dozens you are eating right now.

During the 2012 election, Monsanto, who is the chief engineer and producer of GMO seeds, dedicated millions of dollars to fight California's Proposition 47, the GMO labeling bill that would have forced labels on merchandise that contained genetically modified organisms or plant life on food sold in California. Now, why would they be opposed to you knowing if food was GMO or not? **For one thing, it is already in almost the entire food supply right this second and if people suddenly were afraid to eat it, which they damn well better be, they might not want to buy it.** This is an extreme priority to be concerned about. People are feeding their kids Frosted Flakes loaded with corn that triggers the creation of pesticide in their digestive system.

I've witnessed pictures of the rats entered as evidence in Europe to initiate a ban on GMO corn. The good sized white lab rats had gigantic tumors growing all over their bodies. I've been extremely conscious of my family's "corn intake" since then. No more corn on the cob. No more Fritos. Or Cheetos. Or Doritos. Or corn chips of any sort. No more corn-based cereals, which is a huge amount of them. All those tasty chips are GMO corn products loaded with MSG to get you addicted to eating them in huge quantities. Wash all that down with a fluoridated-water-based Aspartame-Diet Coke and you just hit a home run of toxicity in about 15 minutes, all four highly dangerous substances, all ingested in only 15 minutes. No wonder the cancer rate in the U.S. is rising like clockwork: we're literally poisoning ourselves.

GMO foods are spreading whether farmers want them or not. A gust of wind in the right direction will contaminate an entire "organic" crop with GMO plant-generated pollen, effectively turning the organic crop into GMO foods via the genetic chain. This frankenfood issue and where it is going is anybody's guess, but the scientists working on it were concerned enough to create huge "bunkers" to store seeds in Europe and other places around the world in case GMO foods turn out to be too dangerous and need to be eliminated. Maybe you've heard of this "Doomsday Vault". If **they** are concerned this stuff might turn out bad, so shouldn't **you** be?

You probably thought you were doing all the right things, eating right, living right. The whole time you are being loaded with toxic substances. We are being intentionally misled on so much that it just boggles the mind. This is how badly they've got us.

Chapter 8

AND NOW, A WORD FROM THE PRESIDENT:

"The very word secrecy is repugnant in a free and open society; and we are as a people, inherently and historically opposed to secret societies, to secret oaths and secret proceedings. We decided long ago that the dangers of excessive and unwarranted concealment of pertinent facts far outweighed the dangers which are cited to justify it. Even today, there is little value in opposing the threat of a closed society by imitating its arbitrary restrictions. Even today, there is little value in insuring the survival of our nation if our traditions do not survive with it. And there is very grave danger that an announced need for increased security will be seized upon those anxious to expand its meaning to the very limits of official censorship and concealment. That I do not intend to permit to the extent that it is in my control. And no official of my Administration, whether his rank is high or low, civilian or military, should interpret my words here tonight as an excuse to censor the news, to stifle dissent, to cover up our mistakes or to withhold from the press and the public the facts they deserve to know.

For we are opposed around the world by a monolithic and ruthless conspiracy that relies on covert means for expanding its sphere of influence--on infiltration instead of invasion, on subversion instead of elections, on intimidation instead of free choice, on guerrillas by night instead of armies by day. It is a system which has conscripted vast human and material resources into the building of a tightly knit, highly efficient machine that combines military, diplomatic, intelligence, economic, scientific and political operations.

Its preparations are concealed, not published. Its mistakes are buried not headlined. Its dissenters are silenced, not praised. No expenditure is questioned, no rumor is printed, no secret is revealed.

No President should fear public scrutiny of his program. For from that scrutiny comes understanding; and from that understanding comes support or opposition. And both are necessary. I am not asking your newspapers to support the Administration, but I am asking your help in the tremendous task of informing and alerting the American people. For I have complete confidence in the response and dedication of our citizens whenever they are fully informed.

I not only could not stifle controversy among your readers-- I welcome it. This Administration intends to be candid about its errors; for as a wise man once said: "An error does not become a mistake until you refuse to correct it." We intend to accept full responsibility for our errors; and we expect you to point them out when we miss them.

Without debate, without criticism, no Administration and no country can succeed-- and no republic can survive. That is why the Athenian lawmaker Solon decreed it a crime for any citizen to shrink from controversy. And that is why our press was protected by the First (emphasized) Amendment-- the only business in America specifically protected by the Constitution-- not primarily to amuse and entertain, not to emphasize the trivial and sentimental, not to simply "give the public what it wants"--but to inform, to arouse, to reflect, to state our dangers and our opportunities, to indicate our crises and our choices, to lead, mold educate and sometimes even anger public opinion.

This means greater coverage and analysis of international news-- for it is no longer far away and foreign but close at hand and local. It means greater attention to improved understanding of the news as well as improved transmission. And it means, finally, that government at all levels, must meet its obligation to provide you with the fullest possible information outside the narrowest limits of national security...

And so it is to the printing press--to the recorder of mans deeds, the keeper of his conscience, the courier of his news-- that we look for strength and assistance, confident that with your help man will be what he was born to be: free and independent."
-John F. Kennedy

The above speech was made about 4 months after JFK was sworn in as President on April 27, 1961. He spoke the above words at the American Newspaper Publishers Association meeting to warn patriotic Americans about the conspiracy against them by the Illuminati. JFK followed up on this warning by trying to usurp the Federal Reserve. You now know that he was truly the last President we had that was actually looking out for us instead of the Great Plan. Kennedy was moved to do the right thing when he had the power to do it and was killed for it. May God bless him and thank you forever Mr. Kennedy for showing the bravery to stand against evil. The proponents of the Great Plan were the ones responsible for Kennedy's murder.

Chapter 9

WAR, INC.

There is nothing more profitable, nothing more divisive, and nothing more damaging to societies than war.

Upon completion of this book you will come to the realization that nearly all wars perpetrated throughout mankind's history were a direct result of the proponents of the Great Plan trying to further their agenda, and the 20th century was no exception. In fact, the wars of the 20th century can be easily attributed to the actions of the modern day leaders of the Great Plan, the Illuminati.

Again, it would be impossible to encompass reviews of all the great wars and battles of ancient history, so we will just concentrate on what has happened since the modern day proponents of the Great Plan snatched up the reigns with the founding of the New Babylon and the formation of the Illuminati, both not coincidentally in 1776.

We already went over the founding of the New Babylon, aka the United States of America, and how the Illuminati fomented the French Revolution. We briefly went over aspects of the Civil War, but there is more to that also that you need to be informed of, same as World Wars 1 and 2.

Chapter 9/A

THE REPORT FROM IRON MOUNTAIN

Private capital tends to become concentrated in few hands, partly because of competition among the capitalists, and partly because technological development and the increasing division of labor encourage the formation of larger units of production at the expense of the smaller ones. The result of these developments is an oligarchy of private capital, the enormous power of which cannot be effectively checked even by a democratically organized political society. This is true since the members of legislative bodies are selected by political parties, largely financed or otherwise influenced by private capitalists who, for all practical purposes, separate the electorate from the legislature. The consequence is that the representatives of the people do not in fact sufficiently protect the interests of the underprivileged sections of the population. Moreover, under existing conditions, private capitalists inevitably control, directly or indirectly, the main sources of information (press, radio, education). It is thus extremely difficult, and indeed in most cases quite impossible, for the individual citizen to come to objective conclusions and to make intelligent use of his political rights.
-Albert Einstein, just speaking the facts (as usual)

Before we delve into the facts surrounding the **real** reason why there was a civil war in the United States, where our citizens slaughtered each other at the amusement of the Illuminati, we are going to jump forward to the 1960's, when a paper entitled *"The Report From Iron Mountain"* was published in 1967.

The report is basically a summarization and analysis of how wars over the millennia have been used to control and steer societies, and what kinds of actions besides wars needed to be taken by the proponents of the Great Plan in the future to bring the Plan to completion.

Although the details of the origin of the report are intentionally murky, in all probability it was commissioned by Secretary of Defense Robert McNamara during the Kennedy administration and produced by the Hudson Institute, a Tavistock-affiliated think tank, at the base of Iron Mountain in New York. The Hudson Institute was founded and directed by Herman Kahn of the Rand Corporation, with both Kahn and McNamara of course being members of the Council on Foreign Relations, taking marching orders directly from the Illuminati.

The stated purpose of the report was to propose ways to "stabilize society". Now, that all sounds fine and dandy, until you read the report and find the word "stabilize" actually means to facilitate, and the word "society" used synonymously with "global government". The entire purpose of this report was to formulate a new game plane for the Illuminati and their bought-and-paid-for minions to execute.

The gist of the report is that in mankind's past the fabric that held society together was the omnipresent threat of war and tribulation. Mankind needed to be held constantly on the edge of war with either real or imagined enemies. Only during these times would mankind bear the load of an ever-growing, increasingly-authoritarian centralized government controlled by the members of the occult secret societies. In times of peace, man would become resentful of the largesse and intentionally wasteful habits of big government for the benefit of the few pulling the strings.

According to the report, war or threat of war has always been a required condition for a "stabilized society", with stabilized of course meaning under the control of the members of the Great Plan.

These are the report's exact words:

"The war system not only has been essential to the existence of nations as independent political entities, but has been equally

indispensable to their stable political structure. Without it, no government has ever been able to obtain acquiescence in it "legitimacy," or right to rule its society. The possibility of war provides the sense of external necessity without which no government can long remain in power. The historical record reveals one instance after another where the failure of a regime to maintain the credibility of a war threat led to its dissolution, by the forces of private interest, of reactions to social injustice, or of other disintegrative elements. The organization of society or for the possibility of war is its principal political stabilizer....it has enabled societies to maintain necessary class distinction, and it has insured the subordination of the citizens to the state by virtue of the residual war powers inherent in the concept of nationhood."

The report also theorizes that we are approaching a point in the history of man where war may no longer be necessary, as all the pieces were beginning to come together for "everlasting peace" via a one world government.

Per the report's recommendations, all nations are to be disarmed, including the U.S., and will come under the military "protection" of the one world government through the United Nations' one world army. The report explicitly states: **"The word 'peace', as we have used it in the following pages....implies total and general disarmament."**

Under this scenario, independent, sovereign nations will no longer exist and governments will be stripped of any and all means of conducting war or aggression.

The report then goes on to ponder what can take the place of war as a uniting force for society. According to *"The Report from Iron Mountain"*, there can be **NO** substitute for war unless is meets the following three criteria: It must be economically wasteful, it must represent a credible threat of great magnitude, and it must provide a logical excuse for compulsory service to the government.

This is the origination of the "green movement" that is slowly but surely being indoctrinated into the world societies, with the threat of "manmade global warming" being the chief threat. Manmade global warming is a complete fraud, concocted by the New World Order crowd, and we will go over this later.

The report also considers ways in which the public could be preoccupied with trivial activities such that they would not have the time to participate in politics or resistance to their plans. Recreational drugs, rebellious music, trivial television shows such as sitcoms, and pornography were all lined up to be launched against humanity---and they were---but the best way to preoccupy humans and especially the men who might want to resist the march towards one world government, was to revisit the blood games of the ancient Roman Empire. Blood games are competitive events between individuals or teams that are sufficiently violent in nature to enable the spectators to satisfy their frustrations with how society was going down the tubes.

Enter professional sports in the United States.........

This is when pro basketball, football, baseball, and hockey were all turned into mainstays of the Mainstream Media---shortly after this report was issued in 1967---along with rampant drug use, "hippie" music and the hippie movement, television game shows, sitcoms, pornographic magazines and movies, and the like. All of these new and exciting activities hypnotized the public into a coma, for lack of a better term. Instead of coming home and reading a book or doing some wholesome family activities---or questioning what was going on with their country and government---families would plop down in front of the idiot box for some wholesale Tavistock-based brainwashing.

The result of this program implemented in the mid to late 60's resulted in the societal excesses displayed in the 70's and beyond. These activities set in motion the downfall of the New Babylon, all by design.

These new and exciting activities were enough to pacify, sedate and distract a large part of the population, but wars were still needed in their opinion---albeit smaller wars thanks to the newfound brain-busying activities---at least until such time that a more credible threat could be foisted upon humanity to take us to the next level of the Great Plan.

Per the report:

"Allegiance requires a cause; a cause requires an enemy. This much is obvious; the critical point is that the enemy that defines

the cause must seem genuinely formidable. Roughly speaking, the presumed power of the "enemy" sufficient to warrant an individual sense of allegiance to a society must be proportionate to the size and complexity of the society. Today, of course, that power must be one of unprecedented magnitude and frightfulness."

Enter the environmental movement...now called the Green Movement. This was hatched at the inaugural Earth Day in 1970, 3 years after the report was issued. The first Earth Day paved the way for the UN's Earth Summit in Stockholm in 1972, chaired by New World Order proponent to the extreme, occultist Maurice Strong. Strong is widely regarded as the father of the modern environmental movement, more on him in a bit.

This is all you need to know for now about this. Again, just trying to tell you as briefly as possible the general topics you need to be concerned about and look into for yourself while you can. However, I will explain soon how they are going to use the environmental movement via the Global Warming hoax to crush the United States economy and help bring the entire world under their Global Government. That is, of course, if the coming dollar collapse fails to accomplish this.

"Although war is "used" as an instrument of national and social policy, the fact that a society is organized for any degree of readiness for war supersedes its political and economic structure. War itself is the basic social system, within which other secondary modes of social organization conflict or conspire. It is the system which has governed most human societies of record, as it is today. The precedence of a society's war-making potential over its other characteristics is not the result of the "threat" presumed to exist at any one time from other societies. This is the reverse of the basic situation; "threats" against the "national interest" are usually created or accelerated to meet the changing needs of the war system. Wars are not "caused" by international conflicts of interest... war-making societies require - and thus bring about - such conflicts. The capacity of a nation to make war expresses the greatest social power it can exercise; war-making, active or

contemplated, is a matter of life and death on the greatest scale subject to social control. It should therefore hardly be surprising that the military institutions in each society claim its highest priorities."
-*Report from Iron Mountain, 1967*

Chapter 9/B

AMERICAN CIVIL WAR

"I see in the near future a crisis approaching that unnerves me and causes me to tremble for the safety of my country. As a result of the war, corporations have been enthroned and an era of corruption in high places will follow, and the money power of the country will endeavor to prolong its reign by working upon the prejudices of the people until all wealth is aggregated in a few hands, and the Republic is destroyed. I feel at this moment more anxiety for the safety of my country than ever before, even in the midst of war."
-Abraham Lincoln

"The division of the United States into federations of equal force was decided long before the Civil War by the high financial powers of Europe. These bankers were afraid that the United States, if they remained in one block and as one nation, would attain economic and financial independence, which would upset their financial domination over the world. The voice of the Rothschilds prevailed... Therefore they sent their emissaries into the field to exploit the question of slavery and to open an abyss between the two sections of the Union."
- German chancellor Otto von Bismarck

A strategic opportunity dropped into the Illuminati's lap when social divisions over slavery began to develop as the United States grew more powerful. They fanned the sparks of this issue knowing that they could take control of America through debt if they could divide the North and the South ideologically and then prod both sides into a long and costly civil war---which they would of course be funding from both sides.

"It is not to be doubted, I know with absolute certainty, that the separation of the United States into two federations of equal powers had been decided upon well in advance of the Civil War by the top financial power of Europe."
- Otto von Bismarck

Four years before the war in 1857, the Rothschilds decided their Paris bank would support the South, represented by Sen. John Slidell, a Rothschild agent, from Louisiana; while the British branch would support the North, represented by August Belmont (Schoenberg), another Rothschild "employee", from New York.

The plan was to bankroll, at very high interest rates, the huge war debts that were anticipated, using that debt to blackmail both sides into accepting an Illuminati-owned central bank. Propaganda by their minions pushed the issue of slavery to the public forefront, but the actual purpose behind the war **without question** was to drive both sides to accept a privately-owned central bank---just like we have today.

As in pre-Revolution France, Illuminati agitators were sent to work in the North and the South at all levels of government and throughout society to exploit the divisive issues threatening the nation. In the years following our independence, a close business relationship had developed between the cotton growing aristocracy in the South and the cotton manufacturers in England. The Illuminati decided that this business connection was the United States Achilles Heel.

Their carefully sown and nurtured propaganda developed into open rebellion and resulted in the secession of South Carolina on December 29, 1860. Within weeks another six states joined the conspiracy against the Union, and broke away to form the Confederate States of America, with Jefferson Davis as President.

Even members of then-President Buchanan's Cabinet conspired to destroy the Union by damaging the public credit and working to bankrupt the nation. Buchanan claimed to deplore secession but took no steps to check it, even when a U.S. ship was fired upon by South Carolina shore batteries.

Shortly thereafter Abraham Lincoln became President, being inaugurated on March 4, 1861. Lincoln immediately ordered a blockade on Southern ports, to cut off supplies that were pouring in from Europe. The "official" date for the start of the Civil War is given as April 12, 1861, when Union-controlled Fort Sumter in South Carolina was bombarded by the Confederates, but it obviously began at a much earlier date.

This quote from earlier in the book is worth repeating:

> *"The money powers prey upon the nation in times of peace and conspire against it in times of adversity. It is more despotic than a monarchy, more insolent than autocracy, and more selfish than bureaucracy. It denounces as public enemies all who question its methods or throw light upon its crimes. I have two great enemies, the Southern Army in front of me and the bankers in the rear. Of the two, the one at my rear is my greatest foe."*
> *-Abraham Lincoln*

Lincoln said he feared the money powers (Illuminati) more than the Confederacy, and with good reason as you now know.

After the war, realizing the Union's real enemy was Rothschild and the Illuminati gang, President Lincoln, emphasizing the Constitution, made it crystal clear to Congress that:

> *"The privilege of creating and issuing money is... the supreme prerogative of government!"*

Abraham Lincoln, although never taught in our public schools, fought a legendary battle with the Rothschild bankers after the beginning of the Civil War over who was going to finance the war from the Union side. Lincoln ultimately followed the Constitution and issued money through the federal government---allowing him the financial power to win the war and keep the country intact. As you now know, this is the real reason he was assassinated. If he would have lived, the greenbacks he issued would have become the norm for the United States, and the Great Plan would have been derailed.

For this and other acts of patriotism, Lincoln was shot down in cold-blood by Illuminati agent and alleged 33rd degree Freemason John Wilkes Booth on April 14, 1865, just five days after Lee surrendered to Grant at Appomattox Court House, Virginia.

Booth's grand-daughter, Izola Forrester, states in her 1937 book *"This One Mad Act"* that Lincoln's assassin had been in close contact with mysterious Europeans prior to the slaying, and had made at least one trip to Europe. Following the killing, Booth was allegedly whisked away to safety by members of the Freemasonic Knights of the Golden Circle. According to Forrester, Booth lived for many years following his disappearance, safely hidden away in Europe by the Illuminati.

Truth to be told of the Civil War, and again, this is suppressed history you are not supposed to know about, **the real cause of the Civil War had little-to-nothing to do with freeing the slaves, and everything to do with fighting off the Illuminati and saving the Union**, and it is a FACT that Lincoln made the following two quotes:

"I have no purpose to introduce political and social equality between the white and black races. There is a physical difference between the two, which, in my judgment, will probably forever forbid their living together upon the footing of perfect equality; and inasmuch as it becomes a necessity that there must be a difference, I ... am in favor of the race to which I belong having the superior position."

And:

"My paramount object in this struggle is to save the Union, and is not either to save or to destroy slavery. If I could save the Union without freeing any slave, I would do it; and if I could save it by freeing all the slaves, I would do it; and if I could do it by freeing some and leaving others alone, I would also do that.."

624,511 American citizens died in the Civil War, and 475,881 soldiers were wounded because of the Luciferians attempting to further the Great Plan.

"The death of Lincoln was a disaster for Christendom. There was no man in the United States great enough to wear his boots and the bankers went anew to grab the riches. I fear that foreign bankers with their craftiness and tortuous tricks will entirely control the exuberant riches of America and use it to systematically corrupt modern civilization. They will not hesitate to plunge the whole of Christendom into wars and chaos in order that the earth should become their inheritance."

- German chancellor Otto von Bismarck

Unfortunately, the proponents of the Great Plan were just warming up for something much bigger.....the first truly World War.

Chapter 9/C

WORLD WAR I

"The government of the Western nations, whether monarchical or republican, had passed into the invisible hands of a plutocracy, international in power and grasp. It was, I venture to suggest, this semi occult power which....pushed the mass of the American people into the cauldron of World War I."
-British military historian Major General J.F.C. Fuller, 1941

WWI was planned and fought with the main goal of uniting all nations under a single world authority in the bloody aftermath, and the secondary goal of making money off the loans needed to finance the war, further putting the Western nations on the hook to the Illuminati bankers.

Remember now, throughout history wars are always **started** by the top level of the ruling class, which today is the Illuminati and their puppets. This includes financial oligarchs, major politicians, presidents, major advisers, and wealthy businessmen. Wars are always **fought** by the middle class and lower class, which are forced into service by the governments the Illuminati control.

According to the Great Plan-sterilized "history" books, World War One was started as the result of the assassination of Archduke Franz Ferdinand, the heir to the Austro-Hungarian throne, on June 28, 1914.

The assassination of Franz Ferdinand was what is called a "false flag event", whereby a pre-planned situation occurs in order to trigger another situation that was wanted before the first even took place.

Norman Dodd, former director and chief investigator of the Committee to Investigate Tax Exempt Foundations of the U.S. House of Representatives---the "Reece Commission" we already went over---testified that the Committee had studied the minutes of the Carnegie Endowment for International Peace as part of the Reece Commission's investigation.

The Committee stated: **"The trustees of the Foundation brought up a single question. If it is desirable to alter the life of an entire people, is there any means more efficient than war.... They discussed this question... for a year and came up with an answer: There are no known means more efficient than war, assuming the objective is altering the life of an entire people. That leads them to a question: How do we involve the United States in a war."**

Remember, this idea of taking the U.S. to war is coming from a tax-free foundation supposedly committed to peace, the Carnegie Endowment for *International Peace*, and the betterment of mankind. This quote was from **1909,** five years *before* the "official" beginning of WW I.

It was around the time of this statement in the early 1900's that Illuminati bankers financed and promoted an arms race in Britain, France, Russia, Germany, and America in preparation for the coming World War.

The murder of Franz Ferdinand was enough to excuse the start the war in Europe and it was quickly escalated by Illuminati minions, but the United States had largely followed a policy of non-intervention, and the citizens of the U.S. wanted nothing to do with the events unfolding in Europe. In fact, President Woodrow Wilson, the one who signed the Federal Reserve into law, had as his campaign motto for his re-election in 1916, **"He kept us out of the war"**, when in fact his Illuminati puppet masters and handlers desperately wanted to entangle the U.S. in the pre-planned war.

Enter yet another false flag event......

The false flag attack is based upon the Hegelian Dialectic, which consists of problem-reaction-solution. The Luciferian entities running the government (Illuminati) present the problem in the form of a terror attack against that government's own citizens. The reaction then comes from the terrified public demanding governmental action. The solution to the initial problem, which they created to start with, is presented to the unknowing masses as the best and only response to the initial problem, further placing them under governmental (Illuminati/Great Plan/ New World Order) control.

False flag operations are designed to deceive the public in such a way that the operations appear as if they are being carried out by other entities. The name is derived from the military concept of flying false colors; that is, flying the flag of the enemy combatants.

The term comes from the old days of wooden ships, when one ship would hang the flag of its enemy in order to get close enough to execute an all-out ambush with cannon fire. Because the enemy's flag was hung instead of the flag of the real country of the attacking ship, it was called a "false flag" attack.

Citizens of the U.S. were successfully fooled via false flag to enter the war in 1917 by a series of diabolical efforts, culminating in the sinking of an enormous passenger ship named the Lusitania. President Woodrow Wilson was directly involved in the deceptions and formally sanctioned the U.S. participation in the war in a secret agreement with England on March 9, 1916. We know about this agreement because it was leaked and confirmed by Sir Edward Grey, Ambassador Walter Hines Page, C. Hartley Grattan, and Colonel Edward Mandell House.

In the documented conversation between alleged 33rd degree Freemason Colonel House, President Wilson's Rothschild-appointed adviser, and Sir Edward Grey, the Foreign Secretary of England regarding how to get America into the war, Grey inquired:

"What will Americans do if Germans sink an ocean liner with American passengers on board?"

House responded:

"I believe that a flame of indignation would sweep the United States and that by itself would be sufficient to carry us into war."

Winston Churchill and Woodrow Wilson, in an operation financed by the Illuminati bankers, arranged for the shipment of weapons on the Lusitania in May of 1915. The Lusitania luxury ocean liner was owned by the Cunard Steamship Line Shipping Company and officially part of the British auxiliary navy. The ship's owners were paid 218,000 British pounds a year to keep the Lusitania on the government payroll. As a pseudo-naval ship, the Lusitania was under orders from the British Admiralty to ram any German ship seeking to inspect her cargo. In 1915 it was against U.S. law to put weapons on a passenger ship traveling from the U.S. to England or Germany.

Three German spies attempted to confirm that the 90 tons of unrefrigerated butter destined for a British naval base were weapons and ammunition. The spies were detained on the ship. The weapons loaded on the Lusitania were seen by the German dock workers and reported to the German embassy. In order to warn Americans about the weapons shipment and the perils of traveling on a "military" vessel, the Imperial German Embassy attempted to place an advertisement in 50 East Coast newspapers. The ads were printed with a date of April 22, 1915, but the US State Department blocked all the ads except one. George Viereck, the man who placed the ads for the embassy, protested to the State Department on April 26 that the ads were blocked. Viereck met with Secretary of State William Jennings Bryan and produced copies of the Lusitania›s supplementary manifests. Bryan, impressed by the evidence that the Lusitania had carried weapons, cleared publication of the warning. Someone higher than the Secretary of State, likely Colonel House and/ or President Wilson, overruled Bryan. Nonetheless one ad slipped past the State Department censorship and into the history books.

The warning read: **"NOTICE! Travelers intending to embark on the Atlantic voyage are reminded that a state of war exists between Germany and her allies and Great Britain and her allies; that the zone of war includes the waters adjacent to the British Isles; that, in accordance with formal notice given by the Imperial German Government, vessels flying the flag of Great Britain, or any of her allies, are liable to destruction in those waters and that travelers sailing in the war zone on ships of Great Britain or her allies do so at their own risk. IMPERIAL GERMAN EMBASSY WASHINGTON, D.C., APRIL 22, 1915."**

Captain Dow, the Lusitania captain immediately before Captain Turner, resigned on March 8, 1915 because he was no longer willing "to carry the responsibility of mixing passengers with munitions or contraband." Captain Dow had a close call just two days earlier and was aware the rules of naval warfare changed in October 1914 when Churchill issued orders that those British merchant ships that carried munitions or contraband must ram U-boats. Prior to this change by Churchill, both

England and Germany adhered to "Cruiser Rules". Cruiser Rules enabled crews and passengers to escape in lifeboats before being fired on. With the new Churchill "ram rules", the German U-boats could no longer surface to issue a warning and fired while submerged.

Here, Churchill candidly states his goal of dragging the U.S. into the war:

> *"The first British countermove, made on my responsibility... was to deter the Germans from surface attack. The submerged U-boat had to rely increasingly on underwater attack and thus ran the greater risk of mistaking neutral for British ships and of drowning neutral crews and thus embroiling Germany with other Great Powers."*

The above combined with the next Churchill quote speaks volumes about what really happened and why:

> *"There are many kinds of maneuvers in war...There are maneuvers in time, in diplomacy, in mechanics, in psychology; all of which are removed from the battlefield, but react often decisively upon it...The maneuver which brings an ally into the field is as serviceable as that which wins a great battle."*

On May 7, 1915, the Lusitania slowed to 75% speed hoping the English escort vessel the Juno would arrive. Unknown to Captain Turner of the Lusitania, Winston Churchill had ordered the Juno to return to port. Churchill's order left the Lusitania alone and unprotected in a known area with German U-boats. To really slam the point home, England had broken the German communications code on December 14, 1914. The level of detail known by the British Admiralty was so precise that U boat names and general locations were known and used against the doomed Lusitania and her passengers.

The Lusitania was torpedoed on May 7, 1915, and 1,198 innocent souls were lost in order to bring the United States into the war against Germany. All according to plan......

The official German response was that the Lusitania was acting as a war ship by transporting armaments that would be used to kill German soldiers, which is exactly true. This of course was vehemently denied by the State Department.

The United States entered the war against Germany, and the rest is history as they say.

One of the officers present in the command room in London while the plan for the Lusitania was being cooked up was Commander Joseph Kenworthy, who previously had been called upon by Churchill to submit a paper on what would be the political results of an ocean liner being sunk with American passengers aboard. He left the room in disgust as the plan was unfolding. In 1927 in his book *The Freedom of the Seas*, he states: **"The Lusitania was sent at considerably reduced speed into an area where a U-boat was known to be waiting and with her escorts withdrawn."**

For decades, the British and American governments have denied that there were weapons on the Lusitania. The site of the sinking was declared a protected site, denying divers access. To further frustrate the ability to determine what the Lusitania carried, the Royal Navy, beginning in 1946, repeatedly dropped depth charges on top of the Lusitania as a site for target practice. In 1968, to keep the truth secret, the British Secret Service unsuccessfully attempted to buy the salvage rights to the Lusitania. In 1993 PBS Online visited the wreck and found previous visitors had tampered with the evidence. While the British governments aggressively worked to distort the truth, weapons were confirmed in July 2006 when Victor Quirke of the Cork Sub Aqua Club found 15,000 rounds of .303 bullets in the bow section of the ship, confirming munitions were indeed being transported.

In 1918 World War I ended and in 1919 came the Versailles Peace Conference near Paris. The elite of the Illuminati puppets from Britain and the United States, people like Alfred Milner, Edward Mandel House, and Bernard Baruch were appointed to represent their countries at the meetings which decided how the world would be changed as a result of the war these same people had created.

They decided to impose impossible reparations payments on Germany, so ensuring the collapse of the post-war Weimar Republic amid unbearable economic conditions and thus create the very circumstances that enabled Hitler's rise to power.

While humanity paid the ultimate price with at least 20 million killed, the war industry made a financial killing, as did the Illuminati--who funded both sides....again. No matter who would've won the First World War, the Illuminati would have won and we would have lost.

In the aftermath of the bloody conflict of World War I, the League of Nations, the forerunner to the United Nations, was presented in Versailles as a solution to the horrendous problems that the world had witnessed.

The League of Nations primary function was to keep peace in the world through ordered relationships among the member nations. The only problem with this is that too many nations saw its authority as dangerous to their own countries sovereignty---and rightly so---and refused to join. It was subsequently disbanded, and the Great Plan was dead in the water having failed to spark a one world governmental body they could advance to total control over the world. The Illuminati and their minions immediately went back to work on bringing about the next global conflict, World War II.

In the next chapter, you are going to see how the United States was again tricked into war using a false flag operation, with the full knowledge and approval of President FDR.

Chapter 9/D

WORLD WAR II

"In politics, nothing happens by accident. If it happened, you can bet it was planned that way."
-U.S. President Franklin D. Roosevelt

"The question was how should we maneuver them [Japan] into firing the first shot... it was desirable to make sure the Japanese be the ones to do this so that there should remain no doubt as to who were the aggressors."
-Henry Stimson, US Secretary of War prior to WWII, Nov. 25, 1941 (14 days before the bombing of Pearl Harbor)

Although the following was not conducted by the United States government, it is important to go over for the fact that it is another prime example of a government manipulating public perception. This particular event happened in Germany in the 1930's, and was the false flag operation that installed Illuminati agent Adolph Hitler and his band of Theosophical occultists into power, ultimately leading to World War II.

What the proponents of the Great Plan knew is that the way to gain more power and control over the people is to manufacture a major crisis which makes the people feel insecure and unsafe, and then capitalize on that reaction. After the pre-planned crisis occurs, the "government" then offers to protect the people from this new threat. Problem-Reaction-Solution, aka the Hegelian Dialectic.

Germany was devastated after the First World War, and the Illuminati immediately created and financed the Nazi party beginning in 1919, right after closing out WW I, through the occult Thule Society, of which we already covered. In the phony election of 1932, Hitler and the Nazi party were given large amounts of money by the Illuminati bankers in order to secure a win and their place in Germany's government. The Nazi party "won" the election and Hitler became chancellor of Germany in 1933. The Nazi party seized total power in 1933 after a false flag event, the Reichstag fire.

The Reichstag fire, the pivotal event in the establishment of Nazi Germany, began at 9:14 PM on the night of February 27, 1933, when a Berlin fire station received an alarm that the Reichstag building was burning. The Reichstag was the headquarters of the German parliament, which was Germany's federal government at the time. The fire seemed to have been started in several places, and by the time the police and firemen arrived a huge explosion had set the main Chamber of Deputies in flames. Looking for clues, the police quickly "found" a mentally handicapped man, Marinus van der Lubbe, naked, cowering behind the building. Van der Lubbe was "allegedly" a Dutch insurrectionary council Communist and unemployed bricklayer who had recently arrived in Germany. Most likely he was simply a fall guy to blame the false flag on, someone unable to discern what was really going on.

Adolf Hitler and Hermann Goering arrived soon after and when they were shown Van der Lubbe, Goering immediately declared the fire was set by the Communists and had the party leaders arrested. Hitler took advantage of the situation to declare a state of emergency and encouraged aging president Paul von Hindenburg to sign the Reichstag Fire Decree, abolishing most of the human rights provisions of the 1919 Weimar Republic constitution.

The Nazi party had run on a platform of hysterical anti-Communism, insisting that Germany was on the verge of a Communist revolution, and that the only way to stop the revolution was to pass the Enabling Act. Under this act, the government acquired the authority to pass laws without either parliamentary consent or control, exactly like our Presidents do today in the United States with Presidential Executive Orders. Unprecedentedly, these laws could even deviate from the German Constitution.

The Act effectively eliminated the Reichstag as active players in German politics, and together with the Reichstag Fire Decree, it transformed Hitler's government into a legal dictatorship.

Evidence revealed later showed that the fire was really perpetrated by leaders of the Nazi Party, another false flag attack to further the Great Plan agenda.

After getting their man Hitler into place, the Illuminati bankers financed the massive Nazi military buildup beginning in 1933, setting the stage for the next World War.

So that explains how Hitler got into the driver's seat and got WW II going, but that doesn't explain how **we** got drug into it, so let's get right at it here.

The people of America were war-weary from WWI, and were content to sit on the sidelines and let Europe have it out amongst themselves this go-round. The Illuminati were going to have none of that, as they needed to embroil us in a bloody war to get us to capitulate to their next incarnation of a world governmental body, the coming United Nations. They cooked up an ingenious plan to sucker us in one more time for a shearing.....and to light the fuse on the one world government.

On September 3rd 1939, a U-boat torpedo hit the ocean liner Athenia near Britain with some 1100 passengers, of which 311 were Americans. Sounds like a familiar story.....right? Right. Luckily for the passengers, the sea was calm and *only* 118 people on board lost their lives. This incident wasn't enough to turn American sentiment against the Germans, and the Germans themselves wanted nothing to do with fighting the U.S. and also refused to be provoked by several "American" acts of war. When I say "American" I of course mean what the Illuminati puppets in D.C. were doing to try and incite us to war.

Americans confiscated German merchant ships, and Americans started to support the British with various lend-lease items. United States volunteer pilots joined the RAF and some RAF pilots were in turn trained in the US. The U.S. government gave the British Navy 50 old but usable WW I destroyers and 20 torpedo boats along with tanks, light bombers, fighter aircraft like P-40s and so on. American destroyers also escorted the convoys bound to Britain, and attacked German U-boats whenever they could be located.

In other words, the U.S. government did not maintain a neutral stance towards the growing world war.

Roosevelt and the State Department had gotten their marching orders from the Illuminati, and those orders were to get the United States involved in the war on the side of the allies by any means possible.

Since the Germans weren't biting on going up against the United States, they decided to go after Japan, Germany's ally in the Axis powers of WW II. **U.S. naval intelligence planned and suggested "8 insults", which they felt should bring Japan into war with the United States.** President Roosevelt executed this plan immediately, enraging the Japanese. The most serious one was a total blockade of Japanese oil imports, as agreed between the Americans, British and the Dutch. FDR also declared an all-out embargo against the Japanese and forbade them the use of Panama Canal, impeding Japan's access to Venezuelan oil.

Japan has little natural resources, importing nearly everything they use even today. In other words, we forced their hand into action, appearing as an aggressor in the midst of an ever-escalating world war. The Japanese felt they needed to strike us before we further weakened and attacked them.

Having broken the Japanese encryption codes, Roosevelt's administration knew what was going to happen, when and where, the bombing of Pearl Harbor, but President Roosevelt did not dispatch this information to Hawaii. It was in August, 1940, that the United States broke the Japanese "purple" war-time code. This gave the American government the ability to read and understand all of their recoverable war-time messages. Machines were manufactured to de-code Japan's messages, and they were sent all over the world.....but none were sent to Pearl Harbor.

FDR, knowing the attack was coming months in advance, sent obsolete warships to be bombed in Hawaii as a willing participant of the false flag plan. All the good warships were sent and kept on the mainland, when in fact we should have been maintaining an extremely powerful position in Hawaii.

On December 7, 1941, the Japanese struck at Pearl Harbor, and we immediately declared war on the Axis countries, all according to plan.

Based on the historical evidence, and there is a ton more than I am offering up for you to research, there is no arguing against World War

II being formulated by the Illuminati bankers and their minions. Roosevelt, Churchill, Stalin---they were all alleged 33rd degree Freemasons, and Thule Society member Hitler were all puppets working for the Illuminati. They tried to make a big deal of Hitler being "anti-Mason", but if you aren't in the upper 1% or less of the Freemasons you are just another expendable human to their occult crowd, which encompasses over 99% of unknowing Freemasons today.

At the end of the war, to the "victors" belonged the spoils, and those spoils came in the form of Nazi scientists, geneticists, and weapons engineers and the wealth of research and information they possessed. By all rights most of them should have been sent to prison or worse for the atrocities they contributed to but no, they were instead sent to the New Babylon to become part of our Military Industrial Complex.

The Illuminati literally brought the nerve center of the 3rd Reich to America right after WWII under the top secret Office of Strategic Services (OSS) program called Operation Paperclip, and this is a fact. They were given new identities, new jobs working for the U.S. Defense Department, and shielded from the Nuremburg Trials. Once bleached of their Nazism, the U.S. Government granted the scientists security clearance to work in the United States.

Among the Nazis ferried to America were rocket scientists Wernher von Braun and Arthur Rudolph, the fathers of NASA, and the pioneer of space medicine Hubertus Strughold, each earlier classified by the State Department as a "**menace to the security of the Allied Forces**".

These weren't the only Nazis we brought over here, as an even-more-secret effort to capture German nuclear secrets, equipment and personnel was executed called Operation Alsos.

Ok. That should be enough about World War II to get you pointed in the right direction. Now we need to go over what the proponents of the Great Plan were *chiefly* after all along: the founding of a one world governmental body, known today as the United Nations.

After such a terrible series of events the world had just gone through, the absolute worst atrocities in history, with the Nazi death camps, the incineration of tens of thousands of innocent Japanese civilians through nuclear bombs, and all the rest of the death and destruction, not to mention the First World War, the world was finally ready to capitulate to an organization that would "end all wars"---the United Nations.

Now that statement in itself is a farce, seeing that after the UN was founded the world has been in a perpetual state of war, including the United States/New Babylon bombing over 50 countries since the United Nations inception.

So there it is in black and white. Problem-reaction-solution. World War II was a gigantic false flag based on smaller false flags in order to birth the infant one world government. The Illuminati wanted world government, so they caused those terrible wars and made a ton of money and power off them in the process, the people reacted by wanting no more wars, and they allowed a one world government to come into being, all by the Great Plan. Unfortunately, what is coming down the tracks will make those wars look like child's play and you need to get prepared for it, as we will go over in the conclusion of this book.

On October 24, 1945, the United Nations Charter became effective. Also on October 24, not coincidentally by the way, Senator Glen Taylor introduces Senate Resolution 183 calling upon the U.S. Senate to go on record as favoring creation of a world republic including an international police force. This man Taylor should have been hung for this action, as it spells out the literal end of the United States he was supposed to be representing.

The New World Order had finally been hatched........

Built on land in the city of New York donated by none other than card-carrying Illuminati member **John D. Rockefeller III**, its construction was completed in 1952.

"The United Nations is the greatest fraud in history. Its purpose is to destroy the United States."
- John E. Rankin, U.S. Congressman

"The age of nations must end. The governments of nations have decided to order their separate sovereignties into one government to which they will surrender their arms."
- U.N. World Constitution

"We do not want another committee, we have too many already. What we want is a man of sufficient stature to hold the allegiance of all the people and to lift us up out of the economic morass into which we are sinking. Send us such a man, and whether he be God or devil, we will receive him."

-Paul-Henri Spaak, the first president of the United Nations General Assembly

"No one will enter the New World Order unless he or she will make a pledge to worship Lucifer. No one will enter the New Age unless he will take a LUCIFERIAN Initiation."

- David Spangler, Director of Planetary Initiative, United Nations

Doesn't sound very good for us and our country does it? The United Nations IS the Luciferian one world government referred to in Biblical prophecy, and it is in existence today, right in front of your face.

"For a long time I felt that FDR had developed many thoughts and ideas that were his own to benefit this country, the United States. But, he didn't. Most of his thoughts, his political ammunition, as it were, were carefully manufactured for him in advanced by the Council on Foreign Relations - One World Money group. Brilliantly, with great gusto, like a fine piece of artillery, he exploded that prepared "ammunition" in the middle of an unsuspecting target, the American people, and thus paid off and returned his internationalist political support.

The UN is but a long-range, international banking apparatus clearly set up for financial and economic profit by a small group of powerful One-World revolutionaries, hungry for profit and power.

The depression was the calculated 'shearing' of the public by the World Money powers, triggered by the planned sudden shortage of supply of call money in the New York money market....The One World Government leaders and their ever close bankers have now acquired full control of the money and credit machinery of the U.S. via the creation of the privately owned Federal Reserve Bank."

-Curtis Dall, FDR's son-in-law as quoted in his book, "My Exploited Father-in-Law"

Chapter 9/E

THE COLD WAR

"In the councils of government, we must guard against the acquisition of unwarranted influence, whether sought or unsought, by the military-industrial-complex. The potential for the disastrous rise of misplaced power exists and will persist. We must never let the weight of this combination endanger our liberties or democratic processes... Only an alert and knowledgeable citizenry can compel the proper meshing of the huge industrial and military machinery of defense with our peaceful methods and goals, so that security and liberty may prosper together. "
- President Dwight D. Eisenhower's farewell address, January, 1961

After World War II was put to bed and the framework of the one world government set up via the United Nations, it was time for the Illuminati to go to work getting mankind back to the business of war, or at least the **threat** of it. This was done to keep us distracted and also to build up the New Babylon's military machine in the quest for world domination. This is when the Illuminati ramped up their next "threat" to the Western nations and mankind in general: Communism. Remember, it was the Illuminati who orchestrated the and funded the Russian Revolution.

There was NEVER a chance that we would have had a nuclear war with Russia because it would have contaminated the entire surface of the Earth. The Illuminati wouldn't have wanted to lord over a nuclear wasteland, but it sure made for good propaganda and huge deficit-growing military spending didn't it? If you are old enough to remember the "duck and cover" drills in the schools in the 1950s and 60s you now know this was merely mental conditioning to keep you in fear and in favor of "arming ourselves against Communism". Ducking under a desk in a school when a nuclear bomb goes off is laughable, and these drills were abandoned a long time ago as people finally wised up to this fact.

So, the new excuse for an imminent threat to us was going to be Democracy/Capitalism vs. Communism, and first up to bat was the Korean War.

Korea, under Japanese control since the Russo-Japanese War of 1905 and officially annexed by Japan in 1910, had no choice but to enter the war on the side of the Axis powers with Japan.

After the war, Korea was divided into two parts at the 38th parallel, with the Soviet Union occupying the North and the United States occupying the South.

To make a long story short, **very short**, Communist "agitators" in North Korea started a civil war in an attempt to reunite South Korea under their newly installed Communist government. The newly-formed United Nations immediately stepped in, effectively putting the U.S. military in charge of making sure this didn't happen. Keep in mind the Illuminati are controlling this entire exchange behind the scenes and using their controlled puppets to put on a show for the world of Democracy vs. Communism.

This was the first major event of the Cold War.

The Cold War manufactured an excuse for huge military spending to build the New Babylon into the world police force to combat the 'communist threat', using Federal Reserve fiat currency printed out of thin air, which they put the citizens of the United States on the hook for to pay back. It was also an excuse to create and empower the CIA, who are in effect the secret police of the Illuminati, carrying out their clandestine orders all over the globe.

The United States/New Babylon has **662 military bases in 38 foreign countries**, and a military presence in another 100+ countries. That puts the United States military in about 140 out of 196 countries on Earth. Aggression in or towards any of the 140 countries immediately sets our military in action, and we are footing the bill whether we like it or not.

So what it boils down to is, with the private Federal Reserve in place, we footed the bill for the military takeover of nearly the rest of the world....and our own financial enslavement.

This Cold War distraction/threat lasted for a few decades and then... voila! The Iron Curtain came down and we're all supposed to come together and live happily ever after under UN authority, rallying the countries of the world under the "Green Movement" to face the dragon of global warming, climate change, or whatever they are calling it this year.

Let's briefly go over some more Cold War suppressed history, starting with the Vietnam War.

Here is the "official" story as it was relayed to the American public and Congress in 1964:

> *In early August of 1964, the destroyer USS Maddox, under the operational control of Captain John J. Herrick, USN, steamed along the coast of North Vietnam in the Gulf of Tonkin gathering various types of intelligence.*
>
> *On the afternoon of August 2, 1964 the "Commies" dispatched three Soviet-built P-4 motor torpedo boats against Maddox. The boats reportedly fired torpedoes at the U.S. ship in international waters in the Gulf of Tonkin, about thirty miles off the Vietnam coast, with no hits on the vessel. On August 4, the U.S. Navy reported another unprovoked attack on the USS Maddox and the USS Turner Joy. Torpedoes launched from the P-4s missed their mark. Only one round from enemy deck guns hit the destroyer Maddox, ending up in the ship's superstructure.*

Within hours of the alleged incident on August 4, President Lyndon B. Johnson ordered a retaliatory strike. As the bases for North Vietnamese torpedo boats were bombed, Johnson went on TV and told America: **"Repeated acts of violence against the armed forces of the United States must be met not only with alert defense, but with a positive reply. That reply is being given as I speak tonight."** The next day, Secretary of Defense Robert McNamara assured Capitol Hill that the Maddox had only been **"carrying out a routine mission of the type we carry out all over the world at all times."** McNamara said the two boats were in no way involved with recent South Vietnamese boat raids against North Vietnamese targets.

Officers in the naval chain of command and U.S. leaders in Washington were persuaded by interpretation of special intelligence and reports from the ships that North Vietnamese naval forces had indeed attacked the two destroyers. On August 7 the U.S. Congress overwhelmingly passed the so-called **Tonkin Gulf Resolution**. The resolution pre-approved any military actions Johnson would take. It gave Johnson a free ticket to wage war in Vietnam as long and large as the President wanted. Despite McNamara's testimony to the contrary, the USS Maddox had been providing intelligence support to South Vietnamese boats carrying out raids against North Vietnam. McNamara had also testified that there was "unequivocal proof" of an "unprovoked" second attack against the USS Maddox. In the first months of 1965, the President ordered the deployment to South Vietnam of major U.S. ground, air, and naval forces. By 1969, over half a million US troops were fighting in Vietnam. Millions of innocent Vietnamese citizens were burned, shot, bombed, raped and slaughtered in cold blood by our troops obeying the orders of the Illuminati. Almost 60,000 patriotic Americans lost their lives with hundreds of thousands more injured physically, not to mention the millions who suffered emotional and mental damage that continues to haunt Vietnam Vets today.

It has since come out as **fact** that North Vietnamese naval forces **did not** attack the USS Maddox or Turner Joy that night in the summer of 1964. This event was fabricated in order to excuse all out war in Vietnam. **It was another false flag attack**, an excuse for the military to field test new weapons, spend a bunch of money, distract and divide the country, etc. etc. ad nauseum.

The LBJ Presidential tapes, declassified and released in 2001, prove that LBJ knew the Tonkin incident never happened. **It was factually a 100% false flag event to get the U.S. embroiled in another war.**

In July of 2010 over 1,100 pages of classified documents were finally released by the Senate Foreign Relations Committee, revealing the fact that several Senators knew that the White House and the Pentagon had deceived the American people over the faked Gulf of Tonkin incident in 1964, but kept quiet out of fear of reprisal from the proponents of the

New World Order, who were assassinating political figures left and right in the 1960s.

We have one last conflict to *briefly* review that occurred during the Cold War, and that is the Soviet invasion of Afghanistan in 1979.

The ideal of Communism was not quite ready to throw in the towel heading into the late 1970's and had one tentacle left to reach out with, and that tentacle tried wrapping itself around Afghanistan, a largely Muslim country.

Economic aid and influence had been provided to Afghanistan in an attempt to gain a foothold since around 1919, right after the Communist Russian Revolution. After WW II ended, the Soviets Union began to slowly but surely increase their presence, sending larger and larger amounts of aid, and therefore influence, into the primarily Muslim country.

To make a long story short (again), the atheist Communists pushed too hard too fast and the hard core Muslims rebelled. The Soviets invaded, and it ended up being Russian and the puppet government they had set up vs. the Islamic Mujahedeen, backed by the United States.

Islam is directly opposed to Communism, which is based on atheism, so this particular conflict wasn't so much Communism vs. Democracy as it was Communism (Atheism) vs. Islam. It is worth addressing briefly here just for your own info in case you were wondering. This was the rare occasion of a major event that the Illuminati didn't plan from the start, in my opinion, but they certainly exploited it after the fact nonetheless, turning it into another excuse for mayhem against humanity.

Chapter 9/F

THE DAWN OF WORLD WAR III

So what happened immediately after the cold war ended in 1989? The proponents of the Great Plan wasted no time getting back to the business of war.

In 1990, one year after the official end of the Cold War, they immediately fomented another war in the Middle East against Iraq, which was **again** started by a false flag operation. This false flag scenario tricked Saddam Hussein into attacking and occupying Kuwait in order to excuse the general invasion of the Middle East by New Babylon.

The reasons for the orchestration of the first Gulf War by the proponents of the New World Order are as follows:

-For the New Babylon/United States, the military enforcement arm of the one world government/United Nations, to establish a stronger foothold in the Middle East for future actions, namely WW III. This was established through the setting up of permanent military bases in many countries in the Middle East to protect them from the "marauding" Saddam Hussein

-To display to the rest of the world the awesome military power of New Babylon. Remember watching that war on TV in early 1991? I'll never forget it, just an awesome display of military technology and might for the time.

-To safeguard the oil supply, of which the Illuminati families nearly completely control as you now know, coming out of the Middle East

-To spend a bunch of money and further put us in debt to them, to line their pockets with blood money, to field test new weaponry, to distract our country and the world from the real agenda of the Great Plan, etc. etc. The same old reasons they have always taken us to war

So what was the "false flag" that triggered the first Gulf War?

With former CIA Director/Skull and Bonesman/CFR/Bilderberg/Trilateral Commission member George Bush Sr. at the helm, it wasn't going to be so much a problem taking the U.S. to war as it was how to excuse it.

As briefly as possible of course, Iraq was just coming off the 8 year long Iran-Iraq war and was burdened with $30 billion in debt to its Arab allies, chiefly Saudi Arabia and Kuwait. These countries backed Iraq over Iran in an attempt to contain the radical Islamists running Iran, for fear their ideology would spread throughout the Middle East and topple the power of the elite oil sheiks running these countries. The United States also donated significant support to Iraq in the forms of weapons and intel to try and contain the non-Illuminati-controlled Iran. This is the reason why the UN/United States stood idly by when Iraq first attacked Iran in 1980.

After Iraq and Iran buried the hatchet, Saddam felt that since Iraq took on the job of "containing" Iran that they should be relieved of some if not all of their debt to their Arab neighbors.

Not only did Saudi Arabia and Kuwait not see things this way, Kuwait began oil production beyond OPEC quotas, including continued increased pumping of oil out of an oil pool shared with Iraq on their border, the Ar-Rumaylah oil fields. This had the effect of driving down oil prices AND taking oil away from Iraq, when they were facing a large portion of their $30 billion in debt to Kuwait.

During the Iran-Iraq War, Iraq had ceased production from its side of the Ar-Rumaylah fields while Kuwait continued operations. Kuwait claimed it had taken oil only from its own side of the field, while Saddam claimed it had been poached from Iraq.

On July 15, 1990 Hussein delivered a speech in which he accused Kuwait of continued siphoning of crude oil from the Ar-Rumaylah oil

J. MICAH'EL THOMAS HAYS

fields. He insisted that Kuwait and Saudi Arabia cancel Iraq's $30 billion debt, and accused them of conspiring to keep oil prices low.

This is about the time that Iraq had begun amassing troops on Kuwait's border, our spy satellites watching his every move.

It didn't take a lot of prodding to get Saddam to spring into action, and an advantageous situation was playing right into the Illuminati's hands. The United States had already demonstrated that they weren't interested in meddling in Saddam's affairs, other than some military aid, during the 8 year war against Iran. All he needed was to know was that the United States wouldn't meddle in his affairs again ala the Iran situation.

On July 25, 1990, eight days before the Iraqi invasion of Kuwait, a largely unreported meeting took place between Saddam Hussein and the U.S. Ambassador to Iraq, April Glaspie, at the Presidential Palace in Baghdad. It is here that the "false flag" took place that triggered the entire Gulf War. If Glaspie had told Saddam that the U.S. wanted him to back down, the Gulf war never would have happened, but that wasn't in the plan. The transcript of this meeting is as follows:

U.S. Ambassador Glaspie:

"I have direct instructions from President Bush to improve our relations with Iraq. We have considerable sympathy for your quest for higher oil prices, the immediate cause of your confrontation with Kuwait. As you know, I have lived here for years and admire your extraordinary efforts to rebuild your country. We know you need funds. We understand that, and our opinion is that you should have the opportunity to rebuild your country. We can see that you have deployed massive numbers of troops in the south. Normally that would be none of our business, but when this happens in the context of your other threats against Kuwait, then it would be reasonable for us to be concerned. For this reason, I have received an instruction to ask you, in the spirit of friendship - not confrontation - regarding your intentions: Why are your troops massed so very close to Kuwait's borders?"

Saddam Hussein:

"As you know, for years now I have made every effort to reach a settlement on our dispute with Kuwait. There is to be a meeting in two days; I am prepared to give negotiations only this one more brief chance.

When we meet and we see there is hope, then nothing will happen. But if we are unable to find a solution, then it will be natural that Iraq will not accept death."

U.S. Ambassador Glaspie:
"What solutions would be acceptable?"

Saddam Hussein:
"If we could keep the whole of the Shatt al Arab - our strategic goal in our war with Iran - we will make concessions (to the Kuwaitis). But, if we are forced to choose between keeping half of the Shatt and the whole of Iraq (which, in Saddam's view, includes Kuwait) then we will give up all of the Shatt to defend our claims on Kuwait to keep the whole of Iraq in the shape we wish it to be. What is the United States' opinion on this?"

U.S. Ambassador Glaspie:
"We have no opinion on your Arab-Arab conflicts, such as your dispute with Kuwait. Secretary (of State James) Baker has directed me to emphasize the instruction, first given to Iraq in the 1960's that the Kuwait issue is not associated with America."

Saddam took this meeting as a green light for him to invade Kuwait, and on August 2, 1990 ordered the invasion to begin. Alarmed by this aggression, neighboring Arab countries such as Saudi Arabia and Egypt called on the United States and the U.N. to intervene.

Hussein, being the egomaniacal madman he was, defied United Nations Security Council demands to withdraw from Kuwait by mid-January 1991 and the Persian Gulf War began with a massive U.S.-led air offensive known as Operation Desert Storm. After 42 days of bombing Iraq into oblivion, U.S. President George H.W. Bush declared a cease-fire on February 28.

Saddam was left intact as an excuse for future military action, which you probably well know came in the aftermath of 9/11. Remember the "weapons of mass destruction" which excused another war? They were never found. Just another lie to steer us further up onto the rocks and into the clutches of the proponents of the Great Plan.

However, the "weapons of mass destruction" claim wasn't the false flag that took us to war in Afghanistan and later Iraq again. The false flag that took us to war was 9/11. That's right. 9/11 was a false flag operation, an "inside job" orchestrated by the proponents of the Great Plan. I'm going to prove this to you factually in a couple of chapters. The "War on Terror" **is** the new war by the Illuminati to keep us in line, to keep us in fear, to keep us distracted.

The "War on Terror" is a complete fabrication based on the illusion that one man, Osama bin Laden, outwitted the $40 billion-a-year American intelligence apparatus. The War on Terror is really a war of conquest. Global military domination led by the New Babylon is the final march to the "New World Order", led by the Illuminati-owned Wall Street/U.S. military-industrial complex.

September 11, 2001 provided a justification for waging preemptive war with fabricated excuses. The Illuminati agenda consists of extending the frontiers of the American Empire to facilitate complete U.S. corporate control over the world, while installing within America the institutions of the Homeland Security Police State, virtually identical to Nazi Germany under the Gestapo.

But first we are going to talk about the United Nations and the agenda they are not only pushing but fulfilling day after day, year after year, slowly but surely pushing the Great Plan forward to completion.

The U.N. plans are rarely if ever put out in the Mainstream Media, but are in fact available for all who bother to look, which is hardly anyone. Why take the time to look into these things when "Keeping up with the Kardashians" is on the TV. Or "Dancing With the Stars". Or Monday Night Football. Or any other of the plethora of pure crap turned out by the Illuminati-controlled Mainstream Media to keep you distracted and pacified. Their goal is to keep you in your little comfort bubble while they subvert our Constitution, our country, and our way of life via United Nations/one world government legislation our treasonous politicians have signed us up for.

You didn't bother to look into the United Nations agenda, but I did.

Chapter 10

THE UNITED NATIONS=ONE WORLD GOVERNMENT

To achieve world government, it is necessary to remove from the minds of men their individualism, loyalty to family tradition, national patriotism and religious dogmas ... We have swallowed all manner of poisonous certainties fed us by our parents, our Sunday and day school teachers, our politicians, our priests, our newspapers and others with vested interests in controlling us. The reinterpretation and eventual eradication of the concept of right and wrong which has been the basis of child training, the substitution of intelligent and rational thinking for faith in the certainties of the old people, these are the belated objectives ... for charting the changes of human behavior.

-Brock Chisolm, Director, World Health Organization, a subsidiary of the UN

"It seems to many of us that if we are to avoid the eventual catastrophic world conflict we must strengthen the United Nations as a first step toward a world government patterned after our own government with a legislature, executive and judiciary, and police to enforce its international laws and keep the peace. To do that, of course, we Americans will have to yield up some of our sovereignty. That would be a bitter pill. It would take a lot of courage, a lot of faith in the new order. But the American

colonies did it once and brought forth one of the most nearly perfect unions the world has ever seen."

-Walter Cronkite, from his acceptance speech receiving the "Norman Cousins Global Governance Award" from the World Federalist Association---a proponent of World Government

"We do not want another committee, we have too many already. What we want is a man of sufficient stature to hold the allegiance of all the people and to lift us up out of the economic morass into which we are sinking. Send us such a man, and whether he be God or devil, we will receive him."

-Socialist Paul-Henri Spaak, the first president of the United Nations General Assembly, 1946 to 1957, and former Prime Minister of Belgium. He then went on to head NATO from 1957 to 1961

"No one will enter the New World Order unless he or she will make a pledge to worship Lucifer. No one will enter the New Age unless he will take a LUCIFERIAN Initiation."

- David Spangler, United Nations Director of Planetary Initiative, circa early 1980's

"The planning of UN can be traced to the 'secret steering committee' established by Secretary of State Cordell Hull in January 1943. All of the members of this secret committee, with the exception of Hull, a Tennessee politician, were members of the Council on Foreign Relations. They saw Hull regularly to plan, select, and guide the labors of the State Department's Advisory Committee. It was, in effect, the coordinating agency for all the State Department's postwar planning."

-Professors Laurence H. Shoup and William Minter, writing in their study of the CFR, "Imperial Brain Trust: The CFR and United States Foreign Policy." Monthly Review Press, 1977

"The drive of the Rockefellers and their allies is to create a one-world government combining supercapitalism and Communism under the same tent, all under their control.... Do I mean conspiracy?

Yes I do. I am convinced there is such a plot, international in scope, generations old in planning, and incredibly evil in intent."
-United States Congressman Larry P. McDonald, silenced forever when he was killed in the Korean Airlines 747 that was conveniently shot down by the Soviets in 1983.

"The age of nations must end. The governments of the nations have decided to order their separate sovereignties into one government to which they will surrender their arms."
-United Nations World Constitution

The Luciferian one world government prophesized in the Bible is not coming....it is here. It was founded by the **exact people** who are leading the Great Plan, also as prophesized in the Bible.

The United Nations is slowly being transferred more and more power. Every time the UN gains more power, the sovereignty of the United States erodes ever further, and will continue to erode until it is absorbed into a totalitarian one world government. This is our future, and it is not far off.

It is in the best interest for you and I and our families, friends, and loved ones for the United States to WITHDRAW as a member of the United Nations and kick them the HELL out of our country. It is like playing willing host to a bloodsucking vampire.

On July 20, 1992, TIME magazine published *"The Birth of the Global Nation"* by Strobe Talbott, a Rhodes Scholar, roommate of Bill Clinton at Oxford University, CFR Director, and Trilateral Commission member.

"In the next century, nations as we know it will be obsolete; all states will recognize a single, global authority. National sovereignty wasn't such a great idea after all."
- Strobe Talbott, President Clinton's Deputy Secretary of State, Time Magazine, July 20th, 1992

In this article he writes:

"All countries are basically social arrangements... No matter how permanent or even sacred they may seem at any one time, in fact they are all artificial and temporary... Perhaps national sovereignty wasn't such a great idea after all... But it has taken the events in our own wondrous and terrible century to clinch the case for world government."

Yeah. Terrible as in events orchestrated by the puppet masters of the one world government to further their cause.

The proponents of the New World Order don't even bother to hide their intentions anymore, as they have done a masterful job of distracting you with mindless entertainment and poisoned your mind that anyone who is concerned about these kinds of things is some kind of conspiracy kook. Hopefully by now you realize that there is no theory at all, just a monstrous conspiracy thousands of years in the making.

As an editor of Time magazine, Talbott hyped and defended Clinton during his presidential campaign. Talbott was appointed by newly-elected President Clinton as the number two person at the State Department behind Secretary of State and Trilateralist/CFR Vice-Chairman and Director Warren Christopher.

Talbott was confirmed by about two-thirds of the U.S. Senate despite his statement about the unimportance of the United States' sovereignty.

In 1993 Talbott received the Norman Cousins Global Governance Award for his 1992 TIME article and in appreciation for what he has done **"for the cause of global governance."**

President Clinton even wrote a letter of congratulation and commendation in which he stated:

"Norman Cousins worked for world peace and world government... Strobe Talbott's lifetime achievements as a voice for global harmony have earned him this recognition... He will be a worthy recipient of the Norman Cousins Global Governance Award. Best wishes... for future success."

Keep in mind that these were words **from a sitting U.S. President**, a pro-world government, CFR/Trilateral Commission/Bilderberg member and 33rd degree (alleged) Freemason traitor.

So what is it going to be like under the rule of an authoritarian one world government, let alone one that will be ultimately run by the most deviant, ruthless, tyrannical man in the Bible, a resurrected King Nimrod, also known as the "Antichrist"?

The proponents of the Great Plan are engaged in media treachery right this second to slowly acclimate you into believing that world government is going to be a good thing, a necessary thing. They are telling you that since we live in a "global community" that global government is the next logical step.

The REAL reason behind the planned one world government is the acquisition and consolidation of ever greater wealth and power, control of natural resources, totalitarian political power, and control over those underneath the New World Order power structure.....which will be the whole world. Once the one world government police state is fully operational, all opposition will be crushed......forever. The surveillance systems they are creating and implementing right now are specifically designed for this purpose, an all-encompassing police state.

The toll in human suffering and the loss of innocent lives are non issues for these Luciferians in the name of completing the Great Plan, the Illuminati. Whatever it takes to get mankind to capitulate to their will---they will do it without batting an eye. Hopefully you understand this now.

Chapter 10/A

BIRTH OF THE UNITED NATIONS

"This is an historic moment. We have in this past year made great progress in ending the long era of conflict and Cold War. We have before us the opportunity to forge for ourselves and for future generations a New World Order -- a world where the rule of law, not the law of the jungle, governs the conduct of nations. When we are successful -- and we will be -- we have a real chance at this New World Order, an order in which a credible United Nations can use its peacekeeping role to fulfill the promise and vision of the UN's founders."

-Treasonous minion of the Great Plan and 41ˢᵗ President of the United States George H.W. Bush, speaking on TV to the American people and the world right after we started bombing Iraq in the first Gulf War, January 17, 1991

"Pat Robertson has written in a book a few years ago that we should have a world government, but only when the Messiah arrives. He wrote, literally, any attempt to achieve world order before that time must be the work of the devil. Well, join me. I'm glad to sit here at the right hand of Satan."

-Walter Cronkite, referring to Pat Robertson's 1991 book "The New World Order"

"It is the sacred principles enshrined in the UN Charter to which we will henceforth pledge our allegiance."

-Sitting President George H.W. Bush, addressing the world leaders at the UN

The United Nations was founded on the premise to "end all wars". Well, since the founding of the United Nations the world has been perpetually at war, with the UN/New Babylon right in the middle of it all. Like I said, since the end of WW II, the New Babylon has bombed over 50 countries and built military bases all over the planet in the name of "peace".

The hit men in the mass media have outdone themselves over the last few decades, painting the United Nations as an institution of peace rather than what it really is: the Great Plan's Luciferian one world government.

Here is the timeline of the creation of the UN, right from the United Nations website:

- Signed in London on June 12, 1941, the Inter-Allied Declaration was a first step towards the establishment of the United Nations.

- On August 14, 1941, 33rd degree (alleged) Freemasons President Franklin Delano Roosevelt of the United States and Prime Minister Winston Churchill of the United Kingdom proposed a set of principles for international collaboration in maintaining peace and security. The document is known as the Atlantic Charter.

- On January 1, 1942, representatives of 26 Allied nations fighting against the Axis Powers met in Washington, D.C. to pledge their support for the Atlantic Charter by signing the "Declaration by United Nations". This document contained the first official use of the term "United Nations", which was suggested by Illuminati henchman President Roosevelt.

- On October 30, 1943, in a declaration signed in Moscow, the Governments of the Soviet Union, the United Kingdom, the United States and China called for an early establishment of an international organization

to maintain peace and security. That goal was reaffirmed at the meeting of the leaders of the United States, the USSR, and the United Kingdom at Teheran on December 1, 1943.

- From September 21 through October 7, 1944, the first blueprint of the UN was prepared at a conference held at a mansion known as Dumbarton Oaks in Washington, D.C. During two phases of meetings which ran, the United States, the United Kingdom, the USSR and China agreed on the aims, structure and functioning of a world organization.

- On February 11, 1945, following meetings at Yalta, President Roosevelt, Prime Minister Churchill and Premier Joseph Stalin declared their resolve to establish "a general international organization to maintain peace and security". This was called the Yalta Conference.

- On April 25, 1945, delegates of 50 war-weary nations met in San Francisco for the United Nations Conference on International Organization. The delegates drew up the 111-article United Nations Charter, which was adopted unanimously on June 25, 1945 in the San Francisco Opera House. Alleged 33rd degree Freemason and then current President Harry Truman signed the United States up for the coming world government by pledging the United States full support of the UN.

- On October 24, 1945, the United Nations is created as its Charter is ratified by the five permanent members of the Security Council and the majority of other signatories, and comes into force.

Immediately following the ratification of the U.N. Charter, the first official meeting of the United Nations, with 51 nations represented, opened in Central Hall, Westminster, London.

They would continue to hold the United Nations meetings in Great Britain until their new digs were constructed in the New Babylon.

On December 14, 1946 the United Nations accepted a gift of $8.6 million from card-carrying Illuminati member **John D. Rockefeller Jr.** to buy the land where the UN sits today in New York.

"The concept of national sovereignty has been immutable, indeed a sacred principle of international relations. It is a principle which will yield only slowly and reluctantly to the new imperatives of global environmental cooperation."
-UN's Commission on Global Governance

In 1947 the treasonous U.S. Congress approved a $65 million interest free loan for the construction of the UN buildings. Our bought-and-paid-for elected representatives were actively backing the newly formed one world government, just like today.

The United Nations building was completed in 1952, complete with an anti-gun statue in front consisting of a revolver with its barrel tied in a knot. This statue is meant to represent the United Nations goal of "no more wars", but in reality is a representation of the United Nations/ Illuminati confiscating the guns out of the hands of the civilians of the world, especially the United States' citizens, so they can't resist what is coming in the future.

There are hundreds of UN committees, councils, organizations, etc., all designed to slowly push the Great Plan forward, but we don't have much time or room here to go over them all. We will just focus on the most important aspects of the UN you need to be made aware of.

In fact, the UN holds more than **5,000** conferences a year to slowly guide the global society down the path towards the one world government. That is the entire purpose for the United Nations existence: promote the world government in the name of the Great Plan and its controllers the Illuminati.

Don't forget, the same people who founded and run the United Nations founded and run the Federal Reserve, have assassinated Presidents and anyone else who got in their way, started two world wars and working on the third, most of the rest of the world conflicts, and on and on and on.

These people don't want to help us at all. They want to destroy our country, the United States of America, eliminate most of us, and whoever is left will be their slaves.

I'm sorry. I've got a major problem going along with that.

Chapter 10/B

AGENDA 21

"Effective execution of Agenda 21 will require a profound reorientation of all human society, unlike anything the world has ever experienced. A major shift in the priorities of both governments and individuals and an unprecedented redeployment of human and financial resources. This shift will demand that a concern for the environmental consequences of every human action be integrated into individual and collective decision-making at every level."
   - Excerpt from U.N. Agenda 21, 1992

"We must speak more clearly about sexuality, contraception, about abortion, about values that control population, because the ecological crisis, in short, is the population crisis. Cut the population by 90% and there aren't enough people left to do a great deal of ecological damage."
   -Mikhail Gorbachev, proponent of the Great Plan

Agenda 21 was a major step towards the final phase of the global implementation of the Great Plan, being introduced at the United Nation's Earth Summit held in Rio de Janeiro, Brazil in 1992. Agenda 21 is the official agenda of the UN's goal of a centrally managed global society. This contract literally binds governments around the world to the United Nation's plan for controlling the way we reproduce, live, eat, learn, move and communicate, all under the noble endeavour of saving the Earth from ourselves, when in fact it is the proponents of the New World Order who have done all the damage. When fully implemented, and they are slowly implementing it as you read this, Agenda 21 would have the one world government involved in every aspect of life of every human on Earth.

Again, keep in mind who it was that was responsible for the founding and subsequent control of the UN, the Luciferian proponents of King Nimrod's New World Order. Hopefully by this point in this book you will see that it is all conspiracy and no theory. There really, factually exists a monstrous conspiracy to take over the world and now you know who, what, where, when, why and how it is happening.

Also, before we go forward here, I want to go on record that I am certainly all for being stewards of the Earth, which is part of the reason we are here. This means being environmentally friendly, recycling, keeping pollution to a minimum, etc. What I am against is the using of environmentalism as a ruse to empower the New World Order elites over humanity on the road to completion of the Great Plan; this is exactly what they are doing.

Let's go over how Agenda 21 came into existence, beginning with the birth of the modern environmental or "green" movement on Earth Day in 1970. The name and concept of Earth Day was created in 1969 at a **UNESCO** Conference in San Francisco, with Earth Day originally celebrated at the Spring Equinox around March 20. In 2009 the United Nations officially designated April 22 as International Mother Earth (Semiramis) Day, and this is now the official "Earth Day".

Don't forget the Babylonian Mystery Religion tie-in here. Another title for Queen Semiramis, wife of King Nimrod, is Mother Nature, referred to also as Mother Earth. The environmental movement being pushed by the Great Plan is in actuality a pagan reverence to the co-instigator of the Great Plan, Semiramis.

The first Earth Day led to the creation in the 1970s of the now tyrannical United States Environmental Protection Agency and the passage of the Clean Air, Clean Water, and Endangered Species Acts. You would think with names like this that they would be helping us, but they were in fact put in place to further the UN agenda.

So how do you go from a peaceful hippie-attending love-in called Earth Day in 1970 to a tyrannical plan of culling mankind back to a "sustainable population" of 500 million from 7 billion? And which unbeknownst to 99% of the population is fully endorsed by the bought-and-paid-for traitors staffing nearly every country in the world in the year 2013?

To answer that, I'm going to pick up where we left off regarding "*The Report from Iron Mountain*", with the environmental movement being the proposed new control mechanism for society instead of the many bloody, contrived and expensive wars. Leading the charge of the "sky is falling" is the environmental "threat" of anthropogenic global warming, also known as man-made global warming. This particular environmental threat would affect the entire world whether countries wanted to be involved or not.

The first consideration by the proponents of the Great Plan in finding and promoting this believable threat to manipulate the masses was that it didn't have to be real---just believable. Another "false flag" if you will, an event they could get mankind to believe through the use of their Mainstream Media propaganda machine. Just as they orchestrated and then controlled both sides of nearly every war over the last 300 years, they would control both sides of the "war" between man and the environment.

During the Carter Administration, a task force was appointed to expand upon "*The Report from Iron Mountain*", and on July 24, 1980, a two-volume document called the "*Global 2000 Report*," which had been written by Trilateralist/CFR member and former Secretary of State Cyrus R. Vance, was presented to Trilateralist/CFR member President Carter and then Secretary of State CFR member Edward S. Muskie. Its purpose was to "predict" global economic trends for the next twenty years, and stated that the resources of the planet were not sufficient enough to support the coming increase in the world population.

The report, presented to sitting President Jimmy Carter, **also called for the population of the U.S. to be culled by 100 million people by the year 2050.**

About six months after the Global 2000 Report was released, the Council on Environmental Quality, which is a federal organization, made recommendations based on the Global 2000 Report, called "*Global Future: A Time to Act.*" They suggested an aggressive program of population control which included sterilization, contraception and abortion.

In August, 1982, the private organization, the "Executive Intelligence Review ", published its own report called *Global 2000: Blueprint for Genocide"* which said that the two aforementioned Presidential reports:

"...are correctly understood as political statements of intent- the intent on the part of such policy centers as the Council on Foreign Relations, the Trilateral Commission, and the International Monetary Fund, to pursue policies that will result not only in the death of the 120 million cited in the reports, but in the death of upwards of two billion people by the year 2000."

The next phase of the manufactured war of Mankind vs. Nature came in 1987 through the initialization of something called the Earth Charter.

"The real goal of the Earth Charter is that it will in fact become like the Ten Commandments."
- Maurice Strong

This ongoing "war" against mankind launched in 1970 is currently being masterminded in large part by a New Age occultist named Maurice Strong, widely regarded as the father of the modern environmental movement.

"Isn't it the only hope for the planet that the industrialized civilizations collapse? Isn't it our responsibility to bring that about?"
-Maurice Strong, Founder of the UN Environmental Program, at the opening speech of the Rio Earth Summit in 1992

I'm going to talk for a minute about this character, Maurice Strong, and it is important for you to know not only who he is, but who all the major players of the New World Order are, their backgrounds, what they believe in, who is pulling their strings, and where they want to take us in the future....which is straight into a tyrannical one world government.

Canadian multimillionaire Strong is an Illuminati henchman and one of the power players within the United Nations ranks. He has served as director of the World Future Society, trustee of the **Rockefeller Foundation** (no surprise there) and Director of the Aspen Institute (another Illuminati think tank), and is a member of the Club of Rome, CFR, Trilateral Commission, and Bilderberg Group.

Strong is/was Senior Advisor to the U.N. Secretary General, Senior Advisor to the World Bank President, Chairman of the Earth Council, Chairman of the World Resources Institute, and Co-Chairman of the World Economic Forum.

"It is clear that current lifestyles and consumption patterns of the affluent middle class---involving high meat intake, consumption of large amounts of frozen and convenience foods, use of fossil fuels, appliances, home and work place air-conditioning, and suburban housing---are not sustainable."
-Maurice Strong

Strong is the one behind the UN-enforced, worldwide cap-and-trade carbon-tax scheme to destroy the economies of the Western nations through taxing and limiting factory emissions that is going to begin to affect you and your families' way of life very soon, especially if you are in the middle class as described in the above quote. When the economies of the Western nations are permanently destroyed through the carbon-tax scam, the countries will fall into the hands of the waiting New World Order control grid. They are trying to use the fake Global Warming scare to pull this off, which we will go over soon. This of course is if they get this environmental program in place before the global central bank fiat money pyramid scheme crashes, which at this point looks imminent to me.

"Strengthening the role the United Nations can play...will require serious examination of the need to extend into the international arena the rule of law and the principle of taxation to finance agreed actions which provide the basis for governance at the national level. But this will not come about easily. Resistance to such changes is deeply entrenched. They will come about not through the embrace of full blown world government, but as a careful and pragmatic response to compelling imperatives and the

inadequacies of alternatives. The concept of national sovereignty has been an immutable, indeed sacred, principle of international relations. It is a principle which will yield only slowly and reluctantly to the new imperatives of global environmental cooperation. What is needed is recognition of the reality that in so many fields, and this is particularly true of environmental issues, it is simply not feasible for sovereignty to be exercised unilaterally by individual nation-states, however powerful. The global community must be assured of environmental security."

-Maurice Strong, "Stockholm to Rio: A Journey Down a Generation", 1992

In the late 1970's, allegedly on the advice of a mystic and fellow occultist, Strong purchased the Colorado Land and Cattle Company, which comprised 200,000 acres in Colorado. This mystic/occultist had told Strong that this area would become the center of the New Age movement after the economic collapse and environmental catastrophes that were going to occur in the years to come. Strong named this area the Baca ranch.

As a result of these occult revelations, Strong created the Manitou Foundation, a New Age institution located at the Baca ranch. He then went on to found yet another pro-New World Order organization, The Conservation Fund, with the financial help of **Laurence Rockefeller**.

Fortunately for humanity in 2005, the most influential man in the world in the push to "save" humanity was caught with his claw in the cookie jar......

Investigations into the scandalous United Nations' Oil-for-Food-Program for Iraq found that Strong had received and endorsed a check for $988,885 issued by a Jordanian bank. The man who gave Strong the check, South Korean business man Tongsun Park was convicted in 2006 in a United States Federal court of conspiring to bribe UN officials, including Maurice Strong. Strong resigned from the UN and fled to Canada and thereafter to China where he has been living ever since, but still influencing the United Nations agenda from behind the scenes.

This was of course after he already did a tremendous amount work in the name of the Great Plan during the 1970s through 2005 when he was ran out of town.

During his tenure working with the United Nations, Maurice Strong, fellow Club of Rome member and former Soviet General Secretary Mikhail Gorbachev, and **Stephen *Rockefeller*** co-chaired the committee responsible for drafting the Earth Charter in 1987, which is guide to transition the world to "sustainable development".

Remember, Gorbachev is the same socialist who said the following, and his views on socialism have not changed one iota:

"In October 1917, we parted with the old world, rejecting it once and for all. We are moving toward a new world, a world of Communism. We shall never turn off that road."

He is referring to the Great Plan-caused Russian Revolution, and he feels today he is doing his part to extend that revolution to the entire world. As a reminder, the one world government is a socialist system of government.

His agenda has been and always will be the same, the spread of socialism. The UN agenda *is* world socialism. Gorbachev founded in 1993, and is President of, Green Cross International, whose mission is **"to help ensure a just, sustainable and secure future for all by fostering a value shift and cultivating a new sense of global interdependence and shared responsibility in humanity's relationship with nature."**

"The current course of development is thus clearly unsustainable. Current problems cannot be solved by piecemeal measures. More of the same is not enough. Radical change from the current trajectory is not an option, but an absolute necessity. Fundamental economic, social and cultural changes that address the root causes of poverty and environmental degradation are required and they are required now."
– From the Earth Charter website

At only four pages long, it is tiny compared to the 300 page behemoth plan of action that Agenda 21 is, but it is no less important to the agenda of the one world government. It was an ongoing, evolving document that began in 1987, was adjusted in the 1990s, and was finalized in Paris in March of 2000 at a meeting of the Earth Charter Commission at UNESCO headquarters, and officially "launched" on June 29, 2000.

The Earth Charter is a **"declaration of fundamental principles for building a just, sustainable, and peaceful global society in the 21st century"**.

It is for all intents and purposes the Constitution of the New World Order.....

In between the initialization and finalization of the Earth Charter, the Earth Summit took place in Brazil in 1992, and with it the issuing of the ominous Agenda 21. Agenda 21 is the comprehensive plan of assault on mankind by the proponents of the New World Order on behalf of Mother Nature, aka Queen Semiramis.

> *"Industrialized countries developed and benefited from the unsustainable patterns of production and consumption which have produced our present dilemma. It is clear that current lifestyles and consumption patterns of the affluent middle class -- involving high meat intake, consumption of large amounts of frozen and convenience foods, use of fossil fuels, appliances, home and work-place air-conditioning, and suburban housing -- are not sustainable. A shift is necessary toward lifestyles less geared to environmentally damaging consumption patterns."*
>
> *-Maurice Strong, Secretary General and chief organizer of the UNCED Earth Summit in Rio, June 1992*

The Earth Summit was held over a two week period beginning on June 13, 1992, and 178 currently sovereign governments voted to adopt the main reason for the meeting: to sign on to the plan of action entailed in Agenda 21, which is short for **"Agenda for the 21st Century"**.

Do you remember the goals of the New World Order from the beginning of this book?

1. The abolishment of all individual nations' governments and borders
2. The abolishment of all private property
3. The abolishment of all inheritance
4. The abolishment of all Patriotism
5. The abolishment of all Religion---except the one they are preparing for us
6. The abolishment of all family and marriage
7. The culling of mankind down to a more manageable number of not more than 500 million.

These goals come directly out of the proposed actions entailed in Agenda 21, the game plan for the blossoming one world government.

"... the resultant ideal sustainable population is hence more than 500 million but less than one billion."
- Club of Rome, Goals for Mankind project, 1977

"Generally, more highly educated people, who have higher incomes, consume more resources than poorly educated people, who tend to have lower incomes. In this case, more education threatens sustainability."
-From the United Nations' "Education for Sustainable Development" program

There is a deliberate dumbing-down of the human race, especially Americans. There are deliberate mental distractions being put out there. There is a deliberate poisoning of the human race, particularly in the U.S. These actions are intentional, and perpetrated by the proponents of the Great Plan. If they didn't do these things they quite simply wouldn't be able to get away with what they are doing.

Anything they declare "unsustainable" such as sovereign nations and their laws, private property ownership/rights, livestock production and most meat consumption, personal travel, fossil fuel use, etc. will be outlawed. Agenda 21 is loaded with stealthy and comfortable code words such as "Sustainable development", "Smart growth", "Social justice", "Bio-diversity". Translated these words equate to a totalitarian environmental dictatorship and the elevation of Mother Nature to literal god-status ala pagan ancient Babylon.

Imagine **that**.......

This is a "do as I say, not as I do program". These elitists don't have any intention of giving up their lavish lifestyles, and **we** are supposed to live like serfs on **their** global plantation.

> *"The threat of environmental crisis will be the 'international disaster key' that will unlock the New World Order"*
> *-Mikhail Gorbachev, co-author of the Earth Charter*

The UN *Department of Economic and Social Affairs' Division for Sustainable Development* is in charge of monitoring progress, nation by nation, towards the implementation of Agenda 21, and makes these reports available to the public on its website. They are not particularly trying to hide their agenda; you are just too distracted, intentionally, to notice it. By the time humanity wakes up, the proponents of the NWO will be able to honestly say, ***"We hid nothing. It is your fault for not paying attention".***

And it **will** be **your** fault. How are you going to be able to look your kids in the eyes and tell them you were too busy watching American Idol to pay attention to the destruction of your own country and your current way of life? At this point in this book you should be boiling mad.

> *"The common enemy of humanity is man. In searching for a new enemy to unite us, we came up with the idea that pollution, the threat of global warming, water shortages, famine and the like would fit the bill. All these dangers are caused by human intervention, and it is only through changed attitudes and behavior that they can be overcome. The real enemy then, is humanity itself."*
> *- The Club of Rome, an Illuminati think-tank and regular consultant to the United Nations*

This type of global plan could not be implemented without a large and well-funded group pushing through and implementing its plan of action. Agenda 21 **has** this group, the International Council of Local Environmental Initiatives (ICLEI), and ICLEI is working diligently all over America promoting Agenda 21, aka the Constitution of the Great Plan.

ICLEI USA was created in 1995 through the UN and has grown from a handful of local governments participating in a test pilot project to a **growing** network of over **600** cities, towns and counties actively working to conform to Agenda 21.

Would you support your local government agreeing to rules and regulations set up by a Satanic one world government that is trying to destroy the United States? You may be and not even know it. You should check to see what towns near you are now affiliated with ICLEI and what they are doing working for the New World Order.

Several of our corrupted congressmen and senators have spoken in Congress in support of Agenda 21, including traitors Nancy Pelosi, John Kerry, and Harry Reid.

The United States is home to nearly half of the ICLEI's global membership of 1,200 cities, for it is the United States that most needs to fall under the New World Order ax.

In 2012, at the United Nations Conference on Sustainable Development, the attending countries reaffirmed their commitment to Agenda 21 in their outcome document called *"The Future We Want"*.

If they knew what **you** know now about the real intentions of Agenda 21, the United Nations, and the proponents of the New World Order, the citizens of these countries would probably be rethinking that position.

Chapter 10/C

(ONE) WORLD TRADE ORGANIZATION

The more pro-globalist organizations the proponents of the Great Plan can create and control, the more they are able to entangle the hapless sheeple in their growing world wide web of control. Our bought-and-paid-for members of Congress were nice enough to sign us up for membership in the highly treasonous WTO for example.

Although not a stated goal of the WTO, one of its primary purposes is to help promote the Great Plan. This is accomplished on two fronts. The first is to line the pockets of the owners of the multinational global corporations, aka the stockholders, aka the New World Order crowd, by maximizing their marketing potential. The second way is by the gradual destruction of the Western nations economies by transferring jobs out of high-paying Western nations to slave-wage-paying third world countries. This was also the purpose of NAFTA, the North American Free Trade Agreement, enacted in the early 1990s. NAFTA came before the formal creation of the WTO, but helps accomplish the exact same two goals I just outlined above. We're going to talk about NAFTA here shortly.

The people participating in the Great Plan at the legislative level, whether they are "Americans" placed in our Congress via the money powers, or German, British, French, whatever, don't have a single shred of commitment to the countries they are "from". They are nearly all pro-globalist, bought-and-paid-for-sold-their-soul traitors and whatever it takes to break down the barriers to their precious all-powerful one world government, that they think will have a place for them and their family, they will do.

The "One" World Trade Organization is not a particularly new entity; it just has a more modern sounding name, one that trumpets the fact that we are nearing completion of the Great Plan of global control.

The WTO morphed out of something called GATT, the General Agreement on Tariffs and Trade, which itself came out of the Bretton Woods agreement we already talked about, along with two of the other three pillars of world financial control, the IMF and World Bank, with the Bank of International Settlements the third pillar.

GATT, which was created in 1947 by a handful of countries including the U.S., was never a legally binding contract but merely an advisory organization. The proponents of the Great Plan would have to run with GATT until the societies of the world were sufficiently tranquilized with inane TV shows, drugs, video games, and other forms of pure distraction so they could operate out in the open, but effectively "under the radar" as no one is paying attention to these things these days.

This all changed in 1995 when GATT was replaced by the World Trade Organization. The WTO acts as a global trade Supreme Court, always siding with the multinational corporations over individual countries' best wishes and interests.

The World Trade Organization is purely an Illuminati-controlled elitist group of international economic powerbrokers whose only goals are to grab up as much money as possible, and money equals power mind you, and to break down the economies of the Western nations so they can be absorbed into the global government.

Subjects of interest now falling under WTO authority include but are not limited to intellectual property rights, known to us "patents", all types of agricultural activity (our food and water), and global telecommunications activities, to name but a few economic activities now controlled trans-border by the WTO.

Since the World Trade Organization was able to be pushed through without much if any opposition by the citizens who weren't paying attention, the WTO proponents at the United Nations are now clamoring for a World Development Authority, a formal International Central Bank, an International Development Fund, and a World Food Authority. They are making a grab right this second for as much control as they can get before you and your neighbors wake up and smell what the New World Order is cooking.

So....what has the WTO been up to lately?

The World Trade Organization ruled on June 29, 2012, that United States' country-of-origin labeling provisions violated global trading rules and were unjustly harming agricultural commerce between Canada, Mexico, and the U.S. ala NAFTA guidelines.

The U.S. had been requiring, for consumer safety, that food processors identify the countries from which livestock and produce originate. Canada and Mexico argued to the WTO that the provisions imposed not only prejudice against their products but unfair costs on their exports, reducing their competitiveness. WTO judges agreed that the policies meant beef and pork from Canada and Mexico were treated less favorably than the same U.S. products, and ruled against our country, overriding our sovereignty. See how that works now? Now we're going to have less safe products and increased foreign competition because of the WTO's existence.

This ruling was naturally applauded by Canada and Mexico. **"With this ruling, this process has been concluded in a successful and definitive manner for Mexico,"** Mexico's Secretary of the Economy said in a statement. **"The Mexican government reiterates its commitment to fight any practice that goes against the international commitments that have been made by our trading partners and that unduly disadvantage our producers,"** the government agency added.

"We are pleased with today's World Trade Organization appeal decision in favor of our livestock industry," Canadian Agriculture Minister Gerry Ritz said. **"Our government has always stood with our cattle and hog producers, in order to create a stronger and more profitable integrated North American livestock industry."**

By this ruling, you soon if not already will not know if the meat you are eating was raised on a wholesome family farm in the United States, or in a polluted cesspool somewhere in third world Mexico.

"Today's (June 29) ruling makes very clear that these so-called 'trade' pacts have little to do with trade between countries, but rather impose outrageous limits on the most basic consumer safety policies on which we all rely," said Lori Wallach, director of

Public Citizen's Global Trade Watch. **"The WTO announcing that big agribusiness corporations must be allowed to sell mystery meat here, despite U.S. consumers and Congress demanding these labels, is yet another example of outsourcing our legal system to international commercial bodies that push corporate interests."**

The WTO isn't just stopping there though; they have had an agenda in the works for many years now to eliminate **all** country-of-origin labeling for **all** products, and primarily have this plan aimed at hiding how many of the products we are consuming are coming out of China these days. The more stuff that comes from China = the less stuff being produced in the United States = a continued path to the destruction of the United States as a global power.

How would you like to go shopping one of these days and discover that every product you looked at, the label said "Made in the World" instead of "Made in China," "Made in Mexico," "Made in USA" etc.? The labels on the products we purchase here in the U.S. that names the country of origin may soon be gone.

In 2011, Andreas Maurer, chief of the WTO's International Trade Statistics Section, said **"... in the past two or three years there has been huge momentum to get the necessary information that would be used to rationalize elimination of country of origin labeling."**

On April 16, 2012, the European Commission and WTO held a conference to mark the launch of the World Input-Output Database (WIOD). This effectively moved the WTO another step closer to eliminating "country of origin" labeling.

Since a large amount of today's traded products are not produced in a single location but are the end-result of a series of steps carried out in many countries around the world, the WTO believes the time is right to eliminate country-of-origin labeling. An example of what is happening is that cars and trucks produced by General Motors, Ford, or whoever may have parts and assemblies of parts coming from several other countries, including China.

The WTO wants to adopt the "Made in the World" logo for **all** products on the grounds that global supply chains have made country-of-origin labeling inaccurate and obsolete.

The WTO's "Made in the World" initiative is part of the process of "re-engineering global governance," said WTO Deputy Director General Alejandro Jara, celebrating the launching of the World Input-Output Database. "With the advent and rise of global supply chains it is misleading to rely solely on gross trade flows as a measure" of a country's competitive position. As companies have created global supply chains, "attributing the full commercial value of imports to the last country of origin can skew bilateral trade balances, pervert the political debate on trade imbalances and may lead to wrong and counter-productive decisions."

For consumers in the United States, "Made in the World" labels wouldn't allow you to protect your family from the substandard, tainted, harmful, and even life threatening products coming from China. Remember the toxic Chinese drywall? Remember the melamine chemicals in the Chinese dog food? These labels wouldn't allow you to trace the source of a recalled product, and we would ultimately be left holding the bag of side effects, be they monetary or health related. I could go on for pages listing products from China that have been yanked off the shelves in recent years. If this is implemented, you also wouldn't be able to support American workers and businesses by buying "Made in USA."

These changes are coming....and soon. Bottom line, every action taken by the proponents of the Great Plan are designed to promote and advance the agenda of the one world government.

This is why they started grouping countries together ala the European Union. And the African Union. What? You didn't know that an African Union was already in place? It is. They are currently working on creating the Asian Union, the South American Union and the North American Union. Once the countries of the world have their borders broken down within these Unions, that will make it easier to then merge the Unions into one all-encompassing global body either under the UN or under a newly developed global governmental body.

Chapter 10/D

UNIONIZING MANKIND

"Regionalism must precede globalism. We foresee a seamless system of governance from local communities, individual states, regional unions and up through to the United Nations itself."
-UN's Commission on Global Governance

We're going to run through this sub-chapter as quickly as possible, but I wanted to include this section because the creation of these continental unions is yet another advancement in the breaking down of the sovereign nation's borders on the road to a full-blown, nation-absorbing, borderless one world government.

Let's begin with the first and most well-known of the Great Plan-inspired continental unions, the EU, or European Union, where plans for its existence were batted about at the annual Bilderberg meeting in 1955. Although the globalists already had set in motion the creation of the EU right after WW II, it is significant to learn that what they wanted to happen did.

On May 8, 2009, Wikileaks released leaked papers from the 1955 Bilderberg meeting in Germany detailing the agenda to create a European Union and a single European currency, known today at the Euro.

The released papers detail talks of the **"Pressing need to bring the German people, together with the other peoples of Europe, into a common market."**

The document also outlines the plan, **"To arrive in the shortest possible time at the highest degree of integration, beginning with a common European market."**

Only two years later, in 1957, the globalists formed the European Economic Community (EEC), which comprised of a single market between Belgium, France, Germany, Italy, Luxembourg and the Netherlands. The EEC gradually morphed and grew over the next few decades until it became the European Union, which was officially sanctioned in 1993.

Now, knowing what you've read in the previous 300 pages, here is something for you to ponder: the European Parliament today is housed in what is called the **Tower Building**, and is not only named after **Nimrod's Tower of Babel**, but was constructed to look as close as possible to the most famous piece of artwork that depicts **Nimrod's Tower of Babel**. This is because they are paying tribute to the Great Plan, of which King Nimrod is the most important part. It is also representative of the bringing back together of the various groups of "different languages" that were originally scattered by God in the Book of Genesis, another sign that the Great Plan is nearing completion. The official EU motto, "**United in Diversity**", is certainly fitting. One day, the resurrected King Nimrod may very well be seated in his modern day Tower of Babel, ruling over his empire as he did thousands of years ago. This, of course, would be before he took his destined seat within the rebuilt Temple of Solomon.

So. A European Union is in existence today. Are there any signs of a coming North American Union to merge Canada, the United States, and Mexico? You better believe it.

Just as the European Union was built incrementally, so is the NAU and its proposed currency, the "Amero"....just like the Euro, get it? Just as the European Union evolved through ever more binding trade agreements, so is the North American Union.

The road to merging the U.S. with Mexico and Canada started with something called NAFTA, the North American Free Trade Agreement, which was pushed onto the unsuspecting American public as something that was going to help us. It has, in fact, done us much harm.

Since the establishment of NAFTA, the U.S. trade deficit jumped exponentially from under $100 billion to over $700 billion, not a good thing if you know anything about how economics works.

NAFTA was signed by Skull and Bonesman President George H.W. Bush, Mexican President Salinas, and Canadian Prime Minister Brian Mulroney in 1992. It was ratified by the legislatures of the three countries in 1993. The bought-and-paid-for U.S. House of Representatives approved it by 234 to 200 on November 17, 1993. The bought-and-paid-for U.S. Senate approved it by 60 to 38 on November 20, three days later. It was signed into law by President Bill Clinton on December 8, 1993 after taking the baton of treachery from Bush Sr., and officially began on January 1, 1994.

> *"Why can't we be not only partners in the long term, but a North American Union?"*
> *-Mexican President Vicente Fox*

> *"A convergence of our two economies, convergence on the basic and fundamental variables of the economy, convergence on rates of interest, convergence on income of people, convergence on salaries......erase that border, open up that border for the free flow of products, merchandises, and capital as well as people."*
> *-Mexican President Vicente Fox, speaking of what he sought from NAFTA with regards to the United States*

Now that they had their foot in the door with NAFTA, the globalists set about advancing their agenda towards a fully integrated NAU.

In 2003, two years after the 9/11 attacks, taking advantage of terrorized citizens everywhere, the Independent Task Force on North America was created by the CFR in a joint effort with the respected versions of the Canadian and Mexican versions of the CFR, the Canadian Council of Chief Executives and the Mexican Council on Foreign Relations.

In October of 2004, the ITFNA published *"Building a North American Community"*, which was a game plan for further integration between the three NAU candidates.

The CFR report stated:

> *"The three governments should commit themselves to the long-term goal of dramatically diminishing the need for the current*

intensity of the governments' physical control of cross-border traffic, travel, and trade within North America. A long-term goal for a North American border action plan should be joint screening of travelers from third countries at their first point of entry into North America and the elimination of most controls over the temporary movement of these travelers within North America."

What this report is saying, is that the borders between Canada, the U.S. and Mexico should be eliminated and the border around North America is where the security border should be enforced.

In March of 2005, there were two significant events in regards to the formation of the NAU. First, the ITFNA released a press release calling for expedited implementation of their agenda to create a "North American Economic and Security Community" by the year 2010. This statement was meant to coincide with the second event, which was the fact that at the same time as the release of this statement, the leaders of the three countries signed on to something called the Security and Prosperity Partnership of North America, the SPP. This is just a more advanced version of NAFTA, meant to further break the back of the United States economy.

Fast forward to April 4, 2012, and you will find current President Obama, card-carrying CFR member, picking up where Bush II left off by hosting the "North American Leaders Summit", where they announced further integration of the three countries across a broad range of fields.

"Our integration helps maximize our capabilities and makes our economies more innovative and competitive globally. Working together, we strive to ensure that North American economic cooperation fosters gains in productivity for all of our citizens. By eliminating unnecessary regulatory differences, smaller businesses are better equipped to participate in an integrated North American economy. Success in these efforts opens the way to additional North American regulatory cooperation."

-a joint statement by Obama and the other two leaders

Since ascending the presidency, Obama has also made it clear that instead of arresting and sending home the illegal invaders of the United States, he wants to reward them for breaking our laws by legalizing the tens of millions of illegal aliens, mostly Mexicans, making them, as citizens, eligible to sponsor bringing in the family members they left behind in Mexico, further threatening the stability of the United States.

All in the name of the Great Plan......

People are slowly but surely waking up though:

In September 2006, Patriotic U.S. Representative Virgil Goode caught wind of the NAU plan and proposed, with six co-sponsors, non-binding House Concurrent Resolution 487. This Resolution **specifically outlined** opposition to a North American Union or a NAFTA Superhighway as a threat to U.S. sovereignty. Unfortunately, the bill never left committee.

This same resolution was reintroduced by Goode in January 2007 for the 110th Congress as House Concurrent Resolution 40, this time with forty-three cosponsors, including 2008 Republican presidential candidates Duncan Hunter, Ron Paul and Tom Tancredo, who have all expressed opposition to a North American Union during their campaigns.

Something else to be aware about regarding the NAU is something called the NAFTA Superhighway, or Trans-Texas Corridor.

This was first proposed by Texas Governor and CFR/Bilderberg attendee Rick Perry in 2002. It consists of a 1,200 foot (366 m) wide highway that also carries utilities such as electricity, petroleum, and water, as well as railway track and fiber-optic cables, and would serve to flood the United States with even more cheap, low-quality and often dangerous Chinese products via importation to Mexico, bypassing the United States trade tariffs. In July 2007, U.S. Representative and candidate for the Republican nomination in the 2008 presidential election Duncan Hunter successfully offered an amendment to H.R. 3074, the Department of Transportation Appropriations Act, 2008, prohibiting the use of federal funds for U.S. Department of Transportation participation in the activities of the Security and Prosperity Partnership of North America (SPP).

Hunter stated that:

"Unfortunately, very little is known about the NAFTA Super Highway. This amendment will provide Congress the opportunity

to exercise oversight of the highway, which remains a subject of question and uncertainty, and ensure that our safety and security will not be compromised in order to promote the business interests of our neighbors."

The New World Order is real, and while they are diligently working to create a fully-realized North American Union, the proponents of the Great Plan have already managed to foster the African Union, which you have probably never heard of or knew existed.

The African Union, or AU, came into existence on July 9, 2002, and consists of 54 African countries. This too was the result of years of progressive treaties and agreements. One of their stated goals is the "acceleration of the political and socio-economic integration of the continent".

Onward to Asia, where the Asia Cooperation Dialogue, or ACD, was created in 2002 to promote Asian interest in the growing world of continental unionizing.

And then last but not least, we have the Union of South American Nations, created by the UNASUR Constitutive Treaty signed on May 23, 2008.

When you hear the word "union", it usually brings thoughts to mind of safety, security, and prosperity. When it comes to organizing countries to destroy their sovereignty in the name of the New World Order, the exact opposite is, in fact, the case.

Chapter 10/E

THE REAL "INCONVENIENT TRUTH" ABOUT GLOBAL WARMING

"Now is the time to draw up a master plan for organic sustainable growth and world development based on global allocation of all finite resources and a new global economic system."
-From the Club of Rome's 1974 report "Mankind at the Turning Point"

"Humanity is sitting on a time bomb. If the vast majority of the world's scientists are right, we have just ten years to avert a major catastrophe that could send our entire planet's climate system into a tail-spin of epic destruction involving extreme weather, floods, droughts, epidemics and killer heat waves beyond anything we have ever experienced – a catastrophe of our own making."
- Former Vice-President Al Gore's 2006 "documentary" An Inconvenient Truth

"We've got to ride this global warming issue. Even if the theory of global warming is wrong, we will be doing the right thing in terms of economic and environmental policy."
- Timothy Wirth, President of the UN Foundation and former U.S. senator

"I believe it is appropriate to have an over-representation of factual presentations on how dangerous it is, as a predicate for

*opening up the audience to listen to what the solutions are, and
how hopeful it is that we are going to solve this crisis."*
-Former Vice-President Al Gore, an alleged 33rd degree Freemason

As you can tell from the above quote and others in this book, the agenda of the Great Plan is out in the open for all to see. The quotes from the many evil minions of the Great Plan I've given are unbelievable, but true. The only reason they are getting away with what they are, is that the proponents of the Great Plan have done such a masterful job of setting up a smoke screen in the form of mindless entertainment and brain-numbing poisons foisted on us in our food and water. General humanity is oblivious to the life-threatening changes they are orchestrating for us.

*"Effective execution of Agenda 21 will require a profound
reorientation of all human society, unlike anything the world has
ever experienced; a major shift in the priorities of both governments
and individuals and an unprecedented redeployment of human and
financial resources. This shift will demand that a concern for the
environmental consequences of every human action be integrated
into individual and collective decision-making at every level."*
-Quote from the UN's "Agenda 21" (repeated quote)

So, just to get this out of the way, here is the honest-to-God truth regarding all you've probably heard about Global Warming:

Yes, there is global warming happening, and no, it is not caused by mankind. The Anthropogenic/Man-made Global Warming scare being pushed by the United Nations/New World Order crowd is completely a lie, with the intention of helping to destroy the Western nations' economies, lining their pockets through cap-and-trade/ carbon taxes, and tightening their control grip over humanity. The fact is that we are in a period of increased solar activity, and this is causing the undeniable truth that there is global warming. That's it. That's the bottom line truth.

Global Warming as you have been made to believe by the bought-and-paid-for politicians who do and say what they're paid to, and the Mainstream Media simply doesn't exist. I'm going to explain what is really going on with our environment, and with the Great Plan scam associated with the reality of Global Warming.

The preponderance of factual evidence shows that we humans contribute such an infinitesimal amount of CO_2 compared to natural processes that we couldn't possibly be responsible for global warming. It is a FACT that **mankind only generates 5% or less of all greenhouse gasses and particulates per year.** The main source of greenhouse gases is in fact water evaporation from the oceans of the world. It's very simple: increased solar activity equates to more water evaporation off the oceans of the world. Mankind's contribution to the "problem" is insignificant compared to natural processes such as water evaporation, vegetation decay, dust storms, volcanic activity, etc. that account for 95% or more of all greenhouse gases in a given year.

Global Warming, which **is** occurring, is not due to human contribution of Carbon Dioxide/CO_2, and what is being pushed on us is the greatest deception in the history of science.

What is happening is that we are in a cycle of increased solar activity, and this is the real reason behind global warming trends and climate change in general, which really is happening. The global warming alarmists at the UN have intentionally ignored and clouded the facts surrounding the massive amount of scientific data that clearly shows that warming and cooling of the Earth's climate is directly related to solar activity.

Do you think we had an ice age thousands of years ago because we were lacking mankind pumping out all of those terrible greenhouse gases??? It all has to do with **SOLAR ACTIVITY**; you've got to remember this, because the legislation they are trying to enact at the global level through the UN will be just one more nail in the coffin for our country. By imposing unrealistic emission standards on our industries they will effectively close them down, and those jobs that haven't been shipped to China and India already---who are largely EXEMPT from these proposed standards---will be.

Let me tell you something that happened in the mid-1970s that you may or may not be aware of. The proponents of the Great Plan were rattling our cages that we were in danger of global COOLING---not warming. They jumped the gun on the research looking for another way to control us and got burned. Pro-NWO stalwart *"Newsweek"* ran the story in 1975, among other publications, about the subject. Their incomplete studies of the natural warming and cooling trends of the Earth due to SOLAR activity shot them in the foot, and they immediately did an about-face after figuring out we were actually heading into a NATURAL warming trend that directly correlates with our Sun's solar activity.

Temperatures declined from 1940 to 1980 and in the early 1970's global cooling was the consensus of groups like the Club of Rome and other Illuminati organizations. This proves that consensus is not and never is fact, and is subject to change when faced with undeniable facts---unless the consensus is a pre-manufactured ruse foisted upon an unsuspecting, naïve population. By the 1990's temperatures appeared to have reversed and Global **Warming** suddenly became the consensus and they seized on the apparent trend again as the way to get us under their thumb, pitting man against the environment. The Club of Rome wasted no time in getting the ball rolling on the threat of "anthropogenic (man-made) global warming":

> *"In searching for a new enemy to unite us, we came up with the idea that pollution, the threat of global warming, water shortages, famine and the like would fit the bill....All these dangers are caused by human intervention....and thus the real enemy, then, is humanity itself....we believe humanity requires a common motivation, namely a common adversary in order to realize world government. It does not matter if this common enemy is a real one or....one invented for the purpose.*
> *-From the Club of Rome's 1992 report "The First Global Revolution"*

Our planet has been slowly warming since last emerging from the "Little Ice Age" of the 17th century. Before that came the "Medieval Warm Period", in which temperatures were about the same as they are today. Both of these climate phenomena are known to have occurred for a fact---absent ANY influence by mankind.

"The Climate bill will help bring about global governance....But it is the awareness itself that will drive the change and one of the ways it will drive the change is through global governance and global agreements."
-Al Gore, alleged "expert" on climate change

Global Warming in recent years has been an **undisputable fact**, and no one can reasonably deny that---but it has **nothing to do with human activity.** Don't believe the lies.

We are facing a planetary emergency. The relationship between humankind and planet earth has been radically altered in a very short time..... Yes, Senator, it's a global problem and it has to be solved with a global strategy....and every nation has to be a part of the solution.

I know that CO2 tax is considered wildly unrealistic now. But our pattern of financing our social programs and health and welfare programs on the backs of employment has outlived its rationality and usefulness. We should replace employment taxes with a pollution tax system, principally CO2. I really believe that would help our economy, our competitiveness.
-Al Gore, Congressional Testimony, March 21, 2007

Remember, these quotes are coming from Illuminati minion Al Gore, an elitist who has a **huge** carbon footprint and who lived in a 30,000 sq. ft. mansion at the time he was blowing out these quotes, telling you to "do as I say, not as I do".

"The climate crisis is not a political issue; it is a moral and spiritual challenge to all of humanity. It is also our greatest opportunity to lift Global Consciousness to a higher level."
- Al Gore, Nobel Peace Prize acceptance speech

It was a fitting event for Hollywood, the land of make-believe, to bestow upon propagandist Al Gore an Oscar award for his fictitious fairy-tale "An Inconvenient Truth"---the so-called documentary about the impending global warming disaster that will decimate life on Earth if we don't do what they tell us to do.

But what could possibly be motivating Al Gore to be such a bold-faced liar? This heading from November 2009 in a London newspaper, *The Guardian*, should shed a little light on the subject:

"Al Gore could become world's first carbon billionaire"

.....Al Gore, the former US vice president, could become the world's first carbon billionaire after investing heavily in green energy companies...... Mr. Gore is poised to become the world's first "carbon billionaire," profiteering from government policies he supports that would direct billions of dollars to the business ventures he has invested in.....

Not only this, Al Gore traffics in something called "carbon credits", which are soon to be enforced regulations on U.S. businesses, where they are required to purchase these in order to do business. Gore is positioning himself to profit highly off of this at our expense as he helps to drive the U.S. under.

"It doesn't matter what is true, it only matters what people believe is true."
-Paul Watson, co-founder of Greenpeace

If it is a valid claim that global warming is caused by mankind, then why is it necessary for the global warming alarmists to so viciously attack those who disagree? One of the favorite tactics of the Global Warming alarmists is to throw out a blanket statement calling anyone who doesn't believe in man-made Global Warming to be a tin hat wearing conspiracy theorist, without going into any facts of what they themselves believe.

"Climate change is real. Not only is it real, it's here, and its effects are giving rise to a frighteningly new global phenomenon: the man-made natural disaster."
- Barack Obama, US President

According to the UN legislation they are proposing, the evidence for global warming SHOULD be powerful enough to refute those who disagree---**but it doesn't and falls far short.** They can't factually prove mankind causes global warming because we don't. Instead we find a paranoid fervor inflicted upon society about global warming and man's shameful contribution to it, rather than the facts behind the solar cycle-caused global warming period we are currently going through. That is a major red flag for anyone who is paying attention---like me and millions of other patriotic Americans who know what the real reason behind the scam is: The Great Plan of global enslavement.

> *"A massive campaign must be launched to restore a high-quality environment in North America and to de-develop the United States... De-development means bringing our economic system (especially patterns of consumption) into line with the realities of ecology and the global resource situation...Redistribution of wealth both within and among nations is absolutely essential, if a decent life is to be provided for every human being."*
> *-John Holdren, President Obama's science czar*

We've heard that the "science is settled" from New World Order proponents like Al Gore and Maurice Strong and that it is mankind's contribution to the natural CO2 in the atmosphere that has been the principal cause of global warming. We're also hearing that "all the world's scientists now agree on this settled science", and it is now time to quickly and radically alter our culture in order to prevent a looming global catastrophe. And last, but not least, we're seeing a sort of mass hysteria sweeping our culture regarding the whole "green movement" which is really quite disturbing. Historians ponder how the entire nation of Germany could possibly have been led into Nazism in such a short time. You now know that the **exact** same forces behind Hitler are also the **exact** same forces behind the anthropogenic Global Warming hoax.

"No matter if the science of global warming is all phony... climate change provides the greatest opportunity to bring about justice and equality in the world."
- Christine Stewart, former Canadian Minister of the Environment

"There are too many people, that's why we have global warming. We have global warming because too many people are using too much stuff."
-*Ted Turner, globalist, major UN donor, proponent of the New World Order*

Several well-known names have raised their voices in opposition to the Global Warming scam, but you've probably never heard about them speaking up, because you aren't told what you're not supposed to hear by the Mainstream Media.

Michael Crichton, the scientist, writer and filmmaker (Jurassic Park) was one of the truth-seekers, RIP. In his book, *"State of Fear"*, he explains the flawed science behind Global Warming, and he frequently spoke about his beliefs at various speaking engagements.

Quotes from our own Senators never see the light of day in the Mainstream Media:

I was on a program yesterday with Art Robinson. He was one of the scientists in the Oregon petition, 17,800 scientists, that said that, yes, we understand that we are going through a warming period, but it's not due to manmade gases. And this is ten years after they came out with their report, and nobody ever talks about that. The recent findings up in Canada, when 60 scientists told the prime minister, Harper, if we had known ten years ago what we know today about science, we would never have asked you to sign on to the Kyoto Treaty.
-*Senator James Inhofe*

Who do you think is really telling us the truth about climate change, Al Gore or this guy?:

It is the greatest scam in history. I am amazed, appalled and highly offended by it. Global Warming; It is a SCAM. Some dastardly scientists with environmental and political motives manipulated long term scientific data to create in [sic] allusion of rapid global warming. Other scientists of the same environmental whacko type jumped into the circle to support and broaden the "research" to further enhance the totally slanted, bogus global warming claims. Their friends in government steered huge research grants their way to keep the movement going. Soon they claimed to be a consensus.

Environmental extremists, notable politicians among them, then teamed up with movie, media and other liberal, environmentalist journalists to create this wild "scientific" scenario of the civilization threatening environmental consequences from Global Warming unless we adhere to their radical agenda. Now their ridiculous manipulated science has been accepted as fact and become a cornerstone issue for CNN, CBS, NBC, the Democratic Political Party, the Governor of California, school teachers and, in many cases, well informed but very gullible environmental conscientious citizens. Only one reporter at ABC has been allowed to counter the Global Warming frenzy with one 15 minutes documentary segment.

I have read dozens of scientific papers. I have talked with numerous scientists. I have studied. I have thought about it. I know I am correct. There is no run away climate change. The impact of humans on climate is not catastrophic. Our planet is not in peril. I am incensed by the incredible media glamour, the politically correct silliness and rude dismissal of counter arguments by the high priest of Global Warming.

-John Coleman, founder of The Weather Channel

There are untold numbers of other famous people who have been suppressed by the Mainstream Media when they speak up about the Global Warming scam, but let's hear from someone not-so-famous, who has the credentials to back up his beliefs......

Richard Lindzen is an atmospheric physicist and a professor of meteorology at MIT, renowned for his research in dynamic meteorology, particularly atmospheric waves. He is a member of the National Academy of Sciences and has held positions at the University of Chicago, Harvard University and MIT. In other words he's a pretty smart guy. Lindzen frequently speaks out against the notion that Global Warming is caused by humans, but nobody is listening and the UN agenda thunders forward towards clamping tyrannical carbon limits on United States companies. As Lindzen said regarding the myth of anthropogenic Global Warming: **"the consensus was reached before the research had even begun."** Remember what Maurice Strong said?

"What if a small group of world leaders were to conclude that the principal risk to the Earth comes from the actions of the rich countries? And if the world is to survive, those rich countries would have to sign an agreement reducing their impact on the environment. Will they do it? The group's conclusion is 'no'. The rich countries won't do it. They won't change. So, in order to save the planet, the group decides: Isn't the only hope for the planet that the industrialized civilizations collapse? Isn't it our responsibility to bring that about?"

They are literally ramming this lie down our throats, and most of humanity has swallowed it hook, line, and sinker.

So, now we come to the issue of something dubbed "Climategate" that reared its head in 2009, and was then largely marginalized, buried and finally stonewalled by the Mainstream Media.

The Climatic Research Unit email controversy (dubbed "Climategate" in the media) began in November 2009 with the Internet leak of thousands of emails and other documents from the University of East Anglia's (UEA) Climatic Research Unit (CRU). According to the university, the emails and documents were obtained through the hacking of a server, with 61 megabytes of confidential files released onto the internet.

These files and emails that were released reveal conspiracy, collusion in exaggerating warming data, possibly illegal destruction of incriminating information, organized resistance to disclosure, manipulation of data, private admissions of flaws in their public claims and much more.

A façade of an "independent" investigation into Climategate supposedly cleared the UEA "scientists" of any wrong doing as reported in the Illuminati's Mainstream Media---which is a total farce and slap in the face of any intelligent human who looks into the facts.

We are being taken for a ride here people, and you need to look into these kinds of things.

There is a lot of information and MIS-information about the topic of Global Warming, but I think I gave you what you need to know in a nutshell---the task of looking into it further is up to you.

"Climate Change is the greatest threat that human civilization has ever faced."
- Angela Merkel, German Chancellor

"We have reached the critical moment of decision on climate change. Failure to act now would be deeply and unforgivably irresponsible. We urgently require a global environmental revolution."
- Tony Blair, former British Prime Minister

Chapter 10/F

NEW WORLD ORDER, NEW WORLD RELIGION

"The fate of mankind, as well as of religion, depends upon the emergence of a new faith in the future. Armed with such a faith, we might find it possible to re-sanctify the earth."
- Al Gore, Earth in the Balance

"It is the responsibility of each human being today to choose between the force of darkness and the force of light. We must therefore transform our attitudes, and adopt a renewed respect for the superior laws of Divine Nature."
- Maurice Strong, first Secretary General of UNEP/United Nations Environment Program, which bills itself as "the voice for the environment in the United Nations system"

"The religion of the future will include within its own structure the best of science, art, literature, politics, and sociology. Spirituality is not a blind faith about things invisible. It is an inspired use of things known and available."
-Manly P. Hall, 33rd degree Freemasonic "prophet"

Have you ever seen those "Coexist" bumper stickers? The one where the various religious/humanist symbols are used to form the word coexist? Well, that conglomeration is the exact gist of the coming New Age one world religion.

The proponents of the Great Plan are slowly but surely indoctrinating humanity into believing that "there are many paths to God" and that all religions worship the same God, just in different ways. They tell you things like Jesus Christ was just another in a long line of enlightened humans such as Buddha, or something along those lines in order to marginalize Jesus, who is the #1 enemy of the Great Plan. Jesus Christ is the only one of the supposed "enlightened ones" across the religious spectrum who warns us of the Great Plan, and the only one prophesized to come back and destroy it. This is because Jesus Christ is the only real deal, being the only one aligned with the true Creator, the Most High God.

This is highly significant, and also explains the extreme hatred towards Jesus Christ in particular and no other by the proponents of the Great Plan. Trust me, if they hate something that means it's GOOD for us! What is not good is that there are well-intended Jews and Christians who have been hoodwinked into believing the New Age propaganda and wanting to join hands with the pagan religions fostered by Nimrod's Babylonian Mystery Religion.

There is not much space in this book, as with all topics I've gone over, but this is an important one to understand. Again, scores of books can and have been written about every single topic in this book. It is up to you to do your own due diligence regarding what I've laid out here in these pages.

The coming New World Religion will be a modernized version of the Babylonian Mystery Religion, shrouded in pantheistic environmentalism. Remember, the Babylonian Mystery Religion is itself originally based on nature worship, with the deified King Nimrod originally represented as the Sun, and Queen Semiramis represented as the moon.

"Little by little a planetary prayer book is thus being composed by an increasingly united humanity seeking its oneness. Once again, but this time on a universal scale, humankind is seeking no less than its reunion with 'divine,' it's transcendence into higher forms of life. Hindus call our earth Brahma, or God, for they rightly see no difference between our earth and the divine. This ancient simple truth is slowly dawning again upon humanity, as we are

about to enter our cosmic age and become what we were always meant to be: the planet of god."
- Robert Muller, former UN Assistant Secretary General, its #2 most powerful position and devoted disciple of occultist Luciferian Alice Bailey

The proponents of the Great Plan are going to accomplish this largely through what you may have heard of as the New Age movement, which is in itself the belief that man, through enlightenment gained by the various tenets of the New Age philosophies, can become a god unto him or herself. That's what the bottom line of the Great Plan has been all along: Man turning into a god himself so he won't need the Creator God anymore, being able to live forever via the genetic engineering possible today. As a man or woman who is a member of the inner circle of the New World Order approaches the end of their life cycle, scientists working for the Great Plan occultists can take the DNA and clone that person ala a test tube baby, and through supernatural black magic rituals can, I believe that that they believe this, conjure the soul of one that has passed away into the newly cloned, much younger body. This is obviously conjecture on my part, but this scenario seems logical to me based on their intentions and actions about what they are trying to accomplish, and the sum total of my research. With their thousands-of-years-old occult practices paired with 21st Century technology, they are almost ready to eat from the "Tree of Life" and live forever as gods on Earth.

So. Since the ball for the Luciferian one world government has been set into motion via the United Nations, it would only make sense for the religious counterpart to the one world government, the one world religion, to also be orchestrated through the United Nations.

Well it is, and a prime example of this is the occult-themed Meditation/Prayer Room housed inside the UN headquarters.

In the early 1950s Dag Hammarskjöld, the second Secretary-General of the United Nations, spearheaded a campaign, to create a prayer/mediation room that would welcome **all** religions. He accomplished this with the help of the multi-faith "Friends of the UN Meditation Room" group.

"The stone in the middle of the room has more to tell us. We may see it as an altar, empty not because there is no God, not because it is an altar to an unknown god, but because it is dedicated to the God whom man worships under many names and in many forms."
-Dag Hammarskjold, commenting on the meaning of the altar in the middle of the UN's prayer room

The New Age spirituality promoted in the United Nations Meditation Room is the same as that promoted by many of the UN's religious influences. This includes the coming of a Universal Christ to satisfy all religions. You now know the real identity of this coming Universal Christ as the resurrected King Nimrod, aka the Antichrist, since he was the one who originally spawned all pagan religions; he literally **is** their god. He will deceive all who know not the truth of the facts of **his** Great Plan, including naive Christians and Jews.

The occult is based on the Great Plan, and vice-versa. Occultism originated in the pre-Flood days, and was brought back once again in ancient Babylon under Nimrod, The occult is based on the belief that man, through secret knowledge, can be elevated to god status. This is exactly what the New Age movement is all about. It is the occult coming out of the shadows and being manifested as the New Age/One World Religion whereby man is god, we are all gods unto ourselves. We already have the one world governmental/economical/military systems in place. The **New Age** movement, which encompasses all religions, **is the one world religion.**

The New Age has what it calls the "Christ" but this is not the Christ of the Gospels/New Testament. In the New Age view, Jesus was but one of the many enlightened ones that include Buddha, Confucius, Muhammad, etc. It is this view the New Agers want Christians to adopt. The Christ they will end up with will be the Antichrist/Nimrod. The true translation of "Antichrist" is not "against Christ" but "in the stead of Christ". When Nimrod makes his appearance on the world stage he will claim that he is the real prophesized Christ, but in fact will be an imposter "in the stead" of Christ.

The one religious group who has had more influence on the UN's shaping and pushing of the one world religion is a unique religion we already went over: Madame Blavatsky's Theosophy.

Keep in mind, the spiritual leaders of the New Age movement, Blavatsky, Bailey, Pike, Crowley, and many others admittedly wrote most of their books by automatic hand under the guidance of "ascended masters", which you now know as malevolent interdimension spirits.

The agenda of Theosophy was and is today promoted through the United Nations by a group called Lucis Trust, and for a time Lucis Trust actually had their offices inside the UN building.

The Lucis Trust is a nonprofit organization originally incorporated in the United States in 1922 by Alice Bailey and her husband 33rd degree (alleged) Freemason Foster Bailey, to act as a mechanism for the publishing of Alice Bailey's twenty-four automatic-hand-penned occult books.

"Is it not possible from a contemplation of this side of Masonic teaching that it may provide all that is necessary for the formulation of a universal religion?"
-Foster Bailey, husband of Alice Bailey

Originally founded as the **Lucifer Publishing Company** in the early 1920s, the name was changed to better hide their true intent in 1925 to the *Lucis Publishing Company.*

Here is a quote directly from the Lucis Trust website explaining **why** they changed the original name:

"There are comments on the World Wide Web claiming that the Lucis Trust was once called the Lucifer Trust. Such was never the case. However, for a brief period of two or three years in the early 1920's, when Alice and Foster Bailey were beginning to publish the books published under her name, they named their fledgling publishing company "Lucifer Publishing Company". By 1925 the name was changed to Lucis Publishing Company and has remained so ever since. Both "Lucifer" and "Lucis" come from the same word root, lucis being the Latin generative case meaning

of light. The Baileys' reasons for choosing the original name are not known to us, but we can only surmise that they, like the great teacher H.P. Blavatsky, for whom they had enormous respect, sought to elicit a deeper understanding of the sacrifice made by Lucifer. Alice and Foster Bailey were serious students and teachers of Theosophy, a spiritual tradition which views Lucifer as one of the solar Angels, those advanced Beings Who Theosophy says descended (thus "the fall") from Venus to our planet eons ago to bring the principle of mind to what was then animal-man. In the theosophical perspective, the descent of these solar Angels was not a fall into sin or disgrace but rather an act of great sacrifice, as is suggested in the name "Lucifer" which means light-bearer."

Now, I could ramble on for pages about just Lucis Trust, and their other endeavors such as "World Goodwill", but we'll quote again directly from the Lucis Trust website below to get to the point:

"World Goodwill is an activity of the Lucis Trust, which is on the roster of the United Nations' Economic and Social Council. World Goodwill is an accredited NGO with the Department of Public Information of the United Nations. To support the work of the United Nations and its Specialized Agencies as the best hope for a united and peaceful world"

On the "purposes and objectives" section on the World Goodwill website it states that World Goodwill has three main purposes: To help mobilize the energy of goodwill, to cooperate in the work of preparation for the reappearance of the **Christ,** and to educate public opinion on the causes of the major world problems and to help create the thought form of solution.

Notice they say "the Christ" and not Christ or Jesus Christ. The appearance of their "Christ" refers to the reappearance of the man who was, then was not, and will be again, King Nimrod.

"The beast, which you saw, once was, now is not, and will come up out of the Abyss and go to his destruction. The inhabitants of

the earth whose names have not been written in the book of life from the creation of the world will be astonished when they see the beast, because he once was, now is not, and yet will come."
-Book of Revelation 17:8, NIV

It is the environmental faction of Great Plan globalists that are also the ones throwing the most weight behind pushing this new religion, as evidenced by these quotes:

"It is the responsibility of each human being today to choose between the force of darkness and the force of light. We must therefore transform our attitudes, and adopt a renewed respect for the superior laws of Divine Nature."
-Maurice Strong, wealthy elitist, occultist backer of the Great Plan, and high-ranking member behind the UN global government

"Nature is my god. To me, nature is sacred; trees are my temples and forests are my cathedrals."
-Mikhail Gorbachev, communist and former leader of U.S.S.R, one of the upstanding contributors to the fulfillment of the Great Plan achieved through his leadership position in the "Green Movement"

"My great personal dream is to forge a tremendous alliance between all religions and spiritual groups, and the UN. We desperately need a United Religions Organization to bring reconciliation, unity and peace to all the peoples of our world."
-Robert Muller (again), former UN Assistant Secretary General

Muller was also the co-Chairman of the World Commission for Global Consciousness and Spirituality, and the co-Chairman, alongside (*ahem*) Mikhail Gorbachev, of the World Wisdom Council.

Muller was also active in organizing 1993's Parliament of World Religions meeting in Chicago, an attempt to further corral the religions of the world into a group-think mentality.

The conference hosted more than 8,000 representatives from 150 different religious and spiritual groups around the world. Robert Muller's speech, which received a prolonged standing ovation, was entitled *"A Proposal to establish a United Nations of Religion'"*.

His "proposal" was endorsed in the Parliament of World Religions Joint Communiqué:

> *"Our earth cannot be changed unless in the not too distant future an alteration in the consciousness of individuals is achieved. This has already been seen in areas such as war and peace or economy and ecology. And it is precisely for this alteration in inner orientation, in the entire mentality, in the "heart," that religion bear responsibility in a special way. Religion must be a unifier and peacemaker, not a cause for violence and separation."*

The PWR led to interfaith dialogue initiatives by many religious groups, including the Vatican (no surprise there, right?), and other Great Plan-inspired organizations such as the United Nations, the Gorbachev Foundation, the Clinton Global Initiative, and many other UN-associated, Non-Governmental Organizations, or NGOs as they are referred to at the UN. All NGO means is that they are **private** organizations with **private** funding and **private** agendas that you aren't privy to since they are non-governmental and "private", and you are only told about them what you're supposed to know and not the back-room dealings that regularly go on to formulate their agenda.

The biggest success for the occultists to come out of the PWR was something called the United Religions Initiative, which was proposed, again, by New Age guru Robert Muller.

The URI's stated goals are **"unity among religions** "and **"manifesting love for the Earth"**, which hopefully by now you recognize as a smoke screen for "takeover of the world's religions in preparation of the Antichrist".

Working closely with Muller on the plan to unite all religions is an Anglican Bishop named William Swing of Grace Episcopal Cathedral in San Francisco. Although Robert Muller is the brains behind URI, Bishop

Swing was put in charge as figurehead and spokesperson of this New Age organization.

The URI is and always has been a United Nations-steered project, and therefore just another component of the Great Plan agenda. Bishop Swing stated how Muller had contacted him in 1993 about becoming involved with the founding of the URI: **"Three and a half years ago, a telephone call arrived in San Francisco from the United Nations asking if we, at Grace Cathedral, would host a great interfaith worship service honoring the 50th Anniversary of the signing of the UN Charter in our city."**

This request along with further dialogue with Muller is allegedly what prompted Swing to become involved in the United Religions Initiative. Swing later stated: **"I got out of bed the next day determined to commit the rest of my life to an initiative that would create a United Religions which would, in appropriately spiritual ways, parallel the United Nations."**

Reverend James Davis, an Anglican minister from New York stated **"We've never seen any organization build coalitions as quickly or as successfully as the United Religions Initiative."**

Huston Smith, a scholar of various differing religions and author of *"The World's Religions"*, described the URI as **"by far the most significant global interfaith effort."**

The URI claims that more than 1,000 religious groups, representing over a billion people, have endorsed the URI charter. These include the Vatican and the current leader of Buddhism, the Dalai Lama.

The preamble to the URI Charter is as follows:

We, people of diverse religions, spiritual expressions and indigenous traditions throughout the world, hereby establish the United Religions Initiative to promote enduring, daily interfaith cooperation, to end religiously motivated violence and to create cultures of peace, justice and healing for the Earth and all living beings.

We respect the uniqueness of each tradition, and differences of practice or belief.

We value voices that respect others, and believe that sharing our values and wisdom can lead us to act for the good of all.

We believe that our religious, spiritual lives, rather than dividing us, guide us to build community and respect for one another.

Therefore, as interdependent people rooted in our traditions, we now unite for the benefit of our Earth community.

We unite to build cultures of peace and justice.

We unite to heal and protect the Earth.

We unite to build safe places for conflict resolution, healing and reconciliation.

We unite to support freedom of religion and spiritual expression, and the rights of all individuals and peoples as set forth in international law.

We unite in responsible cooperative action to bring the wisdom and values of our religions, spiritual expressions and indigenous traditions to bear on the economic, environmental, political and social challenges facing our Earth community.

We unite to provide a global opportunity for participation by all people, especially by those whose voices are not often heard.

We unite to celebrate the joy of blessings and the light of wisdom in both movement and stillness.

We unite to use our combined resources only for nonviolent, compassionate action, to awaken to our deepest truths, and to manifest love and justice among all life in our Earth community.

It goes on to say: **The root of this ecological crisis is a spiritual crisis. Just as the religions and spiritual traditions of the world teach respectful interaction with a sacred whole, so must spiritual values and moral imperatives help humanity to rediscover a reverence for all life and respect for the sacredness of the whole of Planet Earth. Therefore, we call for interfaith cooperation in furthering this vision for love and protection of the Earth, reverence for life, and harmony with all living beings.**

According to Bishop Swing, the URI is intended to be to religion what the United Nations is to global politics, unifying the world's religions as the UN is unifying the world's nations. Swing confirmed these plans, **"The URI will be a spiritual United Nations. And what better place to give it birth than the Bay Area, which gave birth to the present UN."**

Bishop Swing also states, **"The URI will offer the world a powerful new vision of hope - the vision that the deepest stories we know can now cease to be causes of separation between people, and become instead the foundation for a reunited humanity. Religions need the URI. Bombs are exploding in the name of God in cities throughout the world, religious persecution is more prevalent now than ever before, religious extremists are demanding and obtaining nuclear weapons, and still there is no neutral arena where all of the religions can engage each other. The URI, in time, aspires to have the visibility and stature of the United Nations. It will have global visibility and will be a vital presence in local communities all over the world."**

The United Nations has granted the URI official "liaison status", which means that in return for UN financial support the URI will "co-operate closely with the UN and its organisations to complement the UN's political, diplomatic and social mandates, influence UN policy and support its programs."

"We stand on the threshold of a New World Order that may be defined either by an increasing polarisation that fuels a spiral of escalating conflict and violence, or by growing global cooperation that calls the human race to work across national, ethnic and religious boundaries to serve a larger global good."
-Bishop William Swing

J. MICAH'EL THOMAS HAYS

Bishop Swing recently made a public apology for 2,000 years of Christian evangelism. His apology included regret for **"proclaiming that Jesus Christ is Lord and Savior of all and for seeking to make the whole world Christian".** These are not the words of a true Christian, but of a New Ager.

The URI's goal is for a New Age spirituality that would unify the planet ala the UN. The URI is the tip of the spearhead of the one world religion right now.

The final form of this New Age spirituality will be a "green" naturalistic/humanistic religion with its roots in the Great Plan/Babylonian Mystery Religion. Anyone who refuses to accept this new spirituality will be labelled an intolerant radical fundamentalist or even a terrorist as things are progressing down the road to a police state in America these days.

"The greatest hope for the Earth lies in religionists and scientists uniting to awaken the world to its near fatal predicament and then leading mankind out of the bewildering maze of international crises into the future Utopia of humanist hope."
- Club of Rome, Goals for Mankind

"What an incredible planet in the universe this will be when we will be one human family living in justice, peace, love and harmony with our divine Earth, with each other and with the heavens."
- Robert Muller, UN Assistant Secretary General

"The spiritual sense of our place in nature...can be traced to the origins of human civilization.... The last vestige of organized goddess worship was eliminated by Christianity."
- Al Gore, Earth in the Balance

Chapter 11

9/11 WAS AN INSIDE JOB

"Our government has kept us in a perpetual state of fear - kept us in a continuous stampede of patriotic fervor - with the cry of grave national emergency. Always, there has been some terrible evil at home, or some monstrous foreign power that was going to gobble us up if we did not blindly rally behind it."
-General Douglas MacArthur

"If tyranny and oppression come to this land, it will be in the guise of fighting a foreign enemy."
- U.S. President James Madison

"A lie, told often enough, becomes the truth."
-Vladimir Lenin

And one more, **VERY IMPORTANT** quote:

"They had as king over them the angel of the Abyss, whose name in Hebrew is Abaddon, and in Greek, Apollyon (Apollo)"
-Revelation 9:11 (9/11 was arguably part of an occult ceremony)

Do you remember where you were when you first heard that a plane had crashed into the World Trade Center on September 11, 2001? Can you ever forget what you were doing when you first learned of the attacks taking place on United States soil? I was managing a construction site in Washington State when the attacks happened. Our jobsite was on a ridge overlooking the town of Issaquah.

Although I had no TV in my job trailer, I was getting updates off the internet---and I was completely awestruck. Just an unbelievable event unfolding right before our eyes. We were under attack, the United States, my country. My patriotic blood immediately began to boil and my guys and I formed a plan of something we could do to show our patriotism. Some of us went to work erecting a 5'x9' United States flag on the hill overlooking all of Issaquah. We ran electrical power over and installed two 500 watt halogen spotlights below the flag and lit it up 24/7 for many months after 9/11. You could see it easily from I-90 both day and night. I bet there are a few people on the eastside of Seattle that remember seeing the lit-up flag on the hill above the Home Depot in Issaquah---you couldn't help but notice it right after September 11.

I gobbled up every bit of Mainstream Media-fed information that came out and took it at face value, as I felt you should be able to at the time. *"Osama bin Laden and the Islamic radicals were attacking our country"* was drilled into our brains relentlessly for days, weeks and months after the attack. I let out a "Hurrah" when I first heard we started bombing Afghanistan and again when we started attacking Iraq. Little did I know the real truth of what was going on, simply because I believed the propaganda of the Mainstream Media, completely naïve of our government's history of false flag operations in the name of the Great Plan.

In other words, I bit on the official story hook, line, and sinker.

Here is the official story we were told and expected to believe:

19 Arab hijackers belonging to Al Qaida and directed by Osama bin Laden commandeered 4 commercial jet liners armed with box cutters. They were able to evade the national air defense system, NORAD, and were able to strike 3 out of 4 intended targets. As a result of the airliner impacts, World Trade Towers 1, 2, and 7 collapsed due to structural failure as a result of the ensuing fires, while the plane that hit both the Pentagon and the field in Shanksville, PA vaporized upon impact. The 911 Commission found that there were no warnings for this act of terrorism, while multiple governmental failures prevented adequate defense.

This blew me away a few years ago because I had never heard this, but in fact a third, 47-story skyscraper that was NOT hit by a jet plane fell in New York much later in the day on 9/11 along with the Twin Towers. Did you know this? I had not even heard of that until I happened across an online documentary about the event. Did you know they found molten structural steel underneath those giant debris piles at Ground Zero, including Building 7 which was not even hit by a jet? The only thing hot enough to melt steel short of a foundry is a demolition product called Thermite.

Fact: **It turns out that evidence of thermite was found by independent researchers at all three collapse areas at the World Trade Center**, including UNDETONATED military-grade nano-thermite. Nano-thermite is a specialized compound created in sophisticated military labs---not in caves in Afghanistan--- meaning someone had to have access to this stuff, and those same people that supplied it wired these three buildings to collapse after being hit by the jetliners.

Osama bin Laden wasn't even tied to 9/11 by the FBI, and that he was not even wanted by the FBI for the events of 9/11 because of lack of evidence, and that is also a fact.

Learning the truth about what really happened on 9/11, what we're going to go over now, is going to be like having the rug pulled out from under you. Like getting kicked in the stomach. Like feeling the worst heartache you've ever felt. This is going to be a terrible chapter for you to come to terms with if you don't know about this stuff, but what I am laying out is the truth and should come as no surprise after what we've already gone over, keeping in mind that the people pulling the strings of events like 9/11 are Luciferians, the most evil, bloodthirsty, sadistic, sexually perverted and reprehensible people on the face of the Earth. Don't be afraid now, not after all we've been through already.

I'm going to show you the mountain of Mainstream Media-suppressed evidence that shows beyond any reasonable doubt that 9/11 not only didn't go down the way we were led to believe, but that it was indeed an inside job orchestrated by the proponents of the Great Plan as an integral part of the final stages of completion of the one world government.

Difficult-to-plan operations such as the events of 9/11 always have loose ends, oversights, and unintended side-effects, and the events of

9/11 are **no exception**. In fact, this was a downright sloppy false flag operation that relied on the complacency of a traumatized population and a controlled Mainstream Media for success.

> *All truth passes through three stages. First, it is ridiculed. Second, it is violently opposed. Third, it is accepted as being self-evident.*
> -Arthur Schopenhauer, German philosopher (1788 - 1860)

Now, here is the cold, hard truth about the events of 9/11:

9/11 was not a terrorist attack orchestrated by Osama bin Laden from some secret cave in Afghanistan. 9/11 was an inside job perpetrated by criminal elements within our federal government, probably the CIA, working under direction of the modern day proponents of the Great Plan, the Illuminati. 9/11 was a "false flag" operation carried out to give them an excuse to launch two wars; one against the resource-rich countries of the Middle East, and one against YOU, John. Q. Public of the United States of America, who would dare stand in the way of the completion of the Great Plan. That is, the events of 9/11 were set in motion in order to excuse the launch of the never-ending "war on terror" against humanity, to further establish the presence of New Babylon in the Middle East, and to set up a tyrannical police state in the United States. They have accomplished all of these things, as you probably are aware of. They needed 9/11 in order to ram through the Patriot Act and Homeland Security so they could better keep an eye on the troublemaking patriots that they KNEW were beginning to wake up to their scheme and cause them trouble in the not-too-distant future, especially as a result of the information pouring out from the internet. They want to know who is planning to rebel against the system, so they can readily be identified when the time comes to try and round them up and put them in FEMA camps as alleged "domestic terrorists".

Chapter 11/A

WHY DID THEY DO IT?

"Sometimes people don't want to hear the truth because they don't want their illusions destroyed."
-Freidrich Nietzsche

Why would the proponents of the Great Plan sacrifice thousands of innocent American lives? Well, to start with, they've been responsible for sacrificing untold millions of people over thousands of years via events from actual human sacrifices in their occult rituals to bloodbaths like the French and Russian Revolutions where millions were tortured, raped and murdered in the name of the agenda of the Great Plan.

The sacrificing of "only" a few thousand American souls was merely a drop in the bucket in the grand scheme of things to them if you look at it from a historical point of view. Unfortunately, they will be sacrificing a lot more of us in the future, so you need to educate yourself about their entire agenda, that which is in this book, as quickly as possible while you are able so you won't be caught off guard like most.

The sheer number of benefits reaped by the agenda of the Great Plan as a result of 9/11 only adds to the sum total of the evidence of their guilt.

I'm just going to flat out list all of the benefits they gained by pulling off 9/11, and then we'll go over them each in a little more detail.

The proponents of the Great Plan/New World Order/one world government orchestrated and executed the events of 9/11 for the following reasons:

-to stun the American Public into believing they need to be unequivocally 100% reliant on the Feds to protect them via the Patriot Act/Homeland Security, when in fact it is the people running the Federal Government that we need protection from, the proponents of the New World Order

*-to shock the American Public so badly that all other domestic issues going on will seem negligible in comparison, such as the day before 9/11 when Donald Rumsfeld was on TV talking about how **$2.3 trillion** couldn't be accounted for at the Pentagon. The money was **missing**. I bet you never heard about that after the tidal wave of 9/11 washed over the media.*

-to excuse injecting our military presence into the Middle East, more so. After the first Gulf War, we set up our initial bases. After 9/11, we fully moved into the Middle East permanently.

-to feed the beast that is the Military Industrial Complex. Untold trillions of dollars have been spent and misspent since we invaded the Middle East in late 2001, lining the pockets of the weapons manufacturers that are largely owned through stock holdings by many of the proponents of the Great Plan.

-to tighten the Illuminati's grip over global energy resources by increased control of Middle East oil via US occupation of the Middle East.

-to reestablish the opium trade in Afghanistan, one of the primary sources of funds for the Illuminati's "black ops" programs carried out by the CIA, etc.

-to excuse the setting up of a police state in the United States via the 21st century Gestapo, Homeland Security.

-and lastly, the new owners of the World Trade Center complex were to collect billions of dollars on a terrorist-themed insurance policy taken out "just in the nick of time"

> *"Fear not the path of truth, for the lack of people walking on it."*
> *-Robert F. Kennedy*

I've explained the CFR, Trilateral Commission, Tavistock, and other groups and their role in expediting World Government, but to help shed some light on 9/11 we need to go over a smaller, highly influential and specialized think tank called PNAC---The Project for a New American Century.

Established in the spring of 1997 and funded largely by the **energy and arms industries**, PNAC was founded as a neoconservative (neocon) think tank whose stated goal was to usher in a "new American century". In other words, the next phase of the New Babylon. The Neocons are literally the Great Plan wing of the Republican Party---**calling** themselves right-wing but in effect the exact opposite of what a real Republican is---someone who promotes smaller, non-empirical federal government.

The neocons want big government and big budget deficits to further the agenda of the Great Plan. They directed and dominated Skull and Bonesman G.W. Bush's policies from 2000-2008, including his "preemptive war strategy" that took us back into Iraq. Dick Cheney. Donald Rumsfeld. Paul Wolfowitz. Richard Perle. They were the neocons forging the Bush policy---all he did was relay their plans as a talking head. Having won the Cold War and no military threat to speak of, this group of ideologues created a blueprint for the future via the Report from Iron Mountain. Their agenda was to capitalize not only on the need of a perceived enemy to keep people in fear and the Great Plan on track, but upon our surplus of military forces and armaments that could be used for conquest and then replenished, and the forcing of New Babylon's hegemony and corporate privatization upon the Arab world.

> *"Further, the process of transformation, even if it brings revolutionary change, is likely to be a long one, absent some catastrophic and catalyzing event like a new Pearl Harbor...(aka a new false flag event)"*
> - *"Rebuilding America's Defenses: Strategy, Forces and Resources for a New Century," This was contained in a PNAC report issued September, 2000.*

It has now been proven, and we will go over this proof, that once Bush had all of his top administration positions filled by PNAC members, who are also all members of the standard Round Table groups, that our guard against terrorist attacks was **intentionally** let down.

The Bush administration not only ignored but later denied the existence of a presidential briefing entitled *"Bin Laden determined to attack inside the United States"* until this document was revealed to the public. Testifying before the 9/11 Commission, Secretary of State Condoleeza Rice referred to it as an "historical document", and during the Commission's investigation we were led to believe this was the only warning, and it had just been overlooked. It has since come out that she was in fact lying. It has also come out that the FAA had in fact received **52** warnings from intelligence operatives that something was in the works in the months leading up to 9/11.

The Illuminati needed a new Pearl Harbor to open up the next front of the Great Plan and the Bush cabal intentionally let down their guard to let the plan proceed.

This "new Pearl Harbor" needed to be something so spectacular, so awesome, so terrifying that the American public would be so stunned and bewildered that they wouldn't know what to do with themselves, other than to blindly rally the troops and rage against whoever it was we were told did this to us.

And so on October 7, 2001, the United States military machine began to wage war on the third world country of Afghanistan by launching "Operation Enduring Freedom". We were told that the Islamic radicals had attacked us because they hated the freedoms and liberties we had in the U.S., and that Osama bin Laden and Al Qaida were an imminent threat to our way of life. This was a pre-fabricated false flag, paired with a pre-fabricated war, sold to the American people via the Mainstream Media.

The bombs began to rain down on the innocent civilians of Afghanistan and then about a year and half later on March 19, 2003 they began to drop on the innocent people of Iraq. Well over a million Afghani and Iraqi men, women, and children died as a result, millions more were maimed or crippled for life, not to mention thousands upon thousands of American soldiers killed and maimed in service in both countries. And for what? All to further the Great Plan, to further the agenda of the Luciferians, paid for with the blood of innocents as has happened for millennia.

And how about profiting from all of this wanton death and destruction? Some of the biggest financial beneficiaries had intimate ties directly to the Bush cabal and stood to reap handsomely from our war mongering. Halliburton, once headed by then Vice President Dick Cheney. Bechtel, once headed by then Secretary of Defense Donald Rumsfeld. Trireme, a military contractor started by then Deputy Secretary of Defense Richard Perle. And the list goes on and on. All members of PNAC who just happened to be in the right place at the right time to reap the benefits of the "new Pearl Harbor".

War means government contracts. Lots of them. Fat and oozing with Government pork and insider deals. War is big business. Forty-six percent of our Taxes go to the Military Industrial Complex. This figure doesn't even begin to account for all of the off-budget, black ops projects, homeland security, or the $60+ billion the United States Government will spend on "intelligence" in 2013 monitoring a non-existent enemy that they tell you is perennially hiding in the shadows. The majority of this $60 billion is in fact being spent watching **you and me**, monitoring as much public sentiment as they can to head off a potential revolt.

To launch an invasion of a country like we did takes time to prepare for. Is it possible there were signs pointing to an upcoming military conflict in the days, weeks, or months before 9/11?

Sure enough, our armed forces were in fact gathered in the Persian Gulf ready to strike before 9/11 even happened under military actions called Operation Swift Sword and Operation Bright Star.

On September 1, 2001, an exercise that had been planned for four years, called Operation "Swift Sword", began. 23,000 British troops deployed for the Middle East. At the same time not one but **two** U.S. aircraft carrier battle groups arrived on station in the Gulf of Arabia just off the Pakistani coast. Also at the same time, some 17,000 U.S. troops joined more than 23,000 NATO troops in Egypt for Operation "Bright Star." All of these forces were in place before the first plane even hit the WTC on 9/11.

And it is certainly no secret that the oil interests were in the pockets of then President G.W. Bush. What is the #1 spoil of going to war and winning in the Middle East? Control of the Oil. After the invasion of Iraq, "we" threw out all the Europeans running the oil show in Iraq and took it over, installing American subcontractors under direction of our military. Oil was one of the primary motives of the Bush regime for allowing and assisting the attacks. Without 9/11, it would have been impossible for the US to invade Iraq and take over their oil fields, which gives the US a dominant military position in the middle of the world's main oil production region. The Bush regime even engineered the rise to power of two former Unocal Oil employees: Hamid Karzai, who was installed as President of Afghanistan, and Zalmay Khalizad, the US envoy to Afghanistan.

Another reason to excuse an invasion of Afghanistan in particular, was that when the Taliban took over Afghanistan, they destroyed the country's opium crop---hindering the money supply for the CIA black ops (underground/off-the-record operations). Implemented in 2000, the Taliban's drug eradication program led to a 94 percent decline in opium cultivation. In 2001, according to UN figures, opium production had fallen to 185 tons. Immediately following the October 2001 US led invasion, production increased dramatically, regaining its historical levels and re-flooding the world market with heroin. According to the UN, Afghanistan supplies over 90 percent of the world's supply of opium, which is used to make heroin............and help fund the CIA's covert operations.

Bringing the reasoning behind orchestrating 9/11 back home to the United States, you have a growing population of people increasingly suspicious and critical of the rampant federal government corruption that they don't even bother hiding anymore. Conflict of interest is the norm in politics these days as our elected officials are purely on the take in our nation's capital. People are starting to wonder just why our government is so corrupt, you now know **exactly** why.

Corruption and waste serve to drive our federal debt higher, further putting us on the hook to the Illuminati bankers who own the Federal Reserve. People are starting to ask questions and look into these matters. They are waking up, and are becoming if not angry yet, concerned over this apparently worse and getting worse-by-the-year situation. And if they are able to dig deep enough into the corruption like I have, you'll run right into the proponents of the New World Order and the Great Plan pulling the strings behind the scenes and this is what they REALLY don't want you finding out about---the exact contents of this book. They don't want this and they can't have this because if humanity gets wise to what they are doing they are liable to rise up and stop them in their tracks. The way they are planning on heading this off is through implementation of a massive Police State and the propaganda through the Mainstream Media to go with it.

I've already heard the term the "age of conspiracy" bandied about the Mainstream Media, implying that there are so many theories about what is really happening in the world that people are becoming brainwashed by lies, propaganda, and paranoia, and therefore a threat to society over all the "evil conspiracy theories" out there. This is literally a pre-emptive strike by the proponents of the Great Plan, because they know what is coming. Planting the seed that: 1. nothing on the internet can be trusted to be true. 2. That people who believe the internet over the Mainstream Media are crazy conspiracy theorists.

I'll tell you something right now that isn't a conspiracy theory but is pure conspiracy, is the fact that the legislation contained within the draconian Patriot Act was written months and years before 9/11, and all ready to be presented and passed by a fear-mongering Congress just weeks after 9/11 on October 26, 2001. We'll go over this in detail in the "Police State" chapter coming right up. The Patriot Act and Homeland Security effectively set up a police state in America, a virtual 21st Century Gestapo right here in allegedly freedom and liberty-loving America. What a sick joke that is.

And last but not least, it is not only possible but probable due to the evidence we will go over that the brand new owner of the entire World Trade Center complex at the time 9/11 happened, Larry Silverstein, was at least aware of if not in on the 9/11 attack plans. This is represented by the facts of his actions about the events of 9/11. How could someone come to this conclusion? Let's take a look here.

The 30 year old World Trade Center had always been publicly owned, and managed by the New York/New Jersey Port Authority.

That is until a businessman named Louis Eisenberg became the chairman of the PA. He personally oversaw negotiations that put the publicly owned WTC into private hands for the first time ever in mid-2001, just a couple of months ahead of 9/11. Those private hands belonged to two Billionaires named Larry Silverstein and Frank Lowy. Even though their bid was lower than other bids for the complex, Eisenberg ensured they got possession of the property. With Eisenberg's help, they landed a 99 year lease worth $8 billion for a bargain price of $3.5 billion dollars.

If Silverstein and Lowy knew about the impending attacks, why did they buy a 99 year lease on the buildings? Because they could do the simple math: Silverstein bought the $3.5 billion lease with only a $15 million down payment. He then took out maximum terrorist insurance coverage only 6 weeks before the attacks...talk about good timing. From an economic standpoint, the World Trade Center, government-subsidized since its inception, had never functioned in the real world real estate marketplace. The complete demolition of the buildings on 9/11 eliminated the needed $1 billion asbestos abatement and facelift. As soon as the brand spanking new WTC is built and expanded to over 11 million sq. ft of rental space, Silverstein stands to pocket billions while the taxpayers and insurance providers cover Silverstein's so-called losses.

Not only this, but Silverstein demanded a **200% payout** from his insurance carriers, citing the two separate planes as separate terrorist incidents, and he got it. A federal jury ruled that the assault on the Twin Towers of the World Trade Center was in fact two occurrences for insurance purposes. The finding in U.S. District Court in Manhattan means leaseholder Larry Silverstein collected up to $4.6 billion, more than enough to rebuild the entire complex and then some.

And why wasn't Silverstein inside the Twin Towers the morning of September 11, 2001 like he normally would have been 99% of the other days he's been in business?

Larry Silverstein spent every morning at the World Trade Center right after he inked a 99-year deal to take over the complex in July 2001. Silverstein would have breakfast at Windows on the World, the restaurant on the 107th floor of the North tower, and then conduct meetings with his tenants. But on the morning of Sept. 11, 2001, he was at home, dressing for a doctor's appointment his wife had made for him, instead of at his usual table at Windows. **"I had said to my wife, sweetheart, cancel my doctor's appointment. I have so much to do at the Trade Center,"** he recalls. **"She got very upset and told me I had to go. As it turns out, that saved my life."**

Talk about being a lucky guy. And why weren't his son and daughter at their offices in the Twin Towers like they would have been 99% of the other days they've been in business? They **both** just happened to be "running late" that day.

All three coincidentally were running late at the same time on the same fateful day of 9/11.

Talk about *luck.*

Silverstein's friends and tenants at Zim-Israel American Shipping Company, which is owned by Zim Israel Navigation, which is owned by the government of Israel, also happened to be absent the morning of 9/11. They suddenly broke their lease, paid a 50k fine, and moved out of the North tower just weeks before 9/11. Talk about luck. When does it go from being lucky to being suspicious is what I would like to know. It turns out that Israel's Mossad, their "CIA", had knowledge of the impending attacks, which we will go over later in this chapter, and probably warned Zim-Israel Navigation to evacuate.

Larry Silverstein, the owner and controller of the destroyed WTC complex, later slipped up and stated in a PBS documentary that **he and the FDNY decided jointly to demolish WTC 7 late in the afternoon of 9/11.** In the documentary "America Rebuilds", aired September 2002, Silverstein makes the following statement;

"I remember getting a call from the, er, fire department commander, telling me that they were not sure they were gonna be able to contain the fire, and I said, 'We've had such terrible loss of life, maybe the smartest thing to do is pull it.' And they made that decision to pull and we watched the building collapse."

There can be little doubt as to how the word "pull" is being used in this context...........to "pull" a building is demolition industry lingo to demolish a building by imploding it. It would have taken weeks to wire up a building with explosives---not minutes or hours. If it were possible to bring down a steel-framed 47-story building perfectly into its own footprint by starting a few office fires, those demolition companies that charge millions of dollars would have been out of business a long time ago. Silverstein slipped up here and luckily other patriots caught this, adding it to the body of evidence of 9/11 being an inside job.

In fact, a bombshell regarding this was released inadvertently on April 21, 2010, when a reporter who was at Ground Zero on 9/11/01 revealed some interesting information he hadn't let out:

> *"Shortly before the building collapsed, several NYPD officers and Con-Edison workers told me that Larry Silverstein, the property developer of One World Financial Center was on the phone with his insurance carrier to see if they would authorize the controlled demolition of the building (7) – since its foundation was already unstable and expected to fall.*
>
> *A controlled demolition would have minimized the damage caused by the building's imminent collapse and potentially save lives. Many law enforcement personnel, firefighters and other journalists were aware of this possible option. There was no secret. There was no conspiracy."*
> *-Jeffrey Scott Shapiro, FOX News, 2010*

This quote is an excerpt from a story where Shapiro is actually taking a shot at the 9/11 Truth Movement. He volunteers information at the time he felt would back up Silverstein's story, but instead he completely torpedoed it. Thank you Mr. Shapiro.

Chapter 11/B

FALSE FLAG HISTORY

If you are having a hard time comprehending that the government that is supposed to be protecting us is responsible for the attacks of 9/11, I don't blame you. That is how compromised our government truly is under the masters of the Great Plan. Let me rephrase that so I can make an important point for the future: **It is not the government the people should be mad at; it's the people _running_ the government you should be taking issue with. The government is like a gun. It is as benign or malevolent as the person or entity wielding it. It would be akin to blaming a gun for a murder instead of the actual killer, the person (people) in control of the gun.**

You don't get much more malevolent than a Luciferian plan thousands of years in the making, willing to do anything and everything they can to fulfill it. This is why we are in such a bad spot today in our country and the world.

Point of fact: 9/11 is not the first time the people running our government planned to blow up our airliners and kill our citizens to further the New World Order agenda. This is something very disturbing and I found extremely unnerving in the course of my research about the events of 9/11. This is all true, found in declassified government documents acquired and put forth by fellow truth seekers.

In the early 1960s, America's top military leaders drafted a megalomaniacal plan and presented it to then President John F. Kennedy.

"Operation Northwoods" was a secret plan to be pulled off by the CIA or other operatives to kill innocent people, commit acts of terrorism in

U.S. cities, hijack airplanes, and plant evidence, among other things. They were then to fire up the Mainstream Media propaganda machine and blame it on Cubans to create public indignation and support an invasion of Cuba. Operation Northwoods is especially notable in that it included proposals for hijackings and bombings followed by the introduction of phony evidence that would implicate a foreign entity for us to go to war against.

Sound familiar?

The plans included the assassination of Cuban political figures, sinking boats of Cuban refugees on the high seas, hijacking planes, blowing up a U.S. ship, and even orchestrating violent terrorism in U.S. cities. The plans were developed as ways to trick the American public and the international community into supporting a war to oust Cuba's then new leader, communist Fidel Castro. America's top military brass even contemplated causing U.S. military casualties, writing: "We could blow up a U.S. ship in Guantanamo Bay and blame Cuba," and, "casualty lists in U.S. newspapers would cause a helpful wave of national indignation."

The plan stated:

> *"The desired resultant from the execution of this plan would be to place the United States in the apparent position of suffering defensible grievances from a rash and irresponsible government of Cuba and to develop an international image of a Cuban threat to peace in the Western Hemisphere."*

The plans had the written approval of **all of the Joint Chiefs of Staff** and were presented to President Kennedy's defense secretary, Robert McNamara, in March 1962. The Joint Chiefs even proposed using the potential death of astronaut John Glenn during the first attempt to put an American into orbit as a false pretext for war with Cuba, the documents show.

"Should the rocket explode and kill Glenn," they wrote, **"the objective is to provide irrevocable proof ... that the fault lies with the Communists in Cuba."**

The plans were motivated by a fervor among senior military leaders to depose Castro, who seized power in 1959 to become the first communist leader in the Western Hemisphere — only 90 miles from U.S. shores. The earlier CIA-backed Bay of Pigs invasion of Cuba by Cuban exiles had been a disastrous failure, in which the military was not allowed to provide firepower. The military leaders now wanted a shot at it. The main proposal was presented in a document entitled *"Justification for US Military Intervention in Cuba "* , which was written by the Department of Defense and the Joint Chiefs of Staff representative to the Caribbean Survey Group .The document was presented by the Joint Chiefs of Staff to Secretary of Defense Robert McNamara on March 13 as a preliminary submission for planning purposes. The Joint Chiefs of Staff recommended that both the covert and overt aspects of any such operation be assigned to them.

Operation Northwoods listed methods, and outlined plans, that the authors believed would garner public and international support for U.S. military intervention in Cuba. These were to be staged attacks purported to be of Cuban origin. Here is the actual wording in the plan:

Since it would seem desirable to use legitimate provocation as the basis for US military intervention in Cuba a cover and deception plan, to include requisite preliminary actions such as has been developed in response to Task 33 c, could be executed as an initial effort to provoke Cuban reactions. Harassment plus deceptive actions to convince the Cubans of imminent invasion would be emphasized. Our military posture throughout execution of the plan will allow a rapid change from exercise to intervention if Cuban response justifies.

A series of well coordinated incidents will be planned to take place in and around Guantanamo to give genuine appearance of being done by hostile Cuban forces.

(a.) Incidents to establish a credible attack (not in chronological order): Start rumors (many). Use clandestine radio.

Land friendly Cubans in uniform "over-the-fence" to stage attack on base.

Capture Cuban (friendly) saboteurs inside the base.

Start riots near the base main gate (friendly Cubans).

Blow up ammunition inside the base; start fires.
Burn aircraft on air base (sabotage).
Lob mortar shells from outside of base into base. Some damage to installations.
Capture assault teams approaching from the sea or vicinity of Guantanamo City.
Capture militia group which storms the base.
Sabotage ship in harbor; large fires—naphthalene.
Sink ship near harbor entrance. Conduct funerals for mock-victims
(b.) United States would respond by executing offensive operations to secure water and power supplies, destroying artillery and mortar emplacements which threaten the base.
(c.) Commence large scale United States military operations.

A "Remember the Maine" incident could be arranged in several forms:
(a.) We could blow up a US ship in Guantanamo Bay and blame Cuba.
(b.) We could blow up a drone (unmanned) vessel anywhere in the Cuban waters. We could arrange to cause such incident in the vicinity of Havana or Santiago as a spectacular result of Cuban attack from the air or sea, or both. The presence of Cuban planes or ships merely investigating the intent of the vessel could be fairly compelling evidence that the ship was taken under attack. The nearness to Havana or Santiago would add credibility especially to those people that might have heard the blast or have seen the fire. The US could follow up with an air/sea rescue operation covered by US fighters to "evacuate" remaining members of the non-existent crew. Casualty lists in US newspapers would cause a helpful wave of national indignation.

We could develop a Communist Cuban terror campaign in the Miami area, in other Florida cities and even in Washington. The terror campaign could be pointed at refugees seeking haven in the United States. We could sink a boatload of Cubans en route to Florida (real or simulated). We could foster attempts on lives of Cuban refugees in the United States even to the extent of wounding in instances to be widely publicized. Exploding a few plastic bombs in carefully chosen spots, the arrest of Cuban agents and the release of prepared documents substantiating Cuban involvement, also would be helpful in projecting the idea of an irresponsible government.

A "Cuban-based, Castro-supported" filibuster could be simulated against a neighboring Caribbean nation (in the vein of the 14th of June invasion of the Dominican Republic). We know that Castro is backing subversive efforts clandestinely against Haiti, Dominican Republic, Guatemala, and Nicaragua at present and possible others. These efforts can be magnified and additional ones contrived for exposure. For example, advantage can be taken of the sensitivity of the Dominican Air Force to intrusions within their national air space. "Cuban" B-26 or C-46 type aircraft could make cane-burning raids at night. Soviet Bloc incendiaries could be found. This could be coupled with "Cuban" messages to the Communist underground in the Dominican Republic and "Cuban" shipments of arm which would be found, or intercepted, on the beach.

Use of MIG type aircraft by US pilots could provide additional provocation. Harassment of civil air, attacks on surface shipping and destruction of US military drone aircraft by MIG type planes would be useful as complementary actions. An F-86 properly painted would convince air passengers that they saw a Cuban MIG, especially if the pilot of the transport were to announce such fact. The primary drawback to this suggestion appears to be the security risk inherent in obtaining or modifying an aircraft. However, reasonable copies of the MIG could be produced from US resources in about three months.

Hijacking attempts against civil air and surface craft should appear to continue as harassing measures condoned by the government of Cuba. Concurrently, genuine defections of Cuban civil and military air and surface craft should be encouraged.

It is possible to create an incident which will demonstrate convincingly that a Cuban aircraft has attacked and shot down a chartered civil airliner en route from the United States to Jamaica, Guatemala, Panama or Venezuela. The destination would be chosen only to cause the flight plan route to cross Cuba. The passengers could be a group of college students off on a holiday or any grouping of persons with a common interest to support chartering a non-scheduled flight.

(a.) An aircraft at Eglin AFB would be painted and numbered as an exact duplicate for a civil registered aircraft belonging to a CIA proprietary organization in the Miami area. At a designated time the duplicate would be substituted for the actual civil aircraft and would be loaded with the selected passengers, all boarded under carefully prepared aliases. The actual registered aircraft would be converted to a drone.

(b.) Take off times of the drone aircraft and the actual aircraft will be scheduled to allow a rendezvous south of Florida. From the rendezvous point the passenger-carrying aircraft will descend to minimum altitude and go directly into an auxiliary field at Eglin AFB where arrangements will have been made to evacuate the passengers and return the aircraft to its original status. The drone aircraft meanwhile will continue to fly the filed flight plan. When over Cuba the drone will begin transmitting on the international distress frequency a "MAY DAY" message stating he is under attack by Cuban MIG aircraft. The transmission will be interrupted by destruction of the aircraft which will be triggered by radio signal. This will allow ICAO radio stations in the Western Hemisphere to tell the US what has happened to the aircraft instead of the US trying to "sell" the incident.

It is possible to create an incident which will make it appear that Communist Cuban MIGs have destroyed a USAF aircraft over international waters in an unprovoked attack.

(a.) Approximately 4 or 5 F-101 aircraft will be dispatched in trail from Homestead AFB, Florida, to the vicinity of Cuba. Their mission will be to reverse course and simulate fakir aircraft for an air defense exercise in southern Florida. These aircraft would conduct variations of these flights at frequent Intervals. Crews would be briefed to remain at least 12 miles off the Cuban coast; however, they would be required to carry live ammunition in the event that hostile actions were taken by the Cuban MIGs.

(b.) On one such flight, a pre-briefed pilot would fly tail-end Charley at considerable interval between aircraft. While near the Cuban Island this pilot would broadcast that he had been jumped by MIGs and was going down. No other calls would be made. The pilot would then fly directly west at extremely low altitude and land at a secure buse, an Eglin auxiliary.

The aircraft would be met by the proper people, quickly stored and given a new tail number. The pilot who had performed the mission under an alias, would resume his proper identity and return to his normal place of business. The pilot and aircraft would then have disappeared.

(c.) At precisely the same time that the aircraft was presumably shot down, a submarine or small surface craft would disburse F-101 parts, parachute, etc., at approximately 15 to 20 miles off the Cuban coast and depart. The pilots returning to Homestead would have a true story as far as they knew. Search ships and aircraft could be dispatched and parts of aircraft found.

Northwoods was signed by Chairman Lyman Lemnitzer and sent to the Secretary of Defense Robert McNamara.

Kennedy personally rejected the Northwoods proposal. A JCS/ Pentagon document dated March 16, 1962 titled *"Meeting with the President"*, reads: **"General Lemnitzer commented that the military had contingency plans for US intervention. Also it had plans for creating plausible pretexts to use force, with the pretext either attacks on US aircraft or a Cuban action in Latin America for which we could retaliate. The President said bluntly that we were not discussing the use of military force, that General Lemnitzer might find the U.S so engaged in Berlin or elsewhere that he couldn't use the contemplated 4 divisions in Cuba."**

Following presentation of the Northwoods plan, Kennedy removed Lemnitzer as Chairman of the Joint Chiefs of Staff.

Kennedy really was our last, true non-puppet President. Everyone since has played the part they were hired to play.

Now I don't know about you, but I'd say that I just showed you concrete evidence that sets precedence that criminal elements within our own federal government think of us as expendable, disposable, stupid sheeple. This is the most iron-clad example to compare to 9/11 to provide merit to the case.

One of the most abhorrent false flag attacks ever conducted against the people of the United States was in fact at the hands of the Israeli military. Keep in mind that the exact same people who control Israel also control the United States, France, Great Britain, Germany, and right on down the line, so don't be mad at Israel over this, just like you hope people don't get mad at us Americans over who or what country the controllers of our federal government decide to blow up next month. It's not the people or the country, it's who's steering the ship. Who is wielding the gun. Who is running the government.

It was the proponents of the Great Plan's intention to sink an American ship and blame it on the Arabs in order to bring the United States into what would ultimately be called the "Six Day War", a battle between Israel and its Arab neighbors from June 5th through June 10ᵗʰ of 1967.

This is just a terribly tragic tale, but it is the suppressed truth, and that's what we're after here:

On June 8, 1967 while patrolling in international waters in the Eastern Mediterranean Sea, the USS Liberty was savagely attacked without warning or justification by air and naval forces of the state of Israel.

Of a crew of 294 officers and men (including three civilians), the ship suffered thirty four (34) killed and one hundred seventy four (174) wounded. The ship itself, a forty million dollar state of the art signals intelligence (SIGINT) platform, was so badly damaged that it never sailed on an operational mission again and was sold in 1970 for $101,666.66 as scrap .

At approximately 6:00 AM the morning of June 8, 1967 an Israeli maritime reconnaissance aircraft observer reported seeing "a US Navy cargo type ship," just outside the coverage of the Israeli coastal radar defense net, bearing the hull markings "GTR-5". This report, made to Israeli naval HQ, was also forwarded immediately to the Israeli navy intelligence directorate.

Throughout the remainder of the day prior to the attack, Israeli reconnaissance aircraft regularly flew out to USS *Liberty's* position and orbited the ship before returning to their bases in Israel. A total of no fewer than eight such flights were made.

From 9:00 AM until the time of the attack five hours later, USS *Liberty* maintained a speed of approximately five knots and a generally westerly-northwesterly course.

At 2:00 PM, while approximately 17 miles off the Gaza coast, USS *Liberty's* crew observed three surface radar contacts closing on their position at high speed. A few moments later, the bridge radar crew observed high speed aircraft passing over the surface returns on the same heading.

Within a few short moments, and without any warning, Israeli fighter aircraft launched a rocket attack on the USS Liberty. The aircraft made repeated firing passes, attacking the USS Liberty with rockets and their internal cannons. After the first flight of fighter aircraft had exhausted their ordnance, subsequent flights of Israeli fighter aircraft continued to perpetrate the attack with rockets, cannon fire, and napalm.

During the air attack, the USS Liberty's crew were unable to contact Sixth Fleet to request assistance due to intense communications jamming.

After the Israeli fighter aircraft completed their attacks, three Israeli torpedo boats arrived and began a surface attack about 35 minutes after the start of the air attack. The torpedo boats launched a total of five torpedoes, one of which struck the side of the USS Liberty, opposite the ship's research spaces. Twenty-six Americans in addition to the eight who had been killed in the earlier air attacks were killed as a result of this explosion.

Following their torpedo attack, the torpedo boats moved up and down the length of the ship (both the port and starboard sides), continuing their attack, raking the ship with cannon and machine gun fire. In Malta, crewmen were later assigned the task of counting all of the holes in the ship that were the size of a man's hand or larger. They found a total of 861 such holes, in addition to "thousands" of .50 caliber machine gun holes.

Survivors report that the torpedo boat crews swept the decks of the USS Liberty with continuous machine gun fire, targeting communications equipment and any crewmembers who ventured above decks.

Damage control firefighters, who had already risked their lives merely by appearing on deck, had to abandon their efforts because their fire hoses had been shredded by machine gun fire.

Survivors also report that the torpedo boat crews fired on the inflated life boats launched by the crew after the captain gave the order "prepare to abandon ship." This order had to be rescinded because the crew was unable to stand on the main deck without being fired upon and the life rafts were destroyed as they were launched.

The defenseless crew, initially unable to report their plight or summon assistance and with only themselves to rely upon, fought heroically to save themselves and their ship. In recognition of their effort in this single action, they were ultimately awarded collectively one Medal of Honor, two Navy Crosses, eleven Silver Stars, twenty Bronze Stars nine Navy Commendation Medals, and two hundred and four Purple Hearts. In addition, the ship was awarded the Presidential Unit Citation.

By patching together different systems, the ship's radio operators had ultimately been able to send a brief distress message that was received and acknowledged by United States Sixth Fleet forces present in the Mediterranean. Upon receipt of that message the aircraft carriers USS Saratoga and USS America each launched aircraft to come to the aid of USS Liberty. The reported attacking aircraft were declared hostile and the rescue aircraft were authorized to destroy them upon arrival. The rules of engagement, authorizing destruction of the attackers, were transmitted to the rescue aircraft "in the clear" (*i.e.*, they were not encrypted).

Shortly after the Sixth Fleet transmission of the rules of engagement to its dispatched rescue aircraft, the Israeli torpedo boats suddenly broke off their attack and transmitted messages asking if the USS Liberty required assistance. At the same time, an Israeli naval officer notified the US Naval Attaché at the American Embassy in Tel Aviv that Israeli forces had mistakenly attacked a United States Navy ship and apologized. The Naval Attaché notified the United States Sixth Fleet and rescue aircraft were recalled before they arrived at the scene of the attack.

At about the same time as the cessation of the torpedo boat attack, Israeli attack helicopters arrived over the ship. Survivors report that the helicopters were packed with men in combat battle dress. The Captain of the USS Liberty gave the order to "prepare to repel boarders" but the helicopters departed without attempting to land their troops.

The official position of the United States of America concerning these events, as contained in a diplomatic note by Secretary of State Rusk addressed to the Israeli Ambassador is partially quoted below:

"Washington, June 10, 1967.
The Secretary of State presents his compliments to His Excellency the Ambassador of Israel and has the honor to refer to

the Ambassador's Note of June 10, 1967 concerning the attack by Israeli aircraft and torpedo boats on the United States naval vessel U.S.S. *Liberty*,

In these circumstances, the later military attack by Israeli aircraft on the U.S.S. *Liberty* is quite literally incomprehensible. As a minimum, the attack must be condemned as an act of military recklessness reflecting wanton disregard for human life.

The subsequent attack by Israeli torpedo boats, substantially after the vessel was or should have been identified by Israeli military forces, manifests the same reckless disregard for human life. . . . The U.S.S. *Liberty* was peacefully engaged, posed no threat whatsoever to the torpedo boats, and obviously carried no armament affording it a combat capability. It could and should have been scrutinized visually at close range before torpedoes were fired.

. . . the Secretary of State wishes to make clear that the United States Government expects the Government of Israel also to take the disciplinary measures which international law requires in the event of wrongful conduct by the military personnel of a State."

No one in the Israeli government or military received so much as a reprimand for their involvement in the attack. The orders to attack came from far above all of that, so there was no one to pin a reprimand on.

Writing in his memoirs, Richard Helms, the Director of Central Intelligence at the time of the attack, explained that the Central Intelligence Agency undertook a "final" investigation after more evidence became available, and he offered the following information concerning the CIA's final finding:

"Israeli authorities subsequently apologized for the incident, but few in Washington could believe that the ship had not been identified as an American naval vessel. Later, an interim intelligence memorandum concluded the attack was a mistake and not made in malice against the U.S. . . .I had no role in the board of inquiry that followed, or the board's finding that there could be no doubt that the Israelis knew exactly what they were doing in attacking the Liberty. I have yet to understand why it was felt necessary to attack this ship or who ordered the attack."

Director Helms was not the only administration official who remained convinced that the attack was deliberate. In 1990, in his memoirs, Secretary of State Rusk observed:

"But I was never satisfied with the Israeli explanation. Their sustained attack to disable and sink Liberty precluded an assault by accident or some trigger-happy local commander. Through diplomatic channels we refused to accept their explanations. I didn't believe them then, and I don't believe them to this day. The attack was outrageous."

The Executive Branch of the United States Government undertook no further review of the attack. Similarly, the United States Congress has never investigated the attack, making it the only attack on a United States Navy ship involving significant loss of life that has not been properly investigated.

This attack was ordered by the proponents of the New World Order in an attempt to force the United States into the 6-day war on the side of Israel and attack Egypt. At the time they had no idea that Israel was going to completely annihilate their Arab enemies so quickly---hence trying to bring us in as backup muscle right away. I had not even heard of this event before I started investigating 9/11.

Let's go over one more terrorist incident that happened, one more highly probable false flag attack that happened to our country: the Oklahoma City bombing. These are politically-motivated events, meant to further an agenda, which in this case is the Police State in America. Now bear with me, all we're going to do is analyze the facts that raise the suspicion that what we were told happened in fact isn't the case.

The April 19, 1995 Oklahoma City Bombing was a highly suspicious event on many fronts, and I felt it needed to be included here. This is particularly true after just going over the plans contained in Operation Northwoods, the attack on the USS Liberty, and of course 9/11. I will tell you that the evidence is strong pointing to an inside job, which would certainly be the norm after all we've gone over regarding false flag history.

I'll tell you right now why "they" were probably responsible for Oklahoma City:

President Clinton's 'Omnibus Counterterrorism Bill' was introduced into Congress in February of 1995, two months BEFORE the bombing, **and was having difficulty passing as what was in it was a throwback to the Gestapo of Nazi Germany.** This is when the real New World Order Police State began to come out of the shadows. Clinton's bill was a death knell to the Bill of Rights and was designed to grant sweeping powers to the executive branch in the name of fighting domestic "terrorism".

Included in the bill's provisions was a much broader wiretapping authority for law enforcement with negligible judicial oversight and access to personal and financial records without a warrant. Most of all, included in the bill were sweeping powers granted to the President to designate certain groups as "terrorist" organizations. The bill also authorized the feds to seize the assets of said groups and their supporters, and to imprison U.S citizens, denying them due process under the law.

It was one of the prime directives of the Illuminati to head off any organized resistance to them at the root---this was prior to the advent of the internet and the current flood of suppressed history now surging forth. They have recently been working on something called "Internet II", which would basically transfer over all the big internet service providers to a "new" internet that would be heavily filtered, but that has stalled as of now. The Illuminati's stance now is to just let the information flood out and pretend it's all fake "conspiracy theories", even mocking it in the Mainstream Media, hoping that they did a good enough job of brainwashing the sheeple so they either won't believe the facts about the New World Order, or they just won't care.

Congress passed Clinton's bill just days after the bombing in the form of "The Antiterrorism and Effective Death Penalty Act of 1996". Clinton signed it into law on April 24, 1996.

One of the new laws considered for passage immediately after the Oklahoma City bombing was the gross destruction of the First Amendment advocated in Senator Charles Schumer's bill, HR 2580. **In this bill, a five-year prison sentence would be given for publicly engaging in unseemly speculation and publishing or transmitting by wire or electronic means baseless conspiracy theories regarding the federal government of the United States.** This is clear evidence to me that the proponents of the New World Order are beginning to fear those who are waking up. Looking into Schumer's other treasonous actions betrays his true loyalty, and it's not to the citizens of the United States.

The Oklahoma City bombing killed 168 people and injured more than 800. It was the worst terrorist attack on US soil up until 9/11. The government and media attributed the bombing to right-wing, anti-government domestic terrorists. But the official story that Timothy McVeigh and Terry Nichols were solely responsible is contradicted by independent research as well as nuggets of truth mined from the mainstream news coverage.

Strange how every "terrorist" event benefits the moving along of the Great Plan, whether it is getting us into wars or tightening the thumbscrews back home on a patriotic population yearning for another 1776-style Revolution to throw the bums out once and for all. These false flag terror operations help them to cement power by spreading terror throughout our nation and fomenting draconian legislation to be passed against us. By spreading the effects of terror--pictures of damage and film interviews of mass hysteria and confusion--the Mainstream Media of our traumatized country serves as an ultra-effective brain washing system. The Mainstream Media acts as a second phase of the false flag operation, by further propagating the terror over and over on the news, the same terrible footage being drilled into your brain. All the while they are muddying the waters on the back end to any conflicting evidence or any truth-seekers questioning the "official" version.

The Oklahoma City Bombing was masked to look like an independent act of terrorism, but closer analysis of the facts reveals numerous suspicious indicators of a false flag operation.

Experts like USAF Brigadier General Benton K. Partin, who saw the bombing site, dismissed the notion that a home-made fertilizer bomb could have demolished a concrete reinforced building. His request that the bombsite be preserved for further investigation was completely ignored by the U.S. Government; instead the site was covered over with dirt three weeks ahead of schedule, effectively burying the remaining forensic evidence. General Partin, who has 25 years experience in the field of weapons research, wrote a letter to Senator Donald Nichols stating, **"From all the evidence I have seen in published material, I can say, with a high level of confidence, that the damage pattern on the** reinforced concrete superstructure could not possibly have been attained from a single truck bomb without supplementing demolition charges at some of the reinforced column bases. The total incompatibility with a single truck bomb lies in the fact that either some of the columns collapsed that should not have collapsed or some of the columns are still standing that should have collapsed and did not."

General Partin even submitted a report to the US Congress detailing the case for secondary explosives---which was completely stonewalled. There were in fact multiple eyewitness reports of multiple explosions going off when the truck bomb detonated.

The Oklahoma City bombing screamed false flag, then and now. The intended results they were after? To vilify patriotic militia groups and millions of law-abiding patriots and Constitutionalists whose numbers had grown significantly as people are beginning to wake up to the fact that something is terribly wrong in America. These are the people who were beginning to sound the alarm about the New World Order en masse. The second intended result was to force through Police State legislation to monitor and suppress these exact types of resistance to the New World Order agenda.

A pre-programmed patsy, Timothy McVeigh, was tied to a militia group and blamed for the entire massacre. We don't have time to go into CIA/Mi6/MK ULTRA mind control, but just know that it is used throughout secret government espionage operations. This is how they set up Lee Harvey Oswald to kill, or at least get blamed, for killing Kennedy. Google and research "MK ULTRA".

Let's jump right into the FACTS surrounding the events of the Oklahoma City bombing, shall we?

Take this odd piece of evidence for example. What was the Army doing with a Ryder Truck just before the Murrah blast?

There are photos of just this scenario. The pilot who took the photos wishes (for obvious reasons) to remain anonymous, but these photos are purported to be of an area near Camp Gruber-Braggs, Oklahoma in early April of 1995. Needless to say, just days after the photo was taken, the Murrah Building in Oklahoma City was destroyed by a "Ryder truck full of explosives".

In a news article written by the Washington Post on June 17th, 1997, the Oklahoma National Guard authenticates the photos as being exactly what they appear to be: photos of a Ryder truck in a clandestine base at Camp Gruber-Braggs.

Another interesting piece of the pie is that McVeigh had been filmed by a security camera at a nearby McDonald's 24 minutes before the time stamped on the truck rental agreement, wearing clothes that did not match either of the men seen at Elliott's Hertz truck rental—the supposed origination of the truck used to bomb the buildings. There is no plausible explanation of how he traveled the mile and a quarter from McDonald's to the rental agency, carless and alone as he claims, without getting soaked in the rain that was falling that day.

The three people interviewed from the rental agency agreed John Does 1 and 2 were dry. According to researcher Stephen Jones, who has seen the interview transcripts, it took 44 days for the FBI to convince the car rental agency owner that John Doe 1 was Timothy McVeigh. At McVeigh's trial, they didn't dare to put the rental agency owner on the witness stand, for fear of what would happen under cross-examination.

On that fateful day, local live news broadcasts reported numerous eyewitnesses that heard *multiple* explosions, and more than one source reported that unexploded bombs even bigger than the truck bomb were being diffused in the unbombed part of the building. This is impossible. If McVeigh and co. had planted other bombs, we would have heard about it through his trial. According to the official story we are supposed to believe, a **single** homemade bomb in the Hertz truck did the damage to the Alfred P. Murrah building.

Throughout the events surrounding the OKC bombing the mainstream media has ignored some serious oddities about what really happened.

For example: some of those killed in the Oklahoma City bombing were not killed in the blast itself but died later under highly suspicious circumstances. One such was Mike Loudenslager who was responsible for saving the lives of many children in the Murrah Building's day care center.

Allegedly, in the weeks prior to the actual bombing, Loudenslager, a GSA employee, had been complaining about the large amounts of ordinance and explosives being brought into the building by the BATF. and DEA, who had offices there. Supposedly others had been complaining too, including the building's security director who filed a formal complaint and then promptly lost his job. Thereafter fire marshals were denied access to the building when they arrived to inspect some remodeling that had been done to the day care center. We need to have another investigation into this event obviously, and the people who need to do it are the people who want the truth instead of the people who want to cover up the truth.

Loudenslager and the day care operator even went so far as to begin warning the children's parents not to bring their children into the building. Had they not done so, the death toll would have been far higher.

Shortly after the actual bombing, Loudenslager was seen by many witnesses, including police officers and rescue workers, involved in a very "heated confrontation". Much of his anger being due to the fact that he felt that the BATF and DEA were responsible for the majority extent of the blast damage.

However, to the astonishment of those who had seen him in the immediate aftermath of the bombing, it was later reported that Loudenslager was found dead at his desk, a victim of the 9:02 AM bombing. This was reported only AFTER he had been seen alive and well by numerous rescue workers. Despite this he is now on the official list of victims claimed by the blast.

His death was to play a part in the demise of another patriotic American seeking the truth: Terry Yeakey. Yeakey was at the Murrah Building that fateful morning. Yeakey had been trying to deliver evidence that Loudenslager was alive AFTER the bombing which is said to have killed him.

Yeakey was a heroic first responder at the scene of the bombing. Apparently, he saw some things that he wasn't supposed to see. He called his wife that morning saying, **"It's not true. It's not what they are saying. It didn't happen that way."** Over the next year, Yeakey was compelled to begin his own investigation into the bombing. Yeakey told friends he had important information that showed the government's story to be a lie, and that he was being intimidated and tailed by federal agents. In May 1996, three days before he was scheduled to receive the Medal of Valor from the OKCPD, **he was brutally murdered.**

Despite the fact that his injuries included eleven slashes to both forearms, two cuts to his throat, what appeared to be rope burns and handcuff marks, and a final shot to the head, and the fact that he was found more than a mile away from his car, his death was quietly ruled a *suicide* after the **FBI** took over the case.

All of the security videotapes from surrounding businesses were confiscated by the FBI immediately in the aftermath of the bombing---just as the feds did with the businesses around the Pentagon when Flight 77 allegedly hit the Pentagon on 9/11. Long-secret security tapes that were finally released showing the chaos immediately after the 1995 bombing of the Oklahoma City federal building are blank in the minutes before the blast and appear to have been edited said an attorney who obtained the recordings on September 28, 2009. **"The real story is what's missing,"** *said Jesse Trentadue, a Salt Lake City attorney who obtained the recordings through the federal Freedom of Information Act as part of an unofficial inquiry he was conducting. Trentadue gave copies of the tapes to The Oklahoman newspaper, which posted them online and provided copies to The Associated Press. The tapes are blank at points before 9:02 a.m., when a truck bomb carrying a 4,000 pound fertilizer-and-fuel-oil bomb detonated in front of the building, Trentadue said.*

"Four cameras in four different locations going blank at basically the same time on the morning of April 19, 1995. There ain't no such thing as a coincidence," Trentadue said.

He said government officials claimed the security cameras did not record the minutes before the bombing because "they had run out of tape" or "the tape was being replaced."

"The interesting thing is they spring back on after 9:02," he said. "The absence of footage from these crucial time intervals is evidence that there is something there that the FBI doesn't want anybody to see."

Just some interesting points to ponder. Although there is not nearly the mountain of evidence pointing to a false flag as 9/11, I would lean towards believing OKC was also a false flag operation to initiate the New World Order police state in America.

Chapter 11/C

AL-QAIDA AND OSAMA BIN LADEN

"The FBI has no hard evidence connecting Bin Laden with the
9/11 attacks on America"
- FBI spokesman Rex Tomb, June 5, 2006

As far as accusations of 9/11 Truthers being "conspiracy theorists" goes, it seems that the real conspiracy, given the preponderance of factual information, was manufactured on the other side of the debate, the side of the Great Plan. As of this day, **the FBI still has no evidence regarding the events of 9/11 to implicate Osama bin Laden in the planning and execution of attacks on 9/11.**

Again, just to ram this point home here: **Osama bin Laden was never wanted by the FBI for the events of 9/11 due to lack of evidence tying him to the orchestration and execution of the terrorist attacks on 9/11, and that is a fact.**

If the FBI is not satisfied with the U.S. government's explanation for the events that transpired on 9/11, blaming bin Laden and using him as an excuse to launch two wars, three if you count the war against us, why should the American public be satisfied?

We were certainly led to believe that he was to blame by the immediate cheerleading of his alleged guilt by the Mainstream Media just hours after the attacks happened.

Immediately after Flight 11 hit World Trade Center 1, CIA Director George Tenet fed the media machine some blood to get the frenzy started: **"You know, this has bin Laden's fingerprints all over it."**

The Mainstream Media took the ball from there and not only con-victed but crucified him over the 9/11 attacks in the press in the follow-ing days, weeks, months and now years. Following 9/11, the media was filled with stories alleging links of the attacks to bin Laden. The problem is, *he was never factually linked to the attacks*. Not by the FBI. Not by the CIA. Not by anyone in the federal criminal justice system. It was just a big propaganda ploy. This speaks volumes about the fact that we have been completely misled by the pied piper that is the Illuminati-controlled Mainstream Media.

After logical analyzation of the facts, I believe that *Osama bin Laden was INNOCENT of planning the attacks on 9/11*. The fact is, he im-mediately **DENIED** involvement in the attacks on September 13, 2001 as we will go over. I'm certainly not saying he wasn't a terrorist, after all he factually worked for the CIA, the biggest terrorist organization in the world. I'm just saying with regards to the events of 9/11 in particular, I don't believe he was implicitly involved.

With an ego the size of Mount Everest, Osama bin Laden would have surely taken the credit for such a monumental triumph over the "Great Satan" as some Islamic fundamentalists call the U.S. Instead he denied in-volvement in it and blamed the United States Shadow Government.........who are the exact proponents of the Great Plan, and he knew this.

Something you need to factor into this equation is that Osama bin Laden was an operative of the Central Intelligence Agency in the 1980's as a leader of the Mujahedeen fighting the Russians in Afghanistan. He ultimately was turned into a CIA scapegoat, a disposable asset, by the real planners of 9/11. They needed someone nefarious to pin 9/11 on and he fit the bill perfectly.

It was revealed on October 31, 2001 by the French daily Le Figaro, that while in a Dubai hospital receiving treatment for a chronic kidney infection in **July 2001**, Osama bin Laden had met with a top CIA official. The meeting, held in bin Laden's private suite, took place at the American hospital in Dubai at a time when he was a "wanted fugitive" for the bomb-ings of two U.S. embassies and the 2001 attack on the U.S.S. Cole. **On July 14th he was allowed to leave Dubai on a private jet and there were no Navy fighters waiting to force this alleged terrorist mastermind**

down. They needed him "on the loose" so they could pin 9/11 on him 2 months later.

Al-Qaeda literally translates in English to "the database", and was in fact a creation of our own CIA. Al-Qaeda was originally the name of the computer file of the thousands of Mujahedeen fighters who were recruited, trained, and armed by the CIA to fight the Russians, and that's a **fact**. There is no evidence to suggest that they still aren't controlled by the CIA, and it is highly probably that it is actually the CIA who is responsible for the majority of the terrorist attacks allegedly committed by "Islamic radicals".

Point of fact: *In the immediate aftermath of 9/11, the Taliban offered to hand over Osama bin Laden if the United States could provide the evidence they said they had against him.*

On September 13, 2001, Afghanistan's ruling Taliban says that Osama bin Laden has told them he played no role in the September 11 attacks on the United States. Mullah Abdul Salam Zaeef, the Taliban ambassador to Pakistan, told Reuters, **"We asked from him, and he told us 'we don't have any hand in this action'."** Zaeef says bin Laden had been cut off from all outside communication, including telephone and the Internet, and so it would have been impossible for him to have coordinated the attacks. Zaeef said the Taliban was willing to cooperate with the United States in investigating the 9/11 attacks, stating, **"We are ready for any help according to [Islamic] Sharia law."** But he stressed that if America had any evidence against bin Laden, it should provide it to the Taliban so they could decide what to do with their "guest" bin Laden.

September 23, 2001, Secretary of State and alleged 33rd degree Freemason Colin Powell said that the administration would soon be able to document its case in public against Osama bin Laden and Al Qaeda. Powell is quoted as saying the evidence will be "persuasive". Kind of an interesting choice of words I would say. It didn't take the Bush White House long to backtrack on those statements. The day after Powell's statements, White House Press Secretary Ari Fleischer went on to say at a press conference when asked the question **"Is there any plan to present public evidence so that not just the average citizen, not just Americans, but so people all over the world can understand the case against bin Laden?"**

His response?

"**Well I think as Secretary Powell said, there's hope to do that and to do so in a timely fashion over some course of time. But I think the American people also understand that there are going to be times that that information will not immediately be forthcoming and the American people seem to be accepting of that.**"

The same reporter countered with, "**It seems as though you're asking everyone to trust you.**"

His response to that? He had none. He went to the next question after looking like a deer in the headlights for a few seconds.

Let's review Osama bin Laden's initial denial of any role in September 11, to his astonishing 180 degree u-turn to complete admittance of guilt after our government just "happened" to find a tape of a man who barely resembles bin Laden claiming responsibility for the attacks. This bogus tape was played across the world as "proof bin Laden orchestrated the attacks". You can check youtube.com for this tape to view it yourself, and now that you can look at it without Great Plan-blinders on, you will see that I am speaking the truth.

There has **never ever** been an admission by the real Osama bin Laden that he masterminded 9/11.

The following dialogue is taken from CNN.com, September 17, 2001. Pay special attention to why bin Laden says the perpetrators carried it out.

DOHA, Qatar (CNN) -- Islamic militant leader Osama bin Laden, the man the United States considers the prime suspect in last week's terrorist attacks on New York and Washington, denied any role Sunday in the actions believed to have killed thousands.

In a statement issued to the Arabic satellite channel Al Jazeera, based in Qatar, bin Laden said, "The U.S. government has consistently blamed me for being behind every occasion its enemies attack it."

"I would like to assure the world that I did not plan the recent attacks, which seems to have been planned by people for personal reasons," bin Laden's statement said.

"I have been living in the Islamic emirate of Afghanistan and following its leaders' rules. The current leader does not allow me to exercise such operations."

Asked Sunday if he believed bin Laden's denial, President Bush said:
"No question he is the prime suspect. No question about that."
Since Tuesday's terrorist attacks against the United States, Bush has *repeatedly threatened to strike out against terrorism and any nation that supports or harbors its disciples.*

So there you have Osama bin Laden, reported by CNN no less, saying he didn't do it.

Here is **another** denial of involvement by bin Laden right after 9/11 given in an interview on September 28, 2001 with a Pakistani newspaper called *Ummat.* I am not surprised that bin Laden also knew about the proponents of the Great Plan, and explicitly identifies them as the perpetrators of 9/11, calling them the "government within a government".

The Mainstream Media did not allow bin Laden to plead his case of innocence to the American people---we were simply told he was guilty---and with no evidence whatsoever linking him to the events of 9/11. These blatant denials of responsibility were intentionally never shown to the American public at large, as we are not supposed to see and hear what we are not supposed to know. Again, this is why to this day the FBI doesn't have the evidence to connect bin Laden to the events of 9/11, and this is a **fact**.

Here is a condensed version of the 9/28/01 bin Laden newspaper interview, and of course the entire transcript is available online:

UMMAT: You have been accused of involvement in the attacks in New York and Washington. What do you want to say about this? If you are not involved, who might be?

USAMA BIN LADEN: In the name of Allah (God), the most beneficent, the most merciful. Praise be to Allah, Who is the creator of the whole universe and Who made the Earth as an abode for peace, for the whole humankind. Allah is the Sustainer, who sent Prophet Muhammad---peace be upon him--- for our guidance. I am thankful to the Ummat Group of Publications, which gave me the opportunity to convey my viewpoint to the people, particularly the valiant and momin (true Muslim) people of Pakistan who refused to believe the lies of the demon (Pakistani military dictator General Pervez Musharraf).

I have already said that I am not involved in the 11 September attacks in the United States. As a Muslim, I try my best to avoid telling a lie. I had no knowledge of these attacks, nor do I consider the killing of innocent women, children and other humans as an appreciable act. Islam strictly forbids causing harm to innocent women, children and other people. Such a practice is forbidden even in the course of a battle. It is the United States, which is perpetrating every maltreatment on women, children and common people of other faiths, particularly the followers of Islam. All that is going on in Palestine for the last 11 months is sufficient to call the wrath of God upon the United States and Israel. There is also a warning for those Muslim countries, which witnessed all these as a silent spectator. What had earlier been done to the innocent people of Iraq, Chechnya and Bosnia? Only one conclusion could be derived from the indifference of the United States and the West to these acts of terror and the patronage of the tyrants by these powers that America is an anti-Islamic power and it is patronizing the anti-Islamic forces. Its friendship with the Muslim countries is just a show, rather deceit. By enticing or intimidating these countries, the United States is forcing them to play a role of its choice. Put a glance all around and you will see that the slaves of the United States are either rulers or enemies of Muslims.

The U.S. has no friends, nor does it want to keep any because the prerequisite of friendship is to come to the level of the friend or consider him at par with you. America does not want to see anyone equal to it. It expects slavery from others. Therefore, other countries are either its slaves or subordinates. However, our case is different. We have pledged slavery to God Almighty alone and after this pledge there is no possibility to become the slave of someone else.

Whoever committed the act of 11 September are not the friends of the American people. I have already said that we are against the American system, not against its people, whereas in these attacks, the common American people have been killed. According to my information, the death toll is much higher than what the U.S. Government has stated. But the Bush Administration does not want the panic to spread. **The United States should try to trace the perpetrators of these attacks within itself; the people who are a part of the U.S. system, but are dissenting against it.** Or those who are working for some other system; persons who want to make the present century as a century of conflict between Islam and Christianity so that their own civilization, nation, country, or ideology could survive. They can be anyone, from Russia to Israel and from India to Serbia. In the U.S. itself, there are dozens of well-organized and well-equipped groups, which are capable of causing a large-scale destruction. Then you cannot forget the American-Jews, who are annoyed with President Bush ever since the elections in Florida and want to avenge him.

Then there are intelligence agencies in the U.S., which require billions of dollars worth of funds from the Congress and the government every year. This [funding issue] was not a big problem till the existence of the former Soviet Union but after that the budget of these agencies has been in danger. They needed an enemy. So, they first started propaganda against Usama and Taliban and then this incident happened. You see, the Bush Administration approved a budget of 40 billion dollars. Where will this huge amount go? It will be provided to the same agencies, which need huge funds and want to exert their importance. Now they will spend the money for their expansion and for increasing their importance. I will give you an example. Drug smugglers from all over the world are in contact with the U.S. secret agencies. These agencies do not want to eradicate narcotics cultivation and trafficking because their importance will be diminished. The people in the U.S. Drug Enforcement Department are encouraging drug trade so that they could show performance and get millions of dollars worth of budget. General Noriega was made a drug baron by the CIA and, in need, he was made a scapegoat. In the same way, whether it is President Bush or any other U.S. President, they cannot bring Israel to justice for its human rights abuses or to hold it accountable for such crimes. What is this? **Is it not that there exists a government within the government in the United States? That secret government must be asked as to who carried out the attacks.**

UMMAT: The entire propaganda about your struggle has so far been made by the Western media. But no information is being received from your sources about the network of Al-Qa'idah and its jihadi successes. Would you comment?

USAMA BIN LADEN: In fact, the Western media is left with nothing else. It has no other theme to survive for a long time. Then we have many other things to do. The struggle for jihad and the successes are for the sake of Allah and not to annoy His bondsmen. Our silence is our real propaganda. Rejections, explanations, or corrigendum only waste your time and through them, the enemy wants you to engage in things which are not of use to you. These things are pulling you away from your cause. **The Western media is unleashing such a baseless propaganda, which makes us surprise but it reflects on what is in their hearts and gradually they themselves become captive of this propaganda. They become afraid of it and begin to cause harm to themselves. Terror is the most dreaded weapon in modern age and the Western media is mercilessly using it against its own people.** It can add fear and helplessness in the psyche of the people of Europe and the United States. It means that what the enemies of the United States cannot do, its media is doing that. You can understand as to what will be the performance of the nation in a war, which suffers from fear and helplessness.

"The most important thing for us is to find Osama bin Laden. It is our number one priority and we will not rest until we find him."
-George Bush, September 13, 2001

"I don't know where he is. I have no idea and I really don't care. It's not that important. It's not our priority."
-George Bush, March 13, 2002

For proof of bin Laden's guilt, and to counter what the real bin Laden was saying in the press, the U.S. government released a video tape, allegedly of bin Laden, on December 14, 2001. This tape was supposedly found in a house in Jalalabad, Afghanistan. In this tape, bin Laden, as they would have you believe, basically admits to having planned the attack. This is the tape the Bush administration trumpeted as definitive proof of bin Laden's involvement and guilt.

Only one problem with this, though. Okay. Many problems. Many problems with the ***authenticity of the tape*** that is.

According to a translation of the audio released by the Pentagon, the man they claim to be bin Laden says: "**... we calculated in advance the number of casualties from the enemy, who would be killed based on the position of the tower. We calculated that the floors that would be hit would be three or four floors. I was the most optimistic of them** all.... (Inaudible).... due to my experience in this field, I was thinking that the fire from the gas in the plane would melt the iron structure of the building and collapse the area where the plane hit and all the floors above it only. This is what we had hoped for. We had notification since the previous Thursday that the event would take place that day. We had finished our work that day and had the radio on. It was 5:30 p.m. our time... Immediately, we heard the news that a plane had hit the World Trade Center. We turned the radio station to the news from Washington... At the end of the newscast, they reported that a plane just hit the World Trade Center... After a little while, they announced that another plane had hit the World Trade Center. The brothers who heard the news were overjoyed by it."

The release of this tape turned out to be a huge news story, and the tape was trumpeted by the media as proof of bin Laden's guilt. The Mainstream Media played this tape over and over to ram the point home that bin Laden was responsible for 9/11, drilling it into the minds of the American public.

President Bush commented, "For those who see this tape, they'll realize that not only is he guilty of incredible murder, he has no conscience and no soul, and that he represents the worst of civilization."

British foreign secretary Jack Straw added, "By boasting about his involvement in the evil attacks, Bin Laden confirms his guilt."

The only problem is, is that it is **not** Osama bin Laden in the tape. To start with, the quality of this tape is conspicuously of poor quality. Fuzzy images are all we can see in this tape to try and blur the poorly-cast Osama bin Laden look-alike, a man who is noticeably heavier than the real bin Laden, has a different nose structure than the real bin Laden, and is seen writing with his right hand. The real bin Laden is left–handed according to the FBI's own website. Looking at the actor in the video and a picture of the real bin Laden one immediately comes to the conclusion that we have been fooled again. Another thing: the Osama bin Laden in this video is wearing a gold ring, which is strictly forbidden by Muslim law. A devout Muslim such as bin Laden surely wouldn't blaspheme his faith to those around him. And lastly, according to the actor in the tape, his calculations that the structure would collapse from the fires is based on what? His own experience?? I didn't know bin Laden was a demolitions expert. **Never in the history of the world has a steel-framed high-rise collapsed from fire, but we are led down that path by this imposter.** I myself, before I was awake to the existence of the New World Order, remember seeing this video on the news and thinking to myself, "Hey. There you have it. He did it. Let's go kick some ass in Afghanistan." I was taken for a complete ride along with everyone else who isn't paying attention to what we are being spoon fed.

Bush's insistence that the tape was authentic **was the premier excuse used to invade Afghanistan.** So many people doubted the video's authenticity after it was released that President Bush soon was forced to make a statement about the tape, saying it was <u>**"preposterous for anybody to think this tape was doctored. Those who contend it's a farce or a fake are hoping for the best about an evil man."**</u>

America's top academic bin Laden expert finally went on record in 2007, joining numerous other experts in calling out this fakery---but of course this fact never made it into the Mainstream Media.

<u>**"It's bogus,"**</u> says Professor Bruce Lawrence, head of Duke University's Religious Studies program.

Lawrence, author of "*Messages to the World: The Statements of Osama Bin Laden*", offered his historic debunking of the administration's lie in an interview with Kevin Barrett ("Dynamic Duo," gcnlive.com, 2/16/2007). The interview marked Lawrence's first major public statement since he made headlines in 2004 by suggesting that recent Osama tapes are hoaxes and that the real Osama Bin Laden may be dead.

And on that note, in the time since I first started editing the final copy of this book to the time it was first printed, Osama bin Laden was allegedly found by our Navy Seals and executed. They then took his body, that no evidence exists ever even existed, and dumped it into the ocean. Why would we kill the most important man in history in regards to the events of 9/11? Wouldn't we want to bring him to the U.S. for questioning? For interrogation? For punishment? I don't buy this whole propagandized and fabricated story, and I'll tell you why.

It was reported from sources in both Afghanistan and Pakistan that Osama bin Laden died in December 2001 and was buried in the mountains of southeast Afghanistan. This was reported in Chinese, Indian, Japanese and other media, but was mysteriously absent in the truth-sterile American press. Pakistan's president, Pervez Musharraf, even stated this same information.

After the CIA found out he was dead, they were then free to impersonate him at will to keep him scaring the American public----hence the date of the first tape in which bin Laden "accepts responsibility", December 14 of 2001---immediately after he allegedly died. It went straight from the CIA's movie studio out to the sheeple upon learning of his passing. Operation Keep-bin-Laden-alive was officially launched.

On December 26, 2001, according to the Pakistani newspaper *The Pakistan Observer*, a Taliban official came forward and stated he had attended bin Laden's funeral and that he had suffered from a serious lung complication and succumbed to the disease in mid-December of 2001, in the vicinity of the Tora Bora Mountains. The source claimed that bin Laden was laid to rest honorably in his last abode and his grave was made as per his Wahabi belief, and that about 30 close associates of bin Laden, including his most trusted and personal bodyguards, his family members and some "Taliban friends," attended the funeral rites. A volley of bullets was also fired to pay final tribute to the "great leader." When asked where bin Laden was buried, the source said, **"I am sure that like other places in Tora Bora, that particular place too must have vanished."** Apparently he was talking about the carpet bombing that came soon after.

On October 29, 2004, on the eve of the Presidential election no less to scare the American public and ensure 4 more years of neocon warmongering, the Arab television network Al Jazeera broadcast excerpts from a videotape of "Osama bin Laden" addressing the people of the United States. In this new tape he accepts responsibility for the September 11, 2001 attacks (again), condemns the Bush government's response to those attacks and presents those attacks as part of a campaign of revenge and deterrence motivated by his witnessing of the destruction in the Lebanese Civil War in 1982. This new video is described as the clearest claim yet of bin Laden's involvement in the attacks of 9/11.

The only problem is that it is another fake.

Again we have numerous problems with this tape of "Osama bin Laden". The tape is of conspicuously poor quality (again), and the actor portraying bin Laden looks eerily different than the bin Laden from the first tape, let alone the real bin Laden, and he has vastly different dialect than the real bin Laden according to professional translators. Again, you can view this video for yourself on youtube.com, and now that you can view it with the blinders off, you will see that what I am saying is the truth.

Senator John McCain was quoted a couple of days after this tape was aired that **"bin Laden may have just given us a little boost. Amazing, huh?"** McCain, being a neocon CFR member and New World Order insider, full well knew it was all a set-up.

The following article appeared on a website called infowars.com, which is one of the leading groups seeking to awaken humanity to the Great Plan. I'm just going to quote it verbatim, as it is such a powerful piece of testimony.

Top Government Insider: Bin Laden Died In 2001, 9/11 A False Flag

Paul Joseph Watson
Infowars.com
May 4, 2011

Top US government insider Dr. Steve R. Pieczenik, a man who held numerous different influential positions under three different Presidents and still works with the Defense Department, shockingly told The Alex Jones Show yesterday that Osama Bin Laden *died in 2001 and that he was prepared to testify in front of a grand jury how a top general told him directly that 9/11 was a false flag inside job.*

Pieczenik cannot be dismissed as a "conspiracy theorist". He served as the Deputy Assistant Secretary of State under three different administrations, Nixon, Ford and Carter, while also working under Reagan and Bush senior, and still works as a consultant *for the Department of Defense. A former US Navy Captain, Pieczenik achieved two prestigious Harry C. Solomon Awards at the Harvard Medical School as he simultaneously completed a PhD at MIT.*

Recruited by Lawrence Eagleburger as Deputy Assistant Secretary of State for Management, Pieczenik went on to develop, "the basic tenets for psychological *warfare, counter terrorism, strategy and tactics for transcultural negotiations for the US State Department, military and in-*

telligence communities and other agencies of the US Government," while also developing foundational strategies for hostage rescue that were later employed around the world.

Pieczenik also served as a senior policy planner under Secretaries *Henry Kissinger, Cyrus Vance, George Schultz and James Baker and worked on George W. Bush's election campaign against Al Gore. His record underscores the fact that he is one of the most deeply connected men in intelligence circles over the past three decades plus.*

The character of Jack Ryan, who appears in many Tom Clancy novels and was also played by Harrison Ford in the popular 1992 movie Patriot Games, *is also based on* **Steve Pieczenik**.

Back in April 2002, over nine years ago, Pieczenik told the Alex Jones Show that Bin Laden had already been "dead for months," and that the government was waiting for the most politically expedient time to roll out his corpse. Pieczenik would be in a position to know, having personally met Bin Laden and worked with him during the proxy war against the Soviets in Afghanistan back in the early 80's.

Pieczenik said that Osama Bin Laden died in 2001, "Not because special forces had killed him, but because as a physician I had known that the CIA physicians had treated him and it was on the intelligence roster that he had marfan syndrome," adding that the US government knew Bin Laden was dead before they invaded Afghanistan.

Marfan syndrome is a degenerative genetic disease for which there is no permanent cure. The illness severely shortens the life span of the sufferer.

"He died of marfan syndrome, Bush junior knew about it, the intelligence community knew about it," said Pieczenik, noting how CIA physicians had visited Bin Laden in July 2001 at the American Hospital in Dubai.

"He was already very sick from marfan syndrome and he was already dying, so nobody had to kill him," added Pieczenik, stating that Bin Laden died shortly after 9/11 in his Tora Bora cave complex.

"Did the intelligence community or the CIA doctor up this situation, the answer is yes, categorically yes," said Pieczenik, referring to Sunday's claim that Bin Laden was killed at his compound in Pakistan, adding, "This whole scenario where you see a bunch of people sitting there looking at a screen and they look as if they're intense, that's nonsense," referring to the images

released by the White House which claim to show Biden, Obama and Hillary Clinton watching the operation to kill Bin Laden live on a television screen.

"It's a total make-up, make believe, we're in an American theater *of the absurd....why are we doing this again....nine years ago this man was already dead....why does the government repeatedly have to lie to the American people," asked Pieczenik.*

"Osama Bin Laden was totally dead, so there's no way they could have attacked or confronted or killed Osama Bin laden," said Pieczenik, joking that the only way it could have happened was if special forces had attacked a mortuary.

Pieczenik said that the decision to launch the hoax now was made because Obama had reached a low with plummeting approval ratings and the fact that the birther issue was blowing up in his face.

"He had to prove that he was more than American....he had to be aggressive," said Pieczenik, adding that the farce was also a way of isolating Pakistan as a retaliation for intense opposition to the Predator drone program, which has killed hundreds of Pakistanis.

"This is orchestrated, I mean when you have people sitting around and watching a sitcom, basically the operations center of the White House, and you *have a president coming out almost zombie-like telling you they just killed Osama Bin Laden who was already dead nine years ago," said Pieczenik, calling the episode, "the greatest falsehood I've ever heard, I mean it was absurd."*

Dismissing the government's account of the assassination of Bin Laden as a "sick joke" on the American people, Pieczenik said, "They are so desperate *to make Obama viable, to negate the fact that he may not have been born here, any questions about his background, any irregularities about his background, to make him look assertive....to re-elect this president so the American public can be duped once again."*

Pieczenik's assertion that Bin Laden died almost ten years ago is echoed by numerous intelligence professionals as well as heads of state across the world.

Bin Laden, "Was used in the same way that 9/11 was used to mobilize the emotions and feelings of the American people in order to go to a war that had to be justified through a narrative that Bush junior created and Cheney created about the world of terrorism," stated Pieczenik.

During his interview with the Alex Jones Show yesterday, Pieczenik also asserted he was directly told by a prominent general that 9/11 was a stand down and a false flag operation, and that he is prepared to go to a grand jury to reveal the general's name.

"They ran the attacks," said Pieczenik, naming Dick Cheney, Paul Wolfowitz, Stephen Hadley, Elliott Abrams, and Condoleezza Rice amongst *others as having been directly involved.*

"It was called a stand down, a false flag operation in order to mobilize the American public under false pretenses....it was told to me even by the general on the staff of Wolfowitz – I will go in front of a federal committee and swear on perjury who the name was of the individual so that we can break it open," said Pieczenik, adding that he was "furious" and "knew it had happened".

"I taught stand down and false flag operations at the national war college, I've taught it with all my operatives so I knew exactly what was done to the American public," he added.

Pieczenik re-iterated that he was perfectly willing to reveal *the name of the general who told him 9/11 was an inside job in a federal court, "so that we can unravel this thing legally, not with the stupid 9/11 Commission that was absurd."*

Pieczenik explained that he was not a liberal, a conservative or a tea party member, merely an American who is deeply concerned about the direction in which his country is heading.

Now, I've already explained my view and the facts available as to why Osama bin Laden was not responsible for the events of 9/11. Now, let's look at the actual hijackers themselves to see if anything smells rotten from the official story.

Point of fact: **Many of the alleged 9/11 hijackers are still <u>alive</u>.**

Wail and Waleed al Shehri (two brothers), Abdul Aziz al Omari, Mohand al Shehri, Saeed al Ghamdi, Ahmed al Nami, and Salem al Hazmi.

These are the actual people named and whose pictures were flashed across the Mainstream Media as being the hijackers---and the exact same ones claimed in the 9/11 Commission Report as having carried out the atrocities........yet, they **<u>live</u>**.

Waleed al Shehri actually showed up in Morocco to do a press conference and proclaim he was still alive after friends and family saw his name and picture as one of the 9/11 hijackers. Of course this was completely and intentionally ignored by the American press. This fact was also stonewalled by the 9/11 Commission, contending that al Shehri was indeed the hijacker and that he was dead, when he obviously wasn't.

Not only that, but two more of the "hijackers" went public after 9/11 stating that they were not hijackers and were in fact alive. Saudi Airlines pilot, Saeed Al-Ghamdi, and Abdulaziz Al-Omari, an engineer from Riyadh, were both furious that the hijackers' personal details, including their pictures, names, places and dates of birth and occupations matched their own.

Doing damage control, CNN reported that the men who hijacked the aircraft used phony IDs containing the names of real people living in Arab nations in the Middle East.

In September 2002, FBI Director Robert Mueller told CNN not once but twice that there is **"no legal proof to prove the identities of the suicidal hijackers."**

Now wait a minute here. One fact here becomes glaringly obvious to me: *If those who hijacked the 9/11 airplanes were using stolen identities, then we don't know who they really were or who they worked for.* Yet these 19 men using stolen identities were the ones implicated by the 9/11 Commission as the perpetrators.

Because the IDs used by the hijackers were faked, we cannot know who they really were or who they really worked for, **but that didn't stop the military pathologists from identifying the listed hijackers as dead, including claiming that they had matched their DNA samples. This is an impossibility, but this didn't stop these "facts" from making it into the 9/11 Commission Report as the "truth".**

The 9/11 Commission Report explicitly states that the names given by the FBI originally are the names and identities of the hijackers. This is an outrageous lie foisted on the American public.

We don't know for certain exactly who planned and executed the 9/11 attacks, but we do know who they *wanted* us to *think* they were: Radical Muslims from Middle Eastern Arab nations working for Osama bin Laden.

In the days after 9/11, the Mainstream Media is fed CCTV photos of Mohammed Atta and Abdulaziz Al-Omari allegedly passing through a security check point before boarding their plane. This is the feds' definitive evidence that the two men were "unquestionably" on board America Airlines Flight 11, the first plane to strike the WTC. The only problem is that the then-famous CCTV video shows the two men boarding at **Portland, Maine** and **not Washington D.C.** In fact, in light of being caught in this misrepresentation, the feds released the "real" video from Dulles airport in Boston in 2004, after being afforded plenty of time to create it at CIA Motion Pictures, Inc.

"The Dulles airport video is unlike the Portland video in every way," writes Paul Zarembka in his book, *"The Hidden History of 9-11-2001"*. **"While the Portland video has sharp, clear resolution, the Dulles video's resolution is poor and grainy. While the Portland video was released soon after 9/11, only heavily edited versions of the Dulles video with segments missing were not made available to the American public until almost three years later, on July 24, 2004, one day before the Commission Report's release. It took a lawsuit by families of the victims of the 9/11 attacks to pry the video loose from the government's grip..."**

And how about the advanced warnings I mentioned earlier to our Federal Government prior to 9/11 from agencies within the Federal Government itself? That there were alleged Al-Qaeda terrorists right here in the U.S. planning to execute 9/11-type atrocities?

Not only did other foreign governments know the attacks were coming, and we'll go over the evidence that Israel's Mossad in particular had advance knowledge of the attacks, but the warnings our government was receiving from within were intentionally stonewalled.

A data mining program called Able Danger was set up by US Special Operations Command (SOCOM) in late 1998. It begins collecting data mostly on Bosnia and China but at this time it begins collecting data on Al-Qaeda---**which is essentially collecting data on clandestine CIA black ops**.

Lt. Col. Anthony Shaffer, running a military unit called Stratus Ivy in the Defense Intelligence Agency (DIA), also took part in the effort. According to Shaffer, Stratus Ivy is tasked **"to take on 'out of the box'**

ideas, and develop them into real intelligence operations." So the goal was to use the information gathered by Able Danger to conduct real operations against Al-Qaeda. Using highly-advanced supercomputers, the unit collected huge amounts of data in a technique called "data mining." They received information from such sources as Al-Qaeda internet chat rooms, news accounts, web sites, and financial records. Using sophisticated software, they compared this with government records such as visa applications by foreign tourists, to find any correlations and to cross-reference them for viability.

Capt. Scott Phillpott, who was head of the Able Danger program, asks Lt. Col. Shaffer to talk to a representative of CIA Director George Tenet and attempt to convince him that the new Able Danger program is not competing with the CIA regarding terrorism, but instead should be augmenting it. Shaffer later recalls the CIA representative replying, **"I clearly understand the difference. I clearly understand. We're going after the leadership. You guys are going after the body. But, it doesn't matter. The bottom line is, CIA will never give you the best information from 'Alex Base' (the CIA's covert action element targeting bin Laden) or anywhere else. CIA will never provide that to you because if you were successful in your effort to target Al-Qaeda, you will steal our thunder. Therefore, we will not support this."**

Shaffer claims that for the duration of Able Danger's existence, **"To my knowledge, and my other colleagues' knowledge, there was no information ever released to us because CIA chose not to participate in Able Danger."**

This is because the CIA doesn't work for the citizens of the United States. They don't work for you and me even though our taxes contribute to their being on the government payroll. The CIA works for the people who really pull the strings in this world, the proponents of the New World Order. This is why, in my opinion and a lot of other truth seekers too, **the CIA is the primary suspect in orchestrating the events of 9/11**. Sure they had a handful of Arab patsies as a front, and we'll go over CIA mind control techniques in my next book that will blow you away. The bottom line is, that an extremely powerful and interconnected entity with all the right connections would have had to be able to pull all the strings that they did to pull off 9/11. The CIA is virtually the only organization interconnected yet clandestine enough to do it. This is the bottom line why they wouldn't cooperate with Able Danger, when to not do so defies all logic.

So, in December of 1999, the Able Danger team begins collecting large amounts of data on their own about Al-Qaeda. Their aim is to acquire intel that would allow Special Operations forces to conduct strikes against Al-Qaeda around the world. Major Erik Kleinsmith claimed later that he was visited by Special Operations officials and he gave them a demonstration of what the data mining techniques they've developed could do. He stated that within 90 minutes of the demonstration, his analysts find evidence that al-Qaeda has a "worldwide footprint" including "a surprising presence in the US."

By the spring of 2000, Kleinsmith and others are able to isolate about 20 people who warranted further analysis. The Able Danger team creates huge presentation charts measuring up to 20 feet in length and covered in small type in order to show all the links between suspects that have been discovered.

Able Danger in fact is able to identify five Al-Qaeda terrorist cells. One of these discovered cells has connections to Brooklyn, New York **and includes alleged 9/11 ringleader Mohamed Atta, and three other alleged 9/11 hijackers: Marwan Alshehhi, Khalid Almihdhar, and Nawaf Alhazmi.**

Project Able Danger was running smack dab into the middle of a CIA black op, one that was never supposed to be uncovered.

Getting too close to the truth, the plug was pulled by those higher than they, and Project Able Danger was shut down early in 2001. They weren't, however, able to snuff out the loose ends that lived on after Able Danger was killed off.

A man named James D. Smith was working for the private company Orion Scientific Systems on a contract that assisted the Able Danger project. Smith will later claim that around March or April 2000, armed federal agents came into Orion and confiscated much of the data that Orion had compiled for Able Danger. Orion's contract is nullified at this time and Smith has no further involvement with Able Danger. However, Smith happens to have some unclassified charts made for Able Danger in the trunk of his car when the agents raid his office. The chart with

Mohamed Atta's picture on it, implicating him as a potential terrorist, survived and was remembered well by Smith. This chart was later confiscated and destroyed in the summer of 2004 by the CIA.

Smith will later state, **"All information that we have ever produced, which was all unclassified, was confiscated".**

Now with all the billions of dollars worth of high-tech surveillance the FBI and CIA were doing around the world prior to 9/11, don't you find it a bit odd that the FBI "knew nothing about the hijackers or their plans" but within hours of the attacks on the morning of September 11, 2001, the FBI supplied to the Mainstream Media the identities, **and pictures no less**, of the hijackers? Then stuck with those names and identities all the way through the official investigation by the 9/11 Commission and their bogus, whitewashing report, even though 7 of the alleged highjackers were factually alive?

If you look into the matter even further, it also seems that we have planted evidence regarding the hijackers.

The most prominent of this incriminating "evidence" coincidentally comes from the alleged lead hijacker himself, Mohammed Atta.

For you see, miraculously Atta's luggage somehow didn't make it onto that ill-fated flight that slammed into the side of the WTC, but instead ended up in the hands of the FBI.....what **luck**.

The materials in this luggage were said to confirm by the FBI that the planes had indeed been hijacked by Atta and fellow Al-Qaeda operatives.

Among incriminating items in the luggage, the FBI ***found*** the following:

* A videotape of the Boeing 757 aircraft.

* A flight operating manual for the Boeing 757, which has the same cockpit as the 767.

* An Arab-English dictionary.

* A packet of papers which included a 5-page letter, as well as Atta's last will and testament, which was dated April 11, 1996, and also written in Arabic.

* A chart-plotting ruler.

* A manual slide-rule device called an "E6B," but more commonly known as a flight "computer," which pilots use to measure fuel consumption, weight and balance and other things.

* A folding-blade knife with finger grips on the handle.

Now, I want you to tell me: Why in the HELL would a man on a suicide mission possess **checked luggage,** let alone the absurd items found inside like **a will** and all the rest of the obviously planted items? Unbelievable.

These hijackers apparently had some help, because who had the power to compel NORAD to stand down on 9/11? NORAD, North American Aerospace Defense Command, is in charge of the security of our skies and takes total control in the event of a hijacking. Do you think the hijackers or Osama bin Laden were able to command NORAD to NOT to intercept these rogue planes? Almost one hundred and thirteen minutes elapsed between the time American Airlines Flight 11 lost contact and was hijacked at 8:13:31 until the time United Airlines Flight 93 crashed in Shanksville, Pennsylvania at 10:06:05. One hour and fifty-three minutes went by and the USAF did not intercept any one of these four "hijacked" airliners.

The US military has spent untold billions of dollars developing stealth aircraft which are invisible to radar so they can mount surprise attacks on adversaries, but it seems they should have saved their money and bought a fleet of airliners commanded by Islamic radicals, because they appear to be far more effective at evading "enemy" radar than anything the Military Industrial Complex has invented.

On September 11, 2001 the world's preeminent military superpower was apparently oblivious to the location of 4 rogue airplanes in its airspace for nearly two hours.

All that was required to overcome America's military might on 9/11 were 19 hijackers armed with box-cutters on 4 airliners.

Does this sound plausible to you?

It's what you're expected to believe. It is the excuse they used to enact a gigantic multi-billion dollar Police State to ensure that something like this "never happens again", even if it means stripping **you** of all your Constitutional rights.

The CIA database called Al Qaeda, which has been promoted by the proponents of the New World Order as the cause of all bombings and terrorism since the destruction of the World Trade Center in New York on September 11, 2001, has become a convenient global boogeyman for the 21st Century.

Terrorism is the new manufactured threat that becomes the cohesive glue to hold society together.

Remember the contents of the Report from Iron Mountain? I think you do.

Chapter 11/D

THE WORLD TRADE CENTER

"When you eliminate the impossible, whatever remains, however improbable, must be the truth."
-Sir Arthur Conan Doyle

"We designed the buildings to resist the impact of one or more airliners"
-Frank De Martini, WTC construction manager, referring to the robust construction of the Twin Towers

So, finally we are going to get into the real meat of the matter surrounding the alarming amount of factual implications that 9/11 was an inside job orchestrated by clandestine criminal elements within our own federal government.

So......

Here's how that fateful morning started, September 11, 2001:

7:59 A.M. - American Airlines Flight 11, a Boeing 767 with 92 people on board, departs Boston's Logan International Airport bound for Los Angeles International Airport.

8:14 A.M. - United Airlines Flight 175, a Boeing 767 with 65 people on board, departs from Boston's Logan International Airport bound for Los Angeles International Airport.

8:20 A.M. - American Airlines Flight 77, a Boeing 757 with 64 people on board, departs Washington Dulles International Airport bound for Los Angeles International Airport.

8:40 A.M. - The FAA notifies NORAD's Northeast Air Defense Sector of the suspected hijacking of American Airlines Flight 11.

8:42 A.M. - United Airlines Flight 93, a Boeing 757 with 44 people on board, departs from Newark International Airport bound for San Francisco International Airport.

8:43 A.M. - The FAA notifies NORAD's Northeast Air Defense Sector of the suspected hijacking of United Airlines Flight 175.

8:45 A.M. - American Airlines Flight 11 crashes into the north World Trade Center tower (Tower 1).

9:03 A.M. - United Airlines Flight 175 crashes into the south World Trade Center tower (Tower 2).

9:08 A.M. - The FAA bans all takeoffs of flights going to or through New York airspace.

9:17 A.M. - The FAA shuts down all New York City-area airports.

9:21 A.M. - All bridges and tunnels into Manhattan are closed.

9:24 A.M. - The FAA notifies NORAD's Northeast Air Defense Sector of the suspected hijacking of American Airlines Flight 77.

9:25 A.M. - The FAA orders shutdown of all airports nationwide, banning takeoffs of all civilian aircraft.

9:31 A.M. - President George W. Bush makes a statement from Emma Booker Elementary School in Sarasota, Florida calling the crashes an **"apparent terrorist attack."**

An "apparent" terrorist attack??? How about a definite terrorist attack, the "new Pearl Harbor" that the Project for a New American Century was talking about in order to facilitate rapid change towards a New World Order.

> *"This present window of opportunity, during which a truly peaceful and interdependent world order might be built, will not be open for too long - We are on the verge of a global transformation. All we need is the right major crisis and the nations will accept the New World Order."*
> *-David Rockefeller, September 23, 1994*

But exactly how is that hijacked planes were flying around the country for almost two hours without being intercepted by one of our F-16's, of which some are always kept on high alert, ready to launch in under five minutes in case of national emergency? The cavalcade of facts that uniquely occurred on September 11, 2001 pointing to an inside job is enormous, and far too many to be a coincidence. The facts we are going to go over in this section on the WTC alone add up to 9/11 being an inside job, let alone analyzing what happened at the Pentagon and Shanksville, PA. It is literally the best and only explanation to logically explain what happened that day, something we call 9/11 Truth.

We talked briefly about this in the last section, but there are a couple more facts we need to go over regarding the NORAD stand down that are critical to understand as part of building the case against the proponents of the Great Plan having planned and executed these attacks against the United States, against our country. They got away with killing thousands of innocent Americans to further the Great Plan, and truthfully I'm very angry about it. That was one of the chief motivators to put this book together, to awaken you to the truth of 9/11, that they intentionally murdered our citizens and terrorized our country. They are going to do things like this again to be sure, and you need to get your blinders off and your guard up. Remember the upside down flag on the cover of this book? That is there to sound an alarm that we are literally under attack from within by the proponents of the New World Order, even as you read these words.

We're going to be going over a lot of factual information here, so pay careful attention to the weight of the **facts** as it approaches and exceeds the weight of the New World Order's innocence over the events of 9/11.

Point of fact: On the morning of September 11, NORAD just happened to be conducting exercises that mirrored exactly what ended up happening in real life: a bunch of hijacked airliners flying around our nation's airspace.

There were at least five training exercises in a joint NORAD/CIA arrangement dealing with hijacked airliners happening in the days leading up to and on the morning of 9/11. As part of the simulation, NORAD radar screens showed as many as 22 simulated hijacked airliners at the same time. NORAD had been briefed that this was part of the exercise drill and therefore *normal reactive procedure was forestalled and delayed on September 11, 2001.*

Operation Northern Vigilance, Biowarfare Exercise Tripod, Operation Vigilant Guardian, Operation Northern Guardian, and Operation Vigilant Warrior were all going in the days up to and on 9/11.

The large numbers of simulated and real 'blips' on NORAD radar screens help explain why there was so much confusion going on about scrambling interceptor aircraft and where they should be headed.

The simulations also explain an on-record comment made public between an air traffic control personnel and NORAD. The controller tells NORAD that a hijacked airliner is heading for New York and requests fighter interceptors to intervene. NORAD responds by saying, **"is this real world or an exercise?"** This audio of this comment is on youtube.com to hear for yourself.

There is a bunch of other information about each of these five exercises in particular and how they individually were suspect for having been going on when 9/11 happened, but we don't have the time or space to go that far into it. There were also multiple failures at multiple levels of NORAD that we could spend pages going into and over. Due diligence is on your shoulders if you need to know more on this particular matter.

And one last pertinent thing regarding NORAD to go over here. According to buried testimony at the 9/11 Commission hearings, Vice President Dick Cheney apparently ordered an interceptor stand-down just as NORAD was finally getting the facts sorted out and was preparing to act right before the "plane" hit the Pentagon.

Upon realization we were under "terrorist" attack on 9/11, Cheney had been taken by the Secret Service to an underground bunker in the White House Called the Presidential Emergency Operations Center. From there, according to CNN no less, neocon and New World Order proponent Dick Cheney was in charge of directing the federal government's response to the unfolding attacks.

Secretary of Transportation Norman Mineta was in the Presidential Emergency Operating Center with Vice President Cheney as Flight 77 approached Washington, D.C. On May 23, 2003 in front of the 9/11 Commission, Secretary Mineta testified:

> *"During the time that the airplane was coming in to the Pentagon, there was a young man who would come in and say to the Vice President, "The plane is 50 miles out." "The plane is 30 miles out." And when it got down to "the plane is 10 miles out," the young man also said to the Vice President, "Do the orders still stand?" And the Vice President turned and whipped his neck around and said, "Of course the orders still stand. Have you heard anything to the contrary?"*

As the "plane" in question slammed into the Pentagon, what else can we conclude except that the "orders" were to **not** shoot down the aircraft and to let what happened happen.

In May of 2001, by Presidential order, Cheney was handed direct control of all war-game and drill operations through being appointed head of the new Office of National Preparedness, which controls FEMA. When a national emergency such as a hurricane hits, you probably know by now that FEMA takes charge over the area and the situation affecting it. When the national emergency of the hijacked airliners happened, FEMA took charge, and Cheney was essentially dictator of the U.S. through FEMA the morning of 9/11, calling the shots as needed to ensure 9/11 went off as planned.

Why would they establish Cheney's position of power just months before 9/11?? Could it be that George W. Bush was an incompetent buffoon and wouldn't have been able to be trusted by the Illuminati to do the job needing to be done on 9/11? Just add it to the list of "amazing unprecedented coincidences" swirling around the events of 9/11.

This meant Cheney was put solely in charge of the integrated NORAD simulation operations/CIA war-games on the morning of 9/11 **and** the response to the 9/11 attacks as new head of FEMA. While waiting for the chain of command to step in and direct what they were supposed to do in the unfolding situation, which would be Dick Cheney, a complacent Cheney contributed greatly to preventing Standard Operating Procedure from being implemented on 9/11 and those planes being intercepted. What was being said behind the scenes we'll never know, save for the testimony from Secretary of Transportation Norman Mineta that came out of the 9/11 hearings, and we weren't even supposed to hear about that. In fact, nothing that Bush or Cheney themselves said at the 9/11 hearings was made public, and that's a **fact**.

So, getting on to what transpired at the World Trade Center, it seems that various explosions were not only heard inside the twin towers after the planes hit, but people were standing next to areas within the towers that exploded and maimed/killed people according to multiple eyewitness accounts, including highly credible NYC fire department personnel. The only way for this to happen is if actual bombs/detonation charges were going off. Remember, all the hijackers were supposedly responsible for was slamming jetliners into these buildings, not planting bombs all over the place. This is why the eyewitness testimony of explosions going off **was stricken from the official 9/11 Commission Report**. According to the 9/11 Commission members and not *hundreds* of eyewitnesses who were inside the Twin Towers, there were **no** explosions at the WTC despite hundreds of claims to the contrary.

Barry Jennings, the deputy director of the Emergency Services Department of the New York City Housing Authority, gave a detailed statement of explosions in the evacuated WTC 7. As a result of a major explosion on the sixth floor, he and his colleague were trapped inside the building for about 90 minutes before the firemen were able to get them to safety.

Louie Cacchioli, was one of the first firefighters to enter the south tower as it burned. A 20-year veteran of the fire department, Cacchioli told *"People Weekly"*:

"I was taking firefighters up in the elevator to the 24th floor to get in position to evacuate workers. On the last trip up a bomb went off. We think there were bombs set in the building."

John Bussey, foreign editor for the *"Wall Street Journal"* described the collapse of the South Tower:

"I heard this metallic roar, looked up and saw what I thought was just a peculiar site of individual floors, one after the other exploding outward. I thought to myself, "My God, they're going to bring the building down." And they, whoever they are, had set charges. In fact the building was imploding down. I saw the explosions, and I thought, 'This is not a good place to be, because we're too close to the building, and it's too easy for the building to topple over."

But if there were bombs planted in the buildings, how did they get there? Surely Osama bin Laden wasn't that good that he could have wired up the twin towers and Building 7 with demolition charges to collapse, right? Of course he wasn't, but that's exactly what happened.

If you are to believe the official story, something amazing happened on September 11, 2001. For the first time in history, and never since, a steel-framed building collapsed due to fire. This happened not **once,** not **twice,** but **three times on 9/11** and never before or after in the history of mankind. Three steel-framed buildings collapsed, and the official government report states that it was due to fire. You can research yourself the various high-rise skyscrapers that have caught fire in history and suffered far worse fire damage, and they didn't collapse.

Whoever did plant the bombs needed to get past some of the tightest security on the planet, this dictates that it would have to have been an inside job. Remember, the twin towers had been targeted before by "terrorists" in the early 1990's, so security at the complex was always tight and on high alert.

This would have had to have been a pretty good sized operation, and a cover would have to have been in place to access the restricted areas of the WTC, something like an elevator renovation or something. I almost forgot, they **did** do an elevator renovation at the WTC in the months right before 9/11. There is little information about this available in the public forum, but it is indeed true and this was a fact not investigated by the 9/11 Commission.

Something else that is lacking in information in the public forum, and was not investigated by the 9/11 Commission, is who was in charge of security at the WTC. The picture now begins to come into focus a little clearer as to how bombs might have been able to get by security. The black ops needed a way to get past security to plant demolition charges, and this appeared to be a non-issue due to the company in charge of security, Securacom. Information about this company is spotty at best, and the role of Securacom in providing security to the targets of the September 11th attacks was intentionally not investigated by the 9/11 Commission.

When asked if the FBI had questioned anyone at Securacom about the company's security work in connection with the 9/11 attack, CEO Barry McDaniel flat out said **"no"**.

Securacom, renamed Stratasec after 9/11, in fact provided security services for several facilities that were central to the crimes of 9/11, including the World Trade Center. In the years leading up to 9/11, the company had security contracts with the organization that managed Dulles Airport, where Flight 77 took off that day, and with United Airlines, which owned two of the hijacked planes.

Securacom was in charge at the WTC and was developing the security system for the buildings in the period leading up to, and including, the day of 9/11.

To sum up Securacom very quickly, they had intimate ties to President Bush's administrative cabinet, family, and business associates, including the fact that President Bush's younger brother Marvin was a Director at Securacom all the way into the year 2000 before leaving—probably so he wasn't sitting right in the driver's seat when the event occurred.

All of those people including Marvin Bush and the other upper tier of Securacom are all paid operatives of the New World Order crowd. They run together, they share secrets together, and they stay quiet together. They do this or else, because if one hangs, they all hang---like something over being involved with the events of 9/11.

What I guess I'm saying with regards to Securacom, is that there are an awful lot of connections between Securacom's ownership and upper level management and the exact people running the New World Order.

Using his influence, Marvin Bush could easily have directed Securacom to "hire" some acquaintances of his, like CIA special ops, to become part of Securacom's work force, and then be steered to the WTC job. Don't forget that his dad, President George H.W. Bush, *ran the CIA as Director in the 1970s.*

During the time of the elevator renovations, it is highly probable that the buildings were wired for demolition. Through the elevator shafts access can be gained to 4 foot crawl spaces between floors where explosives could have been planted without workers in the buildings realizing it or seeing what was going on. There was also a sudden, unexplained power loss and evacuation drills being conducted the weekend before 9/11. The usually tight security at the WTC was lightened for some mysterious reason just days before 9/11, including the bomb sniffing dogs being removed at this time, **and that is a fact**.

> *"The World Trade Center was destroyed just days after a heightened security alert was lifted at the landmark 110-story towers, security personnel said yesterday."*
> *- Newsday, the day after 9/11, on 9/12/01*

What makes the removal of bomb-sniffing dogs so important are statements from firemen and other eyewitnesses that they heard and experienced bombs going off in the Towers and Building 7 on 9/11. This matter of the reduced security, including the specially-trained dogs being pulled out, was completely ignored by the 9/11 Commission.

Nobody in the 9/11 Truth Movement's sphere of influence has the legal authority to get subpoenas and fully investigate these people and these situations, Securacom, Ace Elevator, and the eyewitnesses to the explosions. The responsibility rested with the federal government, and they whitewashed all aspects of what we just went over via the compromised 9/11 Commission.

We're going to move ahead here, and I'm going to do my best to go over the WTC facts in as close of a timeline as possible, starting on the morning of 9/11.

There is only one video in existence of Flight 11, which was the first plane that hit the WTC, and it was not made publicly available until later in the day on 9/11.

This is just not the case, according to President Bush himself on two different occasions. If you'll remember, President Bush was reading to a group of elementary school kids when the attacks began. According to Bush's statements, his exact words, he states *that he saw the video of the plane hitting the first tower before he even went into the classroom*. He states this publicly on **two** different occasions. Unless Bush had the TV in his limo on Channel CIA, he couldn't have seen the first plane hit, because the video for the first plane wasn't made available until later in the day on 9/11. The infamous video of his handler coming up to him and whispering in his ear while he's reading to the kids isn't what you think. According to Bush himself, his handler is in fact telling him that a *second plane had just hit a skyscraper at the WTC*. According to Bush himself he knew we were under attack before he went into that classroom. This scenario all by itself raises some troubling questions. How did President Bush see the first plane hit before anyone else in the entire nation, and why, if he knew we were under attack, did he go into the classroom instead of being rushed away to safety? There is the highest probability that Bush did see the first plane hit, courtesy of the CIA's cameras, and that he wasn't worried about his safety where he was because he already knew how the attacks were going to pan out.

Now, there is only one video of the first plane hitting, and multiple videos from multiple angles of the second plane hitting. Upon close examination from all angles of the second plane, there seems to be a glaring oddity about this particular plane, alleged to be United Airlines Flight 175.

Upon inspection of the various independently filmed videos, it appears that "Flight 175" had some kind of apparatus attached underneath the plane, almost like a long pod attached to the belly off-center of the fuselage. There also appears to be some sort of equipment located under the left wing that shouldn't be there. A standard Boeing 757 passenger jet surely would not have extra appendages like this, so what were they and why were they there? As of this time, this question is still unresolved, but is yet another piece of evidence to add to our growing list proving what we were told happened on 9/11 by the feds isn't the truth.

It has even been alleged that Boeing's department of commercial aviation examined the videos and images of the pod underneath flight 175 for ten days after being brought to their attention and ended up declining to make a statement on what they found for "reasons of national security". This particular scenario first turned up in Barcelona, Spain's largest daily newspaper, the well-respected La Vanguardia. Nothing of this was mentioned in the 9/11 Report. Put the pod anomaly on the list of facts.

Through all of the videos and every angle of the second plane hitting, *and even witnesses on the only video of the first plane hitting*, Flight 11, you can see some sort of incendiary flash occurring at the nose of the planes just as they are about to hit the buildings. Was this to help ignite the jet fuel? We don't know. Just another oddity that is a fact, that there is video evidence of, and that was ignored by the 9/11 Commission. Put it on the list of facts.

Another strange coincidence that had to do with not only the two planes at the WTC, but the other two hijacked planes as well, is the fact that all four planes had conspicuously low numbers of passengers for trans-continental flights, with all four planes having well below the industry average. Another coincidence? Coincidence or not, it's another fact to be sure, and that's what we're tallying up here in this chapter. Put it on the list of facts.

It is the contention of the 9/11 Commission that fire and not the impact of the planes hitting the Twin Towers was what caused their collapse, and that fire alone was also responsible for the collapse of Building 7.

They said that those fires burned long enough and got hot enough to raise the temperature of the structural steel girders, made of special steel that is much stronger and more heat-resistant than regular steel, to the point where their integrity was compromised and they failed to be able to hold the load above.

To begin with, the fires that were "raging out of control" according to the 9/11 Commission were in fact generating dark-black, slow-rolling clouds of smoke, inconsistent with being generated by a fire of the degree of temperature that would be required to compromise the integrity of structural steel. Slow-rolling clouds of black smoke are indicative of a low-temperature, oxygen-starved fire that was sustained by the remaining jet fuel, carpeting, office furniture, etc. that was burning inside the towers after impact. The vast majority of the jet fuel was actually burned up *outside* the Twin Towers in the huge fireballs you can clearly see in the numerous videos showing the collisions. **There are in fact pictures and videos of people shown standing in the gaping holes made from the planes entering the buildings immediately prior to the collapses, so there is certainly no raging inferno going on like we are lead to believe.**

Even if there was massive structural damage to the Twin Towers from the jet impacts, and even if that jet fuel did rage out of control and caused the towers to collapse, *that still wouldn't explain Building 7's collapse, which was neither hit by a jet or significantly on fire, and still collapsed perfectly into its own footprint at 5:20 PM on 9/11.*

The fact that all three buildings fell perfectly symmetrical and at virtually free-fall speed is a tell-tale sign of a professional demolition job. Collapsing at free-fall speed with absolutely no resistance from thousands of tons of structural steel engineered and constructed to prevent exactly this from happening is an impossibility. I'm no demolition expert, but to tell me that all three buildings failed at once instead of as a graduated collapse is ludicrous, especially Building 7. You can even see in the video of the Building 7 collapse that there is the classic "crimp" at the top center of the building, showing the telltale sign that the central supports had been blown out, causing the building to collapse in on itself towards the center right into its own footprint. Building 7 was a textbook controlled demolition.

The following is an excerpt from a Dutch TV program called Zembla, on 9/11/2006 whereby they interviewed Daniel Jowenko – a controlled demolition expert for 27 years and owner of Jowenko Explosieve. **He** had never heard about building 7 either, as most people haven't, and was shown the collapse and told about it for the first time. Their cameras and recorders rolled as he was shown the tape of Building 7's collapse:

JOWENKO (in subtitles translated from Dutch): *Does the top go first? No, the bottom. It starts on the bottom, yeah. They simply blew up columns - and the rest caved in..."*
INTERVIEWER (in subtitles translated from Dutch): *So this is different from the WTC?*
JOWENKO: *Don't you agree?*
INTERVIEWER: *Yes, you see the bottom floors go first.*
JOWENKO: *Yes and the rest implodes. That is controlled demolition.*
INTERVIEWER: *Absolutely?*
JOWENKO: *Absolutely. It's been imploded. It's a hired job, done by a team of experts.*
INTERVIEWER: *But it happened on 9/11.*
JOWENKO: *The same day?*
INTERVIEWER: *The same day.*
JOWENKO: *The same day? Are you sure?*
INTERVIEWER: *Yes.*
JOWENKO: *And you're sure it was the 11th? That can't be.*
INTERVIEWER: *Seven hours after the World Trade Center.*
JOWENKO: *Really? Then they worked hard...*

There can be only **one conclusion** as to what happened to Building 7 and the Twin Towers: they were pre-wired with demolition charges and demolished.

This is exactly what was being screamed by emergency personnel just minutes before Building 7 did implode, that there were bombs in the building, that it was going to collapse, and everyone needed to get out and get back. Again, Larry Silverstein, the owner of the destroyed WTC complex, stated plainly in that PBS documentary that he and the FDNY decided jointly to demolish WTC 7 late in the afternoon of 9/11.

Adding to the burden of evidence suggesting the buildings were professionally demolished is the fact that **molten structural steel** was found at all three collapse sites. This molten steel was well documented and found not only in the days after 9/11, but **weeks after** as they were demolishing the debris pile.

Now, I will tell you that without fail, the only way short of a foundry or cutting torch to melt structural steel is through a chemical reaction using something called thermite. When thermite is ignited, it causes a chemical reaction hot enough to go through steel like a hot knife through butter.

Liquefied structural steel was found **weeks later** in pools underneath the rubble. The ongoing chemical reactions from the thermite kept the iron molten for many weeks. Thermal imaging from satellites was released showing the huge amount of heat being radiated up from the debris piles for weeks after the collapses, heat from the ongoing chemical reactions of the burning thermite.

FDNY supervisions reported that as the excavating machines were pulling the debris out of the piles, **"the liquid steel was running down the I-beam channel rails like lava. Like you were at a foundry."**

There is not a chance in **HELL** that the fires from the exploding airplanes could have melted structural steel and kept it molten for weeks, let alone at Building 7's debris pile where no jet fuel was involved. Structural steel melts at around 2,800 degrees Fahrenheit. Under *ideal* conditions, pure jet fuel burning has a maximum temperature of around 1,500 degrees. Can you do the math? *Those fires would have to have been at least 1,300 degrees hotter than their maximum possible burning temperature to have created molten steel*, let alone keeping it in a molten state for weeks after the collapses. Thermite burns at over 5,000 degrees, easily liquefying any metal it touches.

Now we're going to review the evidence found in both molten metal and random dust samples taken from the collapse area, showing the proof of the existence of not only thermite at Ground Zero, but a specialized U.S. military-manufactured product called **nano-thermite**, which burns even hotter and more rapidly than regular thermite. In fact, it seems we have two different smoking guns of evidence contained in the dust in particular.

The first smoking gun is the fact that contained within the dust samples collected from various sites and people are microscopic spheres of metal. Perfect, tiny microscopic spheres of metal only visible under an electron microscope. This occurs only through the liquefaction and subsequent scattering in the air of molten metal.

The second and most incriminating evidence to come out of the samples is the fact that **unexploded particles of nano-thermite were found.**

Now I might be able to bite into believing a combination of an un-controlled fire and structural damage from a crashed jetliner might have been able to bring one steel-framed skyscraper down. But to have three structural-steel-framed buildings fall down perfectly into their own footprint, with the third not even being hit by a jetliner full of fuel? Add to that the steel members in the debris pile that appear to have been partially evaporated in extraordinarily high temperatures and pools of molten structural steel? At all three buildings??? **The existence of un-exploded nano-thermite is direct evidence that 9/11 was an inside job. Nobody could have gotten access to all of these three highly secure buildings unless you were on the inside, and nobody living in a cave in Afghanistan has the technology to create and place charges of nano-thermite in such a precise manner. This was a completely professional black ops job run by the CIA, working at the direction of the proponents of the Great Plan.**

The sum total of the evidence of the existence of nano-thermite ultimately came together in a report that was completely ignored by the Mainstream Media. On July 31, 2009, in *The Open Chemical Physics Journal*, the scientific paper *"Active Thermitic Material Discovered in Dust from the 9/11 World Trade Center Catastrophe"* was published. It was authored by Niels H. Harrit, Jeffrey Farrer, Steven E. Jones, Kevin R. Ryan, Frank M. Legge, Daniel Farnsworth, Gregg Roberts, James R. Gourley, and Bradley R. Larsen, and conclusively shows the presence of unignited alu-minothermic explosives in dust samples from the World Trade Center.

Aluminothermic reactions are a class of energy-releasing oxidation-reduction chemical reactions in which elemental aluminum reduces a compound, typically by stealing the oxygen from a metal oxide. Alumi-nothermics range from low-tech preparations that take seconds to react and therefore release nearly all their energy as heat and light, to advanced engineered materials with accelerated reaction rates that yield explosive powers similar to conventional high explosives.

The proponents of the official account of 9/11, including the Federal Government's National Institute of Standards and Technology, or NIST, who conducted the "scientific investigation" for the feds, have dismissed evidence that aluminothermics were used to destroy the World Trade Center skyscrapers, claiming that thermite's slow reaction rate makes it an unsuitable tool for demolishing buildings.

NIST was placed in the uncomfortable position of arguing that the Twin Towers and Building 7 were brought down by office fires started by jet fuel, which burns 1,300 degrees cooler than the melting point of iron, while denying the evidence that temperatures hot enough to melt iron were present.

Despite repeated requests by scientists and researchers to address the potential role of advanced aluminothermic composites with high explosive power, officials have refused to acknowledge such materials, and haven't even tested for them, fearing what they would have found. It was left up to the private resources of patriotic Americans to try and found out what really happened, and that is what we're summarizing in this chapter.

The implications of the discovery of unspent aluminothermic explosives in World Trade Center dust are disturbing to say the least. There is no conceivable reason for there to have been tons of high explosive nano-thermite in the Towers except to demolish them. Professional demolition is diametrically opposed to the official 9/11 story from the feds that state the skyscrapers collapsed as a result of the jetliner impacts and fires.

The discovery of nano-thermite adds to a vast body of evidence that the destruction of the Towers and Building 7 were controlled demolitions.

People, nano-thermite isn't something you can make in a cave in Afghanistan. We are talking about **MILITARY GRADE NANO-THERMITE** that was produced in sophisticated government laboratories. Very few people on the face of this Earth have access to this, let alone the quantity of several tons of this stuff we are talking. This is not the kind of stuff that could be easily smuggled in by a single person, or even a small group of people. This was a sophisticated operation with YEARS of planning ahead of it. This was a classic black ops program.

It is revealing that the 9/11 Commission, which published its report in 2004, **does not mention in a single sentence the destruction of the third skyscraper resulting from the terrorist attack in New York.** There is nary even a mention about Building 7 in the 9/11 Commission Report. **This is because they couldn't explain logically and factually how it was able to collapse at free-fall speed into its own footprint without the use of demolition explosives.**

WTC Building 5, which had much more physical structural damage from the collapse of the North Tower next to it, burned much more intensely than Building 7. Although this building had weaker support structures than WTC 7, it did not collapse into a debris pile, but remained standing, as did all the other high rises equally close **and closer** to the Twin Towers collapse zones.

Heikki Kurttila, a Finnish Doctor of Engineering and accident researcher, has made detailed calculations about the collapse speed of WTC 7. He concludes that the short collapse time and low structural resistance "**strongly suggest controlled demolition**". Kurttila notes that an apple dropped from the height of WTC 7's roof would have taken about 0.5 seconds longer to reach the ground than it took the skyscraper to completely collapse. The building was imploded and came down at free fall speed.

Building 7's perfectly symmetrical free-fall collapse means that all of its steel supports, 25 central and 58 peripheral columns, were destroyed *simultaneously*. Any asymmetry in the damage to structures would have led to asymmetrical collapse. Localized office fires and structural damage here and there could not have weakened *all* the central and peripheral support structures in a way that would have caused all of them to fail at the same moment. The simultaneous destruction of support structures throughout the building can **only** be explained by controlled demolition.

One thing **is** certain: the decision to 'pull' Building 7 would have been a boon to a lot of people and organizations within the corrupted federal government.

Building 7 contained offices of the FBI, Department of Defense, IRS (which contained prodigious amounts of corporate tax fraud, including

Enron's), US Secret Service, Securities & Exchange Commission (with more stock fraud records), and Citibank's Salomon Smith Barney, the Mayor's Office of Emergency Management and many other financial institutions. Any number of important or incriminating documents against any of the New World Order insiders could have easily been claimed lost in the "accident".

The SEC has not made public the number of active cases in which substantial files were destroyed by the collapse of Building 7. Reuters news service and the Los Angeles Times published reports estimating them at 3,000 to 4,000. They include the agency's major inquiry into the manner in which investment banks divvied up hot shares of initial public offerings during the high-tech boom.

"Ongoing investigations at the New York SEC will be dramatically affected because so much of their work is paper-intensive," said Max Berger of New York's Bernstein Litowitz Berger & Grossmann. **"This is a disaster for these cases."**

Multiple eyewitness accounts state that officials evacuated the area in the hour before the 5:20 PM collapse of Building 7, and that various officials forwarded verbal warnings conveying certainty that a collapse would occur. *Network television broadcasts contained announcements of the collapse at least 23 minutes before the event---and this is a fact,* and you can still view these news reports on YouTube as of the publication of this book.

At least two television networks made premature announcements of the collapse of Building 7. The BBC unequivocally announced the collapse about 23 minutes before the fact, and even featured a New York correspondent speaking of the collapse in past tense with the still-erect Building 7 standing behind her.

CNN anchor Aaron Brown announced that the building "has either collapsed or is collapsing" about an hour before the event.

Just because the Twin Towers had already collapsed, what made them think that Building 7 in particular was going to collapse? Why not Building 5, which suffered far greater damage?

So now we come to covering their tracks in the aftermath of this inside job. All areas at the World Trade Center began to be cleaned up immediately **with no investigation** as to why three skyscrapers collapsed on 9/11.

Some 350,000 tons of structural steel and debris were swiftly hauled away from Ground Zero and disposed of before anyone could bat an eye. Most of the steel was recycled as per the city's decision to swiftly send the wreckage to salvage yards in New Jersey. The city's hasty move outraged many victims' families who believe the steel should have been examined more thoroughly. Fire experts later told Congress that most of the steel was scrapped without being examined because investigators did not have the authority to preserve the wreckage.

The bulk of the steel was apparently immediately shipped out of the country to China and India.

CFR member Michael Bloomberg, a former engineering major, was not concerned about the destruction of the evidence when asked about it after becoming mayor of New York City:

"If you want to take a look at the construction methods and the design, that's in this day and age what computers do. Just looking at a piece of metal generally doesn't tell you anything."

The pace of the steel's removal was very rapid, even in the first **days** after the attack. By September 29, 130,000 tons of debris, most of it structural steel, had been removed.

During the official investigation controlled by FEMA, only one hundred fifty pieces of steel were saved for future study. One hundred fifty pieces out of hundreds of thousands of pieces.

Given that FEMA considered the steel garbage, useless to any investigation in this "age of computer simulations", they certainly took pains to make sure it didn't end up anywhere other than a smelting furnace or a slow boat to China. They installed GPS locater devices on each of the trucks that were carrying loads away from Ground Zero, at a cost of $1,000 each. The securitysolutions.com website has an article on the tracking system with this passage:

"Ninety-nine percent of the drivers were extremely driven to do their jobs. But there were big concerns, because the loads

consisted of highly sensitive material. One driver, for example, took an extended lunch break of an hour and a half. There was nothing criminal about that, but he was dismissed."

Since no steel frame high-rise building had ever been leveled in human history by any cause other than controlled demolition or severe earthquakes, the total collapses of Buildings 1, 2, and 7 of the World Trade Center would seem to warrant a thorough forensic analysis.

Since Building 7 was evacuated over six hours before its collapse and no people were inside, there were no grounds for the rapid removal and recycling of the steel debris. Because Building 7 was one of the three greatest building disasters in recorded history, the other two being the Twin Towers earlier in the day, the debris of this building should have been meticulously examined. Many individuals and publications, such as *"Fire Engineering Magazine"*, protested the rapid removal and destruction of all evidence strongly, but to no avail. Bill Manning, editor of the 125-year-old "Fire Engineering Magazine", wrote in an article condemning the operation:

"Did they throw away the locked doors from the Triangle Shirtwaist fire? Did they throw away the gas can used at the Happy Land Social Club fire? ... That's what they're doing at the World Trade Center. The destruction and removal of evidence must stop immediately"

Dr. Frederick W. Mowrer, an associate professor in the Fire Protection Engineering Department at the University of Maryland, was quoted in the New York Times as saying:

"I find the speed with which potentially important evidence has been removed and recycled to be appalling."

The pile was, in fact, so well confined to Building 7's footprint that the adjacent streets could have been easily cleared without disturbing it.

Engineering is a science that joins theory and experience to create robust structures safe for mankind to use. Unintended structural failures are extremely rare events that warrant the most careful scrutiny, since they literally field test the original engineering theory. That is why the NTSB carefully documents aircraft crash scenes, and preserves the aircraft remains, frequently creating partial reconstructions in hangars. If an investigation reveals a mechanical or design fault, the FAA usually mandates specific modifications of equipment or maintenance procedures system-wide, and future aircraft are designed to avoid the fault.

Unintended structural failures are far less common in steel-framed high rises than in aircraft. Building 7's remains warranted the most painstaking examination, documentation, and analysis.

There was an initial problem, however, in getting the rapid removal of the evidence up and running: Was the air at Ground Zero safe to breathe, given the copious amount of asbestos and other toxic materials contained in the skyscrapers? Absolutely not, and today thousands of first responders and other workers at Ground Zero are suffering more illnesses than I can list here, including multiple cases of cancer.

On September 18, 2001, EPA administrator and CFR/Bilderberg member Christine Todd Whitman told the public via a press release, **"We are very encouraged that the results from our monitoring of air-quality and drinking-water conditions in both New York and near the Pentagon show that the public in these areas is not being exposed to excessive levels of asbestos or other harmful substances"** and that **"Given the scope of the tragedy from last week, I am glad to reassure the people of New York ... that their air is safe to breathe and the water is safe to drink."**

Without her OK, the process to rapidly remove the evidence simply would not have happened, and the proponents of the Great Plan weren't going to have that.

The White House deliberately pressured the EPA into giving false public assurances that the toxic air at Ground Zero was safe to breathe. As of September 11, 2010, the death toll of emergency workers and first-responders stands at over **900** from toxic air exposure, and more deaths are added every year.

In the weeks preceding the second anniversary of the World Trade Center attacks, a federal report charged the Environmental Protection

Agency with covering up the dangers to workers and residents near Ground Zero.

Another report, made public in September 2003 by a team of US scientists who studied air contamination in the area after the attacks, confirmed that the air at Ground Zero was indeed hazardous, laden with asbestos among other deadly compounds.

"The debris pile acted like a chemical factory," according to University of California at Davis professor Thomas Cahill, who co-authored the academic study. **"It cooked together the components of the buildings and their contents, including enormous numbers of computers, and gave off gases of toxic metals, acids, and organics for at least six weeks."**

In late August 2003, the EPA's Inspector General's office released a report that roundly criticized the agency's handling of the World Trade Center disaster, including charges that the agency misrepresented the danger to the public from the toxic debris.

The EPA's initial press releases on air quality near Ground Zero, it said, were first screened by the White House Council on Environmental Quality. The agency then bowed to White House pressure to downplay the potential dangers by adding **"reassuring comments and deleting cautionary ones"** from early press releases, according to the report.

The EPA also misled anxious residents in thinking that they could safely clean the hazardous dust from the debris inside their homes and buildings, according to the federal report. It points to two press releases in particular, sent out in September and October 2001. The agency assured residents and business owners that **"they could clean their own spaces if they used 'appropriate' vacuum filters, and followed 'recommended' and 'proper' procedures"**, without defining what those terms meant.

According to the Inspector General's report, those instructions were wrong: They should have recommended that residents and business owners obtain professional cleaning. Partly as a result of such press releases, the report added, many workers cleaning homes did not wear respirators or use professional cleaning equipment.

Thousands of heroic, patriotic first responders and New York residents have since come down with various cancers, among other debilitating illnesses and have been shunned for help by the feds.

Unbelievable.

The one last thing we're going to go over, that I'm sure you didn't hear about because it was suppressed by the Mainstream Media, is the issue of the "dancing Israelis".

On 9/11/01, a Mossad (Israel's version of our CIA) surveillance team made a public spectacle of themselves after witnessing the first and second jets hitting the towers. The New York Times reported that the group of five Mossad agents had set up a video camera aimed at the Twin Towers **prior to the first jet hitting**. Police had received several calls from angry New Jersey residents claiming "Middle-Eastern" looking men with a white van were videotaping the disaster with shouts of joy and celebration. Witnesses saw them jumping for joy in Liberty State Park after the initial impact and started calling the police, thinking they were involved with the attacks.

An anonymous phone caller put a damper on their celebration when he called into 911 emergency services to report that a group of Palestinians were mixing a bomb inside of a white minivan and had headed for the Holland tunnel. Based on this phone call, police then issued a lookout alert for a white minivan heading for the city's bridges and tunnels from New Jersey.

When a van fitting that exact description was stopped just before crossing into New York, the suspicious "Middle-Easterners" were apprehended.

According to ABC's 20/20, when the van belonging to the Mossad agents was stopped by the police, the driver of the van, Sivan Kurzberg, told the officers:

"We are Israelis. We are not your problem. Your problems are our problems. The Palestinians are your problem."

The police and FBI field agents became very suspicious when they found maps of the city with certain places highlighted, box cutters (the same items that the hijackers supposedly used), $4,700 cash stuffed in a sock, and foreign passports. Police also told the *Bergen Record* that bomb sniffing dogs were brought to the van and that they reacted as if they had smelled explosives.

The FBI seized and developed their photos, one of which shows Kurzberg flicking a cigarette lighter in front of the burning buildings in an apparently celebratory and snide gesture.

These Mossad agents worked for a NJ based moving company known as Urban Moving Systems. A few days after the attacks, Urban Moving Systems Israeli owner, Dominick Suter, dropped his business and fled the country for Israel. He was in such a hurry to flee the United States that some of Urban Moving System's customers were left with their furniture stranded in storage facilities.

Suter's departure was sudden and immediate, leaving behind nearly all the contents of his offices. Suter was later placed on the same FBI suspect list as 9/11 lead hijacker Mohammed Atta and others, suggesting the FBI felt Suter may have known something about the attacks.

The Jewish weekly *"The Forward"* reported that the FBI finally concluded that at least two of the detained Israelis were agents working for the Mossad, and that Urban Moving Systems, the highly suspect employer of the five Israelis, was a front operation.

The "dancing Israelis" were held in custody for 71 days before being quietly released.

Three of the five detainees discussed their experience in America on an Israeli talk show after they returned home. As of the publication of this book, you can still see this interview on youtube.com One of them even went so far as to say, with regards to why they were in the United States to start with, **"Our purpose was to document the event".**

How is it that they knew there was going to be an attack, that they were here "to document the event", and had set up cameras before the first jet hit? How is it that the Mossad knew, but not our CIA, FBI, etc.? Hopefully by now you already know the answer to that question.

9/11 was an inside job.

Chapter 11/E

THE PENTAGON

September 11, 2001, 8:51 a.m.:
American Airlines Flight 77, originating from Washington Dulles International Airport and headed to Los Angeles International Airport, is hijacked without incident and makes an unauthorized turn to the south three minutes later. No mayday, no hijack code, no sign of struggle. Flight 77 will fly all the way back from the Kentucky-Ohio border for another 43 minutes before crashing into the Pentagon without any military interception at 9:37 a.m.

Now....the Pentagon is one of the most heavily guarded and watched sites on the planet. With radar systems capable of tracking objects right down to sea level, it is unbelievable that a rogue Boeing 757 could hit the Pentagon without warning after 2 planes already had hit the World Trade Center. That is, until you start to figure in things like Dick Cheney's comments in the basement of the White House as the "plane" was approaching the Pentagon.

The FBI arrives within minutes of the impact and the site is declared a federal crime scene, becoming their exclusive responsibility. FBI agents immediately confiscate security camera tapes from surrounding private businesses, including a Citgo gas station and the Sheraton National Hotel, among many others. Now why would they do that unless those tapes showed something the rest of the world wasn't meant to see? Video that would contradict the official story of a passenger airliner slamming into the Pentagon possibly?

Eyewitness accounts of the object that struck the Pentagon range from "it was a missile" to "it looked like a small commuter plane" to "a huge passenger jet crashed there", so who's to say what exactly hit the Pentagon. The one way to know for sure would be to release footage of the crash taken from the dozens of security cameras that ring the Pentagon, and from Virginia Department of Transportation ("VDOT") and/or the VDOT "Smart Traffic Center" surveillance videos from the day and time of the attack. Well, you know what? Those good people working for the feds did release some footage, including the Citgo gas station tape and a video taken from a security camera from the Doubletree Inn which was also in viewing distance of the Pentagon. The tape from the Citgo shows mostly the inside of the gas station, and the camera footage of the Citgo camera that would've shown the plane hitting the Pentagon is conspicuously absent. The film from the Doubletree Inn only shows the explosion in a grainy image and is of no use to anyone in clearing anything up. The only other "video release" so far by the feds are some still-frame shots taken from a security camera at the entrance to the Pentagon grounds, which shows an unidentifiable object entering the camera frame in one still image, and then exploding into a fireball in the next one. The FBI has in its possession a total of **85** security tapes gathered (taken) from both public and governmental entities. According to an affidavit by Jacqueline Maguire, Special Agent Counterterrorism Division of the FBI, **"fifty-six (56) of these videotapes did not show either the Pentagon building, the Pentagon crash site, or the impact of Flight 77 into the Pentagon on Sept. 11, 2001."**

Maguire goes on to explain that **"I personally viewed the remaining twenty-nine (29) videotapes."** Yet she concluded that there was "nothing of interest" for the public to gain from having access to those tapes.

I've got an idea: **release the tapes and WE'LL decide that for ourselves.** There has not been one single tape released that definitively shows Flight 77 hitting the Pentagon, and that's a **fact.**

The reason they have not shown these tapes of a jet hitting is quite simple: **they don't have them.** I don't believe the feds have a single tape of Flight 77 hitting the Pentagon. I'm going to lay out the evidence for the cover up at the Pentagon now, and quite the cover up it was.

Before plowing into the Pentagon building, the Boeing 757 allegedly performed a death-defying 270-degree turn at the speed of approximately 500 miles per hour. Experienced flight personnel, however, say that that is impossible.

"That is a really difficult maneuver," commented Robin Hordon, a flight controller for 11 years at Boston Center. "And what I will say to you is that an experienced pilot with thousands of hours probably would have to take between 10 and 20 attempts... before they would be able to pull off that maneuver."

"A 757 is not designed to do that," Hordon continued. "The 757 is designed to be a cruise ship in the sky. It's not acrobatic. So you just can't do that with one of those big airplanes."

"The speed, the maneuverability, the way that it turned," commented Danielle O'Brien, air traffic controller from Dulles airport, "we all thought in the radar room, all of us experienced air traffic controllers, that that was a military plane."

Then there is the assertion of the official story that the aircraft was flying at 6 meters above the ground at 530 miles per hour for a half mile before hitting its target.

This is literally an impossibility. A huge plane can't go that fast down that low. The air is too dense at such low altitudes and the plane would instantly crash at that level according to those experts that would know.

"I challenge any pilot," says Nila Sagadevan, a pilot and aeronautical engineer, "give him a Boeing 757 and tell him to do 400 knots 20 feet above the ground for half a mile. You can't do it. It's aerodynamically impossible."

So given the extreme unlikelihood that even a seasoned, professional pilot would be able to pull off such a maneuver, how could Hani Hanjour, who could not even negotiate a tiny Cessna 172, be the man who performed these next-to-impossible acrobatic flying maneuvers in a hulking passenger airliner before zeroing in on the Pentagon for a direct hit?

"I'm still to this day amazed that he could have flown into the Pentagon," said one of Hanjour's past flight instructors in an interview with The New York Times. "He could not fly at all."

"His instructor described him as a terrible pilot," admitted the 9/11 Commission report, quoting an FBI memorandum. Another flight instructor went so far as to call Mohamed Atta and Abdulaziz Al-Omari, the alleged hijackers of Flight 11, **"dumb and dumber in an airplane."** **"For a guy to just jump into the cockpit and fly like an ace is impossible,"** says Capt. Russ Wittenberg, U.S. Air Force, in an interview with Lewis News. **"There is not one chance in a thousand."**

So, whenever an airplane crashes, we are all familiar with footage of physical wreckage, including engines, seats, luggage, and wheel assemblies. But there is something peculiar about the crash of Flight 77 into the Pentagon: there is practically no sign of a wrecked aircraft after the crash. All that remained of Flight 77 were about a dozen small pieces scattered about the front of the Pentagon, most of which could be lifted by hand.

CNN anchor Jamie McIntyre was at the Pentagon after the crash:

"From my close-up inspection, there's no evidence of a plane having crashed anywhere near the Pentagon," he commented live from the scene. **"The only pieces left that you can see are small enough that you can pick up in your hand. There are no large tail sections, wing sections, a fuselage, nothing like that anywhere around which would indicate that the entire plane crashed into the side of the Pentagon."**

There was also a firsthand report from a fighter pilot who was ordered to fly over the Pentagon after the "crash" by Major General Larry Arnold, the commander of NORAD, the agency that is charged with protecting the airspace over North America.

According to Barbara Honegger, the senior journalist with the U.S. Department of Defense, the pilot made an overpass of the crash zone and reported back to command center that **"there was no evidence, zero evidence, of an impact of a plane at the Pentagon."**

As questions over the whereabouts of the debris from the mysteriously disappearing aircraft began to mount, the Department of the Defense began to support the theory that Flight 77 simply "vaporized" due to the speed that it was traveling.

The engines of a Boeing 757-200 are about 9 feet long and composed of titanium, the strongest metal on Earth. So why was there no evidence of these engines slamming against the wall of the Pentagon? The two big holes that we would expect to see from these massive engines simply are not there. There should have been a line of complete destruction before the collapse of the building's external wall. It just wasn't there, it didn't exist. Where the wings of the aircraft allegedly should have struck the building, there are unbroken windows clearly visible.

Point of fact: Only a small hole, **16 feet (5 meters) in diameter**, was visible in the side of the Pentagon 45 minutes before the outer wall collapsed, and this is the *only* hole. The footage of this was shown once, live, and never broadcast again because this is an impossibility if a huge airliner really hit the Pentagon. The titanium engines surely would have made their own holes, even if the wings did not enter and disintegrated against the concrete facade upon impact. There was only a **single 16-foot hole**.

If there was only one 16-foot hole, then that means the rest of the "plane" should have been in thousands of pieces on the lawn directly in front of the Pentagon. There was in fact hardly anything.

As of the publication of this book, you can still view pictures and video on the internet of the side of the Pentagon immediately after the impact and view the size of the hole and lack of airplane debris for yourself.

"I look at the hole in the Pentagon," said Maj. General Albert Stubblebine, whose former job was to measure pieces of Soviet equipment taken from photographs during the Cold War, "and I look at the size of the airplane that was supposed to have hit the Pentagon, and the plane does not fit in that hole."

"With all the evidence readily available at the Pentagon crash site," concludes Col. George Nelson, an aircraft accident investigator with the US Air Force, "any unbiased, rational investigator could only conclude that a Boeing 757 did *not* fly into the Pentagon."

According to the 9/11 Commission, the ensuing fire from the impact was hot enough to incinerate the titanium components of the airplane, while leaving the DNA evidence intact enough for the feds to not only ID all of the passengers, but the hijackers too, including two of the hijackers who came back from the dead and are alive today. Do you believe this? I sure don't.

Whatever it was that hit the Pentagon on 9/11, it slammed through **6 massive walls amounting to over 9 feet of rebar-reinforced concrete before exiting into the center courtyard, leaving a nearly perfect**

circular exit hole deep inside the military complex that measured approximately 12 feet across.

So if Flight 77 didn't hit the Pentagon, what did? And what happened to the passengers who were allegedly on Flight 77? We honestly don't know the answer to either of those questions. Judging from the damage to the Pentagon, some people in the 9/11 Truth movement believe it was a bunker-buster-type missile in order to be able to go through concrete like that. And the passengers? If the proponents of the Great Plan aren't opposed to killing millions of other humans as they've done throughout history, and thousands in New York on 9/11, they surely wouldn't be opposed to "disposing" of a small handful of people who were unfortunately in the wrong place at the wrong time.

This is only speculation on my part, trying to piece together what really happened on that fateful day.

All I know for certain is that we need a new and independent investigation. That is the only way to put this event to bed with full closure, and the ones who were really responsible can be dealt with appropriately.

Chapter 11/F

SHANKSVILLE, PA.

Before we go into the details surrounding the crash of Flight 93 into a non-governmental target, a vacant field in Pennsylvania, I want to put forth a hypothesis I have not come across in the 9/11 Truth community, but one I believe has merit.

It is my opinion that Building 7 at Ground Zero was supposed to be hit by flight 93, the plane that crashed in Shanksville, hence it being wired to come down like towers 1 and 2. They could not leave it standing, as investigations post-9/11 would have turned up that the building had been wired to collapse.

Something went wrong though on Flight 93: a group of our brave countrymen fought back against the CIA patsies, and it had to be shot out of the air by our military jets. I have not heard this theory from other members of the 9/11 Movement, but I think it is a good possibility, and a probable one in my mind.

Now, onward to Shanksville......

The hijacking of Flight 93 began at 9:28 AM. By this time, Flights 11 and 175 had already crashed into the World Trade Center and Flight 77 was, allegedly, within minutes of striking the Pentagon. The hijackers on these three flights had waited no more than 30 minutes to hijack the aircraft. It is unknown why the hijackers on Flight 93 decided to wait approximately 46 minutes to begin their commandeering of the plane.

Officials believe the hijackers assaulted the cockpit and then moved the passengers to the rear of the plane to minimize the chance of the crew or the passengers from interfering with the attack.

The cockpit voice recorder began recording the final 30 minutes of Flight 93 at 09:31:57. At this moment, it recorded Ziad Jarrah, the dedicated "pilot" for the hijackers, announcing, "Ladies and gentlemen: here the captain, please sit down keep remaining seating. We have a bomb on board. So sit."

Jarrah instructed the autopilot to turn the plane and head east at 09:35:09. The aircraft ascended to 40,700 feet as the flight attendant in the cockpit is heard to say, "I don't want to die, I don't want to die" followed by one of the hijackers saying in Arabic: "Everything is fine. I finished."

At 9:39 air traffic controllers overheard Jarrah say, "Ah. Here's the captain. I would like to tell you all to remain seated. We have a bomb aboard, and we are going back to the airport, and we have our demands. So, please remain quiet." Air traffic controllers did not hear from the flight again.

Passengers and crew began making phone calls to officials and family members starting at 09:30 using GTE air phones and mobile phones. Altogether, the passengers and crew made 35 air phone calls and two cell phone calls from the flight. Ten passengers and two crew members were able to successfully connect, providing information to family, friends, and others on the ground. The passengers themselves were also provided information, namely that they were on a flying missile and that the hijackers intended to crash the plane into an as-yet unknown target.

We'll just go over a couple of the documented calls here to make the case that the patriotic Americans on board fought back against the hijackers and very probably regained control of the airplane.

Flight attendant Sandra Bradshaw called her husband at 09:50:04 and told him she was preparing scalding water to throw at the hijackers. Honor Elizabeth Wainio called her stepmother at 09:53:43 and concluded, four and a half minutes later, by saying, **"I have to go. They're breaking into the cockpit. I love you."**

Flight attendant Sandra Bradshaw, who was preparing the scalding water to throw at the hijackers, was still on the phone with her husband and said **"Everyone is running up to first class. I've got to go. Bye."**

The revolt on Flight 93 began at 09:57. The hijackers in the cockpit became aware of the revolt at 09:57:55, exclaiming, **"Is there some-**

thing? A fight?" Jarrah began to roll the airplane left and right to knock the passengers off balance. He told another hijacker in the cockpit at 9:58:57, **"They want to get in here. Hold, hold from the inside. Hold from the inside. Hold**." Jarrah changed tactics at 9:59:52 and pitched the nose of the airplane up and down to attempt to disrupt the assault.

The cockpit voice recorder captured the sounds of crashing, screaming, and the shattering of glass. Jarrah stabilized the plane at 10:00:03. Five seconds later, he asked, **"Is that it? Shall we finish it off?"** Another hijacker responded, **"No. Not yet. When they all come, we finish it off."** Jarrah once again pitched the airplane up and down. A passenger in the background cried, **"In the cockpit. If we don't, we'll die"** at 10:00:25. Sixteen seconds later, another passenger yelled, **"Roll it!"** Jarrah ceased the violent maneuvers at 10:01:00. He then asked another hijacker, **"Is that it? I mean, shall we put it down?"** The other hijacker responded, **"Yes, put it in it, and pull it down."** Nevertheless, the passengers continued their assault and at 10:02:23, a hijacker said, **"Pull it down! Pull it down!"** The airplane descended with the yoke turned hard to the right.

Amidst the sounds of the passenger counterattack, the aircraft plowed into an empty field in Stonycreek, Pennsylvania, about 20 minutes flying time from Washington, D.C. The last entry on the voice recorder was made at 10:03:09. The last piece of flight data was recorded at 10:03:10.

There is some degree of controversy between some of the family members of the passengers and the investigative officials as to whether the passengers managed to breach the cockpit and take control of the plane. The 9/11 Commission Report asserts that **"the hijackers remained at the controls but must have judged that the passengers were only seconds from overcoming them"**.

Some people, like myself, believe that there is no doubt the passengers breached the cockpit.

The plane crashed into a reclaimed coal strip mine in Stonycreek Township at 10:03:11. The National Transportation Safety Board reported that the flight impacted at 563 miles per hour at a 40 degree nose-down, inverted attitude. The impact left a crater eight to ten feet deep and 30 to 50 feet wide. All 44 people on board died instantly on impact.

This is where the official story propagated by the 9/11 Commission and the truth part ways, in my opinion.

So, while things were unfolding in the air aboard Flight 93, American Airlines Flight 77 streaked, allegedly, toward Washington, D.C., after being hijacked. NEADS – the North East Air Defense Sector of NORAD, received notice of the Flight 77 hijacking at 9:24 a.m. EST. Six minutes later, two F-16s were airborne from Hampton, Va.

The pilots, however, had not received permission to engage and destroy, but to just head for Washington, D.C. Seven minutes after wheels up, the American Airlines passenger jet allegedly crashed into the Pentagon. This was allegedly the third hijacked flight used as a missile to kill and maim that morning, as far as most people knew, and the national air defense was playing catch-up.

Two minutes before the F-16s from NEADS were airborne, the Federal Aviation Administration learned United Airlines Flight 93 had also been hijacked. Approximately 9:35 AM, the hijacked plane began a left turn to the south near Cleveland, Ohio. By 9:39, it completed the turn and Flight 93 was aimed at Washington, D.C.

There would be no excuse for not stopping what had become a terrorist missile apparently aimed at the seat of our federal government. By this time, numerous supersonic, armed F-15s and F-16s were now in the air and within minutes of Flight 93, which would remain in the air for another 29 minutes.

Unprecedented political decisions were now in the process of being made as Flight 93 and multiple United States fighter interceptors headed for a showdown near Shanksville, a small town in Pennsylvania. In Washington, D.C., an electronic conference was in progress.

The conference focused on Flight 93. A White House staffer would keep coming in with updates on Flight 93's progress towards D.C., according to a Sept. 11, 2002, ABC News program. ABC's Charles Gibson asked what **"the target of that airplane might be?"** Vice President Dick Cheney responded, **"I thought probably White House or Capitol."**

U.S. Army Brig. Gen. W. Montague Winfield revealed that a **"decision was made to try to intercept Flight 93"**. Gen. Winfield told ABC News that, **"... the president had given us permission to shoot down innocent civilian aircraft that threatened Washington, D.C. ...The order was passed on to the pilots intercepting Flight 93......**

"We started receiving reports from the fighters that were heading to, to intercept. The FAA kept us informed with their time estimates as the aircraft got closer and closer," according to Gen. Winfield. Then, the official story presented to the ABC audience begins to blur, as Winfield gave the impression that no one knew what happened next.

Gen. Winfield then gave an explanation of how the situation ended that basically said nothing: **"And at some point, the closure time came and went, and nothing happened. So you can imagine everything was very tense in the NMCC. We had basically lost institutional awareness of where this airplane was."**

One more telling quote comes from the ABC program, by Gen. Winfield: **"It was about, you know, 10:03 that the fighters reported that Flight 93 had crashed."** The FBI had seized Flight 93's CVR (Cockpit Voice Recorder) and claims the tape stopped at 10:03 a.m., this is where Winfield was getting his 10:03 number from.

Now, let's throw this into the mix: **"Several leading seismologists agree that Flight 93 crashed last Sept. 11 at 10:06:05 a.m., give or take a couple of seconds,"** according to a Sept. 16, 2002, *Philadelphia Daily News* article. We seem to have a discrepancy of about 3 minutes between what the feds told us, that the plane crashed at 10:03, and what several different seismologists reported as the time of the plane crash. After everything we've gone through so far here, it is not unreasonable to infer that something occurred during those three minutes the feds wish to hide from the public.

According to public records of the air phone calls, several passengers, and maybe all of them, attempted to take back control of Flight 93. By 10:03, they indeed had succeeded in fighting their way into the cockpit. From the time the feds allege the plane crashed at 10:03 and the time the various independent seismologists say it crashed is about 3 minutes. I believe the passengers did take back control of the plane, but the feds, not wanting a bunch of loose lips, *made the decision to shoot it down anyways.*

On Sept. 13, 2001, barely 48 hours after the Twin Towers came down, the Nashua, N.H., Telegraph Newspaper reported that: **"FAA air traffic controllers in Nashua have learned through discussions with other controllers that an F-16 fighter stayed in hot pursuit of another hijacked commercial airliner until it crashed in Pennsylvania ..."**

John Fleegle, Jim Brant and Carol Delasko were about two-and-a-half miles from what would soon become the Flight 93 crash site. According to the Pittsburgh Tribune-Review, they **"heard engines screaming close overhead. The building shook. We ran out, heard the explosion and saw a fireball mushroom ..."**

Delasko **"... said she thought someone had blown up a boat on the lake.'It just looked like confetti raining down all over the air above the lake.'"**

This is a very important observation by Ms Delasko. Within a second or two after Flight 93 passed over the Indian Lake Marina where Delasko, Brant and Fleegle stood, debris from the stricken plane began to fall into the lake. Lots of debris. Some of it on fire. And it was deposited in a compact area rather than as a continuous trail for some period of time.

Seismologists determined that Flight 93 crashed at 10:06 a.m. and 5 seconds. The 757 was perhaps 20 seconds from crashing when observed by Fleegle, Brant and Delasko. Its cargo area and passenger area had apparently been opened by an explosion. Local news reports described a large number of cancelled checks, stock broker documents, pieces of seats, small chunks of melted plastic and small human parts had landed in the lake.

Also adding to the evidence that Flight 93 was shot down after the passengers took the plane back is the fact that a 1,000-pound section of an engine was found 6,000 feet, over a mile, from the crash site. So, an explosion occurred that separated 1,000 pounds of engine, and opened up a hole in the passenger cabin and cargo hold.

When all the evidence is lined up, it is highly consistent with a heat-seeking missile striking Flight 93, probably around 10:05:30. The evidence strongly infers that the terrorists did not fly that jet into the ground as we were told.

It is my opinion that our military shot that plane down after those brave heroes on board had taken over the cockpit. The New World Order's "new Pearl Harbor" plan would not allow that jet to survive nor the courageous people on it, God rest their souls.

Skull and Bonesman President Bush gave the Vice President authority to issue the order to shoot down Flight 93. Col. Robert Marr, United States Air Force, when interviewed by ABC News remembered getting the orders: **"The rules have changed. We could do something about it now."** The words he heard included: **"We will take lives in the air to save lives on the ground."**

There is no reason to believe the cockpit voice recorder did not continue running three minutes past the official stop time of 10:03, until the plane crashed at 10:06.

What if, when the CVR was first played back, the missing three minutes were not missing? What if the CVR recorded the heroic passengers succeeding in taking over the cockpit and celebrating? They were definitely on the offense when the CVR allegedly stopped. They had actually made it into the cockpit.

What if just as these Americans win the fight and begin the process of flying the plane to safety, a heat-seeking missile slams into the plane in order to silence them forever?

What if that is what the missing three minutes actually revealed?

We'll never know.

The evidence for the plane being hit with a missile is also provided by the eyewitnesses who not only saw the debris raining down miles away from the crash site, but they actually collected some items from Flight 93 that the FBI was more than happy to relieve them of.

When investigating any crime scene, one of the most important pieces of evidence, are **witnesses**. There are plenty of these around Shanksville, and they were talking after the plane crash, much to the chagrin of the FBI who collectively told them to "shut up or else".

I have collected up some of that eyewitness testimony thanks to the internet and other vigilant patriots, so let's briefly go over it. Let's begin with the fighter jet that was sighted by numerous people right around the crash site.

Eyewitness testimonies have generally been excluded from the official version of 9/11 via the 9/11 Commission Report, and for good reason. In the Shanksville area, where many of the residents also believe Flight 93 was shot down, there are scores of eyewitnesses whose testimonies contradict the government's claim that courageous passengers fought hijackers, forcing the jetliner to crash rather than be flown into a building.

Eyewitnesses agree that unexplained military aircraft were in the immediate vicinity when a huge explosive fireball occurred at the reclaimed coal mine near Shanksville.

Viola Saylor saw Flight 93 pass very low over her house in Lambertsville, which is a mile north of the official crash site. She was in her backyard when she heard a very loud noise and looked up to find herself nose to nose with Flight 93, which she says was flying upside down as it passed overhead. It was blue and silver, she said, and glistened in the sunlight. It was so low that it rustled the leaves of her 100-foot maple tree in her yard.

It flew southeastward for about three more seconds and even gained elevation before it crashed over the hill with a thud, she said.

It was really still for a second, she said. Then all of a sudden she saw a very quiet and low-flying military plane coming from the area of the crash site, flying toward the northwest.

__"It was flying very fast, like it was trying to get out of here"__, she said. A second or two behind the military plane were two other planes, which Saylor described as normal planes.

Shown a photograph of a Fairchild A-10 Thunderbolt II, a low-flying combat aircraft commonly referred to as a Warthog, Saylor identified it as the military plane she had seen. She said she recognized the two engines on the rear and the distinctive shape of the cockpit and nose of the plane.

Similar eyewitness reports of military planes over Shanksville on 9/11 remain censored by the Mainstream Media, although they were reported in two leading British newspapers.

Susan McElwain, a local teacher, also reported seeing a military-looking plane at the scene of the crash before witnessing an explosion. Ms. McElwain told Great Britain's The Daily Mirror what she saw:

"It came right over me, I reckon just 40 or 50 feet above my mini-van, she recalled. It was so low I ducked instinctively. It was traveling real fast, but hardly made any sound.

Then it disappeared behind some trees. A few seconds later I heard this great explosion and saw this fireball rise up over the trees, so I figured the jet had crashed. The ground really shook. So I dialed 911 and told them what happened.

I'd heard nothing about the other attacks and it was only when I got home and saw the TV that I realized it wasn't the white jet, but Flight 93.

I didn't think much more about it until the authorities started to say there had been no other plane. The plane I saw was heading right to the point where Flight 93 crashed and must have been there at the very moment it came down.

There's no way I imagined this plane....it was so low it was virtually on top of me. It was white with no markings but it was definitely military, it just had that look.

It had two rear engines, a big fin on the back like a spoiler on the back of a car and with two upright fins at the side. I haven't found one like it on the Internet. It definitely wasn't one of those executive jets.

[However,] the FBI came and talked to me and said there was no plane around."

The plane Ms. McElwain describes is similar to the Warthog seen by Saylor over Lambertsville.

"Then [FBI agents] changed their story and tried to say it was a plane taking pictures of the crash 3,000 feet up", she said. "But I saw it, and it was there before the crash, and it was 40 feet above my head. They did not want my story nobody here did."

The Mainstream Media only reported what Bill Crowley, FBI spokesman from Pittsburgh, said about other planes in the area: <u>**"Two other airplanes were flying near the hijacked United Airlines jet when it crashed, but neither had anything to do with the airliner's fate."**</u>

And then there's the debris field scattered over an eight mile area to contend with.

The Pennsylvania state police, who apparently weren't in lock-step with the feds, said debris from the crash had shown up about 8 miles away in a residential area where local media quoted some residents as seeing flaming debris from the sky.

Residents and workers at businesses outside Shanksville reported discovering clothing, books, papers and what appeared to be human remains. Some residents said they collected bagfuls of items that were turned over to investigators. And there were the reports we just went over of what appeared to be crash debris landing in Indian Lake, nearly six miles from the immediate crash scene.

John Fleegle, an Indian Lake Marina employee, said FBI agents were skeptical of his reports about debris in the lake until they traveled to the lake shore to investigate.

By September 12, crash debris began washing ashore at the marina. Fleegle said there was something that looked like a rib bone amid pieces of seats, small chunks of melted plastic and checks.

He said FBI agents who spent the afternoon patrolling the lake in rented boats eventually carted away a large garbage bag full of debris.

Witnesses say they heard the plane fly over and could feel their houses on the lake shake. The debris evidence also supports the plane flying over Indian Lake AND that the plane was falling apart. This debris would have taken 15-20 minutes to float at 10mph and then descend on Indian Lake from the main crash crater. The testimony and evidence do not support the NTSB story that the debris floated over to the lake from the main crash site..

A shoot-down situation is further strengthened by reviewing statements made by people in various positions of power within the federal government after the fact.

Federal investigators said on September 15, 2001, that they could not rule out the possibility that Flight 93 was shot down. **"We have not ruled out that,"** FBI agent Bill Crowley told a news conference when asked about reports that a U.S. fighter jet may have fired on the hijacked Boeing 757. **"We haven't ruled out anything yet."**

Even Secretary of Defense Donald Rumsfeld had a slip-up and said the plane was shot down:

> *"I think all of us have a sense if we imagine the kind of world we would face if the people who bombed the mess hall in Mosul, or the people who did the bombing in Spain, or the people who attacked the United States in New York, shot down the plane over Pennsylvania and attacked the Pentagon..."*

Yet the official story contained in the 9/11 Commission Report removes all evidence of a shoot down. Under the circumstances, I think most rational-thinking people would agree that shooting down a potential flying missile was the best course of action. That is, unless it is true that those brave Americans who were aboard did in fact take back control of the plane and were then executed for it.

Chapter 11/G

ANTHRAX ATTACKS

Since the "terrorist" attacks on 9/11 were an obvious false flag operation and an inside job, what about the anthrax mailings that followed immediately afterwards?

Another inside job? You better believe it. The anthrax attacks came on so quickly that they could only be related to 9/11 and therefore also an inside job. Getting your hands on military-grade anthrax isn't something you just go down to the corner mart and pick up. The anthrax attacks were unequivocally set in motion prior to 9/11, to coincide with 9/11.

If you'll recall, the anthrax attacks came in two separate waves. The first set of anthrax letters had a Trenton, New Jersey postmark dated September 18, 2001. Five letters are believed to have been mailed at this time to: ABC News, CBS News, NBC News and the New York Post, all located in New York City, and to the National Enquirer at American Media, Inc. (AMI) in Boca Raton, Florida.

Robert Stevens, the first person who died from the mailings, worked at a tabloid called The Sun, also published by AMI. Only the New York Post and NBC News letters were actually found; the existence of the other three letters is inferred because individuals at ABC, CBS and AMI became infected with anthrax. Scientists examining the anthrax from the New York Post letter said it appeared as a coarse brown granular material, looking like crushed, dry dog food.

The second wave of two more anthrax letters, bearing the same Trenton postmark, was dated October 9, three weeks after the first mailing. The letters were addressed to two Democratic Senators, Tom Daschle of South Dakota and Patrick Leahy of Vermont. At the time, Daschle was the Senate Majority leader and Leahy was head of the Senate Judiciary Committee. The Daschle letter was opened by an aide on October 15, and the government mail service was immediately shut down. The unopened Leahy letter was discovered in an impounded mail bag on November 16. The Leahy letter had been misdirected to the State Department mail annex in Sterling, Virginia, due to a misread ZIP code. A postal worker there, David Hose, contracted inhalational anthrax.

Remember now, the anthrax attack occurred while Bush was trying to push through the draconian Patriot Act and begin his attack on Afghanistan.

Two possible blockades to getting the Patriot Act passed, coincidentally, were Senator Tom Daschle and Senator Tom Leahy, both of whom received anthrax letters at their DC offices on Capitol Hill. Both were pushing amendments to the Patriot Act to protect U.S. civil liberties which were about to be trampled by Fuhrer Bush.

The anthrax disruption of Congress allowed the U.S. Patriot Act to be rammed through without it even having a chance at being read and debated.

More potent than the first round of anthrax letters, the material in the Senate letters was a highly refined dry powder consisting of about one gram of nearly pure spores. Barbara Hatch Rosenberg, a molecular biologist and research professor at the State University of New York at Purchase, described the material as "weaponized" anthrax during a 2002 interview for the Australian Broadcasting Corporation.

At least 22 people developed anthrax infections from the anthrax attack, with five dead by the inhalational weaponized anthrax.

The FBI knew early on that the anthrax used was of a consistency requiring sophisticated equipment and was unlikely to have been produced in some "cave in Afghanistan". At the same time, both President Bush and Vice President Cheney made public statements speculating about **the possibility of a link between the anthrax attacks and Al Qaeda.** The *Guardian* newspaper reported in early October that American scientists had implicated Iraq as the source of the anthrax, and the next day the *Wall St. Journal* editorialized that Al Qaeda perpetrated the mailings, with Iraq the source of the anthrax. A few days later, John Mc-

Cain suggested on the David Letterman Show that the anthrax may have come from Iraq. The Mainstream Media's propaganda machine was in full swing.

Though the sources claiming evidence that the anthrax came from Iraq were not named, these reports were cited over and over in the press, starting almost immediately, and for several years following. The letters were cited after the invasion of Iraq as evidence that Saddam not only possessed "weapons of mass destruction", but had actually used them in attacks on the United States. **We now know for a _fact_ that none of that was true, and that we were, once again, taken for a ride by the New World Order-controlled Mainstream Media.**

In mid-2008, the FBI narrowed its focus to Bruce Edwards Ivins, a scientist who worked at the government's biodefense labs at Fort Detrick in Frederick, Maryland. Ivins was told of the impending prosecution and on July 27, 2008 he allegedly committed suicide, by an overdose of acetaminophen---at least according to "official" sources, which hopefully by now you will find hard to believe.

More than likely he was a black ops fall-guy and **didn't** kill himself but was instead assigned a new identity. I don't have any hard evidence to corroborate this theory but it seems to me the most plausible explanation for his "ending" and the subsequent wrap up of the farcical investigation.

Ivins was a top U.S. biodefense researcher who worked at Ft. Detrick. It was widely reported the FBI was about to lay charges on him, however the evidence was largely circumstantial and the grand jury in Washington reported it was not ready to issue an indictment. Rep. Rush Holt, who represents the district where the anthrax letters were mailed, said circumstantial evidence was not enough and asked FBI Director Robert S. Mueller to appear before Congress to provide an account of the investigation. Ivins's death leaves two puzzles conveniently **unanswered**.

Scientists familiar with germ warfare said there was no evidence that Dr. Ivins had the skills to turn anthrax into an inhalable powder. According to Dr. Alan Zelicoff who aided the F.B.I. investigation **"I don't think a vaccine specialist could do it...This is aerosol physics, not biology".**

The other problem is the lack of a **motive**, other than to purely be a fall guy for the Great Plan.

Dr. W. Russell Byrne, a colleague who worked in the bacteriology division of the Fort Detrick research facility, said Ivins was "hounded" by FBI agents who raided his home twice, and he was hospitalized for depression earlier this month. According to Byrne and local police, Ivins was removed from his workplace out of fears that he might harm himself or others. <u>"I think he was just psychologically exhausted by the whole process,"</u> Byrne said. <u>"There are people who you just know are ticking bombs,"</u> Byrne said. <u>"He was not one of them."</u>

Days after he allegedly killed himself on August 6, 2008, federal prosecutors put the whole thing to bed by declaring Ivins to be the sole culprit of the crime when Jeffrey Taylor, the U.S. attorney for the District of Columbia laid out the case against Ivins to the public. The main evidence was immediately disputed by the scientific community.

Taylor stated <u>"The genetically unique parent material of the anthrax spores ... was created and solely maintained by Dr. Ivins."</u> But other experts disagree, including biological warfare and anthrax expert, Dr. Meryl Nass, who stated: <u>"Let me reiterate: No matter how good the microbial forensics may be, they can only, at best, link the anthrax to a particular strain and lab. They cannot link it to any individual. At least 10 scientists had regular access to the laboratory and its anthrax stock, and possibly quite a few more, counting visitors from other institutions, and workers at laboratories in Ohio and New Mexico that had received anthrax samples from the flask."</u>

After the FBI announced that Ivins acted alone, many people with a broad range of political views, some of whom were colleagues of Ivins, expressed their doubts. Reasons cited for these doubts include that Ivins was only one of 100 people who could have worked with the vial used in the attacks, and that the FBI was unable either to find any anthrax spores at Ivins' house or on his other belongings, or place him near the New Jersey mailbox from which the anthrax was mailed.

On September 17, 2008, Sen. Patrick Leahy told FBI Director Robert Mueller during testimony before the Judiciary Committee Leahy chairs that he did not believe Army scientist Bruce Ivins acted alone in the 2001 anthrax attacks, stating:

"I believe there are others involved, either as accessories before or accessories after the fact. I believe that there are others out there. I believe there are others who could be charged with murder. "

On February 19, 2010, the FBI formally closed its investigation, declaring Ivins was the sole suspect and acted alone.

Chapter 11/H

THE 9/11 COMMISSION

In the fall of 2002, the *"National Commission on Terrorist Attacks Upon the United States"*, aka the 9/11 Commission, was established, mostly in response to pressure from families of victims of the 9/11/01 attack.

Well, we might as well jump right on the facts surrounding this ridiculous, underfunded, impotent joke of a whitewash....I mean "investigation".

Point of fact: Originally, President Bush had appointed Bilderberg/CFR/Trilateral Commission member, known Rockefeller henchman, notorious war criminal, and alleged 33rd degree Freemason Henry Kissinger, famous for his role in cover-ups, as chairman of the 9/11 Commission.

Go figure.

In addition to the above New World Order steering groups, Henry Kissinger was then, and still is, an important agent in the service of the British Royal Institute for International Affairs, a member of the Club of Rome and a regular attendee of the occult Bohemian Grove group. He is without a doubt one of the most influential men of the modern era working for the Great Plan.

"The New World Order cannot happen without U.S. participation, as we are the most significant single component. Yes, there will be a New World Order, and it will force the United States to change its perceptions."
- Henry Kissinger

The proponents of the Great Plan, however, ultimately decided that he would have been too much of a lightning rod, and not wanting to attract more attention than already was going to happen, Kissinger stepped down. Kissinger was replaced by former New Jersey governor, and Bilderberg/CFR member Thomas Kean, with Bilderberg/CFR member Lee H. Hamilton being selected as the vice chair, so coming out of the gate you already know we weren't going to get a real investigation. All of these Round Table Group members know each other well behind the scenes from attending these meetings and watch each other's backs, because they know their backs will also need watching someday, either through legal or financial scenarios.

The official investigation of 9/11 was closely overseen, managed, and manipulated by the very individuals who themselves toe the line of their Illuminati masters who are in charge of the New World Order agenda. This section will hopefully be a real eye-opener as to how badly we were lied to about what really happened on September 11, 2001.

Senator Max Cleland, who initially served on the Commission, was the only outspoken original member. After learning who was ultimately going to be involved, he compared the Kean Commission to the Warren Commission:

"The Warren Commission blew it. I'm not going to be part of that. I'm not going to be part of looking at information only partially. I'm not going to be part of just coming to quick conclusions. I'm not going to be part of political pressure to do this or not do that."

In November of 2003, President Bush took care of this "minor" stumbling block and appointed Cleland to a position on the board of the Export-Import Bank, prompting him to step down from the Commission due to sudden "conflict of interest". He was then replaced by Vietnam War criminal and CFR member Bob Kerrey.

Chairs Kean and Hamilton served as the public face of the Commission. Their conflicts of interest should have been concern enough, but the real dirty work of the Commission to hide the truth was in the hands of Philip Zelikow, a fact documented by author and researcher David Ray

Griffin in his book devoted to exposing the fraudulent Commission: *"The 9/11 Commission Report: Omissions and Distortions".*

In 1998, CFR member Philip Zelikow published an article in *Foreign Affairs*, the journal of the Council on Foreign Relations, entitled *"Catastrophic Terrorism: Imagining the Transformative Event".* This was the very report **PNAC** picked up and expanded on when they stated that **"Further, the process of transformation, even if it brings revolutionary change, is likely to be a long one, absent some catastrophic and catalyzing event like a *new Pearl Harbor.."*

So now, the **exact** pro-New World Order operative who suggested we needed a new Pearl Harbor, and got it, **was heading the Commission in charge of whitewashing it.**

Zelikow was a member of the Bush transition team in 2000-2001. In other words, Bush was Zelikow's boss at the time he was appointed to the Commission.

As executive director, Zelikow was in charge of the Commission's staff, and it was these staff members, not the Commissioners we saw on television, who did most of the actual work of the Commission. The Commissioners carried out their own distinctive work, their discussions and interviews, **on the basis of the material provided by the staff under direct control of Zelikow.**

Kean and Hamilton refer to this fact in their statement that the **"professional staff, headed by Philip Zelikow, conducted the exacting investigative work upon which the Commission has built".**

As Executive Director of the 9/11 Commission, Zelikow oversaw a staff of 70 "researchers", comprised of ex-FBI, ex-CIA, and ex-Department of Justice employees. In other words, people who made their very livings off of lies, misinformation and disinformation. Zelikow also had the power to determine what would be researched and what would not be researched. The 9/11 Commission Report was for the most part co-authored by the White House; and literally amounted to nothing more than the White House whitewashing itself.

In his book, David Ray Griffin enumerated some of Zelikow's **many connections** to the Bush White House: Member of the National Security Council of the elder Bush administration, aid to National Security Advisor Brent Scowcroft under the elder Bush administration, co-Author of a book with then Secretary of State Condoleezza Rice, National Security Advisor for Bush Jr., Director of Aspen Strategy Group, to which Rice, Scowcroft, Dick Cheney and Paul Wolfowitz belonged, Member of Clinton to Bush Jr. transition team, member of Bush Jr.'s Foreign Intelligence Advisory Board, until being appointed to the 9/11 Commission.

No conflict of interest there, right?

Not only was Zelikow intimately tied to the Bush White House, *look with your own eyes at these terms laid out by President Bush and VP Cheney in order for them to cooperate to testify:*

-They would only be allowed to testify jointly
-They would not be required to take an oath before testifying
-The testimony would not be recorded electronically or transcribed, and that the only record would be notes taken by one of the commission staffers
-These notes would not be made public.

Huh???? Kind of makes you think they had something to hide, right? There is not a doubt that they did. At the very *least* they knew about the impending attacks and allowed if not helped them to happen. At the very *worst*, they were involved with planning and executing the attacks.

Congress originally allotted only $3 million for the investigation. This figure was later increased to $15 million. By contrast, **$50 million** was allocated for the Challenger disaster and the Clinton Whitewater scandal, whereas **$40 million** was allocated for Ken Starr's "independent" investigation of Clinton's sex scandal. It was intentionally underfunded from the get-go. They wanted people to believe that the Commission was just a waste of time and taxpayer money, and that they already had their perpetrators, Osama bin Laden and his fellow cave-dwellers from Afghanistan.

The committee had **no subpoena power**, little staff support, and was unable to obtain basic information like detailed blueprints of the buildings that collapsed. The White House released only about **25% of some 11,000 documents requested by the 9/11 Commission**, and the documents released were often **heavily blacked out**, thus offering zero information.

Other Bush administration officials also refused to testify under oath. Eventually, Bush, Cheney, and Rice did meet with the commission in secret, behind closed doors, but again, they were not under oath, and no tape recorders or transcripts of the conversations were allowed. The government has still not released much of the forensic data, which is either classified, concealed, or has been destroyed.

The 9/11 Commission has earned the designation by the 9/11 Truth Movement as the **"Omission Commission"** due to its *refusal to even consider the vast body of evidence contradicting the official narrative of the attack*. For example, the Commission decided not to hear from any of the fire fighters who witnessed the destruction of the World Trade Center. The exact same firefighters who would have testified to hearing explosions, seeing molten steel, and knowing that building 7 was going to collapse after being tipped off. The body of oral history testimony from the FDNY and EMS personnel remained suppressed until after the Commission had closed the doors and rubber stamped the report.

The agenda of the Commission to confirm the "official" story, evident in the conduct of its hearings, became crystal-clear with the publication of its final report. **The report is full of outright lies and contradictions, but its principal method for avoiding troublesome facts is through omission.** In essence the Commission performs sleight of hand, diverting attention from the many red flags in the official story by spinning a detailed narrative about the alleged hijackers, terror networks, and breakdowns in systems that were supposed to deal with the threat.

The Report became a best-selling book and was hailed in the Mainstream Media as the definitive report on the attacks. However, the Report is more accurately characterized as the definitive narrative of the official **myth** of 9/11, systematically excluding every fact that doesn't support the official story.

Some of the more glaring facts not covered in the report? And this list is *far from complete* to save time and space in this book:

-The Report fails to acknowledge that no steel-framed high-rise building before or after 9/11 has ever collapsed due to fires.

-The Report fails to mention the total collapse of 47-story steel-framed skyscraper Building 7 at 5:20 on the day of the attack.

-The Report contains no mention of the interview in which the owner of Building 7 states that he and the Fire Department decided to "pull" Building 7 -- an apparent admission of a conspiracy to destroy the building and its contents.

-The Report fails to mention the rapid removal and recycling of the structural steel from the collapsed World Trade Center buildings, the protests against that action, or even to make excuses for it.

-The Report makes no mention of a statement by then-Mayor Rudolph Giuliani to Peter Jennings indicating he had foreknowledge of the collapses: **"We were operating out of there when we were told that the World Trade Center was gonna collapse, and it did collapse before we could get out of the building."**

-The Report contains no mentions of eyewitness accounts of explosions

-The Report fails to mention that George W. Bush's brother, Marvin Bush, and his cousin, Wirt Walker III, were principals in the company that had the contract to provide security for the World Trade Center, Securacom, nor does it even mention the company.

-The Report makes no mention of the fact that a new owner, Larry Silverstein, took control of the World Trade Center complex just six weeks before the attack, obtained an insurance policy covering terrorist attacks, and successfully sued the insurance companies to obtain twice the multi-billion-dollar value of the policy.

-The Report repeats the list of 19 suspects identified by the FBI within days of the attack, while failing to mention that seven of them reported themselves alive after the attack.

-The Report fails to mention that the airlines' published passenger lists contained no Arab names.

-The Report fails to ask why the plane that crashed into the Pentagon was not stopped by anti-aircraft missile batteries that presumably ring the building.

-The Report fails to mention that no credible footage of the Pentagon attack has been made public, despite public knowledge that the FBI seized footage of the attack from nearby businesses.

-The Report does not ask why the Secret Service did not obtain air cover for the President's motorcade from the Sarasota school to the airport, nor for Air Force One, which took off at about 9:54, until about 11:10.

-*The Report avoids mentioning several reports that government officials and business leaders received warnings and avoided targets of the attacks, including:*

A warning by the FBI advising Attorney General John Ashcroft to avoid flying on commercial airlines.

The report that Pentagon officials suddenly canceled travel plans the evening before the attack.

The cancellation of plans by Ariel Sharon to attend an event in New York City on 9/11/01.

A warning to San Francisco Mayor Willie Brown to avoid flying from Condoleeza Rice

-*The Report does not mention that letters with weaponized anthrax were sent to the two most powerful senators attempting to slow the passage of the 9/11/01 attack-predicated USA PATRIOT Act.*

-*The Report states that the Commission was "chartered to prepare a full and complete account of the circumstances surrounding the September 11, 2001 terrorist attacks, including preparedness for and the immediate response to the attacks," but fails to mention that it makes no attempt to meet its charter.*

Finally, the families of the 9/11 victims called for the resignation of Executive Director Philip Zelikow, a Bush insider, and were duly snubbed. Commission member Max Cleland resigned, calling the entire exercise a "scam" and a "whitewash."

If it was such an open-and-shut case on 9/11, why would anybody need to twist the truth and ignore all of the available evidence? There is a legal term to describe this, and it is called **obstruction of justice**, which is a federal offense in the United States.

The bottom line is, if the public cannot place its trust in the very 9/11 Commission that was supposed to investigate the attacks, then how is it supposed to trust the official version of 9/11? For most individuals, expressing any sort of doubt about the official version as to what occurred on 9/11 would mean confronting demons that few people are prepared to or would even want to face....**and that's what they are banking on.**

The official story has been questioned, and many of the points I've made here were raised by members of the US Congress, retired high-ranking officers of the US military, the three leading third-party candidates for President in the 2004 election, a member of the 9/11 Commission who resigned in protest, a former high-ranking adviser to the George W. Bush administration, former ministers to the German, British and Canadian governments, the commander-in-chief of the Russian air force, 100 luminaries who signed the "9/11 Truth Statement," and the presidents of Iran and Venezuela. Not all of these people agree fully with each other, but all would normally be considered newsworthy. Why has the Mainstream Media remained silent about these statements? Hopefully you already know the answer to that by now.

The 9/11 Commission Report ignores the historical record of US covert support to international terrorism via the CIA, while creating the illusion that America and "Western Civilization" are threatened by terrorists. Video and images of the events that day were played over and over to further traumatize us. The various terrorist warnings and code red alerts they flashed on TVs across the nation immediately after 9/11 also served to instill in our country an atmosphere of fear and intimidation, not to mention the police state in America that they have rolled out with greater and greater force since 9/11.

How about what some of the 9/11 Commissioners said themselves about the whole deal:

- The 9/11 Commission's co-chairs said that the 9/11 Commissioners knew that military officials misrepresented the facts to the Commission, and the Commission considered recommending criminal charges for such false statements

- 9/11 Commissioner Timothy Roemer said <u>**"We were extremely frustrated with the false statements we were getting"**</u>

- 9/11 Commissioner Max Cleland resigned from the Commission, stating: <u>**"It is a national scandal"**</u>; <u>**"This investigation is now compromised"**</u>; and <u>**"One of these days we will have to get the full story because the 9-11 issue is so important to America. But this White House wants to cover it up"**</u>

- And the Senior Counsel to the 9/11 Commission, John Farmer, who led the 9/11 staff's inquiry said "At some level of the government, at some point in time...there was an agreement not to tell the truth about what happened", He also stated: "I was shocked at how different the truth was from the way it was described .... The tapes told a radically different story from what had been told to us and the public for two years.... This is not spin. This is not true." He also stated: "It's almost a culture of concealment, for lack of a better word. There were interviews made at the FAA's New York center the night of 9/11 and those tapes were destroyed. The CIA tapes of the interrogations were destroyed. The story of 9/11 itself, to put it mildly, was distorted and was completely different from the way things happened"

If even the 9/11 Commissioners don't buy the official story......do you?

Chapter 11/I

THE WAR ON TERROR = POLICE STATE USSA

"An evil exists that threatens every man, woman, and child of this great nation. We must take steps to ensure our domestic security and protect our homeland."
-Adolph Hitler, when announcing the Gestapo to the citizens of Germany

If you'll remember from earlier in this book, Adolf Hitler staged a false flag attack and blamed it on communist terrorists. Shortly after, he passed the Enabling Act, which completely eradicated the German constitution and destroyed people's liberties. Hitler then led a series of preemptive wars that were justified to the German people as necessary to maintaining homeland security.

"Naturally the common people don't want war; neither in Russia, nor in England, nor in America, nor in Germany. That is understood. But after all, it is the leaders of the country who determine policy, and it is always a simple matter to drag the people along, whether it is a democracy, or a fascist dictatorship, or a parliament, or a communist dictatorship. Voice or no voice, the people can always be brought to the bidding of the leaders. That is easy. All you have to do is to tell them they are being attacked, and denounce the pacifists for lack of patriotism and exposing the country to danger. It works the same in any country."

-Nazi Kingpin Hermann Goering, founder of the Gestapo, Commander of the Luftwaffe, and Hitler's right hand man

We know one of the intentions of the 9/11 false flag attack: to invade the Middle East. Now we need to go over the other reason: to wage war against the patriotic citizens of the United States of America. The ones like me who not only are questioning their motives but speaking up about it, resisting what they are trying to put over on our country by educating others to the truth of what is really happening, **exactly** what is contained in this book.

Many people do not know that the Patriot Act was already written and ready to go long before September 11th, but at the same time, according to the Bush administration, they knew nothing about terrorist attacks that were pending against us. After all, that is why 9/11 happened right? We, according to them, we were "caught off guard" and the only way to protect us is through the legislation contained in the Patriot Act.

The USA PATRIOT ACT is an acronym that stands for Uniting (and) Strengthening America (by) Providing Appropriate Tools Required (to) Intercept (and) Obstruct Terrorism Act of 2001. It was passed on October 26, 2001, in the wake of the September 11th terrorist attacks, granting sweeping new powers to law enforcement and intelligence gathering authorities, and establishing the Gestapo of the 21st Century, **The Department of Homeland Security**, which is the enforcement arm of the Patriot Act.

The Patriot Act offers a broad definition of terrorism which subjects non-terrorist political groups to government surveillance, wiretapping, harassment, and criminal action. In other words, anyone who questions the actions of the Illuminati-controlled federal government is targeted as a terrorist. **THIS** is the **primary reason for 9/11** and the subsequent immediate ramming through of the Patriot Act and Homeland Security---to monitor and attack the rising "patriot" movement in the U.S., people who are waking up to the slide into a one world government.

By waking up other patriotic Americans as to what the hell is really going on with our country and the world, these "radicals" by definition of the Patriot Act become enemies of the federal government they want to take back control of from the proponents of the New World Order.

The Patriot Act increases the ability of state and federal law enforcement agencies to search and monitor telephone, e-mail communications, medical, financial, and other records; eases restrictions on foreign intelligence gathering within the United States; expands the Secretary of the Treasury's authority to regulate financial transactions; and broadens the discretion of law enforcement and immigration authorities in detaining and deporting immigrants suspected of terrorism-related acts. The act also explicitly expands the definition of terrorism to include *domestic terrorism*, thus enlarging the number of activities to which the Patriot Act's expanded law enforcement powers can be applied.

The Act was passed by wide margins in both houses of Congress and was supported by members of both the Republican and Democratic parties. Remember, this thing got rammed through right in the midst of the Anthrax attacks, so no one in Congress was going to so much as utter a peep in resistance and look like they were sympathetic to terrorism.

Opponents of the law have criticized its activities through which law enforcement officers can search a home or business without the owner's or the occupant's permission or knowledge; the expanded use of National Security Letters, which allows the FBI to search telephone, e-mail, and financial records without a court order; and the expanded access of law enforcement agencies to business records, including library and financial records.

Many of the act's provisions were to expire beginning December 31, 2005, approximately 4 years after its passage. In the months preceding the expiration date, supporters of the act pushed to make its provisions permanent, while critics sought to revise various sections to enhance civil liberty protections. In July 2005, the U.S. Senate passed a reauthorization bill with substantial changes to several sections of the act, while the House reauthorization bill kept most of the act's original language. The two bills were then reconciled in a conference committee that was criticized by Senators from both the Republican and Democratic parties for ignoring civil liberty concerns. The bill, which removed most of the changes from the Senate version, passed Congress on March 2, 2006, and was signed into law by Skull and Bonesman President George W. Bush on March 10, 2006.

Under the Patriot Act, civil liberties, especially privacy rights, have taken a severe blow, as witnessed by the following actions allowed under the act: dramatically expanded ability of states and the Federal Government to conduct surveillance of American citizens, **any** crime can now put you under the microscope of Homeland Security, foreign and domestic intelligence agencies can more easily spy on Americans, eliminated government accountability, authorized the use of "sneak and peek" search warrants in connection with any federal crime, including misdemeanors, and on and on.

And if that wasn't intrusive and draconian enough, the Patriot Act has been revised in the last few years into an ever more intrusive and Constitution-annulling piece of legislation, with all changes signed off by the puppet-President Obama.

Now, who exactly is a "potential domestic terrorist" under the Patriot Act? Although I'm not listing everything that classifies you as a potential terrorist, you may very well find yourself on the list below and suspected of terrorist activity by the feds:

-if you are a libertarian

-if you have political statements or political bumper stickers on your car

-if you are pro-Second Amendment and/or own a gun or guns

-if you buy or possess survivalist literature, whether fiction or non-fiction

-if you are a "prepper", as in you buy food in bulk (shop at Costco), stockpile food, guns, ammunition, hand tools, medical supplies, etc. in case of an emergency

-if you have fear of economic collapse

-if you own gold and/or silver coins and bullion

-if you have religious views concerning the book of Revelation (apocalypse, anti-Christ). In other words, if you are a *Christian*, you are considered a potential terrorist under the USSA police state.

-if you have expressed fears of Big Brother or big government

-if you home school your kids

-if you believe in conspiracy theories that involve grave threat to national sovereignty and/or personal liberty....like exactly what is contained in this book

-if you are an American who believes your "way of life" is under attack or threatened

- if you are "fiercely nationalistic" (as opposed to universal and international in orientation) like being opposed to the United Nations agenda of eliminating all sovereign countries borders and weapons

- if you are a former police officer, veteran, or returning active duty soldier

-if you supported Ron Paul for President

-if you fly a U.S. flag at your house, or have U.S. flags in or on your vehicle or place of employment

-if you are pro-life

-if you pay cash for anything rather than be electronically monitored by the banking cabal/government of your purchases

–if you value privacy on the web when using the Internet in public places

–if you use a device to record video

–if you talk to police officers

–if you wear a hooded sweatshirt, a "hoodie"

–if you drive a van

–if you write on a piece of paper in public

–if you use your cell phone to record anything

And on, and on, and on, and on. Virtually every American in the country violates at least one item off this list alone every single day. I personally am guilty of most of the above actions, and I'm about the most patriotic guy you'd ever meet in your life. Not a danger to the United States, but an **extreme danger to the completion of the Great Plan**.

Are you getting it yet? *The people the police state was intended to target from the get-go are the exact people who not only know about the New World Order and are trying to wake other people up about it, but those who are preparing to deal with what is coming our way in this country: a complete and utter economic collapse that will turn into a tyrannical police state.*

They don't want you to be prepared when this collapse happens. What the Federal Reserve is doing right now, "printing" billions of dollars every month and injecting it into the financial system will factually crash our nation's economy, there is no way around it, and we are past the point of no return. At this point they are just trying to buy time, to stave off the inevitable, to get as tight of a grip as possible on the country via this police state they are assembling right this second.

They want you to be 100% reliant on the government to save you, to be your "savior" when this economic event occurs, and it will. You saw how well the feds took care of those people in Louisiana during Hurricane Katrina. This time it will be a nationwide meltdown and there will be little to no help for you and your family **at all**. This is the exact reason that people in the know about the New World Order agenda are prepping for this exact scenario. You can't depend on the feds, nor trust them at this point. Our federal government has been completely co-opted by the Luciferians running the Great Plan/New World Order/ one world government agenda.

Everything I've told you in this book was as factually correct as possible and this is what they are afraid of: humanity learning the facts of what they are trying to do and standing up to them.

So. We have the Patriot Act, which is "enforced" by the now $60 billion-a-year behemoth Homeland Security, with most of that money going towards the USSA police state here at home to target the most patriotic of Americans, the people opposed to the New World Order.

I don't know if you've flown recently, but if you've gone through a cancer-causing full body scan or been groped by a TSA lackey, you are now feeling the initial effects of the progressing police state, and this is just the beginning.

Here is a quick rundown of some of the facts of the Homeland Security Police State compiled, surprisingly, by the *Washington Post*, dated July 19, 2012:

The USSA police state is comprised of some 1,271 government organizations, and 1,931 private companies work on programs related to Homeland Security, counterterrorism, and intelligence in about 10,000 locations across the United States. Over 200,000 people alone work just for Homeland Security.

*In Washington and the surrounding area, 33 building complexes for top-secret intelligence work are under construction or have been built since September 2001. Together they occupy the equivalent of almost three Pentagons or 22 U.S. Capitol buildings - about 17 million square feet of space.

*With the sudden availability of billions of dollars as a result of the Patriot Act, military and intelligence agencies multiplied. Twenty-four organizations were created by the end of 2001, including the Office of Homeland Security and the Foreign Terrorist Asset Tracking Task Force. In 2002, 37 more were created to track weapons of mass destruction, collect threat tips and coordinate the new focus on counterterrorism. That was followed the next year by 36 new organizations; and 26 after that; and 31 more; and 32 more; and 20 or more each in 2007, 2008 and 2009.

*In all, at least 263 organizations have been created or reorganized as a response to 9/11. Each has required more people, and those people have required more administrative and logistic support: phone operators, secretaries, librarians, architects, carpenters, construction workers, air-conditioning mechanics and, because of where they work, even janitors with top-secret clearances.

Add to all the above even more aggressive police state legislation, the National Defense Authorization Act or NDAA, created by President Obama via Executive Order on December 31, 2011. "Executive Order" means that the President bypassed Congress, which is purely against the Constitution. It was signed by the President at 9:00 PM on New Year's Eve while virtually nobody was paying attention to much other than the approaching New Year. This Executive Order was written and signed in complete secret and then released by the White House on its website without comment. All this was done under a President who allegedly studied Constitutional law while at Harvard. What a joke.

I bet you've never even heard of the NDAA, let alone what kind of new powers it gives the feds.

The NDAA basically carves up the United States into individual pieces, each to be under the authority of one of the President's cabinet members, with the President having the ultimate authority over all. Here is how it breaks down:

- The Secretary of Defense has power over all water resources in the U.S.
- The Secretary of Commerce has power over all material services and facilities, including construction materials, in the U.S.
- The Secretary of Transportation has power over all forms of civilian transportation in the U.S.
- The Secretary of Agriculture has power over all food resources and facilities, livestock plant health resources, and the domestic distribution of farm equipment in the U.S.
- The Secretary of Health and Human Services has power over all health resources in the U.S.
- The Secretary of Energy has power over all forms of energy in the U.S.

Not only this, but the NDAA gives the President the power to not only detain any American citizen without just cause but to **execute them** if he wishes. This is how Obama is getting away with assassinating American citizens allegedly working for the Taliban in Afghanistan using those unmanned drones you probably haven't heard about. The ones that kill about 20 innocent civilians for every single "bad guy" they take out.

We are essentially under martial law right this second. The Illuminati are creating a police state in America right under your nose.

But how are they going to round up all those troublemaking patriots I was talking about? And what are they going to do with them to keep them from making more trouble?

That's where **FEMA** comes in.....

A manufactured crisis is all the federal government needs to enact FEMA, the Federal Emergency Management Agency. In 1979, by Tri-lateral Commission member President Jimmy Carter's Executive Order, FEMA was given tyrannical powers. It has the power, in case of "national emergency", to suspend laws, move entire populations, arrest and de-tain citizens without a warrant, and hold them without trial. It can seize property, food supplies, transportation systems, **and can suspend the Constitution indefinitely.**

Not only is it the most powerful entity in the United States, but it was not even created under Constitutional law by the Congress. It was a product of another Presidential Executive Order. An Executive Order becomes law simply by a signature of the U.S. President; it does not even have to be approved by the Representatives or Senators in the Congress.

A state of "national emergency" could be a terrorist attack, a natural disaster, or a **currency crash** for example. The currency crash of our dollar is probably going to be the excuse to declare martial law in America, mark my words, and it is coming within just a few years, and possible just a few months.

Here are just a few Executive Orders associated with FEMA that would suspend the Constitution and the Bill of Rights. These Executive Orders have been on record for over 30 years, and could be enacted by the stroke of a Presidential pen:

Executive Order Number 12148 created the Federal Emergency Management Agency that is to interface with the Department of Defense for civil defense planning and funding. An "emergency czar" was appointed. FEMA has only spent about 6 percent of its budget on national emergencies. The bulk of their funding has been used for the construction of secret underground facilities to assure continuity of government in case of a major emergency, foreign or domestic.

Executive Order Number 12656 appointed the National Security Council as the principal body that should consider emergency powers. This allows the government to increase domestic intelligence and surveillance of U.S. citizens and would restrict the freedom of movement within the United States and grant the government the right to isolate large groups of civilians. The National Guard could be federalized to seal all borders and take control of U.S. air space and all ports of entry. Here are just a few Executive Orders associated with FEMA that would suspend the Constitution and the Bill of Rights. These Executive Orders have been on record for nearly 30 years and could be enacted by the stroke of a Presidential pen:

EXECUTIVE ORDER 10990 allows the government to take over all modes of transportation and control of highways and seaports.

EXECUTIVE ORDER 10995 allows the government to seize and control the communication media.

EXECUTIVE ORDER 10997 allows the government to take over all electrical power, gas, petroleum, fuels and minerals.

EXECUTIVE ORDER 10998 allows the government to take over all food resources and farms.

EXECUTIVE ORDER 11000 allows the government to mobilize civilians into work brigades under government supervision.

EXECUTIVE ORDER 11001 allows the government to take over all health, education and welfare functions.

EXECUTIVE ORDER 11002 designates the Postmaster General to operate a national registration of all persons.

EXECUTIVE ORDER 11003 allows the government to take over all airports and aircraft, including commercial aircraft.

EXECUTIVE ORDER 11004 allows the Housing and Finance Authority to relocate communities, build new housing with public funds, designate areas to be abandoned, and establish new locations for populations.

EXECUTIVE ORDER 11005 allows the government to take over railroads, inland waterways and public storage facilities.

EXECUTIVE ORDER 11051 specifies the responsibility of the Office of Emergency Planning and gives authorization to put all Executive Orders into effect in times of increased international tensions and economic or financial crisis.

EXECUTIVE ORDER 11310 grants authority to the Department of Justice to enforce the plans set out in Executive Orders, to institute industrial support, to establish judicial and legislative liaison, to control all aliens, to operate penal and correctional institutions, and to advise and assist the President.

EXECUTIVE ORDER 11049 assigns emergency preparedness function to federal departments and agencies, consolidating 21 operative Executive Orders issued over a fifteen year period.

EXECUTIVE ORDER 11921 allows the Federal Emergency Preparedness Agency to develop plans to establish control over the mechanisms of production and distribution, of energy sources, wages, salaries, credit and the flow of money in U.S. financial institution in any undefined national emergency. It also provides that when a state of emergency is declared *by the President, Congress cannot review the action for six months. The Federal Emergency Management Agency has broad powers in every aspect of the nation.*

On January 22, 2009, a new bill introduced in Congress **authorized the Department of Homeland Security to set up a network of FEMA camp facilities to be used to house U.S. citizens in the event of a national emergency.**

The National Emergency Centers Act or HR 645 mandated the establishment of "national emergency centers" to be located on military installations for the purpose of providing "temporary housing, medical, and humanitarian assistance to individuals and families dislocated due to an emergency or major disaster," according to the bill.

The legislation also states that the camps will be used to "provide centralized locations to improve the coordination of preparedness, response, and recovery efforts of government, private, and not-for-profit entities and faith-based organizations".

Ominously, the bill also states that the camps can be used to "meet other appropriate needs, as determined by the Secretary of Homeland Security," an open ended mandate which many besides myself fear could mean the forced detention of patriotic American citizens in particular in the event of widespread rioting after a national emergency via total economic collapse.

As the world economy continues its downward spiral, many credible forecasters have predicted riots and rebellions in America that will dwarf those already witnessed in countries like Iceland, Spain, Greece and others.

With active duty military personnel already being stationed inside the U.S. under Northcom, partly for purposes of "crowd control," fears that Americans could be incarcerated in detainment camps are very real.

The camps will double up as "command and control" centers that will also house a "24/7 operations watch center" as well as training facilities for Federal, State, and local first responders.

The bill also contained language that will authorize camps to be established within closed or already operating military bases around the country.

The language of the preamble to the agreement veils the program with talk of temporary migrant (illegal alien) holding centers, but it is made clear that the camps would also be used "as the development of a plan to react to a national emergency."

As far back as 2002, FEMA sought bids from major real estate and engineering firms to construct giant internment facilities in the case of a chemical, biological or nuclear attack or a natural disaster.

For those that think concentration camps will never come to America, they need to be educated to the fact that we've already had them. During WW II, thousand of patriotic Japanese-Americans were uprooted from their homes and stuck in these camps for the duration of the war with Japan because "they couldn't be trusted" and were potential "enemies of the state". I went to school with some of the children of these people, and they literally lost all their possessions, unable to make house payments, tax payments, etc....the banks took it all.

The Illuminati are factually waging war against those who would resist their evil plans.

Consider yourself warned.

Chapter 11/J

THE 9/11 TRUTH MOVEMENT

"I am a firm believer in the people. If given the truth, they can be depended upon to meet any national crisis. The great point is to bring them the real facts."
-Abraham Lincoln

I want to take some valuable space here to line up in a contiguous row, all of the pertinent details surrounding the events of 9/11 so you can take them all in at once and weigh them in your own mind to determine if you think you still believe the "official" story of 9/11 the proponents of the New World Order want you to believe, or if you believe that we weren't told the truth and we need a new investigation by a private, independent, non-partisan, non-governmental entity.

Here is what we know:

-The proponents of the Great Plan proposed the immediate need for a "new Pearl Harbor" in the late 1990s to happen in the near future to help usher in the final stages of the New World Order, and then miraculously got it

-The proponents of the Great Plan wanted to and did in fact gain a larger military presence in the Middle East

-The proponents of the Great Plan wanted to restart their black ops opium cash cow in Afghanistan, and did

-The proponents of the Great Plan wanted to establish a police state in America, which they did and is continuing to unfold today

-The proponents of the Great Plan wanted increased control over Middle East oil reserves, which they got

-The proponents of the Great Plan wanted to reap the financial rewards of invading two Middle Eastern countries via the Military Industrial Complex they substantially own, and they did

-One (1) of the participants of the Great Plan wanted to collect on a multi-billion dollar insurance policy he "luckily" put into place just weeks before 9/11, and was even able to collect on twice as much insurance money through his lawyers convincing the jury that 9/11 was "two separate terrorist attacks" at the WTC

-This same proponent of the Great Plan, "Lucky" Larry Silverstein, and his kids who seem to be incredibly lucky also, all just happened to be absent from the Twin Towers the morning of 9/11 when all three would have been there 99% of the other times

-This same proponent of the Great Plan, Larry Silverstein, was caught talking to his insurance carrier about the collapse of Building 7 before it happened, and then later on PBS admitted that he authorized it's "demolition"

-False flag attacks are the norm, not the exception, of governments trying to steer the nations they control towards an agenda, especially the government of the United States/New Babylon under the flag of the Illuminati families and the Great Plan

-the FBI had no evidence tying Osama bin Laden to the events of 9/11 and still don't (their words, not mine)

-Egomaniac Osama bin Laden himself denied involvement in the attacks at least twice in the public record and explicitly blamed the proponents of the Great Plan, when if he did do it he surely would have taken the credit and notoriety for it in the press immediately

-Various video tapes of Osama bin Laden have been called out as fakes by people far more knowledgeable than I in regards to bin Laden's looks, habits, and mannerisms

-Seven of the FBI-identified hijackers are factually still alive, an impossibility if you believe the official story and the 9/11 Commission Report

-Project Able Danger tried to warn the feds but was scuttled by the CIA

-Apparent planted evidence in Mohammed Atta's checked luggage that **miraculously** didn't make it onto the doomed airliner, falling right in the lap of the FBI

-The NORAD stand down at the direction of Vice President Dick Cheney

-Drills mimicking a 9/11 scenario just happened to be underway the day of 9/11 by the feds, injecting phantom hijacker radar blips and contributing to the overall confusion by the flight traffic controllers and NORAD

-Dick Cheney was handed control over all wargame and military drill operations just months before 9/11

-Explosions were heard, seen, and experienced by hundreds of eyewitnesses on 9/11 at the World Trade Center in all three affected buildings

-For the first time in recorded history and never since 9/11, not one, not two, but **three** steel framed buildings collapsed due to fire, according to the feds

-Operatives of the Great Plan including the sitting President's brother were in control of the security at the World Trade Center in the months and years prior to 9/11

-Neither the FBI nor the 9/11 Commission bothered to interview the security firm Securacom over their role at the WTC according to the CEO of Securacom himself

-An elevator renovation just happened to have taken place in the months before 9/11 at the WTC, injecting workers into the crawl spaces where access to the structural columns was possible at all three buildings

-Security was normally extremely tight at the World Trade Center, except for the few days leading up to 9/11 when security and bomb-sniffing dogs were mysteriously removed

-President Bush said on two different occasions that he saw the first plane hit the first tower before the video was even released, an impossibility unless he had his TV on Channel CIA

-The second plane, flight 175, to hit the WTC had odd appendages on its fuselage and wing that a normal passenger plane wouldn't

-Upon review of the videos of "Flight 175", Boeing refused to make a statement about the pod mounted underneath flight 175 because of issues of national security

-*Every video of both planes hitting the Twin Towers, from all angles so it wasn't a reflection, show some sort of incendiary flash right before impact*

-*The fires burning at all three buildings that collapsed were not nearly hot enough to create the molten steel found days and weeks after the collapses*

-*All three buildings fell at nearly free-fall speed right through the path of most-resistance into their own footprints*

-*Unexploded nano-thermite and microscopic metal spheres (caused by airborne molten steel) were found in multiple dust samples and presented in a peer-reviewed publication by a handful of highly intelligent and competent scientists and engineers*

-*Multiple written records of SEC fraud contained in Building 7 were conveniently disposed of forever, benefitting the financial vampires associated with the Great Plan*

-*Two different television networks made premature announcements of Building 7's collapse*

-*A rapid removal and clean-up with no significant investigation at the WTC, under protest from victim's families and many professionals in the fire and engineer-related trades*

-*The feds told everyone the air was safe to breathe in the days and weeks after 9/11 when it is patently obvious that it wasn't*

-*The Mossad clearly knew about the impending events of 9/11 because they sent their agents "to document the event" (their words, not mine)*

-*We have never seen a single videotape of a plane hitting the Pentagon, while dozens of them factually exist showing **something** hitting the Pentagon*

-*Initially there was only a **16-foot wide hole in the side of the Pentagon**, with no holes from the huge titanium twin engines of the passenger jet*

-*There was hardly any debris at the Pentagon crash site. If there was in fact only a 16 foot wide hole, which there was, that means that most of the stuff inside the plane, let alone the plane itself, didn't go inside the Pentagon and should have been blown all over the front lawn when there was in fact hardly any debris at all. No seats, no luggage, no bodies, etc.*

-The alleged leader of the Flight 77 hijackers was a terrible pilot, but managed a death-defying acrobatic 270 degree corkscrew maneuver to come in and hit the Pentagon perfectly

-Flight 77 allegedly flew at a height of 20 feet for a half mile right before slamming into the Pentagon, something professional pilots say is an impossibility

-Whatever hit the Pentagon had the force to go through over 9 feet thickness of reinforced concrete interior walls and punch a nearly perfect 12-foot wide hole as it exited into the center courtyard

-Eyewitness accounts at the Pentagon say everything from "it was a missile" to "it was a huge passenger jet" that hit

-There is a 3 minute discrepancy between when the feds told us Flight 93 over Shanksville crashed and multiple independent seismologists, who have no reason to lie

-Documented air phone calls from the passengers detailed that they were going to try and take control of the jet back from the hijackers and apparently did enter the cockpit

-Military jets were seen and had allegedly followed Flight 93 before it crashed

-The military had in fact been given permission to shoot down Flight 93

-Flaming debris from Flight 93 rained down on the ground miles away from the crash site, including a large part of a jet engine. This was documented by multiple eyewitnesses.

-Secretary of Defense Donald Rumsfeld slipped up on an interview and stated that Flight 93 had been shot down

-The anthrax attacks that came right on the heels of 9/11 would have taken weeks if not months to prepare, so whoever orchestrated 9/11 was also responsible for the anthrax attacks

-The guy the feds pinned the anthrax attacks on not only didn't have a motive, he didn't have the expertise to do it, this according to multiple professionals in his field

-The guy the feds pinned the anthrax attack on conveniently killed himself, allegedly, thereby closing the book on the investigation

-The man first chosen to lead the 9/11 investigation, Henry Kissinger, was intimately tied to the Great Plan, so much so that his choice of being the man to lead it had to be abandoned

-The people who ended up heading up the 9/11 Commission were all Great Plan minions, belonging to all the major Round Table Groups

-Nearly every single thing on the above list was ignored or omitted by the 9/11 Commission

-The 9/11 Commission was severely underfunded, had no subpoena power, and set up to fail from the get-go

-Even though 7 of the hijackers were alive, the 9/11 Commission stated that according to DNA testing, those were in fact the exact men who were responsible for hijacking and flying those planes

-Bush and Cheney would only testify under special conditions or not at all. What were they hiding? You already know: the truth about 9/11

-The 9/11 Commission members themselves stated after the fact that the 9/11 Commission was a joke. If they said it wasn't a good investigation, do you believe the 9/11 Commission Report?

-The rapid rise and continued escalation of the police state in America following the events of 9/11

Now, I need to make you aware of multiple attempts by the Illuminati-controlled Mainstream Media outlets to discredit the 9/11 Truth Movement, including hit pieces in both Popular Mechanics and Scientific American magazines. I **personally** have researched what they had to say and they completely whitewash the truth ala the 9/11 Commission, using bait-and-switch tactics to make it appear they are addressing the 9/11 Truthers' claims when in fact they only offer red herrings and distractions. You don't know how badly I wanted to prove the claims of the 9/11 Truth Movement wrong in the beginning of my research, but everything I have stated in this chapter, and this book, is to the best of my knowledge the truth so I became a 9/11 Truther myself.

I researched not only these articles but multiple web sites claiming to counter what I've listed above, and found only BS time after time after time. There is a ton of intentionally-manufactured disinformation to try and cloud the waters of truth surrounding this false flag operation. There are also people aligning themselves with the 9/11 Truth Movement who are convinced that the planes were holograms and nothing hit the Twin Towers, and other theories that really are non-factual nonsense. If you focus on just the facts you get a good picture of the real truth.

A lot of people try and discredit the facts surrounding 9/11 not because they don't believe it, but because they simply can't handle the truth of the real facts and how they add up. It would shatter their reality bubble, and they just wouldn't be able to cope with it. They would literally lose their minds, so they put up fronts to convince themselves that these facts don't exist or aren't real.

I've got an interesting story to tell you now. There was a man named Aaron Russo, a very patriotic American who has since passed away. Mr. Russo made one of the best documentaries of all time about the New World Order agenda entitled *"America: Freedom to Fascism"*, and I highly recommend you see it. It is available, for free, on youtube.com as of the printing of this book.

Aaron Russo was an acclaimed Hollywood producer who made the movies *"Trading Places"* (Eddie Murphy/Dan Akroyd) and *"The Rose"* (Bette Midler) among other big-name successful movies. He got into a disagreement with the IRS over some issues, which were complete BS on the part of the IRS after I learned the background facts of his story. To vent his anger he made a movie called *"Mad as Hell"* slamming them. **Nicholas Rockefeller**, son of current Rockefeller family kingpin and "head" of the American branch of the Illuminati **David Rockefeller**, found the movie intriguing, and after learning Russo was a big roller in Hollywood, decided he wanted to meet Aaron. The two met and became very close friends very quickly, with the friendship lasting for a few years. During this time, and approximately 11 months before 9/11 happened, Nicholas revealed to Aaron Russo the entire New World Order plan, that they were trying to implement a one world government ran by the banking industry, of which the Rockefellers are intricately part of, as you now know.

Russo, being the truly patriotic American he was, was horrified to learn the details about this, but he knew Rockefeller was telling him the truth. He ended their friendship over this information, and then went public with it after Nicholas' prophecy about 9/11 came to pass. According to Russo, Rockefeller's words on 9/11 were something along the lines of **"There is going to be an event soon. We're going to invade Afghanistan and our troops will be looking for terrorists in caves over there, and then we're going to invade Iraq."** Remember now,

Russo says that Rockefeller told him this months in advance of 9/11, and it all came to pass exactly as he had said. You can hear and see Russo speak about this on a handful of clips on youtube.com.

He didn't tell Russo exactly what the event was, but it is not hard to deduce when he tells of the end result of it. He also foretells of the coming "war on terror" and how it is going to be a farce but the Mainstream Media will convince the people that it is real, and that the coming "event" is going to enable the federal government to take more and more of our liberties and freedom away. Rockefeller also revealed that they were behind the formation of the European Union, and that they were trying to form the North American Union next, by which the United States, Canada and Mexico would form a borderless community. The ultimate goal, according to Rockefeller, was to implant all people of the world with RFID chips, and have all of your money and personal information contained in these chips, which they would control through the banking system that they (Illuminati) owned.

One other interesting tidbit that Rockefeller revealed to Russo, and I 100% believe it, was that the women's lib movement of the 60's was a fabrication of a Rockefeller think tank operation, under the Tavistock Institute's guidance. There was two primary points to women's lib. One was to average down the wages of the middles class workers by furnishing tens of millions of new competing workers. The other reason was to break up the American family structure in order to weaken the United States. The kids would no longer be raised by "mom", but raised by the "state" through daycare and agenda-schooling. Kids would start looking at the "system" as their family, instead of their real family. After learning about how evil Rockefeller and his cohorts were, a good-hearted man like Russo had no choice but to terminate their friendship.

Aaron Russo has since passed away, but his legacy lives on though videos of him speaking on youtube.com. I suggest you listen to what this patriotic American had to say and what he put out there in his own personal fight against the agenda of the New World Order.

There are other Hollywood high-rollers and celebrities who are on board the 9/11 Truth Train, but before we get to them, I want to bring to your attention a hugely patriotic American and the virtual leader of not only the 9/11 Truth Movement, but the entire anti-New World Order movement, a man named **Alex Jones**. I won't go into a bunch about him, but his name has cropped up multiple times in this book and you need to be aware of him and his endeavors on behalf of the citizens of the United States of America. He is certainly to be admired for his untiring work to wake up humanity to the New World Order plan of enslavement.

Let's go over some more recognizable names to you here, since there is nary a mention of these patriots and their opinions of 9/11 in the Mainstream Media.

The opinions of these patriotic Americans are largely kept out of the mainstream press unless it is unavoidable, and in those cases the Mainstream Media goes on the attack against the truth coming out every time, insinuating that the celebrity is a "conspiracy theorist", their favorite saying to nullify the truth and discredit the messenger.

Actor **Charlie Sheen** is one of the most high-profile celebrities to question the official story. Speaking to The Alex Jones Show on the GCN Radio Network, the former star of the hit comedy TV show *"Two and a Half Men"* and dozens of blockbuster movies including *"Platoon"* and *"Young Guns"*, Sheen elaborated on why he had problems believing the government's version of events:

"We're not the conspiracy theorists on this particular issue," said Sheen in 2006.

"It seems to me like 19 amateurs with box cutters taking over four commercial airliners and hitting 75% of their targets, that feels like a conspiracy theory. It raises a lot of questions."

Sheen described the climate of acceptance for serious discussion about 9/11 as being far more fertile than it was right after 9/11:

"It feels like from the people I talk to in and around my circles, it seems like the worm is turning."

Sheen even went so far as to make a video directed at President Obama and post it online, challenging him to address the many questions and concerns of the 9/11 Truth Movement. Again, you can see this video for yourself on youtube.com

Filmmaker **Michael Moore** is an outspoken critic of the official story, but his film "Fahrenheit 9/11" barely even scratched the surface of the evidence pointing to an inside job. Moore once stated, <u>"I've had a number of firefighters tell me over the years and since "Fahrenheit 9/11" that they heard these explosions, that they believe there's much more to the story than we've been told. I don't think the official investigations have told us the complete truth, they haven't even told us half the truth. I've filmed there before down at the Pentagon before 9/11 and there's got to be at least 100 cameras, ringing that building, in the trees, everywhere. They've got that plane coming in with 100 angles. How come we haven't seen the straight -- I'm not talking about stop-action photos, I'm talking about the video. I want to see the video. I want to see 100 videos that exist of this. I believe that there will be answers in that video tape and we should demand that that tape is released."</u>

Actor **Ed Asner** is also a proponent of 9/11 Truth, stating <u>" I would like to suggest to you emphatically that the 9-11 truth movement is the most pressing issue of the peace & justice movement today. There are many disturbing issues around 9-11 that have yet to be examined in any meaningful way by our media, Congress, and even by the 9-11 Commission. These include accountability for the massive breakdown of air defense and plane intercept procedures as described in FAA and DOD regulations, which were violated on 9-11. This breakdown and astounding unpreparedness by U.S. domestic defense agencies is puzzling to say the least, given the detailed reports our government had of the coming attacks, that were bizarrely suppressed by key officials."</u>

Actress and talk show host **Rosie O'Donnell** lost her job soon after bringing up 9/11 Truth on the daytime TV talk show *"The View"* and had this exchange with a co-host:

Elisabeth Hasselbeck: <u>Do you believe that the government had anything to do with the attack of 9/11? Do you believe in a conspiracy in terms of the attack of 9/11?</u>

Rosie O'Donnell: **No, but I do believe that in the first time in history that fire has ever melted steel. I do believe that it defies physics for the World Trade Center Tower 7, Building 7, which collapsed in on itself. It is impossible for a building to fall the way it fell without explosives being involved -- World Trade Center 7. World Trade 1 and 2 got hit by planes. 7, miraculously, the first time in history, steel was melted by fire. It is physically impossible.**

Elisabeth Hasselbeck: **And who do you think is responsible for that?**

Rosie O'Donnell: **I have no idea. But to say that we don›t know; that it imploded, and it was an implosion and a demolition, is beyond ignorance. Look at the films. Get a physics expert here from Yale from Harvard. Pick the school. It defies reason.»**

Television and movie actor **Woody Harrelson** of "Cheers" fame went on record and said this:

"The media won't ask the obvious questions. For example, when they had loads of information coming in from several FBI agents as well as warnings from Russia, Britain and several other foreign intelligence agencies before 9/11, predicting what would happen, why were reports stifled and investigations stopped? I am reading a book now called '_The New Pearl Harbor_' by David Ray Griffin. I've been stuck in the position of ignoring my gut -- knowing things don't stack up. Even though our government obviously took advantage of 9/11 by making it their "Reichstag", I told myself, "Surely they weren't involved". After reading this book I can't doubt that our government was at least complicit in allowing 9/11 to happen. Get a copy and pass it to all your friends, the evidence is irrefutable."

Former Minnesota Governor and motion picture actor **Jesse Ventura** is another one to question the official story.

Appearing on The Alex Jones Show, Ventura said that his initial reaction to 9/11 was much like most people at the time, and he accepted the official story outright, a response he now regrets because he was in a position of power and could have used it to raise a lot of pointed questions about 9/11.

"I kicked myself when it initially happened that the light didn't go off but I was so shocked that this thing had even taken place that I apologize for not being more aware," said Ventura, adding that watching the internet 9/11 documentary *"Loose Change"* at the insistence of his son was part of the catalyst for his wake up call.

"When I finally did watch it I went through every emotion you could imagine, from laughing, crying, getting sick to my stomach, to the whole emotional thing," said the former Governor.

"To me questions haven't been answered and are not being answered about 9/11," said Ventura, referring to the mysterious collapse of Building 7.

"Two planes struck two buildings .... but how is it that a third building fell 5 hours later?" asked Ventura, **"How could this building just implode into its own footprint 5 hours later - that's my first question - the 9/11 Commission didn't even devote one page to that in their big volume of investigation,"** added the former Governor.

"How could those buildings fall at the speed of gravity - if you put a stopwatch on them, both of those World Trade Center buildings were on the ground in ten seconds - how can that be?" asked Ventura.

"If you took a billiard ball and dropped it from the height of the World Trade Center in a vacuum it would hit the ground in 9.3 seconds and if you took that same billiard ball and dropped it 10 stories at a time and merely stopped it and started it it would take 30 seconds - if you dropped it every floor of the World Trade Center to the ground, simply stopping and starting it on gravity it would take over 100 seconds to reach the ground," he surmised.

Having undergone Basic Underwater Demolition Seal training, Ventura is speaking from an experienced standpoint and he unequivocally stated that he thought the buildings were deliberately imploded.

"Upon looking at the film in super-slow motion and the way the buildings fell and comparing that to the way that they do like a controlled demolition of a hotel in Las Vegas, they both fell identical."

"I did watch the film of Building 7 going down and in my opinion there's no doubt that that building was brought down with demolition," said the former Governor.

Ventura also questioned the lack of wreckage outside of the Pentagon after Flight 77 allegedly struck the building.

"When I was watching _Loose Change_ with a friend of mine - he happens to work for a company that helps build the Boeing airplanes and they said that when the engines completely disappeared and were destroyed, his response was, excuse my French - bullshit!," said Ventura.

"I turned to him and said why and he said because they're made of titanium steel - they can't disintegrate."

Musician **Willie Nelson** is also a 9/11 Truther. He went on record on the Alex Jones show on 2/4/08 and said the following:

Alex Jones: **What's your take on 9/11? Do you question the official story?**

Willie Nelson: I certainly do. And I saw those towers fall and I've seen an implosion in Las Vegas. There's too much similarities between the two. And I saw the building fall [Building 7] that didn't get hit by nothing. So, how naive are we? What do they think we'll go for?

Alex Jones: **Are you saying you started having questions -- the little voice in your head -- I mean did you have a bad feeling the day it happened? Is that what you're saying?**

Willie Nelson: **The day it happened. I saw one fall and it was just so symmetrical. I said, "Wait a minute, I just saw that last week at the casino in Las Vegas." And you see these implosions all the time and the next one fell and I said, "Hell, there's another one." And they're trying to tell me that an airplane did it? And I can't go along with that.**

There are hundreds of other professional entertainers who have everything to lose by going public with their claims, to be ridiculed in the Mainstream Media where most of them make their living. Here are a handful, just to name a few of the truly brave and patriotic: Kevin Smith, Sharon Stone, Martin Sheen, Ed Begley Jr., Daniel Sunjata, Janeane Garofalo, David Lynch, James Brolin, Eminem, Corey Taylor from the band Slipknot, Margaret Cho, and the list goes on and on, there are plenty more I don't have space for. All of these people are doing their patriotic duty by standing up and questioning an obviously flawed 9/11 Commission Report.

In addition to celebrities speaking up, there are literally thousands of architects and engineers standing up and saying they don't believe the official story either. In fact, one man has organized all of them into a group called *Architects and Engineers for 9/11 Truth*, also known as ae911truth.org.

This group of **over 1,750 professional architects and engineers** have banded together under the guidance of a man named Richard Gage, a San Francisco Bay Area architect and a member of the American Institute of Architects.

Mr. Gage became interested in researching the destruction of the WTC high-rises after hearing the startling conclusions of 9/11 researcher David Ray Griffin on the radio in 2006, who then launched his own quest for the truth about 9/11.

On his website, Gage states **"We call upon Congress for a truly independent investigation with subpoena power. We believe that** there is sufficient evidence to conclude that the World Trade Center buildings #1 (North Tower), #2 (South Tower), and #7 (the 47 story high-rise across Vesey St.) were destroyed not by jet impact and fires but by controlled demolition with explosives.

We believe that our website, our DVD "9/11: Blueprint for Truth", and the other referenced material, contain the information necessary to demonstrate to all with an open mind that this is the case, and that such an investigation is warranted and overdue. We believe that the available evidence invalidates the government's official conspiracy theory."

So. We have a hundred plus celebrities questioning the official story, almost a couple thousand professional architects and engineers questioning the official story, and *millions* of ordinary Americans who are questioning the official story.

The most notable group involved in 9/11 Truth activism at the grassroots level is called wearechange.org, founded by patriotic American Luke Rudkowski. I'll let them explain what they are about, from the website wearechange.org:

"We Are Change is a citizens based grassroots peace and social justice movement working to reveal the truth behind the events of September 11th, as well as the lies of the government and corporate elite who remain suspect in this crime. In addition, we are here to aid the sick and dying first responders through fundraising and social outreach programs in order to promote awareness of those who suffer from physical, emotional, and psychological traumas they received in the aftermath of 9-11. We also seek to meet other local citizens who are interested in educating the public while engaging in peaceful demonstration about the pertinent issues that are affecting our lives each and every day. Furthermore, We Are Change is a nonpartisan independent media organization comprised of patriot journalists working to hold those engaging in activities that do not represent the wishes of "We the People" - by asking the hard questions that the controlled mainstream media refuses to do.

We Are Change has arisen from the remnants of our republic to fill the vacancy left by those who swore to preserve, protect and defend The Constitution against all enemies – foreign and domestic. We seek to expose the fraud of the left/right paradigm and reveal that the world truly functions on a top/down hierarchy that threatens to destroy free society as we know it. We Are Change works to educate, motivate, and activate those striving to uncover the truth behind the private banking cartel of the military industrial complex that is directing the majority of U.S. policy, and that is actively seeking to eliminate national sovereignty and replace it with a "one world order." We will also continue to move in a direction that reconnects "We the People" to our nation's founding principles laid out in the Constitution and the Bill of Rights.

We Are Change also seek an uncompromising and independent investigation into the crimes of 9-11, with subpoena power granted to obtain a long-overdue resolution for the survivors and families of the deceased. We reject the official explanation of the events leading up to, during and after the attacks of September 11th, 2001 as well as the fear-based politics and state mandated propaganda being disseminated by the Corporate Media which has facilitated the cover-up of 9-11.

As we establish citizens groups throughout the country and world, we wish to inspire a community of truth-seekers and peacemakers through creative campaigns with a commitment of nonviolence. We Are Change is not so much a group but an idea, an idea that "We the People" are the vehicles of these "ideas" and of the freedoms, liberties, and truths we are seeking all across the globe. An idea that captures the spirits of our forefathers who just desired freedom; that together, as residents of this planet, we grow like a snowball of truth and justice rolling down a mountain of tyranny growing bigger and stronger, recognizing the beauty in our differences and the diverseness of each other, but at the same time strengthening our cause because we learn and grow from each others individuality. Then as we learn to come together, that as one, you, me, him, her, us...will realize that WE ARE CHANGE."

There are wearechange.org chapters in nearly every state and in every major city in the United States, and also in over 40 foreign countries, trying to wake people up to the real truth about 9/11.

A good read about 9/11 I came across recently is a fictionalized version of the true events of 9/11 written by an airline insider. She came upon multiple smoking guns helping to prove that 9/11 was an inside job and doing her patriotic duty she wrote a book to wake people up. That book is 'Methodical Illusion' by Rebekah Roth.

Educate yourself. Knowledge is power, and they seek to keep the power away from us so they can fulfill their Great Plan, the New World Order. I can't emphasize enough how important it is for you to do your own research on the various subjects covered in this book, and to tell others about what is going on. We have reached a point in the history of our country that silence and inaction on the part of the American public is complicity in our government's wars of conquest and general crimes against humanity. "We" bombed Afghanistan and Iraq back to the Stone Age and killed millions of innocent men, women and children, and maimed millions more for life. That fact makes me just sad to the brink of tears, to see video of those little Iraqi kids with their legs blown off being carried down the street by their parents, still barely alive, screaming for someone to help them. **It's time decent Americans did help them, and it's time we help ourselves before it's too late for the United States.**

The greatest threat to our freedom isn't radical Muslims; it's a war-mongering New Babylon out for world conquest in the name of the New World Order. Our military isn't over there defending our freedom, they're spreading our tyranny. That is the bottom-line FACT.

Educate yourself and learn as gospel about the FACTS of what happened before, on, and after September 11, 2001.......our future literally depends on it.

Chapter 12

WHAT DO WE DO?

"Two centuries ago our forefathers brought forth a new nation; now we must join with others to bring forth a New World Order.... Narrow notions of national sovereignty must not be permitted to curtail that obligation."
    -Declaration of Interdependence, January 20, 1976, signed by 32 treasonous U.S. Senators and 92 U.S. House of Representatives in Washington D.C.

"It calls for the surrender of our national sovereignty to international organizations. It declares that our economy should be regulated by international authorities. It proposes that we enter a 'New World Order' that would redistribute the wealth created by the American people."
    -U.S. Congresswoman Marjorie Holt's statement as to why she refused to sign the Declaration of Interdependence. This woman is a patriot and a hero to me and all Americans for this.

So, you've just taken in all the main components of the grand conspiracy that is the Great Plan's agenda to create a New World Order. The final version we are getting close to will be a one world government under the rule of the resurrected founder of the Great Plan, King Nimrod, aka the Antichrist, aka the Beast. Let's quickly summarize how we got to this point in mankind's history.

An ancient plan to take over the world was set into motion thousands of years ago, and is referred to as the Biblical "fall of man". The "fall of man" is a metaphor for the most powerful of the malignant interdimensional entities, known as Satan/the Devil, instilling in mankind the belief that if he could gain enough knowledge he could become a god himself and live forever. At this time he also offered his and his fallen angels, aka demons, help via communication and guidance through occult black magic rituals. This plan of action and the occult knowledge of interacting with highly intelligent and malevolent beings was passed down through the millennia, through the many incarnations of the Luciferian secret societies. Currently, the Great Plan is being helmed by the Illuminati families and secretly orchestrated through the upper **UPPER** echelons of the Freemasons, then executed by the public-face organizations such as the Tavistock Institute, tax-free foundations, central banks, CFR, Trilateral Commission, Bilderberg Group, RIIA, Club of Rome, United Nations, etc.

They currently control our President, Congress, and Federal Government in general. They control and/or own the Mainstream Media, the oil, our military, the CIA, most multinational corporations, the Federal Reserve and the rest of the European central banks, with the central bank control equating to their governments also being on the Illuminati payroll.

They feel that they are so close to completing the Great Plan that it cannot be stopped and announced this by arrogantly putting their occult symbolism on our money starting in 1933, the year they officially took over our country via USA Inc. declaring bankruptcy, and thereby being repossessed by the Federal Reserve. The money we use that is in your wallet or purse, is marked with ancient Luciferian symbolism that until recently only they understood the meaning of. Now you do too.

Nearly every war, recession, depression, political assassination or other major political or societal event, the events of 9/11 among other false flag attacks, and the Great Recession we're currently in have been caused by these evil men. They control the world economies and row them up and down in cycles to fleece us of wealth, knowing in advance which way the cycle is going to go and making appropriate investment decisions before the rest of the public. They plot against us using tax-free foundations and think tanks. They poison us at every opportunity through the water we drink, the food we eat, and the dangerous medicines we are convinced we need. They flood our country with illicit drugs and then take that money and use it against us again by funding CIA black ops such as 9/11 and others. All this in an attempt for this tiny minority of diabolically evil people to gain control over the entire world, culminating with the setting up of a one world government totalitarian police state which will allow them and their descendents to rule over the Earth forever. That's not even mentioning that they are working on bringing King Nimrod, their "founder", back to life, who is called out in the Bible as the Antichrist.

The skeleton of their Biblically-prophesized Luciferian one world government is currently in place via their founding of the United Nations, and they are currently working through the UN on the one world economy, army and religion.

This is exactly where we are headed: a literal Hell on Earth, just as prophesized in the Bible.

"For more than a century, ideological extremists at either end of the political spectrum have seized upon well-publicized incidents to attack the Rockefeller family for the inordinate influence they claim we wield over American political and economic institutions. Some even believe we are part of a secret cabal working against the best interests of the United States, characterizing my family and me as 'internationalists' and of conspiring with others around the world to build a more integrated global political and economic structure - one world, if you will. If that's the charge, I stand guilty, and I am proud of it."

-Head of the "American Illuminati" David Rockefeller, in his book of memoirs, 2003

Chapter 12/A

WHERE WE'RE AT RIGHT NOW

"The technetronic era (New World Order) involves the gradual appearance of a more controlled society. Such a society would be dominated by an elite, unrestrained by traditional values. Soon it will be possible to assert almost continuous surveillance over every citizen and maintain up-to-date complete files containing even the most personal information about the citizen. These files will be subject to instantaneous retrieval by the authorities. "

-Zbigniew Brzezinski, co-founder with David Rockefeller of the Trilateral Commission in his book "Between Two Ages: America's Role in the Technetronic Era", 1970

Where are we at right now? We're in a bad spot, and about to get worse. **Much worse.**

Our economy is teetering on the brink of another crash, the **BIG CRASH**. Economies in Europe are in the process of going into this crash right now and Great Britain will probably go over the cliff before we do, but since the Mainstream Media doesn't emphasize how significant this is, most people don't know or don't care. They think everything is going to be alright as it has been in decades and centuries past.

Unfortunately for us, what we are going through now, and will go through in the near future is drastically different than any of the recessions in history. What we're going through is an engineered financial implosion of the entire world's financial system by the proponents of the Great Plan.

After the crash, they will rebuild and consolidate what remains of our banking system into a global central bank with a one world currency.

To put it simply, we've got two main issues, and dozens of secondary issues. The first main issue is the flood of fiat money that has been pumped into our financial system over the last few years. Our economy, as well as the world economy, has grown addicted to cheap, inflated money like a heroin addict. Now we're in a spot where if the Fed raised interest rates at all, it would completely kill the economy, so we're stuck at low interest rates and inflating our currency with nowhere to go but over the hyperinflation cliff. This has the effect of flooding our economy and the world with United States dollars whose value is ever-declining simply due to the dynamics of supply and demand. This is reflected in the valuation increases of precious metals over the last few years. As our dollar declines in value, it takes more of them to equal the same amount of gold or silver, pushing their prices ever higher. Our dollar will probably collapse when the bond bubble bursts in the next few months.

The second main issue is something you have probably never heard of: the derivatives bubble that is also close to popping. This will be the biggest bubble in history. This bubble-pop will trigger the bond bubble popping, or vice-versa, in my opinion, whatever happens first.

A derivative is a paper investment, basing its value on another paper investment, basing its value on a further down the line paper investment, etc., until you reach the original tangible item that the first derivative was based on, like a mortgage-backed security, or a commodity, or whatever. And these inflated derivatives aren't even paper-based; they are all electronic in cyberspace, with little to no regulation or oversight. It is literally a feeding frenzy, chiefly by the Illuminati families.

It actually came out in the Mainstream Media a couple years ago that Bank of America alone was sitting on over **$50 trillion worth of derivative exposure**, with only about $1 trillion worth of deposits and other assets to back it up, and those deposits aren't even their money, *it's their depositors'* **money.**

The top five banks in the U.S. account for nearly 100% of the **$250 trillion in derivatives exposure in this country, let alone the world**. The global exposure to the derivatives debacle has been estimated as high as **$1.5 quadrillion**, that's with a "q", and that's equal to **1,500 tril-**

lion dollars in purely black-hole debt based on absolutely nothing more than entered numbers on a computer screen.

We are talking about huge numbers here, monstrously huge. Our national debt pales in comparison, and that's probably why the politicians don't even care about it anymore. Current Treasury Secretary Timothy Geithner recently came out and said it's time to abolish the nation's debt ceiling altogether, essentially raising the feds credit card limit to "infinity", which they will need immediate access to when hyperinflation hits.

The financial vampires of Wall Street were playing with fire, and managed to set the global economy ablaze. They tried to batten down the flames after the 2008 crash with a flood of fiat money, and were only marginally successful. Right now, that derivatives fire is burning and gaining strength every day. A time will come soon when it will suddenly turn into an inferno that can't be put out. Once it gets going, this towering inferno of debt will take down the entire global financial system. Don't expect to hear anything about preparing for this out of the Mainstream Media until it is too late for Joe Average investor to get out of the market and into tangible assets that won't lose their value in this type of crash, such as physical gold or silver bullion.

Warren Buffet once called derivatives **"weapons of mass financial destruction"**, and those words will ring true very soon when they detonate and bring the entire world to its knees.

When this massive economic crash happens, you will know that is was coming, who did it, how it happened, and why.

The Federal Reserve has been trying to keep the fire under control since 2008 by throwing money on it via something they call "quantitative easing", which is just a more palatable way of saying they are printing billions of electronic dollars and pumping them into the system to keep the flames at bay. Sooner or later this is going to cause massive inflation, especially since announcing in mid-2012 that they will pump $40 billion a month into the financial system *indefinitely.* This will eventually turn into hyperinflation, as it always does when you print money with no tangible backing.

Right now they are doing a good job of hiding the early stages of hyperinflation by not including energy or food prices in the federal Consumer Price Index or CPI. I'm sure you've noticed that gas prices have significantly gone up and stayed up, and they will stay up permanently and go higher. I'm sure you've noticed that portions of processed food have gone down while prices have gone up. A simple way of confirming this is that you can't buy a half gallon of ice cream anymore, it's now 1.5 quarts for the same price or higher, a reduction of the size of the container by a full 25%. What that really is saying is that your money is now worth 25% less than it was a couple of years ago.

Now let's talk about President Obama, who fully knows about this coming financial Armageddon and what's going to happen, and is content to let it happen because that's what his bosses, the Illuminati, want.

President Barack Obama/Barry Soetoro/whoever-he-really-is, is nothing more than a paid actor. Without his scripted teleprompter lines he is nothing. He is a pathological liar who speaks out of both sides of his mouth, and the people are so dumbed down and distracted that they just don't catch on to this. His staff is loaded to the brim with CFR/Trilateral Commission/Bilderberg/Club of Rome members, a fact you can easily check on Google.

Obama's first job was in fact working for **Henry Kissinger** no less, who himself is an agent of **David Rockefeller**. Obama was groomed behind the scenes for a few years by the proponents of the Great Plan to serve a purpose, which is to be at the helm of the United States when the whole thing comes crashing down, doing exactly as he is directed from behind the scenes, and if he resists them he would be either publicly humiliated, or killed.

If you'll remember, or not, Obama was awarded the Nobel Peace Prize not long after he was elected. This is the same man who today authorizes hundreds of airborne drone strikes in Afghanistan, killing hundreds and even thousands of innocent civilians in the attempt to "get Al-Qaida". What they are really doing is practicing for when it is time to bring those drone strikes home to America to take care of those pesky patriotic Americans.

He campaigned in 2007 that he would close the CIA's Guantanamo Bay torture facility. It's still open.

He campaigned in 2007 he would get all GMO foods labeled. They still aren't.

He said he was going to get us out of NAFTA. He didn't. And on . And on. And on.

I could literally go on for pages about what he said he was going to do if elected, and what he's actually followed through on after being elected, which is instead the New World Order agenda.

It really doesn't matter who is in the Presidential seat, Obama or anyone else, they all work for the Illuminati, hands down. The last real President we had was Kennedy, and you know what happened to him when he tried to buck the Illuminati masters after he go into office. Elections back then weren't computerized and much harder to rig, and Kennedy received an insurmountable amount of votes to get past the Illuminati sentry.

Backing up Obama are the (mostly) traitorous Congressmen and women, the entrenched political elite in D.C. that the uninformed sheeple just keep electing over and over and over and nothing gets done and nothing changes unless it is in the best interest of the Great Plan. Those most valuable to the Illuminati get financial backing among other help, including a compromised electronic voting system for backup if needed.

One of the only members of Congress who actually is on our side is Congressman Ron Paul. Do you ever wonder why he was so vehemently attacked and degraded by the Mainstream Media? It's because he's not part of the Great Plan. He's not a member of the CFR or any of the other Round Table Groups, and this makes him an outsider in D.C. Ron Paul's agenda probably makes total sense to you now at this point in this book. He wanted to abolish the Federal Reserve, shut down all of our overseas wars and bring our troops home, reign in spending, etc. etc. All things that are detrimental to the Great Plan. Do you get it now? Do you now understand why he was so maliciously attacked by the Mainstream Media as a kook for wanting to do these things that would actually help our country?

Our country is in an advancing state of decay at one end of the spectrum, and an advancing state of scientifically-driven, constantly-evolving Fascism at the other. Yes, that's right, I said fascism. The very definition of fascism is the merging of the state with the nation's biggest corporations, which are the investment banks, insurance companies and the oil conglomerate. You already know who the fascist leader will be soon, King Nimrod.

At one end of our society you've got a seemingly uncivilized world where kids have no value of life and shoot each other dead over a pair of sneakers. At the other end you have a "1984"-type of existence coming into focus, where cameras, satellites, and GPS units in the phones and vehicles are tracking your every move and feeding this information into a massive federal database. You probably don't even realize it, but you are being tracked like the owned property you are right this second. All of your financial records are tracked. If you have a modern phone with GPS you are being tracked. If you have Onstar in your vehicle you're being tracked. Every phone call you make is screened for certain words and then stored. Virtually everything you do these days is monitored and stored in giant federally-controlled supercomputers by Homeland Security, and that's a fact. The cost of this storage is negligible, after all, **you** pay for it, and if they need tons of info on a particular "domestic terror suspect" all they have to do is pull up your e-file.

On one end of society, you have Homeland Security demonizing the use of cash as a "potential sign of a domestic terrorist". At the other you have the sheeple corralled into the net of an electronic cashless society with the government and corporations analyzing your purchasing habits and making corporate decisions to try and increase profits, not to mention monitoring things you're buying to see if you fit the "domestic terrorist" profile, such as buying bulk food, guns, ammo, etc.

Super computers, plant genetics/Monsanto/GMO, Nuclear/biological weapons, genetic engineering/cloning, abortion/euthanasia, vaccines/medical advancements, etc. are all the norm in the year 2013, but are they really helping humanity.....or the Great Plan?

Computers and the internet are extremely powerful tools in today's world, and it was important for the agenda of the Great Plan to bring the heads of the main internet and computer corporations into their elite inner circle to get them to toe the line of their agenda. This is why the CEOs of Google, Facebook, Microsoft, etc. have all been summoned to the Bilderberg meetings over the last few years. **In fact, Mark Zuckerberg, the CEO of Facebook, gave the keynote speech at 2011's Bilderberg meeting.**

The Illuminati have turned our country into the most hated country on the face of the Earth due to our military aggression, our export of pornographic filth, our meddling in other countries affairs through our military and the CIA, pushing the gay agenda on religiously fundamental nations, etc. and on and on. People don't like us. This is why the United States is referred to as the "Great Satan" by some countries, and with who is running the show in our country, the Luciferians, I can see why and would generally agree with that assessment.

Our country was founded and is ran today by the proponents of the Great Plan.

They are depending on the apathy they've instilled in you to not think outside the box, to not question what is presented to you in the Mainstream Media, and to not rise up against them. Remember, they have multi-billion dollar think tanks whose only mission is to promote the completion of the Great Plan at any and all cost to humanity.

"Tolerance" is the new buzzword being promoted by those who don't want you to question what is happening in the United States. Political correctness is actually the enemy of free humanity. You should be saying what you think, instead of what you are told to think.

We don't live in the Information Age; we live in the Disinformation Age. This of course courtesy of the Mainstream Media, which pushes the agenda formulated by the tax-free foundations, the Great Plan think tanks, the Round Table Groups, and the occultists at the top of the global power pyramid.

When they jerk the rug out from under humanity in the very near future, you can either be one of the uniformed and unprepared, or you can be informed and prepared via the contents in this book.

Chapter 12/B

WHAT'S GOING TO HAPPEN

Today Americans would be outraged if U.N. troops entered Los Angeles to restore order; tomorrow they will be grateful. This is especially true if they were told there was an outside threat from beyond, whether real or promulgated, that threatened our very existence. It is then that all peoples of the world will plead with world leaders to deliver them from this evil. The one thing every man fears is the unknown. When presented with this scenario, individual rights will be willingly relinquished for the guarantee of their well being granted to them by their world government.
-Henry Kissinger, Bilderberg meeting, 1992

Thanks to Kissinger and the rest of the proponents of the Great Plan, even with our Constitutionally guaranteed First Amendment rights it won't be long before they **criminalize** dissemination of the type of information contained in this book. In fact we are right on the threshold of it, as one of the "signs" of a potential domestic terrorist according to the Patriot Act is belief and talking with others of exactly this type of information, the intimate details and components of the Great Plan.

"To learn who rules over you, simply find out who you are not allowed to criticize."
-Voltaire

History repeats and has for millennia. Since ancient times, the proponents of King Nimrod's Great Plan would get control of a civilized society, build it up until it took over the surrounding lands, corrupt it through pure evil, then institute a police state as it was starting to crash and burn. Babylon. Persia. Greece. Rome. All built up and then fell like clockwork. The Fourth Reich is becoming a reality in the United States of America in the year 2013. This shouldn't come as a surprise to you, now that you know that the proponents of the Great Plan were also responsible for what happened under Hitler.

They are doing it again.....

As you read this, the people running the Great Plan are trying to instigate a war with Syria and/or Iran. You can expect this to possibly happen within the next five years depending on how this economic crisis unfolds, but let's concentrate on what's going to happen here in the United States for right now.

Nearly every American citizen is suspect under the Patriot Act. Cameras are everywhere if you take the time to look around and notice them, tracking everything you do. Just look up at the traffic signals the next time you are in any decent-sized town. A good deal if not all of these cameras are equipped with facial-recognition and license plate-reading software. These are not only monitoring but recording everything that comes into the lens and stored, just in case they need it. It costs next to nothing to store information these days, and they are storing as much information as possible.

We are constantly pushed to stop using cash or checks and to go with "automatic debit" to pay our bills, and on the other end "automatic credit" for our paychecks, whereby we don't even hold in our hand the money we earned from working an honest day's labor—it's just numbers on a computer screen, all tracked by "big brother".

Virtually your entire life has been recorded and is on computer records somewhere, and if you are suspected to be a combatant against the New World Order agenda, these records will be assembled together in some Homeland Security office, and your case will be assigned to one of the HS lackeys to "keep an eye on you", which means this person will be constantly reviewing everything you do, everything you buy, what websites you go to, where you drive your car and what places you visit, looking for anything to build a case against you as a domestic terrorist.

If they feel they have enough "evidence" that you are a threat to the Great Plan agenda, and if you haven't fallen into one of their pitfalls, they will just flat out arrest you with no reason needed or given, and send you to a FEMA camp, or worse to Guantanamo, probably never to be heard from again and all "legal" under the NDAA signed by Fuhrer Obama at the end of 2011.

We are also headed for a national ID card system complete with RFID location-tracking chips. Once that is implemented and accepted by the sheeple, they will take it to the next level: Personal RFID microchipping, either by implantable chip or RFID tattoo, with both of these options in existence right now. RFID stands for Radio Frequency Identification, and allows you to be tracked by GPS anywhere on the planet. I'm not talking about injecting a small chip under your skin either, they can in fact do it now with an RFID tattoo, and if you don't believe this you better Google it, because that is a fact. Be vigilant for false flag events concerning information security that could make RFID chipping **mandatory by law**.

There are about 900 drone (unmanned) airplanes flying over the U.S. at the beginning of 2013, and that number is projected to skyrocket to *30,000 within 10 years*. Why so many drones over the U.S.? It's part of the Homeland Security police state they are implementing. And they are all already equipped with facial recognition software and......maybe assassination implements for the most patriotic dissenters in the future? That's what they are doing right now in Afghanistan: assassinating the "troublemakers", and any men, women, and children who happen to be in the immediate vicinity. Look for this to start happening in the U.S. at some point in the future, literally "Death from above".

The way they are going to excuse quickly bringing in this tyrannical behavior is through declaring martial law in the United States. There are a handful of scenarios laid out in the FEMA guidelines that allows the federal government to declare martial law and suspend the Constitution. This will be accomplished with one of many different false flag scenarios that we already know are in the works due to vigilant people researching these kinds of things. Remember what a false flag is: an orchestrated event to get the people to capitulate to what the Great Plan needs to advance, but otherwise wouldn't go along with it. An orchestrated event like the coming economic collapse most likely, but time will in fact tell.

It was actually made public in the Mainstream Media recently that Homeland Security had purchased 2 billion rounds of 9 millimeter and .40 caliber hollow-point bullets specifically to arm their employees with and also to distribute to other federal agencies across the country. Hollow-point bullets are made to do one thing: inflict maximum tissue damage to a human in the hopes of a single shot being a kill shot. Now why would they be doing this? Is something going to happen that the feds know about that hasn't been put out in the Mainstream Media to alert the public? They wouldn't keep us in the dark would they? You already know the answer to that question. 2 billion bullets is enough to pump 6 rounds into every man, woman, and child in America. What are they planning on doing with all of this ammo except to use it and soon.

Let's go over some of the potential scenarios that I feel are possible, or probable, so that when the next false flag event happens, you will know the truth of what is really going on.

We already went over the economic crash that's coming, the likes of which has never been seen before. The dollar is currently the reserve currency of the world and won't be in the near future. This spells disaster for the citizens and country of the United States of America.

As the derivatives pyramid comes crashing down, the Federal Reserve will begin to "print" money en masse to try and contain the fire. This will not work, hyperinflation will ensue, and the dollar will crash. This means that the dollar will become worthless, and if you have your wealth in the form of United States dollars, you will be financially ruined.

The economic conditions that gave rise to Hitler are coming again x 100. The reason for the crash will be blamed on the Federal Reserve and the other central banks. The Federal Reserve and the rest of the individual nations' central banks will implode or be abolished. This will pave the way for the introduction of the ultimate one world central bank, of course owned by the Illuminati families.

Again, when this massive economic crash happens, you will know that is was coming, who did it, how it happened, and why they did it.

As the worldwide central-bank pyramid scheme falls like a house of cards, bringing worldwide economic and societal collapse, expect pestilence and disease to go off the chart as the power grids break down, sewers quit operating, drinkable water quits flowing into the cities and countries, and generally unsanitary conditions explode. This would probably be a good time for the operators of the Great Plan to introduce a worldwide flu pandemic.....or worse.

Another way, all by itself, to introduce martial law is through a massive pandemic. Military scientists exist whose sole job purpose is to create deadly bioweaponry for the New Babylon's military use. This is where that anthrax came from immediately after the attacks on 9/11. If you research what our military is in possession of in terms of weaponized biological agents intended to be used against human beings, it is truly frightening.

A massive outbreak of an engineered, highly contagious, highly deadly virus would not only excuse martial law to "limit the spread of the disease", it would eliminate millions, if not ultimately billions of humans from the planet. Remember, the elimination of 90% of the Earth's population is one of the goals of the Great Plan.... the Culling of Man. Don't worry though, I'm sure the Illuminati and their families will have the needed vaccines to be able to live and carry on for us all.

The military, under the direction of the proponents of the Great Plan who run the government, have built massive underground cities for the elites to go and hide out in just in case something like a massively deadly and contagious pandemic breaks out. There are over 100 of these multi-billion dollar "hideouts" in existence in the U.S., called DUMBS or Deep Underground Military Bases. Just something else to Google and research for yourself.

Something else to consider as a possible false flag scenario to implement martial law is through the effects of an EMP event. EMP stands for Electro Magnetic Pulse. EMPs occur naturally when a large burst of solar energy hits our planet. If this burst is large enough, it could have the effect of knocking out delicate electronic circuitry that runs our modern day world. Although a significant burst of solar energy and subsequent "crash of the grid" is a low possibility, a manmade EMP through the airburst of a nuclear bomb or other apparatus is a very real and much more possible event. A single nuclear device detonated 250 miles above the center of our country would crash the grid in the mainland United

States, and this is a fact. This would be an extremely easy false flag for the operatives of the New World Order to facilitate and blame on **Iran**, for example, or even North Korea.

The "grid" is representative of the supply/distribution lines of food, energy, water, sewer etc. that we use every day to maintain life. The interlocking grid that enables us to live as a first-world country would be severely disrupted if not outright obliterated by the sudden destruction of nearly every computer within the range of the EMP. 95% of vehicles would suddenly not work. Airplanes would drop out of the sky like flies. Power stations would self-destruct. Basically, anything controlled by a computer would be rendered inoperable. It would be quite the nasty situation for you and your family to experience, and you probably wouldn't live through it unless you were prepared. Perhaps you've heard the term "prepping", well this is why people in the know prepare or "prep" for exactly this type of situation.

Again, it has been confirmed as a fact by scientists that a single nuclear explosion detonated over the center of our country would cause an EMP and in fact render nearly all computers in this country inoperable. Supply lines for food and energy would be severed for months if not years. Massive starvation would set in within only weeks. If this happened martial law would immediately be imposed.

A crash of the grid is the root cause of all this "zombie apocalypse" talk you may have heard about in the Mainstream Media, but they never explain it. The zombie apocalypse happens **when people run out of food and start eating each other**. Remember, it only took that Chilean soccer team that crashed in the Andes in South America some years ago **a matter of days** before they got so hungry they started eating the dead bodies.

In particular relation to an EMP event, we need to revisit the scientific work and discoveries of a man we talked about earlier in this book: Nikola Tesla.

I can't explain in this limited amount of space how far ahead of his time this man really was. I easily rank him among the most gifted intellects in human history. The work he did in relation to electricity is not only off the chart in relation to the limited body of knowledge regarding electricity during his early days, but his legacy is vastly underrated and blacklisted by the proponents of the Great Plan. They literally don't want you to know what his inventions were truly capable of. When he died it is a fact that agents representing the federal government confiscated all of his research papers and work in the interest of "national security" and those inventions fell right into the hands of the proponents of the Great Plan, who are going to use this technology against us in the very near future.

We're going to go over this suppressed information right now, briefly, because it is intricately intertwined with what is coming down the line in terms of worldwide catastrophic events.

The knowledge Tesla had was almost prophetic, and I bet he had some very significant information besides his knowledge of inventing that was never let out after his personal papers were confiscated by the feds after he died.

Tesla's technology could have given mankind free, pollutionless, and unlimited energy. Giving man free and clean energy would have released him from one of the primary bonds placed upon him by the Illuminati, and that is our dependence on the oil they control. This is one of, but not the primary reason, he has been blacklisted from history.

Allowing Tesla glory in the annals of history in the U.S. would have shown him to not only have been one of the greatest inventors in history, but also that he was a highly patriotic man who believed in God and was most likely a Christian, seeing as how his father was an Orthodox Christian priest, knowing and testifying to the true source of his intellectual prowess. Remember his quote from earlier in this book?

I could not find with certainty using Google search that Tesla was a Christian, just something else they would not want us to know about this genius and was stricken from the public record as his inventions.

His inventions transformed the world, with AC power being chief among them. The arrival of AC electricity, in my opinion, was the trigger to what is referred to in the Book of Daniel as "knowledge will increase", which is also a harbinger of the End Times. The advent of consumer electricity in the form of Tesla's Alternating Current allowed mankind's technological advances to rapidly grow by leaps and bounds.

Tesla was not only an inventor with over 300 patents to his name; he was an electrical engineer, mechanical engineer, physicist, and futurist.

Here also invented or discovered radio, radar, radiation, x-ray devices, wireless transmission of communications and energy, hydroelectric power, fluorescent lighting/neon, robotics, superconductors, lasers, and many other subjects far, far ahead of his time.

Tesla not only contributed a huge body of inventions that were beneficial to mankind, he also discovered the ultimate means of power and destruction, and stated that if he wanted to, among other things, he could use that terrible power to literally split the Earth in half. After reviewing the facts behind this statement, I believe he **wasn't** kidding.

This multi-faceted technology with the means of not only helping but possibly destroying mankind is in existence today and the primary location for the exploration of the various uses of this technology is in Gakona, Alaska, and it is called HAARP. HAARP stands for High-frequency Active Auroral Research Program. There are also HAARP-like apparatus' set up at various locations throughout the globe, and both Russia and China now also possess this unbelievably powerful technology, and Russia has in fact used it against us already during the Cold War.

The facts surrounding HAARP are so numerous and detail-intensive that entire books have been written about it. It is critically important to understand that this technology is factually in existence and is in use today. I am going to give you a crash course in only a couple of pages, telling you what it is capable of with as minimal as possible details. Due diligence for the nuts and bolts regarding it are up to you.

Right off the bat, HAARP can be targeted to any area on the face of the Earth and deployed at the push of a button. It can be used to cause DNA damage to humans, cause and/or accelerate cancer, weaken the immune system, create feelings of uneasiness, depression, irritability and foreboding in the minds of mankind, can cause a person to hear "voices" inside their head, can create "Global Warming" side effects in our environment to convince the world we need to pay carbon taxes, can tap into the Earth's magnetic field as an unlimited source of free energy, can harness the power of the Earth's magnetic field to create explosions larger than the biggest thermonuclear bombs in existence, can shield our country from incoming missiles, can cause earthquakes, and can create and/or alter the weather, can cause small or gigantic EMPs. This can all be done from a single "research facility" in Alaska, but also **all of the**

above can be inflicted upon our country by both Russian and China without warning as of the publication of this book.

One other important event that I believe the HAARP technology could be used for is the incineration of an incoming meteor or asteroid, an "extinction event" that would otherwise decimate life on our planet.

Depending on what frequencies, degree of power, and other variables you are applying, and where you are sending the energy, it can be used to create all of the listed situations we just went over. It is truly the power of the gods, and it is in existence **right now.**

What if HAARP falls into the wrong hands? It's already too late to think about that, as it's in the most diabolically evil hands in the history of the Earth: the hands of the Luciferian proponents of the Great Plan. It is also in the hands of two countries that could very well stand up to the Great Plan and wipe the New Babylon, aka the United States, right off the map. Literally. When the world economy crashes, the entire world might blame the United States, triggering a HAARP attack from both China and Russia. Suddenly the quotes from the Book of Revelation regarding the instant destruction and burning of the New Babylon of the End Times might make uncomfortable sense.

The patents for the HAARP technology are held by Military Industrial Complex kingpin Raytheon, and the authority to do the experiments they are conducting are authorized and overseen by the Pentagon, so you know this isn't just a friendly science experiment they are working on up there.

Another, and possibly the most nefarious use of HAARP I need to make you aware of so you don't fall for a deception, can be achieved through the projecting of 3D holograms into the night sky.

"I occasionally think how quickly our differences, worldwide, would vanish if we were facing an alien threat from outside this world"

-President Ronald Reagan said this in a joint speech with President Mikhail Gorbachev, in 1988 on the floor of the UN. He made almost the same comment on many occasions that year, as if to plant a seed for the future.

Now, whether or not this deception is man-made via holograms, or supernaturally based having to do with malevolent interdimensionals manifesting themselves physically for us to see is anyone's guess. I'm just throwing out some possibilities of what might be in our future so you will not blindly accept what you are told by the Mainstream Media.

It says in the Bible that going into the End Times that God will send a strong deception that will fool all but the most ardent, informed Christians. The reason that God is credited with being the one who sends the deception is that He is the one who has to allow it, perhaps Himself opening the dimensional porthole to let those particular demons out of their spiritual "prisons" that is prophesized to happen in the End Times. Or, it may have to do with what I alluded to earlier with Tesla receiving the knowledge from God to create the technology to accomplish this.

According to the Book of Enoch, these malignant interdimensional beings ran rampant right up until the Biblical flood-event, when God was forced to act to keep them from completely destroying mankind and all life on Earth. He imprisoned these beings somewhere in another dimension and wiped their offspring the "Nephilim", plus other DNA-corrupted creatures from the face of the Earth, and basically started mankind over with Noah and his family.

Is the story of the flood a simple metaphor for a much deeper thought process explanation of what happened? I believe it's possible, but I also do believe that interdimensional beings who were not supposed to interfere with mankind did in fact do so. The Creator God had to intervene as a result of these beings screwing up the natural process, placing them in a spiritual prison and wiping the slate clean on the Earth to begin again. According to the Bible, a different faction of these interdimensionals also interacted with the humans after the "flood" and continue to do so to this day, advising the human leaders of the Great Plan through interactions via occult black magic rituals.

There is something else going on to throw into the mix you need to take note of, and I believe it has to do with various applications of the HAARP technology, and this is a phenomenon called "chemtrails".

Chemtrails are chemicals that are apparently being sprayed into our upper atmosphere by military jets. Most people pass these off as harmless jet "contrails", but it is a FACT that genuine jet contrails are only made of water vapor and dissipate within a few seconds or minutes of being generated, unlike these chemtrails that do not dissipate at all and actually spread out over time and grow larger and larger as they drift across the sky. The next time you see a jet laying down an apparent exhaust trail behind it, spend a few moments and watch that trail behind it to see if it dissipates. Again, a water-vapor-based contrail will dissipate within a few seconds or minutes, but if it sticks around and **DOESN'T** dissipate but grows larger and larger, that is a **chemtrail.** Some of the substances of these "chemtrails" have been collected and tested by patriotic Americans and it has been found that these chemtrails are composed of barium and aluminum dust---both toxic to breathe in.

Why are they doing this? Since no one knows for sure, including me, I'm just hazarding a guess that since HAARP has mainly to do with various forms of electricity interacting with our atmosphere, and since these chemtrails are being laid down in our atmosphere, they are related. Barium and aluminum are both highly conductive of electricity, and HAARP is an electricity-based operation. I have already seen Al Gore and others on video stating that one way to "combat global warming" would be to inject some sort of reflecting material into our atmosphere to deflect the sun's rays. There may be a degree of truth to this, but you now know these people are liars and can't be trusted at all. It is my position at this time that the chemtrails have to do with the HAARP project, injecting metals into our atmosphere to probably enhance the capability of various HAARP applications. My view on this may change if presented with **facts** to the contrary, but this is where I'm at on "chemtrails".

So back to the "great deception", one of the rumored mechanisms of triggering the World Government if all else fails is either a simulated **alien invasion**, and/or a simulation of the **return of Christ/the messiah**--- and I am being very serious here. Right now the military has, through HAARP, the technology to project 3d images up into our atmosphere, possibly using the reflective metal particles of aluminum and barium as part of the operation.

In 1974, noted physicist, genuine rocket scientist and co-founder of NASA Dr. Werner von Braun stated that "**when the Cold War ended with the USSR, America would need a new enemy to continue to manufacture arms for, so a fake 'war on terror' would be created,**

When this was seen for the fraud that it is, the next step would be a False Flag event of a so-called "alien attack", which could then keep the war machine going forever".

The Cold War ended in 1989 and over 20 years have passed, so the scenario I've laid out not only with the events of 9/11 and the subsequent launch of the "war on terror", but with what I believe will be a false-flag event to try and convince the world we are being invaded by aliens would fit right in with what Dr. von Braun was warning us of.

To plant the seeds of this, society needs to be conditioned to the existence of UFOs/Extra Terrestrials. The **Rockefellers** in the early 90s, right on the heels of the ending of the Cold War, wasted no time in going to work on this **exact scenario**.

From September 13-15, 1993, leading UFO researchers met at the Wyoming ranch of **Laurence Rockefeller**. They decided on a plan of "approaching" President Clinton about a mutual cooperation of releasing information to the public about UFOs in order to "prove" their existence to mankind. A collection of the "best available evidence" was funded by Rockefeller and written by two leading UFO researchers, finished at the end of 1995, with 1,000 copies of it sent to various U.S. Senators, Congressmen, and Clinton White House personnel. Some of these were also sent to key European politicians.

To discuss the implications of open contact with an advanced extraterrestrial civilization, the Human Potential Foundation, again funded by the **Rockefellers**, organized an international conference in D.C on May 27-29 of 1995.

Another group funded by the **Rockefellers** was the "Center for the Study of Extraterrestrial Intelligence", CSETI, and its founder Steven Greer. He also started something called Project Starlight, whose goal was to present the "best available evidence and witness testimony in a manner which would constitute a definitive disclosure regarding the reality of the UFO/ET subject."

CSETI organized the "Washington Briefings", which was a series of presentations given by 20 firsthand witnesses of UFO encounters and UFO related events within the U.S. government. These briefings, under the chairmanship of Apollo 14 astronaut Edgar Mitchell, were conducted between April 7-11 of 1997 in the Westin Hotel in D.C., with a second, smaller briefing following at the Pentagon.

Greer has since organized another group called the Disclosure Project in 2001 and presented multiple eyewitnesses, broadcast on the Mainstream Media, about alleged "ETs" here on earth, etc. You are going to hear more from **Steven Greer** in the future, so make a mental note of him and who he is working for, the **Rockefellers.** I've seen various interviews with Greer, and his mannerisms set off a character alarm in my mind, not only because of the Rockefellers being involved, but his strong anti-Christian views in particular. For someone to be so open-minded on one end and to be absolutely close-minded and hostile towards God on the other smacks of an agenda, and it's because it is part of the agenda: the final push to fulfill the Great Plan.

It is my **opinion** that we are not being and have not been visited by beings from another planet in our galaxy. This is based on countless hours of research, and I'm not the only one with this opinion. We have been, in my opinion, interfered with by beings from what I believe is the fourth dimension, or possibly higher, who manifest themselves physically in this dimension, and this is where the discussion would lead into scenarios along a much deeper realm of thinking that what I want to go into in this book. Leading UFO researcher Jacques Vallée basically believes the same things I do, that ETs are really EDs.

The nearest possible inhabitable planet to us that science knows about is over 20 light years away. That's over 20 light years in one direction, let alone a round trip "back home" for an alien being. You would have to have an enormous vehicle capable of carrying or generating over 20 years worth of living supplies to make the trip, and that's figuring travel at the speed of light, which is a physical impossibility. This is a phenomenal distance for a small spacecraft to travel, even at or above the speed of light, and that's even if life at that closest planet was planted by other beings, or evolved along far enough on its own to be able to leave their own planet, let alone come all the way out here to see little ol' us.

Very quickly to rehash, here is what I believe is the truth about "Extra Terrestrials" and UFOs. I believe that beings that people have seen and interacted with throughout mankind's history are Extra *Dimensionals*, not Extra *Terrestrials*. I also believe that there are two distinct types of UFOs that people see sometimes in the night skies, and sometimes during the day too. The shiny metallic looking ones you may have seen various pictures of are not manned by ETs but probably are the latest generation of military vehicle technology. It has been alleged that the Nazis invented anti-gravity technology and actually had a small number of "flying saucers" in their arsenal at the end of WW II. This technology would have been **confiscated** by the allies and sent to the U.S., along with people like Werner von Braun, the chief founder of NASA with the quote a few paragraphs above warning us. Secret technologies held by our military are **always far advanced of what is let out in public.** They don't want to bring us too far forward too fast, however, as they want to be able to make the money off of building just the threshold of the latest technology to keep us ahead of our "enemies" and then spend the money to replace it in just a few years. That is my explanation of the clunky-looking metallic craft that certainly did not travel over 20 light years to get here.

The other UFO phenomenon has to do with the objects that are going thousands of miles an hour and then can suddenly do a 90 degree turn, which goes against the laws of physics. Well, if you are an inter-dimensional entity, you don't have to obey the laws of physics because those laws only apply to the 3D dwellers. Again, this is far too deep for this book to get into, but I need to at least let you know where I'm at. I certainly don't believe the UFO community is "crazy", but I think they have been, as everyone else, intentionally misled from what I believe is the truth. The various angels and demons described in the Bible and other religious works are really interdimensionals who I believe are in the presence of **all of us, all the time.** We occupy the same space; they are just in another dimension of it. I'll certainly elaborate more on this topic in a later book.

So, to summarize HAARP, the last thing that HAARP could be used to accomplish is an event that I consider to be the one warned about in the Bible about the grand delusion sent by God. The last Great Plan-executed significant nationwide or global event that could result in martial law is perhaps the most diabolical of all: a faked alien invasion using 3D hologram technology available through the HAARP technology. Again, it is possible that God sent this delusion by bestowing upon Tesla the knowledge to come up with the technology needed to create the delusion. That would explain the delusion quote in the Bible regarding the End Times and what was going to happen. Tesla himself said that his intelligence came directly from "God, Divine Being". Was he trying to tell us something? God only knows.

HAARP is something so powerful and deadly that it needs to be carefully scrutinized and monitored by the public, but in order to do that the public needs to be made aware of it. Please research this subject, HAARP, in particular as it is going to have huge ramifications on our future and if you know what this technology is capable of you can watch the nightly news and view what is happening around us with the blinders off.

Chapter 12/C

WHAT DO WE DO

"During times of universal deceit, telling the truth becomes a revolutionary act."
-George Orwell

Have nothing to do with the fruitless deeds of darkness, but rather expose them.
-Ephesians 5:11

So now that you know what is happening and what we are up against, what are we supposed to do?

The very best thing to do to start with is to educate yourself and those around you to what is really going on behind the façade presented to us by the Mainstream Media. I **rarely** even watch TV anymore because I know for a fact that it's just a bunch of brainwashing crap.

"The CIA owns everyone of any significance in the major media."
– William Colby, former CIA director

"We'll know our disinformation program is complete when everything the American public believes is false."
– William Casey, former CIA Director (from first staff meeting, 1981)

"Deception is a state of mind and the mind of the State."
– James Angleton, head of CIA counter intelligence from 1954-1974

I don't have a video game system in my house, I don't watch TV, and I rarely go to the movies. All I do is spend my time researching this New World Order business because it is so important, and the implications of it are going to affect not only me but my kids and their **future**. Right now, their future looks pretty bleak to me under the New World Order system of Luciferian one world government and the tyranny needed to enforce its rule.

Some people are going to call the sum total of the contents of this book complete lunacy. Those people are the human sheep desired by the New World Order system, the "sheeple" as I and others who are awake to the real truth call them. The sheeple are the people who can look right at the facts of what is happening and the gravity of our situation, and have the gall to say it isn't true. ***"It can't be true. Stuff like this is in the movies or on TV, not real life."*** Now think about THAT statement for a minute after just learning the truth of the diabolical forces behind the Mainstream Media in our country.

"It's easier to fool people, than to convince them that they have been fooled."
-Mark Twain

The most important points you need to take away from this book, points you should investigate for yourself, are as follows:

1. The origin of Abraham/the Hebrews/Judaism/Christianity was brought about by God as the original opposition to King Nimrod's Babylonian Mystery Religion, aka the Great Plan for global enslavement.

2. All of our "holidays" are based on glorifying the story of Nimrod/ Semiramis/Tammuz.

3. *King Nimrod is the Biblical Antichrist/Beast. He is the founder of the Great Plan and he will be brought back to life using modern DNA technology to once again rule over the world.*

4. *Freemasonry, at its upper, upper echelon, is the modern day incarnation of the Great Plan.*

5. *The Federal Reserve is a privately-owned, for-profit corporation, owned by the very people who are steering the Great Plan today. The power of money is the main control mechanism for implementing the completion of the Great Plan. The IMF, World Bank, and Bank of International Settlements are also owned and controlled by these people.*

6. *Most of the tax-free foundations were started and owned by the proponents of the Great Plan to shield their wealth from taxes, and to be able to use this money to promote the Great Plan.*

7. *The various Round Table groups were started and controlled today by the very people who are steering the Great Plan and use them to facilitate the completion of the Great Plan.*

8. *A large number of the most important think tanks in the world, including Tavistock and its subsidiaries, were put in place specifically to steer society towards completion of the Great Plan.*

9. *The Mainstream Media is completely co-opted and should not be believed. **At all.***

10. *Nearly all of the Presidential assassinations and attempts had to do with opposition to a Great Planner-owned central bank.*

11. *There are many poisons intentionally put into our water and foods. Be vigilant about knowing what you and your kids are putting into your bodies.*

12. *All of the wars/revolutions that have happened since the founding of the Illuminati can, in fact, be blamed on the Illuminati, including our Civil War and World Wars I and II.*

13. *The United Nations was founded by the proponents of the Great Plan as the infant Luciferian one world government.*

14. *Agenda 21 is the blueprint for completely tyrannical global enslavement.*

15. *Global Warming as it has been presented to us by the Great Planners* **is an outright lie.**

16. *9/11 was an inside job by the proponents of the Great Plan in order to excuse two wars: one in the Middle East and one here at home in the United States against* **us.**

17. *I believe there is the highest probability that the societal grid will collapse in the near future, and you and your loved ones should be prepared for the worse. This is an extremely important issue and should be addressed* **immediately.**

18. *I believe Jesus Christ is the real deal, and that is why He and only He is so hated by the proponents of the Great Plan. They don't hate Buddha. They don't hate Krishna or any of the rest. They hate* **Jesus.** *They hate Jesus in particular because it is He who is to be sent back to Earth to smite the resurrected Nimrod and his Great Plan entourage consisting of the Illuminati families and their minions.*

Now, the points I just listed are only the most important. Everything else in this book should also be further researched by you, my newly-awakened friend. Don't take my word for anything I've said as the gospel truth. Turn off your TV. Shut off the video games. Put down your handheld devices, and get on the computer and start researching this stuff. Knowledge is power, and you have been denied the real knowledge of what is going on. You have been denied the power you and the rest of humanity deserve. This is why the world is such a messed up place today. The time to research the contents of this book is short, so I highly suggest you get on it.

If you truly understand what is in this book, you should feel just like I did when I found out about it: like you just got kicked in the stomach. The last thing you should try to feel, and this is what the proponents of the Great Plan are counting on, is to be paralyzed with fear. You've still got to live your life. You've still got to go to work. You've still got a family to raise and look after. And now you've got some "homework" and that is how you should look at the sum total of this book as: an outline of subjects you need to look into.

I want you to pick yourself up, dust yourself off, and educate yourself while you can, because this type of information is soon to be outlawed as "inciting or promoting domestic terrorism". That feeling in your stomach will go away, trust me. Let it be replaced with what you **should be feeling** over finding out about the Great Plan: **Anger, and the motivation to do something about it in the name of your family, your country, and hopefully your God.**

Remember the quote from the start of this book:

"The world is a dangerous place to live; not because of the people who are evil, but because of the people who don't do anything about it."
-Albert Einstein

Our first and second amendment rights are soon to be on the chopping block, as the 4th amendment already has and others, under the ever-growing threat of "domestic terrorism" i.e. people waking up to the truth of the Great Plan and wanting to do something about it.

"How fortunate for the leaders that the masses do not think."
–Adolph Hitler, one of the greatest leaders of the Great Plan

Sooner or later good and decent men and women are going to have to draw a line in the sand and stand unflinchingly behind it or they are going to steamroll right over free humanity and it will all be over. Unfortunately for you and me, this is an impossibility at this time **because most people are "asleep".** Hopefully at this point in this book you are now "awake", and I highly recommend you go back and re-read this book at least one more time, if not more, to better understand what the tangled, interconnected web of the New World Order really is. The time to act is now or never because it will be too late for you to educate yourself and others if you procrastinate.

The most effective thing you can do to fight back against the New World Order is to educate others as to what is going on that they are not told about---or intentionally mislead about--- by the Mainstream Media.

I love my country, the United States of America, and I will not stand idly by and watch as she is ravaged in a gang-rape by the proponents of the New World Order. The people who are running our country are purposefully attempting to take her down and be absorbed into a one world government. I couldn't stand idly by knowing this is going on if my life depended on it, it's just not in me.

There was an old typing class exercise in school that you may or may have not come across in your life, but it is worth bringing up here: **"Now is the time for all good men to come to the aid of your country."**

That time is **now....or never**. We are at the threshold of the totalitarian one world government, and if we allow the United States to fall, our lives will all change for the worse. **Much, much worse.**

Are you going to be on the side of those who cause wars, mass murders, recessions, depressions, starvation, environmental catastrophes, and general malevolence, or are you going to be on the side of good, caring, moral, and decent humanity? Even if you are not religious, you have to agree that what they have done throughout history and continue to do today would be considered "evil".

The proponents of the New World Order are nearing the goal they have been after for thousands of years: a Luciferian One World Government. They have pulled out all the stops in order to fulfill this, using their many secret and not-so-secret societies to orchestrate their master plan. They have shoved the New World Order agenda down our throats, and we've meekly accepted it after being brainwashed and co-opted by their "methods of madness". They have control over our government, our schools, our churches, our economy, our society, and us. They literally OWN US. We have stood idly by as they have dissolved our Constitution, our morals, our values, our patriotism, and our country. We should have stood up to them long ago and said "no", but didn't because there was no way of knowing their secretive agenda. Thanks largely to the advent of the internet, suppressed information and history has flowed forth that the Illuminati-controlled Mainstream Media could not filter or stop, so now they have to do damage control and discredit it the best they can. Ultimately they will outlaw transmission of this type of information, mark my words. We now know that we don't have leaders, we have mis-leaders. We have the best government corrupt money can buy, and that is who rules us. It's time to take the reins of the country back from the robber barons and place them firmly in the hands of patriotic Americans like you and me, friend.

The people running this Luciferian End Time Show obviously aren't going to admit to being a part of it, but will sure do everything they can to muddy the water of truth and discredit or kill those who would try to expose it and oust them. It is proven that the Illuminati/Rothschild interests are involved in all these events because their involvement can be traced factually through the monetary paper trails, just follow the money. A man named G. Edward Griffin did an outstanding job of just this in his book, the literal "Bible" about the Federal Reserve, called *The Creature from Jekyll Island*. I highly suggest you read it.

They draw their power from **us**, and **without us** they are **nothing**. Those diabolical pieces of crap actually made us fight and kill each other in the Civil War, remember?? They pitted us against each other and do it today through the false left-right political paradigm. Divide and conquer. They need us naïve and stupid to their plans or they won't work, it's that simple.

Remember though, **the government is not our enemy, and people who say they hate the government have got it wrong**. Government is merely a tool, and in the wrong hands does much harm, much like a gun. No, our enemies are the people behind the curtain of government, those installing the puppets who have allowed a price be put on their souls.

If you nudge society just a little bit every year so nobody notices, over centuries and millennia a society is WAY off course from where we could be or should be, and this is where we are today: way off the course God intended us to be on.

The last people who should be entrusted with fixing the problems of the world should be the ones who intentionally caused them to start with, but that's exactly where we are today.

> *"To oppose corruption in government is the highest obligation of patriotism."*
>
> *-G. Edward Griffin, author of "The Creature From Jekyll Island", which is the best book available to explain the Federal Reserve and central banking in general, including how it ties to the Illuminati families*

There's nowhere on the planet to run from these people, so you better start educating yourself as to what they really have been up to and where our future lies under their leadership.

People are waking up in droves, but **we need a mass awakening,** an enlightenment by education if you will, of humanity as to how things really are.

You need to be eternally vigilant in your quest for the truth as I have. This is the first edition of this book and I've done as well as I can with the time I have invested into it with well over 6,000 hours of research into the New World Order agenda. Be very careful of your sources and cross-reference everything. Anything proven to be factually wrong in this book will be changed in future printings, but as of right now, as far as I'm concerned, this book is the truth in print.

Do **not** use propaganda-based websites like Wikipedia in particular to verify the contents of this book. When you Google something, Wikipedia entries are usually at the top of any search list you might look up not only because they are paid to be, but because Google has been corrupted via their leaders being sucked into the New World Order agenda. As long as you vigilantly cross-reference your research you should get to the truth.

Educate yourself about all things New World Order before they literally pull the plug on this suppressed information stream that is

flowing from the internet in particular. After they pull the plug they will outlaw even talking about this stuff. Virtually all of the information that is pertinent at this time to the New World Order is in this book. If you have this book and they pull the plug on the internet or the power grid goes down, you will be able to alert others by reading or sharing this book about what is really going on. I will list my website where you can find how to purchase copies of this book to give away to friends, family, or anyone you care about. I have also been obligated to give the contents of this book away for <u>free</u>, and I will put a PDF containing this entire book for <u>free</u> for all to have access to on my website. Download the PDF onto your hard drive or a hard file storage unit, because if they shut off the internet you won't be able to retrieve it, but you will still be able to download onto others' computers if it comes to it. You can also <u>email the downloaded PDF</u> out to friends, family, or anyone you want to wake up. I not only highly encourage the free electronic distribution of this book, I am pleading for it. Life, liberty and the pursuit of happiness will come to an end if <u>you don't act</u>. I am just one motivated American and I need <u>millions of patriotic Americans</u> to step up to the plate and take a swing at the New World Order.

Here is a short list of online documentaries on Youtube.com I've seen/ recommend for further education. This is a **small** sampling of some of the more popular ones, but there are literally hundreds and thousands more than I listed to try and wake you up.

I have all of these and many more listed on the "documentary links" page at my website, **samaritansentinel.com**

<u>New World Order in General:</u>
"Freedom to Fascism" by Aaron Russo
"Endgame: Blueprint for Global Enslavement" by infowars.com (Alex Jones' website)
"The Obama Deception" by infowars.com
"Fall of the Republic" by infowars.com
"Wake-Up Call" by John Nada
"Esoteric Agenda" by Ben Stewart
"Know Your Enemy" by the Fuel Project

Financial:
"The Money Masters" by William T. "Bill" Still and Patrick S. J. Carmack
"Money as Debt" by Paul Grignon
"Monopoly Men" by Liberty International

Methods of Madness:
"The Fluoride Deception" by Christopher Bryson
"Sweet Misery", about aspartame, by Cori Brackett and J.T. Waldron
"The GMO Threat" by Jeffrey M. Smith
"Wake Up America, #1,2,3" about poisons in our food, by Peter McCarthy and Radhia Gleis

9/11 Truth:
"Loose Change" by Dylan Avery, and produced by Korey Rowe, Jason Bermas and Matthew Brown
"911: In Plane Site" by David von Kleist and William Lewis

There are also a handful of highly intelligent anti-New World Order activists who give daily broadcasts of the **real** news you need to be hearing on youtube.com and you should be listening to them. People like Alex Jones, Gerald Celente, Max Keiser, Peter Schiff, Jim Rogers, Mark Dice, and Mike Adams are all good people to be listening to on a regular basis to get the truth in news.

There are also many, many books that have been written about the New World Order and its various components besides this one, some of them listed in my bibliography. The book that you have in your hands, however, **is the most comprehensive book to explain the _entire_ New World Order conspiracy that I know of**, and is the exact book I wish I'd had at the start of finding out about the existence of the Great Plan.

"The only thing necessary for the triumph of evil is for good men to do nothing."
-Edmund Burke

Once you educate yourself to what is going on, then you can act accordingly. They have the "Great Plan", I propose the "Great Solution", and that is to break their stranglehold over humanity. The only way to initiate this is to educate yourself and others.

So there you have it: the *first* thing you should get cracking on is educating yourself. Once you are enlightened you can speak with authority on these matters to others and not sound like a crackpot with some whacked-out "conspiracy theory".

Here is an example of how I strike up a conversation with someone who I don't know is awake or not:

> *"The Federal Reserve really messed up the economy this time. Too low of interest rates for too long blew up the economy. Do you know about the Fed being a privately-owned corporation? Did you know that the same people who founded the Federal Reserve are also the same ones who founded the United Nations? What does that tell you about what's going on? Thers is some bad stuff going on you should know about."*

Then you can take it from there, **if you know the rest of the story**. Wage an information war. This is why Alex Jones named his website infowars.com, that says it all right there.

The *second* thing I would recommend you do is to **immediately go and take your money out of the Illuminati-owned banks, because you are paying for your own enslavement**. There is no reason for you to wait to do this. We need to break the back of the International Banking Cartel. As long as they control our money they will push for a one world government and the fulfillment of the Great Plan. If you bank with Chase, Bank of America, Citigroup, Wells Fargo, or any big bank you are helping the New World Order. Immediately take your money out and move it to either a credit union or a small, local bank. By banking with the big, international banks you are helping to expedite the destruction of the United States and the onset of full-blown world government.

Not only this, but make sure to not keep valuables in **any** banks in safe deposit boxes. In the event of martial law, the feds can and will legally confiscate all the wealth contained in the banks. Get yourself a secure safe to keep inside your home where you can physically protect it if needed. I also recommend turning some of if not most of your paper dollar assets into gold and silver bullion. When the worldwide central bank Ponzi scheme crashes down, all those paper dollars will be good for is toilet paper, and the digital money you have in cyberspace? You have been warned.

Gold and silver have held their value for thousands of years and will continue to do so. This is why the owners of the banks themselves, the Illuminati, have traded trillions of dollars worth of paper and digital money over the many years for physical gold, which they keep in huge underground vaults on their estates, complete with armed guards.

The *third* thing I recommend is to not enlist in the armed services, and if you're in there, get the hell out. Why would you want to contribute to or even get killed or maimed just to promote the New World Order? Why would you want to contribute to the murder of innocent humans, especially women and children? You're not living in a video game as they'd have you believe, this is real life we're talking.

> *"In the beginning of a change, the patriot is a scarce and brave man, hated and scorned.*
> *When his cause succeeds however, the timid join him, for then it costs nothing to be a patriot."*
> -*Mark Twain*

The *fourth* thing is to be proactive against this plan to take over the world. Research who you're voting for, and if they promote the New World Order don't vote for them and back someone who is pro-humanity instead. You can also vote with your wallet. Buy stuff made in the USA. Try and buy stuff from non-multinational companies to keep the money here in our country. They tell us trade is good but not when all our country is doing is importing crap and exporting our jobs and way of life.

The *fifth* thing I recommend is to **take care of yourself and your health**. Learn about fluoridated water. Learn about Aspartame. Learn about MSG. Learn about GMO foods. Learn about all of the terrible side effects to your health these things cause and avoid them if at all possible. Taking care of yourself also involves something we talked about earlier: **prepping for a disaster**.

You should be prepped anyways. All of us live in earthquake/hurricane/disaster zones, its part of living on this planet.

You do not want to be waiting on federal aid that will not even show up if a natural disaster occurs, or worse yet if the grid crashes, so for the sake of not only yourself but your family, you need to take the initiative to be prepared for the worst.

You should store enough non-perishable food for you and your loved ones and the means to prepare it for a minimum of **one year**, preferably more. **You probably don't realize how heartbreaking it would be to watch your children slowly starve to death if it came down to it and you were powerless to stop it, but had been warned in advance about what you should do to prepare.**

"The prudent see danger and take refuge, but the simple keep going and suffer for it."
-Proverbs 27:12

Being prepared also involves owning and being proficient in the use of firearms. Firearms are a uniquely American heritage. Firearms are as American as baseball, apple pie, and Chevrolet no matter what the alarmists in the Mainstream Media try to tell you, that you "don't need them".

There is a giant anti-gun statue on the grounds right in front of the United Nations spelling out their intent to disarm humanity and the United States in particular, because people who own firearms are a threat to their totalitarian one world government. **One of their top-of-the-agenda items they want to accomplish is to confiscate the guns of Americans.** There is surprisingly **little** gun violence in the U.S. for the number of guns and gun owners. **Those mass shootings that are happening need to be scrutinized for false flag clues, including CIA-mind control of the shooters.** We have had semi-automatic guns in our country for decades without a problem, and now suddenly there is a problem? In countries where gun confiscation has occurred crime did not go down but up, and now the people can't defend themselves against criminals with guns who weren't going to obey the gun ban laws anyway.

The way they are going to attempt to confiscate our guns will go like this, so pay attention and mark my words: They will require every gun in America to be registered with the Feds in order to "protect us". This will not protect us. How will this stop gun violence? It won't. This is a ruse for the Feds to identify who has what so they can make ownership lists. The value of life in not only our country but the world has been nearly nullified by the proponents of the New World Order, so people killing people is not such a big deal these days---unless you are using it to excuse a gun grab by the Feds. The random gun shootings will continue and probably escalate by crazy kids hopped up on mind-altering prescription drugs like Ritalin, the same kids who then play the latest life-like video games where you murder in cold blood other human beings, and these same kids then snap and get their hands on their parents' guns and go on killing rampages. This is the real problem, not the guns themselves. The Feds will then ultimately declare an all-out gun ban in the United States because of these mass-shootings and then use those gun registration lists to come to your house and collect up what you told them you own.

"The two enemies of the people are criminals and government, so let us tie the second down with the chains of the Constitution so the second will not become the legalized version of the first."
-Thomas Jefferson

You now know that the Constitution has effectively been nullified by the Patriot Act and various other pieces of traitorous legislation, most of them having circumvented the Congress due to Presidential signing statements and Executive Orders by the puppet-Presidents that were installed to promote the New World Order agenda to start with.

The Second Amendment to the Constitution was put there for a reason. People who have the means to protect themselves are less likely to want to be "saved by the government", and they want you 100% dependent on the government so you can be their slave. At a minimum you should have a pistol, a rifle, and a shotgun, and the ammunition and knowledge to use them to protect yourself and your family from the threat of a "zombie apocalypse", and it is a very real threat unfortunately.

You should also store water, but more importantly is the means to collect and store water after the fact, and the chemicals or systems needed to treat it so it's safe to drink. If you get giardia or other water-borne illness from contaminated water you will probably die, unless you are in possession of the next line item here, antibiotics and other prescription drugs.

You should store prescription drugs for yourself and your family. I myself am an asthmatic, and have enough medicine to get me by for awhile, at least a couple of years. Without it I could easily die from an asthma attack. You won't be able to get any medicine, let alone your specific medicine, if the grid collapses. You should also research and store antibiotics, which you can get without a prescription thanks to a current loophole under the pretense of buying them for various fish and farm animals. This loophole will probably close within only a couple of years of you reading this, so time is short. You can get the medicine to treat giardia for instance right now, and you should get not only this but other antibiotics. Something as basic as a respiratory infection can easily turn into pneumonia, which will lead to possible death if untreated. First aid kits and books about how to treat various ailments are also a necessity.

You should also try and keep your teeth in as good of shape as possible, including having any metals in your mouth removed that are filled with toxic substances. Have the metals removed and an epoxy put in place if you're financially able. You might have to go for years without a dentist if the grid collapses, so if you're able, keep your teeth in good shape.

Another thing to think about if you are able is to move out of the cities. Highly populated cities will turn into death traps if the grid collapses and food, water, sanitation and generally safe conditions immediately disappear. On that note, clean water will be scarce and more valuable to drink than to do laundry or dishes. Have extra socks and underwear in particular, feminine hygiene products, toilet paper, paper towels, etc. Also disposable paper plates, cups, flatware, etc.

There are hundreds of websites and books dedicated to prepping for disaster, and I highly suggest you not only educate yourself about this aspect but to prepare for the worst, because it is coming.

When all those third world countries who depend on the United States for supplemental food and water suddenly find no more aid coming in due to martial law in the U.S., those countries will descend into absolute anarchy, and the elites will get the billions of humans culled from the Earth that they are after in only a matter of weeks. Don't let that happen to you here at home by being unprepared.

Your legacy can be that you stood up to evil while others around you stood idly by and watched it viciously attack your country, family, and fellow man. The actions of the proponents of the New World Order directly affects you, your kids, your family, your friends, your finances, your retirement, your rights, your **future**. This stuff is real, and it's not going to go away by sticking your head in the sand.

We are literally at war with these people whether you want to accept it or not. **They are waging war against us, so either get behind me or get the HELL out of my way. Humanity has turned the other cheek to these diabolical madmen for too long; it is time to make a stand.**

It is only when the public rises up that real change occurs, and the dirty little secret they are afraid of getting out is that **we have the real power. They derive their power by manipulating us**.

They number less than 10,000 conspirators leaching off decent humanity according to some estimates. Humanity numbers around 7 billion.

Do the math.

Chapter 12/D

WHY I BELIEVE IN GOD

"In the last days, God says, I will pour out my Spirit on all people. Your sons and daughters will prophesy, your young men will see visions, your old men will dream dreams."
-Acts 2:17

"The gift of mental power comes from God, Divine Being, and if we concentrate our minds on that truth, we become in tune with this Great Power".
-Nikola Tesla

"I have a fundamental belief in the Bible as the Word of God, written by those who were inspired. I study the Bible daily."
- Sir Isaac Newton

"I am a Jew, but I am enthralled by the luminous figure of the Nazarene......No one can read the Gospels without feeling the actual presence of Jesus. His personality pulsates in every word. No myth is filled with such life. How different, for instance, is the impression which we receive from an account of legendary heroes of antiquity like Theseus. Theseus and other heroes of his type lack the authentic vitality of Jesus........No man can deny the fact that Jesus existed, nor that his sayings are beautiful. Even if some of them have been said before, no one has expressed them so divinely as he."
-Albert Einstein

If someone as smart as Einstein, or Tesla, or Isaac Newton believes in God, to me that just adds to the totality of the evidence pointing to the existence of God. To believe in God in the manner that they do is to acknowledge that the Bible is truly the word of God, even if it was intentionally left open to individual interpretation. It certainly does tell us in both the Old and New Testaments of the Luciferian Great Plan, how it started, who formalized it, who is running it today, and where it is taking us in the future.

The process of researching and writing this book was literally a spiritual journey for me. When I started, I was a militant atheist. When I finished, I was a convinced Christian.

In the early stages of my research and from an atheist point of view, I could not understand why so many people who were smart enough to know the New World Order was real were professed Christians. How could people who were smart enough to believe the facts surrounding the New World Order and think outside the box be themselves trapped "inside the box" I viewed religion as?

When I started researching for this book, I kept running into a brick wall because you simply cannot explain *all* facets of the New World Order conspiracy without factoring in the existence of God and everything that goes along with His supernatural existence. You can explain some of it, but not all of it. To simplify, the supernatural is merely that which is not of our world, our 3-dimensional universe. The supernatural is the only way to explain the origin of our 3D universe in my mind. Even when I was an atheist, the notion by scientists that there was nothing in our universe to begin with, and then that "nothing" exploded via the Big Bang to create our universe just never sat well with me. You can't get something as vast as our universe from nothing. It is impossible. It is my belief that the Creator God created the 3D world, which is the universe we live in, as the lowest plane of the multiple dimensions of reality.

It is my belief that both the Big Bang theory and the Creation theory are correct at the same time. The Big Bang was the instant materialization of the third dimension, the infant 3D universe which then spread out according to plan and continues to expand today. Our 3D universe was put in place by the Creator God, the God of the Bible, from a dimension above us, **far** above us. He "created" our dimension and is the creator of our 3D universe.

Not only this, but the existence of beings from other dimensions interacting with our dimension explains the convoluted story of history the proponents of the Great Plan have been feeding us. It would certainly explain such mysteries as how the pyramids and other ancient structures were created, when modern science can't explain today how they were able to move blocks of stone weighing hundreds of tons, let alone place them hundreds of feet up in the air. To supernatural beings who the laws of physics don't apply, this was probably quite an easy task.

Stories abound how King Solomon, considered to be the greatest black magician in history by the occultists, was allegedly able to summon "demons" to work on his temple. What he was really conjuring, using occult black magic, were interdimensional beings.

The "Unfinished Obelisk" at Aswan, Egypt measures 120 feet (42m) long and would have weighed nearly 1,200 tons when complete. Although it was never erected, they had planned it to be. Now how do you expect that the ancient Egyptians would have been able to move this thing, let alone stand it straight up in the air when modern machinery today wouldn't be able to accomplish this? The **only** way they could have attempted this and been successful would have been with supernatural help.

The supernatural is also the way the world is run today through the agenda of the Luciferian Great Plan. Since discovering that we were warned of the Great Plan in both the Old and New Testament, it wasn't a hard leap at all for me to begin believing that Jesus Christ was indeed the real deal. Jesus Christ is God's designated supernatural, interdimensional representative for mankind in the 3D world here on Earth. Jesus Christ is part actual human being, and part Creator God. He is literally the unique link tying mankind to God. It is through Jesus Christ, and only through Jesus Christ, that we can 100% get into God's good grace. Once I came to that conclusion, that's when I had my own supernatural experience with what is called the Holy Spirit.

I remember vividly that day after I gave myself over to believing in Jesus Christ. I remember springing out of bed that morning feeling like a million bucks, just ready to take on the world. Minutes later I was standing in the shower and thinking to myself, "What is going on? What is happening to me? Why do I feel like I'm high on some kind of drug?" A feeling of complete and unconditional love descended on me that day and I felt the happiest I've ever been in my life, even in the face of discovering the ugly facts and reality of the New World Order. Over the next couple of days I felt myself falling in love with my wife all over again. All thoughts of disdain for mankind in general left my being, where before I felt that mankind was a cancer and the Earth would be better off without him.

I felt a whole new respect for the Earth also, and found myself uncontrollably picking up garbage in public and throwing it away when before the thought wouldn't have even crossed my mind. I know that sounds sappy, but it's the truth. A few days after receiving the Lord my family and I picked up two garbage bags full of trash that had washed up on the Washington State coastline while on a trip out there, where before I wouldn't have bothered.

I also felt an overpowering urge to spread the Gospel of Jesus Christ, and I completely understood why people who were really filled with the Holy Spirit did the same.

To make a long story short, the feeling of universal love that had come over me lasted unabated, non-stop, 24/7 for a couple of weeks until I, being the kind of person I just am, just had to test it to see if it was really the Holy Spirit I was experiencing, or if I was just tripping on religion. So I did, and that supernatural feeling of universal love went away, and I'm sad to say I've never been able to get that same degree of universal loving-feeling back. It still makes me shake my head today that I would do something so foolish as to test God, but it is what it is and I accept that I blew it. Today, when I'm truly making an effort to be in touch with God, trying to live right and do the right thing by the Lord, I get a taste of what I had, but I'll never forget those two weeks I literally felt like I walked with God. I'm actually hoping and praying to receive some redemption with Him through procuring this book for Him, by explaining to others how I was brought into His light through the discovery of the facts surrounding the New World Order. I still feel His presence in me, and I still try to be a good representative of God and a steward of our planet, but those two weeks were something I'll never forget and will always long for that very special feeling again.

"This book had to be written by one of three people: good men, bad men or God. It couldn't have been written by good men because they said it was inspired by the revelation of God. Good men don't lie and deceive. It couldn't have been written by bad men because bad men would not write something that would condemn themselves. It leaves only one conclusion. It was given by divine inspiration of God."
-John Wesley, 1703-1791, British religious leader who founded Methodism, referring to the Bible

Beyond any doubt I would say that I have a much different relationship with God than your average Christian. A friend of mine explained it to me, that as we are heading into the End Times, God is calling out His people, those who were put here to serve Him but had strayed from the flock. I've had some odd things happen in my life when I was very young, and even before I was born, that always led me to believe that "aliens" or "ETs" were somehow guiding my life, watching over my reckless hedonistic lifestyle to make sure no harm came to me either from the law or from injury. By all rights I should have been dead years ago the way I had indulged in extreme reckless behavior, but I had always felt the presence of these "ETs" around me, both good and bad, and that I felt that the bad ones were always trying to destroy me, and the good ones finagled situations to keep me out of serious harm's way.

After becoming a Christian and finding out about everything in this book, my life makes a whole lot more sense. And whatever happens in the future? I'm just glad to know the truth of it all. That's all I ever wanted. If anything significant becomes of the assembly of information in this book, I would hope that it did more to bring people to the truth of Jesus Christ than it did to wake them up to the reality of the New World Order, although the two are intricately intertwined. What happens on Earth in the short time our souls exist in the 3D world pales in comparison to an eternity in the higher dimensions in the presence of the Creator God, but remember, that's only if you are **accepted.**

My faith in Jesus Christ is the glue that holds my family together in the face of such a monstrous conspiracy as the New World Order. It is also what holds my sanity together, for we are in a bad spot with little hope for a promising future once you factor in the contents of this book. That is, until you figure Jesus Christ into the equation. He not only gives you the hope you need to keep going in these treacherous times we live in, but He gives us hope that things will work out for the powers of good in the end, and to not dwell on the negative aspects of the New World Order, other than to educate others and just to survive as best we can in the face of what's coming.

Keep in mind, the entire reason for Jesus Christ's return to Earth is to specifically smite the Luciferian Great Plan and those who run it.

We live in times of extreme temptation as never before in mankind's history. What was largely set in motion in the 1960s is today full blown ancient Babylonian-style hedonism, especially in the New Babylon, the United States. Rampant drug use including "designer" drugs made of synthetics, sexual promiscuity, extremely deviant pornography on the internet at the push of a button, rebellious music across the spectrum of styles, chemicals in foods like MSG to make us gluttonous, weapons of mass destruction to murder people by the billions if desired, a hugely materialistic and greedy society due to the free flowing monopoly money scheme from the Federal Reserve, etc.

> *"There will be terrible times in the last days. People will be lovers of themselves, lovers of money, boastful, proud, abusive, disobedient to their parents, ungrateful, unholy, without love, unforgiving, slanderous, without self-control, brutal, not lovers of the good, treacherous, rash, conceited, lovers of pleasure rather than lovers of God— having a form of godliness but denying its power."*
> *-2 Timothy 3, 1-5*

What if instead of creating and spending those trillions of dollars to foster wars, death, destruction, perversion, terrorism and tyranny, they used that money for the benefit of mankind? This is the difference between the Great Plan's world, and a world following the teachings of Jesus Christ.

The only path to the Creator God is through His designated personal representative, who is Jesus Christ, and is the one and only true path we should be following. This is why the proponents of the New World Order have done so much to separate us from Jesus Christ in particular, while promoting the other religions that are merely offshoots of the Babylonian Mystery Religion.

They have their supernatural-interaction rituals via black magic and the like, but we too have the power to call upon the supernatural to help us in this messed up world. **It's called prayer, and it is the most powerful supernatural ritual in the world**. The most powerful supernatural interdimensional entity in existence is **Jesus Christ**, because Jesus is of God and wields the power of the Most High God, our ultimate Creator. This one interdimensional being, Jesus, is more powerful that all the rest of the "angels and demons" put together. Jesus **is** Lord.

Jesus Christ makes it crystal clear that Satan and his demonic entourage are liars to the extreme. The proponents of the Great Plan have fallen for their lies since we were planted on this Earth, that if they follow and promote the Great Plan agenda while living in this 3D world, they will be taken care of when they pass on into the next dimension after they die. They are dead wrong, and they will be justly punished by the Creator God when they die.

Jesus Christ is the antidote to the malevolent interdimensionals' evil, and they seek to deny you the life-saving gift from God Himself that is Jesus Christ, our lifeline to God. The very reason the Illuminati perform black magic rituals is to gain power from the supernatural.

I would make a personal request from me to you to go ahead and try it yourself---- What have you got to lose? Try talking to God, alone and in a quiet, private place. Tesla was right; you too can also gain spiritual and mental power from the supernatural through prayer to God and Christ. I like to go up into the mountains, by myself, when possible, alone, just me and God, but you can be anywhere private as long as you can concentrate and be respectful and believe that He is hearing your words. Trust me, **He will hear you** and you will feel His presence from that point on in your life **if you are indeed sincere**. You have to be sincere and you have to believe He hears you. This is the very definition and context of the word "faith".

"Had the doctrines of Jesus been preached always as pure as they came from his lips, the whole civilized world would now have been Christian."
-Thomas Jefferson

I was having the worst time writing this book because I was fiercely trying to build a wall to keep religion out of the New World Order conspiracy---but when you boil it down, **the New World Order would not exist without the existence of God, and Christ, and Satan, and what is in the Bible**. In my opinion, what is happening on Earth is all a test by God for us as humans, His very special creation. We are given free will to do as we choose, and what we choose is either beneficial to the New World Order, represented by Satan, or is truly beneficial to mankind, represented by Jesus Christ.

The first time Christ came to Earth He was meek as a lamb, not because He was destined to be killed, but to set an example for humanity to live by. He came humbly, born in a manger to a humble family, worked a very humble blue-collar job as a carpenter until the time arrived for Him to begin His full-time ministry. He lived humbly as a representative of the Most High God with a message of pure love for mankind, and left humbly, nailed to a cross and left to die. When He comes back, it won't be as a lamb **but as a Lion sent back to Earth to put an end to the New World Order.**

"Do not think that I came to bring peace on the earth; I did not come to bring peace, but a sword."
-Matthew 10:34, the words of Jesus Christ

Here are just a quick handful of Biblical examples of signs that the End Times are indeed imminent: the resurrection of Israel, technology for the mark of the Beast is in existence today, one world government is in place via the United Nations, modern media technology can now transmit images worldwide of the two witnesses of Revelation 11, vast increase in knowledge and speed of travel per Book of Daniel in the 20th Century, signs of wars and rumors of wars (20th century worst in history), with the invention of the internal combustion engine and the discovery of oil in the Middle East the world spotlight is suddenly back on the land from the Bible = the Middle East is the main stage for the End Times events. Prior to the 1960's you could hardly find a book on the occult. Today there are thousands of books promoting it and is a multi-billion dollar industry, not to mention all manners of magic, sorcery and general occult themes are the norm coming out of the Mainstream Media.

The New World Order is real. I humbly suggest you make peace with God, because the very near future is going to get **downright ugly**.

"Do not lay up for yourselves treasures on earth, where moth and rust consume and where thieves break in and steal, but lay up for yourselves treasures in heaven, where neither moth nor rust consumes and where thieves do not break in and steal. For where your treasure is, there will your heart be also. The eye is the lamp of the body. So, if your eye is sound, your whole body will be full of light; but if your eye is not sound, your whole body will be full of darkness. If then the light in you is darkness, how great is the darkness! No one can serve two masters; for either he will hate the one and love the other, or he will be devoted to the one and despise the other. You cannot serve God and mammon."
-Matthew 6:19-24, the words of Jesus Christ

The proponents of the Great Plan are going to be most unhappy that I put all of this information into a book and am seeking to awaken humanity to the truth of what is going on. I will go on record right here and now and state that I would never kill myself, and if my untimely death occurs it will be because I was removed by the exact same people I have reported on in this book. I love my family, friends and country way too much to take my own life, and my work is far from over. It's just **beginning**. The Lord has seen me safe to this point; God willing He will see me safe in the future.

If this book has touched your life in a positive way, please let others know by posting a review of this book so that others may see what is in store for them if they take a chance and read this book. I appreciate you helping me to spread the truth of what is going on in our world. Please let everyone you can know of the existence of this book as I'm self-published and I need all the help I can get!!!

My website is **samaritansentinel.com**. There are images located at my site you can download and spread around to let others know about my works. My email address is there if you want to say 'hi', and my Facebook/YouTube info is there also. Please join me in trying to wake up others to what is really going on in our world.

I am currently working on the next book, *Rise of the New World Order 2: The Awakening*, and will release it May of 2016......please watch for it. What is in this next book will take your understanding of the New World Order, your 'awakening', to the next level.

Hope and pray for the best, but prepare for the worst my friend. God bless you for having the courage to want and know the real truth and to stand with me for what is right and true in this evil world.

Thanks for your support!

In His service,
J. Micha-el Thomas Hays

Bibliography:

Although a large portion of the contents of this book was gleaned from the internet using Google, which was in turn used to access thousands of books and websites online, the following books were also influential in the composition of this book, coming into my possession during the many years constructing this book:

Albrecht, Katherine and Liz McIntyre *"Spychips"*
Allen, Gary *"None Dare Call it Conspiracy"*
Barlett, Donald and James Steele *"America: Who Stole the Dream?"*
Barlett, Donald L. and James B. Steele *"America: What Went Wrong?"*
Bates, Larry *"The New Economic Disorder"*
Bergen, Peter L. *"Holy War Inc."*
Breese, Dave *"7 Men Who Rule the World from the Grave"*
Brzezinski, Zbigniew *"Between Two Ages"*
Cook, Terry L. *"The Mark of the New World Order"*
Cooper, William *"Behold a Pale Horse"*
Daniel, John *"Scarlet and the Beast,"*
Day, Marcus *"Aliens: Encounters with the Unexplained"*
Dean, John W. *"Worse than Watergate"*
Estulin, Daniel *"The True Story of the Bilderberg Group"*
Figgie, Harry E. with Gerald Swanson *"Bankruptcy 1995"*
Finsterbusch, Kurt *"Taking Sides"*
Flynn, Ted *"Hope of the Wicked"*
Goldberg, Bernard *"Bias: A CBC Insider Exposes
    How the Media Distort the News"*
Griffin, David Ray *"The New Pearl Harbor"*
Griffin, G. Edward *"The Creature from Jekyll Island"*
Hall, Manly P. *"The Secret Destiny of America"*
Hawking, Stephen *"A Brief History of Time"*

Hesemann, Michael *"UFOs: The Secret History"*
Higham, Charles *"Trading With the Enemy: An Exposé of the Nazi-American Money-Plot 1933-1949"*
Hightower, Jim *"Thieves in High Places"*
Kah, Gary *"En Route to Global Occupation"*
Kah, Gary *"The New World Religion"*
Korten, David C. *"When Corporations Rule the World"*
LeMay, Lucien *"The Last Generation"*
Meir, Golda *"My Life"*
Paul, Ron *"The Revolution"*
Perry, Marvin *"Western Civilization: A Brief History, Vol. 1"*
Quigley, Caroll *"Tragedy and Hope"*
Renner, Rick *"Seducing Spirits and Doctrines of Demons"*
Riemer, Neal and Douglas W. Simon *"The New World of Politics, 4th Edition"*
Robertson, Pat *"The New World Order"*
Robinson, John *"Born in Blood: The Lost Secrets of Freemasonry"*
Sarkett, John A. *"After Armageddon"*
Smith, Jerry *"HAARP: The Ultimate Weapon of the Conspiracy"*
Smoot, Dan *"The Invisible Government"*
Stewart, David J. *"The Plain Truth About Christmas"*
Sutter, Keith *"50 Things You Want to Know About World Issues..."*
Sutton, Antony C. *"Wall Street & the Rise of Hitler"*
Sutton, Antony C. *"Western Technology and Soviet Economic Development"*
U.S. Government *"The 9/11 Commission Report"*
Unger, Merrill F. *"Demons in the World Today"*
Von Daniken, Erich *"Chariots of the Gods"*
Von Daniken, Erich *"The Gold of the Gods"*
Weldon, John with Zola Levitt *"UFOs: What on Earth is Happening?"*
Wolf, Naomi *"The End of America"*
Wolfaardt, Wilhelm J. *"The Story Of Nimrod, As It Relates To Christmas And Easter"*

Printed in June 2021
by Rotomail Italia S.p.A., Vignate (MI) - Italy